History of the 72D Indiana Volunteer Infantry of the Mounted Lightning Brigade...: Especially Devoted to Giving the Reader a Definite Knowledge of the Service of the Common Soldier. with an Appendix Containing Complete Roster of Officers and Men

Benjamin F. McGee

Your Comrad
A. O. Miller Col
72nd Ind Vol

HISTORY

OF THE

72d INDIANA VOLUNTEER INFANTRY

OF THE

MOUNTED LIGHTNING BRIGADE.

A Faithful Record of the Life, Service, and Suffering, of the Rank and File of the Regiment, on the March, in Camp, in Battle, and in Prison. Especially Devoted to Giving the reader a Definite Knowledge of the Service of the Common Soldier. With an Appendix Containing a Complete Roster of Officers and Men.

WRITTEN AND COMPILED BY B. F. McGEE, SERGT. OF CO. I.
Regimental Historian.

EDITED BY WM. R. JEWELL, LIEUTENANT OF CO. G.

LAFAYETTE, INDIANA:
S. VATER & CO., "THE JOURNAL," PRINTERS.
1882.

PREFACE

AND

PERSONAL SKETCH OF THE AUTHOR.

A paraphrase of the 31: 35 of Job would read thus: "O, that mine enemy would write a book!" And no doubt the old patriarch verily believed that in no other way could his enemy so completely give himself away.

In early modern times, becoming an author was considered the greatest misfortune that could possibly befall any one, as it laid him open to the attacks of friend and foe alike. Like the unfortunate novice of the present day who runs for office he must make up his mind to have his motives impugned, his character assailed, and himself distrusted by every one. Whether my comrades who unanimously elected me to the position of Regimental Historian, at our first reunion in LaFayette, September 19th, 1878, and at our every reunion since have without a dissenting voice continued me in that position, for a moment thought of the misfortunes they were heaping upon me, I know not. But certain it is, that from the very first my position has been a most unenviable one. Comrades will never know with what feelings of utter helplessness and inefficiency I began the work of preparing a history of our noble old regiment; of the most utter chagrin and disappointment that has followed me all along the course of its preparation; nor of the terrible and overwhelming trials that have assailed me from every side. And now, after four years of arduous toil, in which I have waded through almost insurmountable difficulties and drained the cup of misfortune and disappointment to the very dregs, and have had plenty of time to realize all there is of honor or pleasure in it, I am compelled to say that no amount of money would ever induce me to undertake another such job.

I shall not attempt to enumerate the many difficulties under which I have labored, but justification of myself, and the refutation of the ideas of some others who think they could write a better book in two or three days than this one is, require a few explanations.

Primarily this book has been written for the surviving members of the Seventy-Second Indiana, 450 of whom are still alive; but right here comes *one* of the numerous difficulties under which I have labored.

There were thousands of incidents occurring all along through our eventful service which were of deepest interest to the comrades participating, and the author already realizes the bitter disappointment those comrades must feel, when reading the book, to find those incidents barely mentioned, or left out altogether. Although those incidents may be of very little interest to the general reader, I am persuaded that no apology I could make would ever satisfy those who participated in them, for leaving them out.

Again, comrades get in the habit of telling things in a certain way, and the story has so often been repeated in the same way and in precisely the same words that they think it utterly impossible that other comrades, with equal chances with themselves of seeing and knowing whereof they speak, should see it with different eyes or tell it in different words. To all such, of course, the book will be a disappointment. But, my dear comrade, let me remind you that you and I will soon have to answer to our names where the accidental circumstance of our having seen things in a certain light will pass for but little, but the rectitude with which we *acted* for ourselves, and the charity we *felt* for others, will go for much.

Again, the wants of the general reader have been largely considered in the writing of this book; and I am well satisfied that if I could have had, when young, a chance to read such a book as this, I should have gone into the army a *veteran* in comparison with my greenness on entering the service; and yet I am satisfied that the general reader will find a great deal of prominence and space given to things the details of which will be of little interest to them—such as the specific service performed by individuals upon certain occasions; *who* did this, or *who* did that. For this very reason, gentle reader, this book will be preserved as a sacred relic by the children of those heroes long after you have ceased to take an interest in any history of the war. The thoughtful reader can now see *some* of the difficulties under which I have labored. It has been a divided subject all the way through; an effort to please two parties whose tastes are widely different.

Again, I presume it will always be a matter of opinion with every one as to just what is *the history of a regiment;* and it is barely possible that some names may occur, or some incidents may be noticed, that never had any connection with the regiment. These are certainly very rare, and I wish it distinctly understood that those names have not been used either in disparagement or praise, but simply in a general way to illustrate a principle.

But you ask, "Why write a history at all? Are there any members of the Seventy-Second whose characters need vindication?" *Most* certainly not. "Then is it the design to make a hero of any one?" Nothing could possibly be further from the author than such an idea as this. The only object of the author has been to simply state the facts and let the world award the meed of praise where it belongs. "What then?" Well then, to go back to the first expressed desire for a regimental history, we state that on the 19th of September, 1878, in the city of LaFayette, the Seventy-Second met in its first annual reunion. At this reunion permanent officers were elected and the machinery set up for subsequent reunions. Col. Thomson was elected president, Col. Robinson vice-president, Capt. Rice secretary, and Sergt. Dan. W. Moore corresponding secretary. Considering the competency of the comrades just named, it would seem that they were officers enough to run any ordinary business machine. But comrades present thought best to elect an executive committee of one from each company, just to keep them straight, you know. This, in all conscience, seemed officers enough for every emergency. But to some there seemed something lacking; some great void or vacuum was yet to fill up; and it was attempted to fill this up by electing a *Regimental Historian.* Shades of the departed! Hadn't we already made a history we were all proud of? Hadn't we gone into the thickest of the fight, along with "600,000 more?" Hadn't we kept closest to the enemy for three long years, and left our dead comrades all over the South? Were we not *in* at the death struggle, and didn't we help to capture Jeff Davis? And wasn't our regiment the first free white Yankees to ride in to Andersonville? O yes, all this and a thousand times more. But who knew anything about it?

Modest as we were; we had never blown our own trumpet abroad. No friendly correspondent or paid reporter ever spread on the wings of the wind, or hearalded all over "God's country," the daring achievements of our noble old regiment. While the valiant deeds of other regiments were paraded from Maine to Oregon, and from the lakes to the gulf, *our* regiment worked on quietly, steadily, faithfully, and without recognition. But what of it? Did other regiments get more than their meed of praise? No; but ours got less. W. H. H. Terrell, the adjutant general of the State of Indiana, in his report of Indiana soldiers, furnishes the only history, so far as we know, of Indiana regiments. This, of course, is simply a rehash of the reports furnished him by the commanders of regiments, and through no fault of his is very partial and incomplete. Take for example the two Indiana regiments that served in our brigade. While one of them is given credit for doing as much work, capturing as many prisoners, etc., as was done by the entire brigade, the other one appears as a mere figure-head, of no earthly use but to be looked at. For 13 years, as the comrades of the Seventy-Second moved among the happy results of peace, they had ample time to calculate all the forces brought to bear in the great struggle for National preservation; time to weigh well all the forces of the war; but to their utter astonishment they could not find that the Seventy-Second had any hand in it, or anything to do with it. And I suppose it was partly to supply this great neglect, or injustice, that a Historian for the regiment was first thought of, and your humble servant unanimously elected to the position.

For four years now I have worked constantly, faithfully, earnestly and persistently, and at my own expense, to gather together such facts and incidents as would place the real character of the Seventy-Second Indiana properly before the world; conscious that only the real facts need to be known in order to place the Seventy-Second where she justly belongs—in the front rank of all the regiments that went from the noble old State of Indiana.

When I began the work, with the exception of Corpl. Records, of Company I, I had, as I supposed, the only complete and continuous daily record that had been kept in the regiment. This embraced all the events that took place in the regiment each day, as I saw them, knew them, or believed them to be; embracing our camps, marches, pickets, foraging, scouting, skirmishing and battles; together with the face of the country passed over, direction of roads, names of places, miles traveled, etc. But after I had entered upon my work I found that numbers in each company, like myself, had set out with the determination of keeping a correct record all the way through. But, alas for human hopes! Many who had undertaken it died of disease early in the struggle, others were killed, and still others lost their notes or were captured when the war was nearly over; and besides myself, only five, of all the regiment, ever succeeded in getting a complete daily record home with them. Of the fortunate ones, the first to place his notes at my disposal was Sergt. Remley, of company E, a most complete and valuable diary. The next was Surgeon

Wm. C. Cole. No money estimate can be placed upon the value of his journal to the history of the Seventy-Second. These two comrades have my warmest thanks for the moral and material aid afforded. John G. Hall and John B. Davis, privates of Company D, have also furnished complete daily records; though they are very brief they are full of just the kind of information needed, and they are entitled to the thanks of every comrade, especially those of Company D. But Corpl. Records, of Company I, has kept the most full and complete daily record of any comrade contributing, and he is oftener quoted than any other except Dr. Cole. Records' dates are simply perfect. While most all others have varied a little, his are always correct as sustained by the majority of contributors. Stephen Aiken, of Company K, has furnished a complete diary for the time he was with the regiment. After an honorable service in the 10th Indiana, he came to us on being mustered out with that regiment. Of the partial diaries, none are entitled to more credit than the most complete one, so far as the time extends, kept by Lieut. W. R. Jewell, of Company G, and aside from the vast help afforded by comrade Jewell himself, the book owes much of its value to his notes. I have been permitted to cull from partial diaries kept in every company in the regiment. As it would take too long to mention each one separately, I take this method of thanking each one of them for the great help so kindly afforded.

At our second reunion at LaFayette, on the 7th of October, 1879, a historian for each company was elected to aid me in the work, and each was to be responsible for the history of his own company, as a company. Of the full and complete reports furnished by these historians, Sergt. Samuel Stewart, of Company A, has furnished a most valuable one, and is entitled to the hearty thanks of his company, and he most certainly has mine. Corpl. John M. Riddle, Company G, was next to report. His report is not so full, but contains much of interest. Sergt. Lewis E. Wilhite, Company E, was next. His report and Remley's diary leaves but little lacking for that company. Lieut. Charles D. McClure, Company H, has furnished the best company report that has come to hand, and that is certainly honorable for him, as all are good. Of the partial reports of companies, I have one from Capt. Glaze, Company C, Sergt. A. M. Cory, Company D, Basil Lamb and Hiram Bright, Company B, John Hornaday, Company F, Lieuts. E. B. Martin and A. W. Lane, Company G, and Capt. George W. Brown, Company K, for which their respective companies will no doubt feel under obligations, as I most certainly do. The special contributors are too numerous to mention; but I can not forbear speaking of Col. Thomson, Col. Robinson, Maj. Pinkerton. Maj. Kilborn, Lieuts. Jas. A. Barnes, E. B. Martin and A. W. Lane. Sergts. Dan. W. Moore, Jas. A. Mount, Samuel B. Johnson, and numerous others, to all of whom I feel under lasting obligations.

But to Col. A. O. Miller, above all others, I feel under most obligations. He has, from the very first, been the fast friend of this book, has placed his full and complete diary at our disposal, and this diary covers all the ground from the time he came to us as our Colonel at Lebanon, Ky., until he was wounded at Selma and left in the hospital at Montgomery, Ala. He has furnished us with the official orders and reports which make this book *the history of the regiment*.

Now, comrades and readers, you can see from the foregoing that the following pages are not speculation, or the guess work of an irresponsible party; but they are plain, unvarnished facts. If they are not presented in a style to please, the fault lies in the author, and not for the want of facts, nor in the facts themselves. As to the author's ability to *write* history, it is not necessary to say one word by way of argument, as the book itself must furnish the evidence.

My grandparents on both sides of the house were Scotch-Irish. My father was born in New Jersey, in 1803, came to Ohio in 1812, and emigrated to Indiana and settled in Warren County in 1828, when there were but very few white families west of the Wabash, and when there were vastly more Indians than white folks. He was a Whig of the old school, but for many years an Abolitionist. He opposed the war with Mexico, as a war of conquest in the interest of the extension of slavery. He was most conscientious in all his opinions, and dealings with his fellow men. My mother was a woman of most extraordinary force of character, of great strength of body and mind; a faithful and devoted Christian, and passionately fond of her children; and was the mother of four boys and four girls, eight of whom became the heads of families. When called upon to part with two of her boys, as they enlisted in the army, she said: "My dear boys, for the sake of the love I have for you I would rather not see you go; but I suppose the country needs you; therefore go and fight like men, and never show your backs to the enemy, and the blessings of God and your mother go with you." I was born in 1834, and with my mother's milk sucked in the love of freedom, in its very broadest sense, for all of God's creatures, and from my earliest training learned to hate the tyrant and oppressor. My education was begun in a log school-house where there were but four slab benches reaching the entire length of the house. Those benches were so high that it was with the greatest difficulty I climbed upon them, and then my feet would not reach the floor by a foot or more, and my bones ache yet when I think how I sat on those hard slabs for 10 long hours in a day.

My first vote for president was for Fremont, and my last one for Garfield. In the interim I voted for Lincoln, Grant and Hayes. Early in April, 1861, I enlisted in Col. Bryan's company that went from Williamsport, Warren County. (This company served in the 10th Indiana.) That company arrived at Indianapolis with men enough for two companies, and I was one of the unfortunate ones marked as the excess of numbers over the prescribed 64 for each company. I then joined two other companies with no better success, and my first discharge is dated May 1st, 1861, and signed by J. M. Wallace, Adjutant General of the State of Indiana.

The anthor's education was completed at Hartsville University, where philosophy, chemistry and the higher mathematics, were his chief delight, and in which he greatly excelled. While he well understands the rules of grammar and rhetoric, he makes no pretensions to literary excellence. Indeed, his business, occupation, habits and thoughts of life, have all been in a different direction. Born on a farm, and brought up with the ax, the hoe and plow, in his hands, and surrounded by all the domestic animals, it is not surprising that with him life has been real and earnest. So earnest has been his whole life that it would be almost impossible for him to do or say a funny thing. In the preparation of this work no effort at spread eagle style has been attempted. It is written in plain soldier language, for soldiers, and it is confidently hoped that soldiers will appreciate it. All extravagant expressions, such as sanguinary conflicts, gory fields, and rivers of blood, have been scrupulously avoided. The writer's imagination, never strong and never cultivated, has not been drawn upon for a single item in the book. The editor, in a very few instances, has made me say a few things not intended, for which I freely forgive him. As to him I am under a thousand obligations for suggestions that have helped me over many difficulties.

As none of the Seventy-Second ever sought office, and scarcely a man of the survivors has become wealthy, it has been for two years a matter of the most serious consideration where the money was to come from with which to publish the book. Various means of raising the money have been tried, only to be abandoned as failures; and the writer, who had spent so much time and money in the gathering of the material, was more than once upon the verge of despair. But finally Col. Thomson, with a large heartedness and generosity characteristic of the man, and worthy of the noble cause he has fostered, and the everlasting gratitude of every comrade of the regiment, came to the rescue, and advanced the money to insure its publication. This is a clear case of disinterested benevolence, as the book cannot possibly be sold for more money than will pay the cost of publication, and reimburse him for his outlay. Indeed, he will do well if he is so fortunate as to get all his money back.

And now, my comrades, in taking this my final leave of you, as the Historian of our grand old regiment, I ask your kind forbearance and most charitable construction of everything contained in this book. As before stated, I was elected to this position by you, and I beg to assure you that all along through these years I have not, for a moment, forgotten I was your servant, and from the first have endeavored to bring to the discharge of my arduous duties the most conscientious impartiality; and I shall be pained to know that any comrade feels himself aggrieved.

God, in His abundant mercy, has been kind to us as a regiment, and there are, perhaps, 450 of us yet alive; and while we thank Him for His unbounded goodness, and rejoice in all the blessings of life and peace, let us not forget those who have dropped out of our ranks by the way. From the very day we crossed the Ohio River going South to the day we left the Ocomulgee to come home, disease and death hovered upon our track, and with some our *first* day's march was *their* last. The first victim of disease was discharged at Louisville, September 1st, 1862, and the last one claimed by death, while yet in the service, was drowned in the Eachaconee on the 8th of May, 1865. Year after year many of those who were so fortunate as to get home, have been dropping here and there; and those of us who are left have been scattered all over the West, and will never more meet at the sound of the reveille, as we once did; and we cannot restrain the bitter tears of regret for those who have answered to their names at the roll-call that finally awaits us all. But for none are the fountains of sympathy and sorrow so broken up as for our poor unfortunate comrades who starved by inches and rotted in Andersonville and other prisons of the South. And to all those of our regiment who thus gave up their lives for their country—"with malice toward none, but charity for all"—is this book most respectfully dedicated by the author.

B. F. MAGEE.

Your Comrade B. F. Magee

A FEW WORDS BY THE EDITOR.

To what Comrade Magee has said I have but little to add. To him belongs the honor of the hard and faithful work which has resulted in compiling and publishing this history. To those who have given him so much aid he has returned his hearty thanks. His courage in this enterprise has been as unflagging as it was in the many hard battles in which he participated, and he comes out of his long book-battle as he did out of the long war for the Union—victorious and glorious.

For many weeks the Historian worked at this history in the office of the Editor, and made his home in the Editor's family; and we feel it proper to say that there is no man on earth we love and respect more than we do Sergt. B. F. Magee. He has put as much conscientious work into this history as any man ever put into a book of its size. His great anxiety has been to make it as correct as possible in all its facts, and he has certainly succeeded admirably, considering the time given him.

In obedience to the wishes of my comrades, expressed by electing me Editor, I have wrought with Comrade Magee, regarding him as my captain. He has furnished or approved all the facts. I have also mainly followed his style of composition in editing, and as he freely used the language of the Union soldier of the war of '61—'65 in camp, march, and battle-field, I have thought best to follow him. I admit that a more dignified and elegant style could have been adopted; but I do not admit that any other style would have been more powerful or accurate in conveying facts or ideas. The words "rebs," "Johnnies," "gray-backs," "body-guards," "skedaddle," "you'uns," "we'uns," "contrabands," "Yanks," etc., etc., are of the war dialect, and used in these pages because they were current and significant words of that remarkable period. Stately historians will reject them, but this history will help to preserve them. Old soldiers will like it much the better because these words of the war are used, and others will understand it just as well.

It has been the joint aim of Historian and Editor to make this an accurate book in all the details of the history of the soldiers who did the actual service of the war; to show how the rank and file of our regiment lived, in camp and on the march; how they fared in hospital; how they fought and died upon the field, and how they were buried; how they were captured and escaped, and how they were taken to and suffered in the prison-hells of the South. In a word, the history of fighting soldiers from the time they volunteered until mustered out.

We have never seen a book so full and accurate in all its details of actual soldier life as this is, and we have seen a great many so-called histories. The book will also be found to possess much merit as a history of the campaigns of Buell, Rosecrans, and Sherman; for, while giving particular attention to the history of our own regiment, all general movements of the army of which it formed a part are carried along very accurately.

The work which I have done on the history has been during such hours as I could snatch from a very busy life while editing the Danville (Illinois) Daily *News*, active participation in the large business of the Illinois Printing Company, and participation in politics. That I have done imperfect work, I admit; but that it has been hard and long work, I know.

I must thank Comrade Magee for his great kindness and frankness to me in the delicate task assigned me by my comrades; and also Mr. S. Vater, Editor of the Lafayette *Journal*, who, as proof-reader, detected and corrected many errors.

With wishes of health, long life and prosperity to living comrades, immortality to those dead, and perpetual peace and prosperity to the Union we fought to preserve,

I am your comrade,

Danville, Ill., July 12th, 1882. WM. RAY JEWELL.

HISTORY OF THE 72D REGIMENT.

TABLE OF CONTENTS.

CHAPTER XXII. [Page 164

CHAPTER XXIII. [Page 190

CHAPTER XXIV. [Page 208

CHAPTER XXV. [Page 229

CHAPTER XXVI. [Page 254

CHAPTER XXVII. [Page 280

CHAPTER XXVIII. [Page 311

INTRODUCTION.

BY COL. THOMSON.

The Seventy-Second Regiment Indiana Volunteers made a history in their three years' service of which every member is justly proud; and the recollection of having faithfully performed every duty to make the regiment so efficient, is the highest reward the gallant soldier can wish. During the service, while in camp, on the march, and on the battle-field, a number of soldiers kept a diary, carefully noting down events as they transpired, for the benefit of their friends and posterity, little thinking of the importance of their note-books for compiling a history of the regiment to be published in book form. For years our faithful historian, Sergt. Magee, has been collecting this material and arranging it for publication, and with the aid of comrade Jewell, now presents the book with the hope that it will fully meet the expectations of the friends of the regiment. Every possible effort has been made to secure something from every comrade of the regiment—in the way of personal incidents, reminiscences, &c.—that it might be truly a soldiers' history, interesting to every member of the regiment, and to the friends of those who have passed away. The historian having been of the *ranks*, and faithfully carrying his gun and knapsack throughout the entire service, and depending largely upon the diaries of private soldiers for material for the history, it will present army life from the standpoint of the common soldiery, and perhaps contains more of real war history than any other book published. No one realizes the labor and expense it has been to prepare and publish this book; and the faithful historian will never be compensated, unless it may be in that highest reward, the consciousness of having done his duty. I know not what is in the book, having read but a few pages of proof-slips. But an intimate acquaintance with Sergt. Magee, during the service and since the close of the war, assures me it is a faithful collection of actual regimental history, such as surviving comrades and friends of the regiment will wish to keep in their libraries and hand down to future generations, and I most earnestly commend it with the hope that his faithful services in preparing it will be appreciated.

Very truly,

C. G. THOMSON.

History of the Seventy-Second Regiment.

CHAPTER I.

CAUSE OF THE WAR.

While there were many minor causes of the war, there was but one great cause—African slavery. Early in the history of the country there arose a conflict between the Free and the Slave States. Hon. John C. Calhoun taught the doctrine of State Sovereignty; that each State was supreme sovereign over its own territory, to the exclusion of the authority of even the United States. In the heated contests of the period South Carolina passed resolutions of nullification and secession as early as 1828, in which it was elaborately set forth that a sovereign State had the right to annul a law of Congress, or to secede from the Union, if its people so determined. Gen. Jackson, then President of the United States, issued his celebrated proclamation in 1832, in which he plainly told the people of South Carolina that he would use the military power of the United States Government to compel obedience to the laws of Congress, and to preserve the Union; that he would meet secession by coercion. President Jackson also embodied in this proclamation a constitutional argument for the sovereignty and perpetuity of the Union, which has never been surpassed, if indeed ever equaled.

The President prevailed, and the nullification and disunion projects of South Carolina were, for the time, deferred, but the baneful doctrines were not abandoned. As time passed, the conflict between Slavery and the Free States, in efforts to obtain territory for new States, became very fierce. The Union doctrine of Jackson spread and strengthened in the Northern Free States, while the secession doctrines of Calhoun were generally received in the South. From 1828 to 1861 there were frequent threats of secession. The contest over the admission of Kansas into the Union intensely excited both the North and South, and threats of disunion came more emphatic from the Slave States. All the efforts of the wisest men failed to pacify.

The Presidential contest of 1860 was the most remarkable in the history of the country. The Republicans nominated Abraham Lincoln. The Democratic party divided. The Union wing nominated Stephen A. Douglas, a Jacksonian Democrat, of fame and ability, who held the Union dearer than his political success or his own life. The Calhoun Secessionists would not support Mr. Douglas, and nominated John C. Breckenridge, a rabid Secessionist. The canvass was bitter, especially in the Southern States, where the supporters of Lincoln and Douglas were nearly equally obnoxious. Many outrages were committed in the South during this canvass, in which both Union men and women suffered severely, often losing their lives.

The Secessionists declared, from first to last, that if Lincoln should be elected the Southern States would secede from the Union in a body. Union men, Republicans, Democrats, and Old Whigs, thought this but a frenzied repetition of an old threat, and an effort of the minority to gain by bullying what they could not gain by votes. Every man went right on and voted the ticket he preferred. The result was the election of Abraham Lincoln.

As soon as it was known that Mr. Lincoln was elected, South Carolina, the hot bed of disunion sentiment and treasonable plots, proceeded openly to make preparations to secede from the Union. How rapidly these preparations were pushed, how wildly and widely the fires of Secession spread, we have no space here to detail. By the 4th of March, 1861, seven States had passed secession ordinances, had formed an independent Government, called "The Confederate States of America;" had adopted a constitution, elected a President and Vice President, and set in motion all the machinery of Government. This was the state of things when Mr Lincoln, escaping the bloody villains who lay in wait to take his life, arrived in Washington and was inaugurated.

In his inaugural address, Mr. Lincoln clearly announced that he had no desire to interfere with Slavery where it was then existing, and no power to do so if he had the desire. He spoke in a spirit of reconciliation, yet was quite distinct in declaring that he would enforce the laws of the United States, in all the States.

Most prominent among the distinguished men present at that inauguration was his great but magnanimous political rival, Stephen A. Douglas. As soon as the President had concluded his address, Mr. Douglas extended to him his hand, and assured him of his sympathy and support in efforts to preserve the Union.

Floyd, Secretary of War under Buchanan, a rank rebel, while acting under a solemn oath to preserve and defend the Union from all foes.

dispersed the Navy, transferred most of the arms, troops, and munitions of war, to the Southern States, where the troops were surrounded by rebel officers as soon as the war broke out, (or virtually before,) and all the arms and forts seized, except Fort Sumter. Thus Mr. Lincoln found a rebel government established, with about all the arms and troops of the United States at its command, and actually making war upon the United States authorities.

The cause of the war was unquestionably Slavery. The object of the war was simply to put down the rebellion; not to abolish Slavery, but to put down treason. The Slaveocrats believed that the spread of slavery in the territories yet to become States had become an impossibility if they remained in the Union, for the Free States had gained control of the Government. They hence determined to secede from the Union, make Slavery a perpetual institution in their new Government, acquire all the territory possible, and spread Slavery to its utmost limits.

In the progress of the war, the emancipation of almost 4,000,000 slaves became a military necessity. It was early seen that the rebels were using their slaves to aid them in the war against the Union. President Lincoln was urged repeatedly to make proclamation that all slaves of rebels should be free. He had great caution and patience, and waited until to wait longer seemed useless. He issued his first proclamation 100 days before New Years, 1863, in which he stated that on January 1, 1863, he would issue another proclamation, declaring the slaves in all States, or parts of States, free after that date. The proclamation was issued, and it will shine as a fadeless star of Liberty on the earth forever.

CHAPTER II.

From 1860 to 1862—Progress of the War to the date of Enlistment of the Seventy-Second.

On January 9, 1860, the steamer "Star of the West" was sent with reinforcements and supplies for Major Anderson, who was holding Fort Sumter with a small force. When the steamer, flying the United States colors, attempted to land at the Fort, she was fired on by Rebel troops, and forced to retire, without effecting her purpose. This, perhaps, was the first hostile shot at the flag. No more were fired until the 12th of April, 1861, when the Rebels, hearing that a fleet was sailing to the relief of Sumter, opened fire on the Fort by order of the rebel Government, and on the next day its brave commander and garrison, being able to hold out no longer, surrendered.

The insult to the flag and the fall of this Fort ran like mad fire through the North, exciting intense indignation. In the South it was hailed with wild delight—by the ringing of bells, firing of guns, bonfires, and other extravagant manifestations of joy. It had directly opposite effects in the two sections. In the South it intoxicated the rebels with enthusiasm, and they believed the war would speedily terminate in their favor—some actually thought that it had been decided, and the Yankees would make no further resistance. It hastened the secession of other States, and stimulated the volunteering of rebel troops. The gallant Southrons were anxious to be in at the defeat and death of the "Northern mud-sills."

In the Northern States the attack on Sumter convinced the people that war was inevitable, and they resolved that as the rebels, in their foolhardiness, would accept nothing else, they should have war to the knife and the knife to the hilt.

On April 15, 1861, President Lincoln made his first call for 75,000 militia, to suppress the "insurrection," as he mildly termed it, and also called an extra session of Congress, to convene on the next 4th of July, to provide ways and means for the war. Another proclamation was issued on the 19th of April, blockading the ports of the rebellious States. Other determined war measures were speedily adopted. The fight was on. It was sure to be fierce and bloody, and no one could tell how long.

It has been remarked that when Lincoln was inaugurated Douglas was present and offered his assistance in that portentous hour. It was the act of a magnanimous man and pure patriot, and was accepted by the President in the spirit it was proffered, and with thanks for the wisdom and influence of such a man in such an emergency. On May 1st, 1861, while all the country was in a tumult, and when even some Northern men were halting as to the policy of making war on the South, and some doubting even the constitutionality of it, and thinking that compromise measures might yet be adopted, Judge Douglas spoke in Chicago. The speech sounded like the key note of patriotism. It was able, uncompromising, convincing, and Jacksonian in every sentence. "The Union, it must and shall be preserved," said Mr. Douglas, and in this contest "every man must be for the United States or against it. There can be no neutrals in this war—ONLY PATRIOTS AND TRAITORS."

This speech consolidated patriotic Democrats and Republicans. Party lines disappeared, except with persons who were actually rebels at heart. Lincoln and Douglas were on the same side, and so were the people of the North, with the exceptions named. Let the memory of Stephen A. Douglas, the Little Giant, be ever green and glorious, and let immortelles forever wreath his brow. Not only great, but a true patriot was he, whose country was his first and last love.

No State in the Union was more thoroughly aroused than Indiana. No Governor in the Nation was more prompt in offering troops to the President than Gov. Morton. On April 15th, immediately on the reception of the news of the fall of Sumter, he telegraphed to the President: "On behalf of the State of Indiana, I tender to you, for the defense of the Nation, and to uphold the authority of the Government, 10,000 men." That tender was made on the very day that the President issued his call for 75,000 men. It is but one of hundreds of proofs of the fact that from the very first Gov. Morton had a clear comprehension of the magnitude of the war, and of the necessity of meeting the rebels promptly and with large bodies of troops.

The day after the call for troops was made—April 16th—500 men were in camp at the fair grounds—Camp Morton—at Indianapolis, and were coming like a tide. From morning until night were seen columns of men marching the streets from the cars to camp, colors flying, drums throbbing, fifes screeching. When night came the stream was not broken, and in less than seven days from the call 12,000 men were in camp, almost three times the quota of Indiana, and the cry was, "still they come." As Adjutant Noble in his report says, "the question was not who will go, but who will be allowed to go."

In five days after the tender of 10,000 men made by Gov. Morton, he tendered the Government six more regiments, without condition as to term of service, to be raised within six days after accepted. So fully impressed was the great war Governor that the troops would be needed, that, not getting a reply from the War Department, he took the responsibility of organizing, drilling, equipping and holding the troops ready at the call of the Government. The patriotic men who were anxious to enter the service were as much gratified at this wise act of their Governor as was President Lincoln.

But of course we cannot follow the movements and fortunes of the Indiana troops. Having said enough to show that the State met the great crisis with a bold and ready spirit, we must hasten to put our own regiment in the field.

The three months troops from Indiana made a splendid record, and were almost all in battles or skirmishes in which the rebels were defeated. The defeat of the Army of the Potomac at Bull Run in 1861, startled, thrilled and chilled the country, and no State felt it more keenly than Indiana and her noble Governor. Meetings were held and speeches made by the ablest men in every neighborhood, town and city. The people were now more fully informed as to the magnitude of the war, and given plainly to understand that it might require years instead of months to crush the rebellion. Many of the most ardent Union men had supposed, before this terrible defeat, that a few thousand men from each loyal State could "flog out the rebels in a jiffey," as the expression went, and the time had come to undeceive this confidence and let the people know that it was Greek meeting Greek—that though our enemy was erratic, he was strong, full of desperate courage, and now in the flush of victory would be more troublesome to subdue than ever before From the date of the first Bull Run defeat the war took on a more serious and permanent aspect.

Gov. Morton, ever keen of foresight, vigorous and prompt of action, sent messengers to all the three months Indiana regiments, whose time was about to expire, and exhorted officers and men to retain their organizations by re-enlistment as soon as their term of service was out. He was successful, and the regiments were speedily reorganized, most of the officers and men enlisting for three years; and the second call of the President was virtually met by Indiana in advance, a large number of the regiments having the advantage of a three months' active service in the field.

During the first four months of 1862 the Union forces gained many important victories, as Mill Spring, Fort Donelson, Pea Ridge and others. The terrible battle of Shiloh was simply a repulse of the enemy at a heavy loss to the Union troops. By midsummer our troops had been so wasted by war and sickness that Gen. Buell was in full retreat from the heart of the South to the Ohio River; the Army of the Potomac was driven staggering back from its lines before Richmond, and the year that had opened so full of promise for the Union cause was clouded before half gone; and President Lincoln called for 300,000 more.

This is the call that caught the Seventy-Second Indiana, and brought out some of the best troops who served during the war. We do not mean braver men, but men more advanced in years and settled in the business of life. It was a proverb, during recruiting under this call, often repeated: "The boys have been going to the war; now the men are going to help them."

CHAPTER III.

From July 7th to August 12th, 1862. Col. Chris Miller commissioned to enlist the Seventy-Second. Alex. A. Rice made Adjutant. Prizes offered for the first Company to report—Competition and rapid enlistment—Camp Tippecanoe—Regiment full—First Cooking—Marching Orders—First March.

On July 7th, 1862, Governor Morton issued a colonel's commission to Capt. Chris Miller, of Lafayette, to recruit the Seventy-Second Indiana Volunteer Infantry, in the Ninth Congressional District, to rendezvous at LaFayette. This brave officer was barely able to keep alive, so severe were his sufferings from a wound received in the three months' service, July 11th, 1861, at the battle of Rich Mountain, while leading Company A of the Tenth Regiment. While his health was feeble, the fire of patriotism burned in his eye; the people had confidence in him, and soon began to flock to his standard. There were numerous applications for permits to recruit, and he issued from three to four for every company to be recruited.

The camp to receive the recruits must be selected and put in order, and the recruits received and assigned to their places in camp as they came in. This would require a man of some military discipline and judgment. On the 7th of July, Gov. Morton telegraphed Gen. Joseph J. Reynolds, of LaFayette, to name a man for adjutant of Camp Tippecanoe, who should take charge of the camp and discharge the duties above named. Gen. Reynolds named Alexander A. Rice, of Attica. Mr. Rice was a young man of much promise, who had, at the beginning of the war, just completed a course of law study and been admitted to the bar. When Father Abraham called for 75,000 men, in April, 1861, Mr. Rice enlisted a company at and in the vicinity of Attica, and reported at Indianapolis about the 20th of April, with almost men enough for two companies. Like 20,000 others, they were too late to get into the three months' service; but being determined to enter the service, he was assigned to the Fifteenth Regiment, George D. Wagner, colonel. Capt. Rice was a man of more than ordinary intelligence, but in "matters military" his greenness was conspicuous and prominent. But with a worthy ambition to surmount every obstacle, he determined to make his company the first in morale and discipline in the regiment. In drawing lots for position he got A, the first in the regiment. To make his company all he had determined it should be, he hired a drill-master to drill himself and company, paying him $60 for his services. In a short time there was not a man in Company A but knew more about tactics than the Colonel commanding. It is no disparagement to Col. Wagner's bravery, and the service he rendered in putting down the rebellion, to say that he never did understand the tactics, and it is no wonder he gave many ridiculous commands, all of which Capt. Rice and his men would execute to the letter. As the command was often the reverse of what was intended, it soon caused difficulty in the regiment, and, as they were frequent, it may be proper to give a specimen command:

"Head of column to the right or left, as the case may be!"

In which case, of course, Company A would move straight forward. On one occasion it climbed over a big stake-and-ridered fence, and moved right out into a field of corn. Of course the Colonel became furiously mad, while Company A insisted it was executing its last intelligent order. A row ensued, and they became of such frequent occurrence that Capt. Rice's patience became exhausted, and he resigned, which of course militated against his military aspirations for all time to come; but about the 21st of July he got his commission from Gov. Morton as Adjutant of Camp Tippecanoe, and immediately reported for duty. Here he had ample opportunity for testing his patience and energy.

With the exception perhaps of the three months men, no regiment in the State enlisted more speedily than the Seventy-Second. Camp Tippecanoe was opened in the latter part of July, and by the 11th of August 11 companies had reported. As but 10 could go in one regiment, the odd company was assigned to the Eighty-Sixth. The companies were lettered as they entered the camp—the first to enter was made A, the second B, &c. A few that came in at the same time drew lots for position. The camp was regularly laid out, and each company was assigned to the position it held throughout the service.

With patriotism pitched to the great emergency, Moses Fowler, Esq., of LaFayette, offered a prize of $500, and James P. Dugan, Esq., of Delphi, a prize of $200, to the first company that should go into camp at LaFayette in answer to this call. The patriotic liberality of these gentlemen is an index to the spirit and conduct of men of means throughout the State in seconding the efforts of Gov. Morton to promptly fill Indiana's quotas without a draft. The contest of the various companies enlisting to obtain these prizes was stirring, and greatly facilitated the enlistment of the Seventy-Second.

Company A secured these prizes, being rapidly recruited in Carroll County, by Nathaniel Herron, Lewis Gros, James H. Barnes and others, organized at Delphi, and brought into Camp Tippecanoe on or about the 28th of July, before any other company. At the organization Nathaniel Herron was elected captain, Milton Newton first lieutenant, A. J. Klepser second lieutenant.

We have not exact dates when each of the companies entered Camp Tippecanoe, but know that all were in camp by the evening of August 9th, and those that had not previously organized held elections on the 10th.

Company B was enlisted at Crawfordsville, Montgomery County, by Henry M. Carr, Oliver P. Mahan and Wesley C. Gerard. At its organization Henry M. Carr was elected captain, Oliver P. Mahan first lieutenant, Wesley C. Gerard second lieutenant. This company entered camp on the afternoon of the same day Company A entered. It was a close race between them in the contest for position and prize.

Company C was enlisted at LaFayette, Tippecanoe County, by James E. Robinson, Frank B. Everett, George Geiger, Daniel W. Moore, George Ruger, John Glaze. William Thieme, and others. It organized by electing James E. Robinson captain, Frank B. Everett first lieutenant, George Ruger second lieutenant. The company went into camp July 29th.

Company D was enlisted at Thorntown, Boone County, by Robert H. LaFollett, Chester G. Thomson, Robert M. Simms, Lewis B Garrett, and others. It was organized by electing Robert H. LaFollett captain, Chester G. Thomson first lieutenant, David H. Ashman second lieutenant.

Company E was enlisted at Linden and Ladoga, Montgomery County, and Sugar Grove, Tippecanoe County, by Dr. J. B. Johnson, Lawson S. Kilborn, Harvey B. Wilson, and others. At its first election Dr. John B. Johnson was elected captain, but never mustered as such, being commissioned and mustered as first assistant surgeon. The commissioned officers mustered in with the company were: Harvey B. Wilson captain, Lawson S. Kilborn first lieutenant, Wm. H. Mahan second lieutenant.

Company F was enlisted by the commissioned officers and others, at Williamsport, Warren County, It organized by the election of Moses Burch captain, James L. Dalton first lieutenant, Orrin E. Harper second lieutenant.

Company G was enlisted at Dayton, Clark's Hill, Stockwell and Culver's Station, Tippecanoe County, by Samuel C. Kirkpatrick, Adam Pinkerton, John B. Crick, Wm. R. Jewell, and others. At its first election Samuel C. Kirkpatrick was elected captain, but was commissioned and mustered as major. The officers mustered in with the company were: Adam Pinkerton captain, John B. Crick first lieutenant, Wm. R. Jewell second lieutenant.

Company H was enlisted at and in the vicinity of Attica, by Jas. M. Stafford, Augustus Zerse, and others. It organized by electing Robert B. Hanna captain, Dr. Wm. C. Cole first lieutenant, who was commissioned and mustered in as second assistant surgeon. James M. Stafford was mustered in as first lieutenant, and George F. Ward as second lieutenant.

Company I was enlisted at Pine Village and Milford, Warren County, and Montmorency, Tippecanoe County, by Jesse Hill, Robert A. Vance, George J. Foster, and others. It was organized by the election of Jesse Hill captain, Ira Brown first lieutenant, John Watts second lieutenant.

Company K was enlisted at Frankfort, Clinton County, by the officers who were elected at the organization of the company, viz: Hiram B. Collins captain, George W. Ross first lieutenant, James H. Whitcomb second lieutenant.

IN CAMP TIPPECANOE.

Here we are, in Camp Tippecanoe! It would be a mild expression to say there was confusion—at times almost a mob—not violent, but noisy. Very few knew anything of what might be required of them as soldiers, and, while all were willing and anxious to learn, there were few to teach. While Col. Chris Miller was nominally commandant of the post, his feeble health allowed him to be there very seldom, and the work of laying off the camp, assigning companies to their camp grounds, procuring cooking utensils, provisions, blankets, etc., devolved upon Adjt. Rice. Everybody wanted something, and wanted it just now. In all this confusion Adjt. Rice was cool. If he answered one question he answered thousands, and many questions he answered a thousand times. His patient, good nature and determination soon brought order out of confusion, and in less than two days he had every soldier provided with everything that could possibly be procured for duty and comfort, the camp established under guard by day and night, quarters policed, and all moving under as regular discipline as if the regiment had been in service months instead of hours.

Adjt. Rice was now reaping the benefit of the $60 he paid the drill-master in the Spring of '61. An incident is here to the point: The Adjutant had a brother in Company F, Capt. Burch commanding; on the second morning after all the companies reported, while Adjt. Rice was mounting guard and giving them their instructions, Capt. Burch, who was standing near, all attention and admiring the ease with which the instructions were given, turned to the adjutant's brother and asked: "What military school did your brother attend?"

The members of the regiment, from expectant officers to many non-expectant privates, had provided themselves with copies of the tactics, or procured them as soon as possible; and began the hard study of them immediately at every spare moment of time. But there was little time in this camp; friends were going and coming, and all was humming with those preliminary transition details inevitable when citizens suddenly become soldiers. There was some effort at drill by a few of the companies, but little could be accomplished in that line.

On the night of the 9th of August, Gov. Morton made a speech in the public square, LaFayette. The members of the Seventy-Second were invited to attend in a body, which they did. It was one of the Governor's grandest efforts, and was greeted by round after round of applause. His grand spirit penetrated, cheered and strengthened every one who heard him. To the men just entered into camp, having left the peace of home and their dear ones for the strife of war, it was medicine to the bones, and all marched back to camp with calmer and more reconciled hearts.

On the evening of Monday, the 11th, orders were given to be ready to move at 6 the next morning, and our hopes that we might remain in this camp for some time were nipped. The camp was situated on a beautiful hill south of the city, and as other regiments organ zed here had been permitted to remain for some weeks or months to drill and get ready for the field, we had indulged a hope that such might be our fortune. Besides the desire to be near our families and friends, and to secure sufficient drill to feel safe in the enemy's country, most of the men had left their business in a very unsettled condition. Farmers had left their wheat unthreshed, and no arrangements for the care of their farms. Some merchants had turned the key in the doors of their stores and made no arrangements about selling their stocks or employing clerks. Doctors had left their practice, and some patients at death's door whom they hoped to visit again. Mechanics had locked up tools and shops and were anxious to make some arrangements by which tools and shops could be sold, or the business carried on by some one else. As in the days of the Revolution men left plows standing in mid-furrow to join the patriot forces, so had men dropped their business in the middle of the furrow to answer this call, which came when the army was in great straights, and when the Union was trembling in the balance.

This camp will be remembered by almost all the original members of the regiment the longest day they live, as being the place where they made their first attempt at camp life. Brought up in a land of peace and plenty, with mothers, sisters and wives, as good as the world affords, few of them had ever undertaken to provide a meal's victuals for themselves, and had they undertaken it at their own homes would not only have failed, but amused the "women folks" almost to death. But here in camp, where the materials for a square meal were neither varied nor abundant, and the means for preparing it neither convenient nor extensive, their failures were ludicrous and laughable in the extreme. A thousand incidents of these first attempts might be written, and the thousand failures, with the most utter chagrin and mortification, would make an amusing and often sad chapter in the history of the Seventy-Second. Just imagine, reader, that you see a mess of farmers whose wives could make a cup of coffee fit for the gods to sip, and dress it with pure white sugar and golden cream, so that its richness excelled the purest Rhenish wine—and to such delicious coffee their palates have been educated from youth up; now the mess sit upon the ground, their legs coiled up before them, and in their midst lies their first spread of hard-tack, sow-belly, and their own make of coffee. Of course they can't attack the s. b. and h. t. without a sip of coffee as an appetizer. They pour the coffee, which runs out grounds first, daub some commissary sugar into it, and say, as they stir, "how I *do* wish I had some cream;" then see them as they taste, working their mouths, licking out their tongues, and each acting just like a young colt at weaning-time when he lays hold to suck as usual and finds the udder soaped from end to end.

If there ever is a time when a great big man feels his utter helplessness, it is when he begins to cook for himself in the army. He wants to jam both fists into his eyes, howl like a booby, and say, "I want to go home!" Of course we always said on such an occasion, "the smoke hurts my eyes."

No raw soldier should attempt to cook a goose. It requires great skill, attained only by frequent practice, on different geese, to cook a goose well. On their way to camp from Pine Village in wagons, a squad of Company I, called Pinevillians, caught a lot of geese at the farm of Judge Rowe, of the West-Side, and brought them into camp—because it was Sunday, the 10th of August, and so great was their hurry that they left home without rations. Under no other circumstance would they have taken the geese in a Northern State. When they got to camp they found plenty of bread, but little meat, and being ravenously hungry, they proceeded to skin and try to cook their geese. From 3 P. M. to almost sundown they boiled the pot like fury, until it sung and danced upon the fire; but the longer they boiled the tougher the geese got. As the sun sunk in the west, their hunger became unbearable. They tore the geese from the pot, rent them asunder, seized a piece of bread in one hand and a "hunk" of goose in the other, and began to eat. But, horror! what faces! And to this day if you want to ruffle the calmness of the stomach of a Company I man, ask him how he relished his first gander supper at Camp Tippecanoe. Yet, with such a discouraging beginning, the men of the Seventy-Second could cook any rebel's goose neatly inside of six months from enlistment.

The night of the 11th, after receiving marching orders, was one of much excitement and little sleep. The word flashed out by telegraph and sped by couriers to the friends of the regiment, and long before daylight wives, mothers, fathers, brothers, sisters and sweethearts, began to arrive, and by sun-up numbers of them were in camp, bringing such articles as they thought we might need, and to bid us good-bye. The occasion is a sad one to call to mind. There were so many mothers with babes on their bosoms, and little children clinging to their skirts—for, as before said, the fathers went in this call. In spite of their brave efforts, many could not refrain from sobs. Some ladies and gentlemen, who had come out from Dayton to see us off, sang the following song a little while before we took the cars:

Heavily falls the rain, wild are the breezes to-night;
But 'neath the roof, the hours, as they fly,
Are happy, and calm, and bright.
Gathering round our fireside, though it be Summer time,
We sit and talk of brothers abroad, forgetting the midnight chime.

Brave boys are they! gone at their Country's call;
And yet, and yet, we cannot forget,
That many brave boys must fall!

Under the homestead roof, nestled so cozy and warm,
While soldiers sleep with little or naught to shelter them from the storm:
Resting on grassy couches; pillowed on hillocks damp;
Of martial fare how little we know till brothers are in the camp.

Brave boys are they! &c.

Thinking no less of them; loving our Country more;
We sent them forth to fight for the flag their fathers had borne before.
Though the great tear-drops started, this was our parting trust:
"God bless you, boys! we'll welcome you home when Rebels are in the dust!"

Brave boys are they! &c.

May the bright wings of Love guard them wherever they roam;
The time has come when brothers must fight, and sisters must pray at home!
Oh! the dread field of battle! soon to be strewn with graves!
If brothers fall, then bury them where our banner in triumph waves!
Brave boys are they! &c.

While this was a patriotic song, it was not the most cheerful that could have been sung at that hour of excitement, when the fountains of every heart were ready to break through its wounds. Before the verses were half finished, many of the listeners and singers were in tears; it was too true, too vivid a prophesy of the fate that awaited many. We hasten to a more cheerful subject, if that (to us) remarkable day affords any.

This being our first and in one respect the most important march we ever made, it is strange that among the voluminous material for this history furnished by comrades, not one of them says a word concerning it, as if there was something about it the comrades would gladly forget. As most of the companies had an excess of from three to twenty men, there were in camp on the morning of the 12th 1,200 men. With the excitement above named, getting breakfast, taking down tents, and packing up for the first time, there was a storm of wild confusion reaching up to 10 A. M. There was ample time, and with the means at hand "old sogers" would have enjoyed a good, hearty breakfast; but with the novelty of the situation and incident excitement, it is doubtful whether a single man got half enough to eat. By the time the sun was an hour high an effort was made to get this mass of confusion into line preparatory to moving "off for the war."

As we had not yet a single regimental officer, and our captains and lieutenants were as green as the greenest, the scene can be better imagined than described. Specimen commands of officers on that memorable occasion are here given, as they may be useful to rising generations:

"Get in two lines, one behind the other!" "Fall in here, boys, in two rows, like ingerns!" "Come up sideways, with your faces in this direction!" "Get in two ranks!" "Step over sideways, Lige, and march backwards four feet!" "Now, march in a string!" "Come around to the left, like a barn door!" By a sort of mutual understanding of each other, the officers and men, assisted by the adjutant, got into a pretty fair line of three to five deep, and as we were not to receive a charge from the enemy, we cared less for its military exactness than for its rugged outline. It looked as ragged and grand as a mountain range.

We marched forward promptly at the command, but as we had no music each took his own step, and at every slight turn in the line of march we telescoped into each other liberally, and when the leading company was halted it was almost blotted out by the others rushing pell-mell down the hill and piling on to it. We were "gwine to the war," and didn't stop for trifles. We were untangled at the foot of Third Street about 9 A. M., and told that the cars would soon be along. Then we began to kiss our wives, sisters, sweethearts, and other women, in a great hurry, as we supposed the cars would be along before the last sweet but sad duty could be deliberately performed. However, the cars delayed their coming, the kissing was ended, the sun was boiling hot, and we simpletons stood in it while there was an abundance of shade close by. Some of the newly-elected officers became suddenly inspired, perhaps by the presence of the ladies, or his Satanic majesty, with the importance of their offices, and kept us standing there by the side of the railroad track in the hot sun, and would keep marching up and down the line commanding us to stand up straight and keep in our places, for, said they, "the cars will be along in two minutes, and you may be left."

We cannot now help thinking how natural it would have been for an old soldier to have deliberately walked to this shade, spread out his blanket, laid down and gone to sleep. But there we stood, like blockheads, until after 12 M., when we heard the cars whistle, and once more began to kiss the women and babies farewell; but before we got fairly througn the cars came, and we all got on with the greatest haste for fear we would be left.

It was an hour before the train started. Every effort was made by the departing soldiers to keep up a cheerful exterior, and those who stood near the cars, waiting to see us off, reciprocated the effort. Reader, may you never know what an ordeal we passed through at that train. A mother with her babe on her bosom, and three little ones hanging to her skirts, stood near the car, when the little ones stretched out their hands, some saying, "Papa, papa, tum back, tum back!" and another began piteously to plead, "Papa, take me wid 'oo!" The poor mother's heart could bear no more and she wept bitterly—the father sobbed like a child. It was con tagious, and not only wives and mothers wept, but many a stout frame shook with emotion. As the cars rolled slowly away, both those going and those staying looked at each other with tearful eyes as they waved adieu. Those were the days that tried the souls of men and women. What was suffered that day, thousands of others suffered during the war.

CHAPTER IV.

August 12th to August 18th, 1862—From Lafayette to Indianapolis—Camp Chris Miller—Attempts at drill—Making out Muster Rolls—Being mustered—Drawing pay, bounties, clothing and guns—March to Union Depot—Night Ride to Jeffersonville.

While the ride from LaFayette to Indianapolis was devoid of incident, save the groups that gathered at the stations from which men had joined the regiment, to cheer them on their way, it was one of interest to us all, who had left our loved ones on that day whom we might never see again. The trip gave time for serious reflection and composure. The sun was more than an hour high when we arrived at Indianapolis, but we were marched and countermarched until sundown, when we were put on a piece of ground in the northwest part of the city, between the LaFayette Railroad track and the canal, which we christened at once "Camp Chris Miller." A permanent camp was subsequently made of the ground, called Carrington.

The novelty and excitement of the first days of camp life had died away; the men were worn out with fatigue, disgusted with the day's work, and sadly out of humor. When they were told that it would be impossible to get rations for them that night, their cursing was not so loud as forcible. The prospect for a general stampede to the city to find food became more than probable. Adjt. Rice, with admirable tact, assured them he had done what he could, and plenty of rations would be in camp by morning, and prevailed on most of the men to lie down and go to sleep. Some refused to do so, and went into the city, imbibed bad whisky, and came back in the night melodiously drunk. Just at daylight we saw Jeddiah Killin, of Co. I, come into camp with a chicken, which he skinned, roasted and ate without salt or bread, remarking as he did so, "Uncle Sam has taken a contract to board me for three years, but is making a bad job of it so far."

Early on the morning of the 13th we drew rations, eat, laid off a regular camp, dug sinks, and went to regular soldiering. The officers applied themselves to tactics. Capt. Samuel C. Kirkpatrick, company G, was promoted to the majority of the regiment, and ordered squad and company drill every day. During this first day at Indianapolis some efforts were made at company drill, but they were generally failures. Drillings could be slobbered over or slighted, but a muster roll was a matter-of-fact piece of work, which would not "get up into two rows endways." They were ordered to be made out immediately, for each company, and signed. Now comes the tug of war!" It was found upon investigation that there were, perhaps, on a fair average, less than three men in each company competent to this exacting work. Day and night the laborious work went on. Many rolls were spoiled, and had to be begun *de novo*. Some officers laboring over them for 24 or 48 hours, almost turned gray, and many from that time forth would prefer to enter a hard battle rather than make out a muster roll. All day of the 14th, and day and night of the 15th, and even as late as the 16th, these rolls were wrought upon. They were finally done, and the companies ready for muster.

The muster rolls were left long enough for us to assemble in a body and receive a flag made for the regiment by a lady 93 years of age, named Nancy Green, of Waveland. The presentation speech was made by United States Senator Henry S. Lane, and was as magnificent as the flag was beautiful. Major Kirkpatrick responded. Senator Lane said he knew the regiment would never let this flag trail in the dust, and Major Kirkpatrick assured him that we never would. Let the reader follow us, and see if that pledge was redeemed.

The inspection of the men by the surgeons began on the 15th, and was completed in the afternoon of the 16th. As the men had to strip to the skin, it was amusing what tricks some of the patriotic resorted to that they might hide some minor defect. All wanted to go, but in spite of every effort to pass a few were rejected in each company, and in some as many as 12 to 15.

The 16th and 17th were among the busiest days ever experienced by mortals. We were in line almost constantly for the 48 hours, with scarcely time to eat. On the afternoon of the 16th we were mustered into the United States service by companies, by Col. J. S. Simonson, for three years or during the war; terms of service $100 bounty—$25 down, and $75 at expiration of term of service—and pay one month's in advance. We knew nothing then of the great straits to which the Government was reduced to furnish this money, nor of the herculean efforts of Gov. Morton to enable the Government to fulfill its obligations to Indiana soldiers.

Sunday, the 17th, was, if possible, the busiest day we had yet seen, and was emphatically a day of drawing, but not of draw poker. We first drew wood to cook breakfast; next, rations to cook; next we were drawn up in line early in the morning and drew our bounties: first $25 from the Government, and receipted for it; next, $10 offered by the county, and receipted for it; next, some of the companies drew local or township bounties, amounting in some cases to $10; next, we drew our clothes, a complete outfit—dress coats, pants, shirts, socks, shoes, and caps; next, knapsacks and haversacks, but no canteens; and just at sundown we drew the most important draw of all, our Springfield rifles and accoutrements. We had not been off our feet 20 minutes that whole day, and when we were released if we didn't draw down our throats an enormous supper, then some one has made a false record.

We had been ordered to cook two days' rations on Saturday, the 16th, and to be ready to move on the morning of the 17th, but on account of the absolutely necessary duties above noticed, it had been impossible to get ready. The order was now repeated to cook supper and pack, ready to move immediately. By the time supper was over it was dark, but the work of packing went forward with determination. We were now soldiers, uniformed, armed and equipped, under orders to go to the front—although without ammunition—and we were ready. Having pulled on our new uniforms, we for the first time packed our knapsacks, and oh, what loads! It would make an old soldier smile the bark off a tree to see the variety shops we filled to carry in mid-August. We went into camp with good clothes on; we now had our uniforms, but we had no way to send our citizens' clothing home, and they were too good to throw away, so, of course, we would rather carry than to lose them. Let the sequel show whether we lost them.

In regard to the clothing we drew much might appropriately be said. Uncle Sam in all cases *aimed* to supply us with the very best clothes that could be procured; but he was not always successful in getting those made of the best material. All our clothes were designed to be made of wool, but the unprecedented demand for wool, necessitated by the vast amount of clothes to be made, soon exhausted the supply, and the price soon run up to $2.00 per pound—a price so high as to induce unscrupulous manufacturers to mix in materials of much less value, and after the first year of our service we got but few articles of clothing that were wholly of wool. Our dress coats and jackets, or roundabouts, were more nearly of pure wool, and were the subjects of little complaint. Our kersey overcoats and pants contained a large per cent. of what we called horse hair. Our underclothes were of various material and of various kinds and styles. Our first shirts—as analyzed and reported upon by the boys—were composed of two parts wool, one part Lin bark, and one part hog hair. As we never saw one of them entirely worn out we suppose they might have lasted to the end of the war. These shirts, like all the wise and bountiful productions of the God of battles, had many redeeming and compensating qualities. While they invariably took the skin off—a part of it at least—of every one who first attempted to wear them, they, always kept the pores open and encouraged the freest perspiration while they afforded a comfortable breeding place for the myriads of graybacks with which we sometimes unavoidably became infested, and which often frisked and played up and down between our shoulders like spring lambs in a meadow, and tickled us in every fiber. A few shrugs of the shoulders furnished all the scratching necessary, and in our efforts to rid ourselves of this pestiferous pest they would bear almost any amount of scorching without danger of burning the shirt. Whether the supply of Lin bark and hog hair ran entirely out we know not, but this first outfit of this kind of shirts was all we ever drew. Our next shirts, and from that on till the close of the war, were of a material that defies description. The most prominent feature of their make-up was their elasticity. They would stretch equal to the conscience of a Jew. But this also had its compensating features. After they had stretched till they reached to the wearer's heels, the lower end of them made capital gun slings, and upon cases of emergency served as halters to bring in captured horses or to tether the pack mules. But the army sock was the institution among all our clothes. Its biography will never be written. One of its most prominent peculiarities, after being worn a few hours, was to turn down over the shoe, flop around over the toe, and so expand and dilate as to be able to hold most any thing from a spring chicken to a ham of meat, and by night were ready to be cut off—one end sewed up, and used as forage sacks.

Just as the street lamps were lit up we for the first time strapped on our new knapsacks and began to move to the Union depot to take cars. Like other green troops we took the longest road to get there. Did somebody want to show what a fine body of men we were? Did the citizens want to see how soldiers looked by lamp light? Or did some one make a thoughtless mistake? This Indianapolis night march must be regarded as one of the most foolish and fatal we ever made. Straight down the railroad track, or by the nearest street, the distance was about three quarters of a mile, and the march might have been made in fifteen minutes and not have heated or worn the men It was 8 o'clock when we started. We marched down by the State House, around the Governor's Circle, and through street after street, till we finally halted at the depot at just 11 o'clock, having marched three hours. We were very tired when we started, and when we stopped we were heated to the boiling point, our limbs weary and feet sore.

We immediately took the train awaiting us, made up of coal, box, flat and cattle cars, just as the cattle had been taken out of them. It was our fortune to get into one of the cattle cars with about six inches of the droppings in it. This looked like it was intended to test our endurance and make soldiers of us in the least possible time. Many not 'mild mill-dams might have been heard. The cars soon moved at a lively rate, the road was very rough, and we bounced about like so many rubber balls, sometimes one on top of t'other and sometimes t'other a-top of one. In two hours we were shivering with chilliness, and we verily believe, that night's ride was the cause of untold suffering and the death of many of its participants. The misery lasted until 8 o'clock the next morning.

CHAPTER V.

August 18th to August 19th—Crossing the Ohio—March Through Louisville to Oakland—Ammunition Issued—Load Guns the First Time—Night Ride to Lebanon with Incidents—First Cooking in Dixie—Into Camp Lucy Carson—Summing up Results.

Arrived at Jeffersonville we tumbled out of the old cars as bruised and limpy as any lot of pigs or calves ever shipped over that rough road. As we tried to get the string halts and kinks out of our limbs and come into some sort of line, we noticed a small, smoothly shaven, elderly man, mounted on a very quiet horse. The old gentleman wore a linen coat, a white hat, indefinite colored pantaloons, and a carbine strapped about his shoulders. He rode up and down the front of the regiment and squinted at us as if trying to ascertain how many there were of us. He spoke a time or two to Major Kirkpatrick, and seemed to know one or two others in the regiment. We came to the conclusion that he was a wealthy old Unionist who lived in the suburbs of the city, followed squirrel hunting as a pastime, had heard of our coming and had come to invite us to breakfast.

"Who is that old skeesix?" asked some of us of the Major.

"Why, that's our General, Ebenezer Dumont; you must be careful how you talk about him," replied the Major.

It was General Dumont, and though the brave man now sleeps the sleep that knows no waking, it is not derogatory to his memory as a brave soldier and a wise and witty man to say that there were numbers of our boys who had never seen a live General before, and to them he was a terrible disappointment in size, dress and style. "Why, I'd look that well myself on old black, with dad's squirrel gun," said pony Ashly.

From the cattle cars we were marched to the river to see the ferry boat pulling out for Louisville, leaving us to stand in the sun for full an hour. We were hungry, thirsty, tired, sleepy, sore and faint. Finally the ferry boat is here; it is the old Isaac Bowman; and we proceed to board her pell-mell and stretched out on the decks for a little smooth rest. Just as we got down on the floors with our heads on our knapsacks, our limbs spread out, and began to think of feather beds, home, and mother's delicious coffee, the steam calliope of the boat began to howl, "Home, Sweet Home," like a big boy baby lost in the woods and crying for his mama. Was it a wonder that some of the boys—and married men were boys also—turned their hands over their eyes and shed a tear or two? William R. Stewart said he "believed the engineer was a rebel and wanted to make us all too home sick to be able for service;" but the Seventy-Second had started for rebeldom and was determined to go.

No spavin ever came limping from the stables more haltingly, or feeling and looking more woe-begone, than did the Seventy-Second from the Bowman. Their feet touched Dixie soil with but a slight thrill; as they fell into line every motion was slow and dull, and indicative of exhaustion. Without ceremony each company formed in the best order possible and followed into the dusty, hot, narrow streets of Louisville. Our regimental musicians furnished their best marching music. In a trice the streets windows and doors were thronged with people, and in many places the house tops were loaded, who greeted us with hearty cheers of welcome. Stars and stripes were flung out, and waved from many windows. The limps and lags left the regiment in a twinkling, and the men became erect and elastic, and greeted the stars and stripes displayed by the people with round after round of applause. The negroes and whites were about equally divided, and while the demonstrations of the whites were very hearty, those of the negroes were often extravagant and ludicrous. Almost the entire march of five miles was an ovation, and had it not been for dust, heat and thirst, would have been rather pleasant. While this hearty reception of the Louisville-ians was a stimulus, for we had supposed that city to be a den of rebels, it could not prevent the heat, dust and thirst, from causing us great distress. To Broadway we marched through very narrow streets and could get no water, for it was scarce and the men had no time to fall out and look for it. We mention with pleasure that the Louisville people, when they found out how terribly we were suffering from thirst, made haste and got buckets full of water and ran after the regiment and gave the men to drink.

In spite of this some were smitten by the heat and tumbled over the curb stones and against the fences. B. F. Magee fell from a sun stroke, the blood bursting from his mouth and nose in streams, which doubtless kept him from smothering. He rallied and came up at Oakland. Under our new uniforms, knapsacks and guns, this five miles was one of the harestd, most painful marches, the regiment ever made, and its memory is yet full of horror for some of the comrades. Six men never got further than this place.

Oakland, a station in the suburbs of Louisville, on the Louisville & Nashville R. R., was reached at 2 P. M. The order was to get something to eat, immediately, which many of the men could not do from sheer exhaustion and blistered feet. Since they had put on their new army shoes they had made two hard marches and had not had time to take them off, and now their feet were so galled blistered and skinned that locomotion was very painful. Water and fuel were quite scarce. Little coffee was made. Most of us lay down, took a slice of raw s. b. upon a hard tack from our haversacks, and with our heads on our knapsacks ate it, and it was "sweeter'n de honey, or de honey gum," as de darkey said of "de 'possum."

While composing ourselves for a nap, or to write a few lines home, the order was given to cook two days rations and be ready to move at a moment's notice. Speedily following this order a lot of ammunition was dumped into the camp accompanied by an order to draw 20 rounds of ammunition to the man. We had expected to remain here a few days, rest, drill and become more fully inured to camp life, but these orders put an end to this hope and we knew we were to soon be off to some point requiring the immediate aid of troops.

The afternoon was made busy with opening ammunition boxes and issuing this first ammunition to the men; with distributing to them their canteens and getting the two days rations provided, and with almost every one writing a brief line home and informing anxious friends of the situation. At 5 P. M. we were ordered out to the railroad to take the train. Presently General Dumont rode up, ordered us to load our pieces but not to cap them, previous to taking the train. He told us that we were going to Lebanon, Ky., that Morgan had lately captured a garrison there and we had to go down to attend to him. After delivering this order and information he rode away very leisurely.

Here we waited, waited, waited for the cars. Every toot or whistle of locomotive or steamer elicited the remark "here they come." Nature overcame some, and stretched on the ground, or leaning against trees, they snored like steam boats. A soldier of

Company B. lay sound asleep on the flat of his back some three rods from the track, one leg drawn up and the other resting on it, his foot sticking up three feet high. Capt. Carr was also asleep near this soldier. The cars came thundering along, Capt. Carr took fright, jumped up, ran against the soldier's exalted foot, turned him a summerset, the Captain pitching ten feet, falling on his belly like a frog, trotted off on his all fours three rods to a tree, ran behind and threw his arms around it, while his eyes bugged out like saucers. The impression was that the Captain was frightened in his sleep.

The cars drew up and we were commanded to load our pieces before entering the cars, but not to cap. This was the first time our regiment ever put powder and ball into their pieces. Considering all things it was well and quickly done, and we were soon on the cars. It was another mixed train with a large number of dirty cattle cars. Narrow boards were laid at right angles on boxes for our seats, giving each man a space of about six inches to put his feet and legs through to the floor. This was so miserable, and worse than no seats at all, that much of it was cast out of the cars soon after starting.

Off into the darkness of Kentucky woods and hills we shoot, at a terrible speed, for the first 20 miles. The road is so rough that at times the cars seemed to stand still like mad mules trying to throw their riders, and jump straight up and come down stiff legged. Crash came a fearful bounce that almost pitched us through the tops and ends of the cars. The train had run over something or run off the track and stopped almost at once. We had run over a piece of timber put on the track by the rebels to wreck the train. As soon as this was ascertained many of the men capped their guns quietly without orders. They felt certain that if rebels put the timber on the track they might be in force in the vicinity and ready to attack us if the train was thrown from the track. Men had been seen standing near the track, at several places, with guns in their hands, and some of our boys at first took them for rebels, but soon became certain they were Union soldiers guarding the track.

The engineer got scared and would go no further without a guard to go before the train some distance, to see if there were any more obstructions. The guard was furnished and marched in front of the train Each bridge was inspected before crossing, and the remainder of the trip was made with caution. It was well known that Morgan was on the wing and that a new regiment was a tempting bait to him.

When the train stopped after running over the rail, or timber, the Seventy-Second boys did their first foraging. Some of them expressed the belief that the people near that place had put the obstruction on the track, that they were rebels and their stuff ought to be confiscated. They sallied forth, capturing a lot of butter, apples, peaches, chickens, potatoes, geese, &c. Often as the train poked along after the guard, these boys who had been so nearly used up that day, revived by the cool night air, would leap from the train, shoot off to a house and bring in something refreshing to the inner man. You see how naturally they took to "sogering" in Dixie and how deftly they did it. They improved to the end of the war!

As the sun pushes his fiery face above the forest the train slowly pulled into Lebanon. We have been five hours in running some 65 miles. We left the cattle cars and marched on to a common, rank with dog-fennel and smart-weed, but bare of shrub or tree to shelter from the sun, whose heat intensified as he ascended the clear sky. We looked at Lebanon with a deep interest, as we knew we were to defend it, and knew that Morgan had captured a Union force there a short time before and burned part of the town. The chimneys were standing like exclamation points after his dashing deeds.

We were ordered to stack arms and get breakfast on the dog-fennel common. It was a joyful sound to the weary and hungry, but there were a few difficulties in the way of its execution. First, there were not three men in each company, on an average, who knew how to stack arms. Adjt. Rice, the patient father of the regiment, came down the line and showed the boys how to accomplish that military feat, and soon there was a row of stacked rifles in front of the regiment, bayonets gleaming in the sun, of which the men felt proud. Ranks were broken and the next difficulty was encountered—wood and water, where were they to be had? The men displayed their native genius in this case, needing no assistance from any officer. Some went for the water and some for the wood, and they brought both.

"Well, those sticks look very much like rails," said Capt. Pinkerton to Lieut. ——, as the Lieutenant tossed half dozen dry sticks about 10 feet long from his shoulder.

"Yes, they do, Captain, but they are not," replied the Lieutenant, "they are sticks from the abolition tree which grows down here. It grows up in this shape without limbs, leaves or sap, and all you have to do is to go and get it."

"Ah, that's good; the Lord provides for all emergencies; come show me where it grows," said the Captain, "and I'll go with some of the boys and fetch a load also." And so he did. The Captain was a most devout and practical elder in the Presbyterian Church.

and quickly discerned the hand of Providence in all His works. The smoke of abolition wood ascended towards the skies, bearing the perfume of sow belly and coffee, that morning, and we must think it pleased Him who ruleth in justice, even if the old rebels did make discords on the air with their d—ns about the Yankees burning up their rails. When the coffee was poured from boilers into tin cups it was immediately covered by thousands of little weed hoppers. After vain efforts to skim them off and keep them out the men yelled out, "well, we can stand it if the bugs can," and drank it bugs and all. 'Twas death to the bugs but refreshing to the soldiers.

We remained on this common in the scorching sun, whose heat came down with a scorching, sickening power, until noon. Many were overpowered by heat and forced to seek protection from it. The diarrhœa on that day began its malignant attack on the regiment, and many became quite ill. At noon, when the stoutest began to fail, as they sweltered in their uniforms, an order was given to march, we knew not where, but were soon informed that we were to go into camp near town. We marched up through Lebanon and from the windows of some houses the stars and stripes were displayed. On this march many began to fail and their guns and knapsacks were seized and carried by their stronger comrades to enable the failing ones to keep up with the regiment. This noble charity of comrade sharing strength with comrade and bearing each others' burthens began that day in the withering heat, and lasted to the end of the war. Well we know that many noble deeds of this sort shine like gems on the pages of the recording angel's book.

At 1 P. M. we drew up in line in our new camp, were assigned grounds and ordered to pitch tents. It was Hood's Meadow, cleanly mown and reflecting the sun from the bright surface as from a mirror, intensifying the heat. Not a tree or object to give shelter was near. In the oppressive heat the weary men began to pitch tents and perform the other duties of camp—getting wood and water, digging sinks, doing guard duty, &c. Our regiment was General Dumont's whole brigade when we reached Lebanon, and had a vast deal of hard work to do, and considerable responsibility resting upon it. By night matters were in tolerable shape, and except the men who were on guard duty, there were never a lot of mortals slept more soundly. Exhaustion was about complete. We should remark that in almost every tent there was one or more sick men.

While we rest a little here let us sum up, and see if there has not been enough to make men sick. On the 16th, at Indianapolis, we were ordered to cook two days' rations, and be ready to march at noon. We had not been mustered or drawn anything. The hard work occupying day and night of the 16th and 17th has been told. Then followed the march from camp to the Indianapolis depot in new shoes and new shirts, under enormous loads, the ride to Jeffersonville, the march through Louisville, the night ride to Lebanon, the march to this camp, and the hard work of setting it in order done this afternoon—three days and nights of incessant work and hard marching, with little to eat and less sleep.

Is it a wonder we left men exhausted all along the way? Is it a wonder that numbers are sick and groaning to-night, and that some are in the hospital over there in Lebanon? There were 62 men died or discharged before the end of the first year, and most of them from the effects of that rough initiation. There is little or no grumbling; the men take it as a matter of course; they know soldiering is severe and nothing is worse than they expected; yet it wears them out rapidly. We rest, and like the old fellow who had lost his coon dog, his fish-hooks, his gun, shot pouch and powder horn, we thank the Lord that it is "no wusser with us than it is."

CHAPTER VI.

August 19th to August 23rd—At Lebanon—Camp Lucy Carson—Why we were so Hurried—Battalion Drill—Confiscation of a Tavern for a Hospital—Picket Duty and Incidents—Negroes on Picket and in Camp.

We at first called our camp in Hood's Meadow "Camp Dumont," and some letters written to our homes on the first few days we were there are dated "Camp Dumont," &c. The name was finally changed to Camp Lucy Carson, which became official. Had it been named for man, woman or angel, it would have been a villainous hot place all the same. Before we resume duties let a word be said in explanation of why we were so hurried into military birth and so hurried after born and so hastily tumbled down to this place. Buell was in full retreat before Bragg, and Morgan's raiders and other small bands of rebels, as well as non-militant rebels, were doing all they could to destroy the Union wagon trains, capture artillery and annoy and impede the progress of the retreating army. We were hurried forward to help guard the railroad over which the retreating army was receiving its supplies—for Buell didn't know how to live off of the country—to aid in checking Bragg's advance and attend to Morgan. Lebanon was an important post and must be held until our retreating army could get between it and Louisville. The enemy was making a desperate effort to flank the army of Buell and capture both Louisville and Cincinnati, and for a few days it seemed that he might succeed. It was a perilous passage in the history of the war. Troops were hurrying from other States to the rescue, and Governor Morton, ever first in filling the quotas of Indiana, had hurried forward the Seventy-Second, as one of the best of the new regiments, some weeks before it would have been sent to the front had there been no such crisis.

That General Dumont, a brave and experienced officer, was given command of us; that we constituted his sole command until, after Lebanon was reached; that we were sent to so important a point directly in the face of the enemy; that Col. A. O. Miller, another brave and experienced officer, was made our Colonel in a few days; shows what reliance was placed in our regiment in its infancy. Comrades, those of you whom God has given to survive those fiery days, and the days since the close of the service, it is some compensation to know tnat our initial service was hard because our country had to have such service or perish; and because our immortal War Governor, O. P. Morton, believed the material of the Seventy-Second to be of the best quality, and that it would stand the test of such a trial. He was not deceived.

Here we are in the very front of the army, liable to attack any moment, and have never had battalion drill, and but few of the companies have made attempts to drill. We are very raw troops—almost raw all over in our new shoes, and socks, and hog hair shirts—and rawest of all in drill. Gen. Dumont determined that he would at once give us drill enough to hold together. So on the 20th, the very next day after we got into camp, he ordered battalion drill. The company officers got their companies together as well as possible, and much better than at LaFayette, for each had been studying Hardee with all energy. Adjt. Rice formed the battalion in his quiet, exact manner, giving each officer and non-commissioned officer all the instructions possible in so short a time. He marched to his post in front of the regiment, saluted the General, and said, "the battalion is formed."

The General looked at the battalion for a little while, as he sat on his horse with drawn sword, and then sang out in nasal accent:

"Officers and non-commissioned officers to the front and centre—March!"

Capt. Heron, of Company A, and Capt. Carr, of Company B, memory serves us right, were the only officers who responded to the command and went to the front. The other officers stood in bewilderment as if willing to run or do anything else if they only knew what to do.

The General could not restrain himself and yelled at the top of his voice, "Why don't you obey the command?" No movement, and he again yelled, "Well, if you aren't the d—dst greenest set that I ever saw in all my life;" and as no one disputed his word he proceeded to belabor us more heavily. Adjt. Rice suggested that perhaps if he should go and give a little aid there would be a general response. The General told him to go and "get them up here some way or other, I want to tell them something." The Adjt. came along the line and a few words from him brought all the officers to the front, where they saluted the General and awaited his "few words." He proceeded to tell us that few of us knew anything about drilling, and to impress upon us the necessity of learning how to execute some battalion movements immediately, as we were in front of the enemy and liable to attack at any time. "A regiment can not hold together when not under fire if it has no drill," said the General, "and without it will become a panic stricken mob under fire." He then told us what our respective duties would be in a few simple movements he wished to make, and sent us back to our places. The command was given, "by the right of companies into column—March!"

Two or three companies executed the command pretty well, but all the others became as miserably tangled as a six mule team hitched up for the first time; company cut company in two; company telescoped into company; officers were cut off from their companies, and what should have been a column was a torn and tattered mob. Capt. Hanna was roaring out "here Company H, where the d—l are you?" Capt. Carr was requesting Company G to untangle and get out of Company B, while Capt. Heron, of Company A, was making similar requests of Company I, and Capt. LaFollett was hustling around like an old hen that had lost her chickens. Gen. Dumont made music to this confusion by piping out red hot oaths from his horse as he rode up and down the tangled battalion. The sun was hot, and in their confusion the officers sweat until the perspiration poured down in blinding streams over their faces. The Captains sweat most of all, because they were cursed most by Gen. Dumont. Again the battalion was placed in line, again the officers were called to the front and centre, again instructed and sent back to their places, and again the command, "By the right of companies into column—March!" was given. This time all came up pretty well. But we can not follow all the details of this first drilling. One time Capt. Hanna plunged his company through two or three others. Gen. Dumont roared out, "Capt. Hanna, what the h—ll *are* you doing?" The Capt. yelled back, "I don't know what the h—ll I *am* doing, do you know, General?" Capt. Hanna could swear just as viciously as Gen. Dumont could, and hence had some self-protection; but Capt. Hill used no oaths and was open to the terrible attacks of the General's curse batteries. One day, in executing a movement, Capt. Hill missed it altogether, and as the battalion was moving in one direction, Capt. Hill led his company off towards the woods in a north-westerly direction. Gen. Dumont sat and looked after him a moment and then yelled out, "Capt. Hill, where in God's creation are you going—out into the woods squirrel hunting?"

Another day, while on battalion drill, the General gave the command "Right wheel by companies," Capt. Hanna forgot the tactical expression, and yelled to his men, as he marched backwards in front of them, holding his sword by the two ends and wheeling it around as if his company were in his hand, "Boys, come round here like a barn door." But we can not give all the very laughable incidents of men and officers who were as green as a six mule team just learning to pull. Every day in the blazing hot sun the persevering Gen. Dumont put us through the battalion drill, and when not on battalion drill we were drilling by squad or companies. The General himself instructed the officers at his headquarters, or had Adjt. Rice do so when he could not; and once more we must say that no man could have shown more uniform patience or courtesy towards so many men with so many wants than did Adjt. Rice. In a few days we could execute the simple battalion and company movements pretty well, and Gen. Dumont said to us, "I think you could now hold together like two tom kittens tied by the tails and hung over a pole." Every officer and man was making his best efforts to learn, for we were seriously impressed that our lives and safety depended on our rapid progress in drill. And here be it said that Gen. Dumont could be as serious and civil as any one when occasion required.

The sick were increasing on our hands daily and a regimental hospital must be established where they could be properly treated. Major Kirkpatrick commanded Capt. Robinson to take a detail of men and go into Lebanon and select a proper building—such a one as Surgeon Johnson should think proper. The Surgeon selected a tavern kept by a lady whose husband was in the rebel army at that time. She was respectfully informed of the determination to convert her house into a hospital, and thereupon lost reason and raved and railed. Capt. Robinson proceeded to execute the order in a quiet but firm manner under the direction of the surgeon, and the landlady, finding she could not stop him and his men, flew to the Major, who heard her patiently until she launched into unlady like abuse of the Union soldiers, when he informed her in a sentence that was spiked, that as long as ladies keep their place and use proper language they are respected, but when they depart from either they are not, and told her to at once leave his quarters. Of course the tavern was used as a hospital as long as we remained at Lebanon, and when we left the lady was given a statement of the fact, which has no doubt been made the basis of a heavy claim against the United States Government, and perhaps she has "proven her loyalty" and gotten her money.

On the 21st, the second day after we entered Camp Lucy Carson, there was an order for 125 men and three commissioned officers to be sent out to picket the various roads. This again was bran new business of which we had heard mueh but experienced nothing. Most of those that were ordered on this duty were pleased with the idea of getting out of the hot dusty old camp, the drill and other routine, to forests and more freedom. They indeed found it quite pleasant on picket duty except when night came, and then there were incidents which made the hair crawl and the blood run cold.

Officers and men knew that the great duty on picket was to keep wide awake and a sharp lookout. The instructions were to allow citizens to pass through to Lebanon single or in numbers of two to five together, but to separate into smaller groups, or arrest and send into camp, at our discretion, any number of unarmed persons above five, especially men; and, as Gen. Dumont said one day while visiting a post, "if there are a number of women in one group, any of whom have big feet, short hair or beards, separate them from the delicate looking ones; you can't tell what the dashed rebels will be up to, and they may steal the livery of angels to steal into these lines."

After getting into the lines no one, man or woman, could pass out without a pass from provost marshal Col. Owen. This was very vexatious and caused many a stubborn old Kentuckian to roost on the picket line all night mad as a storm and too spunky to turn back and get a pass. But about 12 hours would unbend the dignity of the stoutest, and they would quietly return to Lebanon, procure a pass, return to the picket, present the paper and go through uttering a good many cheap oaths at such tyranny. The ladies were more offended at this rule, apparently, than the men, and often rallied the pickets about being afraid of women, and would remark in the most elegant Kentucky irony, "when Mo'gan was hea'h he nevah axed us fo' a pass; he was not so afea'd of Kentuckians as you ones from the

No'th." Officers were so prudent and gallant as to simply demand passes and not discuss the merits of "Mo'gan."

At night no one was allowed to pass either way without the countersign. This instruction was very strict. At headquarters, before we started out, we were solemnly instructed that we should, after night, conceal ourselves in fence corners or bushes, and if any one came near, to challenge, "Halt! who comes there?" If the answer was "a friend," then we were to demand, "advance friend and give the countersign." Holding our gun in the position of charge bayonet, at a half cock, if we had doubt of who it was, and a full cock if we had strong suspicion it was an enemy, we were to compel the person to advance near enough for the bayonet of our piece to be placed to the pit of his stomach, and then require him to lean forward over the bayonet and whisper the countersign into our ear. Very naturally there were not many friends fooling around the picket line, for friends don't like cold steel so near the seat of digestion. If on being challenged thrice there was no halt or answer of the person or thing challenged, we were to fire to kill. We say "or thing" not upon authority of headquarters, but from the fact that in actual practice cows, horses, hogs &c., were sometimes challenged and fired upon. Horses were rarely killed, hogs and cattle almost every shot.

Instructions like these necessarily led the men to be apprehensive of attempts by the enemy to get through our lines, and every unusual noise heard after nightfall created the suspicion that a sly rebel was approaching, rifle or revolver in hand, looking for a Yankee of whom to make a corpse; and it was a Yankee trick the Seventy-Second boys took to from the very start to make the other fellow a corpse.

One night a brave corporal was doing duty on picket with a squad of men. It was the first night for them all and their hair was tumbling about as lively as if they had been in the service three months and the graybacks were on a spree. They were not afraid, but very attentive to every sound. The corporal heard the tread of some one approaching, pierced the darkness with eager eye, and beheld a dark form plainly moving between himself and the sinking moon, but much nearer to himself than to the moon. "Halt! who comes there?" he called in a clear voice. The form moved on, and the challenge was repeated more imperatively, but still no halt or attention. He raised, cocked and leveled his gun, but just before the trigger was touched the old horse "nickered," as if indulging a hearty laugh at the greenness of the corporal, who, had he not known he would never hear the last of it, would have shot the old scamp for revenge.

We give a graphic and true relation of an incident on picket while at Lebanon, written by W. H. Records, of Company I:

"Just then a few *old soldiers* came to see us. These o. s.'s were very candid, as old soldiers usually are to raw recruits, and told us that just a short time before this a battle between some Union forces and Morgan's cavalry had been fought here, in which case the former were *utterly* defeated and all of the United States property taken and destroyed, and the air was full of rumors of his intended return. These things only tended to increase our apprehension, for we had not had a single battalion drill. And as discipline is one of the most essential things to the soldier to render him efficient in battle, we felt ourselves rather unequal to the occasion. While these things were weighing upon our minds with ponderous magnitude we were detailed for picket. It was our lot to be assigned to the Danville road three miles from camp, when General Dumont came to us and began to dilate upon the situation in his own peculiar style and accent, which tended in no degree to lessen our apprehension. It was represented that Morgan and his band of rebels were not very far away and were hourly expected on that road. Well, nothing of importance happened until we went out to stand our third and last "trick" for the night, when we got the order for increased watchfulness and above all to not let the enemy take us so by surprise that we would not be able to fire the signal of alarm. The night was very dark and still, and the very stillness was alarming. The intenseness of our anxeity is better imagined than described. So careful were we to note every sound that our breath was suppressed, and the rustling of leaves by some birds or little animal was magnified until it appeared to be the movement of men or the tramping of horses Then with breathless suspense and trembling nerves we stood with our finger on the trigger of our guns, when the cause of our alarm would be discovered, and we relaxed our vigilance —when hark! what's that? Horsemen coming upon the road? Yes, we can hear the clatter of their hoofs distinctly. On and on they come nearer and nearer. There were only three of us on that post, and there appeared to be a host coming upon us. We flew to the shelter of some large trees by the road side, and crouched behind their massive forms we awaited the attack. On they came nearer and heavier; when near enough one of our number called out in a clear and distinct voice, "*halt!*" They halted. Then the challenge "who comes there" was given. We were answered by a growl that told us they were of the canine instead of the human species. Fearing we could not justify our selves for firing upon dogs, and yet anxious to be revenged for the needless alarm, we charged bayonet and "put them all to flight without the loss of a single man."

Other incidents could be related of a like character, but these are sufficient to give the nature of the duty and the faithful manner in which it was performed. This picket drill under Gen. Dumont, which was continued under Col. Miller, was a fortune to us. The regiment was as wakeful as a cat and was NEVER SURPRISED, *never "slipped up on,"* during its long and eventful service. Indeed, the regiment was never fired upon day or night but what it was ready to return the fire immediately and effectively; hence it was never captured.

The negro, that singular and ubiquitous creature of the war, put in an appearance in camp and on the picket line. Men and women came to sell pies—such pies—corn bread and other negro commodities. The women came to solicit washing, sewing and mending. Almost as soon as we were in camp a mulatto woman with a daughter almost as white as any lady of the fairest complexion came around soliciting washing.

"Are you slaves?" asked one of the regiment.

"We are," replied the mother.

"Why, then, are you not at work for your master?"

"Our master is in the rebel army, and our missus has ordered us to come here and see if we can get some washing."

"Will your mistress get the money?" persisted the soldier.

"Yes, she gets the money for all we do," rejoined the mother with much embarrassment.

"Well, you give your mistress our compliments and tell her we'll see her upon a long and hot march before we'll furnish you work to support herself while her husband is in the rebel army."

"This is shameful and sinful, and heaven will avenge the outrage," said the just and sympathetic Priest. He was correct.

While there were many darkies in whose statements little or no reliance could be placed, there were others who spoke with great candor and truthfulness. They were generally densely ignorant. We heard a soldier ask one who came to the picket line why he didn't run off. He said he was afraid he could never reach the Ohio River. "Why, it's but a short distance," said the soldier; "you can walk it in two nights." The negro explained that he understood it to be a thousand miles to the Ohio, that the stream was ten miles wide, that there were a lot of terrible men with terrible dogs to catch or shoot every darkey that crossed, and that it was 20,000 miles from the Ohio to the Canada border, and many big rivers to cross, and that no black man had ever got there alive.

Some one spoke to one old and quite intelligent negro about there being so many Union people around there. He replied, "Yes, dar seems to be, massah, but it's mighty hard to tell. Ye see day keep a sesesh flag to stick out when de sesesh comes, an' a Union flag to stick out when de Union's come, and dat way day please bof sides. Days mos'ly fur Jeff Davis, now, dats a fact."

So much to introduce the negro. We shall meet him often.

CHAPTER VII.

August 23rd to August 30th, 1862—Col. A. O. Miller Takes Command—A Short Sketch of Our Colonel—Elections—First Alarm—First Prisoners—Scarcity of Water—The Mess and Sibley Tent—Are You a Preacher?

On the 23rd of August, while we were in camp Lucy Carson, Lebanon, our new Colonel, A. O Miller, joined the regiment and immediately took command. As this gallant and able officer was with us all the time, participated in all the hardships, fights and skirmishes of the regiment, it is proper to introduce him more fully, as we must meet him often.

Abraham O. Miller was born in Madison County, Ohio, October 3, 1827. His parents removed to Clinton County, Indiana, in 1830, and both died in 1833. Young Abraham found a home with David Clark, a farmer, on the Twelve Mile Prairie, with whom he lived and worked on the farm. When he grew up he determined to be a doctor and read medicine, attended and graduated from the university at Louisville, Ky., in 1856, when Gross, Flint, Yandell, Miller and others, were professors in that institution. He was never a politician, but voted for Pierce, Buchanan and Douglas, for President, before the war.

He was a true Jacksonian Democrat, holding the preservation of the Union as the sacred duty of every American citizen, and when the rebels assailed that Union, A. O. Miller, on the first call for troops, raised a company of three months men for the 10th Ind. Vol Inft., and served the full three months with it. After the battle of Rich Mountain, he made the following report:

RICH MOUNTAIN, VA., July 16, 1861

COL. M. D. MANSON—DEAR SIR:—In obedience to your order, on the morning of July the 12th, 1861, I proceeded in the rear of the cavalry down the road towards the enemy's camp. After passing the pickets of the 13th Regiment, the cavalry halted. I took Sergt. Allen and Privates Yargus, Amos and others, throwing them out on the right as skirmishers. We ascertained that the enemy had fled from their works on the hill. Being well convinced that there were no enemy in ambush from the fact that we found a large amount of camp equipage, two boxes of cannon ammunition, several horses hitched, and everything indicating that the enemy had fled, I then sent Lieut. Schertle with others to the camp; he soon reported the enemy gone; my company then took possession of the camp and some prisoners. One Surgeon Taylor informed me that Lieut Watkins wished to surrender everything to me Watkins came forward and gave me his sword, at the same time saying there were a number in camp whom he would surrender as prisoners of war. I took down the only flag I saw floating; I saw several in tents.

I left Lieut Schertle in charge of the camp and proceeded with the balance of the company to our camp left the day before, one quarter of a mile from the works. We met the German regiment of Ohio troop in their rear, and Gen. McClellan and staff. I informed the General of the condition of affairs; turned 21 prisoners and the camp over to the authorities, and further saith not.

A O. MILLER, Capt. Co. C, 10th Ind. Vol.

Gen. Manson claims that this was the first flag taken from rebel works at the commencement of the war, and that Capt. Miller and his company, of the 10th Ind., had the honor of taking it.

At the expiration of the three months' service, Capt. Miller was mustered out with a splendid record as a brave, calm, discreet officer. At the reorganization of the 10th Regiment for the three years service, he again raised a company and went into camp at LaFayette, was made Major of the regiment, went with it to the front, and in the battle of Mill Springs, Ky., was in command of three companies when the battle opened, and in the hottest of it all, and saw the rebel Gen. Zollicoffer fall from his horse when pierced by the fatal shot.

Maj. Miller was in command of the 10th Regiment from February, 1862, to the time he left it, commanding it in the Buell campaign, at the battle of Shiloh, at the siege of Corinth, and the falling back of the regiment to Winchester, Tenn., in Buell's retreat before Bragg At Winchester, the Major was informed that he had been made Colonel of the Second-Second. That was in August, 1862. He had been promoted to the Lieutenant-Colonelcy of the 10th April 5th, 1862, and as he was much attached to that regiment and was held in high esteem by his command and commanders, it was natural that he should hesitate to exchange his present and established position for a new and untried command, simply for the sake of one grade in rank.

He sought the advice of that prince of men and soldiers, Gen Geo. H. Thomas, and asked the General whether he should accept the Colonelcy of the Seventy-Second or remain Lieut. Col. of the 10th. Gen. Thomas said, "Do always what is asked of you, if it is right. Gov. Morton gave you the regiment and duty says for you to take it." This was on August 14th, 1862. With such an answer there was no parley, and the young Lieut. Col. sorrowfully bade adieu to the gallant 10th, in which he had done all his service and gained all his promotion, and returned to Indiana to resign his Lieut. Col.'s commission and accept a commission as Colonel of the Seventy-Second. This he did from a sense of duty and not desire. Yet we believe he never regretted it.

While making this important change in his military life, he thought it an opportune time to make even a more important one in his civil life, and was married to Miss Mary Zion, one of the fairest and most accomplished ladies of the State, at Lebanon, Ind., on August 21st, 1862, Rev. John L. Smith officiating. He immediately joined his regiment, reported to Gen. Dumont at Lebanon, Ky., on the 23rd of August, 1862, and assumed command. It is not amiss to say that Mrs. Miller accompanied her husband, the Colonel, to Lebanon, Ky., and that the regiment became somewhat acquainted with her and ever after took a deep interest in her welfare.

The sort of commander Col. Miller made the following pages will disclose. It had been very much desired by many in the regiment that all its officers, from the Colonel to the corporals, should be selected from its own ranks. It is but fair to say that there was a slight feeling of disappointment when a man from another regiment was made our Colonel. The fact that he was a tried and brave man was most satisfactory to the great majority The officers called and paid their respects, and the Colonel at once made the rounds of the camp, inspected it and set at rights whatever was wanting. In a few days it was conceded that we had in him the right man in the right place.

We shall be safe in asserting that soldiers look more carefully to their physical than to their spiritual wants. In the Seventy-Second both were considered of consequence. It was not long until many wished for a sutler who could supply them with some articles not furnished by Uncle Sam—for while the army rations were substantial, they did not embrace every delicacy. Those who were religiously disposed, soon met and held services, and decided that we ought to have a chaplain. There were two very good preachers in the regiment, Capt. Hill, of Company I, and Sergt. Priest, of Company E, both of whom were willing to be chaplain of the regiment. The matter was to be settled by vote of the commissioned officers, and they met on the night of August 28th, and elected Spence sutler and Louis C. Priest, chaplain. The latter was elected by a small majority, and several officers being on picket, and Company K having yet to report—for it had remained to be mustered at Indianapolis—enough votes were secured from these absent officers after their return to camp, to elect Capt. Hill chaplain, and he was soon after commissioned. With a sutler and chaplain, the regiment was not far from the kingdom.

On the night of the 29th of August, the officers met at Col. Miller's tent and elected Major Kirkpatrick Lieutenant Colonel, and Adjt. Rice, Major. Of course this action was subject to the ratification of the authorities at Indianapolis. Col. Kirkpatrick got his commission, but we know not why Adjt. Rice did not get his. But one thing we do know, it was not because he lacked in solidity of character or soldierly qualities.

A few days after we went into Camp Lucy Carson, there was alarm that Morgan was coming, and without an order the men immediately, but quietly, got their arms ready to give him a warm reception. The alarm was false, and is noted to show the spirit of the regiment. Morgan did not come, but on the 27th there were 20 live rebels brought in and put under guard, who had been captured some place in the vicinity. Our boys paid them a visit and gave them close inspection. They were the sort of fellows we were to fight, and we were anxious to measure them as accurately as possible. It may be that the poor fellows were cowed and showed to disadvantage, but it is certain that their appearance very much reduced our dread of the "Johnnies." These men were poorly uniformed, dirty, lousy, and looked absolutely "onery," as the men expressed it.

We were pretty well settled down to camp life. The greatest trouble was the water, which was bad and scarce, and as some other troops came up, including cavalry, the little springs along the branch near the camp were almost exhausted in spite of the most vigilant guard duty. For several days there was not water enough for cooking and drinking, to say nothing about bathing, and the prospects were that we should soon become as dirty as the rebel prisoners. You will remember, comrades, that this slippery soapstone water, dipped up from the little springs that stood almost boiling in the sun, felt like hot castor oil in the mouth, and it was almost impossible to swallow it. No wonder the camp diarrhœa made progress with such stuff to drink.

We will have time here, aud may never have it again, to speak of that great company institution the "Mess." Each company, for the convenience of drawing rations, cooking and tenting, was divided into four messes, and each mess had a non-commissioned officer at its head. The messes were numbered one, two, three and four. The men of the company formed their own messes on the principle of "birds of a feather." If a man was known to be disagreeable, it was pretty hard for him to get into any mess at all, and often he could not, except to get tent room. Each mess governed its own internal affairs, and could exclude from their mess what was distasteful to them, as gambling, drinking, or any manner of disorderly language or conduct.

The mess, in short, was the company family, and many of them were about as well regulated as the best of families are. To each mess for cooking there were issued three camp kettles of different sizes, three mess pans, three frying pans; a knife and fork, tin plate and tin cup to each man, and to some regiments a spoon to each man, but we got none. The men generally carried water in the larger kettle, boiled beans and s. b. in the medium sized one, and made coffee in the smallest one.

Cooking was done in various ways in different messes. Some would select a cook and do his duty, except in battle, as a compensation for his culinary services, but as a general rule it was not satisfactory. Some messes cooked by turns, each man taking a pull at it, and in some messes each man did his own cooking. We have known instances where fellows who were perpetual grumblers were compelled to cook and eat and grumble by themselves. Sometimes a lot of this sort would form a mess, which those acquainted with their grumbling proclivities would dub "the grumblers' Eden," or "the happy family." But cooking, like drilling, was soon reduced to a science, especially when the cooking utensils were reduced to a single coffee pot and frying pan to the mess.

The Sibley tent, which we first drew and held for almost a year, was a peculiar institution. Each tent was composed of 26 pieces, a yard wide at one end, tapering to a point at the other, and about six yards long. The tent was erected by placing the top of the pole into a socket in the centre of a hoop to which the narrow ends of the tent cloth were sewed; the pole was then hoisted up, taking the tent withit, until the bottom of the pole rested in a socket on the top of a tripod about three feet high, set in the centre of the place the tent was to occupy; it was then stretched, staked through the loops at the bottom and declared pitched, or "up."

To put up, take down, and newly pack, these complicated tents, was hard work and quite a trick. When up, each man was assigned a strip and one strip was used for a door. Each man had to keep his "traps" under his own strip, and sleep under it at night. It was a common occurrence to see a soldier come in and order another, "get from under my strip." When we slept, we lay with our heads to the tent cloth and our feet all pointing to the tripod in the centre. When it was cold, fires were built in the centre of the tent between the feet of the iron tripod. It was intended by the inventor of this marvelous military tabernacle that the smoke should go out at the round hole left in the top, but it generally went into the eyes and down the throats of the men.

Company K, which had remained at Indianapolis to fill up, joined the regiment at this place on the 13th of August. Gen. Dumont perpetrated so rich a joke on one of the officers of this company on the evening of its arrival, that we cannot forbear telling it. The regiment was under marching orders to move the next morning. The baggage of Company K was hauled from the cars and dumped out in the place assigned it in the regiment. Amongst other things a tremendous trunk was flopped down upon the ground. Dumont, who was standing near, eyed it a moment and asked:

"Great Cœsar, whose trunk is that?"

The officer to whom it belonged promptly answered, "General, that is my trunk."

Dumont looked at him all up and down for the quarter of a minute, and asked, "Well, sir, are you a preacher?"

"No sir, I am not. Why did you ask?" replied the puzzled possessor of the big trunk.

"Why, I didn't know but you were a preacher carrying your church around with you, and had the steeple inside. You should be a preacher."

CHAPTER VIII.

August 30th to September 5th, 1862—Our First March Towards the Enemy—Getting Ready all Night—Pressing Teams—An Officer Wants His Shirts—"Where are we Gwine, Ginr'l?"—The Oppressive Heat—Scarcity of Water—Gutting Knapsacks—Rain and Camp for Night—Return to Lebanon—Fortifying—Sickness Greatly Increases—Capt. Carr to Muldraugh's Hills with a Battalion—Return Teams to Owners and Draw Our Own.

On the afternoon of August 30th, we got orders to cook two days' rations, draw 20 rounds of ammunition, and be ready to march at a moment's warning. "Ah, there was hurrying to and fro," and the camp hummed and roared again. In addition to cooking the rations and putting them into the haversack, filling canteens with water, scouring up the guns, and the other *et ceteras* of preparation to march, letters must be written home by almost every man. It was after midnight before the camp settled to rest. The air was full of rumors that the enemy was advancing in heavy force, and at headquarters we ascertained that we would march towards Danville or Lexington and perhaps engage the enemy the next day.

We had scarcely got to sleep before reveille was sounded, and we were all up getting breakfast, which we dispatched with much speed by the light of our camp fires, for, to tell the truth, we were a little bit nervous. Breakfast over tents were struck and tied up. We were ready to load, and not a wagon, not a mule, for the regiment. Details of men and officers were made to press teams and drivers from citizens, and this consumed much time, for we had an immense amount of equipage. We smile to think of what the great tents of the men and officers—two officers' tents to each company headquarters—the great trunks of the officers, cooking stoves, camp chests, camp cots and camp stools, looked like in the fitful light of the camp fires that night. It was almost like a city with all its families and household goods turned suddenly out doors

The teams began to arrive, driven by negroes, many of them without hats, looking as astonished and frightened as if called to judgment. Here they come by dozens in a long trot or in a gallop. Loading begins and is hurried with all speed. It takes three and often four wagons to the company.

Col. Miller said to Capt. LaFollett, "How are you getting along?"

He replied in all seriousness, "Why, just *tolerably* well, Colonel. If I just had about two more wagons I think I *might* get along."

"How many wagons have you?" asked the Colonel.

"Why, only three," said the Captain.

As the veteran Colonel rode away, it was quite plain he had heard something that sounded very funny. All can see the broadness of the joke when it is stated that, on our last campaign, a single wagon was all that was allowed for a whole brigade headquarters, and a single pack mule for the whole regimental headquarters.

Following almost every team was the owner of it, praying and beseeching that it should not be taken away from him, with his slave driver also, without any sort of compensation. "My God, sah, it will ruin me," the poor fellows would say. They were assured that teams and drivers should be returned, but they must be used just now. Some went dejectedly back home feeling that their property was probably "done gone," while others actually followed the army all day.

By 7:30 A. M., after being up almost all night, we got out upon the Danville Pike and started. At this juncture a young and stylish officer hastened up to Gen. Dumont and said:

"General, I really don't see how I can go. All my best shirts are down in town to be washed and done up. I *must* get them."

The General yelled to Adjt. Rice, "Here, Adjutant, stop this army until this d—d fool goes and gets his biled shirts!"

The young man saw the temper and point of the words and evaporated.

The force now moving towards Lexington, under the command of Gen. Dumont, was composed of the 60th, Seventy-Second and 75th Regiments Indiana Infantry, Nicklan's 13th Indiana Battery, and a battalion of cavalry. Adding to this column the baggage train, it was five or six miles long. The day became intensely hot by 9 A. M., and water was very scarce. The men had filled their canteens last night, but now almost every one is dry. By 10 o'clock many of them showed signs of rapid exhaustion and began to gut their knapsacks and throw away all surplusage. Most of the citizens' clothing packed at Indianapolis was heaved out by the road side on this march, with other things ornamental.

While halted to rest a little under the shade of some trees, Gen. Dumont came riding slowly along telling the officers to stop their men from straggling for water. A large, raw-boned soldier, who had been born and bred in the vital air of freedom in a sparsely settled district, and who felt on an equality with any man that lived, because he "had been raised that way," deliberately walked to the middle of the road, laid one hand upon the mane of the General's horse, while holding his gun with the other, the breech resting upon the ground, and thus accosted the General:

"Wall, Jin'r'l, whare do you think we are goin', any how?"

Gen. Dumont looked in his face a moment, and reading its innocent verdancy, quietly beckoned him to one side of the road into a fence corner. When the General was as close to the fence as he could get, he took hold of the soldier's shoulder, drew him up close to his horse, stooped over as if to whisper confidential information into his ear, but instead of whispering, roared out in his keenest, nasal accent: "God Almighty only knows where we are going." This climax of the ridiculous scene convulsed with laughter all who witnessed it, while the General rode slowly away.

After this trip Gen. Dumont was never seen to wear his carbine, or squirrel gun, as the boys call it, and some of the men were of the opinion that he threw it away on account of the intense heat.

Water in canteens being exhausted, men began to run in every direction in quest of it, for in the heat and dust they were almost perishing of thirst. The stronger men taking a half dozen canteens would run a mile to a farm house, and often find no water when they reached it, for most of the springs were dry. By 10 A. M., the heat had become intolerable, and straggling became so general that orders were issued to stop it, for they were wearing themselves out more by running for water which they did not find, than to move along with the command and endure the thirst. The march continued until 3:30 P. M., many men giving out, some suffered sun strokes and lay by the road side unconscious, foaming at the mouth. The officers displayed their kindness that day by aiding their flagging men in carrying their guns and knapsacks. By noon it was so intensely hot that it seemed we should all perish. We never had a hotter, more trying march, than this.

At 3:30 there came up a little shower of rain, a gracious boon. When we were halted, a messenger came to Gen. Dumont and informed him that the Army of the Potomac, under Gen. Pope, had gained a great victory at Bull Run. It was something to be glad about, and we cheered lustily over it, though it turned out to be the very reverse of victory when fully heard from.

We were soon ordered into camp, after having marched 10 or 12 miles, where we built fires in a fine poplar and sugar tree grove and rested for the night We had a fine field of roasting ears at hand and but for the water, which was strongly sulphurous and tasted like gun powder and rotten eggs, we would have been very comfortable.

It had been a very severe day on the men. There were no ambulances, and all night long men who fell out through the day were arriving in camp and hunting their regiments and companies. We were up early the next morning, and after a hasty breakfast returned by the same road to Lebanon and went into camp near Camp Lucy Carson, in a wooded place. The cause of the return was the defeat of our troops at Richmond, Ky., under Gens. Nelson and Manson, by the rebels. The Union forces were severely handled, and many killed and captured.

We at once began to fortify against the enemy, of whose approach there was no longer a doubt. He was coming in force and preparations to meet him were rapidly pushed. Sickness increased rapidly after this march, some of the strongest men, who had run for water with 10 to 20 canteens, and who had seized and carried three or four knapsacks and guns of failing comrades, were taken sick, and many died or were afterwards discharged. We lay on our arms for two days and nights at Lebanon, not putting up tents, but fortifying all the time. On Wednesday and Thursday the work was pushed with great energy. The crash of falling trees was heard all day, and earth works were thrown up with great rapidity.

The day after we returned to Lebanon, Capt. Carr, with a battalion of infantry, was sent to reconnoiter and to guard the pass at Muldraugh's Hills, accompanied by Assistant Surgeon Cole. This was a

old venture, as Morgan was expected to approach from that direction.
One day Capt. Hanna was ordered to make out a detail from his ompany and report to work on the fortifications at Lebanon. The en were almost all worn out with hard work or sickness. He left them rest and gathered up a squad of negroes that were about camp, rmed them with picks and shovels and set them to work. Every ody said bully for Hanna.

On Thursday morning, the 4th of September, the baggage was un-aded and the teams and the colored drivers turned over to their espective owners, who had been waiting and watching for them, and eceived their property with great delight and struck off for home in a urry. We had drawn our own mules and wagons, and needed no onger to press teams. Before the tents were up, an order was given o prepare to march immediately, as the rebels were moving on us in great force, which we could not resist. The baggage was packed that afternoon and put on the cars for shipment to Louisville, and it was understood that the whole command would immediately move on foot for that point. Every moment of time was given to breaking the mules and fortifying; but the mule breaking business, including shoeing them, was the slipperiest job the regiment ever had on its hands. Artemus Ward could not do the subject justice in time of profound peace; and with the enemy pressing upon us in force, the subject must be dropped with a mere allusion. We regret that nature has not endowed us with that mulier genius which would give us power to write in fitting song or prose the history of that wonderful creature, the army mule. Some day a historian or poet may arise equal to the subject, and then will the mule be exalted to his proper rank and dignity, and the scrolls of fame will bear the name of another immortal author. The coming mule historian or poet must have been a mule driver, and write from association and sympathy. And no doubt this accounts for the fact that, in all his poems, the poet of the Seventy-Second sang not of the mule in a single line.

CHAPTER IX.

From September 6th to September 22nd, 1862—From Lebanon to Lebanon Junction—First Long Roll—In Arms All Day—Rebels Momentarily Expected—Compliments from Our Commanders—Company A sent to Muldraugh's Hills—Extensive Fortifications and Constant Drill—Capt. Carr and Battalion Return—"A Sutler and a Jew"—Part of Our Brigade Captured at Mumfordville—"No Traveling on Sunday!"—Orders to Move and Destroy Commissary and Quartermaster's Stores—Company A Comes in—Lie in rain All Night—Move to Shepardsville—Capture of Prisoners—Major Kirkpatrick Drills the Battalion.

On Friday morning, the baggage of the regiment was sent to Louisville, the regiment got ready to move, but was held until the next day, when it boarded the cars and evacuated Lebanon, leaving just at sundown, September 6th. We made a rapid run, arriving at Lebanon Junction at 11 of the night, and were ordered to get out and lie on our arms. The order was executed with some confusion, and the regiment lay near the railroad track and slept until morning. Breakfast was eaten, and the companies went out to drill in different directions, when, about 10 o'clock, the long roll was beaten furiously, and the companies re-assembled in hot haste. As the long roll was beaten in each regiment, it is impossible to describe the confusion it caused in the men making haste to gather around their respective regimental standards. The Seventy-Second was speedily formed in line, with Col. Miller at its head, awaiting orders, in just 15 minutes from the time the long roll was first sounded. Splendid time for a new regiment which had never heard the long roll before. As we stood in line we could see the General's orderlies flying from one regiment to another, and could hear the Colonels of other regiments hurrying their men into line. Col. Miller called his officers together and spoke a few words to them of the necessity of being cool and setting a good example for their men. Gen. Dumont rode up and told us to follow him, and we did so. As we marched up the railroad, we passed the 60th Ind., an old regiment which was just falling into line, although they got the alarm before we did. We moved up opposite the Junction depot and took our position on the right of the line facing north-east, with a battery in our rear as support. We threw forward two companies as skirmishers and awaited the attack. It was reported that the rebels, 7,000 strong, had got between us and Louisville, and were moving on our position. It was not possible to ascertain the exact cause of the alarm until 2

P. M., when the cavalry came up and informed us that the alarm was caused by three or four hundred rebel cavalry making a dash on Shepherdsville, 12 miles north of us, capturing the garrison and burning the railroad bridge over Salt River at that place. This was done by part of Morgan's men. They didn't care to visit Dumont's camp, but retreated with all speed on the Bardstown road as soon as their mischief was done.

As soon as the cause of alarm was ascertained, Gen. Dumont rode to our regiment, massed us in column, and made us a speech congratulating us on the promptness with which we got into line in the morning, and for our cool and soldierly bearing throughout the day. He had told us on the hot drill ground of Camp Lucy Carson, some 20 days ago, that we were the dad-dastedest greenest set he ever saw. He remembered it, too, and now he said emphatically "you are not so green a set, after all, but behaved like veterans."

This speech was received with hearty applause. It took all the old stings out. It mollified every bruise. It went like strength to the marrow. It was the expression of confidence by an old and tried soldier. When we arrived in camp, Col. Miller also made a few remarks, commending our promptness and cool bearing, and we again cheered. These two little speeches by these two brave veteran soldiers did us a vast deal of good. From that day forth we felt that we were a fighting regiment, and averaged our fighting weight pretty high. We were dismissed to get supper and rest with stacked arms. It was almost sundown; we had been in line of battle almost the entire day, and yet no regiment ever felt more cheerful and happy. We had worn the green off. We were soldiers now and no mistake, and had the approval of our commanders. What an advance in less than a month!

We spoke of a battalion going from Lebanon to Muldraugh's Hills on the 3rd, under command of Capt. Carr, of Company B, to picket the pass through it. The distance was six miles. The battalion was drawn up in line on report of Morgan's approach, but he did not come. On the 4th, the battalion marched to Raywick, arriving at midnight. The Captain called on a wealthy old farmer named Cecil, and inquired for forage and provisions, but found him very ignorant in regard to them, until he was told, with more cunning than truth, that we were a part of Morgan's command on our way to surprise the Yankees at Lebanon. This brought the old gentleman down, and smiling he told us to help ourselves to all we wished, and coolly informed us that he had just been praying for Morgan's success. Our boys were not sparing with the poultry, which the darkies, who understood the joke, cooked in style. The battalion, after refreshments, proceeded to Chicago Station, took cars and joined the regiment on the night of the 6th.

On Mondav morning, September 8th, Gen. Dumont set forward fortifications all along our line, which was literally all around the Junction for a circumference of about four miles. The 68th, Seventy-Second and 75th Ind. Infantry regiments, and the 98th Ill. Infantry, were organized into a brigade at this point, Gen. Dumont in command. Work and drill was systematically pushed, only time being given for meals and sleep. No set of harvest hands were ever busier. When the men had not axes, mattocks or spades in their hands, felling trees or digging trenches, they had their muskets in their hands learning to handle them effectually. The spirit of energy and pride was fully aroused, and the noble fellows bore their toil with high courage. About as soon as we arrived at Lebanon Junction, Company A was detailed to guard the tunnel at Muldraugh's Hills, and at once left for that point, about nine miles from the Junction.

That we were becoming very military, is shown by this incident. One day, a Lieutenant of Company H was sent with a detail to report to Gen. Dumont. Each man had an axe on his shoulder. As the Lieutenant, who felt the pressing dignity of his office, marched his men up to the General's headquarters, the doughty chief was sitting on a stool in front of his tent watching the details from the various regiments as they came up and reported. Our Lieutenant halted his detail in front of the General and called out, "Attention battalion! right dress!" Dumont sent him to his company to study the tactics. This same detail were felling trees for dear life that day, and as a man of Company H had just bit the last stroke on a monarch of the forest, and it was fast bending to the earth, he noticed an old man dressed in citizens' clothes, on a black horse, gawking around, and saw the tree must certainly kill him unless he quickly got out of the way, and roared out, "You d—d old fool, get out of that." One of his comrades just then recognized the man on horseback as Gen. Dumont, and informed the man who had called him the unsavory name who it was. As the General rode up, the man stood like a condemned criminal, and the General reproved him thus: "Why the h—l didn't you let it fall on me if I am such a fool as to be a drone in this busy hive."

Hornaday, of Company F, said the rebel farmers at the Junction were glad that we came, as we cleared all their land for them, and that Company F, having been raised with axes in their hands in the woods, were just at home here. We may say that we had a very good schooling in fortifying at this point, which was of importance to us ever afterwards. There were rumors on all sides that the rebels were closing in on us, but we kept on working. Water was very scarce and very bad, and the soldiers suffered severely from thirst. Almost every drop used was carried two miles from a branch of the Salt River, and was so filthy and muddy that it could scarcely be used.

If the water was bad, the living was pretty good. By some means the men found such things as chickens, turkeys, geese, pigs, milk, mutton and vegetables, besides more than full rations. The citizens in the vicinity had a good supply of produce, and the men had been paid large sums of money at Indianapolis, and why should they not live well. In this camp they "got the hang" of army life; their association with older regiments no doubt helped them, and from that date they never stood in need of anything where anything was to be had.

Orders issued by Gen. Dumont were very strict to arrest every person found about the picket lines who had not a pass from himself. One day a little Jew was picked up on the lines. He could give no account of himself, except that he was "selling tings to de poys." He was taken before Dumont, who heard a statement of his arrest near the picket line and his excuse for being there.

"What is your occupation, sir?" demanded the General in his most emphatic nasal accent.

"I am a sutler," stammered he, trembling like an aspen.

"What is your nationality—that is, to what people do you belong?" continued the General with increased severity.

"I am a Jew," replied the little fellow.

"Great God! A sutler and a Jew! Here, officer of the guard, take him out and hang him. If it hadn't been for just such d—d cusses as he is, our Lord Jesus Christ would have been alive and well until this day!"

The sentence was emphasized by the General bringing his clenched fist down on the table. The officer of the guard led the trembling victim out of the General's tent, and told him he had better make his way to Louisville as fast as possible before the General's order was executed, and he went like a scared hare.

On the 14th, Sunday, we heard that our forces at Mumfordville, south of the Junction about 40 miles, had been attacked by the rebels, and we were ordered to hold ourselves in readiness to go to their relief ata moment's notice. On Monday we learned that our forces had repulsed the attack; but asked General Dumont for re-inforcements, thinking they could hold their position with a little aid. On account of our position in the line, we were ordered to remain, and the 60th and the 68th Ind. Infantry, and two guns of the 13th Ind. Battery, were sent, arriving on the morning of the 17th, just in time to be captured before they got off the train, as our forces had been completely surrounded and overpowered, and forced to surrender just at daylight Gen. Dumont, who followed the above named regiments on a special train, got in sight in time to see them surrender to the rebels, and ordering his engine reversed with all speed, he returned to the Junction with his hair bristling, and swearing like a steam whistle at the loss of so many men of his brigade in such a contemptible way.

We must give place to another anecdote. On the 14th, Sunday, while the excitement was high over the report of the fighting at Mumfordville, and the troops under marching orders, an old citizen came to the depot where Gen. Dumont had his headquarters. The citizen first addressed Capt. Braden, the General's Adjutant, a very fine looking military man, and asked if he could get a pass to go over the lines to attend church that day. The Captain referred him to the General, who sat on a stool in the sun, leaning up against the side of the building, his legs and arms crossed, his head bowed and eyes shut. In his white hat, white coat and neuter colored pants, he looked more like a whippoorwill than a military commander.

"General, this man wishes a pass to go over the lines to church," said Capt. Braden.

"He does, eh?" drawled the General, raising his head a moment and taking in the man with a glance out of one half open eye, and added, "Well, sir, why do you want to go to church in this country?"

The citizen said, "Well, sah, Gin'ral, my favorite preacher preaches at de church jist acrost de lines down thar. I want to hear him moughty bad. I'll jist go and come right back arter church is out, and not tell nuthin' to nobody ef you'll let me have a pass."

The General seemed to have gone to sleep during this brief speech of the religious Kentuckian, and after it was ended, made no manner of movement. The citizen stood before him for a minute and a half, and getting no answer, ventured once more to ask, "Gin'ral, can I have de pass?"

Again slightly raising his head and half opening one eye, he answered in his emphatic nasal: "No sir, you can't; we are religious ourselves at these headquarters, and e-gad we don't allow any traveling on Sunday."

On the 17th we received orders to prepare to march immediately; the rebels were reported at Elizabethtown, and rapidly moving towards Louisville, and we had to evacuate the Junction. We burned all the camp and garrison equipage of the captured regiments, including their wagons. The men just loaded themselves with sugar, coffee, &c., before these stores were burned. We remained under arms at the Junction all day the 17th and all night. It began to rain early in the night and gave us a thorough drenching.

While we lie here in the rain wondering if Capt. Heron and Company A were not captured by the rebels, we have a moment to look after their welfare. They had several very pleasant days at the Muldraugh's Hills Tunnel. Peaches, chickens, potatoes, and all the means of subsistence, were cheap, and could be had on very reasonable terms, and the company was exempt from the hard work of fortifying in progress at the Junction, and had about come to the conclusion that they would be willing to take a contract to put in their term of service at that place. Their minds were changed, however, on being made certain that the enemy was approaching in force, and receiving orders from Col. Miller to come on the next train. They made fully ready to board the train, but it went thundering through, and heeded not their shouts and signals, leaving them to foot it or be gobbled. They didn't choose to be gobbled, and proceeded to foot it through the heavy rain. They had to wade Salt River in the night, and after a hard march of nine miles, came in to the Junction at 2 o'clock of the night, wet, muddy all over, and as tired and hungry a set of mortals as ever one saw. They had lost a good deal of baggage, mostly by falling down in the river on the slick stones. The Captain lost his blankets and tent. The company got in just in time to take the train for Shepardsville with the regiment.

On Thursday morning, September 18th, we left the Junction and moved on the cars 12 miles to Shepardsville, on the Salt River, 18 miles south of Louisville. Gen. Dumont reported to Louisville to take command of a division, and Col. Miller took command of the brigade. At this place, Gen. Granger joined us with two regiments. Reports of the crushing advance of the enemy was the camp talk. The fact of our terrible defeat at Bull Run had gradually become known, and also that the enemy were besieging Covington, Ky., and Cincinnati, with some prospects of capturing them, while all the citizens were pressed in to their defence. From all points the news was unfavorable, and well calculated to inspire a feeling of gloom amongst the troops.

On the 21st, Col. Miller sent a scouting party to reconnoiter, which. making a dash on Lebanon Junction, captured and brought back 20 prisoners. This achievement overbalanced all the bad news we had heard, and as we once more gazed on these rebels, miserable in their dirt, we felt the blood rise to the point which said, "we can flog a world full of such fellows." It was at this point the chaplaincy question was decided, and Capt. Jesse Hill resigned to become chaplain of the regiment, having been duly elected.

Maj. Kirkpatrick was as brave and generous a man as ever buckled on a sword, but military tactics, to use his own words, always "got away" with him. He was resolved to conquer, and when Col. Miller assumed command of the brigade at Shepardsville, the Major was left in command of the regiment. He had never had charge of the regiment on drill or on dress parade, and on the evening of Sunday, the 21st, Adjt. Rice formed the battalion under his eye, saluted him and said, "the parade is formed," and marched immediately to the rear and right of the Major. It was the military custom for the commanding officer to put the regiment through the manual of arms, then call the commissioned officers to the front and centre, and give them any instructions he might have, and after the officers returned to their places, the parade would be dismissed, each company, returning to its quarters, where the commanding officer would give the company any special order he had to communicate before the company was dismissed. Well, Maj. Kirkpatrick stood before the battalion in full uniform, even to the buckskin gauntlets, drew his sword and assumed command quite soldier-like. He looked at the battalion a little while, then glanced around at Adjt. Rice, who moved his lips a little, and the Major looked back at the battalion and shouted:

"Order arms!" and kerthump went the butts of the guns upon the ground, for we were pretty good in drill already.

The Major again glanced from the battalion to the Adjutant, and again shouted:

"Shoulder arms!" and up went every piece in a twinkling. Again the Major glanced at the Adjutant, whose mouth moved, and the Major commanded:

"Right shoulder——," then he paused for some time and turned to the Adjutant and said, "What's the balance, Rice?"

This raised a good laugh, in which none joined more heartily than the jovial man the joke was on, and who quietly told the Adjutant to dismiss the parade.

CHAPTER X.

September 22nd to September 30th, 1862—From Shepardsville to Louisville—500 Men on Picket Duty Eating Sweet Potatoes—Rumor that we were Captured—Moving Through Louisville all Night—City Crowded with Troops, Artillery and Wagons—500 More Men on Picket and More Sweet Potatoes—Fortifying Through Cave Hill Cemetery—Buell's Troops Coming in—Bragg Asks Buell to Surrender and is told to go to ——. —Men, Women and Children in Fright Flee the City—Gen. Nelson Killed—Gov. Morton Comes to see us—Incorporated into the Army of the Ohio.

On the 22nd of September, we took cars and went to Louisville, a detail marching through on the dirt road, felling trees across it and making it in every way difficult for the rebels to travel. We marched through Louisville for the second time in a little over a month, and were again greeted very cordially by the citizens as we marched through the city to our camping grounds on the Louisville & Portland Horse Railroad. On the very next day, a detail of 500 men went out on picket duty under Maj. Kirkpatrick down below the city, near the Ohio River, and were not relieved until on the 25th. As we took rations for but 24 hours, we were forced to shift a little for the extra time, but experienced no serious difficulty in so doing, as sweet potatoes were plenty and we boiled them by the bushel in a big kettle which a lady near the post kindly lent us, and which we religiously left. It was too big to carry.

Our regiment had been the last one to get in from the south, and fears were entertained that we were captured, and a rumor got afloat to that effect, which caused our friends at home some uneasiness. Louisville was now all in commotion. As soon as we returned from picket we removed to a new camp in the night. We started soon after supper, and were all night making about eight miles. The streets were so jammed and packed with wagons, artillery, ambulances and men, that it was impossible to make any sort of progress; we were not more than started until we were halted, and the whole night we were marching a few rods and halting several minutes or an hour, until the men were almost worn out and their patience exhausted.

As day begun to dawn, the Seventy-Second was marched out into a potato field full of rank weeds and told to lie down and rest. They did so, but the stench was horrible, yet so tired were the troops that they could not be dainty, and rolled up in their blankets and slept soundly until sun up, when they were called up to go into regular camp. The stench which came up from the ground was caused by its having been carelessly occupied by troops for a day or two before.

We went into camp at the head of Broadway, near Cave Hill Cemetery, put things in tolerable order, but in a few hours 500 more men were detailed for picket duty, which left but a few hundred in camp. This was the last time that 500 men were ever detailed at one time from our regiment for picket duty. In six months from that time there were not 500 men fit for duty in it.

When we returned from picket duty, we made another move and went into camp, forming a part of the outer line of Buell's army, which was rapidly fortifying for the defence of the city. The fortifications were constructed directly through the beautiful Cave Hill Cemetery without regard to graves.

The old troops were now arriving from the south; members of the 10th, the 40th, the 61st, and other regiments in which we had acquaintances. They came to see us and were dirty, lousy and foot-sore from their long forced march. They told us some tremendous yarns of their sufferings and adventures during the retreat, which we didn't more than half believe at the time, but think all true now.

Bragg had sent in a demand for Buell to surrender, and had received as reply to "go to Hill's," and pushed his fortifying with more vigor, and extended and strengthened his lines as his veteran troops arrived. Men, women and children, in a panic of fright, were fleeing from the city, and Louisville was in a howling uproar, filled with troops, teams, dust, and clatter-bang of arms. On the evening of the 28th, firing of cannon from some point of our fortifications led to the rumor of an attack, and again every man of the Seventy-Second quietly examined his gun and saw that it was ready for service. Buell was determined not to be surprised, and for several nights we were called up at 3 A. M., and made to lie on our arms until 5 A. M., in the chilly morning air. This was very trying on the men who had hard duty drilling and working on their fortifications every day They did grumble at it, and no wonder; the order was utterly useless if the approaches to the city were properly picketed. But even Generals learned slowly, and wore out thousands of men in learning a very little.

On the 29th, news spread through our regiment that Maj.-Gen. Wm. Nelson had been assassinated by Jeff. Davis. This caused great excitement and confusion, as it was at first understood that Jeff. Davis, President of the Southern Confederacy, had slipped in and murdered the General, who was regarded as one of the ablest Union commanders. We presently got the story straight and understood that Gen. Jeff. C. Davis and Gen. Nelson had quarreled, and the killing grew out of it. We were too busy to have a continued interest in the matter, and as soon as we found that the head of the Southern

Confederacy was not in the city, we proceeded with fortifying, drilling and cooking.

While we lay at Louisville, Gov. O. P. Morton visited the city and every regiment from Indiana, inquiring into their wants and making notes of them that he might have supplied to the extent of his ability. He visited the Seventy-Second and was heartily received. He was much pleased to learn of our improvement in discipline, but very much concerned to learn that sickness was thinning our ranks so rapidly.

At this city we were incorporated into the Army of the Ohio, in the 12th division, 40th Brigade; the division under the command of Gen. Dumont, and the brigade under the command of Gen. Granger.

CHAPTER XI.

September 30th to October 5th, 1862—To the Mouth of Salt River on Boats—March to Elizabethtown, 21 Miles, in Good Order and Complimented by Our Colonel—Carrying a Grind Stone—To Elizabethtown—What we Come for—Return to West Point—Slow Crossing of Salt River—Hard and Cruel March by Gen. Granger and Many Give Out—Tenderness of Comrade for Comrade—Return to Louisville—Friends Come to see us—"The Lord will give the Boys Manna and Quails."

On the 30th of September, Tuesday morning, we were ordered to prepare three days' cooked rations for our haversacks and take five days' raw rations in our wagons, and prepare to move right for the mouth of Salt River, on the Ohio, at a moment's notice. Our regiment was becoming accustomed to this sort of orders and obeyed with promptness. We had all things in readiness some time before the order to move was received. At 10 A. M., the command to march was given, and leaving the camp in charge of those not able to go, to guard it until our return, we set out in high cheer, glad to get out of the dust and confusion of the city, and most of all to escape the vexatious and useless order of lying on our arms from 3 to 5 A. M. A march of seven miles brought us to the landing opposite New Albany, Ind. The 74th and 75th Ind., 98th Ill. and 13th Ind. Battery, were with us. After long waiting on the landing, we boarded the steamer Excelsior and went grinding down the Ohio, for the river was so low that the keel of the vessel could be heard rasping over the gravel almost constantly. At 9:30 the brigade disembarked from the steamers, climbed to the top of the bluff at the little town of West Point, and rested several hours, if lying on sharp rocks can be so called.

Our wagons and battery had come through from Louisville to this point under escort of cavalry, and early on the morning of October 1st, we started for Elizabethtown. The day was pleasantly cool, water was tolerably plenty; we marched on a pike, halting a little for rest about every two hours, and at night we went into camp near Elizabethtown, having marched 21 miles. The regiment was in excellent condition, few men having fallen out, and almost every gun was stacked. This so pleased Col. Miller, that he complimented us highly the next morning, when we formed to resume the march, assuring us that the march had been severe, and that veteran soldiers could not have made it in better time or condition. Many of our feet were blistered all over the bottoms. During the march, we often heard men remark, "there, I felt another blister smash on the bottom of my foot," but they neither winced nor halted, but marched right on. Just before going into camp, Capt. Robinson jocosely accused Wm. Relph with being almost "played out." William denied the charge, and to prove that his vim was abundant, he seized a grindstone weighing about 100 pounds, which stood near a house we were passing, and carried it three quarters of a mile into camp. He was always known after this exploit as Grindstone Bill.

The next morning we marched to Elizabethtown and halted for some time. We had come down to aid in protecting Buell's army train as it made its way to Louisville, the troops having beaten the train in the race and left it somewhat exposed to Bragg's advancing force. We learned that the train we came to guard into Louisville was passing up next to the Ohio, and we about faced and marched towards the mouth of Salt River again, over the same road we had trodden the day before. Our feet had become very sore and our joints jammed. A pike is very hard to march over, and we began to feel its effects, but our pluck was uppermost and the regiment was kept in remarkable good order. Of course a dash from Bragg was probable at any moment, and all was kept solid for his reception.

On the evening of that day, a soldier of the Seventy-Second went into a front yard, seized a bee hive, threw it on his shoulder and ran away with it, while the bees swarmed in a cloud about his head and streamed out from behind like smoke from the stack of a locomotive. He succeeded in getting the hive from the bees and safe into camp with him. That night the odor of honey mingled with that of coffee and s. b. on the balmy air of the Kentucky autumn.

On the 3rd of October, we marched to the 21 mile stone, within four miles of West Point, and had an hour or two to wash and repair our blistered feet and bathe our dirty flesh. The next morning we drew half rations, for we were entirely out, and resumed our march. There was a long delay at West Point in crossing the Salt River, over which was but one little pontoon for all the trains. At 1:15 we finally succeeded in getting over and taking up the line of march on the river road for Louisville. We didn't get to go back on boats as some expected. This afternoon we marched very rapidly, passing over about three miles to the hour on the average, and moving 19 miles before going into camp. With their sore feet, jammed joints and short rations, this was a very hard march on the troops, and to add to its hardships, water was not to be had. When we went into camp on the banks of the Ohio, 21 miles from where we had started, many of the best men were left behind, and not more than two-thirds of the guns were stacked. Water was hard to get, but with great resolution those who got into camp began to get coffee for themselves and for their comrades who had fallen behind, and whom they expected to come up almost famished.

We cannot refrain from speaking of this brotherly and devoted attachment of comrade to comrade, on such a march as this, when a soldier like Bob Cann would say to his messmate Tom Bailey, "Well Tom, I'm played; I'm bound to stop and rest; I'll come up with you in camp to-night if possible;" then Tom would not only get coffee and supper for himself when he got into camp, but also for his exhausted comrade; would manage to keep it warm, and would also prepare the softest possible place for him to sleep when he should arrive. This is but a specimen of the universal noble conduct of messmate with messmate under all such circumstances. And no husband or son ever came in sight of the light in the window, set there by a mother's hand, on a cold, dark, wet night, with more certainty that fire and food and cheer were ready, than did the weary soldier who came in sight of the camp fires of the Seventy-Second after a day's march like this. The devotion to each other was not only brotherly, it was, in its warmth and beauty, motherly.

For hours after going into camp that night, the weary comrades came limping in to find that their messmates had prepared refreshments for them. This uselessly hard march was no fault of Col. Miller. It was a useless exploit of folly by Gen. Granger. He could kill more troops by marching than the enemy could by fighting. At 4 o'clock the next morning, reveille sounded, and we were up and off after a hearty breakfast; making another forced march, we reached Louisville at 11 A. M., having moved 15 miles in six hours. The last part of this march was conducted by Col. Miller. He knew how to handle troops, and would halt them for a short rest every hour and a half or two hours, making as much speed in a given time as Granger did who never halted for rest.

We find that all comrades who kept notes of our movements during our service concur in saying this was the hardest marching we ever did, and that it was as useless as it was cruel. The immediate result was many sunstrokes and exhaustion, followed by sickness of long duration, discharges and deaths.

On this march we had no tents; slept in the open air; were marched hard, ran short of rations, and tasted soldier life fully and stood the test splendidly. When we got back, we were almost as dirty as the old soldiers, and could almost tell yarn about with them. Buell was all in safe now, and the next thing was to be besieged by Bragg or to get out after him, smash him up or force him back.

We found many of our citizen friends from home in the camp when we returned, amongst them Mrs. Maj. Kirkpatrick and Mrs. Col. Miller. But some, not being able to hear from us, and not knowing when we would return, had left their presents and regards, and returned home. All these noble friends brought something to make our soldier life more comfortable—articles of wearing apparel, home made socks, one of the greatest comforts to the soldier's feet, fresh butter, fresh home made bread, cakes, and all the dainties that the good hands and noble hearts of the loved ones at home could prepare. To us these presents were at once strength and comfort to muscle, mind and heart. To know that those at home were thinking of and praying for us, was half the battle to many a soldier.

Of course our Indiana friends went to Gen. Dumont to inquire about us, and the General kindly gave them all the information he had, and said he didn't know just when we would get back to camp.

"Why, General," said one of the citizen visitors, "They only took three days' rations in their haversacks and have now been out almost five days. What *will* they do for something to eat?"

That brought out the General's most ironical nasal, and he replied with a most puzzled expression: "Lord have mercy on them, my friends, I hadn't thought of this until you suggested it. I don't see what those honest, innocent Seventy-Second fellows will do for something to eat. May be the Lord, in his goodness, will rain down some manna or blow some quails into the camp for the boys!"

The citizen saw the point and quietly stole away.

CHAPTER XII.

October 6th to October 18th, 1862—General Forward Movement—Trunks Sent Home—March to Shelbyville—First Graybacks—Songs for the Rebels and Darkies—Hard March for Frankfort—Skirmish on Entering the City—First Rebel Blood—Into Camp near the Cemetery—400 Men for Picket—March to Versailles—Capture of Rebel Soldiers.

Arrived at Louisville, October 5th, we found most of the troops gone, and learned that they had marched in the direction of Bardstown. The streets we left so thronged, were almost empty. As soon as we got into camp, orders came to cook two days' rations for our haversacks, to put four days' raw rations into our wagons, and be ready to move early next morning. We had enough of Louisville and were anxious to be off after Bragg, as we heard he was retreating. Our only dread was that horrible Gen. Granger, who had almost worn us out on the Elizabethtown march.

The very important order was also issued that line officers should dispense with trunks, .and they all brought carpet bags and sent their "meeting houses" home, steeples and all. One trouble with Buell had been too much baggage train, too few ambulances. We were to have less baggage train and more ambulances from this time. It was a most important step in the right direction.

On October 6th, about noon of as beautiful a Fall day as one ever saw, we shouldered our knapsacks and guns, and marched out on the Louisville & Frankfort pike, through a delightful country. We understood that we were going to Shelbyville, some 32 miles distant. Our march was again very rapid that afternoon, and we made 17 miles before going into camp on Floyd's Fork of Salt River. The water was very bad at this camp. Many men whose feet had been skinned on the Elizabethtown march, had to fall out, but fortunately, now, and for the first time since we entered the service, we have ambulances with us to aid the men in keeping up with their regiments.

On the 7th, the march was resumed, and we reached Shelbyville at 4 P. M., and went into camp on the grounds which a rebel force had occupied a few days before. We found, to our horror, before morning, that the ground was alive with graybacks—the name given by the soldiers to the army body louse. We had seen old soldiers picking them out of the bristles of their hog hair shirts, but we had never enjoyed that distinction, being "too new." After this night we were veterans, having received the finishing touch on that camp ground, and you ought to have seen us scratch. From that night we could tell as big a yarn as any veteran, and do as much scratching to the square inch.

On the 8th, we formed and marched up into Shelbyville, where we remained until 1 P. M. While here the boys sang many patriotic songs, to the great annoyance of some bitter secessionists, near whose house we were halted. The one that made them maddest was:

> Say, darkies, hab you seen de massah
>   Wid de mufftache on him face,
> Go down de road some time dis mornin',
>   Like he's gwine to leab de place?
> He seen a smoke way up de ribber,
>   Whar de Linkum gun-boats lay,
> He took his hat an' left berry sudden,
>   An' I 'spec he's rund away!
>
> De massa run? ha! ha!
>   De darkey stay? ho! ho!
> It mus' be now de king-um am a commin, an' de yar ob Jubilee!

This song delighted the darkies who had flocked to see us, as much as it exasperated the white rebels, and it was too funny to see the rebels raving in front yards, on porches or at windows, while around the corners of the houses the darkies were rolling their great white eyes, bending their bodies and beating their woolly heads in deliriums of joy and laughter. They at once caught the melody and spirit of the song, and for their sake it was sung about a dozen times, and the tune stayed with them, and most of the words, too.

When the brigade did start it went almost in a run, as if our little Gen. Granger had just aroused from a sleep, and realized that he was some miles behind. On we went over the hard pike at the rate of three and a half to four miles an hour, halting but briefly once or twice until 10 o'clock of the night, when we were ordered to get over into a field, lie down on our arms, and go to sleep, which we speedily did. We knew we were within six miles of Frankfort, and at that place, report had it, we would meet the rebels strongly fortified and be stoutly resisted by them. It is no boast to say that we were willing to meet the rebels, if it was their pleasure, and many expected it would be their pleasure to keep us out of Frankfort, and we knew if they made a stand at that place after burning the bridge, the city would have to be shelled and battered with artillery, as the river and bluffs would make it impossible to charge and take it at the point of the bayonet.

After resting about three hours, we were called up by the long roll, told to see that our guns were ready for action, and hurried off.

Many of us were so stiff and foot sore, having lain down hot in the chill of the night, that we shuffled along like ducks after over eating pumpkin seeds. We could hardly lift our poor swollen, blistered, peeled feet, from the ground, or step more than 15 or 18 inches.

Soon after we started, the cavalry dashed by, and soon after that we heard the roar of cannon and a slight clatter of small arms in front. Our patriotic hair bristled, our blood had a quicker circulation, and we were ordered to take a double quick step, and did it at a lively rate, forgetting all about our sore feet for the nonce, not from fear but desire for the fray. (Historic lie-sense allows the last statement.) We got in sight of the bridge over the Kentucky River at break of day. It was a long, covered structure; our cavalry had charged upon the rebel pickets as the battery let a few shots fly over the city, and the rebels cut sticks and left "berry sudden," and ran away, leaving a considerable part of their effects behind them.

One rebel was killed in the charge on the bridge, and the blood was dark on the floor and the sides of it. This was the first rebel blood we saw. After sleeping around upon the pavements and cellar doors until about 8 A. M., we were marched to the top of a high hill east of town. near the beautiful cemetery, and went into camp. Our camp ground overlooked the city, which is built on a little table land on the river bank, at the foot of towering hills that fence it in; and we could look right down into the penitentiary walls and see the convicts in their striped clothes at work.

On the afternoon of this same day, October 8th, the Seventy-Second furnished 400 men for picket, and it took so many of those able for duty that battalion drill was not possible until the pickets came back to camp. Our ranks were visibly thinned, and many of those ablest of body when the regiment was first formed, had gone to the crowded hospitals, and some to the grave. Over-marching had done a terrible and sad work. While there was no large force of rebels in that section, there were many small bands, and skirmishing often occurred as we were establishing our picket lines.

On this day also the battle of Perrysville was fought, and though full forty miles away, we could hear the roar of the artillery.

On the 11th of October, we were ordered to get ready to move as lightly as possible, with two days' cooked rations in haversacks. It was now evident that when any rapid movement was to be made, the Seventy-Second had to participate. We were also fully posted as to what these orders to move light at a moment's notice, with cooked rations, meant, and we laid aside every weight, and big knapsacks, which so easily upset us, and, each with a single blanket rolled up as hard as a cable and swung around the shoulders, his gun, haversack, canteen and tin cup, were ready before the order to move came, and quietly resting to the last moment. What a change from the first order to march, at Lebanon, when it took some fifty teams to haul our camp equipage, and when we almost wore ourselves out getting ready, and were tired when we started. Here we all were, in an hour after receiving marching orders, fully ready and serenely waiting, and not a team to accompany us, save a few ambulances.

At 2 P. M., the order "March!" was given, and we moved out on to the Versailles pike and faced for that town. We sailed along at a rate of over three miles the hour on a solid pike and through a splendid country, part of the blue grass region. It was understood that our brigade was to make a dash on the rebel force at Versailles. Before 6 P. M., we entered the town, having marched 14 miles in four hours, and hardly a man fell out by the way. All the rebel soldiers that were able, fled the town at our approach, but we captured 300 sick and convalescent rebel soldiers and paroled them. We mingled with and talked freely to these prisoners, and most of them expressed themselves as glad to be captured. They represented the condition of the South as deplorable. The supply of food and all other supplies in most of the rebel states were about exhausted. Bragg had forced his way north, hoping to invade Indiana and Ohio, plunder food, horses, &c, from them, to get heavy reinforcements from Kentucky, Indiana and Ohio, dishearten the North, and compel the Union Government to ask for an armistice and a compromise. Instead of accomplishing his purpose, he was being driven back at every point, and his army, so lately full of vim, courage and expectation, was now on the retreat to the destitute states disheartened and half demoralized. This news was bracing to us, who had a short time before been falling back before this same army, and we felt pretty well, as we were now chasing them before us.

It was Saturday evening as we entered Versailles, and it seemed that all the negroes for miles around had assembled to see us march in. Their demonstrations of joy as we filed by them were enthusiastic, quite amusing and often touching. They shouted, danced, leaped, yelled and prayed for us. One old lady expressed her delight by first yelling out a blessing on us, and then butting a gate post over and over, with all the force of an old ram. The boys asked for corn bread, and the negro women ran quickly and got all they had and brought it to them, and said "If you 'uns 'ill wait we 'uns 'ill go an' jist bake cords uv it fur yeh." But we 'uns could not wait.

We camped over night near the town, and the next morning

extended our reconnoissance towards Nicholasville four miles, took ten prisoners, returned by the same road through Versailles two miles on the Frankfort road, and went into camp. On this afternoon, the first negroes that ever left their masters and followed us, got down from the fences along the side of the road and joined the regiment. Most of them were returned to their masters. Next morning we returned to camp at Frankfort, but had not more than stacked our arms before we were ordered to draw five days' rations, and be ready to march in the morning. When morning came, we were ready, but marching orders were countermanded. We remained in camp from the 13th to the 18th without incident. The weather was beautiful, and battalion and company drill was the daily routine. As long as we had been in the service, we had never seen a military funeral until the 15th of October. A soldier was buried who was followed to his grave by the fife shrieking out the dead march, accompanied by muffled drum, while comrades followed the slow moving ambulance with reversed arms. When buried, shots were fired over his grave. All who witnessed it were deeply impressed with the solemnity of this unique funeral; and it was especially depressing on those who had a touch of the jaundice and home sickness, and for them the fewer such funerals they witnessed the better.

One day, while lying at Frankfort, Gen. Dumont met a Seventy-Second man carrying a mackerel, and said, "My man, what have you got?" "I have a mackerel," said the man. "What do you intend to do with it?" asked the General. "I'm going to broil it and eat it; I've heard that broiled mackerel is good for the diarrhœa." "Young man," said the General, very gravely, "Go, broil that mackerel well, eat it and report the result to me; if it cures you, I will have a keg of mackerel issued to every man in the Seventy-Second Regiment."

CHAPTER XIII.

October 18th to October 23rd, 1862—After Morgan in Mule Wagons with one Day's Rations—Capture Rebels at Versailles—Find Morgan Asleep Just in the Right Place—Col. Norton, a Military Ass, Wakes Him up with Cannon—Morgan Runs and we Stay on a Hill—Wrath of the Men at Norton—Gen. Dumont a Little too Late for Morgan, but not for Norton—The Seventy-Second Continues the Chase two Days to Bardstown—Draw Rations, Eat Raw S. B., &c., at Bardstown—Return to Frankfort.

On the afternoon of Saturday, October 18th, we had orders to draw one day's rations and get ready to move as light as possible. The word soon got out that it was to be a scout after Morgan, who was said to be in the vicinity of Versailles. We were delighted to get off on such an errand, and the regiment turned out 600 men. We marched out to the road, where we were ordered to get into the wagons, which were drawn up in line. Sixteen men got into each wagon. The Seventy-Second took the advance, and at sun down, off we went at a gallop over the pike What a noise, what a dust, what jolting! The regiment was in high spirit and merry as robins in spring: 14 miles, 14 miles, 14 miles, onward; 14 miles, 14 miles, rode the 600! The whole brigade was in mule wagons except the 13th Battery boys, who were mounted on their guns and caissons. At 9 o'clock, we dashed into Versailles and captured a squad left there by Morgan to watch and give him notice if Union troops advanced. From these prisoners we ascertained that Morgan had taken the Lawrenceburgh road. We followed immediately and rapidly. Upon entering the ravine, which had very steep banks, leading down to the Kentucky River at Shryock's Ford, the advance guard took another rebel sentinel who was fast asleep.

The brigade was halted, our regiment was ordered out of the wagons, and cautioned to be as still as possible. Just then there was a discharge of three vollies of musketry. Then a pause and deep silence. Then thundered the cannon once, twice, thrice, each one making an echo so distinct in the hills that many thought six shots had been discharged. In the crisp, clear air, the shots were heard shrieking as they sped away. We instantly formed on the narrow bit of road along side of the wagons, and went to the front in double quick. We were ordered to climb up the side of a very steep hill, which we speedily did. Then we were ordered to sit down, or lie down gun in hand, ready to get in line at the command. The hill was so steep that we could not sit on it without slipping down unless we each took a sapling between our legs, which we did, and sat there nursing a gun between our arms and a tree between our legs. Steep as the hill was, the cavalry began to climb it, the horses slipping and stumbling over the rocks, and the men swearing like sinners. We supposed the cavalry were passing around to the rear of Morgan, as we heard commands, men mounting, the clatter of horses' feet and cavalry swords, and expected we should soon be commanded to dash down on his camp; but we soon learned that the cavalry were dismounted and asleep on top of the hill, while we heard Morgan's men running away.

The explanation of all this is, that we had come upon Morgan's pickets and captured them. We had slipped up to the very border of his camp, where the chief and his men lay sound asleep. Dumont was moving to Lawrenceburg on another and shorter road, with a brigade on foot, and when there would have turned into the road we were on, come to meet us, and between his force and ours, Morgan would have been bagged and doubtless captured, as he could not have gotten away. The great mistake was made by Col. Norton, of Ohio, who commanded our brigade Instead of keeping perfectly quiet and waiting for Dumont to come up, as he had been ordered to do, and as Col. Miller begged him to do, he ordered the shots spoken of above to be fired into Morgan's camp, which awoke him and his men. In a minute after the first shot, we could hear the voices of the rebel commanders hurrying up their men, hear the men mounting and dashing away for dear life. Soon all was still and the rebels were gone.

Here was a chance for our division, including the Seventy-Second, to reap laurels of fame and take one of the most pestilent rebel raiders. We could see into his camp and almost reach the prize, when the fool commander, Norton, ordered us on to a hill side, set us astraddle of the bushes; sent the cavalry up the same hill to go to sleep, aroused the enemy and let him go.

O, but we were a mad set of men, from Col. Miller to the least of us. Next morning, after many useless delays, we moved at 9 o'clock, and when we came to Morgan's camp and found saddles, guns, spurs, sabers, provisions, clothing, and even pack horses, our wrath became hot as a furnace, and we breathed curses upon Norton's head for his base folly or treason. When we met Gen. Dumont with his force at Lawrenceburg, and found that he arrived at the mouth of the road by which the rebels escaped just thirty minutes after they got out of it, we were more fierce in our wrath than ever. When Dumont found out the facts, put on all his steam, stood up in his stirrups and cursed Norton for a fool and a rebel with all his fierce invective, we enjoyed it beyond measure. That was one time when swearing was allowed on Sunday, and traveling too.

Morgan had six hours the start of us, was fearfully scared and moved rapidly. All that 19th day of October we pursued him over the roughest roads we had ever traveled, being almost jolted and pounded into mince meat.

One of the incidents of this rough day's drive in a sweeping trot over the breaks of Salt River, was the running away of the mules which drew the wagon in which Capt. Watts, of Company I, and his detachment, were riding. The wagon wheel hit a rock or stump, threw the bed into the air, men and all going up with it towards the moon, looking like the boats and men do in the pictures when a furious whale has hoisted them with its tail The bed turned upside down and lit on the men. Great confusion all along the lines. The mules brought up against a tree, wiggled their tails and subsided. The wagon bed was lifted off the men, who crawled up, none of them much hurt, except a few square feet of their bodies a little worse bruised than before; the wagon was reconstructed, the mules reorganized and started off on the long trot again. It was a common sight that day to look from a wagon, as we halted on the brow of a hill to give time to teams ahead to get out of the way, and see men tossed three or four feet into the air as the wagons went at full speed down the hills and over the rough rocks—for we were on no pike now, but a common country road. Men were often thrown out of the wagons and considerably bruised. Capt. Pinkerton tried to get into a wagon while it was in motion and got his foot almost pulverized.

The weather became quite cold for that time of year, and we went into camp at about 10 o'clock at night on the south bank of Salt River in one of the windiest, bleakest, coldest, rockiest places, we ever saw. We had but a blanket each and no overcoats. It was too cold to sleep, and we gave the whole night to keeping up fires. We were also out of rations, and so sore from bruises that we could hardly walk. But like Mark Tapley, we were cheerful and resolved to come out strong.

We had learned from prisoners taken that Morgan's force broke up into squads, after passing Lawrenceburg, so they might elude pursuit, and being in the rear of our main army the more easily rejoin Bragg. The Seventy-Second and some cavalry were alone on this scout, Gen. Dumont and the other troops having turned back to Frankfort.

Next day, the 20th, we still pushed on, taking now and then a jaded prisoner who could go no further, and in the afternoon arrived at Bardstown at 3 P. M., out of rations and hungry as wolves. We had learned at Bloomfield that Morgan was 24 hours ahead of us, and the statement being confirmed at this place we found a commissary, drew rations and ate out of all reason.

We had started with one day's rations, and had been on the move day and night for two days, with no time to forage. The pork we drew was very thick and fat, yet the men were so hungry that they did not wait to cook it, although wood could be easily obtained, but bolted it down raw in great quantities, with hard tack. We have never seen so much fat meat eaten as that evening in the hickory grove near Bardstown. The result was a very restless night in camp. In all directions were heard groanings and explosive sounds of stomachs unloading their enormous weight of pork. The next day it was necessary to lay quietly in camp for the men to recuperate from the effects of this gorge. On the 22nd, we started back to Frankfort and camped for the night on Salt River, opposite Taylorsville. On the 23rd, we pushed ahead and reached Frankfort at 10 in the night, tired enough, and slept soundly in our tents once more.

The explanation of this affair, given in Basil M. Duke's history of Morgan's Cavalry, is, that Morgan had been covering the rear of Kirby Smith's column of Bragg's army in his retreat out of Kentucky in 1862, when, at Gum Springs, about 30 miles south-east of Lexington, he started with 1,800 men and two howitzers to raid our lines, and to pass into Tennessee at Gallatin. He arrived at Lexington just at daylight on the 18th of October, and captured the 4th Ohio Cavalry, and left Lexington for Versailles at 1 P. M. of the same day. How Dumont ever learned of his whereabouts in time to do anything, is more than we can tell, unless it was by some of the fugitives from the fight at Lexington, about 30 miles from Frankfort.

The rapid pursuit of Morgan, and the plan for attacking and capturing him, were admirable, and would have been perfect but for the blunder of Col. Norton, and reflected great credit on Gen. Dumont. Col. Norton was arrested, tried by a court martial, and dismissed in disgrace for his incompetency or baseness. Gen. Dumont was given a larger command.

The greatest mischief Morgan did on this raid was the burning of some 80 wagons belonging to Buell's army. He hustled into Tennessee as fast as he could scamper.

This was always referred to as the raid of the mule brigade. We conclude the account with a quotation from T. W. Milligan, giving an account of his experience in mule driving, as it is a fair specimen of the driving done on that raid.

Mr. Milligan says: "On our return from Bardstown, we called a halt about sunset to take our refreshments. When we were ready to march again, our teamster was missing, and the Lieutenant called for a volunteer mule driver. I was heartily sick of my position in the wagon, and volunteered. No one was aware of my ignorance of how to steer the mules. Darkness soon set in, and I felt rather uncomfortable, seated on the saddle mule, the reins tied fast to the saddle. The mules started up a little brisk, the boys in the wagon told me not to drive so fast; I hallooed, whoa! whoa! and they went faster. I jerked the rein and yelled, gee! gee! and pulled haw! haw! whipped them over the head, then over the rump, but all my attempts to halt were a sad failure I looked back to see how the boys in the wagon were enjoying the ride, and found that the old wagon was bounding like a ship in a storm without helmsman. Lieut. Crick was standing in the front end of the wagon holding fast to the box with one hand, and the other high above his head, swearing that Buck Milligan was no more fit for a teamster than he was for a chaplain. I stuck to the mules like grim death until they were ready to slack their pace, when I slid off and left them to go at will, and they trotted into camp at Frankfort in good order and halted at the proper place. I then and there swore never again to take hold of a string that had a mule at the end of it."

The result of this raid was a very large increase of sickness, both from the exposure and over-eating at Bardstown, where we drew the thickest, fattest, meat, we ever saw, which the men, who were ravenously hungry, ate raw in large quantities. We never saw them eat so much raw s. b. before or since. On our arrival at camp at Frankfort, the diarrhœa raged with increased violence, for the rations were so bad —the meat so rotten and maggoty, and the crackers so full of big white worms—that the boys declared we were using rations Uncle Sam had left over from the Mexican War. To cap the climax, measles broke out among the troops and spread to our regiment, taking to hospital and to the grave some of the best men. No disease in the army was more destructive to the health and life of soldiers than the measles.

CHAPTER XIV.

October 25th to November 11th, 1862—Orders to March—Striking Tents in the Snow—Cry for Overcoats—Order of March—Hard March Through Snow—Sleeping in Hog Beds and Barns—Weather Becomes Fair and Dusty—Burning Rails—Plenty to Eat but Bad Rations—March Through Bowling Green—Into Camp at Lost River—Reviewed by Gen. Rosecrans—More Graybacks.

After the battle at Perryville, Bragg got out of Kentucky with all speed, Buell was succeeded by Rosecrans, and a vigorous forward movement begun. On Friday evening, October 25th, we were ordered to prepare to march, and were called up next morning by daylight to strike tents, pack up and be off. Snow had fallen rapidly all night and about three inches lay on the ground. As the men hauled down tents and packed up, they cried as dolorously as Pharaoh's locusts, "o-o-o-o ver coats!—o-o-o-o ver coats!" The cry spread from camp to camp, until there were thousands repeating the sad refrain. Dumont's division, consisting of four brigades and three batteries, was soon on the Bardstown road moving through the snow. As this is the first time our division had moved together in perfect order, it may be of interest to give the regulations that govern the movements of a division.

Each brigade is numbered according to the seniority of rank of its commander, one, two, three, four. Each regiment in the brigade is numbered in the same way. On the first day's march, the first brigade has the advance, and the first regiment in the brigade acts as advance guard. On the second day's march, the second brigade has the advance and the second regiment in that brigade is advance guard, while the first brigade falls to the rear and the first regiment becomes rear guard. On the third day's march, the third brigade comes to the front, its third regiment being advance guard, and the second brigade falling to the rear, its second regiment becoming rear guard. And so on until all have held the advance and rear When not near an enemy, each brigade train, together with its Quartermaster's teams, artillery attached to the brigade and ambulances, march just in the rear of the brigade to which they belong. A division of four brigades and three batteries, and all wagon trains, makes a line full five miles long on the road, and presents quite a formidable appearance.

In the vicinity of an enemy, when expecting an attack, the line would be arranged thus: First, infantry; second, artillery; third, infantry; fourth, artillery; fifth, all teams in rear of the division under a strong rear guard.

On this first day's march on that snowy 26th of November, our brigade had the advance, and our regiment, headed by Col. Miller, was advance guard. We had to break the road, the snow thawed and knotted and balled upon our shoe soles, and towards evening froze on our feet and pantaloons, making marching disagreeable and exhaustive in the extreme, and two-thirds of the men gave out before night and failed to stack arms. The ambluances were all full; some crept to straw stacks or hay stacks, barns, and other out-houses, to screen themselves from the cold while they rested; some found resting places in negro cabins, and some on the floors of the houses of the whites. One man said he drove up a lot of hogs from a hollow tree and took their bed. Corporal Riddell, Company G, crawled into a stable loft and got under the fodder to keep himself from freezing. During the night, a squad of rebel cavalry, which was following our rear, came and took nearly every blade off of him. This was a close call.

On the 27th, which was Sunday, we made but a Sabbath day's journey, eight miles. The snow melted away, the day was beautiful, most of the men came up who had fallen behind, we had a good night's rest, and on the morning of the 28th, started out in good cheer, passing through Johnsonville and Chaplin Hill, We were highly complimented for this and all subsequent days of this march to Bowling Green. On the 29th, we passed through Bloomfield and Bardstown, encamping on the south of the latter place.

On the 30th, we marched to New Haven, went into camp on the south of that place on a fork of Salt River; were ordered to put up our tents and to make out our pay rolls. This latter order was a welcome one, especially to the officers, who had not received a cent from the Government since they had entered the service, and who had been borrowing from their men or drawn on the reserve at home. All haste was made to gett.he pay rolls made out, but as it is as hard and delicate a piece of work as to make out a muster roll, but few of the companies succeeded before the order was given to march the next day.

On the 31st, we passed President Lincoln's birth place, between New Haven and Elizabethtown, which most of us viewed with reverence, as if it were sacred and classic ground.

About noon of the same day, Corporal Magee got badly hurt. While sitting on a low fence eating his dinner, Corporal Geiger, of Company C, a big stout man, fell out for walnuts. There were plenty on the ground, but he wanted some fresh from the tree, and picked up one-third of a fence rail, walked up a hill, threw it over the top of the tree, thirty feet high, and it fell upon Corporal Magee, the end striking his head, mashing through his sole leather cap crown and cutting a gash in the scalp three inches long. This was a "rail" ugly accident. That night we camped at Nolin's Creek, getting in late. The month had been one of great activity with us, but on the whole it had been a very agreeable one to those who kept well, for we had been all the time on chase of the enemy, having captured almost a thousand prisoners, and were now in full pursuit of Bragg's great army, driving it as chaff is driven before the strong wind.

On November 1st, we marched to Bacon's Creek, a short easy march. The weather was glorious Indian summer; the roads were so dusty that our clothing, beards and hair became white with the fine limestone dust of the pike. Water was pretty plenty in pools or sinks in the ground, and pretty good, too. We were holding out well, and could only complain of the rations, which continued to be bad. The worms were so thick in our coffee after we had broken a cracker into it that we had to skim them off. The boys often yelled out, while cooking, that a skipper had kicked their skillet over. We burned thousands of rails each night to cook and warm by; for though the days were pleasant, the nights were frosty, and every morning we would arise with the side of the head that was uppermost covered with frost. What appetites we had! And every day we ate a greater variety than our rations, and fresher food, too.

On the 2nd, we crossed Green River at Mumfordville, and marched to Horse Cave, where the first mail since leaving Frankfort was received, which caused great rejoicing, for letters from home were indispensable to a soldier's happiness. On the 3rd, we passed Cave City and Pruitt's Knob, and camped at Dripping Springs, having made a hard march all day.

On Monday, November 4th, we marched through Bowling Green, and went into camp three miles south-west of that place at Lost River, having marched 180 miles in 10 days, an average of 18 miles per day. We were highly complimented for our discipline and endurance, both by Col. Miller, our Brigade Commander, and Gen. Dumont, our Division Commander. The latter always had a fatherly pride in the Seventy-Second, at whose birth he officiated.

While on this march, Gen. Dumont had gone home to arrange some private affairs, he having been elected to Congress. A few days before reaching Bowling Green, while we were halted for our noon lunch and were lying at will, we saw a one horse buggy coming up from the rear, and soon a yell went up. It was Gen. Dumont come back. He was dressed in that same old white hat with other clothes to match, and was driven by a very black little negro boy, and had no other attendant. As soon as the Seventy-Second recognized him, they got on their feet, swung their caps and raised the yell, calling for a speech The buggy halted a moment, the General took off his old hat, bowed, smiled, and said, "Boys, d—n it keep still, you bother me," and was off again in a round of applause all along the line.

Our camp grounds at Lost River were unlevel and dusty. The weather became raw and cold, and the wind blew furiously almost every day, carrying clouds of dust into our eyes and cooking food, so each got about a peck of dirt per day plus the worms in our meat and bread. We put up tents, and the officers built chimneys to their tents, which smoked at the wrong ends. The men in their Sibleys were a little better off, but in any of them was a famous place to smoke bacon. In a few days we all had colds, sneezing, with watery eyes, and wishing we could go on another march. The truth is the Seventy-Second never liked camp life and duty. Here we found the 70th Ind., which had been in camp at Bowling Green for three months, and we were veterans compared with them.

Cave Spring, or Lost River, or Mill Spring, near which we were camped, deserves a word, as it was a great curiosity to us Indianians, who had never seen a deeper hole in the ground than a well. It was a large deep stream, three or four rods wide—we never knew how deep—which came out of the ground at the foot of a low hill, ran six or eight rods, ran under the ground again, and finally came out into the Big Barren River some six miles below Bowling Green. Some of our boys, with a spirit of exploration largely developed, followed the stream through all its windings, some eight miles, to the Barren River The water was then low, but the worn rocks showed that the channel was often quite full.

While in camp in this old dusty field, which had been pulverized by both armies, and the very dust of which was almost all alive with vermin, we learned that Gen. Rosecrans had superseded Buell in the command of this army, and that he was to review us soon. Then we began to scour brass buttons, scabbards, blades, guns and bayonets, and get everything ready for the eagle eye of the great commander.

On the 6th of November, in the cold air and dust of the afternoon, our division was drawn up in splendid order. The Seventy-Second was out with every available man, knapsacks and haversacks on as if to start on the march; guns and bayonets polished until they shone like silver; buttons shone like fine brass—everything in perfect trim. Gen. Rosecrans was making a very careful inspection of his forces, and reviewed by regiments, riding very deliberately around each. When he rode slowly down the front of the Seventy-Second, he repeated several times:

"Aim deliberately, aim low." As he rode up the rear of the regiment he repeated, "Eat well, sleep well, keep well."

He made us a little speech which we cheered to the echo, advising us to take care of ourselves, become well drilled, and to be cool in action. We find in Col. Miller's notes, made at the time, the statement that Gen. Rosecrans told him that the Seventy-Second was one of the finest regiments he had reviewed for many a day.

When we reached Bowling Green, we found the main body of the Army of the Cumberland, for so it was called now, moving through it marching for Nashville. The 10th Indiana contained many of our home acquaintances, and we had a pleasant time visiting with them. On the 9th, Rosecrans' division passed us moving southwards. On the 10th, a man in the 108th Ohio accidently shot and killed himself near our regiment, and on Company I was laid the unpleasant duty of burying him. About the same time a man in Company C had a finger shot off. He claimed that a bushwhacker did it, but his bunk mates said he did it himself to get a discharge, but shot the finger from the left hand and failed. A man in Company I was more successful. He had fits, and after he was discharged his messmates said he ate shaving soap to make him froth at the mouth. There are some such frauds amongst the best men that ever got together, and home sickness and dread of battle had a fearfully demoralizing effect on such.

CHAPTER XV.

November 11th to November 28th, 1862—March to Scottsville—Dumont Ordered to "Go Home"—A New Place—Col. Miller's Description of the Natives—Drill School—An Abundance to Eat—Lousy as Lazarus—Trading Lids From Pill Boxes and Cancelled Postage Stamps for Chickens, &c.—The Negro Gallows—Capt. Hanna's Vest Swap—March to Gallatin—Spoon to the Right or Left, as the Case May be—Draw Overcoats at Gallatin—Go Into Camp.

On the 11th, the regiment moved for Scottsville, Ky., 25 miles from Bowling Green, making 18 miles over roads that were little traveled, but well cushioned with autumn and other large forest leaves. On the 25th, we arrived about noon in a driving wind and cold rain, and took up the day in trying to find a camping place, and in building fires and fixing temporary shelters, only to be ordered to another place. Before we settled the camp, a detail of 100 men from the Seventy-Second was made to go back and repair the roads so that rations could be hauled from Bowling Green.

While the regiment was being settled, some of our men built a fire, and a man dressed in citizens' clothing came up and stood warming himself, and finally turned around and gave the fire a kick. This made one of the men who had helped build the fire very mad, and he raved out, "You dashed old fool, what did you do that for? what are you fooling around here for anyhow? I think you'd better go home now, we don't want any more of you."

When the angry soldier stopped his clatter, the old fellow said, with a peculiar nasal that every man in the regiment would know on the darkest night that ever blew, "Well, e-gad, I expect you're about right, soldier, I han't got any business here, and I'll go." As Gen. Dumont stalked away with his old shawl over his head, the laugh was on the soldier who had mistaken his General for some old citizen, and ordered him home.

This Scottsville was a new place. No soldiers of either army had been there before. Situated 25 miles from a railroad, in a hilly, heavily wooded country, the people were intensely rural even in the little town itself. In the woods were chestnuts, hickory nuts, persimmons, haws and grapes, pigs, mutton, sheep, milk—all that heart could wish—and had these things been temperately used, they would have greatly benefited us, as we had been so long on hard army rations that scurvy had begun to appear. But with the soldier it is always a feast or a famine, and most of them ate so much as to make themselves sick. On the day after we arrived, Maj. Carr, who had recently been promoted from Capt. of Company B, a most accomplished drill master, organized a school for the instruction of commissioned and non-commissioned officers in tactics, including skirmish drill. This was of great advantage and improved us rapidly. Squad, company and battalion drill, was pushed every day the weather would permit, and the Seventy-Second was the best drilled regiment in the division, and officers from all the other regiments often came to see us drill.

With over-eating and with the unhealthy location of the camp, and the cold rains that fell about every other day, "home-sickness" and physical ailment increased to an alarming extent in the brigade, and touched the Seventy-Second a little. Coughs and colds became fearful, and the picket post could be located for miles around by the incessant coughing of the pickets. Here some of the companies became thoroughly lousy. We had a sprinkle at Shelbyville, a shower at Bowling Green and a deluge at Scottsville. We made a desperate effort to get rid of them, for they are too lively to sleep with. Some scorched their hog hair shirts over the fire, but graybacks hid down deep between the bristles and could stand it better than the shirts could. Some hung their hog hair out on a pole to freeze them out, but you might as well try to freeze Esquimaux. Some seated themselves on logs in the sun, stripped to the waist, and tried to pick them out from amongst the bristles, but you might as well try to pick the drops from the ocean, for the "cattle" bred faster on one shirt in the sun than five skillful nigger cotton pickers could pick them off. Some borrowed big kettles from the natives and put their shirts in them and boiled them all day and all night. This process killed most of the graybacks, and it drew up the hog hair shirts until they were not large enough for a doll baby's dress; and many of them fell apart like sand as soon as the "stiffening" was out These wretched vermin got into every stitch of clothing a man wore. When a company set about it in earnest, they could keep them pretty well subdued, but always retained enough in a dormant condition to seed the whole regiment in a few days of favorable neglect and dirt. The boys had a saying that if there ever came a time when a grayback could not be found in a company, some one in that company was going to die, sure.

We called these pestiferous vermin "graybacks" because we called the rebels that name, and because we got them from the rebels, and because there was no other creature on earth as mean as a rebel but a body louse. But we have lo(u)st the subject and must return.

A country is a pretty sure index to its people. This country was poor and the people were also, and the most ignorant of any we had yet seen. Col. Miller says in his notes of November 15th:

"Went to town to-day and saw a lot of the natives They are of the real butternut stock. The men are long, gangle-kneed, and look as though they had lived on raw persimmons all their lives; while the women are just as scrawny, but seem to have children by instinct, intuitively, or some other process."

One day while out on picket, we saw "Limber Jim" of Company F buy five roasted chickens and twenty pies for $20 in confederate money, and get $2 good money back in change. Web. Reed, of Company F, bought a basket full of corn bread with the lid off of a tin pill box. This was about the time that postal change came into circulation and the natives were not well posted as to its appearance, and we have seen the men on picket buy any amount of corn bread, apples, potatoes, chickens, &c., with canceled postage stamps which had been carefully removed from old letters. Of course we did not endorse this method of putting down the rebellion, but as faithful chroniclers of events gives these facts as examples of Yankee shrewdness over Southern chivalry.

There was one picket post south-east of Scottsville about two miles on a lonesome country road which lay through a deep forest. The picket post was on a little branch which crossed the road. In a small opening near the road and branch, stood a large upright post from which projected a great beam, at a hight of about 10 feet from the ground. Through this beam was bored a large hole. This was the negro gallows. We learned from an aged negro man many facts about this gallows and the victims hung on it. He said the gallows had been standing for several years, and that many negroes had been hung on it. "Da is deir graves, massah," said he as he pointed to some graves near the gallows. The graves had all been covered over with rails, but on many the rails had rotted and fallen into the sunken graves. Some of the graves were not more than a year old.

"What were the negroes hung for?" we asked.

"O, I dunno. We black 'uns done neber knows nuffin 'bout sich 'fairs. But we feels purty sartin most ob 'em was hanged case day was ole."

He proceeded to explain that often when a negro became old and worthless, some sort of charge was trumped up against him in the courts, and if the master could get the court to allow a fair price for the negro, he was hanged, and the master got the cash for him. We do not know that there was the least truth in the statement. He said a young negro was condemned to be hung, and his master, "A big man," got him "loose" because the price fixed on him was not enough.

Capt. Hanna, of Company H, was detailed as provost marshal of Scottsville. As there was an abundance of apple-jack in the country, the Captain was soon "hail fellow, well met," with all the leading citizens, and one day while in his balmiest mood, he traded his military vest with one of the largest citizens for a home spun home made vest of dark material with red stripes running across the breast. It was a wonderful garment, reaching from the Captain's chin almost to his knees. The vest trade passed as a good joke until we got to Murfreesboro, and the Captain one day reported to Col. Wilder for duty. The eye of the doughty chief scanned the vest and blazed with indignation, and he roared, "Captain, how dare you come into my presence with that vest on! You know that is not the regulation garment. Leave me at once and do it quick!" The Captain went away and remarked, "I don't believe

Wilder likes my vest a d—d bit from a few remarks he made about it."

Several men deserted at this place. The country around being sparsely settled and heavily wooded, was a good place in which to hide. While here we did more and better drilling than ever before or afterwards. At this place Adjt. Rice was promoted to be A. A. G. on Gen. Joseph J. Reynolds' staff with rank of Captain, and to our regret left us. Sergt. Maj. William K. Byrns became acting Adjutant of the regiment, and was subsequently commissioned as Adjutant, and made a very excellent officer. Captain Hiram B. Collins, Company K, was made Adjutant of the Brigade, and Lieut. John B. Crick, Company G, was made Brigade Inspector. Our 13 days at this place were quite remarkable. We had more to eat, more drilling, more sickness, than at any other camp in our service. More than half the regiment were sick aud many died.

On Tuesday, November 25th, we struck tents and took up the line of march at 7 A. M. for Gallatin, Tenn., 35 miles south-west. Little of interest occurred on this march. The weather was quite cold of nights, freezing the ground two inches deep; and as we had only our summer clothing, neither overcoats nor blankets, we suffered intensely. On the night of the 25th, we camped at the Rock House. The night was so bitter cold that the men, to economize blankets, slept six in a squad or pile. They pinned two blankets together to lie on, and pinned four others together to cover with, thus giving every man the benefit of three blankets. This is not the most pleasant way to sleep, but it is better than freezing.

The men, in such a bed, have to all lie with their faces the same way, which makes it very warm for the four between the two outside men, but cold for the two on either flank. All had to turn over at once, and when some fellow would lie until the lower side was almost freezing from the cold ground, he would yell out, "Spoon to the right," and all six would flop over on to their right sides. About the time one got sound asleep, some one else would call out "Spoon to the left!" and over would go the pile on to their left sides. And thus, upon the frozen ground, the night would be worn away. That night many sheltered themselves in the leaves of the forest on the hill, and many others in the clefts of the rocks which projected from the hills. That night some Company I men who could not sleep determined to forage a little. They lit out and soon found a plantation that promised plenty, but nothing that could crow or squeal was found. After scouting about the premises awhile, they heard a chicken crow, which sounded as if under the house, and inspection proved that it was there with others. The question was how to get them out, as a large family was in the house, not yet gone to bed. Part of the boys agreed to go into the house to warm and others agreed to go under the house and get the chickens while those within talked, laughed, and clattered their feet upon the carpetless floor to drown the noise of the chickens. The plan worked like a charm, and the chickens went into camp.

Next morning, 26th, just as we started from the Rock House, two cavalrymen rode up to the house from which the Company I men had taken the chickens. One of them dismounted and took after a turkey, which ran under the house and he after it. Just then the old woman came out with a big heavy split broom, and as the fellow undertook to come out with the turkey, she belted him over the head. After making two or three unsuccessful efforts to get out, he drew his cheese knife (saber) and began to tickle her ankles, and cried out, "If you don't get away from there I'll cut your old legs off." She fled, and the scamp having overpowered the broom with the sword, galloped away with the turkey. On this morning, as soon as the men got up, they began the old and dolorous cry, "o o-o-vercoats, o-o-o-vercoats," and kept it up all day. Especially when over Quartermaster, Lieut. Dewey, passed, the shouts for overcoats were deafening, and in disgust he put his spurs to his horse and ran to Nashville, got our overcoats and brought them to us speedily.

On that same 26th of November, we passed the Tennessee line and camped at Gallatin, late at night. On the night of the 26th, a soldier named Geo. W. Dodd, of Company B, who had marched all day, died in his tent.

On the morning of the 27th, we went into regular camp, pitched tents and had a grand jubilee, drawing our blue, long forked tailed, heavy caped, horse hair overcoats. Every fellow got a fit. The coats of the tall men reached to their calves; the coats of the short men reached to their heels or swept the ground. They had no pockets in them, but the boys soon inserted a pocket on each side as big as a bag, and some put a big breast pocket on each side. When a fellow stole from one place all he could carry away in his overcoat pockets, there was little left but the women and babies.

CHAPTER XVI.

November 28th to December 25th, 1862—March from Gallatin to Castillian Springs—Go into Camp—An Exposed Position—Rumors of Morgan's Threatening Movements—Fortifying—Rain and Snow—Attack on Hartsville, and a 10 Mile Run to that place—Scenes on the Fiery, Bloody Battle Ground—Removal to Bledsoe's Creek—The Great Battle Approaching—The Emancipation Proclamation—Wilder Assumes Command—Move Camp again—Go in Swimming on Christmas Day.

On the 28th our brigade moved from Gallatin about 10 miles southeast, to Castillian Springs, and camped in the most beautiful place we had yet occupied. The ground was high and rolling, covered with beautiful timber and blue grass. This place is about half way between Gallatin and Hartsville, the latter being the extreme outpost on the east of Rosecrans' army. We moved to Castillian Springs to support Col. Moore's brigade of our division, which was at Hartsville. Bragg's army had made a stand at Murfreesboro, 20 miles due south of Hartsville; hence both Hartsville and Castillian Springs might be attacked at any time.

We devoted the first few days in this camp to fixing everything up in neat order, having hints that we would most likely remain in it all winter. The inevitable drill was again instituted. On the 30th we had our first brigade inspection, and invoiced to the satisfaction of Lieut. Crick. He simply remarked that some of the men were careless in numbering their knapsacks, and that if he were not well acquainted with the character of the Seventy-Second for taking care of their property, he would be led to think by some of the numbers that somebody had stolen something. But as he found other regiments afflicted with the same carelessness, it was not best to attempt to correct the mistake.

On the 29th of November the 10th Indiana marched from Hartsville and camped near us, having been relieved at that place by Col. Moore's brigade of our division, consisting of the 106th and 108th Ohio infantry, the 105th Illinois infantry, and two guns of the 13th Indiana battery. The infantry were so largely composed of Germans that we called them the Dutch brigade. When the 10th left Hartsville they told the Dutch brigade that Morgan would get them inside of a week, if they did not look a "leedle out." We shall see what we shall see.

On December 6th P. S. Nowlin died in camp of congested measles, which he took at Frankfort. He was the first man in the regiment, and, so far as we know, the only one, buried with the honors of war. The poor fellow was a loyal Tennessee refugee, who lived at Carthage, only 30 miles from where he died.

Rumors of Morgan dashing hither and thither are in the air again, and again our blood is up, as we remember how near we were to the old fox once, and every man is on his mettle to prevent a surprise. Every gun is quietly loaded and ready. We begin to fortify our camp with big log breastworks, the pickets are doubled, videttes thrown well out, and every man ordered to remain in camp, where he can seize his musket and fall in at the sound of the long roll Lieut. Ruger, of Company C, while working on the breastworks was ruptured, and resigned on December 1st.

It was hourly expected that Morgan would cross the Cumberland River at the ford between Hartsville and Castillian Springs and attack one or the other of the posts, but no one knew which he would choose. On Friday, the 5th, it rained, hailed and snowed. On Saturday, the 6th, it was cloudy and quite cold, with three inches of snow on the ground, under which was a crust of ice.

On Sunday morning, the 7th, just at daylight, we were aroused by the sound of cannonading in the direction of Hartsville. Instantly every man is up and all know that the post at that place is attacked. The men of the various companies seize their arms and fall in without orders from their officers; the officers buckle on their swords and join their companies without orders from the Colonel. In five minutes from hearing the first gun, the regiment is ready to march. Col. Miller dashes over to the tent of Col. Harlan, commanding the brigade to which the 10th is attached, and tells the Colonel that Hartsville is attacked, and suggests that as Harlan is the senior Colonel, he take the lead and march at once to its relief.

Col. Harlan replies, "Yes, I guess it is attacked; and you, Col. Miller, had better march to its relief, and I'll follow as soon as I can get my men up."

Col. Miller says, "No, you have been there, know the ground, and can go quicker."

"My men are not up yet; you go on and I'll soon follow," replies Col. Harlan.

All this time the cannon roared louder on the crisp morning air. Every minute was an hour to the Seventy-Second, and a fatal delay for the attacked post. Col. Miller dashed back to the regiment and shouted, "Forward, march!" and we were off on double quick, in less than 25 minutes from the firing of the first gun, through the snow, moving for Hartsville.

The ground was not only covered with snow and ice, but also

rough with stones, many of which were flat and loose, and would turnand slipunder our feet. As the sun came up the snow began to melt and clogged on our feet, and the road became sloppy and slippery. Some times we marched with lines extended on either side of the road, upsetting fences as we came to them to get them out of the way, for the ground was new to us, and once or twice word came that Morgan's force was dashing down upon us. When five miles from Hartsville, a force of the enemy's cavalry are seen up the road, and we suppose the attack will be made. Our line of battle is quickly formed, a shell or two thrown amongst the rebels, and they put out for Hartsville with all speed. When we saw these rebels, we were commanded to load, (though most of the guns were already loaded) and Capt. LaFollett commanded, "Attention company; load by the nine commandments—load!" The men knew what he was driving at and drove their balls well home. Then falling into column in the sloppy road, we hurried forward again, the field officers exhorting us to greater speed. Close to Hartsville we meet a squad of darkies bare headed, bare footed, and almost naked, their clothes in ribbons. "Where is Morgan?" we shout to them. "Da—da—da!" they reply as they point their fingers towards Hartsville.

On we go--on! on!! on!!! until many a man falls headlong from utter exhaustion and can not get up. We are at the foot of the hill near Hartsville. "For God's sake, hurry up, do hurry up!" shouts Col. Kirkpatrick, as he gallops along our column. We see a great smoke burst from the woods above us, and make another desperate effort to go faster. Capt. Pinkerton, in running up the hill, steps upon a rock, his foot slips and he is sent forward upon his hands and feet, and finally flat into the slush, but the brave fellow gathers up, seizes his groin with his hand, and is off again. We run through a thick wood, burst into an open field, and behold! the tents are on fire, the flames shooting high into the air, and the dead are strewn so thickly on the ground that we stumble over them. The cries from the tents attract our attention and we begin to rescue the wounded and sick from the flames. The Seventy-Second is called upon to support two pieces of Capt. Nicklin's artillery, which command the Cumberland ford, and which open fire upon Morgan's forces as they hasten over the river, and one shot sends one of his wagons high into the air and makes his forces scamper off at full speed. His artillery send two or three shots of grape and canister back, but soon limber up and get out of the way of our artillery. Once more we see Morgan running from us.

The Seventy-Second had made 10 miles in two hours, getting in ahead of Harlan's veterans full a half hour, though they made remarkably good time.

To explain. This was one of Morgan's dashes. Half his force crossed the Cumberland between Castillian Springs and Hartsville, and quietly surrounded the camp in the night on the west and north. The other half crossed above Hartsville, and came quietly in on the north-east, and when the attack was made others crossed at the camp. So noiselessly was this done that the camp was completely surrounded before the attack was made. The attack began at daylight. The pickets of Col. Moore's forces were thrown out but a little distance, and when the attack was made, there was little time to form and make resistance, as the rebels came in on all sides with their fearful yell and volleys of musketry. The Illinois regiments made out to form a line and make considerable resistance; and the men of Nicklin's two guns had made a brave fight. One of the Lieutenants lay dead were the piece stood, with his six shooter in his hand, the chambers empty and several rebels dead around him. He had sold his life dearly. On the west of the camp there had been hard fighting, and the lines of battle of both forces could be traced by dead rebels and dead Union men. The whole affair was the result of a sad piece of carelessness in not keeping the picket force strong and thrown well out from the camp, and not keeping videttes well out, and all around, Not a particle of fortifying was done, and the camp was exposed on all sides. Some of the wounded men told us that on account of the nights being so cold and snowy, it was thought impossible for the enemy to move, and there was but a very light camp guard on.

Some of the rebels who were wounded and fell into our hands, said that Morgan had intended to attack Castillian Springs, but on reconnoitering, found the picket line so heavy, well advanced and wide awake, and found the fortifications so strong, that he concluded to fall upon the careless fellows at Hartsville.

The rebels captured some 2,000 prisoners, and almost all the arms of the brigade, including two guns of Nicklin's 13th Indiana Battery. Morgan's force in this action consisted of five regiments of cavalry, two infantry regiments and one battery. The rebel loss was 125 killed and wounded, 40 of their dead and some wounded being left on the field. The Union killed and wounded were considerably more.

As soon as the enemy is gone and the fire extinguished, we proceed to the burial of friend and foe, digging long graves and laying in each six or eight side by side, wrapped up in their blankets; when it was possible to find a man's name, we wrote it on a pine stick, in large plain letters, and carefully wrapped it up to preserve the pencil marks and put it in his blanket. We ascertained the names of most of the Union soldiers, from letters or memoranda on their persons, but we could ascertain the names of but few of the rebel soldiers, for they had few letters or memoranda on their persons. We laid the Union soldiers in graves by themselves, and the rebel soldiers in graves by themselves. This work occupied the whole day. and until after night. The wounded were cared for as far as possible, and removed to Gallatin. There was one poor fellow through whose head a ball had passed just behind his eyes and thrown both eyes out upon his cheeks. He was perfectly conscious. A little rebel, in a neat butternut suit, lay with his face on the ground, his hands spread out, and in the right hand a common hunting rifle, with wooden ramrod, while about his shoulders was the home made powder horn and shot pouch. We turned him over to carry him to his grave; on his fair young face was the enthusiastic smile he bore in the charge when a ball pierced his heart. He was a mere boy, with flaxen hair, and had no doubt furnished his own arms from his father's gun rack. In front of him lay a young Adjutant of an Ohio regiment, also on his face, his head pierced with a ball, his revolver in his hand. Little doubt these two had fired simultaneously and each killed the other. Another poor fellow had one fourth of the top of his head shot off with a grape shot, or piece of shell; he had crawled to the side of an old stump, where he sat shivering with cold, and singing and talking in wild delirium. He was alive the last time we saw him late in the afternoon.

The rebels left behind them an old country doctor, with long red tangled hair and beard. He was dirty, ignorant and bigoted, a fine specimen of back-woods butternut rebel. We made him our prisoner and treated him kindly. As he walked over the battle field he came to a place where lay a number of dead Union soldiers who were pierced with balls, their blood coagaluted in pools in the mud and snow. He halted, lifted up his hands, and said, with an expression of great delight: "Thank God for this! It has been a glorious day for the Southern cause." Several guns were leveled at the old brute's breast, and but for the interposition of an officer, he would have been shot dead in his tracks. He had to be taken out of sight to be kept from death.

This was our first experience on a bloody battle field, where fire and sword had done its work; where the blood was smoking, the wounded groaning and writhing in agony; and to tell the truth, it had a very serious effect. We all concurred in the sage remark of "Buddy Burns," Company G, the big mule driver, who solemnly said, "Well, boys, too see sich a sight as that, makes a feller feel d nged glad that he's religious."

About 8 o'clock at night, we started back to our camp at Castillian Springs, as tired a set of troops as ever tried to march. The night was cold and the road icy and slippery. Some got back about midnight, but many others did not get in until daylight. We spoke of Capt. Pinkerton slipping and falling. He ruptured himself seriously in that fall, but the brave fellow kept up and did duty all day in burying the dead, and marched back to camp, and was severely attacked by erysipelas next day. The sick list was largely increased by this trying affair.

On the next day, the 8th, all was quiet, but a sharp lookout was kept. On the 9th, we began in earnest to fortify more extensively, as Morgan, flushed with success, might dash down upon us.

On the 10th, Gen. Dumont, who had been with us for six months, was relieved by General Joseph J. Reynolds, and went home. We were sorry to lose the brave, wise and witty Dumont. We shall never see his like again. He carried with him the warm affection of every man in the division, and especially in the Seventy-Second. He had been elected to Congress, where he did as noble service as he had done in the field.

Before the witty and gall nt General leaves, we must tell his last passage at arms of wit. One day, Lieut. Col. Kirkpatrick, who commanded the regiment while Col. Miller was commanding the brigade, was directed by Gen. Dumont to take the Seventy-Second to a certain place on the line. The Colonel rode up to the regiment, which stood at an order arms and faced to the front, and without ceremonies said, "Attention, boys! follow me to the place the General has pointed out;" and started to ride to the place himself Gen. Dumont said, "Colonel, had you not better command your battalion to shoulder arms and right face?" Col. Kirkpatrick said, in a good natured, careless manner, "It don't make a d—d bit o' difference, General: don't you see they are coming all right? they know just what I want 'em to do, and will do it, too." The Colonel was correct. The regiment had promptly shouldered arms, faced about, and was at his horse's heels when Gen. Dumont spoke. "Well, if there's a mutua understanding between you, it don't make a d—d bit o' difference, sure enough," said Gen. Dumont, with his inimitable squint and nasal, and rode quietly away, fully satisfied that the Seventy-Second and her brave Lieutenant Colonel understood each other in plain English, and were not going to balk over a pebble of tactics in the way of duty. There is more than a mere witty passage between the General and the Colonel in the above. It illustrates the secret of the strength and discipline of the volunteer troops of the United States. They were not long in the field before intelligent officers comprehended what should be done and how to do it properly; whether they understood the language of the tactics or not, they made their intelligent soldiers understand them; there was "a mutual understanding" and hence a unity of action and effective execution. The Seventy-Second always understood the gallant Col. Kirkpatrick, as the sequel will show.

On the 11th. we were called up and formed line of battle long before day, stacked arms and went to work on the fortifications. Hall's brigade, of our division, and Wolford's cavalry, reported to Col. Miller for duty. Since the fate of Hartsville, we are on the extreme left of the army, and the way into Kentucky *via* Hartsville is open to the enemy. On the 12th, we were still under arms. On the 13th, Gen. Reynolds visited the camp and pronounced it untenable, there being some high points from which, he said, the rebels could shell us out in two hours. We hardly thought so, and hated to lose all our hard work, but we must obey our General, and he ordered us to move about two miles west on to higher ground, near Bledsoe's Creek, to which place we removed camp on the 14th of December. Here we lay without fortifications, being often called up in the night to form line of battle and lie for hours on our arms; and frequently we could hear the clatter of the hoofs of the rebel cavalry on the pike in the vicinity of our camp. On the night we left our old Castillian camp, rebels came into it. They were hovering about thick as flies in August watching their opportunity to pounce down upon us

On December 14th, Sergt. McClure, with 36 men, was put on picket between our present camp and the one just vacated at Castillian Springs, and they formed a part of a chain picket on that and the south side of our camp. They had a corn field in their front, and after night were ordered to fire on (with halting) anything that approached from that direction. About midnight a movement was heard in the field, and the men began firing and kept it up at intervals till morning, when, just at daylight, Capt. Hanna, who was officer of the day, came tearing out to see what was the matter and to cheer us up, when we found out in the field a gang of jacks and jennels quietly feeding on the corn stalks.

It seems amusing now, but we failed to see the fun then.

The main topic amongst the soldiers was the advance of Rosecrans from Nashville on Bragg's army at Murfreesboro. We all knew that a great battle was soon to be fought there. It was in those days of folly when the Generals of our great armies told all the newspaper correspondents what they were going to do, and how they were going to do it, and thus notified the rebels in advance of all our movements. This was very convenient for the rebels, but death on Union soldiers. This battle was approaching, and day by day we could hear the firing of the artillery skirmishing of the two great armies, and day by day we expected to be ordered to the front. Another topic of conversation was the 100 day emancipation proclamation which was to go into effect by the issuance of another on the next New Years, now almost come, proclaiming all the slaves of rebels free. Would the President adhere to his purpose, or would he recede? Some thought he ought to recede, as the attempted enforcement of such a proclamation would only make the rebels resist more desperately to save their millions of dollars' worth of slaves. Others held that the President should be firm in his purpose, and as the slaves were the property of the rebels, and a source of strength to the Rebellion, he should confiscate them and put them in the Union army to work and to fight. What he did, the world knows, and the world and Heaven approves his noble act.

On the 20th of December, Col. Woolford made a reconnoissance towards Hartsville and found the rebel pickets occupying that place. At this time it had been quite well ascertained that when the battle should begin between Rosecrans' and Bragg's armies, Morgan would be sent with a heavy and fleet force to play havoc in the rear, destroy trains, capture and destroy supplies, cut the railroad and telegraph, and interrupt communication in all possible ways.

On the 22nd of December, Col. Wilder, of the 17th Ind., joined our brigade and took command. The Seventy-Second always regarded this as an insult to Col. Miller, who had commanded the brigade from the time we left Frankfort, and had commanded it well, being liked and trusted by all the regiments of the brigade; but rank was rank, and Col. Miller came back to the regiment, which had been commanded all this time by the brave and generous Lieut. Col. Kirkpatrick.

As soon as Wilder assumed command, (25th,) he ordered us to move camp further south-west on to the top of the hill in the woods, which was, we think, a good position.

On the 25th, Christmas day, it was as warm and pleasant as a May day. The birds sang, the spiders, flies, gnats, mosquitoes, and all their kin folks, were out in force, and several of the Seventy-Second went in swimming, and reported the water very pleasant.

CHAPTER XVII.

December 26th, 1862, to January 8th, 1863—The New Reveille—Ordered to March—Forced March Through the Rain to the Rock House and Scottsville—A Two Days' Wade—Frozen in the Mud—Clothes up and wade Big Barren River—We may Forage a Little—At Glasgow—Fresh Mutton and Pork, Chickens and Apple Jack, and a Regimental Spree—To Bear Wallow—Mule Brigade that Didn't Chase Morgan—To Cave City and the Storm that Upset Tents—News from the Great Battle at Stone River—A Victory on the Emancipation Proclamation—March to Murfreesboro—On the Battlefield—Limbs Found in Tents, Bodies in the Waters, and Devastation Everywhere—What's de Matter, Dah?—Into Camp at Murfreesboro on the Hickory Flats.

Up to this time all our movements had been regulated by fife and drum. On the morning of the 26th, just before day, a bugler at Col. Wilder's headquarters blew reveille. The men bounced up at once at this new sound, supposing it might mean that the rebels were coming in fury upon us. Before fully dressed, the breakfast call was blown, and before breakfast a furious blast was blown which we were informed, meant to strike tents and prepare to march. Breakfast was not half eaten, but we arose and promptly hauled down tents, and before we had them ready, the regimental teams came up in a sweeping trot. Something was up we knew. Before the wagons were loaded, the drums rolled out orders to fall in, and before the sun was up, we were moving out to the pike, wondering whether we were to go to the main army now advancing on Murfreesboro, or to Hartsville and attack Morgan.

At the pike we were halted and company commanders ordered to send every man not able for a forced march, to Gallatin. Many were really sick, and many who were not sick were not able for a long forced march; and some few played sick and fell out, which left each company about 50 men—half the number at muster-in. Of the number who fell out and were sent to Gallatin Hospital, 27 died. What a terrible mortality!

We were to chase Morgan once more, and turned our faces northwards. Reynolds' whole division was in the column. Just then a cold rain began to fall and continued all day. We moved directly north to the Rock-House and went into camp on the ground we had occupied just a month before. The marching had been miserable, the mud ankle deep, water often knee deep, and we went into camp wet, muddy and very tired.

On the 27th of December, we moved on to Scottsville, that famous rural town. We marched all day in rear of our train, and the rain came down in torrents. We had to march much of the time right up little branches through water from six inches to a foot and a half deep, and through mud from three inches to a foot deep. When we went into camp at Scottsville, many of us were so coated with mud to the waist, that we waded into the creek where it was two feet deep and washed the mud off our clothes. The whole regiment wore shoes, and as we had marched 40 miles in two days through rain, mud and water, and over sharp stones, the condition of our feet might be better imagined than described. Some of us had worn our shoes out, and our feet were raw and bleeding at every step. Almost every one's feet were very much blistered and sore. With but little cooked rations—for it was difficult to get wood, everything was so wet--we wrapped up in our blankets to spoon to the right or left, as the case might be, until morning. During the night it turned cold, the rain turned to snow, and by morning the ground was frozen an inch deep.

It was hard to pull out of the frozen earth on the 28th and resume our march; but it had to be done, and we struck out early on the Glasgow road, tarrying not in old Scottsville. We made another 20 miles that day, which was clear and cool, but quite muddy. About an hour before sundown, we came to the Big Barren River, where we were commanded to strip and wade. The river was swollen, and ice an inch thick had formed along the shore. We stripped off our pantaloons and began to yell, "Close up!—close up!—close up!" With pants, shoes and socks, gun and haversack, elevated in air, we waded into the water and modestly elevated our hog-hair shirts as the water encroached on the lower borders thereof. The water was almost to the armpits of the short men, and cold—booh! Just as we were wading in, a smart orderly rode up and called out, "Col. Wilder says for you to close up here." Some fellow who had his shirt up to his neck yelled out, "Bear my compliments to the Colonel and tell him I can't get clothes an inch higher without tearing them off." There was many a slip and tumble in getting into the bluff banked stream, and the officers and orderlies formed a line below to catch those who might be washed down by the water, which ran as swift as a race horse. We crossed without serious casualty, though many got handsome duckings and wet hog skins.

As soon as we crossed the river, we went into camp, where dry rails were abundant, and if we didn't burn thousands of them that night, then we are no historian. And if the country round about was not foraged thoroughly for something to eat, then we were not good soldiers. The rain had spoiled all our rations and we were in a manner out.

On the morning of the 29th, before we marched, Col. Miller told us that as our rations were out, we might forage some, but to be moderate and discreet. We had anticipated him a little, but cheered as though it was a new born privilege. We availed ourselves of it during the day but little, as we moved rapidly, making 20 miles through forests, over hills and rocks. We crossed the Little Barren River on a log in the forenoon, and went into camp near Glasgow late in the afternoon.

When we got to Glasgow, our rations were utterly exhausted, and we had to forage. Some of us remained in camp and built fires while others went out to bring in something to eat. They found sheep, hogs, chickens and turkeys, in abundance, and also "bought" large quantities of meal, corn bread, biscuits and flour, from citizens. A mill was pressed to grind meal and flour for the boys. Soon the camp smelled as savory as Jerusalem of old on burnt offering day. Hundreds of fires smoked with fresh meats. Mingled with this odor of meats was one never smelt in Jerusalem—the odor of apple jack. The boys had found a still house full of this jolly Kentucky beverage and almost every man in the regiment got drunk. Of course there were exceptions, but it was called a general and glorious drunk by the oldest judges of that article. 'Twas a night of feasting, frolic, fun, song and dance. Every fellow seemed to forget his sore feet, his tattered shoes, and all his ills, and go in for a good time. Those that were not drunk laughed themselves almost outside in. This was always referred to as the general drunk of the regiment. There were times afterwards when two or three companies would get well filled, but this is the only time when every man in the regiment, who would indulge, got "three sheets in the wind." Yet, be it said to the credit of the regiment, there were many men who could, under no circumstances, be induced to touch a drop. And the boys didn't get on much of a high, after all. The fiddler of Company I felt pretty well, and to his music hundreds of the boys danced in their tattered shoes and stockings until there was scarce a bit of either left.

We remained at Glasgow all day the 30th, and on the 31st we started north again before daylight. We marched 15 miles to a place called Bear Wallow, a mere sign of a cross-road town, getting there just after noon. Here it first became known to the men generally that we were after Morgan, who had been raiding upon the Louisville & Nashville Railroad, our main line of communication in Kentucky.

On January 1st, while at Bear Wallow, we learned that Morgan was making his way back into Tennessee. That evening, just after sundown, the long roll beat, and we were just three minutes forming line, being in line several minutes before any other regiment. The enemy did not come and we lay on our arms all night. The movements of Morgan were closely observed and reported by scouts, and we knew he was hovering around us and measuring our strength and position.

On this very evening of January 1st, 1863, near night, when firing was heard north of us and the report came that Morgan was passing around our right flank, Col. Wilder, anxious to give chase, attempted to mount a lot of men on the team mules of the division. The mules were brought out in great haste, each one shaking his tail as if he knew there was extra duty demanded. Not more than one mule out of six had ever had a man on its back, and never wanted to have. The order to mount was given, and the bold men and officers each leaped upon his mule; each mule gave a bray, brought his head between his fore feet as his heels flew high into the air, and each man also flew high into the air and flopped down in the mud. The mules wiggled their tails, shook their heads, and became as demure as Quakers. The brave men picked themselves up out of the mud and each went for his mule again, and sprang upon their backs. The mules turned a hand-spring as before, sending the men tumbling into the air. Scarcely a man stuck except those that got on to the saddle mules. Soon the mules seemed to understand the game and began to jump on to each other's backs, some of them climbing on behind the men that had stuck and knocking them off; some ran under the bellies of other mules and hoisted them from the ground, and in a minute they were as badly tangled as a den of snakes, braying piteously, shaking their tails and kicking up and down, right and left. In vain those holding the bridles while others tried to mount shouted, "Who-o-o-a!" with a chorus of mill dams, coffer dams, and all sorts of dams. It was worse than a battery of grape and canister, and the mule line had to be abandoned, upon which they untangled, shook their tails, and were soon at their respective wagons eating hay as solemnly as hypocrites. The Seventy-Second had no part in this farce except to do the laughing. The 17th did the swearing.

It is said that this attempt to form a mule brigade to chase Morgan was the conception of the idea which resulted in Col. Wilder having the brigade mounted some months afterwards. We had been chasing Morgan's force, which was mounted on the best blooded horses of the South, in mule wagons and on foot, and the Colonel seeing the futility of such chases, determined that he would try and have a brigade mounted so as to travel as rapidly as Morgan could. So the attempt to form the mule brigade was prolific, if not successful at Bear Wallow.

When Hartsville was abandoned, the way was left open into Kentucky, and Morgan, with 6,000 cavalry, eight pieces of artillery and two howitzers, marched rapidly on the 24th of December, for Bowling Green, tore up the railroad, and did a great deal of mischief; but being assailed in front, rear and flanks, he fled towards Tennessee. Reynolds' division had been hurried forward to intercept him, but although we marched 20 miles a day, the old fox flanked around and got away. An old Kentuckian who came into our camp to protest against our burning his rails, was treated with marked civility by officers and men. He was asked why this place was called Bear Wallow. "You see that thar pond up yander, don't you?" We said, "Yes sir." "Well, long time ago, when I fust settled hare, b'ars used to come an' waller in it; and when the Post-office was made at these cross rods in my house, we called it B'ar Waller."

While we were on this march, the great battle of Stone River was being fought, and but for the chase after Morgan we would have participated in it.

January 2nd, in the afternoon, we moved some 14 miles from Bear Wallow to Cave City on the L. & N. Railroad, to take the cars for Nashville. We were very anxious to learn the result of the battle of Murfreesboro, and also of what had come of the emanipation proclamation, as we had heard nothing from the world since the 25th. We moved through woods and fields, over a mere country trail, to Cave City, arriving in the night and rain. Our wagons were there and tents were hastily put up to keep off the rain. Just before daylight, a most terrific wind and rain storm struck the camp. The tents flopped and rattled; men jumped up to hold them down, some with no garment on but their shirts, which cracked and popped in the storm like vollies of musketry. Hallooing, braying and confusion was in the air, and down came almost every tent. The air was full of hats, caps, breeches, drawers, and everything that a mighty wind could move, chased by men in their shirts. It was the most ridiculous scene ever witnessed in the regiment. Men were hunting pantaloons and other articles for some time after daylight. It was the first night for over a week that we had an opportunity to sleep like white folks, and to be raided by a rebel wind in that style was too vexatious.

The sun came up bright and warm, and gave the men a chance to dry blankets and clothing. Near our camp was a peculiar cave, the mouth of which was funnel shaped, 50 feet across at the top, just as deep as wide, a deep pool in the centre of the bottom, where a hydraulic ram worked and pumped water to a railroad track a mile distant. From the pool, a cave ran to the north-east no telling how far; some of us followed it a mile. We had to get into the cave by passing over some slabs that lay over the pool. Some of the 17th Ind. men squatted down on the slabs, and as we attempted to pass them Capt. Watts, Company I, accidentally pushed one of them in, which made lots of fun, and lots of cursing, too, from the fellow that got ducked.

We lay at this camp until the 5th of January, during which time we heard that Rosecrans' army had gained a great victory over Bragg, compelling him to evacuate his works at Stone River, leave Murfreesboro, and flee for Duck River. This gave wonderful cheer to the troops. We also learned that the President had issued his emancipation proclamation. While we lay here the inevitable drill was attended to for part of each day, and getting wood the other part of the day. One day Maj. Carr was drilling the battalion, and Capt. Hanna, getting a little tangled, disputed the correctness of one of the Major's commands and refused to execute it. This astonished every one, for the Major was very bright in the tactics. After some parley, Capt. Hanna, who was notorious for knowing very little of the tactics, executed the command under protest. After going off drill, the Captain went to the Major's quarters and offered an apology, saying that he was wrong and the Major was correct.

"Well, why didn't you say so on drill?" asked the Major withwarmth

"Why, do you suppose, Maj. Carr, that I'm such a dashed fool as to acknowledge before my company that I am wrong?" replied the Captain with solemn emphasis.

On the afternoon of the 5th, we began to pack up and but our equipage on the train to go to Nashville. The hardest things to load were the mules, many of which had to be literally lifted up and shoved into the doors despite their kicking and braying. We ran to Nashville that night, and it was a miserable duplicate of the ride from Indianapolis to Jeffersonville. It was a box and flat car train; the artillry was put on the flat cars and half our regiment on top the box cars. It was our fortune, as usual, to be put on top. The first part of the night was bitter cold, and about midnight it began to rain, and soon we were wet to the skin. We were so overcome with fatigue that we could not resist sleep, and taking our gun slings we strapped ourselves to the foot board to keep from rolling off, and were thumped and banged until daylight, when we arrived at Nashville, running 100 miles in a little over 14 hours. The miserable old train just flew down some of the grades and crawled up others.

That morning, (the 6th), we marched through the muddy streets of Nashville, and to camp three miles south-west of it, expecting to stay a few days, but that very night, we got orders to draw clothing and prepare to march in the morning. As we had not drawn any clothing since we enlisted, except overcoats, and as we had just had one of the muddiest marches soldiers ever made, we were dirty and ragged beyond description, and as previously hinted, some were a little graybackish.

The whole regiment drew a complete new outfit, except dress coats, and we also drew new gum blankets. This work was not finished until midnight, and yet there were several men in each company for whom there were no pantaloons big enough, and a special requisition had to be sent to Nashville to get harness they could work in. There were five sergeants in Company I, whose combined weight was 1,000 pounds.

At 2 A. M. of the 7th, reveille sounded. We got up in the snow and took breakfast at 4, got into Nashville by dawn, and learned that we were to go to Murfreesboro with the 17th Indiana and 19th Indiana Battery, as advance guard for a train of 3,000 wagons that were loaded with rations for the army at that place. There was a thin snow on the ground, which melted as the sun arose and made walking sloppy. We had all drawn new shoes, the pike was torn to pieces by the movement of heavy artillery over it, and full of sharp stones and immense mud holes. The shoes pinched and blistered our feet—for a pike is far worse than a dirt road to march over—we moved very rapidly, and before night, almost half the men had fallen out of ranks We marched 35 miles that day, including three miles from camp to Nashville, and the last 10 of it was exquisite torture. Blisters formed and bursted upon the feet that day by scores. But the brave victors at Stone River needed food, and we would not halt as long as we could move one foot after the other. Many of the teams gave out, and several mules smothered in the mud holes in which they fell exhausted The poor mule is odd, but he has never had a proper eulogium pronounced up his service, his sufferings and his patriotism, and we are sorry to say there is no space in these pages for so great a spread.

We went into camp three miles from Murfreesboro on one of the battle fields, every foot of which had been fought over. Indeed, all the way from Nashville to Stone River was scarred by the great struggle, but as we neared that river, the evidence of the fearful conflict became more ghastly and startling. Many pages could be taken in describing the ravages of the battle. In many places the hedges and underbrush have been mown down like weeds by the leaden storm of musketry. In other places great trees were torn limb from limb, and some even blown up at the roots. One large tree had been perforated by seven large shells; huge pieces had been torn out of it, but it still stood like a scarred veteran. The ground in the forest was covered by limbs cut from the trees by cannon shot and shell. Hundreds of horses lay upon the ground torn and mangled. It was after dark when we got into camp; when we built our fires, a man's leg was found in our quarters—cold comfort. A Company C man picked up a rebel canteen and threw it in the fire, and in a few minutes it exploded and wounded a man seriously. This was hot comfort, and convinced us of the truth of the statement we had often heard, that rebel soldiers had gun powder and whisky furnished to them to make them fight furiously. Indeed, we afterwards picked up many a rebel canteen which had gun powder in it and smelled of whisky, which leaves no doubt of the fact in our mind.

In hunting for water, we found a pond and filled our camp kettles and did our cooking with the water. Next morning we went to that pond for more water, and found two dead rebels lying in it frozen in the ice. We went to Stone River, nearly a mile away, to get water, and when we got to it, there lay anotner dead rebel in the edge of the water. The reflection that we had drank coffee made from the wasting of dead rebels was not pleasant. But such is war. Many men from that bloody field were buried hurriedly in out-of-the-way places, and often not very deep. We know of several instances where wagons would pass over the bodies, and the head, hands or feet, would fly up out of the soft ground as ghosts rising from the earth. We shall never forget a horrible incident where a wagoner accidently drove over one of these shallow graves and a man's hand flew out of the ground. "Look at that fellow grabbing at my wagon wheel," roared out the rough soldier.

On the 8th, we started late and moved leisurely over the battle field of the second day's fight, noting with curiosity and deep interest the many scars and seams of the terrible carnage. After crossing Stone River, we went into an old field on a high ground to rest. The pioneer corps were very busy felling trees, just north of us, to be used in building a bridge. A lot of teams were waiting to haul away the timber. A negro who drove a team had lain down in his wagon and gone to sleep; a large tree began to fall near his six mule team, creaking and crashing as it came down, the mules sprang forward and began to run at full speed; in 10 rods the front axle hit solid on a big stump, every mule broke loose, faced square about and stood still as if amazed; the wagon bed flew 10 feet into the air and came down with a crash. We expected the negro was mashed into jelly; but he "kind 'o" roused up a little, looked around and said, "What's 'a matter da'r." When our regiment roared with laughter, he looked at us with a bewildered expression, as if we were all fools.

We moved through Murfreesboro, a mile east on the McMinnville pike, and went into camp south of the road, in a very flat piece of ground heavily wooded—hickory flats, that's precisely what it was. This was a week after the battle, yet everything was in confusion. We were now encamped in line by brigades along with all our division, and were for the first time regularly incorporated into the Army of the Cumberland.

CHAPTER XVIII.

From January 8th to February 19th, 1863—Recapitulation of Result of First Six Months Service—Resignations, Deaths, Discharges and Desertions—Our Sick and Dead Left all Along our Line of Hard Marches—Hard Duty and Short Rations at Murfreesboro—The Endless Chain of Mules—Tardy Repairing of the Railroad—Officers Dismissed—Scouts to Franklin, Liberty and other Places—"A Hoss! A Hoss! my Kingdom for a Hoss!"—Talk of Mounting—Capt. Pinkerton's Prayer—Discouraging and Encouraging Letters—The Power of our Heroic Women—Testing the Seventy-Second by Two Paces to the Front—A Hypocrite and Spy Shot—Deserter's Head Shaved and Cheek Branded with a Red Hot Iron—First Pay Day—An Incident—Move Camp from the Old Death-Pit Into an Open Field—The Seventy-Second Sent for a Little Lumber and Brings in a Saw Mill—"Surrender! you d—d Yank—Surrender! you d—d Reb!"—The Rebels Attack Hall's Brigade and are Defeated—Imposing Funeral Ceremonies.

We have now been in the service five months from enlistment, and this point marks an epoch in the history of our regiment. From the day of our entering Camp Tippecanoe, and our muster at Indianapolis, we have been constantly on the move, hardly staying long enough in any one place to get our camp fitted up and our clothes washed. Here we begin a season of camp life which lasts almost six months. It seems but yesterday since we left our homes of peace and plunged into the midst of the strife. But let us take a brief retrospect and we shall see what sad changes have been wrought in those short—to us long—months.

Adjt. Rice, who, if not the father of the regiment, was a father to it, has been promoted to Adjutant General on Gen. Reynolds' staff; Maj. Samuel C. Kirkpatrick to the Lieutenant Colonelcy; Capt. Henry M. Carr, Company B, to the Majority, and Capt. Jesse Hill, Company I, to the Chaplaincy of the regiment. The following had resigned: Capts.' Henry Wilson, E; Robert LaFollett, D; First Lieutenants, Ira Brown, I; George Ross, K. Second Lieutenants, George Ruger, C; George W. Ward, H; James H Whitcomb, K; David H. Ashman, D; a total loss of nine commissioned officers, one of whom, Capt. Wilson, had died after resignation.

The losses of non-commissioned officers and privates by death, discharge and desertion, for the same period, were as follows:

	Died	Discharged	Deserted
Company A	2	4	1
" B	5	2	1
" C	6	1	1
" D		2	
" E	4	5	1
" F	10	1	1
" G	4	4	3
" H	3	2	2
" I	4	6	1
" K	5	2	4
Totals	43	29	15

Making a loss of nine officers and 87 men, a total loss of 96 in five months. But this loss of one-third of the commissioned officers and one-tenth of the men is but a faint representation of the terrible suffering and losses which our short service had caused. We had left our dead all along the line of our marches, and our sick and exhausted in every hospital. Many were lingering in the hospitals at the date of this recapitulation who died afterwards from the effects of the hardships of our first five months' service. To prove this, it is only necessary to go back to the starting point and note the deaths in the various hospitals: Two died at Jeffersonville; seven at New Albany; 13 at Louisville; two at Frankfort; two at Bardstown; seven at Bowling Green; six at Scottsville; 27 at Gallatin; four at Nashville; 24 at Murfreesboro, making a total of 94 who died within six weeks after we got to Murfreesboro. That is, 43 men had died by January 8th, 1863, the date of our going into camp at Murfreesboro, and 51 died in the next six weeks!

The Hartsville run and the Morgan chase had in six weeks been more fatal than all the battles our regiment was ever in. In the first six months of our service, three times as many men died as were killed during the whole three years service of the regiment.

We have no data from which to calculate the number finally discharged for disability contracted before we reached Murfreesboro; but asuming that the rate of discharge was the same as the death rate, the result is 70 discharged; a loss of some 189 men and 10 commissioned officers, a total loss of 199—one fifth of the regiment—as the result of the first five months' service. Had this rate of loss been continued, the entire regiment would have been dead or discharged in 25 months. Few will differ from the statement that the severest period on the health of the regiment had been almost passed.

Gen. Rosecrans' whole army of 47,000 was lying in and around Murfreesboro, and with all speed the proper points were strongly fortified and all approaches were picketed. There were details for fatigue duty on fortifications, and hard work for many days after we pitched camp, in those miserable hickory flats. The question for getting rations forward from Nashville, a distance of 35 miles, was a very serious one. The railroad had been torn up by the rebels during the late battle and was in a painfully slow process of repair. Every day 300 wagons loaded with rations, each wagon drawn by six mules, left Nashville for Murfreesboro; every day 300 such teams left Murfreesboro for Nashville, to be in their turn loaded and sent back with rations. Thus an endless chain of mule teams was moving on this pike all the time, drawing supplies for this great army; and as it rained a great deal, no wonder that the pike became next to impassable. Teams were three days regulary, and often four days, on the road from Nashville to Murfreesboro. It required a long time to get enough provisions up for full rations for the army, though the teams at first brought in 2,000 loads a week. It took about three months to put the railroad in running order, and five months to accumulate military stores sufficient to move on Bragg at Shelbyville, Tenn., who, during this delay, had grown stronger than ever before. What a contrast between the manner in which the army was supplied at this time and during the last two years of the war, when Sherman would have had the cars running in two days, and his men would never have lost a ration, as he did on the Atlanta Campaign. All this time we were hard at work on fortifications and picket duty, and in addition scouring and scraping the country for forage, and the rebels were bolder and more defiant than every they had been before, and hardly a day passed that they did not attack some post or foraging party, and often with success.

The first day we were at Murfreesboro, a detail of 100 men from our regiment was sent on picket, Capt. Watts in command. He was ordered to picket in front of our division, and to connect his lines with the pickets on the right and left. It was very dark and rainy, and he could find no lines to connect with, but posted his men the best he could and waited for daylight to find the other pickets. We were very short of rations, and Capt Watts had none at all, except what the men of his company gave him. Just at daylight, he went to a house to get something to eat, and while gone, the officer of the day, the Major of the 17th Ind., came and found him off his post, and as soon as he returned put him under arrest and subsequently preferred charges against him for which he was dismissed on the 20th of January, by order of Gen. Reynolds.

Col. Miller says, "this was all wrong;" and it was so regarded by everybody in the regiment, as by it Company I lost its best officer. We may also here speak of Lieut. Orrin E. Harper, Company F, who was dismissed the service on March 2nd of the same year, and of whose dismissal Col. Miller says, in equally emphatic terms, "It should never have been done." And Hornada, of Company F, says that "Lieut. Harper was at once father and brother to the company."

On the 23rd of January, our regiment went out fifteen miles in the direction of Franklin, to guard a forage train. We became aware that the enemy was making a movement for our capture, and began a speedy return to camp, bringing in our train all right, and making a 30 mile march. Just as we got back, we met a force going out to our relief, as Gen. Reynolds had been apprised of the movements of the enemy and feared we would be cut off. That was as brisk a march, especially returning, as the regiment ever made, except when it ran to Hartsville. In going out, before danger was apprehended, we passed through a section where things were pretty plenty, and the boys managed some way (bought them, we suppose,) to get hold of hams, shoulders, fresh side meat, cabbage, chickens, geese, turkeys, &c., &c., which were stuck on to, or hung on to, thier bayonets. And, although the return march was very rapid, not a man would part with any of this newly acquired property, and brought it all into camp. We have known of soldiers throwing away, blankets, clothing, knapsacks, and even guns, on occasians, but who ever heard of a soldier throwing away a ham, a chicken, a cabbage head, or any such thing? Very few.

It will be impossible to mention all the scouts we made while lying at Murfreesboro, and therefore we select the most important ones.

On the morning of February 3rd. Reynolds' division started to Liberty, the object being to make a forced march and surprise the enemy at that place. The division moved briskly to Auburn, near which one of the enemy's pickets was captured, and it was learned that the rebels had a force of about 1,500 at Liberty. On Wednesday, the 4th, it was clear and cold. We got ready to move on the enemy at daylight, the first brigade having the advance, and moved so cautiously that it took all day to march seven miles; and when we got to Liberty, we found the enemy had been gone some time. We might as well have surprised and captured them. When we got to Liberty, we marched eight miles in pursuit on a road the rebels did not take, and camped at Alexandria. It was a very severe night of rain and snow. On that night two of our brigade were captured by the rebels.

On the 5th, we moved 20 miles, the rebels following in our rear closely all the time to pick up any unfortunate man who could not keep up, or any stragglers. On the 6th, it was clear and cold; we passed through Lebanon, Tenn., and went into camp at Bird's Mills, on the Murfreesboro road, six miles from Lebanon. On the 7th, we got on the road early, Hall's brigade taking the front, the wagon trains following, and the Seventy-Second some half mile behind the train. While passing through a dense cedar thicket, which had once been infested by robbers, but now by guerrillas, the latter swarmed out from the thicket and attacked the train furiously. The train would have been captured, too, had it not been for some men of Company I, who being foot-sore had been permitted to start in advance. They were right at the place the attack was made and opened fire on the assailants, driving them into the woods. The Seventy-Second quickly formed line of battle and came to the rescue, and Lilly's battery shelled the woods, which were too dense for troops to penetrate in any sort of order. The rebels lost two killed and five captured in this little affair.

Sergt. Sam. Taylor, of Company I, played a clever piece of strategy on this occasion. His feet were so crippled that he could hardly walk at all. He had strapped his gun on his knapsack, and with a cane in each hand was moving along with the greatest difficulty; but when the rebels attacked the train, he threw both canes away and ran like a buck back to the regiment. When the boys raised a great laugh at this sudden cure, he said: "Well, what the deuce could I do but run; my gun was strapped to my back so I could not get it off, and the way the Johnnies were peppering them old wagon boxes, I was afraid they might hit me." "But how about your feet?" asked the boys. "O, they don't hurt me a bit now; I don't think I shall need a cane any more to-day," he replied. Taylor was a good soldier, and ever after was always ready.

Another little incident to show the spirit of the Seventy-Second. When near Murfreesboro, late in the evening, something obstructed the movements of Hall's brigade, and our regiment had to stand in column until their legs ached and their patience was exhausted, moving a rod or two and waiting. When they reached the obstruction which had so long detained them, they found it to be a big mud hole, over which Hall's brigade had passed single file on a rail When our men saw what it was, they called out to Col. Miller, "If your horse can go through it we can." The Colonel rode through it and the mud and water was only knee deep to the horse. At once the men raised the yell that they used on charging rebel works and dashed through it double quick, four abreast. We crossed Stone River on a bridge of wagons drawn up side by side, and got into our camp at Murfreesboro at 10 o'clock at night, muddy, tired and ravenously hungry. The result of the trip was 50 prisoners and three rebels killed.

During this month there began to be considerable talk about mounting the regiment. At first there were a large majority of men and officers opposed to it; they said they had enlisted and been drilled as infantry, and they didn't want to become cavalry. But the many scouts we had to make through the mud and over the hills, fording mud holes and streams on foot, brought us to the conclusion that if we had to do cavalry duty, we would prefer to have horses to ride. This was especially the case on a scout begun on February 17th, and continued to the 19th, towards Trinne, about 12 miles from Murfreesboro. It rained very hard, the streams became high and the roads desperately muddy, and the cry of Richard could be heard all along the line at every stream and extra bad piece of road, "a hoss! a hoss! my kingdom for a hoss!" This trip was prolonged to the 19th, on account of the high waters, and when the men got back to camp they were for mounting by a large majority.

After arriving at Murfreesboro, there were some who expressed dissatisfaction with the President's emancipation proclamation. One day a Lieutenant visited the headquarters of Company G, was invited to stay and take dinner, and accepted. Dinner was spread on a table made of ammunition boxes in the little tent; the outlay was plain and the beans not over done. While eating, the question of the proclamation came up. The visiting Lieutenant said, in a fretful, com plaining spirit:

"Well, if I were living here in the South, and such a proclamation should be issued, I'd feel like fighting the Government forever before giving up my property."

"You don't quite approve the proclamation, then?" quietly suggested some one.

"No sir, decidedly I don't. I think it an outrage upon the rights of property—"

Capt Pinkerton could stand it no longer, and brought his fist down with violence upon the table. knocking a tin platter of beans and s. b. to the top of the tent, as he said with such emphasis as to blow the beans out of his mouth until they rattled like musket balls against the side of the tent: "Lieutenant, I say any man who will talk that way 'damn him!—damn him!!—damn him!!!' (hitting the table to emphasize each damn.) I'm not swearing, now, either, I'm praying! —I'm praying!!—I'm praying!!! Such disloyalty is contemptible."

The Lieutenant didn't pursue the subject. but did very soon pursue his way from that tent of earnest, pointed prayer, not caring to be prayed for after that fashion. In this connection we mention that there were many discouraging letters sent to many of the men by those at home who opposed the Administration. The emancipation proclamation, and the talk of arming negroes, were seized upon to encourage desertion. Some men received letters telling them if they would desert and come home they would be protected against arrest and punishment. But we say, with pride, that these letters were almost universally spurned. Many of them were handed over to the officers, and some of them sent home to be filed with the county officers of the counties from which they were sent. In this hour of peril to the Union cause, many thousands of the wives, mothers, sisters and sweethearts, of our soldiers wrote them letters exhorting them to be firm, gallant and hopeful; to not waver in the least degree in facing all the dangers and hardships of field and camp. These letters were a power for good which can never be fully measured. We have many such letters before us which show what heroines our women were in those fiery, bloody days. Had not the women been brave, and ready to suffer privation with patience and courage, we are candid in saying that the Union cause might have failed. We speak from personal knowledge when we say, that many a soldier was led to desertion by letters from wife, mother, sister, or some lady friend. Others who were too honorable to violate their oaths became heartbroken, and died of home sickness—pining away in unutterable anguish—dying by inches. We know of such cases and mention a few. One day we were asked to walk with a noble soldier; we had been in the field but four months. When some distance from camp, he pulled a letter from his pocket which he asked us to read. It was, indeed, a pitiable document. The wife of the man had written it, and filled it with the most agonizing entreaties for him to get off, in some way, and come home. She told of how she dreamed of seeing him dead when she fell asleep, and awoke screaming with anguish; how she wept by day and by night; how her three little children joined in her sorrow and refused to be comforted. The poor fellow sat on a log and shook with emotion. We told him to write her cheerful letters; to insist on her believing that he would come out all right, and that he was not in half as much danger as she supposed. "I have done all that," he replied; "I have written to her over and over, but to no purpose. She began to write me in this way as soon as I had left for the front, and twice a week, on an average, I have such letters." The letters grew worse; his wife became so weak from grief that she was bed fast. The poor fellow could not get home; he became melancholy, took sick and simply perished—slain by grief.

Many similar instances we knew, and give one more. A young man entered the service as a line officer, leaving a young wife at home. For two years she wrote him brave, cheerful letters. The fearful campaigns of 1874 came on; the line officer had become a field officer; his wife read in the papers of the fearful carnage, and her heart became heavy with an awful dread that her husband's name might be in the next list of killed. She began to write the most depressing letters to her husband. Her health was delicate; the officer idolized his wife. His courage failed; he became cowed if not a coward; he was now in command of the regiment, but he rode at its head no more. He was not sick enough to be in hospital, he was not well enough to be in the front. He lost reputation amongst those who had admired him for his courage, and went out of the service almost in disgrace, and quite in contempt of his command. It is proper to say this officer was not a Seventy-Second man. Wonderful was the power of a brave, sensible wife, mother, sister, or sweetheart, over a soldier in the field! Such women could make first rate soldiers of men who, without such a power over them, would have been very poor military material, if not worthless.

Good letters from home would often make a sick man almost well. It was a reply often given, when one soldier would say to another who was not well, "How are you to day?" "O, I'm almost well; I got a bully letter from mother, or sister, or wife, to-day; it does me good all over." At the risk of being tedious, we give a few quotations from letters. A mother, who had been left with five little children, in a log house on a rented farm, in the forest, writes to her husband, who was a private:

"Well, when you left home you know we both promised that we would tell each other, once a week, if possible, all that had happened. I have your last letter, and I thank our Father which art in Heaven that it is so well with you. When I think of your exposure and hardships on these cold nights, and your dangers beside, I know that I am blest with ease and comfort, and feel that I have hardly any right to so much ease, when you and others have so many hardships. It snowed hard last night, and when I got up in the morning I found snow three inches deep all over the floor. Little Mattie looked out of the bed, from under cover, and said, 'Mamma, do 'oo fink it 'nowed on papa last night?' She is so sweet! Frank said, 'No it didn't either; for he's got a tent and God covers him up with a blanket every night.' I had sent to mill for meal three days ago, but hadn't got any yet, and I had but little breakfast for the children and myself, but we all ate it with thanks, only hoping that you had as much and as good. I am now at uncle's and we are all right. I walked through the deep snow and carried Katie on my shoulders and the baby in my arms; the other children walked. We pray for you all the time. We think you will come home. Be cheerful and happy about us, take care of yourself. I know we will conquer, and am glad we are doing all we can," &c.

While passing through a hospital, one day, a soldier boy called to us to come and read a letter from his mother. The letter was written by his mother after the reception of the news of the loss of her son's leg in battle. It was as full of consolation as the famous dialogue of Hugh and his mother, in the old school readers. When we had done the reading, he eagerly asked, "Isn't that a good letter?" To this we replied affirmatively, and he said, "I tell you I feel proud of my mother, and I just wish I had a dozen legs to lose in the defence of my country, just because she loves it so well. She has always written me the bulliest letters you ever read. I have a big stock of them, and when I used to get cowardly or blue, I would take one of these letters and read it, and I'd be all right again."

A sister wrote to her brother in almost these words: "Well, Scott has finally gone to the war; he got into the 73rd Indiana some way or other; he must have told a fib about his age, as he is not old enough by at least 18 months. You know Seth and Taylor went into the 7th Indiana Zouaves; John went into Col. Coburn's regiment; James went into the 143d Indiana, and you into the Seventy-Second Indiana This takes the six boys--every boy in the family. We all thought father would be greatly broken down when his last and youngest son left him, but it is not so; he really wants to go himself so much that he can hardly sleep. If he could get in by a little fib about his age as easily as Scott did, I really do think he would hardly hesitate to tell it. He now puts his age five years younger than he did before all his boys went into the army. I really believe that he is prouder of these six sons in the army than he would be of a big bag of gold. We women folks help father do the out-door work, and we will do our part gladly, and pray for you all, and send you all the little favors we can. We know "the time has come when brothers must fight, and sisters must pray at home—and work as well as pray."

The following is part of a letter written by his sweetheart to a member of the Seventy-Second, Company I: "*Dear Friend:*—It may be that we shall never meet again on earth, and that I shall never again see your dear face, or hear your words assuring me of your affections. It may be that your body, enervated by disease, weakened by privation or smitten by the enemy, shall be left to moulder on the battle field, or in a strange land; yet in your last moments—though left to die on the cold ground, pierced by the enemy's balls, with no friendly voice to soothe your last moments, no kind hand to close your dying eyes—I know your last thoughts will be of her who writes these lines to you. Such a fate would indeed be hard, and would cause me unutterable pain and long sorrow. Yet, she who wishes you happiness and prosperity on earth, and a home in heaven, writes to say that with all her love for you, with all her desire for your safety, she thinks it is better for you to go and fight for your country, share the toils and hardships of those who are in the field, and the worst fate that could possibly befall you, than to remain at home with kindred and friends, and all that the heart holds dear, and see the old flag trodden under the feet of traitors, and our splendid Government destroyed. What are home and friends without liberty? I love you all the more because you are a patriot soldier. The braver you are the more will I love you. Be assured that the few hours we have passed together will never be forgotten by me, whatever befalls you. If you die like a brave soldier, I will ever hold you sacred in memory. If you return safe from the field, having done nobly your duty, I will receive you with delight."

We might multiply these specimens of heroism displayed by our noble women during the war, but it is useless. Before the mind of son, husband, brother and lover, in the toil and conflict of camp, march and bloody field, stood the fair angelic forms of those dear ones whose love and esteem was more precious than life. In such presence none but cravens could be cowards. Every brave soldier will say, God bless the noble Union women for their grand words and deeds during the war. They were equal to legions of angels.

While we lay at Murfreesboro, some time after the battle of Stone River, Col. Miller got a hint that there was considerable discontentment in his regiment. He could have no patience for a soldier who made the course of the Government a pretext for not fully doing his sworn duty. He therefore determined that he would "sift out the souls of his men." Accordingly, one evening on dress parade he made a short statement to the regiment of what he had heard but did not believe. He said he would ask—not command—those who were determined to stand honorably to their oaths and do their sworn duty, to step two paces to the front; if there were any in the regiment who desired to violate their oaths they might stand still, that he and all others might see them. He then requested all who were determined to stand by their oaths and do their duty to step two paces forward. The whole noble old Seventy-Second bounded two steps to the front, with a promptness and energy that satisfied its brave Colonel that there was not a man in it who was less than a whole loyal man. The Colonel said he knew he was not disappointed in his regiment, and that this action gave the unanimous d—d lie to its slanderers. The Colonel, like Capt. Pinkerton, and sundry other officers and men, prayed a little sometimes, and this was one of the times.

Shortly after we went into camp at Murfreesboro, there came into camp a strange kind of man, dressed in citizens' clothing, who pretended to be very religious, saying he had been sent by the Christian Commission. He carried a good supply of paper, stamps, envelopes and other notions, which we very much needed, and gave them to all who could not pay for them. For a time he came into our camp nearly every day, talked, sang and encouraged us to be good men and soldiers. His manner was to get upon a stump and sing patriotic songs, many of his own composition, about Morgan and Bragg, Rosecrans' great victory over Bragg, and other epics. He had a good voice, a pleasant address, and we enjoyed his visits. The regiment would gather around him in large numbers, hear his songs and exhortations, receive his notions, and then he would go to the next regiment and repeat; and so he put in his time. After keeping this up for about two weeks, Gen. Negley had him arrested on suspicion of his being a spy. He was put into the provost guard house in Murfreesboro, which was a long store room. One dark, rainy night, the guard fell asleep and the fellow slipped by him. A Seventy-Second man who was present gave the alarm and told the guard to go after the fellow and bring him back. The guard was afraid to leave his post, and the rascal would soon have escaped had not the Seventy-Second man seized a gun, ran after and bid him to halt; but he would not halt, and the soldier shot him dead. On examination of the body the next morning, a complete map of the fortifications about Murfreesboro was found on it, even to the positions of the various regiments. He was one of Bragg's spies and met a spy's fate.

On Sunday, March 1st, a man in the 75th Indiana who had been tried by a court-martial for desertion and an attempt to kill an officer, received the execution of the sentence. Reynolds' whole division was drawn up in line, without arms, on the McMinnville Pike, to witness the deed. The condemned man, hand-cuffed, was marched to the front and centre of the division, where a fire was burning briskly. He was seated on a stool near the fire. A barber lathered his head until it was white as snow, and then proceeded to shave it until it was as bare as the palm and as slick as an onion. This done, his head was firmly held, while Col. Wilder took a red-hot iron from the fire and pressed it against the right cheek—a siz and jet of steam—the iron is withdrawn, and there is a large red D upon the cheek. The bands all began to play the rogue's march, while the deserter was taken to the extreme left of the division and marched along its front, bare headed, the great D showing fiery red, two soldiers following him with bayonets pointed at his hips; a drum and fife in rear playing the rogue's march. Stripped to the waist, with a single blanket rolled up and swung about his shoulder, a canteen of water and one day's rations—the wretch shivered as he passed along before us, and most of the men will say that during their service they never saw a more revolting, pitiable spectacle. He was taken beyond the Union lines, north of Murfreesboro, and set adrift with the assurance that if ever he came back he would be shot.

This was severe, but it became necessary to preserve the discipline of the army. Others, in other corps, were treated like this man. Some were shot and others hung, and yet there were still some cases of desertion and criminal conduct.

On the 3rd of March, our division started on a scout towards Woodbury, taking nine days' rations, and the first night out, camped at Reddyville. The next day we went out on a forage scout and got forage off of ground where never before had forage been got without a fight for it. While taking forage, we saw a soldier undertake to get a horse from a house in the hills—for it was a very hilly country. He had bridled the horse and was leading it away, when a young woman of the house got a hickory gad and belabored him so unmercifully over the head that he had to let it go. The brave girl seized a 10-year-old boy, threw him on the horse and told him to "skip out quick," and in a twinkling he was out of sight. This brave act of the girl was greeted by rounds of applause by our soldiers. On the 5th, our brigade remained quietly in camp at Readyville, while Hall's brigade foraged.

On the 6th, we marched rapidly to Woodbury to surprise a reble force, a detachment of Morgan's command, the Seventy-Second in advance. We left on our advance and escaped, as was usually the case when infantry undertook to capture cavalry. There was a heavy rain during that day and a furious storm at night, resulting in much suffering and subsequent illness. The expedition returned on the 8th to the old camp at Murfreesboro, with 500 loads of forage, with blistered feet, shouting "a hoss! a hoss! my kingdom for a hoss!" They were wet, muddy, tired, hungry and generally out of fix. At this time some of the 17th Indiana had been mounted, and the Seventy-Second had become convinced that it was "easiest walking when a man has a horse in his hand;" and as there seemed a determination to use us as horses, we decided to have horses to help us out.

While absent on this march, a lot of Indiana troops were captured at Franklin, including John C. Coburn's brigade, of which we heard when we returned to camp.

Pay day came at last, and for the first time, on the 10th of March. It rained the whole day, and many of us got soaking wet as we waited patiently about the pay-master's tent. We were paid to the end of the year, December 31, 1862.

The men and officers settled all their bills to that date with the Commissary and Quartermaster. And what was of most inportance to the men, the officers paid them all loans. This left the men in funds and most of them happy, especially those who had families and who needed money very much to send home for the actual wants of their wives and children.

We here mention what one of the officers wishes spoken of, (but does not want his name used) that had it not been for the generosity of the privates and non-commissioned officers, who got a bounty and advance pay, many of the commissioned officers could hardly have remained in the service, for it would have given them much trouble to have gotten uniforms and swords on entering the service, and provisions to this date. There never were a more generous lot of men mustered than were those of the Seventy-Second. There was scarce a man so mean that he would not pay his debts on pay day.

There was a wonderful amount of settling and balancing all round to do that night, and it was after midnight before the adjustments were made and the men lay down to rest. The chuck-a-luck men didn't lay down at all—they ran all night and almost perpetually until the greenbacks were exhausted.

On March 12th our regiment furnished 300 men for picket, and it took almost every well man in camp.

On the 14th of March, we moved out of the camp in the hickory flats into the field near the pike, about two hundred yards north, on to the ground for a long time occupied by the 18th Indiana Battery. Although this was but a very slight move, it was like passing from one world to another. It is putting it gently to say that that old hickory swamp camp was a death-pit. It rained much while we lay in it, and the water could not be drained off, and the best policed tents were often overflowed. And the sinks—excuse us, comrades, for naming those horrid pools of putridity, surrounded by those treacherous poles in treacherous wooden forks, and the more treacherous earth at the edges; those horrid pits in which many a luckless soldier has received the baptism of total depravity—sent up their noxious vapors day and night to poison the air. Often in that camp at night, while lying with the ear near the ground, have we heard a chorus of "grave yard coughing," as the men called it, in which three to four hundred men joined. This camp, with the hard scouting, picket and fatigue duty that had to be done, broke many an iron constitution and sent many to the grave and hospital. The strong will and frame of Col. Miller could not stand it, and he was very ill for a time. The memory of that camp is a misery. Men often died in their tents who were able to get about a little; and many died suddenly in hospital. Camp diarrhœa in its most malignant form prevailed; men would pass from their bowels from a pint to two quarts of bloody matter, or pure blood; their bowels literally decomposed. Many comrades, who have survived to this day, (February 1882,) almost 20 years, still suffer from disease contracted in that camp, and which will yet take them to the grave. Many a brave man and officer was forced to leave us that would have given "half his head" to have gone through the service with the regiment.

But here we are, out on a rolling piece of ground, where the sun shines on us; and it is now so warm that the peach bloom is already out and the swelling buds are giving a sweet tinge of green to the woods. The winter is over, and if it does rain the water runs from our camp and is not mixed with snow.

On the 17th of March, the Seventy-Second was sent out after some lumber and brought in a saw mill. Men were dying very rapidly, and there was not lumber enough in the army to make them rough coffins. When we got out to the mill, the thing looked so small and so handy, that we just thought we'd put the lumber on our wagons and borrow an ox cart and bring in the mill, which we proceeded to execute in neat style. While the mill was being loaded, one of the pioneers felt the power of the sun—or the gray-backs in his hog hair shirt felt it—and he slipped off into the woods, sat down on a log, drew off his shirt and began to "skirmish for graybacks." While thus intently engaged, one of Morgan's mounted graybacks rode up, covered the half naked pioneer with a pistol and demanded, "Surrender, you d—d Yank!" Of course the pioneer could do nothing but comply with his order, and threw up his hands in token of surrender. But the tables turned on the rebel just then and there. Just behind the fence Corporal H. W. Monroe, of Company H, lay with a squad of six men, and they all raised with rifles cocked and leveled at the rebel, and Corporal Monroe sung out, "Surrender, you d—d rebel!" which he proceeded to do without parley, to the great delight of the pioneer. The rebel said his first impulse was to run, but when he looked into the muzzles of six guns covering him at short range, he thought he'd better climb down and stay awhile.

On March 19th, Hall's brigade of our division made a scout to the vicinity of Liberty, where they were attacked by and had a hard fight with Morgan. Our brigade was ordered to hold itself in readiness to march to the relief of Hall at a moment's notice. His brigade repulsed Morgan with a loss of six killed and 40 wounded. The dead and wounded were brought into Murfreesboro, and the dead buried with the honors of war. The whole division turned out to take part in the solmn ceremonies. The division, massed by regiments, formed a hollow square around the large grave in which the dead were buried. A funeral sermon was preached by one of the chaplains, to at least 10,000 men, before the bodies were covered with earth. After the bodies were covered, the battalion, formed of details taken from the regiments to which the dead belonged, fired three rounds over the fresh made grave of their comrades. This was the heaviest firing by volley we ever heard; and taken all in all, was the grandest funeral we ever saw. There was scarcely a day passed without some one being, killed. Soon after the above funeral, a Colonel of cavalry was killed and buried with the honors of war, a full brigade band taking part in the services. We never heard such music before or since. Smith's march was played; each instrument played a solo and played in response to each other; and when all joined in the full chorus, the outburst was grand and thrilling, going to the very fountains of the soul. A detail of men bore the Colonel's body on a catafalque slowly to the grave, and just behind it came the Colonel's horse saddled, bridled and equiped with his revolvers, boots, spurs and sword; the horse followed without any one leading him, and the noble animal seemed the saddest mourner in the funeral train. It was truly such a funeral as the poet speaks of:

And when the hero dieth—his comrades in the war,
With muffled drums and arms reversed,
Follow the funeral car.
They tell the banners taken, they tell the battles won;
And after him lead his masterless steed,
While peals the minute gun.

CHAPTER XIX.

March 17th to June 24th, 1863—To Horse! Mounting and Incidents—Scouting for Horses, Mules, Negroes, &c.—Two Seventy-Second Men Captured and Cruelly Shot—First Fight and Flight after Mounted—Capture and Escape of Dick McCann—Filth and Sickness—Scouting Improves Health—Sibley Tents Exchanged for Shelter Tents—Various Scouts—The Lightning Brigade Draws its Lightning Guns, the Spencer Rifles—Description of the Spencer Rifles—Bold Reconnoissance—Scouts to Readyville, Woodbury and Liberty—Last Scout North-east of Murfreesboro—That Section Utterly Impoverished—Wilder's Report of Operations of the Brigade—Ordered for the Forward Movement of the whole Army—Chaplain Eddy's First Sermon—Writing Home Before the Battle—Reflections.

On or about the 17th of March, the Seventy-Second voted for and against mounting, and decided in favor of it. The 17th Indiana had already voted for mounting, and had drawn part of their horses. We proposed to cease peeling the bottoms of our feet on Tennessee and Kentucky rocks, and ride from this time forward. The 75th Indiana voted not to mount and was put into Hall's brigade, and the 123rd Illinois, of that brigade, voted to mount and took the place of the 75th Indiana. The brigade, after this most important epoch of mounting, was composed of the 17th and Seventy-Second Ind., 98th and 123rd Illinois Regiments, and Nicklin's 18th Ind. Battery. These four regiments remained in the same brigade to the close of the war, and were as solid in attachment and action as brothers.

After deciding to mount, the next thing was to get horses to mount. One or two companies were mounted on convalescent horses—a feeble sort of animal—which they drew on the 18th of March. For a few days we were occupied in details necessary to the great change which had taken place in our military mode of locomotion. We drew cavalry uniforms, but cut off the yellow stripe from the legs of the pants and jackets so that we might not be taken for regular cavalry. We were a new branch of the service; simply mounted infantry.

On the 26th, our division was reviewed by Gen. Reynolds and made a very imposing appearance; and on the 31st of March, the whole corps was reviewed by Gen. Rosecrans. By the 1st of April, the brigade was all mounted except Companies H, I and K, and that day it started on another raid, backed by the rest of the 14th division, which was joined in the vicinity of Carthage, Tenn., by Stokes' Tennessee Cavalry. Companies H, I and K, of our regiment, who were not yet mounted, were commanded on this expedition by Capt. Hanna. We camped that night on the banks of Stone River. On the 2nd of April, we arrived at Lebanon, county seat of Wilson County, Tenn., and found the mounted portion of our brigade there. Capt. Hanna took command of the three dismounted companies as a provost guard and made his headquarters in the Court-house. Near Lebanon the mounted men captured a lot of rebel prisoners, which they turned over to Capt. Hanna at this place.

On the 3rd, about 4 P. M., an alarm was sounded and we got rapidly into line of battle. Capt. Hanna was one of those men who could not see fighting going on without his taking part in it. On seeing the brigade rallying for a fight, he mustered his provost guard, prisoners and all, and marched out to the front to participate. To the great relief of the prisoners he was ordered back to his provost duties. "O, d—n it," said he, "I thought when there was a fight going on a fellow had a right to take part in it." There was no fight.

On this same day, a detachment was in the vicinity of Taylorsville, Tenn., assisting to destroy a lot of commissary stores, wheat, bacon, &c. Capt. Herron, Company B, was on picket duty with part of his company. He threw out Elma P. Wright, Wm. P.

Montgomery and John W. Vance, as videttes. A superior force of rebels made a dash at them with the object of cutting them off. They were on a by-road leading off at an angle of about 20 degrees from the main road, and the rebels came down the main road, horses in a full run. Vance and Montgomery were cut of; but Wright, being in advance, urged his horse to utmost speed, hoping to reach our picket at the forks of the road before the rebels should cut him off from the post. The "Johnnies" rode after him furiously, pressing him hard and hallooing, "Halt! halt! you d—d Yank." But Wright halted not, but only struck the rowels deeper into the flanks of his horse, which was flying before the foe when the poor animal ran its head against a tree and fell dead; Wright shot through the air like an arrow some 20 feet, lit on his feet, never halted nor looked back, jumped a fence, ran with all speed and saved himself. The exploit was hailed with applause and laughter by his comrades, who were galloping to his relief, and the rebels were compelled to turn and fly to save themselves.

But what of Vance and Montgomery? Let Vance himself tell the bloody story, and then let the reader say, whether in any civilized country its wanton cruelty has been surpassed. Their comrades made a long and anxious search for the captured men that night and the next day, but in vain, and supposed they were taken to Southern prisons. After returning to camp at Murfreesboro, the facts which follow were ascertained from Vance himself. They were taken to Lebanon that night, and the next morning were ordered to be taken out and shot. They were led out of the town by men who tied them to a tree, and heeded not their manly protests that they were prisoners of war, and should not be murdered in that cruel manner. They were only answered that they were d—d Yankee dogs, and ought to be hanged. Finding protests vain, they met their fate with brave resolution, commending their spirits to God.

When the ruffians had tied them hand and foot to a tree, two rebels stepped close to them and each rebel fired three shots into their heads. When they were untied, both fell forward on to their faces; but their fiendish foes, not being content, came up to their victims, placed their revolvers to the backs of their heads and sent another ball through each, and then left them for dead. The first three balls had pierced the head of Vance, and the fourth shot entered above the left ear and came out at the left eye, tearing the eyeball out of the socket. When Vance fell from the tree on to his face, he was still conscious, and had so much presence of mind that he tried to control his muscles and lie as still as if dead. He heard the murderers talk, and heard them determine to give both himself and Montgomery another round; then the revolver was pressed to the back of his head and he expected to pass into eternity. He heard the pistol almost in his ear, felt the ball crush through his head and tear out the left eye ball and throw the dirt in his face, and yet, to his astonishment, he retained consciousness, but it was as in a troubled dream of terrible pain. He still lay perfectly quiet. The bloody devils who had perpetrated this heartless work muttered curses upon the bodies and souls of their victims, and mounting their horses dashed away, leaving the bodies to "rot and be eat by buzzards and hogs," as they expressed it. As soon as Vance was sure they were gone, he attempted to raise his head, which was honey-combed by bullet holes and clotted with blood. After much effort, he succeeded in cleaning the mud and blood from his face, so he could look about him. He saw no one near and heard no sounds. The first effort of the noble soldier was to ascertain whether his comrade, Montgomery, was alive or dead. He crawled to the body, examined it, and found, alas! that life was extinct. Not being able to do anything for his comrade, he affectionately pressed his feeble hand upon the head of the noble dead, and began to crawl away, bleeding profusely, to a place of concealment, near the road on which he had left his comrades, the pickets, the night before. He expected every moment to die from loss of blood. After lying by the road for some time, he saw a white man on a load of wood, and lay down till he passed by; for almost every white citizen was an enemy. After a while, a negro came along, and as every negro was the Union Soldiers' friend, Vance succeeded in attracting his attention. The wounded soldier was not mistaken. The old negro compassionately and tenderly helped him to the Murfreesboro pike, and there he was taken up, the same day, by the Union Cavalry, carried to Murfreesboro and cared for. Notwithstanding his terrible wounds, and that all thought he would die, he got well—almost miraculous—and 12 years afterwards he served two terms as Recorder of Tippecanoe County, Ind.

Remember, kind reader, that this was but one of hundreds of simiiar atrocities committed by the heartless creatures known as "bushwhackers," who were really rebel robbers and murderers; but they were countenanced and encouraged by the regular rebel troops and the rebel civil authorities. Remember, too, that this act of kindness by that truly Good Samaritan, the old negro, who helped Vance to our lines at the peril of his life, is but one of thousands of such deeds of kindness which will shine as the stars forever, and which prove the manly grandeur and tenderness of the African race. Thanks to God that the North gave such a people freedom.

Major Adam Pinkerton says: "This almost incredibly cruel affair gave us of the Seventy-Second to understand with what fiends we had to contend. Prisoners taken by us, in open fight, were treated as kindly as if they were brothers; but after that barbarous atrocity, "Bushwhackers" were turned over to Co. B, the company to which Vance and Montgomery belonged, and the Provost Marshal's list was never cumbered with their names."

One can very well understand, after the above relation, why the members of the Seventy-Second dreaded being captured. We were a terror to the natives and as widely known as the command of Morgan. It was our business to scout for supplies, not only for ourselves but other commands, and also to destroy supplies when we could not take them. Hence we were dreaded and hated, and liable to cruel treatment if captured by rebel home guards; but they got very few of us, while we got many of them.

On the night of the 3rd our regiment camped on the farm of the rebel Gen. Anderson, and got enough horses in the neighborhood to mount one company, and also took away seven negroes. The next morning we moved to Rome, Tenn. On this march large amounts of tobacco, forage, horses, mules and slaves, were captured. We were now right in the muscular part of the rebellious ham, carving out large slices. Many incidents are related by the various members of the regiment, of the efforts the people made to hide and save their horses. There was not a noble man in the regiment but regretted the necessity of taking the property of these people and leaving them in destitution. But "war is cruel at best," and we very well knew that the rebels would use all these things for their own troops, and our object was not only to supply ourselves, but to impoverish the country. Horses were found hidden in the woods, in ravines, in caves—every place that they could be secreted. On this scout Lieut. Glaze and Corp'l Fisher, of C, found a horse in a lady's back parlor, and a noble animal he was too. He was tied to a bed post and standing on a pile of straw. It is impossible to draw, with pen or pencil, a sketch of the rebel lady's wrath when the noble animal was found, led out and taken away. If "the powers that be" heard her prayers, then, from that day to eternity, no Yankee will "enter in through the gates into the city."

On the 5th the brigade moved to Carthage, which was garrisoned by Crook's brigade, of our own division, and to him all prisoners and surplus were turned over. We went into camp about two miles from what is called the upper ferry. At this post we drew five days' rations and were joined by Speer's brigade of Negley's division, which had come via Liberty, where they had, in connection with a heavy cavalry force, attacked Morgan and driven him to Snow's Hill, where he made a stand and where he was given the neatest whipping he ever got, according to the rebels' own account of it.

On this same day some members of company D, got after some rebels, and while A. M. Cory and John B. Davis were chasing them down hill full tilt, Davis' horse turned a complete sommerset, pitching him more than ten feet, and he came down sprawling in the road. This was fun for his companions if not for him; for everything that did not kill outright was always taken for fun, even though the effect might subsequently cause death. On this day company E captured two rebels and brought them in.

By the 6th enough horses had been pressed to complete mounting the brigade, and were turned over to the dismounted battalion of the Seventy-Second, at New Middle Town, a town on the road from Carthage to Liberty. As we had few saddles and bridles, and that few of the citizen pattern; and many of our horses were untamed, we had a gay time riding the "brutes." Bridles and saddles were improvised of gun-straps and blankets, and for the first time the Seventy-Second was fully mounted!

That night we encamped in the Alexandria, Tenn., Fair grounds. The fence around the grounds was supposed to be high enough to keep our stock inside, and they were not very well fastened; as the night advanced they began to get loose and wander about. We were sleeping on the ground, inside the same inclosure, and in the midst of the night some of the stock were stampeded and ran over some men who were sound asleep, and they sprang up yelling, "Rebels! Morgan!!" alarming the whole camp. The moon was shining, the real cause of the alarm was soon seen, and with a hearty laugh, the men were soon sound asleep again.

On the 7th we proceeded towards Liberty. The mounted force proper were going by a route east of us, which would strike a road leading from Liberty to Smithville, on which they would approach Liberty opposite to the road we were on. A brigade of infantry and the Seventy-Second constituted the force advancing from Alexandria. As we neared Liberty the advance was opposed by rebel cavalry. The officer in command thought the proper thing to do would be to send cavalry after cavalry; so he ordered us front, and such another performance as was then enacted never occurred again during the war. We were ordered to move quick; but equipped as most of us were—

a strap tied around the jaw of our steed and no saddle—made it "mighty uncertain" whither we should go when we started. We were almost a match for the Bear Wallow mule brigade. Nevertheless, we all "lit out" at a sweeping gallop, and with a grim determination, some of our horses going side-wise and some behind-wise. This terrific charge was sufficient to scare the enemy into falling back on Liberty, where they made a stand. As soon as we came up we dismounted, formed on foot, moved into town and found the enemy also formed on the opposite side of Dry Creek. We opened fire by volleys; on the second round they broke and ran away on the road towards Smithville, meeting our mounted force previously mentioned as coming on that road, got into a trap, and a company of fifty men and two commissioned officers were taken.

Just here an affair occurred which might have counterbalanced our success. The officer sending us ahead failed to inform us that another Union force would enter the town opposite to where we entered it; and before we began to retire on the column which was now moving towards Murfreesboro, we saw a column of troops approaching upon the Smithville road, upon which the enemy had just retreated. We naturally supposed the rebels had been reinforced and were bearing down upon us to make a vigorous attack; the dust they raised veiled them from sight and imagination did the rest. We opened fire on them, but they neither halted nor changed formation, but advanced steadily in columns of fours. We began to fall back, but on they came; once more we fired, still on they came, only a little faster—at least we thought so. The order was given, "boys, to horse, and get out of this!" The scene which ensued beggars description. Our saddles having no stirrups we could not mount encumbered as we were with arms and ammunition. The efforts we made were truly ridiculous failures. Jumping upon our horses, our breasts would rest almost on their backs, and down we would go, flat upon the ground. All this time that awful column was advancing like an avalanche. We could stand the pressure no longer, for our fear was as intense as was that of Icabod Crane, as the headless Hessian bore down upon him in the darkness of the night. The clatter of the hoofs of the horses, and the clash of the swords of the advancing column, were in our ears; we abandoned our horses and skedaddled—men and horses mixed and mingled, and it is averred that no man let a horse get ahead of him; everything that we could throw away except arms, was abandoned in the flight.

Soon we came to a gorge in the hills, called a gap, and here formed and determined we would hold the gap. We sent back to the main column for reinforcements Just then a flag of truce was displayed at the head of the advancing column; a parley ensued, and the fact that our supposed enemies were friends was discovered. We learned from them that they had captured part of the rebels we had driven out of town. Of course we proceeded to get together our stock and stuff, like a joint snake that had been knocked to pieces with a club, with a sense of meekness over what had happened, and a conviction that some means of more certainly and speedily mounting, when pressed, was an absolute necessity.

On this same day company A captured ten rebels, who said that Morgan had sent them to examine our picket posts, get the position of pickets and report to him. They saw the posts but failed to report.

On the 8th, the brigade returned to Murfreesboro. The result of the trip was 196 horses, 110 prisoners, 35 slaves and a large lot of forage. On the 9th, companies H, I, and K drew saddles and cavalry equipments, and the regiment was now fully mounted; and we may remark, what no doubt the little affair of confusion at Liberty has suggested, that while we were well drilled as infantry, on our undrilled horses, we were little less than a mounted mob for a little while; but we soon gave our horses a saddle, bridle and spur drill which led them to understand pretty well what we were up to.

On the 11th, we were called up at 2 a. m. and moved at 4 a m. We went towards Lebanon and then returned towards Levergne, crossed Stone River at Buchanon's Mill and taking a by-path we came suddenly upon some rebel cavalry, emptied some guns at them, captured two, but the others scattered into the dense cedar thicket. We camped six miles from Levergne.

On the 12th we moved via Levergne and Nolinsville, to Franklin, Tenn, and on the 13th, returned to Murfreesboro again.

At this time our assistant surgeon, Dr. Wm. C. Cole, as brave and noble a man, and as good a surgeon as was ever in the service, who had been detailed at Castillian Springs, by Gen. Dumont, December 13th, 1862, for duty at the Gallatin hospital, returned to the regiment. On his way from Gallatin to Nashville he came near being gobbled by John Morgan. As Dr. Cole was so well known and highly esteemed in his regiment, and indeed, in the brigade and division, we deem it proper to give him a fullerintroduction here. In the course of the history you will often meet him, always in the line of his duty at his post; always kind, always brave, always skillful.

W. Carnahan Cole, M. D., was born July 16th, 1828, in Washington, Daviess County, Ind., of English and Scotch-Irish ancestry.

In his 18th year, enlisted in New Orleans, La., in the regiment of Mounted Rifles, Smith's brigade, Twiggs' division, and with that command, under Gen. Scott, participated in all the battles in the Valley of Mexico, entering the city September 14th, 1847, and remaining until the close of the war. Discharged at Jefferson Barracks, Mo. Graduated in Medicine from the Medical College of Ohio. In August, 1862, he assisted in recruiting company H, Seventy-Second Indiana, and was elected First Lieutenant. On the arrival of the regiment at Indianapolis, Dr. Cole was commissioned by Gov. Morton Assistant Surgeon; and after a little over one year's service in the field, and in charge of Hospital No. 5, Gallatin, Tenn., he was commissioned Surgeon of the regiment. Serving during the last year of the war as Surgeon-in-Chief of Wilder's brigade of Mounted Infantry; and at the close of the last campaign, while at Macon, Ga., he was detailed with Dr. Groves, of the 98th Illinois to accompany the 4th Michigan in pursuit of Jeff. Davis. Dr. Groves was present at the capture of that noted individual.

He was mustered out at Indianapolis. The Doctor is a member of the American Medical Association, Indiana State Medical Society, and Fountain County Medical Society, of which last he is an ex-President He is also a member of the National and State Associations of Mexican Veterans. The Doctor is a man of splendid physique, with a lofty but not ostentatious bearing. His mind is large and well cultured; in his profession, as in his citizenship and among his comrades, he stands very high and above reproach. His views are comprehensive and liberal, his heart large and warm. All who know him love and admire him. He was always with us, and of all the officers of the regiment he kept the only complete diary; it is very full. As we have never had access to morning reports of companies we are under obligations to Dr. Cole for most of the information in regard to the sick and wounded, and feel sure that it is accurate.

From April 14th to 20th the regiment was constantly on picket and fatigue duty.

On the morning of the 20th the Wilder brigade and a large force of infantry, accompanied by cavalry, moved east of Murfreesboro to Readyville.

On the morning of the 21st we were in Woodbury by sun up. The regiment took a by-road and was in the rear of McMinnville shortly after noon, but found the place already in possession of Union troops, the balance of the command having moved directly on the place. We quote from comrade John Davis, company D:

"On that afternoon our force had a lively chase after Morgan,

W C Cole
Surg 72 Ind

capturing Morgan's wife and the notorious Maj. Dick McCann, of Morgan's staff, a wagon train loaded with bacon, 130 prisoners, a train of cars loaded with fat hogs, 300 woolen blankets, 30,000 pounds of bacon, 2 hogsheads of sugar, 3 hogsheads of rice, and 8 barrels of whisky. We also burned a large grist mill, a train of cars, a railroad bridge, a cotton factory and 2 bales of cotton."

Sergt. Stewart, company A, says: "the next morning McCann was missing, and when the guards were asked what had become of him one of them sang out,

Oh, he went up the rope.
And came down a slope,
Into the happy land of Canaan.

But the truth is, McCann's guards had got their canteens full of apple-jack during the day, and when they were put on guard they were afraid the officers would take the tangle-foot away from them. McCann being aware of their fears sympathized with them and proposed that they give their canteens to him, and they did so. During the night the sly rebel gave the guards liquor as often as they wanted it, and each time pretended to drink with them. Before morning the guards were so drunk that they could not tell McCann from a two dollar dog, and the rebel slipped out and got away. That is the history given of McCann's escape in Basil M. Duke's history of Morgan's Cavalry. The Seventy-Second had nothing to do with McCann at that time; Minty's brigade captured him and the 4th Regulars guarded him. Sergt. Records says that at Peach Tree Creek he fell in with one of the men who guarded McCann, and he admitted that they were so drunk on the night he escaped that they didn't know they had ever had him. The only connection the Seventy-Second had with the McCann affair was that we passed the placed where the rebels had been whipped a few minutes before, and Will Harvey, company I, got McCann's hat, and *it* never got away.

On April 22d we moved to Smithfield. No fires were allowed, consequently no supper. On the 23d we moved so early that we took no breakfast, marching via Snow Hill, we reached Liberty, where we fed the horses and took dinner. At this place we destroyed a large flouring mill.

While company D was getting corn out of a large bin they found some nice hams; this led to further search and two rebels were found under the floor. We camped that night near Alexandria, and here, again, the enterprising John Davis and Jimmy Hall, of company D, succeeded in getting more hams, and as they were running off with them the landlady exclaimed, "there, the villains are carrying off my meat!"

On the 24th we stayed near Alexandria and scouted eight miles east, capturing a rebel team and wagon, and also some horses, mules and some stragglers from the enemy. On the 25th the command moved to within eight miles of Lebanon, scouting parties scattering all over the country, bringing in cattle, horses, mules, slaves and rebel prisoners.

On the 26th we moved on to Lebanon scouring the country, as yesterday, with liberal success. Company I got nine rebels. We again quote from comrade John Davis, of D: "Here a detail was made to hunt the body of Montgomery, who was captured and shot by the rebels on the 3d of April, (the particulars of which have been given). While Vance and Montgomery were being led through Lebanon a certain tavern-keeper shouted out, "hang the d—d sons of b—s, I'll find the rope." The detail did not find the body, but proposed to hang the tavern-keeper to make him tell where it was, and it is presumed they did their duty.

27th. The same duty as yesterday with varied success. A heavy rain storm, and picket firing at night.

28th. The Seventy-Second started for Murfreesboro with all the captured stuff, horses, mules, negroes, rebels, etc., arriving in the evening, but the brigade did not get in until the next day. This was a long and successful scout during which the men were in the highest spirits and best of humor. We quote from Dr. Cole's journal of April 15th: "Sickness in the regiment prevails to an alarming extent; average attendance at the sick call, 100, and perhaps 100 more are not fit for duty. This army of 40,000 men is encamped on a space so small that it is utterly impossible to keep the camps clean. Thousands of dead horses, mules and offal of every description, literally cover the whole face of the earth inside our picket lines; and each emits a thousand stinks, and each stink different from its fellow. The weather for months has been almost one continual flood of rain, and now, as the sun comes up more nearly straight over us, and pours down his boiling rays on this vast, sweltering mass of putridity, the stinks are magnified, multiplied and etherealized until the man in the moon must hold his nose as he passes over this vast sea of filth."

On the 29th of April Dr. Cole says, just after the scout above mentioned, "the health of the regiment has rapidly improved on the scout, owing to a change of air, and from salt army rations to fresh diet."

On May 1st we turned over our Sibley tents and drew French Shelter tents, called by the men "dog tents," on account of their smallness and lowness. These were stout sheets of duck canvas, six feet square, and so arranged, with buttons and button-holes along the edges, that any number of pieces could be buttoned together, either forming long strips, or large square sheets. Perhaps these tents, as much as any other mechanical convenience began immediately to contribute to the health of the army. We quote from Sergt. Records, May 1st: "The stench of this great encampment is becoming utterly unendurable, and these scouts are hailed with delight. The health of the regiment is rapidly improving, and the morale and discipline of the brigade are in a high state of perfection."

On the 2d we moved our camp two miles north-east of Murfreesboro, near the picket lines, and close to the boiling springs. We were delighted when the wind came from the north-east; we could then get a breath of fresh air.

On May 6th we moved to Levergne through a heavy rain, and remained there until the morning of the 9th, when we moved on by-roads in a north-east course, passed through Silver Springs and camped on the Lebanon road. About 10 a. m. the column was fired upon and company D was detached to give the rebels chase, which was an exciting one, resulting in the capture of a few prisoners. In the evening of this day Madison Barton, company E, accidentally shot himself in the knee, and his leg was taken off by Dr. Cole. The accident to this faithful soldier, and his loss to the regiment were deeply regretted.

On the 10th company I went across the river, north-west, as a guard for a supply train and took Barton, the wounded man, with them. He got well. In the afternoon the command went to Lebanon, and on the 11th returned to Murfreesboro.

We were now well mounted, and our rapid movements soon gave us such notoriety that we were called "The Lightning Brigade." It was part of the original plan that when mounted we should be armed with repeating rifles; accordingly, on the 15th of May, we turned over our old companions, the Springfield rifles, and drew the famous Spencer repeating rifles. These rifles were of so much importance in all our subsequent movements, and were so conspicuous in making the brigade distinctive and successful in the service, that we here give a description of the Spencer, and compare it with some other repeating rifles. Up to the breaking out of the rebellion, all the armies of the world, so far as we know, were armed with a muzzle-loading, single shooting gun. The percussion cap was a great improvement over the flint; yet a gun using the flint could be loaded as quickly, fired as rapidly, would shoot as far and as accurately as a gun using the percussion cap. Citizens of the United States were not a fighting people, hence her inventive genius had never been pressed to produce anything better than the common sporting rifle, used in hunting game. There had been some improvement in projectiles—The minnie ball, with a hollow, expansive base that would catch and hold all the force of the powder, was a vast improvement over the round bullet that permitted one-third of the force of the powder to spread around the ball, and even to get past it before leaving the muzzle—But as before stated, when our war broke out, our soldiers were armed with the same muzzle-loading gun with which our forefathers fought the battles of the Revolution. With these guns it was impossible for the most experienced soldier to load and fire more than twice per minute. This, for a *fast* people like the Americans, was entirely too slow. And acting upon the principle laid down by Sherman in his "Memoirs," that "the more destructive you can make war the more humane it is," genius began to invent guns that could be more rapidly loaded and fired. A gun was greatly needed that would shoot accurately at long range, that could be fired a number of times without stopping to load, and that would not get out of repair. To invent such a gun many unsuccessful attempts were made. Among the first of these attempts was "Colt's repeating rifle," which was made with a barrel of the usual length of army rifles. Instead of loading at the muzzle it had a revolving cylinder at the breech containing five chambers, into which as many loads could be placed; but it took quite as long to load one of these chambers as it did to put in a single load from the muzzle, so that there was no *time* gained in loading; but after the chambers were all loaded they could be fired very rapidly. But as there was a possibility of two or more chambers being discharged at once, thus crippling about as many of those using them as of the enemy, few regiments were ever armed with them. They were very heavy and clumsy to handle, and were soon abandoned.

The next candidate for favor was the "Henry rifle." This was a vast improvement over the "Colt." It was short in the barrel and light in the breech—on the under side of the barrel was a chamber into which could be placed 16 metaliic cartridges. In order to get these cartridges into the barrel of the gun, a light lever which was also a guard for the trigger was thrown forward—this threw the breech-pin (we call it that for the want of a better name) back far enough to admit one cartridge to pass up opposite the hole in the barrel, and as the lever was pulled back it was pushed in ready for firing; the usual motion of hammer and trigger completed the work. Every time the lever was moved it also threw out the metallic shell that had contained the powder. This gun could be loaded and fired 16 times in a minute; but easily got out of repair, and was, from its shape, entirely unfit for the "manual of arms." Aside from "scouts" and "sharpshooters" it was never used by the army.

Next came the Spencer rifle. This, to our mind, was so nearly perfect, that after using it for two years, our brigade had not a single change to suggest; and after a lapse of 20 years we have seen nothing equal to it. The barrel of the Spencer rifle was two feet eight inches long, cased on the under side with a light strip of walnut, held in place by three rings or thimbles, This barrel screwed into a heavy piece of iron, which had a slot or mortice in it from top to bottom. In this mortice was the breech-pin, worked up and down by a lever much the same as the Henry rifle. The stock was of walnut, much the size and shape of the Springfield or Enfield rifles in common use in the army. In the centre of this stock was a cylinder, or barrel, which also screwed into the heavy piece of iron at the other end. This barrel would hold seven metallic cartridges; these cartridges were pushed up and held in place by a spiral spring. The hammer and trigger worked just like any other gun. To load, after the chambers were filled up, all you had to do was to throw the lever or trigger guard forward, which would throw out, on top, the empty cartridge shell from which the ball had been fired, and as you drew the lever back to its place another cartridge slipped into the barrel, ready to fire. This gun could be loaded and fired seven times in a minute. It *never got out of repair.* It was put together entirely with screws, and any body that had sense enough to be a soldier could take one all to pieces and put it all together, just as well as the man that made it. The gun shot a forced ball; that is, the bore in the barrel was smaller at the muzzle than at the breech. It would shoot a mile just as accurately as the finest rifle in the world. When held in the hand at a "ready" the weight was exactly balanced between the two hands; it was the easiest gun to handle in the manual of arms drill we have ever seen. It could be taken all to pieces to clean, and hence was little trouble to keep in order—quite an item to lazy soldiers.

We are safe in saying that another great war will never be fought by the United States with muzzle-loading guns. The Spencer rifle demonstrated the superiority of breech-loading repeaters. This, or an improved repeater, will be the rifle of future wars in the United States, and perhaps in Europe.

About this time the regiment began a system of instructions in the management of their horses in evolutions in squad, company and batallion drill, and of movements in line and skirmish drill, which perhaps had never been attempted by Federal troops before. It is safe to say that in this drill we had learned many valuable lessons from the rebel John H. Morgan; for this was actually his system of drill which we adopted. This system was afterwards modified and simplified a little, and adopted by all the cavalry service in the Army of the Cumberland, and is the basis of Gen. Upton's tactics now used by the United States Army, both infantry and cavalry.

We were not cavalry, but simply mounted infantry, a new branch of the service, which of course required new methods. Also about this time there was organized a corps of scouts in each regiment of the brigade, by taking one picked man from each company; all the scouts of any one regiment were under command of one Sergeant and one Corporal. Afterwards all the scouts of the brigade were placed under the command of a Commissioned officer.

On May 21st we turned over all extra baggage and had orders to move at a moment's notice, and Col. Miller says that the whole army had the same orders. Our picket lines had been frequently attacked during the last few days.

On the 22nd our brigade, and two guns of the 18th Indiana battery, made a reconnoissance, in force, of the enemy's front, and the left moved out south-east on the Manchester road. When near Hoover's Gap, the rebel videttes were driven in, the picket post was charged and some prisoners taken from two Georgia cavalry regiments. Company C was left here to menace the rebel camp, which was in plain view, and the column turned east. At every road leading toward the enemy the videttes and pickets were driven in and a company left to watch them; in the afternoon the head of the column reached the McMinnville road, where the command concentrated and moved back to camp, having reconnoitered one-third of the rebel front, causing great consternation in the whole rebel army. We had killed a few, captured a few and driven off the rest. Col. Miller said we returned to camp in fine style, which remark had a most exhilarating influence on the regiment. We were agreeably surprised to see what damage we could inflict on the enemy, and retire from our exasperated foe without being punished.

On May 24th we moved east to Readyville, and on the 25th made a march of 30 miles, captured a few prisoners and returned to camp on the 26th. On the 25th, private William Swift, company C, had half his head shaved, was drummed in front of the division, and sent to the penitentiary to work out the balance of his term of service, for deserting his post while on picket.

On June 1st companies E and B, under command of Capt. Kilborn, went to Readyville, and at midnight started to Woodbury to surprise a camp of rebels. While on their way a most terrific rain and thunder storm came upon them, which those on the expedition will never forget. When they reached Woodbury the rebels were gone.

On June 4th we moved early, taking the road to Liberty, regimental scouts in advance; we captured the rebel pickets at Auburn without making any alarm, and the column moved into Liberty. Two miles out the only rebel vidette on the road was shot and killed, leaving the rebel camp to our mercy. The brigade moves swiftly in a column of fours, the Seventy-Second in advance, Col. Miller at its head. The Scouts are thrown forward right and left as flankers, and rush into Liberty full sweep. The rebels are taken completely by surprise; their horses are unsaddled, they are quietly getting supper, and our sudden appearance causes a wild stampede. Our scouts did most of the firing. The brigade halted, but the Seventy-Second pursued. The rebels attempted to rally in Liberty; but they were so closely pressed that they broke and fled to the opposite side of Dry creek and began forming. With Col. Miller at our head, and never changing formation, we rushed down upon them in a steady gallop. This sort of tactics was new to them, and without waiting to fire a second shot they broke and fled from the field; we pursued them some distance and captured twenty of them. At sundown we abandoned the pursuit, returned to the brigade and went into camp, having marched 30 miles that day. The rebels left an immense amount of stuff in their camp, and strewn along after them in wild confusion.

On the 5th the Seventy-Second lay in camp, and the 98th Illinois went to Dark Bend on the Cumberland river. The 123rd Illinois took after the rebels that we ran out of camp last evening, had a fight with the enemy and drove them beyond Snow Hill, to Smithsville.

On the 6th of June we moved to Auburn, where Col. Miller made his headquarters. A detail of 20 men from each company, under Lieut. Col. S. C. Kirkpatrick, were ordered to scout towards Woodbury; deploying on each side of the road, they went to within five miles of Woodbury. The scout was lively and successful, resulting in the capture of a lot of stock. Company I broke a rebel soldier's thigh, and captured three others. The expedition returned to camp that evening. While we were out the teamsters and camp guard had a lively adventure. A party of rebels dashed into camp and tried to capture the trains. The men rallied and drove them away, but they carried one of our men with them. Our men mounted and gave chase with such zeal that they rescued their comrade, wounded three rebels and captured three others. When the rebels first charged on the camp, two burly fellows dashed up to John Hamelton, company I, regimental teamster, and ordered him to hitch up quick and drive out. "I won't do't" said John in his Irish brogue, "for this is Col. Miller's wagon, and I'll be dom'd if yees shell have it." At the mention of Col. Miller of course they wanted it all the more, and leveling their guns at John they said, "hitch up quick, or we'll shoot you." "Shoot an' be dom'd wid yees," said John, as he dived under the wagon bed. Two bullets crashed through the wagon bed as he popped up on the other side, but it was a clear miss. Swearing by all the Saints, he yelled out, "ye dom'd buggers!" seized his Spencer and brought it to a ready. and the rebels "left bery sudden," while John sent two or three shots after them.

On June 7th we returned to Murfreesboro with 60 prisoners, 320 horses and mules, and part of a captured wagon train. It would be impossible to name all the incidents connected with this scout, or the result of each company's work separately. All entered into the work with a zest, and each company was about equally successful.

June 10th. At six this morning a detail of an officer and 15 men from each company, started under command of Lieut. Col. Kirk, as we always called him, for Lebanon, while the remainder of the brigade moved on the road to Liberty; one north, and one northeast, and both 30 miles from Murfreesboro. The brigade got near Liberty half an hour by sun, and the Seventy-Second dashed into the place to find the enemy gone. Only one rebel was killed that day; the Seventy-Second went back and eamped with the brigade. According to Col. Miller's notes an attack from Morgan was expected that night.

Lieut. R. C. Clark, commanding scouts on this occasion, says: We encountered the rebel pickets about two miles from Liberty, routed them and pursued them hotly, and were right upon them when we reached a point, just before entering town, where the creek is on the right of the road, and a very high precipitous cliff on the left with only a wagon road between. When we were fairly in this position we were fired upon from the cliff, which was so steep, and the enemy being directly above us, over shot us. There were 200 on the cliff commanded by a Major. To stop, or to try to turn and retreat, was certain death; so we dashed through and around the foot of the cliff, and came out right amongst them. Our men deployed, and as our Spencer rifles were fully loaded we did very good execution. The rebel Major called out that he surrendered, but our men were too much deployed to hear what he said. To enable them to hear, we gave the command to cease firing, and the rebels mounted and retreated, pell mell, we after them; we ran them through town and about two miles into the country, taking several prisoners. The number of old rebel haversacks and amount of corn bread scattered by the flying foe, along the road and through town, was immense. If my men had ceased firing when the order was given we could have marched the two hundred men in as prisoners.

We were called up before day (11th) saddled immediately and waited till noon, but no rebels came. In the afternoon we moved to Alexandria and camped over night. On the next morning (12th) we went on to Lebanon, where we met the detachment under Col. Kirkpatrick. They had been successful in collecting a very large lot of forage, horses, cattle and negroes. The negroes had recently taken to gathering in the vicinity of roads, and when the Yankee troops would come along would fall in and go with them. They had learned to take advantage of the emancipation proclamation. Some of these negroes were taken into the service of the officers, and some employed to cook and groom horses for the messes, and made themselves very useful, taking many a burthen off the soldiers. One man captured on this occasion, named Wyatt, or "Wallick," as we called him, stayed with company F until we were mustered out, and then crossed the Ohio river with us, at Jeffersonville.

We returned to Murfreesboro on the 13th. This was the last scout of the Seventy-Second north and east of that place, and Dr. Cole remarks that "the country is in a most deplorable condition, there being neither horse, forage nor provisions of any kind left in it." Duke's history of Morgan's cavalry says the same thing.

From the 1st of February, 1863, the brigade has been through the rebel lines 28 times, has taken 1,157 prisoners, 4,000 horses and a small army of slaves. In the last expedition we took 600 prisoners, 800 horses and 250 slaves; killed 10 guerrillas and mortally wounded Col. Grant. We have hung five and shot 15 rebels, including a Second Lieutenant, caught with our uniform on, as it was the order of Gen. Rosecrans to take the lives of all rebel soldiers found wearing Union uniform. The above is from Col. Wilder's report; in all this work the Seventy-Second had done its full share.

On the 20th we moved camp north-west of Murfreesboro, close to Stone River, and were busy until the morning of the 24th, in active preparations to take part in the forward movement of the Grand Army of the Cumberland. On the 23rd we were ordered to be ready to move next morning, at daylight, with 10 days' rations and 80 rounds of amunition. Everybody in camp knew what this meant. We had been for months waiting and expecting the army to move forward, and the order for 80 rounds of cartridges assured us that the time had come at last.

Gentle reader, please imagine yourself in a position where you know that on the morrow you may enter into mortal eombat with an enemy your equal, in which you know that the chances are that you instead of he may bite the dust. And suppose, too, that behind you are wife, children, father, mother, sister, brother and sweetheart, whom you have not seen for months, and may never see again. How you would like to give them a glimpse into your inmost soul! How you would like to assure them of your love and constancy as you stand upon this border of death-land! But you hesitate. You would not, for one moment, have them think that you even dream of such imminent danger, lest you give them anxiety and pain.

Whatever the feelings may be, or however different in different individuals, such orders always brought out the materials for writing; and on this evening, under the pressure of marching orders, thousands of tender missives were written to beloved ones at home. To write a few lines to their beloved ones was one of the last duties performed by soldiers in the field, before facing death. It seemed like speaking what might be our last words to them, and then we were braver, and could face death firmer. Often the order would come from our considerate commanders, who themselves were like us, "one half hour for letter writing," and then in two minutes thousands of pens were in motion, not writing of the perils of the situation, but speaking words of love and all the encouragement possible. It was amazing what cheerful letters could be written in the very face of death!

To our regiment the circumstances were peculiarly impressive. Our chaplain had resigned and gone home, and for months we had not heard the gospel of peace. But on the 14th of this month a new chaplain had come to us, and this evening preached his first sermon. How fully he realized the necessity of preparation for to-morrow! With what earnestness he presented to us the way of life! But we must not anticipate. Suffice it to say that, when the last notes of the bugle that sounded tattoo died away in the hills, and when the last light was put out in the lonely tent, each soldier lay down to sleep, well understanding what was expected of him on the morrow, and as well understanding what might happen to him ; but ready for duty at all hazards.

In order that the movement, about to be made, may be more clearly understood, and the part taken by the Seventy-Second made plainer, a few remarks, as to the relative positions of the two great armies, are necessary.

When Gen. Rosecrans drove Bragg out of Murfreesboro, January 1st, 1863, Bragg fell back to the south side of Duck River, almost due south from Murfreesboro, and made that river his line of defence; and his front, or line of battle, took the general direction of that stream, which at that place is almost due west. The headquarters of Bragg were at Shelbyville, 12 miles south of Murfreesboro, his right wing rested on Winchester, and his left extended towards Farmington.

At the same time Gen. Rosecrans disposed his army as follows: The centre, the 14th corps, commanded by Thomas, in and about Murfreesboro. McCook's 20th corps as the right wing, to the south-west of Murfreesboro; and Crittenden's 21st corps as the left wing, to the north-east of Murfreesboro. The army had a general front to the south-east, or a little east of south. The pickets between the two armies, on the road from Murfreesboro to Shelbyville, were in sight of each other; while Morgan, during January and February, constantly scouted about our camp, often passing entirely around our army.

The scouting in which we had taken part, up to this time, had been directed to breaking up Morgan's command, and impoverishing the country, so that he could not subsist to the east and north of Murfreesboro. We had quite thoroughly done this, and now other work is before us.

Rosecrans opened the campaign by moving his right wing, McCook's 20th corps, south, making a strong feint on Bragg's centre at Shelbyville. The left wing, Crittenden's 21st corps, moved straight east, to Readyville, and thence south-east, to McMinnville. The centre, Gen. Thomas' 14th corps, moved south-east on the Manchester pike. Reynolds' division belonged to Thomas' corps, and Wilder's brigade to Reynolds' division. Our division moved first in the corps; our brigade in advance, and our regiment advance guard. This gives you the position, as nearly as possible, and shows you that we are directly in front. We now return to arouse the men we left sleeping in camp at Murfreesboro.

CHAPTER XX.

June 24th to August 16th, 1863—Rosecrans' Army moves forward—Lightning Brigade in advance—Charge and capture Hoover's Gap—Brave dash led by Col. Kirkpatrick—A bloody battle in the rain—Thrilling Incidents—Babes in the Wood in the storm of battle—Sergt. Pike's face shot off—A cannon shot passes through Chaplain Eddy—Casualties of battle of Hoover's Gap—Raid on Decherd—Capt. Rice in a close place—Sleeping and slipping up and down a mountain—Bragg scared and evacuates Tullahoma—In camp near Wartrace—Filth, Green flies and maggots—How dirty the rebels could be—Camp at Rowe's Hill—Fourth of July in camp—Thompson, our poet—Scouting, and details of how it was done—When the Union split, I split, too—Move to Decherd—Summary of first year's service—The Regiment reduced almost one-half.

On the 24th of June the bugle sounded the reveille at 3 in the morning. Up, feed, get breakfast and move at daylight. We reach Murfreesboro and find that the whole army of 50,000 men have struck tents. What a change in one short night! One can never realize it till one sees it. Everything is loaded on wagons, and the regiments, brigades and divisions are rapidly taking their places in line. We move right on through the town, passing the horrible old camp in the hickory flats, and take the road for Wartrace, moving south-east on the Manchester pike. Companies A, F, D and I were advance guard of the regiment.

The weather was cool and lowering, and rain began to fall in the forenoon and continued all day, pouring down in torrents in the afternoon. The men were cheerful for all that, in broad contrast with the weather. We strike the rebel videttes ten miles out from Murfreesboro, and five miles from Hoover's Gap. We promptly charge the picket post, and they as promptly set out to spread the alarm. Soon a company of cavalry attempts to check our advance, and they, too, are driven as chaff before the wind. We kill one man, capture others, and take a flag inscribed: "Presented by the Ladies of Selma, Alabama." A coincidence: that in our first battle we should capture this flag, and almost two years after, in our last battle, we should capture Selma, and ladies who presented the flag, too, perhaps.

We press on. As the rebel force opposing us increases, we strengthen our skirmish lines, and bear down upon the retreating rebels with such impetuosity that the motion of our column is not checked until we near the mouth of Hoover's Gap, where we find a line of rebel cavalry extending from one hill top to the other, across the little hollow through which we are moving. They open and keep up a constant fire on us from one end of the line to the other. Here Company C comes forward, and with A, F and D in line, and I and C in column, we give them such a push that they fail to rally at a line of breastworks and a cannon they had planted in the Gap, but run on at a fearful rate.

Company C here turned attention to some camps on the hill to the left, and captured a signal station with all its train, camp and garrison equipage. This station had first signaled Gen. Hardee that the attack was only by a small reconnoitering party of cavalry—a lucky mistake for us, leaving us in undisputed possession of the Gap. But we did not stop here. A, F, D and I, just charged right on in column after the retreating fugitives, who scarcely took time to fire a gun, chasing them into the little village of Beech, two miles beyond the Gap. Here the column checked up, and Lieut. Col. Kirkpatrick, who was in command, went into Jacob's store to get some caddies of tobacco, brought them out and began to distribute the tobacco to the men, while firing is still going on in the front between the regimental scouts and the enemy.

But hark! Just to our right and rear, a half mile away, a hundred drums begin simultaneously to sound the dread long roll. A Staff officer comes dashing down the road and yells to us, "get out of this as quick as God Almighty will let you!" We about face and move briskly towards the Gap, the rebels following and encouraging our efforts with repeated shots.

During the melee in which the four companies were engaged the head of column of brigade had passed through the Gap by the earthworks, and captured the piece of artillery. Col. Miller grasped the situation in a moment. This was the key to the whole position, and two hours later could scarcely have been charged and taken with 10,000 men. Col. Miller immediately sent Company H out on picket to the right of the road, and Company E on the same duty to the left, on a by-road, and formed the other four companies on the brow of the hill to the right of the road. All this time the rebel drums are beating the long roll furiously, which gives Col. Wilder the situation of their camps. The 17th is hurried up to form on the right of the Seventy-Second, the 98th Illinois still further to the right, and the 123d Illinois to the right and rear in reserve; our battery of mountain howitzers in front of the Seventy-Second and the 18th Indiana battery directly in our rear upon the highest ground.

The four companies come back in a hurry and take place in line;

the rebels following us cut off Companies H and E from the road. By this time two divisions of Hardee's corps, encamped to our right-front, scarcely a mile away, have gotten in line and send forward a cloud of skirmishers who soon strike Company H, and for a time its situation is perilous in the extreme. Just as the company began to fall back W. R. Clark was shot in the abdomen, the ball coming out at his back. Three or four comrades quickly dismounted, helped him on his horse and hurried him to the rear. The company by a circuitous route gained the rear, and took its place in the line.

By this time rebel skirmishers are at short range with our line; they come up in splendid style and in plain view. Our howitzers and four pieces of artillery open on them and pour volley after volley of grape and canister into their ranks, as they rush upon us with hellish and deafening yells. On they come, as if determined to take the battery without firing a gun The Seventy-Second opens upon them with our seven-shooting Spencers, and for the first time they seem to wake up to the fact that they are not fighting cavalry. They stagger and fall back in confusion. The weight of the charge has struck the 17th The sharp clatter of rifles is deafening. From some cause the 17th is soon out of ammunition and some commotion is visible. Now the 98th Illinois change front and come to the rescue, and the rebels are hurled back. Now the 123d Illinois move to the support of the 98th, and the rebels open on our mountain howitzers with a battery of rifled guns. Three shells in quick succession pass through our regiment: one cuts one of the gunners in two; another tears off the face of Sergt Pike, of Company D, and another passes through the neck of an artillery mule.

As the rebels have more and heavier guns than we, our battery of howitzers limber up and get out of the way, and it seems now but a question of a little time when the 18th battery six-pounders will have to do the same. At this juncture the rebel infantry move upon us, outnumbering us five to one, but our splendid Spencer repeaters more than compensate for the disparity in numbers. When they close upon us the clash and crash of small arms is added to the deafening roar of artillery, and the din is terrific in the extreme. The struggle was desperate but brief. The rebel infantry are again sent staggering back. Their artillery yet hold supremacy and every shell they send over us and at our guns increases our anxiety and the peril of our situation; for if they silence our guns there's nothing to prevent them from shelling our ranks at their leisure. We are in extreme peril A large chunk of railroad iron, thrown from a rebel cannon, strikes in front of Company D, near Sergt. Garrett's head, throwing mud all over the company. Another large shell strikes just in front of the colors, and before it has time to explode, Corpl. Drummond, Company I, one of the color guard, jumps to his feet, seizes and throws the shell down the hill, which explodes as soon as it touches the ground! Brave and timely deed. Our peril increases with every moment.

At this critical moment the 19th Indiana battery, Capt. Harris, with guns one-half caliber larger than those of the 18th, ten horses to the gun, came thundering down the road to our relief, the drivers urging the horses with whip and spur until they were frantic with fury. For once artillerymen are permitted to ride on their guns. Capt. Harris takes position and opens immediately on the rebels. As the guns belch forth fire and shot over our heads we feel great relief, and anxiously watch the telling effect the shots have upon the enemy, and in a short time the rebel guns are seen to limber up and move to a more respectful distance.

It is now almost sundown; we have been lying in the mud and water for nearly four hours—for the rain has come down in torrents all the time. We were not heavily engaged any more that day, and at dark were relieved by Crook's brigade.

It would take many more pages than we have to spare to note half the incidents of this battle, yet we cannot forbear speaking of a few. After dark we fell back and lay on our arms in reserve. All had done their duty so well that it is not possible, without being invidious, to give special praise to any. We have not yet ascertained what became of Company E, and will give their experience. Soon after they found that they were cut off two rebel officers came up to them, supposing they were part of the rebel force, and did not discover their mistake until it was too late for them to escape. Just then the rebel artillery began to rake their position and the skirmishers also began to fire on them. The company started to move across the woods and immediately came upon three little children who were bewildered in their efforts to escape from the dangers and awful noise of the battle; two little girls aged about seven and nine, and a little boy aged five. These were veritable babes of the woods The girls could out-run the boy, but every minute would stop, turn and cry, "come on, bubby, come on!" Sergt. Wilhite, amid a shower of bullets, dismounted, helped them over the fence, placed the boy between the girls and started them towards a house, out of the range of the fire, remounted his horse while the bullets rattled against the fence and rode away unhurt. At such an act of tenderness would not the angels smile through the smoke of battle and protect the brave man who did it? Company E got out in safety and took place in line while the battle raged. There is not space to speak of hair-breadth escapes.

The mortal wound of Sergt. Pike, in the face, has been spoken of, and to see him lying in the mud and rain, clawing the mud with his hands and ever and anon picking at the shreds of flesh and shattered bones of his face, was horribly distressing. His face was all shot off. It sickens us to write of it. Death soon came to the brave man's relief, and we all thanked God to see our poor comrade out of his agony. Lieut. Cravens informs us that he stood over Sergt. Pike, a short time before he died, and said, "Pike, don't you know me?" The poor fellow muttered, "O, mother, poor mother! What will she do?" He spoke no more, and soon expired. He was a noble man and the support and pride of his widowed mother. He was buried near the line of battle where he fell.

Clark, of Company H, has been mentioned as being shot in the abdomen; Dr. Cole says: "The ball went through the skin on the abdomen but did not penetrate the muscles; passed round his body and came out at the back, exactly opposite the point it entered, just as though it had gone straight through him. He soon got well and served out his time." Other casualties were Sergt. James O. Peed, Company G, a good and brave man, mortally wounded in the left lung. Private Peter Moore, Company A, musket ball through the left shoulder. Daniel Long, Company E, broken right fore-arm. P. C. Burnham, Company D, bayonet wound. John R. Bennett, C, musket ball through left lung. E. Banister, D, slight wound on knee. A. J. Hubbard, B, musket ball in left shoulder. Wm. Grismar, K, wound in thigh. J. R. Rutherford, B, slight wound in head. J. K. Sheets, K, wound on shoulder.

The most impressive event of the day was the killing of Chaplain Eddy. The regimental hospital was established over the hill, in rear of our regiment, and the Chaplain was near it helping with the wounded; a shell of the enemy fired at the 18th battery passed over it and over the hill, and through the Chaplain's body, killing him instantly. We have said that the night before he had preached his first sermon to us in camp at Murfreesboro, exhorting us to be prepared for death. To be taken from us thus, on the first day of service, in the brave discharge of his duties, was a matter of sorrow to every heart. His name will be ever dear to the Seventy-Second.

We quote from Col. Miller's notes: "We were under fire for five hours. This was our first battle and the men stood well. We had three men killed and 20 wounded, some of them mortally. We were relieved by Crook's brigade after dark, and lay on our arms in the mud that night."

On June 25th the whole of the 14th army corps came up and formed line where we were yesterday. Skirmishing commenced early, but our troops were content to hold the splendid position gained, for the capture of which we claim the honor belongs to our brigade. We lay in reserve all day and the rebels showed their spite by throwing shells at our forces, while the clouds poured down rain.

The 26th opened with rain, and we moved east and south up a fork of Duck River, passing through some narrow defiles where we pick up a few prisoners. The rebel army seems to be falling back. We camp for the night in six miles of Manchester.

On the morning of the 27th we were in the saddle early, and dashed like fury into Manchester, surprising the place and capturing 300 prisoners and a lot of Commissary stores. We remained there all day while part of the brigade made a reconnoissance towards Tullahoma. The 14th corps came up in the evening, and the rain continued.

On the morning of the 28th we set out from Manchester to raid on the Chattanooga railroad, going by way of Hillsboro, Pelham and Hawkinsville, 45 miles to Decherd. Duck and Elk rivers were so swollen by the rains as to swim all the mules and small horses; at one place we carried the artillery ammunition across on our horses, and at the other made a raft to ferry the artillery over. We reached Decherd at nine o'clock at night. The bulk of Bragg's army was at Tullahoma, 15 miles north of this place, and hence we are right in the rear of Bragg's army. We found Decherd garrisoned by a small force of rebels in stockade, and scattered them with a few shots from our howitzers—Lack-een-guns, we always called them, because we used mules to haul them, and often took them to pieces and strapped them on the backs of mules when we traveled very hilly country, as was frequently the case.

While this was going on Capt. Rice started through the village to give directions to scouts who were burning the water tank, tearing up the railroad and working all possible mischief in a great hurry. He had dismounted and was quietly leading his horse when suddenly some rebels began to fire on him from a stockade; the bullets rattled against a fence and scared his horse, which jerked loose from him, leaving him in quite an unpleasant predicament, and his chances for Libby prison good. His horse did not run from him, but just as he caught the bridle another volley, and another rattle of balls against the fence, and again the horse broke away. This was repeated, the Captain's hair standing on end, until the horse got out of range of the bullets, and then the Captain mounted and went out of there like a bird flying. He regards this as his most daring feat during the war, but confesses that he was a little scared.

The first thing captured was the rebel mail. The depot was burned, a short section of the railroad torn up and a bridge burned. The command then hurried away six mile, north-east, to a point on the Cumberland Mountains, and as Records has it, "ambushed for the night;" that is, simply stopped in the bushes and lay down to sleep, holding our horses' bridles in our hands. We had put in another hard day's work in the rain, and our beds were on the mountain side on the sharpest of rocks. The mountain was so steep that we had to get our feet against the trees or rocks to keep from slipping down. And had not the surroundings been so desperate it would have been funny to see us try to sleep. You see a big, stout, long-legged soldier lay down flat of his back, his legs stiff and his feet braced against a tree; in two minutes he is asleep, his muscles begin to relax, his knees fly up, and down he goes a-straddle of the tree. With many the remainder of the night is worn away in sliding down the hill and climbing up again; while others more fortunate, find a hole or depression, the rain still pouring down, and two hours later they are called up to find themselves in water six inches deep.

On the 27th we were in saddles by daylight and moved on a by-path to the top of the mountain, as we were apprehensive that the enemy had thrown a force between us and Pelham. When near the top of the mountain a fearful thunder storm came upon us. We were so high, or the clouds so low, that we were in the clouds, and the thunder was as often below as above us. The average soldier took but little interest in this grand sight, knowing only that the situation was uncomfortable. To many of us the sublimity of the scene dispelled thought of discomfort or danger. God seemed very near.

The want of rest and sleep was telling on us, and we were constantly falling asleep and reeling in our saddles like drunken men. The route was almost impracticable, and the howitzers had to be pulled up by hand. When we got to the top of the mountain we could see reinforcements pouring in to Decherd. The rebels had been struck suddenly there and were fearfully scared, not knowing whence the Yankees came, or whither they went.

On the top of the mountain each man was ordered to take a sheaf of wheat for his horse, and the column moved forward on the trot to University Hights, whence a detachment of the Seventy-Second and 98th Illinois, Col. Funkhouser in command, hurried to Cowan, to burn the trestle work of the Memphis, Chattanooga & Charleston railroad, but on getting in sight of the place found rebel troops pouring into it by thousands, and returned to the column. While Col. Funkhouser's detachment was gone the brigade tore up the railroad at Tracy City; as this was a short road, running to a coal mine, the object of tearing it up was never visible to the naked eye.

It still continued to rain. Many horses gave out and were killed, while others were left to fall into the hands of the rebels. The constant rain had swollen the Elk River out of its banks and the bridge at Pelham was our only chance of crossing; and should the enemy destroy that, our chances of escape were slim. Just before going down the mountain a detail from Company I, Lieut. Vance in command, was pushed forward to the bridge and arrived in time to drive off a rebel force that had just reached the bridge. Our boys tore up the floor of the bridge, carried the boards to our side, built breastworks of them and held the fort until morning. We remember the names of but Munson, Wyatt and Allen, of Company I, who took part in this brave and important work. The brigade went into camp immediately on coming down from the mountain, and for the first time since leaving Manchester we had a chance to make coffee.

On the morning of the 30th we succeeded in getting across the bridge with but one man wounded, although Wheeler's rebel cavalry were pressing us hard. In actual damage done to the enemy this expedition was a failure, but in nnifying the brigade and giving each man confidence in himself and his officers, it was a grand success. The rebels had hitherto had it all their own way in raiding railroads; this expedition demonstrated that we were just as competent to raid rebel railroads as rebels were to raid Union railroads. This raid had a very demoralizing effect on Gen. Bragg, and he began to evacuate Tullahoma in two hours after he heard the report of our guns at Decherd, thinking he had been flanked by the whole army. We failed to say it rained all day the 30th.

July 1st was the first day since we left Murfreesboro that it had not rained. The brigade scouted towards Wartrace, in the rear of the retreating army. Having traveled 300 miles in a little over three days, and lost over 500 horses, we were told we could have a short time to recruit up a little.

On July 3d we went to Wartrace and went into camp on the ground recently occupied by the rebels. The strongest imagination could not exaggerate the vast accumulations of filth which we saw here and at many other places. Our men often remarked that it seemed as if the rebels expected us to drive them away from their camps, and for our especial discomfort left as much filth behind as possible. Looking back over nearly a year's service we see that the very first thing we have done, on going into camp, even for a few days, has been the digging of sinks; and from our first entrance into the service until now we have digged enough sinks to make a respectable Suez Canal, were they all joined together; or a ditch of sufficient capacity to drain the Kankakee swamps. But up to this time we had never seen a rebel sink; they seemed to revel in filth, and a thousand mingled stinks must have been sweet perfume to their nostrils.

The deluge of rain which had fallen in the 10 days past had soaked the ground until the whole face of the earth was a reeking sea of carrion; in many places, as we walked over the ground, we could hear and see the sputtering water through which the noxious gases arose to high heaven, blending a thousand filthy smells into one, which no christian olfactory could withstand. Countless thousands of green flies flitted about with nasty, lazy drone, like the hum of a thousand spindles. These flies were constantly depositing their eggs on the ground, on the leaves, on everything—which the broiling sun soon hatched into millions of maggots, which wiggled until the leaves and grass on the ground moved and wiggled too; and in a short time they hatched into flies and added to the swarms in the air, and laid more eggs, &c. We are willing to risk our reputation as a faithful recorder of historic facts in saying that we have seen acres and acres of ground covered with leaves that were in a constant quiver from the motions of the maggots that infested them. Every member of the Seventy-Second will remember our camp on "Maggot Hill" as long as he lives. There is an abundance of evidence to prove all we say. The nuisance was so intolerable that we were given permission to clear off a new camp a mile away, which was done by details on the 5th of July. This camp was near Rowesville, and we moved to it on July 6th.

For several days we did little but forage for horses. Shortly after moving to Rowesville our good Dr. ——— went to a house near camp and spoke for his dinner. By good luck the lady of the house had a chicken to fry. The air around the cabin was filled with the savory smell of the frying chicken, and the Doctor's mouth began to water in anticipation of the change from h. t. and s. b. to such a delicacy. But unfortunately for the Doctor, just when the fowl had reached the stage of brown that indicated a job well done, the lady of the house stepped out of the door, and so did the chicken, skillet and all. There was some foul play in the matter, and a man in Company H could tell who did it, but as he didn't sign his own name we will not give it.

The whole country was full of wheat and oats standing in the fields uncut, and foraging for feed for the horses was a matter of pleasure and a light duty; but food for ourselves was scarce; aside from a few apples, potatoes and blackberries, the country afforded nothing. All our government rations had to be hauled from Murfreesboro in wagons, the roads were a vast swamp, and it was next to impossible to get any hauling at all done. Blackberries were fortunately plenty, and with these, and what hard tack we got, we could manage to live.

On the 4th of July there was hardly a cracker in the regiment—and it is a dry Fourth without crackers—so we sought to make up our deficiency in rations by an extra issue of o-rations. This Fourth will long be remembered as one of the bright days of the gloomy years of the rebellion. We were in very high spirits in our Tennessee camp, even if the maggots and green flies were sporting in "shoals and oceans;" and had we known that Lee had been defeated at Gettysburg, and that Vicksburg had surrendered, our joy would have been unbounded. Perhaps we sniffed the good news from afar, and inhaled the spirit of rejoicing which made the loyal North ring and roar with delight and thanksgivings.

We gathered in the afternoon at headquarters, and Col. Kirkpatrick, who was the only politician in the regiment, was called out for a speech. He responded in one of his happiest efforts. When he spoke of the "dear old flag, the stars and stripes" in a grand burst of eloquence he said, "they should wave over the land of the free and the home of the brave when the last mother's son of the rebellion should be dead and rotten, damned and forgotten." We cheered him to the echo. He was followed by Sergt.-Maj. B. M. Thompson, and for an hour we had a grand oration. This occasion was an oasis in the many dreary days of our service.

While having a few days quiet in camp in this sweet-scented country, we have leisure to state that at Murfreesboro the Seventy-Second conceived and brought forth a poet, in this same Sergt.-Maj. Thompson, who became an institution in our history. From the opening of this campaign to the close of the war the regiment made no important move that he did not reduce to song, in such lively verse that, if published, would hand the regiment down to posterity as the embodiment of all that is chivalrous, generous, dashing and good. His poetry is not in elegant style, but quite forcible in expression. It would be a pleasure to insert it all in this volume, in connection with the circumstances described in each piece; but poetry fills space so rapidly that we are compelled to leave it out. We have it all before us, and should the sale of this book justify another edition we promise to insert it in full.

On July 10th we moved camp to near Normandy, on Duck River, nine miles from Tullahoma.

On the 13th Col. Miller took a detail of 20 men from each company in the regiment and went on a scout, north and west through Shelbyville and Unionville, to see if the rebels had all left the country. We traveled 75 miles, captured a few rebel prisoners and returned on the 15th.

On the 16th we scouted to Elk River to see if the rebels had all crossed, and found none. Also on the 16th the Seventy-Second and 98th, Col. Wilder in command, went on a scout to destroy some saltpeter works near Lynchburg, Tenn, and returned on the 17th. It was on this scout that Corp'l John T. Haynes, Company I, captured the famous old fighting cock "Methuselah" which was never whipped in many fights. The old bird furnished much amusement to those who enjoyed it, and many a rooster went down before his gaffs, after he became a member of the Seventy-Second.

On the 18th of July the Regiment was paid off from January 1st to the 1st of May, four months.

On the 21st Col Wilder, of the 17th, went home and left Col. Miller in command of the brigade.

On the 22d a detachment of the brigade under the gallant Col. Funkhouser, of the 98th Illinois, who was always on hand for his share of the hardest and most dangerous duty, consisting of part of the 92d and 98th Illinois, and 10 men and a non-commissioned officer from each company of the Seventy-Second, Capt. C. G. Thomson in command, went on a scout to capture horses for the 92d, and also to fill up losses of horses in the brigade. This detachment passed through Shelbyville, Unionville, Chaplain Hill, Bythursday, Columbia and Hunt's Store, part of the country where our troops had never been, and secured stock and forage in abundance.

As this was a very important scout, in which Sergt. Steward of Company A says 1,154 horses and mules were captured, we record a few of the many exciting personal incidents, begging pardon for not giving all the vast pile that lies before us. The command moved at 8 a. m., passed through Shelbyville and camped four miles from Unionville. After the precautionary information that we were to move through a section of the country infested by bushwhackers—furloughed rebel soldiers—we were commanded to begin to forage for stock and able bodied negroes. Each non-commissioned officer was train as a guard, and a rallying point for the bands of scouts. The allowed to take all his 10 men except two, who were left with the pack train and guard moved along the main road while the scouting detachments took any direction they preferred, all to report to the officer in command at the train at certain points agreed upon for camping over night. Sergt. Steward, commanding the detachment from Company A, reports the capture of 30 horses and mules during the scout; taking this as an average for the capture of each detail from the Seventy-Second, would make their aggregate capture of horses during the trip 300, or three horses for each man on the scout, which is about correct. Records, of Company I, furnishes the best account of this scout. Of the work on July 23d he says: "My detail had to serve as rear guard for the column until late in the afternoon when scouts began to come in. when I got permission from Capt. Thomson to draw from detachments of other companies and go foraging. I had just learned that some men were running a threshing machine on the south side of Duck River. Taking two of my own men and two others, our whole party being five, I started. Several parties that day had tried to get on the south side of Duck River but failed on account of high waters. We reached a point from which the machine could be seen in the distance. I told the men I wanted to go for that machine. Otherr of our regiment came up at that point and said they would go and see us try it, but didn't feel like running any risks themselves. We struck the river at Maury's Mills, but the bridge was in ruins. A man at the mills told us that there was a ford just below, but it was deep and dangerous. Just then I saw a horse hitched which I was told belonged to a boy who was then in the mills. By this time several squads had come up and we went down to the ford. The river looked so formidable that I wished the men would decline to go further, but one of them said, "go in and try it," and rather than back out I put into it. The water run over my horse's back but I pushed ahead and called out, "come on!" With a whoop they dashed into the river and all got speedily over in safety. The boy had crossed in a canoe and was flying off on his horse to alarm the threshers; but we pursued and soon overtook him, and learned from him that the threshing was on Grey's plantation, that Grey was a Captain of company of rebels and that his company was guarding the threshing. I directed some of the men to take charge of the horse and boy, but we had not gone far until I saw the boy running across a cornfield, and saw in a moment that this was likely to spoil the arrangement if we failed to reach the machine before the boy, and that we might get our hair raised. We dashed off in a gallop, and as we neared the machine raised a whoop and cheer, making as much noise as a regiment.

The noble guards, three times our number, broke for the cornfield, jumped the fence and disappeared in a trice. We stripped the horses and mules, 12 in number, put the darkies upon them, and fearing the rebels might find how few we were, slip back through the corn and pay us their respects, we dashed back, crossing the river in safety." The rebels having lost their negroes and animals were left to their own reflections, and we never heard how Capt. Grey finished up his threshing. We moved on through Unionville and Chaplain Hill and camped that night on Rutherford Creek.

On the 24th (we quote John B. Davis, Company D,) our advance was fired on by bushwhackers, two of whom we captured. We advanced to Columbia, where we had a slight skirmish, and turning back camped on the farm of a Maj. Allen, who was then in the rebel service On this march we were instructed to state to all persons from whom we took property that if they would come to camp and establish their loyalty their stock should be returned to them. We had native guides with us who knew those who were loyal.

We give a sample day's scouting by the detail from Company D, which illustrates the work of the whole command. On leaving Spring Hill we came to a house where a young lady was holding a horse by the bridle. On entering the house we found a revolver, and saddle pockets filled with apples. Coming out we asked the lady for the horse; she threw her arms around his neck and declared we never should take him. We disengaged her arms, took the horse and moved on. The next place was a large plantation where we found three mules, two in the gin house and one in the lot; we unhitched the two from the gin and went for the one in the lot, when the old lady came out and said, "Lo'd A'mighty! you'uns don't want that mule, he's done 25 years ole!" We took him for eight years old, and moved on.

We next secured a fine horse, the owner seeming to care very little about it. One of the native guides came up and told us that the owner of the horse and himself had hidden together from the rebels in a cave for six months. We wouldn't take such a loyal man's horse and returned it to him. We next took a horse from the rebel Col. Haines. Next came to an old woman who was weeping bitterly; it wouldn't be so bad to take her horses but we had taken her negroes too. We asked her if she was a Union woman "No," said she, "when the Union split I split too!"

This scouting party returned to camp at Roseville, on the 27th found the brigade had gone to Decherd, followed and reached them on the 28th, bringing in 1,000 horses, 1,500 mules and 1,000 negroes

We lay in camp at Decherd from July 27th to August 16th, the longest period of inactivity since we were mounted. Aside from a little skirmish drilling and foraging we did nothing. The 10th Indiana was at Winchester, a few miles from us, and we had a pleasant season of inter-visiting.

As this date completes our first year's service and marks an epoch in our history, we note the changes in our regiment since our last review up to January 8th, when we went into camp at Murfreesboro:

Capt. R. B. Hanna, Company H, had been detached as Provost Marshal, on Gen. Reynolds' Staff. At Decherd station, Company H was detailed as Provost Guard, at Gen. Reynolds' head quarters. Sergt. Maj. W. K. Byrns, has been promoted to Adjt. of the regiment, to succeed A. A. Rice, who has been previously mentioned as promoted to the rank of Captain and made A. A. Gen'l. on Gen. Reynolds' Staff. Chaplain Jesse Hill resigned April 13th, succeeded by Rev. John Eddy, of whose brief service and death by a cannon shot at Hoover's Gap we have spoken. John B. Johnson, Assistant Surgeon, resigned May 3d. Capt. Milton Newton resigned February 1st, and Andrew Klepser succeeded him. Frank B. Everett, 1st Lieut. Company C, resigned February 16th, and Edward A. Cutshaw succeeded him. Jno. N. Insley, 1st Lieut. Company E, resigned February 9th, and Lewis C. Priest succeeded him. Capt. Moses Burch, Company F, resigned March 23, and James L. Dalton succeeded him. Orin E. Harper, 2d Lieut. Company F, dismissed March 1st, and Johnson Parker succeeded him. W. R. Jewell, 2d Lieut. Company G, resigned from sickness, May 19th, re-entered service in July next as Captain of a Company at Indianapolis; the company not being ordered to the field, he resigned and accepted the Chaplaincy of the 7th Indiana Infantry, and served until its time expired. Jacob Gladden succeeded him. James M. Stafford, 1st Lieut. Company H, resigned Juue 11th, and John C. Scott succeeded him. John Watts, Captain Company I, dismissed January 19th, and Wm. H. McMurtry succeeded him. Capt. Hiram B. Collins, Company K, resigned April 21st, and Richard H. McIntire succeeded him. John W. Gaskill, 2d Lieut. Company K, died at Murfreesboro, February 20th, succeeded by James W. Davis. Making 11 commissioned officers resigned, one died and one killed.

In Company A, non-commissioned officers and privates, died 2, discharged 6. Company B, died 6, discharged 19, killed 1. Company C, died 3, discharged 6, drummed out 1. Company E, died 10, discharged 12, killed 1. Company F, died 6, discharged 9. Company G, died 4, discharged 11, deserted 1. Company H, died 1, dis charged 11. Company I, died 4, discharged 10. Company K, died 2, discharged 6. Total for the Regiment: died 38; discharged 90; killed 3; deserted 1; drummed out 1. Making the total loss of the Regiment, from January 8th, 1863, to August 16th, 1863, in officers, non-commissioned officers and privates, 146. To this add the loss of the first six months, 98, and the total loss for the year is 244 We left Indianapolis with 978, and in this first year we have lost just two more than one-fourth of our entire command.

With perhaps one or two exceptions, every officer had resigned on certificates of disability, precisely the same ground upon which non-commissioned officers and privates were discharged. Perhaps 90 per cent. of this heavy loss was caused by the horrible filth pit at Murfreesboro, before spoken of. In addition to the losses above alluded to, there were enough absent in hospitals to make a total loss of full 300 men and 9 officers; deduct those transferred and on detached duty and there are about 500 men in the regiment for service.

At Castillian Springs, in 1862, there was a general overhauling of the non-commissioned officers of the entire regiment, nearly one-half being dropped from their places and others substituted; but after that, in most cases, officers were advanced in regular order of promotion.

CHAPTER XXI.

August 6th to September 14th, 1863.—Begin Second Year's Service at Decherd—Beautiful Camp, Good and abundant water—Comrades join us—A Big Mouse—Bragg's Retreat from Tullahoma—Lightning Brigade move over the Mountains, attack Chattanooga and Bragg evacuates the City—Dry Valley and Racy Incidents—Big Corn, Big Sheep, Big Eating—How we got our Mutton—A Tussle with the Bell-Wether—Hard on the Old Sow—Crossing the Tennessee River—The Feint deceives Bragg, He Retreats and the Lightning Brigade flashes after Him to Tunnel Hill, Striking the Rebels in Force—Bad Mistake of Rosecrans, who will not be Convinced that We have found the Enemy in Force in Front—We are Ordered to LaFayette—Bloody Battle of Rock Springs—We Escape from the Enemy after Night—Seventy-Second Foragers taken before Gen. Rosecrans—Sergt. Wakeman Introduces Capt. Smith to Col. Miller.

We begin our second year's service in our camp at Decherd. Our summer's service on horse back in the pure air, and on fresh rations most of the time, has worked out the poison of Murfreesboro from our blood. The camp at this place was a beautiful one, situated on a gently sloping hill-side abundantly shaded, near a clear stream of water, which flowed from a large fountain which was almost bottomless and burst up from a fissure in the rocks, furnishing water for bathing, washing, and all other purposes.

Many of our comrades who had been left behind sick came back to us at this camp, and bathing in the pure water and the abundant use of peaches and blackberries, which were plenty, soon put them all in the best of fighting trim. We never saw the command in better spirits. We cannot forbear relating an anecdote, showing on what intimate terms the men and officers were. The stream above mentioned ran between our horse quarters and regimental headquarters. Wm. Grismar, Company K, was put on guard by the side of the creek. Col. Miller was then in command of the brigade and Lieut. Col. Kirkpatrick in command of the regiment. Just at daylight Col. Kirkpatrick came out of his tent, stretched himself and caught sight of Grismar, who immediately cocked his gun and pointed to a big drift pile in the creek, and called to the Colonel to come there. The Colonel started and Grismar motioned for him to keep as quiet as possible. The Colonel came up on tip toe, Grismar still holding his gun leveled at the drift, and motioned for the Colonel to get down; and all ears, eyes and attention the Colonel got down on his knees, began to peer under the logs and whispered, "what is it?" Grismar whispered back, "just tear that drift pile open and you will find the d—dest biggest mouse you ever saw." The Colonel said, "that'll do," tossed Grismar his pocket-knife and told him to say no more about it.

Bragg began his retreat from Tullahoma on the night of June 28th, and never stopped until he put the Cumberland Mountains between Rosecrans and himself, making his headquarters at Chattanooga. Rosecrans followed and camped his army at the western base of the mountains, his left resting on Manchester, centre at Decherd and right south of Winchester. It took Rosecrans until the middle of August to get up supplies enough to justify him in climbing the mountains.

On August 16th we broke camp at Decherd, moved along the base of the mountains four miles north and began the ascent. Every man was ordered to dismount and lead his horse. It was two miles from where we started to the top, steep and rocky. As we had not walked so far for a long time we were very tired when we reached the summit. All the lovers of grand and beautiful scenery were richly paid by the sublime and far-reaching view spread out in the direction whence we had come. We passed University Hights and camped at Tracy City.

It may be proper to state that the plan of the campaign was to make a strong feint at and above Chattanooga, while the main body of our army was to cross the Tennessee River away below Chattanooga, and come up on the east side of the river. The portion of the army making this feint was our brigade, now composed of the 17th and Seventy-Second Indiana, the 92d, 98th and 123d Illinois, and the 18th Indiana battery; and Gen. Wagoner's brigade of infantry. Gen. Wagoner started from Manchester when we started from Decherd, but we had to lie in camp at Tracy City and wait for him to catch up.

On the 18th we moved forward, and on the 19th, near noon, reached the edge of the mountain bordering the Sequatchie Valley, which is one of the finest and richest valleys in the world. The rebels had every road and crossing leading out of it to the west strongly picketed, and the valley was full of the enemy. We struck the valley at Sherman's Crossing. the 92d Illinois in advance. The rebel vidette on the hill reported our advance in time for the rebels in the valley to concentrate and get ready for us by the time we descended the mountain.

When the 92d struck the rebel pickets it came promptly to a halt. This so exasperated Col. Wilder that he ordered it to stand aside and ordered the Seventy-Second forward. As soon as we reached the head of the column Col. Miller took Companies A, F, D, and I—

Company I, Capt. McMurtry, advance guard—and struck across the valley. The command had not gone far until the road forked and it was necessary to send a company on each branch. Company I kept straight across the valley, which was about three miles wide at this point, while Company A made a lively chase after some rebels on the other branch of the road, in which Albert Sigers killed a rebel. Company D run on to a school-house where some rebel soldiers were holding a conference over some Union Home Guards they had just captured. The rebels had decided that the home guards should die, but Capt. Thomson came upon them so suddenly that it "broke up the meetin';" turned the tables completely, and the Captain left the home guards guarding the rebels. When Capt. McMurtry, with Company I, reached Sequatchie River, they found it a wide, deep stream, having bluff banks, each side skirted with thick brush and timber; the road struck the creek and turned squarely to the right, passing down the stream some distance to a ford. Here the rebels undertook to make a stand, and opened fire on I, as they came around a curve in the road, but the Company without a halt or a return of a shot dashed like furies down to the ford, across the stream, up in the rear of the rebels, opened on them with their Spencers, killed one, captured five, and chased the terror stricken enemy north-east, through the open country, until they reached the foot of the mountain, where the rebels scattered and hid in the brush. That was a brilliant dash performed in less time than it takes to tell it.

This rapid movement brought Company I across the valley in a brief time and with little noise, and left the next rebel post, further up the creek, in ignorance of our movements; this post was on a road leading north-west; they had dismounted, barricaded the road with rails, and were behind them with their backs toward us, eagerly straining their eyes watching for the Yanks to come, but, Yankee like, we slipped up behind them and they knew nothing of our approach until we were covering them with our fatal Spencers and demanding their surrender. They made no resistance and were all captured.

The brigade went into camp at Dunlap. Kings never lived better than we did here, for grapes, peaches and roasting ears, abounded. At Dunlap we left all our trains and loaded all our traps and five days' rations upon our pack mules, and early on the morning of the 20th of August, we started up another range of the mountains, called Waldron's Ridge, which runs straight south to the Tennessee River, at Stevenson and Bridgeport. This range was much higher, steeper and more difficult of ascent than the other one had been; and as we had to walk and lead, it was an uphill business, and very exhausting before we got to the top. We moved rapidly, and as the ridge is only 20 miles across the summit, we reached the eastern brow that day by 4 p. m.

Clark, in command of the Seventy-Second scouts, says: On this march, and when within about a mile of the foot of the mountain, Col. Wilder gave me a guide and told me to take my scouts and those of the 17th and go down the mountain, by what is known as "Wild Cat Trace," and get in the rear of the rebel pickets at the foot of the mountain on the road. He said that he would hold the command one hour for me to get position. I did so. I placed the 17th scouts on the first road and my scouts took the second road. We dismounted, got ready, and had just got position when the advance of the column was fired on by the pickets. The fire was returned and here came the pickets, pell mell, past us; well, not exactly past us, for we fired into them, and some were wounded and a great many thrown from their horses and captured. I remember one who jumped over the fence into a clump of bushes, when Amos Hollingsworth jumped over after and caught him by the coat collar and seat of his trowsers and threw him out in the road. We learned by the people whose houses the frightened rebels passed after being fired on, that there was not a man of them wore a hat, but that their hair stood as erect as porcupine quills.

The Seventy-Second was in advance, A, F, D and I, advance guard. We struck a heavy picket post just at the foot of the mountain, and as we charged them about one-half ran up the valley and the other half down it. The four companies above named chased the squad that turned north 12 miles before we stopped, but as our horses were already tired and theirs fresh when we started, we didn't catch any of them. Soon after we started in pursuit of the rebels the horse of John Young, of I, dashed ahead of all others and came close up to the fleeing foe. One rebel halted and leveled his gun at Young; and Young, without halting his horse, brought his Spencer to his shoulder and fired at the rebel. At this instant Young's horse stumbled and fell, and the rebel fell from his horse severely wounded by Young's shot. Young was not hit by the rebel's bullet, but he was almost crushed by his horse falling on him; his leg and arm were broken and he was otherwise bruised. As soon as Young and the rebel recovered they talked the matter over very cooly, as they lay near each other, until they were taken up. The rebel died of his wound, and Young is badly crippled for life, yet by his energy and tact he makes his way very well in the world and has a good business at his home in Oakwood, Illinois.

We remained all night on picket right where we stopped. The remainder of the brigade went into camp soon after getting down from the mountain, at Poe's tavern, 15 miles above Chattanooga.

At daylight on August 21st the brigade moved very rapidly down the valley to Chattanooga, the Seventy-Second scouts driving before it the pickets of the enemy at several points, captured 30 prisoners and came near capturing the steam ferry boat which carried the retreating pickets across the river, killing the ferryman. The regimental scouts captured 100 horses and mules that day.

The brigade came up and took position on the bluffs overlooking the city, on the north-west. Capt. Lilly immediately opened fire on the city with two guns. That was some sort of fast day or holiday in Chattanooga, and when our shells began to drop among them there was such a stampede for the fortifications as you never saw. The rebels replied with a battery of 32 pounders, a shell from which killed four horses and shattered the leg of a gunner, all belonging to the same section. Dr. Cole amputated the leg, but the soldier never rallied and soon died. Our brigade kept up a strong demonstration in front of the city until dark, and then fell back five miles and camped in Dry Valley.

Companies A, F, D and I, which chased a squad of rebels 12 miles and picketed the road on the night of the 20th, moved early on the morning of the 21st, being 27 miles above Chattanooga; we scouted slowly down the river hunting all the fords and crossings, and getting acquainted with the country generally. We reached the camp of the regiment at nine o'clock that night.

Dry Valley was not so very dry after all, for numerous beautiful mountain streams meandered through it, the land was rich and forage abounded. We remained here until the 29th of September, and enjoyed as much solid fun as we ever did during the same length of time while in the service. Every afternoon our battery would go to the bluff overlooking the city and shell it vigorously; the regiments of the brigade took turn about going down on foot with the battery, leaving our horses behind to give the rebels the impression that we had an infantry force as well as artillery and cavalry. We constantly kept a strong picket force all along the river.

The ridge our battery occupied each day was nearly a mile from the river. Off to the right of our position, and about half way down the hill, was a little frame house. After a few days' shelling with but an occasional shot from the rebels, the thing became monotonous and our men and officers became saucy and venturesome. About the 23d, Col. Wilder and his Staff Officers, in order to get a better view of Chattanooga and surroundings, concluded to go down and get into the house. In the squad were Col. Wilder, Capt. Shields, Lieut. Crick and Lieut. Newell, of the Topographical Engineers. This was rather a bold adventure, but they succeeded in getting into the house from the back way, as they supposed unobserved. The back of the house sat on the ground, and the front part, next the river, was three or four feet from the ground. Everything was quiet about the house, but the officers saw under it a very large old sow, serenely sleeping. The Johnnies had observed all their movements and turned a 32-pounder upon the house, and just as our heroes had secured the best positions at crack and crevice with their field glasses, and had begun to survey the situation, the Johnnies let drive at them. The 32-pounder was well aimed and well timed, and came under the house "thud," literally blotting the old sow out of existence, and at the same instant exploding, and quicker than you could wink, pieces of the floor, hair, entrails, fresh pork and old iron came boiling out through the roof of the house like lava from a crater. To say that the officers rolled out of that house faster than hornets ever tumbled out of a nest, would be putting it rather mildly; and to say that they made good time up the hill would be *true*. Lieut. Newell jumped out of the window, and in just two minutes by the watch was going over the brow of the hill, when Capt. Rice hallooed "hello, Newell, what's the matter with you?" Without checking up Newell hallooed over his shoulder as he ran, "O! there's nothing the matter with me, but it was terrible hard on the old sow."

On August 25th our regiment went on a reconnoissance to Friar's Island, 12 or 15 miles from our camp. At this place there is a ford that can be crossed at ordinary stages of water. We found the ford strongly picketed and guarded by a battery of artillery protected by earthworks. We exchanged shots across the river, which is at this point three-quarters of a mile wide, but did not attempt to cross.

When we marched from Dunlap we left our teams behind and Company E to guard them. About the 26th Capt. McMurtry gathered together all the pack mules of the brigade and started back over Waldron's Ridge for rations. From our camp, straight across to Dunlap, it was 30 miles; we made the trip across and back in two days. This was repeated several times by other companies, till the fourth of September, when our teams also came across. Reconnoissances and scouting up to Friar's Island were made every day by some of the companies. On the 29th Col's Wilder and Miller went up and talked with the rebels across the river. Companies B and I went up there one day, dismounted, left our horses out of sight and slipped down close to the river to see what chance there was of getting across. The enemy discovered and fired on us awhile with their muskets, but did us no harm, and when they saw that we didn't mind it they turned a piece of artillery on us and we hastily got out of the way. Two or three miles further down we saw a man washing his feet on the opposite side, and as he didn't know we were about, we fired a shot or two simply to impart to him a knowledge of our presence. He received the news violently and tore up the earth as he pawed up the hill. Again, two or three miles below this, we saw some rebel pickets on the other side and began to talk with them and ascertained what regiment they were of, how long they had been stationed there, and various other bits of information. They were so friendly that we invited them to come over, pledging ourselves not to harm them. They at first agreed to come, and we dismounted, left our guns and went down to the river to receive them. They modified their proposition and said they would meet us half-way; we also accepted this proposition. The river was a mile wide and seemed very shallow, and Sergt. Magee pulled off his clothes and waded to the middle of it. The men who were doing the talking now said that their officers would not let them come. We may here mention that our guns were so superior to theirs that our balls easily went over the river, while theirs rarely came across.

We have been a farmer all our life, and point to the prairies of Indiana and Illinois with great pride as producing the best corn in the world; but we saw corn on our trip down the river on that day beside which the best fields of Illinois and Indiana are dwarfs. The rows were three and a half feet apart both ways, two stalks to the hill, and such stalks we have never seen since. As we rode between the rows on a large horse with a forage sack before us, most of the ears were just a convenient hight to gather, but to reach many ears we had to stand up in the stirrups. One ear cut in two four inches from the butt measured four inches in diameter, and each grain was three-quarters of an inch long. We were getting our entire living off the country, and in such a valley neither man nor beast was likely to suffer.

The geological formation of this valley is peculiar, and we have seen nothing like it anywhere else. Right at the base of the mountain is the beautiful little Dry Valley in which we are encamped; between this and the river is a range of hills, many of them almost as high as the mountain itself. These knobs are chiefly composed of a species of quartz-rock, nearly square in shape, from the size of a walnut to that of a man's head. These rocks make the hills the most difficult to climb of any we ever ascended. When the scouting party above named got opposite Chattanooga we climbed a hill till we could look down into the rebel works, and could tell by the columns of dust that the rebel troops were moving east.

Returning to camp that evening we noticed a fine lot of sheep in a field near the picket post. We had strict orders not to leave camp after night, but the fat sheep were too great a temptation, and a party of us determined to risk a venture to capture some mutton. In going to the field a point of the mountain had to be climbed to avoid the pickets, and the square stones rolling under our feet with their sharp corners made the trip so toilsome that we had earned the mutton before taking it. The sheep had lain down very near the picket post, and the puzzle was how to get them away without alarming the picket. After a few whispers we crawled up near the sheep and began to toss pebbles at them; when a sheep was struck it got up; when about half were up a stone struck the bell-wether and he jumped up in fright, rattling his bell like the beat of a long roll until it reverberated among the hills. The pickets were up and all attention in a moment, and we thought our mutton prospects withered as we heard the pickets speculating as to what was up. We lay as flat as snakes in the grass and still as stones until the pickets got over their alarm; the sheep in the meantime had all come to their feet, and by skillful tossing of stones we got them away from the picket post and drove them to the further end of the long field. There were six of us. We cornered the sheep and each made a dive for one. It was our fortune to seize the bell-wether by the collar. At a single bound he jerked us off our feet, and we fell sprawling on the ground, holding to the bell-collar like grim death as we went rolling with the sheep down the steep, rough hill for some rods—the sheep on top half the time—but we were a full match for him, being on top the other half, but were terribly bruised on the square rocks. Our grip was failing, but two comrades came to the rescue and the prize was secured. Three others got good ones. We skinned them in a twinkling—practice makes perfect—but now the question is how to get them into camp. They were big, fat and heavy—the bell-wether being the fattest sheep we ever saw. When strung on a rail it was all two of us could do to carry one of them. As we went to the field the side of the mountain to be ascended was not so steep as the one to be descended, and we reached the top without serious mishap; but the trouble began when we began to descend. Lights were all out in camp and we were not certain of the direction. We began to descend, and every little bit the man at the front end of the rail—and we happened to be at that end—would find himself sitting down and scooting down the mountain on the half-sole of his pantaloons, the sheep lapping about his neck, and the man who should be at the upper end of the rail lapping round the sheep. Such service tried a soldier's bottom. When about fifty feet from the foot of the mountain the men at the upper end of the rails seemed to let all holds go at once, and men and sheep came rolling down upon us like an avalanche, and before we could check up we came down in a heap against Col. Miller's tent, bruised, bleeding, and almost as badly skinned as the sheep. When we struck the tent the Colonel started up in a terrible fright and hallooed, "*Ha, there!*" We held our breath for a moment, and the Colonel concluded that a convalescent horse had stumbled over the tent ropes, and he fell asleep again. We picked up our bruised and mangled forms, and also our sheep, and silently stole away. We had mutton for the inner man and mutton suet to mollify our wounds as long as we remained in camp.

On the 26th of August Wagner's brigade came into the valley at Poe's Tavern, and made the strongest possible demonstration on the enemy along the river. On the 28th Wagner moved down near us and shelled Chattanooga, the rebels replying but once with a small gun, and from the little attention paid us we were led to think that they had decided our attack was but a feint, and were concentrating against our main army that was now across the river at Shell Moun, Bridgeport and Stevenson, 35 miles below. In order to disabuse the rebels of this idea our trains came over the mountain and Gen. Wagner moved his brigade to the top of the mountain opposite the city, put up tents in plain view of the rebels, and burnt brush and log heaps as if a whole corps were in camp.

On the 5th of September, to add to the demonstration, Gen. Hazen's brigade was sent into the valley at Poe's, and shelled the woods across the river. This seemed to have the desired effect, and our pickets early that night sent information to camp that the rebels were preparing to cross. This was a cause of serious alarm to our brigade, as Wagner was on a mountain two miles high, and could not possibly get down in time to aid us, while Hazen, 15 miles above, could give us no immediate aid. In this situation a corps of rebels, crossing in the night, might drive us from the valley and capture the two other brigades.

The night was dark and favorable for the rebel advance. Our wagons were all loaded and the teams hitched to them; the pickets were doubled and a regiment sent to the river in front of the city.

An unusual amount of hammering and noise continued on the rebel side opposite to us, and our teams were hurriedly started up the mountain. It was our lot to be on picket; the noise continued late into the night, our brigade lying on arms; but the day dawned and no attack was made. We afterwards learned that the confusion was made by the rebels preparing to evacuate the city.

The solid comfort we had in this valley, notwithstanding our exposed position, has been spoken of, and also the square stones, and the fun we enjoyed. We will now relate an incident that combines all these, and then we are ready to go out of this valley of fatness.

After leaving Decherd, on the 16th of August, we never had our tents up until we reached Maysville, Ala., October 24. Each mess, or camp family, would hitch their horses in a circle in the woods and cook, eat and sleep in the center of the circle, so in case of alarm each could mount most speedily. To get a shady place to hitch we had to go on to the hillside, the level ground being in cultivation. Company I was encamped in regular order, mess 1 up the hill about 100 yards from the road, 2 about 25 yards further down, 3, to which we belonged, 25 yards further down, and 4 next the road; the hill was so steep and rough that we had to scrape away the rocks to get a place level enough to sleep on. Every night numbers of horses would get loose and wander about in the camp; besides there were scores of convalescent horses that had given out and were turned loose to live or die. One night one of these horses stumbled over some fellow, away up in mess 1, and he jumped up in a fright and ran for his life; this scared the horse and it came down through mess 2, in a full run. We were awake when the man in mess 1 scared the animal and knew from the rattle and crash of rocks that it was coming straight for our mess, who were all sleeping in a row—we in the middle—and as the horse swept over mess 2 they all jumped up and hallooed as if Satan himself were after them. We jumped up and called to mess 3 "for God's sake save yourselves." From the additional fright given the horse in mess 2 he came upon mess 3 like a whole regiment of cavalry; the men jumped up half awake, the horse stumbled and fell right into our bed, rolled over and went rolling down through mess 4, landing in the road at the foot of the hill. For a moment the hair stood straight up on top of our heads as we realized how near we came to being crushed to death; but in a moment more the thought of the ridiculous figure we cut in jumping out of bed with nothing but our hog-hair shirts on and running till our banners cracked in the wind to get out of the way of the old horse, overcame our fear, and we all roared with laughter and hallooed like Indians. Other companies joined in the jollity and kept it up for half an hour.

On September 7th our brigade moved up to the mouth of North Chicamauga Creek, near Friar's Island, and Wagner's brigade moved off the mountain to the river in front of Chattanooga. In the night our brigade dug some trenches and built lunettes for the guns, and made every possible preparation for crossing at the ford just below the point of the island. Our battery shelled the enemy and they replied with an energy that let us know they were ready.

On the morning of September 8th the brigade made ready to cross, the 17th having the advance. Its scouts undertook to swim to the island, which is about 80 rods long and 20 wide, and covered with timber, which screened our movements. The object of the scouts was to get on the island and pick off the rebel gunners. The channel on our side was not so wide as on the other, but quite deep except just below the point of the island. The river just below the island is nearly a mile wide. In the efforts of the brave scouts to get over, their leader, Joseph C. Wilson, was drowned, but the others gained the island and a vigorous skirmish immediately opened. Our artillery did good work; but in a short time, to our agreeable astonishment, the rebel artillery limbered up and deliberately moved away. The reason for this retreat was that the rebels evacuated Chattanooga on the night of the 7th; Crittenden's corps immediately took possession and began to move east and south, and was about to cut off the rebels in our front; hence they left and we crossed the river at our leisure, Company C in advance. Capt. Glaze says a passing column was reported to the Colonel across the river, and the battery being close at hand opened on them over the trees. In the language of a contraband picked up on the road in the rear of the column, "Sich scramblin' to git away from de shells" was never seen. Company C could not resist the chance for a few shots, but the enemy were in a hurry and did not return the fire. We found a few tents and some camp equipage near the forts which probably belonged to Gen. Hardee, as his name appeared on some of the camp stools, which Capt. Glaze took charge of.

Of the importance of this capture of Chattanooga, with its wealth of saltpetre beds and coal, by a flank movement, we have not space to speak; histories of the war will inform the reader that it was hailed with delight at the North as of little less importance than the fall of Vicksburg, and that it had a most depressing effect in the South, where the position was regarded as invincible. After the fall of this city the Southern people said the great gate to the invasion of the South was opened wide.

The only guns fired on Chattanooga were those of which we have already spoken. Crittenden entered the place without firing a gun. On page 140 of Ridpath's history of President Garfield is the following explanation:

"On August 16th began the movement of the army across the mountains towards the Tennessee River. The paramount effort in the manner of the advance was to deceive the enemy as to the real intention.

"The army made the movement along three separate routes. Crittenden's corps, forming the left, was to advance by a circuitous route to a point about 15 miles south-west of Chattanooga, and make his crossing of the Tennessee River there. Thomas, as our centre, was to cross a little farther down, and McCook 30 miles further to the right.

"These real movements were to be made under cover of an apparent one. About 7,000 men marched directly to the river, opposite Chattanooga, as if a direct attack were to be made on the place.

"The extent of front presented, the show of strength, the vigorous shelling of the city by Wilder's artillery, the bold expression of the whole movement, constituted a brilliant feint. Bragg was deceived again. Absorbed in the operations in front of the place, he offered no resistance to the crossing of the Tennessee River by the main army."

We have already told the part the Seventy-Second took in this famous attack on Chattanooga, by which Bragg was so alarmed that he forgot to guard his flanks. At Decherd, in his rear, we had helped to hurry him out of his stronghold at Tullahoma; at Dry Valley, in his front, we have held him until he is flanked out of Chattanooga. The reader can judge whether the "Lightning Brigade" and the Seventy-Second have a right to be proud of this part of their history. We have helped to open the gate in this Switzerland of America, for the invasion of East Tennessee, Alabama, Georgia, North Carolina and Virginia, and must now "move on."

On the 9th all our trains came up and crossed at the same ford we did, and we drew seven days rations, and on the 10th we moved on Ringgold and camped just inside the Georgia State line.

On the 11th, just as we got in column on the direct road to Ringgold, a brigade of infantry came on to it from Chattanooga; our regiment was in the rear and the commander of the infantry asked who we were, and we told him; he turned to his Adjutant and said, "tell Col. Wilder who is here, and to push them." Our advance was then skirmishing with the rebels at Ringgold, and before the Adjutant had time to reach the head of the column we began to move, passing through Ringgold, where the depot and vast piles of commissary and quartermaster's stores were on fire. We saw no more of the infantry General who said "push them." When through Ringgold we turned east through a gap in Taylor's Ridge where two long trestle bridges were burning. Passing through the gap we turned south and were met by a few shells thrown by the retreating rebels; our battery took position, fired a few rounds, the rebels limbered up and pushed on, we following, our advance and the rebel's rear skirmishing at intervals. As we neared Tunnel Hill, some 10 miles south of Ringgold, the scouts and Company A in advance, the rebel cavalry suddenly came sweeping down upon them in full charge. Col. Kirkpatrick, seeing the dust raised by the advance of the enemy, shouted, "Company A, they are charging us! dismount and give 'em h—l!" Company A, without taking time to form line, dismounted and took to the fence corners, Col. Kirkpatrick shouting his battle cry all the while to cheer them on, "d—n 'em—d—m 'em—shoot 'em in the guts! go for 'em!"

Company A poured such a stream of well directed bullets from their Spencers into the advancing rebels that they quickly wheeled and dashed away beyond the range of the fire. At this point one rebel was killed. Company A met and repulsed them gallantly and handsomely. A mile further on the column came to a halt, the brigade dismounted and formed line of battle, and prepared to fight on foot, the Seventy-Second on the right. The line moved forward until a position was reached from which we could see right into the mouth of the railroad tunnel. Between our line and that tunnel there were thousands of rebels. It was near sun down and our only safety lay in keeping up a bold front. It seems that the enemy had purposely been drawing us on, and were now waiting for us to charge them, with the expectation that they would take us all in. We did not charge, but held them in check until after dark, quietly fell back to our horses, moved back behind a large hill and were ordered not to unsaddle or build fires. Companies E and K of the Seventy-Second were put on picket duty and were in plain view of the rebels all night, and could hear them talking in camp.

On September 12th, by 3 a. m., we were quietly called up and as quietly mounted our horses and rode away, carefully keeping in the pine woods, concealed from the rebels. Companies E and K were left in a very uncomfortable position, for as soon as morning dawned the rebels began to fire on them. Capt. McIntire, of K, was in command, and immediately began to prepare to follow the brigade. Placing part of Company E under command of Sergts. Remley and Wilhite, as rear guard, they slowly retired, the rebels closely pressing them. Our men showed great coolness and courage in disputing every inch of ground and retarding the advance of the rebels until the command got well out of the way. During the gallant affair almost every man in Company E received close calls, but all got off safe. Some may ask, "why did not the rebels rush up and capture these two companies?" The answer to this question covers all such questions. The rebels did not know but these companies were acting as mere decoys to draw them into the ambush of a strong Union force; for that reason the rebels moved cautiously. Had they known that E and K were left alone, and the command on the retreat, they might have charged, surrounded and taken them; but that is just what they did not know. Rash commanders have often dashed on to a little force of the enemy to take it, only to find themselves surrounded by a superior force and compelled to surrender.

Our brigade moved back to Ringgold fully convinced that we had met the enemy in force at Tunnel Hill, and expected to find the infantry there which were following us yesterday, return with them and make a more determined attack on the rebels; but the infantry were gone. It was the belief of Gen. Rosecrans that the rebels were in full retreat and all we had to do was to press them. The magnitude and results of this mistake will be more fully spoken of further on, and it is mentioned to explain the difficulties the Seventy-Second encountered that memorable 12th of September.

At Ringgold Col. Wilder had orders to report to Gen. Reynolds' division, to which we belonged, and was informed that the division was at LaFayette, or would be that night. We immediately marched for LaFayette on the road that runs nearly south, on the west side of Taylor's Ridge, and not many miles from the road we were on the day before, that road being on the east side of the ridge. We knew nothing of the exact situation of the rebel troops, but were confident they were not retreating, but calmly awaiting a favorable opportunity for battle. We proceeded on the road above mentioned, moving rapidly, and by 4 p. m. had made 15 miles, our regiment being rear guard. At that hour we suddenly heard heavy skirmishing ahead, and the column came to an abrupt halt. This was some six or eight miles due west of Tunnel Hill, and at the crossing of the road leading to Lee & Gordon's Mills. The 17th Indiana held the advance, Capt. Boswell commanding the advance guard. After skirmishing half an hour the column was still standing. A staff officer came and told Col. Miller to send forward four companies of the Seventy-Second, and A

F, D and I, were ordered forward under Col. Kirkpatrick, rode to the front in a gallop, on the east side of the road, to near the head of the column, and turned off on a by-path to the east. A half mile out we dismounted, formed line of battle and moved to the south-west, our regimental scouts in advance as skirmishers. It seemed that we had marched almost a mile when we came to a long and rather steep ridge running north-west, the side next to us sparsely covered with stunted jack-oaks. We had moved on pretty quick time till we reached the foot of the ridge and the scouts about half way up it, when the commander, R. C. Clark, Company I, called out, "halt!" We did so, and could hear an ominous noise over the ridge, and we knew the rebels were coming; and the vital question was which should reach the top of the ridge first. Clark sang out, "deploy and charge!" Immediately 10 men were going up the hill like the wind; we followed at double quick. Just as our scouts disappeared over the ridge we heard a volley, and the quick reply of the Spencers bade us hurry up. Company I deployed forward as skirmishers; in two minutes we reached the brow of the hill out of breath and staggering. The first volley from our scouts threw the rebels into confusion, and they hesitated a moment, but seeing the small number of the scouts they again pressed forward. In a minute our scouts must have fallen back or been captured, when Clark again commanded, "dismount and take to trees!"

By this time Company I, on the ridge, had dressed the line and moved forward; at that moment we heard a most fiendish rebel yell, and they came up the hill like a whirlwind; but we had beaten them and were ready to receive them. What were our scouts to do between two forces bent on each other's destruction? We feared to fire lest we should kill our own men. There and then we witnessed an act of the coolest courage we ever expect to see. The scouts fully realized the situation, mounted their horses and dashed out to the left when the rebels were in fifty feet of them; and strange to say not one of them got a scratch. Clark's horse was shot.

By this time the rebels were in fifty yards of us, and Capt. McMurtry, with revolver in one hand and sword in the other, commanded "fire!" and we did, and never stopped until we gave them our seven rounds. That was the last word ever spoken by the brave Capt. McMurtry; for just as he gave the command they raised their fiendish yell and charged us again, and the Captain fell pierced by three balls. George Brooks also fell mortally wounded and Jacob Allen fell severely wounded, his leg being broken. The rebels checked up to reload, and were close enough to see how few we were, then dashed at us again, and we should have been quickly swallowed up had not the three other companies just then come to our relief. Company F was behind and in a few feet of our lines. The rebels belched another volley of death upon us; Company I had almost all gotten behind trees, and F being in plain view at short range received the force of this fire, before which nine strong men fell. Had F wavered or faltered for one moment, under this terrible fire, we must all have been lost; but with Capt. Dalton at their head firmly commanding, "steady, boys!" they never stopped till in line with I, and then every man went to work with such earnestness, and steady, cool determination, that the woods seemed a vast sheet of fire. Companies A and D poured in a steady, destructive fire, from left-oblique, which proved the grain of coffee that broke the camel's back, for the rebels broke in confusion, ran down the ridge, and we poured a leaden hail storm into their backs, sweeping down many of them.

It had not been thirty minutes since our scouts started up that ridge until this fight was over. But what terrible bloody work in that half hour! It was our fortune, in less than a month after this fight, at the battle of Farmington, to capture a part of this same rebel force that fought us that day; and also two years afterwards, just at the close of the war, to pass over this battle field. We do not hazard exaggeration when we say that for disparity of numbers, severity, and loss of men engaged, the whole history of the war scarcely furnishes a parallel to this battle.

On our side there were just the four companies and our regimental scouts engaged; there was scarcely an average of 40 men in each company, or about 160 men all told; while opposed to us was a brigade of four full regiments; estimating 250 men to each regiment would make seven rebels to each one of us. Yet not a man of our little band faltered or thought of danger; and had the host against us been ten times greater, and had they lapped around us and swallowed us up, we doubt if a man had thought of running. A few incidents will show the terrible severity of the rebel fire. The writer was near Capt. McMurtry, who fell at the first fire of the rebels. Our company was on open ground. We opened on the enemy with all the speed we could command, emptied our Spencer of its seven loads, and stepped behind a small white-oak tree less than a foot in diameter to reload; just as we were ready to give them another seven shots, Company F came into line with us, the rebels opened fire again and nine men in F fell within ten feet of us, and our little tree was struck three times at less than our hight. We tell you, if ever there is a time when a man wishes he were as thin as a board, it is when in a place like that was.

In addition to the killed and wounded in Company I, Company F lost Geo. W. Mathis, Thomas Cozod, John A. Nixon and Elisha Holycross all killed; and had the following wounded: Harvey Schoonover, mortally; Geo. B. Stump, severely in right arm; Wm. A. Schoonover, severely in left side of face; John Munson, flesh wound in left hip. The name of the other man wounded in Company F we did not get. In Company A Joseph Edskin was killed, and the following wounded: Sergt. James Robinson, mortally; Harrison Gaumer, left upper arm, severely; John McArdle, left thigh, severely. Two others, whose names we did not get, were wounded slightly. Making a loss of 8 killed and 10 wounded, a total loss of 18, inside of fifteen minutes. Company D fortunately lost none. We killed 30 rebels dead on the field; the number wounded we do not know.

The sun was sinking as in a pillar of blood in the west, and from our position on the high ridge we could see, a half mile over on the road on our right, that the rebels were thick as thieves. We could see their orderlies and officers riding furiously about forming line for a charge on our head of column to our right and rear; and an occasional shot from our skirmishers over there told us that preparation had been made to receive an attack. We had up to this time no opportunity to get the least idea of the situation; but the longer we stayed the more painfully apparent it became that we were in a most dangerous and exposed position, and we marveled that we had been sent out there. Rebels enough were in plain view to eat us up, and a very slight move on their part would have cut us off, and we wanted to be relieved. Our dead and dying lay just where they had fallen. We had straightened up our lines a little in advance of where we fought, and lay on the ground watching every leaf and twig that moved in the wind, expecting momentarily that the "Johnnies" would charge us again. But they didn't come. In a few moments the sun is down and twilight creeps over us in the smoky forest, and we are commanded to gather up our dead and wounded and fall back as noiselessly as possible.

With chagrin at thought of sneaking away from our enemies, and grief at the loss of our comrades, we gathered up our dead and wounded and carried them down to the cross roads. Our wounded we put into ambulances, and our dead we lay in a row on the porch of a large white house which stood near the cross roads. It was dark, and the numerous camp-fires in nearly every direction admonished us that we were in the midst of a powerful enemy and had no time to lose. In this day of peace, when friendships are rarely cemented by dangers shared in common, it will hardly be possible to realize with what overwhelming grief we looked upon that row of nine brave men, with Capt. McMurtry at their head, for the last time, and turned away without the privilege of burying them or shedding our tears over their graves. As to Capt. McMurtry, he was the writer's Captain and particular friend, and we loved him as a brother. He was a brave man and a general favorite in the regiment, and beloved by all who knew him.

The question was, how to get out of this; and it is not too much to say that Col. Wilder was much confused and did not know what to do. Finally Col. Miller got us mounted and moved on the road leading west, the Seventy-Second in advance of the brigade. We had not gone over a mile till we heard a sharp "halt! who comes there?" Before the man who uttered it knew what he was about our scouts relieved him of his gun and brought him to Col. Miller. From this prisoner the Colonel learned that there was a division of rebels camped not more than a mile ahead of us, and concluded that it would not be safe to go further on that road. But what shall we do? Col. Miller rode back to a house and pressed in an old citizen to pilot us out of that. The citizen objected and said he didn't see how he could, as there were rebels camped in every direction we wished to go. The case was desperate, and the number of shooting-irons near the old gentleman's head persuaded him to make the effort. The fence was opened on the north side of the road and the regiment moved through the field, Company E advance guard, Sergt. Wilhite in charge of the advance. When in the field we plainly saw the rebel camp fires to the left on the road we had abandoned. We moved in a north-west course, and when a mile from the road could also see rebel camp-fires on our right, and it was strange that we had not that afternoon run into the rebels camped there. After going a mile further Capt. Kilborn, of Company E, in command of a detachment of prisoners, was ordered to build camp-fires on a high ridge, as if the command were going into camp; everything was dry and the fires were easily built; but we marched steadily and briskly on, and at midnight struck our pickets a mile east of Lee & Gordon's Mills, passed inside the lines and immediately lay down to sleep without putting out any pickets, for the first time in many long months. We felt very sensibly our narrow escape from capture.

And now that we are safely out of it, it is proper to go back and explain how it happened that we were thrown upon the ridge where we had such a sharp fight with the rebels.

The first step in the explanation is, that our brigade had run full into the rear of the rebel Gen. Polk's corps, and Col. Wilder thought we were opposed by but a small number of the enemy. The fight we have described was half a mile southeast of the intersection of the Ringgold and LaFayette road and the road from Tunnel Hill to Lee & Gordon's Mills. We were marching on the Ringgold and LaFayette road for LaFayette when our column met the rebels precisely at Leet's tan-yard, not far from Rock Springs, and the fight was always called the battle of Rock Springs. The first intimation Col. Wilder seemed to have of the whereabouts of the rebels was when his advance guard run on to them at these cross roads. He saw that they were in such great force that he could not attack them with a shadow of success, and to retreat would be equally hazardous. He wanted, just then, to be in supporting distance of the left wing of our army, but how to get there was the serious question, as the rebels were on the only road leading to Lee & Gordon's Mills, and his advance had failed to move them from it. Now, what was to be done? In this dilemma he sent back four companies of the Seventy-Second to guard against attack from cross roads behind, and ordered us to move off to the east, and then to the southwest, and attack the rebels in the rear, in hope of compelling them to abandon their position on the road leading to the mills. The movement was successful, at the fearful cost of blood which has already been told.

We return to camp inside our picket lines. It was about 1 o'clock on the morning of the 13th of September when we lay down to sleep, and about 3 in the morning we were aroused by very rapid picket-firing. We saddled immediately, but the firing ceased. We took breakfast, and shortly after sun-up moved out in the direction in which we had heard the picket-firing. When three miles out we formed line of battle and moved east for some distance, passing over the ridge on which Capt. Kilborn built camp-fires last night. We now had an explanation of last night's heavy picket-firing. The force we fought on the cross-roads did not know we had slipped away from them until we had all gone. They followed, and coming to the camp-fires on the hill they quietly surrounded them, and at daylight charged the supposed Yankee camp with such fearful yell and discharge of musketry as to arouse us in our safe camp within our picket-lines. We could see their tracks in the ashes made as they marched in line of battle, side by side, in regular order. They had an easy victory in capturing Yankee ash heaps, but didn't enjoy the Yankee trick. That was Sunday, and we lay in line of battle all day, skirmishing at times very heavily, while skirmishing and artillery firing was in progress off to the right between the infantry and the rebel division we had seen in our front the night before. Late in the evening we fell back to the west side of Chicamauga Creek and went into camp not far from Lee & Gordon's Mills.

During the day a strong reconnoissance of infantry from Crittenden's corps, to our right, had met the same division we did on the night of the 12th, and had demonstrated that the enemy were in force in front of Lee & Gordon's Mills; therefore our infantry fell back behind the creek and never after attempted to move in that direction.

It must be borne in mind that the last four days have been such busy ones, and so full of interesting events, that we had not had a moment's time to forage. This is saying a great deal, for it must, indeed, be a busy time with a man of the Seventy-Second if he don't find some time to forage; and this evening, as it was known that we were going into camp, foraging parties sallied forth in swarms. The infantry was between us and the enemy; some of the parties had to go a long way, and in their rambles some of them fell into the hands of Gen. Rosecrans' body guard and were arrested as stragglers and taken to the General's headquarters. Without coming out of his tent the General inquired who they were. The officer informed the General that they claimed to be Wilder's men. "Impossible," said the General, "Wilder's whole command is captured and now on the way to Libby prison." The officer told the General that they persisted that they were Wilder's men in fact. The General then came out to see them, and when assured that they were of the Seventy-Second Indiana, he was astonished beyond measure, and said, "Wilder's men beat the devil, anyhow." Turning to the officer he said: "Take them to Wilder; he's the only man in the army who can manage them." In the squad there were some from nearly every company in the regiment, but more from I than any other. These were led by Corpl. (afterwards Orderly Sergt.) Wakeman. On their way to Wilder's headquarters they resolved to get even with the officer. When they reached Col. Wilder he simply asked what regiment they were of, and when told they were of the Seventy-Second he simply pointed and said: "You will find Col. Miller over there," and the officer started in that direction. A happy thought struck Corpl. Wakeman, and when near the Colonel he motioned to his comrades and they closed up on the trot and came to a front face, and, before the officer had time to think, Wakeman dismounted, saluted the Colonel, turned to the officer and said: "Col. Miller permit me to introduce to your acquaintance Capt. Smith, of Gen Rosecrans' staff." Col. Miller caught the idea in a moment, and as he advanced to take the Captain's hand he simply motioned to the boys and said: "You can go to your quarters." This attempt to punish men as stragglers when they were only foraging turned out to be the best farce of the campaign.

On the 14th we made another effort to get to our division, which lay at Crawfish Springs, 15 miles southwest of Lee & Gordon's Mills. We started early and reached the division by the middle of that afternoon, and most of us saw our knapsacks for the first time since leaving the Sequatchie Valley, a month lacking two days. On the 15th, as we had been in the saddle for a month, we were promised some rest, and accordingly washed our clothes for the first time in three weeks, and put up our dog tents. The 16th was spent in foraging and shoeing horses.

CHAPTER XXII.

September 17th to September 19th, 1863—Just Before the Battle of Chicamauga—Rosecrans' Great Mistake—Halleck Confirms it—Bragg's Strategy—He Awaits in the Forests and Hills to Destroy Our Army—Negley Finds the Enemy and Warns Thomas—Rosecrans' Line Extended 80 Miles—The Lightning Brigade Strikes the Main Army of the Rebels—Rosecrans Finds Out His Mistake—Efforts of Garfield to Concentrate the Scattered Corps—The Lightning Brigade Opens the Battle on September 18th—Brave and Bloody Work of Company A at Alexander's Bridge—We Fall Back to the Rossville Road and Repulse the Enemy at Dark—Noises and Reflections at Night—Bragg's Official Report of What Company A Did with their Spencers—Battle of Chicamauga—Perilous Position—A Night of Military Movements—Reflections Before Battle—Position of the Lightning Brigade—Temporary Works—The Beginning of the Battle—Storms and Calms—Yells and Charges—Davis Terribly Handled—The Storm Strikes Us, but Our Spencers Send the Enemy Back with Heavy Loss—Panic-Stricken Soldiers Run Over Us—"Make Way for Sheridan!"—Last Charge and Repulse—We Hold Our Own to the Last—The Awful Night—Shrieks of Wounded and Dying—"O! for God's Sake Come and Help Me!"—On Picket in the Ditch with Dead and Wounded—The Second Day's Fight—Called from Beef to Blood—Hard Fight to Recapture a Battery—Our Army Cut in Two—Lightning Brigade Ordered to Guard Trains to Chattanooga—Our Horses Captured and Recaptured—The Fearful Panic, Rout and Confusion—Our Hospitals Captured—We Find and Save the Army Trains—Col. Miller on the Great Battle.

We have mentioned that Gen. Rosecrans was ignorant of the whereabouts of Bragg's army, but believed it was in full retreat, and that all we had to do was to press it hard. On September 11th, the day before we ran into the rear of Polk's corps and had the battle of Rock Springs, Gen. Halleck had telegraphed to Gen. Rosecrans, with characteristic inaccuracy, that Bragg's troops were reinforcing Gen. Lee on the Rappahannock. This confirmed the deception and completed the confusion of Gen. Rosecrans.

Preliminary to the bloody battle in which we are to take a conspicuous part, and to enable the reader to more fully comprehend the situation before the battle was joined, a few important facts are stated.

By September 3d the main body of Rosecrans' army had crossed the Tennessee River 30 to 50 miles below Chattanooga. Bragg evacuated Chattanooga a few days afterwards, and our brigade, with the other forces engaged in the successful feint, crossed above Chattanooga on September 8th. Two ranges of mountains lie between the Tennessee River and a valley running south from Chattanooga, called the Raccoon or Sand Mountain, and Lookout Mountain. East of the Chattanooga Valley is Missionary Ridge, and east of Missionary Ridge runs Chicamauga, or "Dead Man's River." East of Chicamauga is another series of ridges called Pigeon Mountains. All these mountains and ridges run nearly straight north and south, but the river, from Chattanooga to Bridgeport, runs southwest. When the left wing of Rosecrans' army, Gen. Crittenden's corps, crossed the Tennessee River, it moved to Chattanooga, arriving on the 9th of September. The center, Gen. Thomas' corps, moved nearly straight east, and his advance, Gen. Negley's division, got across Lookout Mountain at Stevens & Cooper's Gap, or Johnson's Crook, as it is sometimes called, on September 12th, being several miles in advance of Gen. Thomas' main command, which was yet west of the mountain, which is but seven miles wide at this place, but very difficult to cross. The right wing, McCook's corps, after crossing the river, started southeast to Summerville, 60 miles from Chattanooga, his advance reaching that place on the 9th.

Thus, on the 9th of September, Rosecrans' line was extended 80 miles from extreme right to left. That is, Thomas was pushing through the Lookout Mountains 25 miles southwest of Chattanooga, and McCook was preparing to cross the same mountains at Summerville, 35 miles south of Thomas, while Crittenden's corps was deployed and pushed forward 20 miles beyond Chattanooga, with orders to "push Bragg." We did push him so hard that on the 12th the Lightning Brigade pushed right in behind Polk's corps, and by marvelous cunning slipped out after the hard battle of Rock Springs. The various corps of the army were deployed in the order above recited on the 12th.

Bragg was not reinforcing Lee's army, but the very reverse was true. The corps of Hill and Longstreet, the very flower of Lee's army, were moving to reinforce Bragg, while Lee made demonstrations on the army of the Potomac, and allowed prisoners to be taken, who were instructed to report that Bragg was reinforcing Lee. Nor was Bragg retreating; he was, in his turn, playing a game of strategy with Rosecrans, and fell back from Chattanooga to LaFayette in such a manner as to impress Rosecrans that he was in full retreat, bordering on panic and rout; hence it was not expected that he would make a stand and give the Union army battle. Bragg had concentrated his army on the east side of Chicamauga River, in a dense woods, the great forests and Pigeon Mountains concealing his forces completely from our signal stations. His position was precisely opposite to the pass in the mountain through which Thomas was to move his corps of 18,000 men. It was the plan of Bragg, who had anticipated just the disposition of forces that Rosecrans had made, and who had learned from spies how the corps were separated, to fall upon the Union forces and crush and capture them by detail while they were thus so far apart that they could not give each other support.

In his strong position, no boa constrictor, hung concealed in a tree over the path of his prey, ever more eagerly awaited the victim's coming than Bragg waited for Thomas to debouch from the mountain pass, cross the Chicamauga and begin the ascent of the Pigeon Mountains. Then the rebel boa would fall upon his victim and crush him in his military coils.

Thomas was a brave General, but very cautious also, and hence had sent Negley's division, as before mentioned, several miles ahead. On the 9th Negley's division passed through the gap, crossed Chicamauga Creek, and came suddenly upon the enemy, to the mutual surprise of both. Negley immediately saw that the enemy was in great force in the woods and hills, and advantageously posted. He rapidly fell back into the pass in Missionary Ridge, took up a strong position, began to fortify, and at the same time sent couriers to Thomas informing him of the situation, and the latter immediately disposed his force so as to defeat the object of Bragg.

On the next day (the 10th, the day we were at Ringgold and the officer told us to "push them,") Bragg attacked Negley with fury, but could not drive him. Bragg, foiled in his plan to crush or capture Thomas, speedily marched his force against Crittenden's corps, which had, as before stated, advanced from Chattanooga after the supposed retreating rebel troops. The object was to take Crittenden in flank and rear, whip, capture or cut him off, but he failed in this also, because our brigade found the rebels in force on the 12th, and on the 13th the reconnoissance in which we took part, and which was made over part of the very ground we were upon the day before, confirmed our discovery so dearly bought; and no doubt this discovery saved Crittenden's corps, as Negley's discovery saved Thomas' corps. Bragg failed for four days to make the attack on Rosecrans' army, no doubt waiting the arrival of troops from Lee's army. This delay was precious time to the Union forces, as the sequel will show.

Up to September 13th Rosecrans still believed that Bragg was in full retreat into Georgia. When he was convinced of the real position of Bragg he was thoroughly alarmed. Gen. Garfield, his chief of staff, at once began vigorous efforts to concentrate the army, and worked night and day until that awful morning of September 19th. Couriers were sent upon the swiftest steeds to McCook, 65 miles away, to tell him of the imminent danger, and to hurry forward his corps. Others sped to Crittenden and told him to concentrate his corps, and to Thomas also were sent orders to hurry forward. From the above it will be seen that on the 12th, when Crittenden moved from Ringgold south-west to Lee & Gordon's Mills, Bragg's way back into Chattanooga was open for him to return on the same road by which he had left it; and that his right wing, Polk's corps, was just as near to Chattanooga as was Crittenden's corps, Rosecrans' left wing. Rosecrans began to concentrate his forces at the wrong wing, moving Crittenden so as to uncover Chattanooga.

On the 17th Forest moved north and made a heavy demonstration on Crittenden's left, and at the same time Wheeler made a demonstration on Rosecrans' right, southwest of LaFayette. The movement of Forest demonstrated the error of leaving the road to Chattanooga uncovered, and on the morning of the 17th the Lightning Brigade was sent to Alexander's bridge, about three miles down the Chicamauga Creek from Gordon's Mills; and Minty's brigade of cavalry was sent to Reed's bridge, three miles further down the creek. The general course of this creek is northeast, and it is very crooked, quite deep, and dangerous to cross. We camped about a mile north of the mill. A and F of our regiment were sent to picket the creek; A was stationed at Alexander's bridge, and F at a ford a mile south. The 123d Illinois were deployed as pickets between the ford and the mill. The night was quiet, and we rested well.

The morning of the 18th opened clear and beautiful, and men from the Seventy-Second were soon in the country foraging, some going over the creek, but they came back before noon and reported rebels over there, northeast of us. Little attention was paid to these reports, and at noon most of the command sat down to a good dinner brought in from the country that forenoon. In our own mess we had eggs, chickens and potatoes, and had just got coffee poured and stomachs fixed for a large, square meal, when to our disgust the bugle began to blow "boots and saddles" furiously, and immediately blew "fall in." We had only time to hastily swallow the coffee, gather our saddle and run. In 10 minutes after the first bugle notes the regiment was mounted and moving out on the gallop to Company F.

The enemy was upon them! Skirmishing had already begun. Company F and the 123d had been driven from the creek by superior numbers, and F was so scattered that parts of the company for some time thought the remainder captured. F was driven northward away from camp and in the direction of Company A. A had also been severely handled, and as Lieut. Barnes and Sergt. Stewart, of A, who were both in the fight, give graphic accounts of it, we con-ense the following from their notes, using what seems best in each:

"The night on picket passed quietly. The first thing done the next morning was the sending of a strong foraging party over the creek, which soon returned laden with good food. A hearty and quiet breakfast was enjoyed. The boys thought they would go across the creek again and get a good supply to take to camp when relieved in the evening. They started south about 10 a. m., but in a few moments they came back like flying birds, with rebel pursuers close at their heels, yelling and shouting at every jump. The rebels got the advantage of them, cut them off from the bridge, and they had to plunge into the creek and swim across. A few shots from the boys at the bridge drove the rebels back. A now realized the situation, and speedily tore up the flooring of the bridge and built a lunette fort of it, and determined to hold it at all hazards. In a short time the rebel cavalry came dashing up to the creek, but from the lunette, the whole company being in it with their Spencers, they drove the enemy back without difficulty, punishing them severely. In the meantime Company F and the 123d Illinois had been attacked and driven from the creek, and soon afterwards a whole brigade of nfantry advanced across the field to attack the position of A. They came up in splendid style, lines well dressed, step firm, even and steady, bayonets fixed and gleaming in the sun. At this imposing advance of superior numbers there was not a tremor in the ranks of A. The company held its fire until the advancing enemy were so close that they could see their eyes bat, then opened upon them with their Spencers, which belched such a constant and awful stream of well-aimed balls that the rebels were completely surprised, faltered, wavered, and then retreated. They soon re-formed, deployed on the flanks, and came at A's position again, determined to flank and surround it. At this critical moment some men of F and the 123d got into a position where they could see that A's horses were about to be captured by the rebels, and fired upon and killed most of the horses.

"About this time Company A found itself without a commissioned officer, but Sergts. Barnes and Stewart were equal to any emergency, and the company was composed of the sort of men that would stand firmly by them—and from their lunettes punished the enemy so severely in front that he gave way the second time, but on the flanks he still continued to advance. At this juncture the Seventy-Second came up, and the rebels were also pouring across the creek, above the bridge, by the thousand; they had an hour before driven our men from the creek below and were crossing in large numbers. Hence it was plain that in a few minutes A would be entirely surrounded. The rebels had also got their artillery in position and began to shell the brigade. Col. Miller saw the condition of A and sent his orderly to tell them to get out of there the best they could. That brave boy Gênio Lawrence, dashed up behind them and called out, "Company A, get out of here, the enemy are surrounding you," and again galloped away amid a shower of lead. But it was not so easy for A to get away; had they undertaken to do so in a body, most of them would have been captured or killed; so they slipped out one or two at a time. You can get some idea of how close was the gauntlet of death the members of A ran when the fact is stated that Sergt. Joseph R. Higinbotham, in running 25 or 30 yards, was shot five times; first in the head, second in the face, third in the right arm, fourth in the left side, and fifth in the right leg. He finally recovered of his wounds, and afterwards died at Corinth, Miss., Jan. 14th, 1864.

All slipped out until only Sergt. Barnes, Stewart and Geo. Baily were left. Stewart says of Baily: "He was a boy 17 years old, had fought bravely, and being the last to get the word to fall back, would not go but turned and shot a rebel who fell; another rebel ran up to aid the fallen man and Baily shot him also. I, having got a shell fast in my gun, kept urging Baily to fall back. I got the shell out and we both gave the enemy a farewell shot and ran. My horse was killed where he was tied, but Baily's was not, and cutting him loose he mounted and rode away in a shower of bullets. Both got out safely."

And thus was begun the great battle of Chicamauga, at noon, on the 18th day of September, 1863. In the fight at the bridge Company A had two men wounded and 31 horses killed out of 37 taken into action. The following incidents of the first day's battle are given: When the shelling was begun by the rebels, our regiment formed line of battle facing east, about 80 rods west of the bridge. A, in leaving their lunette at the bridge, had to pass out nearly northward and were soon separated from each other and lost in the dense forest. John Saulsburg and John Barnard soon found that they were in the rear of the rebel army, and wandered in forest and hills for two days trying to turn its right wing and gain our lines. They succeeded and came in safely just after the battle was over. Sergt. Barnes passed the night of the 18th with the infantry and got with the train on the 19th. When the horses were killed A lost most of their blankets, tents, haversacks and canteens.

As soon as A left the bridge the rebels replaced the floor and immediately ran their artillery across and began shelling us with energy. We fell back to the road leading north to Jay's Mills (a large tread mill.) This was just west of the position occupied in the forenoon by Minty's brigade, at Reed's bridge. We found that Minty had been driven away from the creek, and the rebels opened on us again with shells. The whole of Forest's corps was now west of the creek and Polk's corps were pouring across at more than a dozen places. Forest was 10 miles nearer Chattanooga than our infantry at the mills. The rebels were now pressing us in such superior force that we had no time to form line of battle, but our brigade and battery formed column by regiments and retreated by the right flank, the battery in the centre with two regiments on either side, swinging back to the rear on a line a little west of south toward the camp we occupied in the morning. The rebels pressed so hard and closely that we continued to fall back in this order six miles, till we reached the road leading from Lee & Gordon's Mills straight north to Rossville. We struck this road a mile and a half north of the mills. Here we found a brigade of infantry in line of battle, facing east. We dismounted and formed on the left of the brigade with our line facing north, and the left of our brigade resting on the Rossville road.

It was about sundown when we dismounted, and we immediately went to work with a will and in a few minutes threw up a line of works of old logs and rails. We were not a minute too soon, for just at dusk the enemy came upon us. We opened upon him and in two minutes the cloud of smoke from our rifles made it quite dark. Soon after encountering our brigade he also attacked the infantry on our right. A single volley from the whole line closed the work for the day, and the enemy ceased firing. When we dismounted our horses were taken away, and as our tents and blankets were always fastened to our saddles we never saw horses, tents or blankets again until the 20th. We lay all that night behind our works without blankets, tents or a bite to eat; the night was so cold that frost fell on the leaves and grass and we suffered severely. Sleep was out of the question. The night was clear, and thousands of sounds for many miles around were audible; while those coming from the south were omens of good to us, those coming from the north and east were presages of disaster and defeat. Between these conflicting sounds, and the feelings engendered by each in turn, we wore the hours of night away. We had ample time to reflect upon the result of the bloody battle which had fairly begun the day before.

Before entering upon the history of the 19th of September, we must speak a word more about the gallant conduct of Company A, at Alexander's bridge. In his report of the affair Bragg says:

"The resistance offered by the enemy's cavalry and the difficulty arising from the bad roads, caused unexpected delays. When Gen. Walker's division reached Alexander's bridge they found Wilder's mounted infantry on the opposite bank. Wilder set his light artillery to work and threw such a shower of shells across the stream that Walker's troops recoiled, and under cover of the small arms a squad of Wilder's command rushed down to the bridge and set it on fire, compelling Walker to retrace his steps and cross at one of the fords."

Thus Bragg attributes to the whole brigade what was done by Company A, alone! No artillery was used at all; only the repeating Spencers, in the hands of brave, cool men, who knew how to use them with as much precision and dexterity as they used their right hands. No wonder the rebels thought one company a whole brigade with light artillery and musketry in full play! It was one company defeating a whole division, and the rebels were shown what fearful execution a few determined men could do with such rifles in their hands. We hope this history, if it shall have any influence, will aid to banish from our army and arsenals for ever the old muzzle-loading single-shooting guns.

A few words, while yet the stars twinkle in the clear sky of this September night, above the great hosts that lie in this valley of Dead Man's River, whose waters are soon to be swollen and reddened by blood, making it doubly Dead Man's River forever more. A few words, while we watch for the dawning to break in from the east, and with the dawn the merciless fire of the enemy. A few words to put you more fully upon the bloody ground, that you may watch the gigantic struggle a little better, through forest, and pillars of fire, and clouds of smoke, as it proceeds. Remember what has been said of positions of corps; remember yesterday's struggle with Forest and Polk, and then note that fully 10,000 rebels are now between us and Chattanooga, and are 30 to 40 miles nearer that place than the centre and right of our army, and you will be forced to the conclusion that nothing in the world will prevent Bragg's forces from marching right past us into Chattanooga, and cutting our army to pieces, a division or brigade at a time, as we may try to make our way back over Missionary Ridge, Lookout Mountain, the Sand Mountains and the

Tennessee River. On the 16th the right wing of McCook's corps was at Galesville, 60 miles south of Lee & Gordon's-Mills. On that day Rosecrans began to draw in his right wing, which made it necessary for part of McCook's corps to cross Lookout Mountain twice, and yesterday evening (18th) they were coming up in the rear of Thomas, but the bulk of Thomas' corps was 25 miles from the Mills, Rosecrans believing all the time that the great battle would be joined and fought near LaFayette; and at noon on the 18th, when we sent word to him from our position at Alexander's bridge that the rebels were attacking and pressing us in great force, he persistently refused to believe it.

At sundown, on the 18th, the 14th corps had not moved a regiment. It was only when the infantry on our right became engaged with the enemy on that evening that Rosecrans was *compelled* to believe that Bragg was moving north. Rosecrans being now convinced saw he was a day too late in ascertaining the enemy's movements, and immediately began to hurry his troops north, on the Crawfish Springs road, with all possible speed. All the night of the 18th they marched at the top of speed, and by midnight we could hear the rumbling of artillery wheels, as they came across from the Crawfish Springs road to the road we were on. This was one of the sounds that gave us heart and hope, though they were so long getting across that it was almost daylight before we were sure that they were near enough to give us support and aid in keeping back the foe.

As soon as the firing ceased on the evening of the 18th we could hear at the creek a mile east of us, and for miles to the *north-east* of us, the sound of thousands of axes engaged in constructing bridges across the creek, making roads through the forest and building defensive works. All night long we could hear thousands of troops moving into the woods and taking up positions north of us; while the rumbling of the enemy's moving artillery and ammunition wagons never ceased the whole night. These were sounds of ill omen.

By what had transpired in the past few days every one in both armies was anticipating a great battle, and we now knew the shock must come on the morrow. Do men of affairs ever calculate the chances of failure or success in business enterprises? Then just as certainly do intelligent soldiers weigh the chances of victory or defeat. No doubt there were many who lay behind that line of logs and rails that night who knew much of the strength and position of both armies, and were sickened at the thought of the odds against us. Yet they had the courage to calmly wait for the day, and for the storm of battle to burst in all its fury upon them.

Readers, you who were never in the position we were in that night, can you conceive of the courage that is necessary to meet such a day with self-possession? Consider, what if you had to go out to-morrow morning, and be shot at, at short range, by ten of the most skillful riflemen! What would you take to stand fifty paces from them and let them fire, not only once, but round after round at you? You would not, as you value your lives, permit it for millions of dollars. Yet, well we knew that night, as we lay there listening to the preparations, the marchings and the counter-marchings of friend and foe, that in the morning we should be shot at, not by ten, but by ten thousands, of trained riflemen, supported by cannon, solid shot, shells, grape and canister. That we thought of all whom we held dear on earth at home; that we lifted our hearts to the God of battles and commended both ourselves and them to His keeping, what wonder? That we thought of the old flag, of our oath, our country and our honor, what wonder? But the night is far spent, the day is at hand, and we must up and to arms.

By daylight of the 19th the whole of Gen Thomas' command, the 14th corps, had marched past our left wing (we faced north) and formed line of battle facing east, a short distance east of the Rossville road; the right wing of the 14th corps just reaching our left wing. On the morning of the 19th our whole brigade swung back to the right rear and formed on the right of that corps, we too, facing east, our line forming a right angle with the one we held last night. Our position was a most fortunate one, and had we been permitted to select it ourselves we could scarcely have bettered it. The general line of battle crossed the road just at the left of our brigade, where the road bears to the south-east, the infantry being on the east side of the road and our brigade on the west side. The line of our regiment was straight north and south along a fence, with a heavy forest to our rear, and an open field in our front, which in some places extended a half mile to the east of us. A large deep ditch or ravine extended from the north-west corner of the field, almost south-east, and nearly parallel with the road, the entire length of our front. From our line down to this ditch—100 to 300 yards—the ground sloped regularly but pretty rapidly, while beyond the ditch the bank was more abrupt; but on the east side a little higher than where we lay.

As soon as our lines were straightened, we were told that we had come to stay. We knew that this meant that we must fight on this line. We knew the value of hastily constructed defences, and we all dropped our guns and went vigorously to work piling up rails and logs, and by the time the sun was up we had a line of works from which Longstreet's whole corps failed to drive us that day, after repeated and desperate efforts.

Our temporary works constructed, we had a few moments' leisure in which we could have prepared breakfast, but we knew not where our horses and rations were. Before we moved our line we had heard the rebels preparing breakfast, and they were rested and fed for the day's work before them.

On the 19th, soon after sun up, the rebels began to move forward north-west towards Rossville. The skirmishing soon opened away to the north and east of us, two miles away, yet we heard every shot so distinctly that it seemed to be much nearer. It was the habit of the Seventy-Second to be in the right place at the right time, and we took our places in line behind our works. The skirmishing soon died away and for a few minutes all was still; then suddenly there came a volley as if a whole regiment had fired. Again there is a lull for a little while. Then the skirmishing again opens, now a shot, then a shot, then several shots—gradually the shots increase until there is a crashing as if a whole brigade is engaged. Louder and louder it grows, until there is a continuous roar of musketry, interspersed with an occasional shot from artillery. This continues for about half an hour, and then comes a fearful yell and a charge, and the noise is grandly thrilling—awful for a minute or two—now it drops suddenly to a lull. Of course we are all attention and excitement. It was about nine in the morning when the firing ceased. In half an hour it begins again, and we can tell from our position that it starts about the same place but runs away further north, and we can also tell that the rebels are pushing on towards Chattanooga. The contest is long and terrible; now comes the yell and a charge—for a minute or two we almost hold our breath, so terrible is the crash—then it drops into a lull, almost a calm.

Up to noon this had been repeated three times, each time more men were involved, the fighting more furious, the crash of the charges more terrific and the lull more painful, for we knew they were periods in the progress of this great battle, written in blood. To this time there had not been a shot fired within a mile of us, and did we not think that our troops were being terribly punished the infernal din and roar would have become monotonous. At each round of firing the wave has come a little nearer our position, we are expecting every moment that it will strike us, and the suspense is terrible. Near one o'clock p. m., just north of our brigade, the rebels drove our line back, and Davis' division, immediately on our right, began to move across the field in front of us, seemingly for the purpose of taking the rebels in the flank as they were pushing our men back to the bluff on the left of us. The division moved across the field in a north-east direction till they struck the road in front of us; Davis' left was about 400 yards straight east of our regiment, and 200 yards in front of Davis' division, as it faced east, was a dense woods of jack-oaks and little pines. Just as he got his division in line on the ridge along this road, the rebels poured into his ranks a most destructive fire. From our position we can see his men falling by the hundred; the rebel bullets coming clear over the ridge and droping in front of us. If Davis remains on that ridge long his command will be annihilated. But he stays not; the whole division charge, with a whoop! into the woods, and for a few minutes the crashing is like the rolling of mighty thunder and the smiting of the bolts. The thunder of the rebel artillery, the screeching and bursting of shells, the demoniac yells of the rebels, mingled with the incessant roar of musketry, make such an unearthly din that we clap our hands to our ears and hold our breath. The contest between Davis' division and the enemy is short. In a few minutes our troops begin to fall back out of the woods followed by hundreds of rebels, and simultaneously the enemy to our left-front begin preparations to fall upon Davis' flank immediately in front of us. The excitement in our brigade, as we witness these movements, so close to us, becomes as intense as our suspense through the forenoon had been fearful.

Charge after charge of grape and canister fly shrieking over the field, and crashing into the woods to our right. At this critical moment our brigade is ordered across the field to support Davis. The wounded of Davis' division are crawling over the brow of the ridge and sheltering themselves in the ditch by scores. The rebel bullets have begun to pour across the field from the north, in the rear of Davis' now retreating men. We can see and hear it all, and O! horror!! what an effort it is for us to leave our works and move out into that fiery hell of death. (Bear in mind that we have not fired a shot yet, or done anything to wear off the timidity.) Yet we show no timidity, and without a moment's hesitation we leave our works, move across the field on to the ridge, and check the advance of the rebels who are moving from the north against Davis, and those in front of him also fall back into the woods. Davis' men, who have fought like heroes but been overpowered, as soon as we come to their relief re-form line and start into the woods again, but just now we are ordered to fall back to our old works and hold them way for Sheridan!—make way for Sheridan!" He passes through our line, his men following him like a swarm of locusts. If Davis' division was demoralized and panic stricken, there is no word in the language to describe the most abject fear of Sheridan's command. There is no effort made near us to rally them, and we see nothing more of them. However, the rebels following them remembered the warm reception we gave them a few hours before, and halted just behind the brow of the hill, being content to let their skirmishers crawl up as near our lines as they could and pick off any of us who might expose our heads above our modest works. During all this time the battle had raged furiously just north of us, and the rebels were incessantly shelling us vigorously. In the forenoon the fighting on our left had been east of north, but now it is changing to the west, and the position of our brigade is getting critical. As we lie here patiently under this terrible shelling, we have time to note this and several incidents. Lieut. Priest, of E, as brave a soldier as ever drew a sword, kept cautioning his men to lie low and not expose themselves, but was utterly oblivious to his own safety. Finally the men told him he had better take some of his own advice, and keep down himself. Just then a Minie ball cut a limb off a small tree close by the side of his head. He simply remarked, "I suppose that has reference to me, but somebody must do the watching for the company and I can do it for them and myself both."

We have forgotten to say that on the ridge east of the ravine, and right in front of us, was a log cabin, 400 yards distant, behind which the rebel sharp-shooters had crawled in numbers, and annoyed us considerably. Shortly after Sheridan's men had run over us, a great big rebel who had been plundering our dead and wounded, and had a roll of blankets and overcoats almost as large as a bale of hay on his shoulders, stepped out from behind the cabin to look, and just then some of our boys fired at him. The ball must have passed between him and the house, as he dodged further from the house. Some one else gave him a shot and he again dodged further from the house. By this time there had been a hundred shots fired at him and the dirt torn up all around his feet. He kept jumping and dodging, but all the time getting further from the house, and the whole brigade began to yell, laugh and shoot at him. He finally started to run towards a point of timber 200 yards north of him, and then everybody in the regiment put in his best shots at him, yelling the while as if on a charge. A cloud of dust was raised by the shower of bullets that hit the ground around him, and it seemed that he would reach the woods in spite of everything; but when near there he gave a bound into the air and fell dead, little doubt.

This was at 4 o'clock, and the rebels seemed to be having it all their own way on the left of our brigade, while all in our front was perfectly quiet; so quiet indeed, that the roar and storm of battle on our left seemed to break out afresh. This was correctly interpreted by our officers to be the precursor of a storm. Our brigade line was the only line the rebels had not brok n during the day, and if they could only crush us the day would end with a victory for them.

The sun is now sinking into the tops of the trees of Missionary Ridge behind us, and he looks through the cloud of smoke as if dripping with blood. The rebels see that what they do must be done quickly. While the roar of battle on other parts of the line continues, in our front it is still—*so still!* Ammunition has been carried and poured on the ground beside each of us; our officers ride along and tell us to use the ammunition on the ground first, and keep perfectly cool. Our battery, the old reliable 18th Indiana, is to the left of our regiment, each piece double shotted with grape and canister and ready for the work of death. We await in awful suspense the bursting of the storm of battle upon us, which we know is coming. We are determined to hold that line, and all the more so as the night is at hand and we know the rebels have been victorious at other points, and if we give way the day may be lost to the whole army. To every brave heart it is a crisis of sublime courage! Each resolved to conquer or die.

They come! Out of the woods in plain view, with lines dressed, as steady in motion as a piece of machinery. Just back of the first division is a second for support. The scene baffles description, for who can tell how look and how feel those soldiers advancing upon these that lie behind their frail works, their seven-shooting Spencers leveled at the hearts of the advancing foe, and piles of ammunition at their sides! We momentarily expect a storm of fire and lead and a furious charge from them; and they momentarily expect a storm of well directed lead, grape and canister, to mow down their ranks. On they come as one man, their arms at right shoulder shift, with fixed bayonets, and the sinking sun casts his bloody rays upon their bright guns. Our officers sing out, "don't fire until you hear a shot from the cannon; then go in, show them that you have brought your knitting and come to stay all day!" The sight is magnificent as our brave foe sweeps across the field. They near the ditch in front of us and are startled by a well directed shot from the battery, followed by a volley from our guns. They promptly answer by setting up the rebel yell and charging upon us in double quick, determined to give us a chance for as few shots as possible before closing upon and completely crushing us. Our Spencers are equal to the emergency; we have six loads to use upon the advancing foe, and we cease not to pour the leaden hail with rapidity, cool accuracy and fearful effect, until but a thin, weak line of the enemy wavers in the smoke before us: they stagger, they flee, and take refuge in the ditch! Instantly a section of our artillery runs to the head of the ditch and sweeps its entire length with grape and canister. So fearful is the result that a Lieutenant of the battery begs the Captain not to fire again, declaring it murder.

We have repulsed the enemy! Firm as a rock we have held our position, while all others have changed. We have saved the day!

The repulse of this last charge added materially to saving the whole army. We captured a lot of prisoners, and from them learned that the last charge was made by part of Longstreet's corps, the flower of the Confederate army, which had arrived from Virginia the day before, where they had generally had things their own way. The proud fellows felt much humiliation at being repulsed and "captured by a d—n little brigade of cavalry," as a rebel Colonel expressed it, in language more forcible than elegant. "But," said he, "we just thought we had struck about 17 lines of battle all at once."

We shall never forget, to the day of our death, the splendid charge that the rebels made upon us; nor shall we ever forget how, before our fire, they seemed to sink from sight beneath a sea of flame, over which rolled mountainous waves of smoke in which played the glare of lightning from rifles and artillery.

The sun now sinks behind Missionary Ridge; the vast volumes of sulphurous smoke settle down over the battle field, as a pall upon the dead and dying, and it is night—dark, gloomy, and full of horrors. The roar of the battle's bloody storm has ceased, and all is still save the waves that sob upon the shore—those waves are the shrieks of the wounded and dying—and these are more horrible and trying to our hearts than was the storm of battle. In that storm manly courage bore us up; in this storm of groans and cries for help that come on the black night air, manly sympathy for comrades and enemy makes our hearts to bleed, for we can give no help.

Just in our front there are doubtless more killed and wounded than on any other part of the field, for the ground has been desperately contested four times. The rebels lie on their arms in the woods just in front of us, whipped, yet defiant and spiteful; and while they seem to make no effort to care for the wounded their pickets fire on us whenever we attempt to go to the relief of the sufferers. It is impossible for us to tell the awful horrors of that night. We lay all night precisely where we fought all day, and the air was cold and frosty. The rebel shells had fallen among our horses and they had been taken we knew not whither.

As we lay in the chilly air that long and doleful night, we had ample time to count up the cost to us of the bloody day's work. Company A had but few men in the fight, on account of their becoming so scattered the day before in the fight at Alexander's bridge; but of that few private Joseph L. Hair was wounded in the right leg. Company B, private David Martin wounded, captured and supposed to be dead. Company C, in addition to Campbell, previously mentioned, private Michael Flinn, wounded in right arm. Company D, private Joseph Cain, killed. This brave man had been with the detail to hold horses until about noon, when a detail was sent back for ammunition, and he insisted on his mess-mate, Wallace Hill, taking his place and allowing him to take part in the great fight the remainder of the day. He said he wanted to be in the line where he could be doing something. In less than an hour after coming to the line he exposed his body, in changing position, to the enemy's furious shots that were passing over our works, a Minie ball pierced his breast and he fell dead without a struggle at the side of Capt. Thomson, who says of him: "Joseph Cain was a noble young man, of a good family, the idol of his parents, beloved by all who knew him at home and warmly attached to all his comrades in the service. He was not reckless, but ever ready for duty, however perilous that duty might be. He fully realized what a sacrifice his enlistment was to his loving parents and friends, but was always cheerful in the service, being devoted and conscientious in his patriotism. Only the day before, when contemplating momentarily the perils of a fearful battle, he made the remark to his Captain that he did not expect to get home again, but he had never regretted enlisting, for he felt that it was his duty, and the service had been a great pleasure to him. So cheerful and happy was he in recounting the hardships of the service and the satisfaction resulting from a consciousness of having done his duty, that he did not make the impression on others that he then had the presentiment that he was about to give his life in the service of his country. But at the close of that fearful day, when his manly form, with that of John Campbell, of C, "lay in state" under the old oak, in rear of our line, his comrades remembered his words and noble deeds; and it was with deep regret that we had to leave their bodies for the enemy to capture next morning, in re-forming our lines for the second day's battle. But they were not forgotten, and many weeks after, when the field of battle was between the lines of the two armies, a squad of brave comrades, defended by their trusty Spencers, passed through the lines, and after spending a lonely night on the battle field they found the remains of both Cain and Campbell, buried them, and marked their graves, and they were afterwards removed to the National Cemetery at Chattanooga, where their friends might find and remove them, or let them rest till the last great day in the beds of honor spread by the hands of a grateful Nation.

We return to the field and the wounded. Other casualties in D, were private Charles Taggart, wounded in left fore-finger; private Leander C. Cory, left leg. In Company E, private John C. Wood, killed; Sergt. Lewis E. Wilhite, wounded in left thigh; private Silas W. Albertson, upper lip and jaw; private Francis M. Mason, right thigh. Company F, private John W. Gray, right thigh. Company H, Capt. Robert B. Hanna, severely in hip; Corpl Edward Allen, severely in knee and subsequently died; Corpl. Bromley, severely. Company I, Sergt. B. F. Magee, right hip slightly; Sergt. Samuel Taylor in scalp by Minie ball; private James W. Hawkins, scalp, left side of head; Corpl. Records, Minie ball took off beard from right jaw and grazed neck, blistering the skin; Sergt. Eli W. Anderson, left thigh severely. Company K, Capt. Richard H. McIntyre, thigh severely. John B. Creek, Company G, acting brigade inspector, was also wounded. Making a total of 20 wounded and three killed.

Corpl. Bromley was our postmaster and distributed the mail to us about noon, and in the afternoon, while distributing ammunition to us, he was hit just as the rebels made their last assault on us. In the case of David Martin, of B, as soon as he was shot Capt. Herron put him on Sergt.-Major Thompson's horse and told him to go to the hospital. Neither he nor the horse was ever heard of afterwards. As to Eli W. Anderson, when the brigade was mounted a battery of four-gun mountain howitzers was attached to it, and a detail made from each of the four regiments in the brigade to man the battery, and Sergt. Anderson, of I, was detailed to command the battery; but when the movement began from Decherd, the battery moved with Reynolds' division—to which we belonged—and on this day took part in the fight and did noble execution. "Maj. Anderson," as we always called him, was a brave man, and commanded brave men whom he inspired with his own spirit. As already mentioned, Reynolds got badly punished and driven back, and came near losing all his artillery. In one of the charges Maj. Anderson was badly wounded in the thigh, and the command of the battery devolved on Acting Corpl. Philip A. Miller, of Company H of the Seventy-Second. When Miller was ordered to fall back with his battery, he raved and swore like a mad man, and almost refused to obey orders, declaring that he would like to stay and fight it out, then and there, to the bitter end.

Just here we cannot forbear relating a personal incident illustrative of many other cases During the night our picket or skirmish line was along the ditch so often spoken of, while that of the rebels was just in the edge of the woods. As this was the second night without eating or sleeping, the men were so overcome with exhaustion that the skirmishers would go to sleep in spite of themselves and their critical and horrible surroundings. The men, too, feeling the responsibility of the position, refused to go because they could not keep awake. In this emergency our Orderly called for volunteers, but not a man among the privates would risk it; not for want of bravery, but for the reason above stated. Sergt. Magee and Corpl. Wakeman volunteered to go. This was about three o'clock in the morning. We went down to the ditch and took our places. It was almost pitch dark owing to the heavy smoke that settled down over the field. The point in the ditch was furthest from our lines where it bore to the right, and we were within 50 yards of the log cabin on the ridge. The wounded on the ridge and in the edge of the woods were still uncared for, and we are sure that many of the "gray-back" hearers were dull to the cries of the wounded. We heard that night, immediately after the firing ceased, a loud, clear voice, just in the edge of the woods, calling out: "O, for God's sake come and help me!" This was repeated so often and with such pitiful earnestness that we could stand it no longer, and some of our men undertook to go to his help, but were fired upon and driven back. This piteous plea, like a doleful refrain, was kept up the whole night, but long before we went down on the picket line had grown so weak that we could not hear it from our works; but when we got down into the ditch, from not more than 100 yards north of us came the same pitiful but faint moan, "for God's sake come and help me!" and to this day that dying, wailing petition, is still ringing in our ears.

During the night the whole right wing of the army fell back—part of it as much as three miles—and our little brigade was left for some time alone; but just before daybreak it was also ordered to fall back. Owing to Wakeman and ourself being further out than any of our pickets, we were not called in at all. About four o'clock, and while it was yet very dark in the ditch, we could hear the rebels in the woods north of us rousing their men, "falling in," and "telling off," forming regiments, and finally forming a brigade within 300 yards of us. The brigade commander had a lion-like voice, and we could tell the number of each regiment in his brigade by the command he gave. In half an hour from the time they began to fall in the brigade was formed and moved north-west, and for nearly an hour we could hear that man away in the distance commanding his troops.

All was now still near us. The sun must have been nearly an hour high, though it was scarcely light where we were, and we wondered why everything was so still behind us. Just then the smoke lifted a little and we could hear some one talking on the hill near the cabin. Looking in that direction we could see the sun about as big as a candle in the dense fog, and close to the cabin a battalion of cavalry. Wakeman raised his gun and said. "shall I fire?" "No," we said, "they are too close, and if you do we shall have hornets about our ears; and besides we believe our regiment has gone and left us." After looking about for a few minutes the man at the head of the battalion turned to his comrade and said, "the d—d Yanks lie pretty thick here, don't they?" They turned about and rode away towards the mills, and we picked ourselves up and started back, and found that scores of dead men were round about us. Union men and rebels lay side by side and in about equal numbers. As we approached our lines we were surprised to find dead rebels 50 yards nearer our works than we thought they had at any time got the day before. We found that our regiment had left the works, and were at a loss to know which way to go to find it. There was no road, and the woods were cut by the wheels of artillery and ambulances in every direction. As we were yet undecided which way to take, the battle opened away to the north-west of us, and we moved directly west. It was 9 a. m. before we reached the regiment, and the boys were glad to see us come up, as they thought we had surely been captured.

SECOND DAY'S FIGHT, SEPTEMBER 20TH.

The Lightning Brigade this morning formed on the hill, west of the Widow Glenn's house, and was the extreme right of the army, the Seventy-Second lying on the extreme right of the brigade, so that it was on the extreme right of Rosecrans' forces on that memorable day. This necessitated the detaching of D and F, Capt. Thomson in command of both, and moving them out to the right, at right-angles with our line, as flankers Our line, as on yesterday, faced east, Companies D and F facing south. Our regiment had thrown up a line of rails and logs, and stacked arms; our horses, too, had been brought up behind the ridge, it being the first we had seen of them since Friday night. Our butcher had killed some beeves, and we were ordered to get breakfast. About the time we began to cook, the roar of artillery north of us became terrible and the fighting furious. We could tell that more artillery was being used on our side than on yesterday. For some cause our army did not use much artillery the first day; we suppose it was on account of the nature of the ground and the thick woods. To the left and a little in front of our brigade was a battery of 32-pounder Parrott guns, and every time they fired the earth trembled and shook. Just as we got our beef on to cook, the rebels made a charge on this battery and took it. We were ordered to fall in and take arms, and moved to the left-front for about a half mile in common time, and then to the east, when we wheeled into line and moved forward on quick time for nearly a half mile further, and were ordered to charge, which we did with a will. It seemed to us, just then, that the heavens and earth were certainly coming together, for as we drove the rebels back from the battery the artillerymen flew to their guns and opened fire by volleys. The shots cut the tops from the trees over our heads, the shells bursting in front of us, while each gun was answered shell for shell from the rebel batteries, which shells also burst in and about our lines. To this was added the rattle and crash of our Spencer rifles, and the noise was so deafening that we could not hear ourselves cheer, though each man yelled at the top of his voice. We drove the rebels about a quarter of a mile, took 300 prisoners, fell back on high ground, right in front of the battery we had retaken from the rebels, and re-formed our lines, so close to some large houses which had been set on fire by shells that the right of the regiment had to double on to the centre, and then the heat was so intense that it scorched our clothing. Ammunition had been left in the houses, and the shells began to burst, throwing fire and shingles 100 feet high. The battery behind us continues to belch forth death and destruction. The rebels are coming for us again, and we see their skirmishers and sharpshooters darting from tree to tree, getting nearer and nearer, while from their shots the dead and wounded are falling about us; and altogether, we are as near hell as ever we were or ever expect to be.

Just then we got the word that the army, north of us, had been cut in two, and that the wagon train of our whole army would surely be captured; and immediately following this disastrous news we were ordered to go guard our wagon train into Chattanooga. The rebels were within 100 yards of us when this order came, and we gave them a few rounds to check their advance and moved to the right (taking the battery off the field with us) back to the works we had left an hour before. But where were our horses? Only a few dead ones lay around on the field. Companies F and D were also gone. The explanation as given by John B Davis, of Company D, is that during the absence of the regiment, a squad of rebel cavalry had dashed in from the right, behind Companies D and F, killed five or six head of horses and stampeded the rest. The two companies in turn came in on the rear of the rebels, captured some of them, and moved on after our horses for several miles before they overtook them.

But what were we to do? We knew not where our horses were. Just north of us the rebels were driving everything before them, and we were then in rear of the rebel lines, in a series of broken mountains or ridges covered with stunted trees and jack-oak bushes, without road or by-path. It was after 12 m. when we took the trail of our stampeded horses and moved over the same sort of Rocky-Mountain knobs as those before described in the Dry Valley, north of the Tennessee River. The trail led to the south-west, and as we stumbled along over the square boulders it seemed from the roar of battle that the rebels were getting west as fast as we were.

On the 19th, the trains of our whole army had gathered in the vicinity of Crawfish Springs; but on this morning—the 20th—they had been started to Chattanooga on a road leading down the Chattanooga Valley, west of Missionary Ridge, and if the rebels shall get across the Ridge before the teams get past, all the trains will be lost. As we trudged along over the ridges, with scarcely strength enough to drag one foot after the other, two deer passed before us, coming down from the north, as if frightened almost to death. Under ordinary circumstances the whole regiment would have delighted to fire at them; as it was we let them pass within 100 yards with scarcely a remark. It was 2 p. m. before we met Companies F and D coming back with our horses, and never were soldiers more delighted than we were with meeting the horses then and there. We were almost famished with hunger, worn out with fatigue, and the reaction, after such intense excitement, left us limber as rags. We clutched at our horses like a drowning man at a root or limb of a tree, and like a drowning man had scarcely strength to pull ourselves upon their backs. Those of us who had left our haversacks tied on our horses, explored their utmost recesses in the hope of finding at least a hard-tack. Illusive hope! Not a crumb was left. We must take space to pay a tribute to Number Four, who during these terrible three days and nights held horses. Remember that our rations for both man and beast were exhausted on the 17th, and also that the men who held horses had no better chance to draw food than those on the line of battle. And no one but the man who has held for three days and nights four hungry, starving horses, can ever tell of the terrible and exhaustive labor there is in the work.

By the time we had mounted it seemed that the whole of the right wing of our army had been shattered to pieces, ceased fighting and taken to flight, and that the rebels had little to do but to follow and capture them. The woods were full of the fleeing fugitives, running in every direction; ambulances filled with wounded, the drivers frantically urging the horses on, to they knew not whither; artillerymen were trying to get their guns away, in many cases with but a single span of horses. Caissons, limber-chests, guns, ambulances and men, were wandering in confusion over the hills and knobs like sheep without a shepherd. Though we were entirely worn out and unable to fight more, yet each company was closed up, each regiment compact, and the whole brigade under as quiet control as if on dress parade.

While we fully realized that two-thirds of the army was whipped and scattered to the winds, yet we knew that *we were not whipped*, and had never turned our backs to the enemy. We at once set about gathering up scattered fragments of what, a few days before, was a powerful army. Fugitives were fleeing in every direction utterly demoralized, the one great desire and determination being to get away from the rebels, whom they imagined pursuing them at their heels, and advancing much more rapidly than they in fact were, though, alas! they were coming very fast. Where our trains were, the fugitives did not know; many of them were heading for Crawfish Springs, supposing the trains were yet there, but that place had been captured by the enemy early in the morning, and of course all fugitives going towards it were going right into the rebel lines, instead of escaping. Our brigade went to work vigorously to head off this vast mob towards the Chattanooga road, and we can compare it to nothing more fittingly than to a large herd of cattle stampeded and panic stricken. And in this herd of confusion were many of our friends of the 10th Indiana, and acquaintances of other regiments, who were wounded and lost or bewildered. We got the vast herd turned into the road 10 miles south of Chattanooga, where the great army train was making pretty good time northward. Our brigade moved down the road south five miles further, until we found the end of the train, lapped ourselves around the rear of it, deployed in line across the valley, and like a funeral procession, moved slowly for the Tennessee River.

This grand movement of our brigade, as a special providence, saved our train and thousands of our men who would have fallen into the hands of the enemy. By 11 o'clock at night we got the whole train within 10 miles of Chattanooga, and just west of Rossville, where old Pap Thomas, with the 14th corps, was still standing like a grand rock at the entrance of a harbor, and beating back the fiery billows of battle. We were safe behind his solid lines.

On the 19th our hospitals had been established near Crawfish Springs, west of Lee & Gordon's Mills. Early on the morning of the 20th, our trains were started for Chattanooga, and it was a great mistake that our hospitals were not started thither at the same time, as, about 10 a. m. that day, the rebels made a charge on them and captured tents, ambulances, wounded, physicians, and all stores, &c., in that great hospital camp. Unfortunately, with the rest was captured the regimental ambulance driver of the Seventy-Second, private Richard A. Hatton, of Company H; and his ambulance, containing Dr. Cole's case of instruments and dress sword, was also captured. Corpl. and Regimental Musician Sylvanus C. Wilson, Company G, was also captured, and the brave and good fellow never returned. Drs. Cole and Stearns had just left the hospital to go to the place our lines were yesterday, (19th) and came within an ace of being captured by riding directly into the rebel lines; the Doctors not knowing our lines had fallen back in the night. The rebels that captured our hospitals pushed on after our trains, and we were not a moment too soon in getting between the rebels and the trains, thus saving the latter from capture. The rebels followed us up, skirmishing with the rear guard, till we went into camp, As stated before, we went into camp on the night of the 20th, at 11 o'clock, Company I on picket This company had its headquarters near a house, where we got some chickens and sweet potatoes, and just at midnight Sunday we got the first bite to eat we had since Friday morning's breakfast. And to-day, (March 10th, 1882,) as we think it all over, it is resolved in our mind never to complain of weariness or hunger as long as we live. We cannot more fittingly close this long chapter than by inserting a part of Col. A. O. Miller's speech, made at the reunion of the Seventy-Second at LaFayette, Ind. October 7th, 1878. We feel that we cannot do justice to that masterly effort, and so shall not make the attempt, but shall begin just at the point where we feel the Seventy-Second and its friends are most interested:

"Comrades, we have met to-day to talk about the battle of Perryville, the expulsion of Bragg from Kentucky, and how terribly we suffered for water on that memorable campaign; and it is a matter of fact, though not of history, that had it not been for the possession of a small stream of water, the bloody battle of Perryville would never have been fought. To talk about the new song we learned to sing. We had been singing 'Old John Brown,' and now we went back to Nashville singing 'We are coming, Father Abraham, six hundred thousand more.' To talk about our advance on Murfreesboro, where our new commander, Rosecrans, marshaled his disciplined host along the banks of the meandering Stone River, threading its blue stream through the gloomy vastness of cedars that were soon to become Nature's living witnesses of the bloodly conflict, and one of Nature's most fitting emblems of the solemnity of death. How impatient we got, that winter at Murfreesboro, before we started down the road leading to the blue-hazed mountains between us and the Tennessee. With the wildest enthusiasm we startled Bragg's forces at Hoover's Gap; swept around the beleaguered forces at Tullahoma; crossed Elk River, and bade Hardee's flying squadrons farewell at University Place, on Independence Day. And when autumn came, as soon as our stock could live off the growing corn we started over the Cumberland Mountains. A small force stopped and shelled the city of Chattanooga for a feint, while the main army passed over the Tennessee River at Bridgeport, climbed across the mountains down into the valley, the great thoroughfare to the sea, where lay the sullen and desperate foe, hid behind the ragged banks of the wood-covered Chicamauga.

"To talk about the battle of Chicamauga. How, after an all night's march, Gen. Thomas sent Gens. Bayard and Brannan to take in a force that Gen Dan. McCook had surrounded on one side. How the surrounded force repulsed Gens. Reynolds and Negley, of the 14th corps, Gens. Palmer and Vancleve, of the 21st corps, and Gen. Johnson, of McCook's corps, before noon, and the balance of the army 10 miles away.

"At four o'clock Gen. Sheridan came on the field, with his men on the run, with his Aides crying, "Make way for Sheridan! Make way for Sheridan!" How way was made for him. How in less than half an hour he lost his two batteries, had his men stampeded and corralled in the woods in *our* rear; and how at night, Gen. Crittenden did not know where a single brigade of his corps was.

"We shall never forget the night after the first day's bloody conflict, when the round, full moon rode unveiled over the gory field, the frosty wind moved sighingly through the adjacent wood; how the pickets of both armies kept up a constant interchange of shots, and the artillery an unceasing rumbling during the night, as the guns were hurried past from their positions of the day before to the new places assigned them for the morrow's conflict; yet, above all, and most heart rending of all, were the moans of the thousands dying. The pitiful plea for help, and the cry for water, from the wounded who lay on the field, is still ringing in our ears, with a vividness undimmed by the frosts of time."

CHAPTER XXIII.

From September 21st to October 10th, 1863 —"Forward! the Lightning Brigade!"—Trains Cross the River—Seventy-Second at Friar's Island —The Enemy in Our Front—History of Company H while on Detached Duty—Incidents of the Bravery of Capt. Hanna and his Company—Capt. Hanna's Wound, and his Resignation—Col. Wilder Leaves Col. Miller in Command—Wheeler's Raid into Tennessee, and Our Chase After Him in the Rain—We march Up a Hill and Down again—Two Serpents of Fire—Overtake Wheeler's Rear Guard at Thompson's Cave—Wheeler Captures McMinnville—Fight with and Drive Wheeler in the woods North-west of McMinnville —"Get out of here, You S— b—!"—We Charge and Kill Eighteen Rebels—Rebel Loss and Our Casualties—We Push ahead to Save Murfreesboro—Wheeler Sends in a Demand for Murfreesboro to Surrender, But the Lightning Brigade Hits Him in Rear and Flank and He Concludes not to wait for an Answer—We Save Murfreesboro—Wheeler's Retreat—The Bloody Battle of Farmington—Col. Monroe, 123d Illinois, Killed—Gallant Conduct of Col. Miller and his Brigade—Losses on Both Sides—We Press Wheeler Across the Tennessee River.

The trains we were guarding yesterday moved all night, and at daylight this morning (21st), were crossing the Tennessee River, and we soon followed the trains. Before reaching Chattanooga we passed several lines of provost guards, stretched across the valley to pick up the stragglers. When within a few miles of Chattanooga we passed by the rear of the trains and moved through Chattanooga without stopping. We crossed the river on a bridge, built since our troops occupied the town on the 9th instant. The evidences of defeat and disaster were numerous and painful yesterday, and are still seen to-day. While most of our severely wounded were captured yesterday, thousands able to walk or crawl were to-day making their way across the bridge the best they could. Broken caissons, limber chests, splintered artillery, and other wrecks gathered from the late terrific storm of war, were there. But we were glad to get away from those sad reminders, and moved right on up to the crossing at Friar's, where we had crossed less than two weeks before in such high spirits, and just a month, to a day, since we first came into this valley. How full of thrilling events these few days had been to us!

We should be glad to drop Chicamauga, right here, and never speak of it again, but duties yet before us require further mention. It is true our forces had met partial defeat, and some commands were badly demoralized, but the rebel design to crush the whole army had been foiled. Every intelligent soldier in the army understood that the next move of the rebels would be to cut off our supplies, starve us into surrender, and thus accomplish by strategy what they had failed in on the field. Their nearest and speediest way to do that would be to cross at Friar's Island, make a bold dash on our trains, capture and burn them. Our brigade was sent to the Island to prevent this movement.

On the 22d of September, details from the Seventy-Second were sent across the river to destroy all the rebel works on the east side. These consisted of some lunettes and rifle pits opposite the Island and ford. When the detail crossed, Company D were thrown out as pickets, and were fired on, showing that the rebels were there and ready to cross at the first opportunity. Our men were ordered not to fire or bring on an engagement, but to do their work as speedily as possible, and protect themselves the best they could, and return as soon as the works were destroyed. As the rebels' shots were knocking the earth and dust into the air around them, they wrought with a will, accomplished their mission, and returned without casualty. Our brigade immediately began to build earthworks and lunettes for the battery. The rebels appearing in force on the opposite side, we lay all night in the trenches on our arms. We remained here in camp until the 30th, simply guarding the ford. The enemy occupied the opposite side, and we frequently talked across with each other.

The Historian begs leave, right here, to remark, that there were so many different things done by the regiment, all of equal interest, that it is impossible to carry them all along at once and make a straight, smoothly reading narrative. There must be breaks, somewhere, which, of course, to some extent distract the reader. The history of the regiment would be incomplete without giving, as far as possible, all the incidents generally known in every company. We have already said that Company H was detailed as provost guard at Gen. Reynolds' headquarters, while the regiment was at Decherd. From that date to this, we have said nothing of the company, but it must not be inferred that it has done nothing; on the contrary, its service for that period is of thrilling interest, and we condense the following from Sergt. McClure's manuscript, which is kindly put at our disposal:

Reynolds' division left Decherd on August 16th, passed over the Cumberland Mountains, by way of University Hights, to the mouth of Battle Creek. From the latter place, Sergt. McClure and part of the company were intrusted with the hazardous mission of carrying a dispatch to Stevenson, Ala., which they accomplished in safety. From Battle Creek, Reynolds moved to Jasper, in the Sequatchie Valley; thence to the Tennessee River, and crossed at Shell Moun; thence to Trenton; thence crossed Lookout Range to McElmore's Cove, near Pond Springs, where he arrived September 15th On the night of the 18th the division started for the battle field of Chicamauga. Company H. were thrown out on each side of the ammunition train, as flankers, as an attack was momentarily expected. As the night was dark and the brush thick, they had a very difficult and painful night's march. At daylight they found themselves at that historic place, the Widow Glenn's house, Gen. Rosecrans' headquarters. All through the memorable 19th, Company H followed Gen. Reynolds as his body guard. After the General formed his lines he planted his artillery on a ridge, some distance in rear of the infantry. Near noon the rebels charged the division, and some of the troops in front of the battery gave way; the wounded began to come back in numbers, and things looked squally. This aroused Capt. Hanna's pugilism to its highest pitch, and he determined to take a hand in the fight; he accordingly ordered his men to fall in and help support the battery. Some of the men said, "Captain, what shall we do with the horses?" He replied in his best, briefest English, "Let 'em go to h—l." Some of the men took him at his word and let their horses go, and lost them, while others tied theirs. The Captain meant business, and began to press in all the stragglers he could find as he moved to the front; he found a straggling flag-bearer and made him stand and hold his colors as a rallying point until a respectable regiment was collected, which the Captain stationed in front of the guns of the battery and made them lie down. Soon the enemy had driven everything in front of Company H, and were coming for the battery, when the 16 pieces opened simultaneously right over Hanna's line, and in a few moments the smoke was so thick that they could see nothing in the brush before them; but they knew from the infernal yell just in front of them, that the "Johnnies" were charging on the guns. At this crisis the men of Company H did some of their best and most fatal work with their Spencers, and in a few moments the charging mass of rebels was cut down and hurled back into the forest, and the artillery saved. There were several artillery horses shot; but one man was struck (with a spent ball) the rebels overshooting. It was here that Maj. Anderson, Company I, was wounded. Company H was relieved by fresh troops. On the morning of the 20th, H was still with the General, moving about over the field wherever duty required them. The battle opened at 8:30 a. m., and for a time all seemed to go on well, but at 10 a. m. the left of the division was pierced, cutting off three brigades, which were forced into a narrow pass on the ridge, and unable to do anything more in the fight that day. Thus the help of 2,500 men was lost. Company H was then ordered to guard Reynolds' ammunition trains to Rossville, and its experience in that vast mob was similar to that of the regiment on the same day, before given. Sergt. McClure, however, wishes to emphasize that he never saw anything equal to the rout and panic at Chicamauga.

We must take up another passage in the history of Company H. About the time the company crossed the Tennessee River, Sergt. Joseph Henry and Corpl. Edward Allen and 12 men were detailed at Tracy City to serve on the staff of Col. Carlton, of the 89th Ohio, commanding brigade; and served with him until after the battle. On the 20th, soon after Carlton's brigade became engaged, one of his staff officers had his horse shot from under him. Corpl. Allen gave the officer his horse, went into the ranks with Carlton's men, and fired his Spencer until it got so hot it burst; the gallant Allen threw it away, took the gun and accoutrements from a dead soldier, and continued the fight until he was disabled by a shot in the knee, which sent him to the hospital. What General displayed more bravery on that day than Corpl. Allen? We are sad to record that he afterwards died of his wound in the hospital at Nashville. Sergt. Henry and his men did gallant service throughout the battle, and reported to the company at Rossville, long after night. Bromley, already spoken of as severely wounded across the back, was discharged January 30th, 1865, and subsequently died of his wounds. Capt. Hanna was provost marshal on Gen. Reynolds' Staff, and from the character of the man, as demonstrated on previous pages, he was always where he thought he could do the most good in putting down the rebellion. In passing up and down the lines he had occasion to dismount; he gave his horse to an orderly to hold until called for; the Captain passed on down the line on foot, and had proceeded some distance, when the rebels made a charge on the particular place in the line where he was, and things became wonderfully mixed in the turmoil of battle. The first thing the Captain knew, a mounted rebel officer rode up, presented a pistol at him, and roared out, "surrender!" The Captain in turn roared, "go to h—l!" and started to run; "and then," said the Captain, "the d—d old fool let drive and took me in the stern!" Some one else must have attended to the rebel officer, as Capt. Hanna crawled off the field and joined his company at Rossville, late that night. The brave old Captain went home to Attica, as soon as he was able, and had the ball cut out of his hip; and as soon as it was well enough for him to get about, he rejoined his regiment, Dec. 1st, 1863. Soon afterwards he got a dispatch that his wife was dying. He had faced death often without fear, and borne many hardships without a murmur, but this news bowed his head and rent his stout heart. He did what all wished he would do, and thought he should do—sent in his resignation, which was promptly accepted by the officers, who knew how courageously he had fought, how manly he had endured. Thus Company H and the regiment lost a true and brave man. In many respects Capt. Hanna was peculiar. While rough in manners and language, he was in heart and practice good, generous, brave and kind. While terribly severe on the "play off," (he could never, for a moment, countenance anything low or mean,) the good and faithful soldier always found in him a true and faithful friend. He was known by all in the regiment as an officer who was always looking out for the welfare of his men. He left the regiment with the love, well wishes and sympathy of all.

Soon after our army took Chattanooga, feed become scarce, and Company H was sent to Stevenson, Ala. In a few weeks afterwards there were many changes in the general officers of the Army of the Cumberland, and Company H was released as provost guard and ordered to report to the regiment, and did so at Maysville, Ala., on November 5th. As the company marched to the regiment, private W. H. Loman, was left at a house sick, was captured a few days afterwards, and was a prisoner for over a year.

Our only apology for this extended consecutive notice of Company H is, that it was the only company so long detached from the regiment; that its service was conspicuous and important; and moreover, the data have all been furnished by the efficient historian of that company. Other companies doubtless did as much, and did it as well, and the historian would be glad to give each as extended a notice, but we have not the facts before us. Each company has been invited, nay, urged, to furnish facts, but to our sorrow have not responded.

We quote from Col. Miller's Journal of September 22d, 1863: "Engagement at Chicamauga, killed, 11; wounded, 30; missing, 3."

On the 24th, Col. Wilder went home and left Col. Miller in command of the brigade. On the 26th a large rebel force moved up the river on yon (east) side, and on the 28th a strong rebel force was opposite to us. On the 30th our brigade was relieved by a brigade of infantry and moved up the river to Bly's ford, about 40 miles above Chattanooga, and camped on Sales Creek. Wheeler, with 10,000 cavalry and seven pieces of artillery, had crossed the river at this ford and immediately struck across the mountains for Murfreesboro, with the object of cutting off supplies for the army at Chattanooga.

On October 1st it rained for the first time since we left Decherd, on August 16th, and for 30 days afterwards it rained almost every day, and for nine days at a time we had not a dry stitch on us day or night. It never rains in the South but it pours. During October 1st there was an unusual amount of scouting while waiting for orders and preparing to follow Wheeler. Minty's brigade of cavalry had been stationed at this ford and at Mount Washington, further up the river, and had been driven back and scattered in every direction, one regiment being driven clear up on top of the mountain. In the afternoon at 2 p. m. we got started after Wheeler and moved up the river about six miles. It was raining when we started and continued to rain long after night and blew a hurricane. Just at dark we came to a place where we supposed Wheeler had gone up the mountain, but a torrent of water was pouring down the mountain road as if a water sprite had bewitched it. At the base of the mountain the road forked, one lying on one side and the other on the other side of the hollow, the two roads being but two or three hundred feet apart. We were puzzled to know which one to take, as the beating rain had washed out every trace, so that no one could tell that an army had ever passed over either road. But remembering the guide board at the entrance to the bridge, which says, "keep to the right, as the law directs," we ascended the mountain on the right side of the hollow. We had been over this (Waldron's Ridge) six times before at different places, but at no place where it was so high or steep as here. It was yet pouring down rain; we dismounted, and for hours we toiled up the steep mountain, and when within a half mile of the top we got above the rain. The wind whipped around to the north, blew through our wet clothing and chilled us to the marrow of the bone. The Seventy-Second was in advance, and it was 10 o'clock at night before we reached the top of the mountain. After all the toil and exposure we hadn't gone a quarter of a mile until we found that we were on the wrong road. The other regiments of the brigade were strung along on the side of the mountain from bottom to top following us. We had nothing to do but to wait until a staff officer could be dispatched down the mountain to order the column to march by the other flank, or move with the other end foremost.

The wind continued to whistle around the brow of the mountain with piercing power and as cold as mid-winter. Several attempts at building fires failed owing to everything being so wet, and we were compelled to stand and shiver and suffer until 2 a. m. before we got started down again. As we had to walk it was about as hard on our legs and feet as going up, and day was breaking by the time we got down.

This was October 2d. All the regiments were down from the mountain and had fed before we got down; as soon as we could feed, details were made to pull our battery up the mountain, and as soon as it was out of the way we started after it, on the south side of the ravine, which was more rugged and steep than the north side which we ascended and descended last night. We had read of "Napoleon himself crossing the Alps," and from this experience we decided that we would prefer not to be with Napoleon or any other gentleman on such an expedition. We reached the top of the mountain without accident, about 10 a. m., and it looked like we could throw a stone across to the place we halted in the bitter cold of last night; but between us and it was a great gulf fixed, which was thousands of feet deep, and as impassable (to us at least) as the gulf between the rich man and Lazarus. Once up, we found delightful roads, as smooth as a floor; we were two days behind Wheeler and moved as fast as possible and got down on the west side into the Sequatchie Valley by noon of that day, Sunday, where we fed and ate dinner. Here we learned that Wheeler had burned a large wagon train, down the valley near Dunlap, where we crossed the valley the first time. At 2 p. m. we proceeded west over a high range of hills, Minty's brigade following us; we got over these hills and across a western branch of this same valley, and began to climb the mountain on the other side just at dark. We shall never forget that night. This valley is very rich, well cultivated and well fenced. Our regiment was in the rear of our brigade, and the ascent of the advance slow and tedious, which caused a constant recurrence of checks and stops in the column. Every time the column would halt the boys would bolt off their horses and build fires in the fence corners to warm by; and by the time we got half way up the mountain we could look back over the valley, over the range of hills, over the other side of the hills, clear back to where we came down off the range of Waldron's Ridge, and see two lines of fires, one on either side of the road, six or eight miles long, the whole way across the valley, which looked like two immense serpents of fire following us, curving right and left according to the sinuosities of the road. We never saw so much fire in one night, and we burned up enough rails to fence a county. We reached the mountain summit about 10 o'clock and went into camp. This had been a hard tramp on us, although we were not more than 40 miles from where Wheeler crossed the river, for we had climbed the mountain three times and descended it twice in little more than 24 hours.

On October 3d we started at daylight. The two brigades of cavalry, Long's and Minty's, which were then with us, had moved out in advance of us. We had most excellent roads, as all roads on tops of mountains are, and we tried to make up in speed what we had lost in getting started, and moved 50 miles without stopping to feed, which brought us to the western edge of the mountain, at a place called Thompson's Cove, where we run on to the rear guard of Wheeler's forces, who made a desperate effort to keep us from going down the mountain. As stated, the cavalry were in front, and as cavalrymen never dismount and fight on foot, the rebels worried them considerably, killing two of them before they got down the mountain. The sun was about an hour high when we came to the descent of the mountain, and impeded by the rebels, it was near sundown when we got down. In the cove, where we descended, we found our cavalry all massed in column by the side of the road awaiting us, and the rebels in line of battle stretched across the mouth of the cove to receive us. The 4th U. S. Cavalry, of Minty's brigade, had the advance, and were urged to make a saber charge and drive the rebels out. The cavalry formed line and made ready, but for some cause did not charge. We afterwards learned that it was because they were barefooted, having traded their boots off over at Mount Washington; and upon reflection we remembered that, as we came up the valley, we noticed all the women wore boots. Our brigade was dismounted and we were hurried forward and formed lines in the thickest briars we ever saw. Our skirmishers were sent forward and succeeded in killing and wounding quite a number of the enemy; but by the time we got our lines formed it was so dark (we were still back in the mouth of the cove) that we could not see a rod through the brush and vines before us, and were ordered to keep place in line and lie on our arms. This was the unkindest cut of all, and seemed so foolish to the dullest of us that the expressions of disgust were very frequent and forcible. We were not allowed to build fires, though the night was cold; our horses were in the rear and we had to pass the bitter night without food or sleep, when we might as well have had a good night's rest.

When daylight came on the 4th, we found the rebels had gone, having left their dead and wounded on the field. We moved after them at sun up, crossing the Collins River at Hill's Mills, and marched rapidly till 3 p. m., when we reached McMinnville, 35 miles from where we came down the mountain. Here we ran on to the rebels again—that is, they went out of one side of the town while we went in at the other. The rebels had captured the whole garrison of 400 men, and a vast amount of clothing, quartermaster's and commissary's stores, and burned what they could not carry with them. The cavalry pursued the retreating rebels, capturing 20 or 30 of them, while our brigade, battery and all, kept right at the heels of the cavalry. After a chase of four miles the cavalry ran on to the enemy in line of battle in thick, heavy woods, at the further side of a large field. The position was well chosen by the rebels, and our cavalry, as usual, came promptly to a halt. Our whole brigade, on a keen run, moved up within 400 yards of their line and dismounted behind an orchard, and in 20 minutes had our lines formed for action. Our battery whirled past us up through the orchard, limbered up, and by the time we were even with them they were ready to go to work. Company B, of the Seventy-Second, Capt. Herron in command, are deployed forward as skirmishers; they go for the woods on the run and our line after them in quick time, while our battery knocks the trees to pieces with shells and mows the underbrush with grape and canister, it being on high ground and shooting over us. The rebels open on us with musketry, and everything is lively as we dash into the woods with a whoop and cheer, in the very front of rebel muskets, and in two minutes we have driven the rebels from the fence.

Capt. Herron says that in this charge, he was, for the first time, sure that he saw one man shoot at and kill another. Soon after getting into the woods he saw a rebel dismount to get out of the way of the shower of bullets, keeping his horse between him and us; Sergt. Thos. C. Greene, Company B, also saw the man, took deliberate aim, shot through both jaws of the horse and through the rebel's head, killing him instantly. Before reaching the fence, on that charge, one of Capt. Herron's men had the entire top of his hat shot off and his hair pulled by the passing ball, but it did not break the scalp.

The sun was not more than an hour high when we got into the woods. We found it very difficult to march in line of battle and make much headway, and when the rebels found that we were not coming on them so fast as they at first supposed, they rallied, and from every tree, and stump, and log, gave us a volley and then fell back to the next. We pushed on as fast as we could, paying little attention to the rebels, except to fire at them every time we got in sight of them. We drove them rapidly for about a mile, when we saw a rebel officer coming down the road towards us, his horse in a gallop; he rode a white horse and was waving a white handkerchief. Lieut.-Col. Kirkpatrick was near the road, and when he saw the rebel approaching with the white flag he ran out and said, "What the d—l do you want?" The rebel officer said, "I want to make some arrangements about burying our dead." This made Col. Kirkpatrick mad and he roared out, "This is not the time or place to make such arrangements. Get out of here you son of a b—h!" The officer wheeled his horse and went back like a bird flying. It was now evident that they were doing all in their power to delay us until they could get ready for us some place else; so we made redoubled efforts to push them, and soon came on to them near a house with open ground beyond, where they had taken position and were unlimbering their artillery. We just charged right into the rebel line, killed 18, and without halting charged on the rebel guns. The rebels were too quick for us, limbered up and hurried away for Murfreesboro. It was now dark and we went into camp right on the battle-field, six miles from McMinnville. The rebels left 25 or 30 wounded in our hands. Our only casualties were, private Alfred Love, G, right arm severely; private Simeon Harper, G, right thigh; Wm. Cue, K, right heel severely; Corpl. Jacob Richestine, B, slightly; Samuel H. Rinehart, G, regimental scout, in knee. Total wounded five. This fight lasted but little over 30 minutes, and showed that when we undertook to do a thing we did it quick. We went to bed early and tried to make up in sleep what we had lost the night before. When we started from north Chicamauga, on the 30th, we had rations for but two days. Here we made coffee, the first time since three days past.

On October 5th we again started in pursuit of the rebels, and discussed the chances of Wheeler's capturing Murfreesboro as we pushed after him. We knew not what forces we had at that post, but knew it was of vast importance to us to hold it, and of just as great importance to the rebels to capture it and destroy our stores. We pushed on, hoping to arrive there in time to prevent the rebels from capturing it; moved rapidly and steadily all day; passed through Woodbury, and turned and went north at Readyville until we reached the road from Auburn to Murfreesboro, in order to avoid Wheeler's rear guard, which was strongly posted on the main road from Readyville to Murfreesboro. Wheeler's entire command came in front of Murfreesboro about 3 p. m., and immediately sent in a demand for its surrender; but while he awaited a reply, our cavalry came on to his rear and he learned that the Lightning Brigade was flanking him on the right. In this predicament, with his eyes watering as he looked at the great Yankee prize and the glory to be gained by seizing it, he concluded he had better get out of the way speedily, and he retreated without firing a shot. We went into camp just at sundown, on the banks of Stone River, close to the fortifications north-west of town. We were feeling first rate over the successful movements of the day. Wheeler had crossed the Tennessee and moved rapidly almost 200 miles for the express purpose of capturing this place, and had he succeeded it would have been an incalculable disaster to our army, while his name would have been handed down to future generations glorious with the record of having captured the strongest Union fortification in the South, with its immense stores; and as having dealt the army at Chattanooga a blow little less disastrous than that given it on the bloody field of Chicamauga. We now felt certain that his grand raid was a failure; we had started two days behind him, but had caught up with and whipped him, and felt perfectly competent to do it again.

On October 6th we were up early and ready to march by sun up; but as we had been in the saddle for six days on two days' rations, our officers tried to get some rations. We had not a single team with us except the artillery and ambulances. We drew three days' rations of crackers alone, and did not get started until 11 a. m., and then there seemed to be a great deal of concentrated slowness in finding out on which road the rebels moved their main column. Finally we got strung out on the Shelbyville Pike, moving very slowly, our brigade in rear of column and our regiment in rear of all. About the middle of the afternoon it began to rain, and we could not have been more than six miles from Murfreesboro when night came on, after which we dragged along at a snail's pace for two miles further and went into camp. It was dark as Egypt, and in looking back over the service we cannot remember a single instance where we had a worse time getting into camp. It was 10 o'clock before we stopped, and then it was in the middle of the biggest, thickest, thorniest, most pestiferous patch of green briars we ever saw. Here it was that we first learned how to put up a raider's bunk; and as it served us a happy purpose on many occasions, we describe it here: The raider's bunk was constructed of six rails, and two men could put one up in less than a minute. With the addition of a rail at each side and our gum blankets thrown over them, the bunk had ample room under it for six men to sleep and keep dry, no matter how hard it rained. Lay three rails down parallel with each other and two feet apart. Lay a rail across these a foot from the ends, on top of the two outside ones and under the centre one. Now raise this end of the three rails three feet high and cross two rails over the end of the centre one, and under the ends of the outside ones, and the work is done.

We are now eight miles from Murfreesboro and four from Shelbyville. The rebels are in and near Shelbyville, and have burned the railroad bridge over Duck River, at Wartrace, but have torn up no track, and this is the only damage they have done to the Chattanooga railroad.

October 7th. It rained all last night, but as this was the day for our brigade to take the advance in regular turn, we were up and ready to move by daylight. There never was any "foolishness" or delay about Col. Miller in getting ready to move at the time ordered. When he got orders to move at 6 a. m., at 6 a. m. we moved; and there was no tardiness in removing anything out of our way that obstructed our progress. When we got to Shelbyville we found that Wheeler's forces had torn the whole town to pieces. Notwithstanding that this town was Bragg's headquarters for six months, the citizens were decidedly Union in sentiment, and Wheeler's men, chagrined at their failure to take Murfreesboro, wreaked their spite on the people of Shelbyville, We reached this town early in the day. The rebels had bothered the Union officers yesterday by dividing their forces, and delayed our pursuit, and they followed the same tactics to-day in leaving Shelbyville, part of them going towards Farmington, part towards Unionville and part in other directions. Gen. Crook, commanding all the troops on the expedition, sent Minty's brigade in one direction, Long's brigade in another, and the Lightning Brigade, Col. Miller in command, on the direct road to Farmington, 12 miles west of Shelbyville. This was the road on which most of the rebels had moved. We started about 8 a. m., and Sergt. Remley, Company E, says a boy came into the road at head of column and told Col. Miller that there was a force of rebels on a by-road a mile north of us. As we had been fooling along for several days depending on the cavalry to hunt rebels for us, we had determined to do the hunting ourselves, and as these reported by the boy seemed to be nearest, we turned square off the road and made for them. It is said that Wheeler purposely stationed them there expecting us to move straight on to Farmington and engage his forces at that place, when this brigade, Scott's mounted infantry, were to come up in the rear and capture us. Be this as it may, we charged upon the rebels (Scott's mounted infantry) and struck them in flank, as they were dismounted, the 17th and 98th coming near getting between them and their horses. About 200 of them threw down their arms and were taken in by Capt. Robinson, of Company C.

As the rebels who got mounted undertook to pass through a narrow lane, the 17th and 98th poured in a destructive fire on them, killing a great many men and horses. When our column struck the rebels they were in line facing east on a road which lies north and south. The 98th and 17th struck them first; our regiment being next in column was dismounted, but before we got a chance for a shot they broke through a lane to the west, the 17th and 98th after them at full speed, and the Seventy-Second men putting in their best time to catch up with the 17th and 98th to take a hand in the fight, or have some shots at the fleeing foe. Lieut.-Col. Kirkpatrick was at our head, calling out, "hurry up, boys, or you won't get a smell." At that there was a regular foot-race, and our color-bearer gave out; the flag was hard to carry, but Capt. Thomson gathered it in his stout hands and pressed on. We shall never forget how his example inspired us. We were so completely exhausted that we felt we could run no further, but to see him with the flag in one hand and his sword in the other, shouting, "Come on, Seventy-Second," infused new life and energy into us.

It was soon found that it was no use to try to keep up with the rebels on foot, who were retreating as rapidly as possible through the cedar woods, and making every effort to get back to the main road. So the horses were hurried up, the men mounted, and we pushed them. The whole country seemed full of rebels, and though a constant running fire was kept up with them we did not make very rapid headway.

We wish here to pay a tribute to Col. Monroe, of the 123d Illinois. His regiment this day was in the rear of the brigade; every time the rebels would make a stand he chafed because he could not get to take part in the battle. Just after noon, Capt. Rice, adjutant of the brigade, dropped back to Col. Monroe's regiment. The Colonel complained that Col. Miller was not using him and his regiment fairly, and remarked: "The Indiana regiments are getting to do most of the fighting, and not giving myself and regiment a chance." Of course Col. Miller had never thought of slighting the gallant young Col. Monroe and his regiment. Each regiment had taken its turn in advance, and it was purely an accident that there happened to be more fighting when the 123d was in the rear. This fact would have pleased many a Colonel, but not so with the gallant Monroe; he wanted to be in the thickest of the fray. After talking awhile Col. Monroe told Adjt. Rice he was going to resign; he did not have to be a soldier, as he had just inherited a large fortune; "and besides," said he, "there are lots of men in my regiment who want to step up, and deserve to, and I shall get out of their way." After some further conversation, Adjt. Rice went to the head of the column and told Col. Miller what Col. Monroe had said, hearing which Col. Miller said: "At the next engagement bring the 123d to the front." The running fight continued till about 4 p. m., when our head of column was in about a half mile of Farmington, where we encountered the rebel skirmishers. Capt. Rice rode back to the 123d, saluted Col. Monroe, and said: "Colonel, the brigade commander directs me to have you bring your regiment to the front."

Col. Monroe seemed overjoyed, turned to his regiment and sang out: "*Attention battalion! Forward, quick trot, march!*" The 123d, led by its brave Colonel, dashed past us to the front. We were just then in the densest cedar woods we ever saw. The skirmishing in front became rapid, and we were certain the rebels were determined to make the best resistance they were able. The Seventy-Second was halted and well closed up, and waited for the three regiments in front of us to get their places, which they did—the 123d on the south side and next to the road; the 17th and 98th on the right, and moved out far enough to give space for our regiment. The rattling of the Spencers had become pretty rapid, and were as rapidly answered by muskets from the enemy, and we were presently startled by the boom of cannon, but the sound was so muffled by dense cedar brush that we were not aware it was so close to us as it really was. The fight now opens in earnest, and Col. Monroe is killed as he gallantly leads his command. We hear, just then, the commands of Col. Kirkpatrick, in rapid succession:

Seventy-Second, left into line! Tell off in fours! Prepare to dismount! Dismount!

The commands are executed as rapidly as they are given. An officer comes in full gallop down the lines and shouts: "Don't stop to form, but hurry your men to the front!" Corpl. J. Frank Tolby, Company G, has our colors, and Col. Kirkpatrick hurries him to our place in line as indicated before, and then commands: "Seventy-Second, form on the colors!" Now, as we move into line, the rebels catch sight of the flag and open on it with shells, which at first range high, cutting off limbs and tops of trees, which rain down amongst us; the shells burst above our heads with terrific sound, scattering fragments of iron in every direction. As each company of our regiment comes into its place on the line the rebels catch sight of us, and depress their pieces so as to throw their shells full into our ranks. There never was a piece of cooler courage shown in the world than the forming of the

Seventy-Second just here, under this galling fire. We avoid the effect of the artillery firing as well as we can by falling flat on our faces at the flash of the guns, while the shells, that pass over and so close to us that we hear them shriek like demons and hiss like serpents, and feel them blow their breath on us, make fearful havoc in the timber around and behind us. We are not more than formed before we get the order, "Forward!" We promptly obey, and as we move forward they open on us with grape and canister, which is not so easy to dodge. We are fortunately ordered to halt and lie down, as this hail of battle begins to pour upon us, which we gladly obey. As the rebels have four pieces of artillery, there is thunder to pay all along the line, and the other regiments are receiving the same sort of treatment that we are.

At this critical juncture Col. Miller received from Gen. Crook the following order:

"IN THE FIELD.

"*Colonel:*—From what information I get from you, and what I get from other sources, I am convinced the enemy's forces have made a junction at Farmington. His forces are much larger than yours. I have no word from Gen. Mitchell's division. Minty is 10 miles in the rear. Cannot you keep off an engagement? In less than an hour it will be dark. I am confident an action will be certain defeat with so unequal forces. GEORGE CROOK,

"Brig. Gen., Commanding Cav."

After reading the order, Col. Miller said to the officer: "Tell Gen. Crook it is impossible;" and immediately gave the order, "Forward!" At that command the whole line instantly rise up, as if from the heart of the earth, and move forward. We find great difficulty for some distance in getting over the fallen timber and through the brush. Suddenly we find ourselves in an open field, and there, close to us, is the artillery! "Come on, Seventy-Second!" shouted Col. Kirk.; "let's take that battery!" With the words the brave Colonel starts for the battery and his regiment after him. Double quick and with a shout we dash upon it, and the battery is ours! The whole line charged simultaneously with us, and in less than 15 minutes from the command "charge" the rebels are flying through Farmington, and we at their heels. As we pass over the field we see that the rebel artillerymen have fought their pieces well, and many of them fallen at their posts, where they lay dead. The rebel lead horses were massed in column half a mile beyond the town. We followed the fleeing foe as fast and as far as we could, shooting many of them in the back as they ran. By the time we got a quarter of a mile beyond the town we were out of breath and gave up the chase. But such another uproar as the panic-stricken rebels made getting on to their horses you never heard. Had the cavalry been with us and charged just after we did they could have taken in the whole of them, bag and baggage. It was now getting dark, and we went into camp for the night. Immediately after the battle Col. Miller sent the following dispatch to Gen. Crook:

"*General:*—At the time of receiving your order, to prevent an engagement was impossible; the enemy would have attacked me had I not him. I have whipped him and stampeded all his troops; have taken all four of his cannon and 300 prisoners, but not without loss to my command. Col. Monroe, 123d Illinois, with two other officers, are among the killed. Send forward medical aid as soon as possible.

"A. O. MILLER,
"Col., comd'g Brigade."

Col. Miller further says in his report: "The whole of the rebel division was concentrated here. They had a battery of four guns. I dismounted my brigade, and, after a hard struggle, we charged their lines and drove them through the town in confusion. Our brigade fought them three to one. We killed 100, wounded 150, and have taken 300 prisoners."

Surgeon Cole in his report says: "The fight did not last long, but for earnestness and resolution in giving and receiving hard blows, it was never excelled. In less than an hour from dismounting of first regiment we were victorious and the rebels in full flight. During the day we have captured 500 prisoners. The loss of Col. Monroe is deplored by all. Loss of brigade 12 killed, 67 wounded; and strange as it really is, the Seventy-Second charged and took the battery without the loss of a single man. This we attribute, first of all, to that kind Providence that had been over us from the beginning. Second, the ripe, good judgment of our very careful officers. Third, but perhaps not the least, the efficiency and discipline of the men themselves."

We close our account of this battle with an extract from the report of Maj. Gen. George H. Thomas, published by order of the War Department:

"On the night of September 30 the enemy's cavalry, under Wheeler, crossed the Tennessee River near Washington, and moved thence against Gen. Rosecrans' communications. Wilder's brigade pursued him through Middle Tennessee and drove him back across the Tennessee River without his having materially interfered with Gen. Rosecrans' communications. The brigade had several brisk skirmishes with the enemy, and at Farmington a severe battle was fought with Wheeler's forces, driving them from the field with heavy loss."

After going into camp Company I was placed on picket on the road north to Columbia, and about 1 o'clock at night two rebel soldiers came to the outposts, and our videttes let them pass right into our lines, one of the videttes riding back with them to headquarters. You ought to have seen them stare and look around for a place to get away when they came up to the fire and saw we had blue clothes on. They saw some one had played a practical joke on them, that there was no getting away, and threw down their guns. They said that in the morning, when they left Shelbyville, they had gotten permission of Gen. Wheeler to go and see their families, who lived a few miles north of Farmington, with the understanding that they report at Farmington that night, as Wheeler said he would stay all night there. But Wheeler didn't stay, and they reported at wrong headquarters. We kept them at the post that night, and in a short time we were on most friendly terms with them, and learned that they belonged to the same force that fought us at Rock Springs; learned the man's name who lived at the white house where we left our dead, and many other things we will give when we get on our way home from the war.

Dr. Cole relates that "while riding through the woods collecting the wounded I came upon a six foot Mississippian lying in a thicket, whom I supposed to be wounded, and who, on my approaching him, raised his hands and said, 'I surrender.' This surprised me, and when told that he was not wounded I dismounted and received from him his revolver, loaded and capped; then his gun, a six-shooter, also loaded; after which I had him to arise and took him to our lines. He was rather chagrined and surprised when I told him that this was rather out of my line, being a surgeon, and not armed at all. The fellow was so badly frightened that he had not noticed the green sash I wore. The Colonel and men were greatly amused at my turning provost marshal."

On October 8th we moved at daylight, and passed that morning the place where the rebels had camped the night before, 10 miles southwest of Farmington. Wheeler had concentrated all his trains and forces on this road, and was making all speed to get out of Tennessee We passed through Lewisburg, and about half an hour before sundown came to Pulaski, 30 miles from Farmington. A few rebels were seen, and our regiment was dismounted and we marched through the town in line of battle, which, of course, delayed us considerably, and it was sundown before our horses were brought up. We went into camp as soon as we could find a place to hitch our horses. We picked up 20 or 30 stragglers during the day. Here an incident occurred on this march that was rather amusing. We came upon a rebel major, a conscript officer; he first showed signs of running his horse and getting away, but when ordered to halt he did so. When asked by Capt. Clark, of our scouts, why he did not get away, he answered he was on a borrowed horse and it belonged to a widow woman, and that he did not like to run a borrowed horse, especially a widow woman's. The conscientious fellow was taken with us, horse and all.

On October 9th, as Pulaski is but 35 miles from the Tennessee River, we knew it would be our last day's drive of Wheeler's forces, and moved in good time, as soon as Minty's brigade, which had the advance, could get out of the way. About 10 a. m. Minty ran on to the enemy very strongly posted on Sugar Creek. They had a line of rail works thrown up quite across the mouth of a cove, up which the road ran on the other side of the creek from us. The place was a strong one naturally, and they had it strongly fortified. Gen. Crook had placed Col. Minty under arrest for not coming more promptly to our relief at Farmington. He had just been released, and was burning with wrath at the disgrace, and when he came to this line of works he formed line of battle and charged like a thunder storm, and put his command over the works, on horseback, upon the astonished rebels. This was a most daring feat, and many of the rebels were killed. Here we saw the only rebel that we ever did see that we were sure had been killed by a sabre. His head was split from the crown to the neck. About the middle of the afternoon we came up to a piece of artillery, the wheels of which the rebels had chopped to pieces and left it. When in about five miles of the river we got word that the rebels were yet on this side of it, on hearing which a long, loud cheer went up from the Seventy-Second, and we started on the gallop, never stopping till within a half mile of the river, when we learned that the rebels had all got over, leaving on this side and in the water 8 or 10 wagons and one piece of artillery. About 60 prisoners were picked up to-day. Thus ends the Wheeler raid, which on the part of the rebels was bold in conception, daring in execution, but disastrous to them in results.

Wheeler crossed the Tennessee river 40 miles above Chattanooga on the 30th of September with 7,000 to 10,000 cavalry and 7 to 10 pieces of artillery. He captured 300 of our troops at McMinnville, and burned one bridge at Wartrace. We started after him on the 2d of October and chased him 300 miles in seven days, killed, wounded and captured 1,000 of his men, captured six pieces of his artillery, and 20 wagons. The total Union loss in killed and wounded was

110. Of this number the Lightning Brigade lost 12 killed, 67 wounded, 11 missing—total 90; making the total loss of 20 for the two divisions of cavalry that first and last took part in the chase. The rebels recrossed the river at Lamb's Ferry, four miles south of Rogersville. We went back near Rogersville and went into camp. Near Lamb's Ferry a rebel picket post, with 16 prisoners, was captured by the scouts

CHAPTER XXIV.

October 10th to November 15th, 1863—Rest and Forage—Meet Major Apple Jack Again—A Lice-entious Story—After Rhoddy—The March of the Mud Cavalcade—Dead Horses by the Acre—Capture and Escape of Capt. Kilborn—Capt. Kilborn Captures Gurley and his Brother—Chaplain De La Matyr Joins the Regiment—What Gen. Thomas Expects of Col. Miller—In Camp at Marysville—Capture and Destruction of Boats—Arming the Negroes—Two Regiments Enlisted—Their Dancing and Songs—God is Marching on.

For seven days previous to October 10th we had not been out of the saddle on an average six hours of each 24. Our rations were out; the fatigue of the campaign had been very severe on both man and beast. We were 150 miles from Chattanooga, and neither rations nor forage could be issued. We therefore spent the day foraging and resting. We have failed to note that from the day we struck the rebels at McMinnville we had been constantly picking up loose horses, until at this date each company had from 10 to 50 more horses than men; but we had picked up negroes enough to take care of the horses, and our small brigade had grown until now it seemed as large as a division. Fortunately there was an abundance of forage in the surrounding country for man and beast, and also plenty of that soul-cheering beverage, the life-giving principle of the Southern chivalry, Apple Jack, the elixir of life. We spell his name with capitals, because Apple Jack had the rank of Major in the Southern Confederacy, being the Major drink. He was also a Caput-al drink, flying quickly to the caputs of those who took him, often putting more caput on them than they could carry and stand upon their feet. He kindled their devotions, tickled up their notions, made them merry *caput a navem*—from head to navel—giving them a caput-al time generally. Is it a wonder that some of the boys, after returning from this hard chase after Wheeler, in which every nerve and muscle had been taxed to its fullest capacity, and, meeting with this merry old Major, should turn aside with him for a season of relaxation and hilarity? Not a whit of a wonder. One of the Seventy-Second declares that the following lines of the Bardie Burns to guid old Scotch whisky are equally applicable to Apple Jack:

> O thou, my Muse! guid auld Scotch drink,
> Whether thro' wimplin' worms thou jink,
> Or, richly brown, ream o'er the brink,
> In glorious faem,
> Inspire me, till I lisp and wink
> To sing thy name!
>
> * * *
>
> Food fills the wame, an' keeps us livin':
> Tho' life's a gift no worth receivin',
> When heavy dragged wi' pine an' grievin';
> But, oiled by thee,
> The wheels o' life gae down-hill, scrievin',
> Wi' rattlin' glee.
>
> Thou clears the head o' doited Lear;
> Thou cheers the heart o' drooping care;
> Thou strings the nerves o' Labor sair,
> At's weary toil;
> Thou even brightens dark Despair
> Wi' gloomy smile!

For the day the regiment abandoned itself to a jubilee, in which Co. A seemed to lead, and though there were but nine men of them on this raid (the others having lost their horses in the battle of Chicamauga), their enjoyment appeared to be in the inverse ratio of their numbers, and for several hours they monopolized the business of "raising Cain," till at last every one of them got so limber drunk that he could neither stand nor sit, squeak nor squeal. Lieut. Barnes, in command of the squad, who had never tasted liquor before, and has never been known to taste it since, became as limber as the limberest.

We cannot forbear relating a little incident, as given by Capt. Glaze, in which he, Capt. Robinson and Adjt. Byrnes, were the actors. During the battle of Chicamauga a riderless horse came dashing into our lines from the direction of the enemy, which was fully equipped with saddle, bridle and officer's outfit. The three divided the prize amongst themselves. Adjt. Byrnes took the horse, and Capts. Robinson and Glaze divided between them the contents of the saddle-bags, which consisted of two changes of underclothing and a bottle of brandy. Capt. Robinson got the underclothes, and as he had no other way to carry them, decided to put them all on, and did so. From that time to this date he had no opportunity to wash, and, like old Ten Broeck, he wore four shirts and four pairs of pantaloons, counting each pair of drawers as a pair of tights. He had felt bundled up all the time, and on several occasions felt an uneasiness when awake, and in his dreams had been run over, stamped into the ground and horned and tossed in the air by ferocious herds of cattle, awaking in sweat and scratches of terror. He had grown pale and dejected. So on this day of rest and jollity he determined to bathe his flesh, take off his manifold suits and have some of the underclothes washed and aired. He took off one of his captured shirts and was astonished to find it so lively a garment. This induced him to slip off the twin rebel shirt, which was twice as lively as the first. The third shirt, one of Uncle Sam's veritable hog-hair texture, when taken off, and let go, was as lively as a wild boar of King Egbert's time. When the inner pair of drawers were taken off they raved like a wild wolf. "Creeping alive" was no name for this army of gray-backs that had colonized on Capt. Robinson. He was three times as lousy as any man in the regiment was ever known to be, and that is saying a great deal, for Jim Armstrong has been known to capture 120 at a single sitting. The Captain recovered slowly, but he always believed the horse bearing those underclothes was sent into our lines for the same purpose that the wooden horse was sent into Troy, and congratulated himself on defeating the project by his discovery of the fact, and by giving the graybacks as complete a defeat as we had just given their prototypes, Wheeler's forces. The Historian gives the foregoing as a specimen, and expresses it as a candid opinion that Capt. Robinson was pretty lice-entious at that time.

For our own part, we cannot call to mind any time in the service when rest and good living were so thoroughly enjoyed as at this time and place. As before mentioned, we were 150 miles from Chattanooga, without orders and with no possible chance of getting supplies from our commissaries.

On the 11th of October we marched toward Chattanooga steadily, and without anything worthy of note until the middle of the afternoon, when we went into camp east of Athens, and 20 miles from Rogersville. Our camp was near an old mill, on a beautiful stream of water. Col. Miller took possession of the mill and set it to grinding flour for our brigade, and the flour we got from this mill, together with plenty of pig and sweet potatoes, which abounded in that section, helped wonderfully to make life endurable. This was Sunday, hence we made but a Sabbath day's journey.

On Monday, the 12th, we moved due east through mud a foot deep, and camped at Huntsville.

On the 13th we started for Stevenson, but after going some distance learned that Rhoddy, with a small band of guerrillas, was raiding about through the country, and Col. Miller determined to break up the band, and consequently marched in the direction of Athens. On the 14th we moved toward Winchester. On the 15th we marched through Salem to near Winchester, then countermarched and camped near New Market. On the 17th we passed through Maysville to Brownsburg, a depot on the Memphis and Chattanooga Railroad. Failing to come up with Rhoddy at any time, we gave up the chase. The expedition, however, was not void of good results, as it taught Mr. Rhoddy that he must be more careful in conduct and distant in manners. It rained every day of this march.

As before stated, we had picked up a great many more horses on the Wheeler chase than we needed. Our manner was to always ride the best and lead the worst. When we got to Brownsburg the brigade had 1,000 more horses than men, and Col. Miller determined to have them sent to the railroad, at some point, and shipped back to Nashville, where they could be recruited up a little and made almost as good as fresh horses. Hence early on the morning of the 15th all the surplus horses in the brigade were mustered and a non-commissioned officer and enough men were detailed from each company to lead all the horses turned over by each company, and were sent to Decherd, 50 miles distant, and the nearest point on the railroad. The Seventy-Second turned over 350 horses, and each of the other regiments about as many, making a vast cavalcade. The whole expedition was placed under command of Capts. Thomson, D, and Kilborn, E. This expedition took place while the balance of the brigade went in pursuit of Rhoddy, guerrillas and bushwhackers.

It was the misfortune of the Historian to be on this detail, and as it proved five days of the hardest service we ever saw, we shall go somewhat into particulars. 1st. It had been raining very hard for several days before we started. 2d. It rained hard every day while we were on the trip. 3d. The soil in this country is as red as a brick, and when wet as sticky as tar. 4th. Each man had to lead three horses, besides guiding the one he was on. 5th. Fifty horses passing over a given piece of road, or ground, would tramp the ground into mud a foot deep and about as thin as batter for "flapjacks." Now suppose you start a thousand horses over such roads under such conditions. But you cannot realize the condition of things. You must have seen for yourself before you could possibly imagine the mud—mud—mud!! The mud was under us in rivers; it flew up from under the horses' feet in sheets, pouring up our breeches legs, up our coat sleeves, into our eyes, mouth, nose and hair; it flew high into the air and came down in a pelting shower of mud all the time. Men and horses were mud all over, and the whole long column looked like a lot of men and horses that had been made of mud and were running away from the factory before dried and baked. The sight was miserable, the feeling of it horrible. Each of the three horses being led would pull back as hard as it could, stretch out its neck and stick out its nose, and had to be almost pulled along by the leader. And what is meaner, more vexatious work than leading such a horse? This pulling made the horses to march obliquely, and as one file after another moved along in the same track they cut out four ditches side by side, each a foot deep, full of mud just thin enough to fly from the horses' feet 30 to 40 feet high, and just thick enough to stick The only reason that we were not smothered in mud is that a deluge of rain would pour upon us now and then and wash it off. Our cavalcade was full two miles long, and the pulling, whipping, hallooing and swearing, that were done as we dragged it through the mud and rain, would have done credit to a thousand Indiana ox-drivers breaking raw prairie. "The army swore terribly in Flanders, but nothing to this!" We made an average of about 20 miles a day by greatest exertions, and terrible wear and tear of body and piety. While marching through the day we had to forage for ourselves and all those horses. It makes us tired to think of, and write about, that distressing trip.

We were two and a half days getting to Decherd. A terrible spectacle met our eyes when we got there, which we relate to show what untold losses the Government sustained just for the want of a little attention to details. When we left Decherd, August 16th, to go over the mountains, our brigade had 700 convalescent horses which we did not want to take with us; so we hauled rails and fenced in a pasture of 100 acres, turned the horses into it, and left them. We supposed, of course, that they would be sent back to Nashville and cared for. But it seems that when we moved the whole army moved, and those horses were left in the pasture, had eaten up every green thing, and had died of starvation. We counted 200 carcasses inside of two acres of ground. We had seen numbers of dead horses at Nashville, Murfreesboro and other places, but nothing like this.

When we reached Decherd, with our mud-bespattered cavalcade, we moved out east, to our old camp we had left two months before; but the stench was so intolerable that we had to move further out. At this place we first met part of the 11th and 12th corps, under Gen. Hooker, who were on their way to the relief of our beseiged army at Chattanooga. They were fresh from the Army of the

Potomac, where they had been well supplied with everything that soldiers need, and had never missed a ration since in the service, and were complaining bitterly of their present hardships. This was fun for us, who had not seen a hard-tack for 10 days, and who knew that the army at Chattanooga was on the point of starvation.

We were so completely incased in mud that as we came from Winchester to Decherd, our troops actually thought we were "Johnnies" and were hardly restrained from firing on us. That night some of the 4th New Jersey stood picket near our camp, and took some pains in describing some of the terrible sufferings endured since leaving the Potomac, and among other things said they had not had a bit of butter for a week. We told them it was pretty rough to be without butter to grease the hard-tack so it could be swallowed without cutting the throat in furrows, but their failure to get it was, no doubt, owing to the fact that they were so constantly on the move; that when they got to Chattanooga they would "get dead loads" of butter. We state it as a fact, that we had but one pound of butter while in the service, and for that we paid one dollar.

When we saw what had become of the horses we left at Decherd in August, we thought it a poor chance for those we had brought, and feeling almost certain that if left they would perish, we turned about and returned with them to Brownsburg, where forage was abundant, and where we could feed them ourselves, if we could get the time to do it. We got back on the 20th. There were many thrilling incidents took place on this trip, but so much space has already been taken with it, that we mention but two.

On the 16th, while going up to Decherd, when near Salem, a party of guerrillas swooped down upon the rear of our column and captured Capt. Kilborn, of E, and three of his men. We were at the time moving north-east along the base of the Cumberland Mountains, and from the tops of the knobs these guerrillas could see our every movement. A wagon in the rear got stuck in the mud and Capt. Kilborn and his men stopped to get it out, and fell quite a distance behind, and the first thing they knew, were surrounded and captured. On request Capt. Kilborn has told the story of his capture and escape, so admirably, with the incidents that followed, that we here insert it just as he wrote it:

"The command left Huntsville, Ala., as we all thought to march to Stevenson, but at Maysville we received orders to send our wagons, sick men, led horses, and artillery, to Decherd, Tenn., and the rest of the command to move light, in hopes to intercept the rebel Gen. Rhoddy, who was reported fleeing from Gen. Mitchell. I was put in command of the convalescents of our brigade, and in company with Capt. Lilly, of our battery, and Capt. Stokes, of the Board of Trade battery, the latter in command of the whole detachment, we commenced our march. We camped that night in a small town named New Market, which was said to be a noted rendezvous for bushwhackers.

"In the morning I got the command ready to start, when, just at the time of leaving, I was informed by the Surgeon that one of our prisoners, a rebel Captain, was too sick to be taken farther. Capt. Stokes desired me to parole him and leave him. Detaining a Sergeant and two men, I stayed behind to attend to this duty, and was just leaving the place in some haste, under the friendly admonition of an old negress, who said to me, "You'd bettah git out o' heah, lots o' bushwhacka's round," when I found one of my wagons, containing two saddles and several Spencer rifles, abandoned in the mud.

"I could not bear the thought of leaving these loaded Spencer rifles for the bushwhackers, and so sent one of my men to turn back the teamster, and then hasten on to the command and bring back a squad of men for assistance in case of need. The teamster soon returned, and we got the wagon out of the mud and started on our way. About three miles from New Market we had to pass a strip of woods; I rode ahead, and, as I thought, carefully examined the woods. I noticed the fence down in a number of places, but thought nothing of this, as it was a very common thing, but could see nothing of any enemy. A thick undergrowth prevented my seeing far into the woods, however. I galloped back to the Sergeant and his men who were coming on slowly with the wagon, and told them it was all right. I fully expected to meet the man I had sent on to the command, with a detachment of men, by the time I reached this wood. There were of us, myself, a Sergeant of the 98th Illinois, named Wetherell, one private, my colored servant, named Aleck, and the colored teamster. It was raining quite hard, and the men had their rubber ponchos on, and their guns carefully covered by them to keep them dry. We had passed but a short distance beyond the point where the woods came down to the road, when eight rebels, three in front and five in rear, each with a cocked pistol in his hand, dashed into the road and demanded our surrender. I took in the situation at a glance. They had 48 shots, we had 20. Their weapons were in their hands, ours under our ponchos, while they were at our very sides. It seemed useless to fight, and I threw up my hands in token of surrender. The moment the excitement was over I felt deeply chagrined, and wheeled my horse's head, determined to attempt escape, when one of the rebels put a cocked pistol to my breast, and with an oath told me to "*jest try that.*" They turned off into the woods, and after dividing our pistols and some other articles among themselves, three were put in charge of the wagon and prisoners and the remainder went off to try to capture four more of our men of whom they had heard. The whole party were under the charge of a Lieutenant of the 4th Alabama regiment, rebel cavalry. No words can express the chagrin and mortification I felt at thus being captured, without having fired a shot. Gloomy visions of Andersonville flitted through my mind and I resolved to lose no opportunity of escape. Noticing that the guard by my side seemed to carry his carbine very carelessly, I purposely allowed the wagon to get some distance in advance, and the guard in my rear had also lagged some distance behind. I made a sudden grab for the carbine of my guard and tried to wrench it from him; but he held it firmly, and soon brought the rear guard to his aid, and I was fain to give up the attempt. With many bitter curses and a torrent of vile epithets heaped upon me, I was made to exchange my fine gray mare for the poor rack-o'-bones of my guard. I considered myself lucky to escape so easily, and went on my way, feeling, as the "boys" often expressed it, "glad that I was alive."

"Perhaps I ought to say, in honor to my guard on this memorable occasion, that I talked to him like a father, and we were soon very good friends; and he declared he did uot blame me for trying to escape, and after a while frankly begged my pardon for having applied such abusive language to me.

"We were taken, without further incident, to the house of the father of one Lieut.-Col. Hambrick, of the 4th Alabama Cavalry, situated in what is called Hurricane Valley. After a while three other prisoners were brought in, among them the man I had sent forward for help. We were treated kindly and given a good supper, but closely guarded. Col. Hambrick seemed to be home on a furlough, and as I learned was trying to get together a number of the men and some of the officers of his regiment who were over in this section without leave, and were carrying on a kind of guerrilla warfare, principally for personal profit. During the evening one of the young men brought in one of our Spencer rifles containing its seven charges. After trying all round to load it, he stepped towards me saying, "Perhaps the Captain will show us how to use it." Just as I reached out my hand to take it, the young man who had been my guard in the woods sprang forward and caught the rifle, exclaiming "Not by a d—d sight; we don't want none o' *his* showin'." Thus was lost what a moment before I had hoped would be my second chance for escape. With that seven-shooter in my hands, I had felt certain I could defy them all. We were put in a room and guarded for the night. I proposed to the boys to try for an escape that night, but reflecting that they would be released any way in the morning, I told them I would not ask them to imperil their lives for me, and concluded to bide my time and trust to my own resources.

"In the morning Lieut.-Col. Hambrick said he supposed I was too much of a gentleman to give a parole the terms of which I knew would not be respected, and he would therefore be compelled to send me across the river. My men were turned loose, and all returned safely to the command. I bade them good bye with a heavy heart, and under the charge of two quite youthful rebels, started to cross the Tennessee River, and go to Andersonville. As we rode away, my guard of the previous day yelled after the boys, "Now you keep a sharp eye on that Captain." Amid all my chagrin at my ignoble capture, and my gloomy forebodings of Andersonville, it was some little consolation to feel that one man, at least, was fully fixed in the belief that I was no coward.

"Left to myself, I now set to studying my guards to determine my best means of escape. They were only boys, one 17 and the other 14 years old. Both had run away from home to enter the rebel service, The younger one was the son of a wealthy secessionist in Louisville, Ky. He ran off from home a year before, went first to John Morgan, was rejected by him as too young, and then drifted farther south, and finally joined the 4th Alabama. The elder one I do not remember much about. Both were sprightly boys, naturally kind hearted, quite companionable, seemed to take quite a fancy to me, insisted that I seemed more like a Southern man than a Yankee, and earnestly urged me to desert the Yankee cause, and go back with them and join their free and easy party. I soon learned that they were heartily sick of regular rervice, though quite well pleased with their present mode of warfare; and that they dreaded nothing more than crossing the Tennessee River, where they would at once be put to regular service with their regiment. I found them exceedingly watchful, but soon became convinced that it was not so much to prevent my escape, as in hope of having a good pretext for shooting me and so avoid the necessity of crossing the river and joining their regular command. They were not sufficiently hardened to shoot me in cold blood, but if I would just make an attempt to escape, then they would feel not only justified in taking my life, but would glory in the deed. Believing that I read them aright, and that any show of a forcible attempt to escape would only result in instant death, I determined to try working upon their feelings, and bribery first.

"It had rained incessantly for days, and all the little streams were very high. The air was thick with rumors of "Yanks" in every direction also. These things caused us to go through many by-ways, foot-paths, and devious windings, through the day. We passed the house of the father of Frank Gurley, the man who shot Gen. McCook, in '62, and the spot where his own house had once stood. Ashes and a chimney only marked the place now. The boys told me confidentially that Capt. Gurley was in the neighborhood then. We took supper at the house of a rebel, about half past four o'clock, and again started on our way. The recent rains had swollen all the streams, and we were informed that Paint Rock Creek, which it was necessary to cross to reach the ferry across the Tennessee, was very high, and probably could not be passed for several days. I saw that this and the rumors of "Yanks" in every direction made the boys very uneasy, and after supper I at once opened negotiations for release. It was finally agreed that I should exchange coats with them, and give them my watch, a new Waltham, for which I had paid $10 a short time before, and in return I should be allowed to take my course up the railroad toward Stevenson. The boys assured me there were no bridges burned, and a little after 5 p. m. I bade my guards good-bye and with a light heart started for Stevenson, distant as I learned by the first mile-stone 45 miles.

"The sky was overspread with clouds, the rain soon began to fall in torrents, the night set in dark and gloomy, only lighted now and then by the lurid glare of the lightning. Still I trudged cheerfully on my way until, as nearly as I could guess, about 10 o'clock, when I came to Paint Rock Creek. To my dismay I found the bridge burned, at least the most important part of it. The flash of the lightning revealed the rails fastened together by the chairs through which they had been spiked to the ties, extending across a gap of some 20 feet over the centre of the stream; one side entire, the other parted in the middle. On either side of this naked gap, the half-burned sleepers on which the ties rested extended out some 10 or 15 feet from the part of the bridge yet unburned. Here and there a partially burned tie still hung by the chairs, sometimes to one, sometimes to both rails. It seemed a perilous undertaking to try to cross on that single entire rail. Below was a rushing, roaring torrent, not less than twenty feet deep, and I was no swimmer, and in case of precipitation into the flood, could depend on nothing but the iron rail to float me on its surface. I believed that behind me were rebels, and probably Andersonville before me, and across this perilous bridge, was Stevenson and freedom. I hesitated but a few moments, and then got astride of the entire rail and carefully slid along its surface. It swayed and creaked, and bent well down when I reached the middle, but the chairs held to their places and I gradually ascended the further side, and finally breathed freely as I reached the half-burned sleeper, and a little further on found the abutment to the bridge, sprang to my feet, and eagerly and joyously proceeded on my way.

"No further incident occurred until about one o'clock in the morning. when my ears were saluted by the challenge, "Halt! Who goes there?" I feared I was again about to fall into the hands of the enemy, but I determined to risk the chances, and so replied to the challenge, was soon taken charge of by the guard and marched to headquarters. Believing them to be rebels of Rhoddy's command, I represented myself to be cut off from Wheeler, and trying to get across the river and rejoin my command. The Corporal of the guard quietly told me he guessed I had got into the "wrong nest," but I held my peace until I was reported to the commanding officer. This I found to be Capt. Barth, of the 28th Kentucky. I had papers about me which soon satisfied him as to my identity, and I was furnished comfortable quarters, of which I gladly availed myself for the rest of the night. I had walked 23 miles in about seven hours.

"On the morning of the 16th, Capt. Barth furnished me a squad of a Sergeant and eight men, put eight prisoners captured at this point under my charge, and we set out for Stevenson. Arrived, I went at once to the quartermaster, exchanged my rebel gray for Union blue, and then reported to Gen. Hooker. The General desired me to tell of my adventures, to which he listened very kindly, and then gave me permission to retire.

"On the morning of the 18th I learned that a train was to be sent down the road with provisions for our command. I was soon on board, and found the newly appointed Chaplain of our regiment among those going down. After numerous delays in building burned culverts and bridges, we reached Paint Rock Creek in the afternoon of the 18th. The rails on which I had crossed the burned bridge had fallen into the stream. I was informed by a man living on the bank that they fell about four o'clock on the morning after I crossed.

"On the 19th details from the command began to come for rations, and as soon as it was known who I was, I was cordailly received by all. I stayed with Maj. Patton, of the 1st Ohio Cavalry, that night, and on the morning of the 20th we started for camp. We met the detail from our brigade on the way, and they cheered me vociferously. I reported to Gen. Crook about noon. He received me kindly, and told me he would like to have me go out and try to "take in" some of the fellows who infested that country.

"I went across to my regiment and was warmly received by all, from the Colonel down. I had been reported dead. I found my colored boy Aleck had also escaped his captors, and had told them ever since his return to camp, "dem boys would neber take Cap'n 'cross de riber." Determined to act at once upon the information I had gained during my captivity, I took six men and started out about dark in quest of Gurley. I was dressed in my rebel grey, except pantaloons, and played rebel on secesh people, anxiously seeking Gurley to cross the river with him, and get away from the "Yanks." All advised me to cross the river at once, as the "Blue Bellies were thick around there," but protested they knew nothing of the slayer of Gen. McCook. We finally lay down for the night in an old barn, belonging to the man with whom I and my guards took supper a few evenings before. I had the boys out about four in the morning, and went around and searched old man Gurley's house. We found nothing and learned nothing there. I was about to give up in despair, and return to camp, when I saw a horse by an old house, about a quarter of a mile from the road. I hid my men among some trees and went to examine the house. I peeped through a crevice and saw one man in rebel uniform, and heard him speak to another. I hastily returned to the road, tied my horses, stationed all my men but one so as to cut off retreat, and then throwing off my rebel garments, so as to take no unfair advantage, I took one man and went cautiously around to the door. Both were sitting in the door, and were taken by surprise. The younger of the two surrendered at once; the other, however, made a rush for the timber; my men at once opened fire upon him, nda he fell down in the grass and bellowed loudly that he was shot, and begged them to stop shooting. He was secured, and our prisoners proved to be no less personages than Capt. Frank Gurley and his brother, Lieut. Thomas P. Gurley. I took them to camp and reported to Gen. Crook, who warmly thanked me for my services, and as the capture of Gurley was considered quite an exploit, it effectually silenced those who had been disposed to question my courage in allowing myself to be captured, and for quite a while I found myself the lion of the camp, in a small way.

"The Surgeon of the 98th Illinois, who had been quite decided in his condemnation of my conduct, came to me, acknowledged his error, and told me he had thought I had fully vindicated my courage. There remains but little more to be said. Gurley was sent north, had a trial for murder, I believe, but proved himself to have been in legitimate service at the time of his killing McCook, was exchanged, and since the war has been Democratic Sheriff of his county several terms.

"The command lay in camp at Maysville about a month. During that time I made it too hot for the guerrillas to rest in the Hurricane Valley. I recaptured my wagon, saddles, Spencer rifles, more than twice as many revolvers as I lost, and nearly 20 of the gang that had been bushwhacking through all that region, a number of them being of the party that captured me. My men lived on the fat of the land, yet I gained the good will of the citizens, for I never allowed them abused, and I always gave them receipts for what I took for my men. Quite an amusing incident occurred on my first return to New Market after my escape. I had shaved off my whiskers, so as to be somewhat disguised should I fall in the hands of those who had had me prisoner before; and had directed my men to call me by my given name. I called upon the old negress who had advised me to get away from there, and asked her about bushwhackers. She told me the story of my capture, and "spected likely 'nuff dey'd killed dat Capt'n." I asked her if he looked any like me. She replied, "No, he was a heap taller and had great black whiskers."

"I now look back upon those scenes, and rough, wild adventures, with half regretful memory. But often in my reveries, by the lurid lightning's glare I see the dark roll of the waters of Paint Rock, hear their mad rush below me, and the hoarse creaking of the iron rails as they bend at the joints under my weight, and a shudder passes over me as I think of the dear ones at home, and strain my eyes to catch through the darkness a glimpse of the charred and blackened timbers on the other side."

We have spoken of the rain, and something of its volume can be imagined when we say that there were seven full days and nights that we had not a dry stitch of clothing on us. We have spoken of the mud. When we left the Tennessee River, just three weeks ago, we were ordered to move light, and consequently left our tents, knapsacks and blankets. Now, if you know anything of the affinity of "graybacks" for filth and dirt—and we take it for granted you do from what we have said on previous pages—you can have a slight idea of how these vermin sported and rioted over us in shoals and oceans. They were colonized in every seam of our clothing, and made every loose thread pulsate like an artery of life. They even had colonies of millions planted in the double soles of our pantaloons, between us and our saddles, where any other creatures, even wood-ticks, would have been ground to powder; but the graybacks flourished in that heated seat of action.

We say it rained, but not all the time; between showers the sun would come out as hot as midsummer, and set the everlasting graybacks cantering up and down our backs like a herd of buffalo playing on the western plains. Then you should have seen our boys, officers and men—for graybacks, like death, put all on an equality—begin to "scrooch" up their shoulders, twist and wriggle, and contort their faces. Ordinary scratching was nothing. And finally, unable to stand it any longer, the head of column would halt, every fellow leap from his horse, throw off coat and vest, draw his hog-hair shirt, and begin skirmishing for the biggest ones. The skirmish would grow into a regular battle, with each fellow beating his shirt against a tree until the sound was almost as terrific as an actual engagement. To witness such an engagement, the Union forces stripped to the waist, was very interesting; to engage in it was quite exciting and satisfactory—indeed, a luxury which the itch-loving King would have enjoyed.

On the 23d of October our new Chaplain, Rev. Isaac De La Matyr, joined us. He was a fine old Presbyterian minister from Thorntown, Ind. Since the sad death of Chaplain Eddy at Hoover's Gap we had been without a Chaplain. We were delighted to find Chaplain De La Matyr all that a devoted Christian minister should be, and all that a faithful Chaplain could be. The office of Chaplain, in a volunteer regiment, is a very delicate and difficult one to fill; indeed, we may say, it is the most difficult office to fill acceptably there is in the regiment. In all the other offices the officer knows just what his duties are, for they are defined by regulation; the men of the regiment also look upon all other officers as necessary to the service. The moral conduct of officers, as long as they remain faithful and brave in the line of military duty, gives them no inconvenience by bringing them into contempt. A Chaplain has little of this definite duty laid down. He is looked upon by nearly all as an officer who can be dispensed with without injury to the service, and by many officers and men, in many regiments, the Chaplain was looked upon as a useless, salary-absorbing appendage. A Chaplain, to be of any use to a regiment, and to have a standing amongst officers and men, must have the best qualities of a man, a soldier and a Christian. He must be brave; the brave volunteer soldier will excuse no one for being a coward—except, perhaps, a mule-driver. The Chaplain is not expected or asked to go in the fore-front of the battle; no soldier wants to see a Chaplain or Surgeon in unnecessary danger; but if, as his regiment marches up to take place before the enemy, the Chaplain falls back rapidly as the first shot from the enemy's battery shrieks over his head, or the first rattling musketry is heard on the skirmish, he might just as well send in his resignation and go home; the men who see him beat a hasty retreat at the first signal of danger will hold him in lasting contempt, will doubt his Christianity and his manhood, and will mock at his prayers and sermons. All the brave soldier expects of a Chaplain at such a crisis is, that he will follow his regiment far enough into danger to know where it is stationed, and keep near enough to render aid to the wounded and dying; and this they rightfully expect and demand of him—as rightfully as they expect the colonel, brigade and other commanders, to keep near enough to them to know all about their manœuvres and to direct them. To take such a position often requires the Chaplain to be under fire for a long time, and to be in a place of exposure throughout a hard-fought battle. With the display of such quiet bravery on the field a Chaplain lays a solid foundation for the highest respect; for it is instinctive with men to believe that a true Christian is a truly brave man when his duty calls to face danger, and to believe that a coward is no Christian. After bravery on the field, a Chaplain must be pure in his language and morals. Others may swear, and be obscene, and behave immorally, but the Chaplain never; if he does he is in contempt. He must also be generous, ready to divide all he has with a soldier in need—or more, ready to give all, if all is necessary. Volunteer soldiers are the most generous men in the world to both friend and foe; they hate the least selfishness in man or officer, and detest it in a Chaplain; for, again, instinctively they know that a Christian should be generous, and if a Chaplain is not generous he is no Christian—he is a craven and a hypocrite, and the most detestable of men. A Chaplain must be industrious. We speak not of the number of times he preaches or prays, but of his industry in looking after the many wants of the men of his regiment or his brigade (for Chaplain De La Matyr had a brigade). There are wounded and sick men who need attentions that the surgeon cannot give. They want letters written; they want words of cheer or comfort; they want many delicate attentions which they will gladly accept from a Chaplain whom they hold in esteem. With such duties he can employ his time, do great service for his men and his country, establish for himself a firm standing in his command, and be as popular as any officer in the service. The Editor knew a great many Chaplains, and their fortunes in the service, and will give a few incidents illustrating the foregoing remarks:

A Chaplain came to a certain regiment with the reputation of being an able orator. He was quite a florid speaker, and at first the men and officers of his regiment liked to hear him preach. He held himself in high esteem and wished to be solid at headquarters, and thither he repaired daily and spent most of his time in competing with others who assembled there in telling yarns. The hospitals were full of sick and dying men, who longed in their sufferings for some good Christian man to bend over them and speak comforting words to them as they died, away from their homes and loved ones; some one who could hear their last words of faith and love, write them in a letter, and send them home as a priceless treasure, an unspeakable comfort to mother, wife and children. Men were sick in company tents whose groans this professed follower of Him who healed the sick and helped the afflicted could hear every day; yet he gave them little attention, but stuck to his loafing and yarning. In three weeks he was in utter contempt, was called nicknames, was mocked at when he prayed and preached on Sundays, and soon had to go home as a failure. We knew another Chaplain, who had a regiment composed of the bravest and solidest of soldiers. He had two horses—one to ride and one to carry all his "traps." He had a little negro boy to take care of himself and horses and do all his chores. He worried along with his regiment a year, long before the expiration of which he was hated and despised, and for many months neither preached nor prayed. One day his regiment was marching to take its place in line of battle, moving in column up a road through a forest. Suddenly a 32-pounder solid shot dashed through the tree tops, mowing them like a reaper in its flight. The Chaplain was near the head of column with his little darkey when the ball sped over. He grew pale, turned his horse squarely about, and dashed back to the rear with his little darkey following on the pack-horse, the pans and camp-kettles, on which the darkey rode, rattling and banging like an old-fashioned *charivari*. The regiment set up a yell of derision, which was taken up by all the soldiers as he flew down the road, almost running over some. Of course, he never appeared in official capacity again, and speedily resigned.

We knew many other Chaplains who by pursuing the proper course gained a high standing. Such a Chaplain was Rev. Isaac De La Matyr. Brave, generous, kind, industrious, pious without ostentation, grave without austerity, genial and social without meanness—he soon gained and held to the last the confidence and love of every man. He stuck to us through thick and thin, and was mustered out with the regiment.

About the 25th of October we sent all our pack-mules up to Stevenson for rations, and they returned on the 26th with some crackers, just 20 days from the time we drew three days' rations at Murfreesboro. On October 30th Col. Miller, commanding the Lightning Brigade, received the following order from Gen. Geo. H, Thomas:

"*Colonel:*—I have just telegraphed the authorities at Washington that I would hold Chattanooga or starve. When doing that I allowed you to protect the right of my line and guard the river from Bridgeport to Decatur, Alabama. I know your lines will be over a hundred miles long, and that your horses and men are much fatigued and have been separated from your wagon train for over a month—all of which I take into notice. Knowing your former zeal and integrity,

"I remain yours,

"GEO. H. THOMAS, Maj. Gen'l,

"Com'd'g Army of Cumberland."

The events to follow show how wisely the confidence of the Great General was placed in Col. Miller. The country was still full of bushwhackers, who were constantly picking up our men and killing them after captured, and it was necessary to send out scouting parties every day to punish the desperadoes.

On October 31st our trains came up to us with knapsacks, tents and blankets. It had been a full month since we had a change of clothes or a chance to wash the ones we had on. Never did poor, lice-ridden mortals, enjoy clean clothing more than we did. Our camp at Brownsburg was in a very beautiful place on the Flint River, but was in the bottom and liable to be overflowed at any time. As the order from Gen. Thomas indicated that we might remain in this vicinity for some time, we removed camp to Maysville, two miles north of Brownsburg, as soon as our trains came up. Here we again got a most delightful place for a camp, and immediately went to work to put up comfortable quarters; we erected neat cabins, covered them with our tents, built chimneys to them, and fixed them up quite home-like and comfortable. In such work as this the soldier who has been on the move for months takes a real delight. Some members of Company D excelled all others in building one house of very large proportions and convenient appointments, and, as preaching and prayer meetings were frequently held in it, the boys called it the Chapel.

From this place our convalescent horses were sent to Nashville. Those who took them of course had a hard time of it, but a good deal of fun, too.

After the rebel Gen. Bragg adopted the starving-out strategy to finish the destruction of our army, so well begun at Chicamauga, he began to make efforts to get as much live stock, provisions and forage out of this rich country as he possibly could, and while we lay at Brownsburg his men were constantly employed in getting stock and forage across the Tennessee River. To stop this work of the rebels a detail from the Seventy-Second was sent on the 12th of November to destroy all the boats along the river that we could capture. This detail reached the river at Whitesburg just in time to see the "Johnnies" start across it with a boat load of hogs. As the rebels had got so far out into the river that it was impossible to get them back, we fired into the boat until we killed all the hogs, and also did very fatal work to the rebels. We then moved down the river to Decatur, taking all the boats we could find with us. At one place we saw some boats on the other side picketed by some armed rebels. Without knowing how strong the rebels were, 15 or 20 of our boys got into boats, went across the river, had a lively skirmish with the pickets, drove them away, captured the boats, and brought them over safely. When we reached the mouth of Limestone Creek, below Mooresville, we had 25 to 30 boats, of all sizes from a skiff to a large flatboat, all of which had been used to carry forage across to the rebels. We destroyed them all. This expedition was quite successful.

As long as we lay at Maysville there were parties of rebels in Huntsville—which was 12 miles west—every day. A mountain range ran between the two places. The mountains were close to Huntsville, to which place we sent scouting parties nearly every day, at whose approach the rebels would scamper up into the mountains, look down on our boys until they left the neighborhood, and then come down and go back into the town and stay until the next Union scouting party was announced. Several times our men had lively and exciting chases after these rebels, but as they were real mountain goats the chases were not often repaid by their capture.

On the 12th of November came again the joyful period of being paid off, and as four months pay was due us, and we got it all, there must be the usual joy and jubilee in camp, and "squaring up" all around. The chuckaluck men ran like mills with a fresh head of water; but most of the money was used to good purpose, and the longest half sent home to those who needed it, with letters breathing love and hopes for the future.

At this time the Government had begun the experiment of making soldiers of negroes. This made quite a change in the general treatment of negroes by the soldiers of our brigade. From the time our regiment had landed at Lebanon, Kentucky, negroes had flocked to our camps wherever we had marched, and upon the least encouragement would stick to us and do all kinds of labor and drudgery. They had also been kindly treated by the men of the Seventy-Second. From the time we left Frankfort there had always been an average of five negroes to the company, and while we were not allowed to draw rations for them we freely shared with them, the best we had, considering that they paid well for their board and clothes in the many hardships they relieved us of. We have had occasion to speak of the very wearisome work of leading pack-mules and horses. The negroes relieved us of that exhausting work, and also did our cooking beside. However, our officers always discouraged their coming into camp, as there were many times when we could not get enough to eat ourselves, to say nothing of enough for the negroes. More than once strict orders were issued to keep them out of camp, but the negroes well understood the cause of the war, most of them had heard of the Emancipation Proclamation of the President, clearly anticipated the result of the contest, and they could not be kept out, for they came in spite of orders. It was as natural for them to flock to the Stars and Stripes, wherever unfurled, as for children in a storm to run home to mother and father; and when they came our officers could no more find it in their hearts to drive the poor things away than mother or father could to drive children forth from their home into a driving storm. When they came they stayed, and managed some way to live. But now a happy change of policy for the negroes took place, and they were invited to come into camp.

To illustrate the great change which had taken place in less than a year in the feelings of many soldiers as to arming the negroes, we relate an incident that occurred while lying at Murfreesboro, soon after the Emancipation Proclamation was issued, and at the time the arming of the negroes was first discussed. A teamster detailed from Co. G came to the tent of Lieut. Jewell, bowed his head, looked in and said: "Well, Lieutenant, I hear they are gwine to put niggers in the rig'ment—how 'bout it?" "There is some talk of it," was the reply. "Well, when that's done I want to go home. I didn't come out to have myself mixed up on a eequal'ty with niggers," said the grave and dignified mule-driver. "Well, you needn't be mixed with them; there are 10 or 12 men from G on detail duty, and you are one of them. That's about as many negroes as will be sent to Company G, and when they come we will order you men back to the company to take your muskets, and detail the negroes to take the teams you now have," said the Lieutenant. The stately driver walked slowly towards his mules in the rear of the regiment, with his head bowed in thought. Presently he came back, quietly opened the folds of the tent, peered in, and said: "See 'ere, Lieutenant; I don't care a cent if niggers is put in the rig'ment. I'm useter to the mules than I am to the musket, and I guess I won't resign. Jist give one o'.them niggers my gun when he comes."

This prejudice, so strong in the Union army and amongst Union people one year ago, was now all gone, and the arming of the negroes was so popular that it was almost an enthusiasm. It proved an unfortunate move for many of us, however, for almost every mess in the regiment had a faithful negro to whom the men had become attached, and would as soon have thought of turning out one of their bunk-mates as one of these faithful fellows. But the very first opportunity these noble black men had they went into the army as soldiers for the Union, and our sorrow at parting with them was as genuine as their loyalty and manhood. There were thousands of negroes in Northern Alabama, and as soon as they learned that the Government would accept them as soldiers they came flocking into our camp, and were delighted on finding that they would really be enlisted to fight for Uncle Sam and "Massah Linkum." This readiness of the negroes to become soldiers exalted their manhood in the estimation of the Union soldiers; for, as before said, the volunteer soldier's great and final test of manhood was bravery to face the enemy. When a man had real bravery, whatever his rank or color, the volunteer soldier respected him.

There were two regiments of negroes gathered up and enlisted by the Seventy-Second while lying at Maysville, and for these two regiments Indiana ought to have credit, but we think Ohio had a recruiting agent down there with us, and they were credited to that State. Their camp was near us, and we used to frequently go over and see them, and we think we saw amongst them more enjoyment to the square inch in their dances than we ever saw amongst any other people; and more fervent devotion than was manifest at their prayer meetings and preaching was never exhibited in pulpit or pew. And their singing—well, it seemed that it might charm the very birds of the air—so earnest, so pathetic, so weird, and withal so grandly rugged and yet harmonious. On Sunday the colored women, for miles and miles around, would come into "dem meetin's," and on such days there was one song they used to sing, the chorus of which was:

"Gwine down in de valley on my knees for to pray;"

which was peculiarly impressive and solemn, reaching to and thrilling the hearts of singers and listeners. It seemed the sweetest, saddest music, we ever heard, and still rings in our ears as the notes of a solemn bell just struck and still vibrating. We have seen nearly all denominations worship God, but have seen none who so fervently threw both soul and body into it as did those negroes. To them, indeed, the "Kingdom had come, an' de year ob Jubilo!" 'Twas a grand period when "God was marching on," and with his almighty arm of justice smiting the oppressor and letting the oppressed go free; a period which will rank in history with the liberation of the children of Israel from the bondage of Egypt. It was one of those great epochs when the groaning slave becomes a citizen and a soldier, and takes up arms in the name of the God of Justice against his oppressors. The grand enthusiasm of the transition from bondage to freedom did no more powerfully thrill and stir the souls of the children of Israel, on that morning when the sun arose over the surges of the Red Sea and the billows of that sea rolled over the lifeless forms of Pharaoh and his hosts—when Miriam took the timbrel and led in that song of triumph:

"Sound, sound the loud timbrel, out o'er the Red Sea,
Jehovah has triumphed, his people are free!"

—than did the same spirit of God and pulsations of new birth thrill the souls of those men and women who had just crossed the Red Sea of Bondage. Like the children of Israel, their songs, their prayers, their very dances, were full of religious enthusiasm—full of effort to express a new-found and great joy. Those whom God permitted to see those days and those scenes had before their eyes a splendid testimony of His being, and of His presence and power in human government to smite the wrong and help the right. Let the reader note that from the time the resolution was made to arm the negroes, and firmly adhered to, no great disaster befell our arms.

We were near a very large cotton field, and many of us who had never seen the like had an opportunity of seeing the much-heard-of operation of cotton picking—not by slaves, but by freemen who had learned the art while slaves at the end of the task-master's whip. It was really interesting to see how dextrously they emptied the pods of their contents.

CHAPTER XXV.

From November 16th to January 28th, 1864—Men Sent Home to Recruit—Success of Lieut. Brown and Others—Detailed Men all Come Back—Splendid Health of the Regiment—Extensive Foraging—Sergt. Sigars Killed—A Fight by Moonlight—Surrounded—A Big Drove of Hogs, Horses, Sheep, Mules and Negroes—From Maysville to Huntsville—Big Chapel and Comfortable Quarters—Taking Prisoners to Chattanooga—Capt. Thomson and Comrades go to the Battle-Field, Find and Bury the Bodies of Cain and Campbell—Move From Huntsville to Pulaski—March through Rain and Mud—Vexations of Going into Camp in Darkness and Rain—Start on a Four Days' Scout in a Fearful Storm—The Four Days Lengthened to Three Months—Cold New Year and Great Suffering—Veteran Fever—New Recruits Arriving—We Move Back to Huntsville—Battle and Victory near Florence—Attack on Athens—Gallant Conduct of Capt. Robinson and the Seventy-Second—Col. Miller Compliments the Captain, the Seventy-Second and the New Recruits.

On the 16th of November a man from each company in the Seventy-Second was detailed and sent home to recruit for the regiment. It had gained a good and extensive reputation, and the men were all successful in recruiting. Each was rewarded by a commission as a company officer, or as a non-commissioned officer, according to his success in recruiting. Lieut.-Col. Kirkpatrick went home with this detail. As most of the recruits made good soldiers, whose service was highly appreciated by the regiment, we should like to make honorable mention of all those who helped to fill our depleted ranks; but want of space compels a single case to be taken as representative of all. Company K, it will be remembered, when the other companies of the regiment were mustered, was not full, and remained at Indianapolis for two weeks to fill up; and was finally mustered with 82 men rank and file, being a less number than was in any other company of the regiment. Geo. W. Brown, who had just finished a full medical course, was one of the privates of K. As soon as he arrived at Lebanon, Ky., he was detailed for duty in the hospital, but deserted his post in the hospital to take part in our first march from that place, with his gun on his shoulder. He continued on duty with his company until the regiment got to Frankfort, Ky., where he was detailed by special order from Gen. Dumont to duty in general hospital at that place. While in this service he performed a *post mortem* examination, by order of Surgeon Morrow, in which he received a dissecting wound resulting in *septicæmia* and partial loss of the use of his right arm.

He remained in hospital service until just before the Tullahoma campaign, when he was detailed to the Quartermaster's department, and assigned to duty with Capt. Preston, where he remained until sent home as one of the detail above named, to recruit for Company K. His affable and genial manners made him a favorite with the young men wherever he went, and in a short time he recruited 76 men for the regiment. This was, of course, enough to entitle him to a Captain's commission. He had been previously commissioned as First Lieutenant, and as soon as there was a vacancy, made by the resignation of James B. Davis, of K, he was assigned to the place. As soon as relieved of his recruiting duty, Lieut. Brown reported to his company, and took command in the absence of Capt. McIntyre, who was wounded at Chicamauga, and was with it in every move, skirmish and battle participated in by the regiment to the close of the war. On the resignation of Capt. McIntyre, Lieut. Brown was promoted to the Captaincy of K. As an officer he was brave, and trusted by his company and superiors; as a man he was generous and held in high esteem by all. He was kind and considerate to his men, and no company in the regiment kept more men ready for duty than K. From being the last and the least in the regiment, under the command of Capt. Brown it became one of the best; and on its last muster showed, what no other company did, that there were 101 men, rank and file, on the rolls—which was the outside limit allowed by the regulations—and that there were 12 more men assigned to this company than could be taken by it.

The result of the work of those sent home from other companies was: Company A, 33 recruits; B, 34; C, 26; D, 26; E, 30; F, 33; G, 25; H, 14; I, 29; K, 45; and 42 unassigned—that is, it was not known at the Adjutant General's office which of the companies they went into, some going into one and some into another; some did not reach the regiment at all until it came back to Nashville to be mustered out, and then they were assigned to the 44th regiment with the other recruits.

The battery of mountain howitzers has been mentioned, which was manned by details from the Regiment and attached to the brigade, under the command of Sergt. Eli W. Anderson, Company I, of the Seventy-Second. We have also mentioned that "Major" Anderson was severely wounded at Chicamauga. The result of his wound was his discharge from the service, and the result of his discharge the disbandment of the battery, the men reporting to their companies while we lay at Maysville. At Murfreesboro there was also a detail of two men from each company, to serve with Capt. Lilley's 18th Indiana battery; they were also relieved and reported back at this place. We have also noticed that Company H joined us at the same place, on November 5th. So all there was left of the regiment was together once more.

We were encamped in one of the most beautiful places in the world, and had plenty of wholesome food, gathered from the surrounding rich country—pigs, chickens, onions, potatoes, dried fruit, etc.; with sugar, coffee and salt, and just enough hard-tack and s. b. to fall back on, in case of an emergency. Our rations had all to be hauled in wagons from Stevenson, 35 miles distant, and it was only intended to keep us in full rations of sugar, coffee and salt, and one-fourth rations of hard-tack. The men were all in excellent health and as fat as pigs. We had not heard the sick call since leaving Murfreesboro in last June; and with the exception of a few cases of varioloid and small-pox, there was not a sick man in the Lightning Brigade, and we were all lightning on victuals as well as on the war path.

It is worthy of remark that small-pox was often in the regiment or brigade, yet we lost few men from it; while measles were rare, and yet, when they did attack the soldiers, they died like sheep with the dry rot.

Gen Thomas' order had made it our duty to guard the Tennessee River, from Stevenson to Decatur. As the starving process of Gen. Bragg began to tell on our army at Chattanooga, Gen. Thomas began repairs on the railroad from Stevenson down into this very rich country, that he might have some of the vast amount of supplies, in which it abounded, shipped to Chattanooga for his army. As soon as it was repaired as far as Brownsburg, near our camp, we were ordered to go out at once and gather up all the cattle, sheep, hogs, and negroes too, that we could find, and bring them in. In obedience to this order, on the morning of November 18th the Seventy-Second and the 123d Illinois moved early for Huntsville with orders to press in everything that could possibly be of any service to the rebels, or that would do us any good. After passing through Huntsville our command broke up into squads, the more thoroughly to scour the country, each squad having orders to camp at Whitesburg, on the river, nine miles south of Huntsville. Whitesburg is the landing place on the Tennessee for everything destined for Huntsville, and ever since Bragg had been driven out of Tullahoma, had been the crossing place for much of the forage used by his army. That afternoon's scout was a lively one, into which we all entered with enthusiasm; it looked more like *business* than anything we had ever seen before. The men were sure that this policy would break the back-bone of the rebellion quicker than any ever before adopted; and, dull as we were, we wondered why it had not been adopted by the Government long before. Companies F, D, and I, thoroughly scoured a cove leading from Huntsville south-east down to the river. No one who has never seen a mountainous country can imagine the surpassing richness of these coves. This one was eight miles long by a mile wide, a beautiful mountain stream meandering through it. We got after a band of guerrillas in it, and chased them to the river, but could not catch them. We made a large haul of stock, however.

On the next morning (19th) a detail was made to drive stock already collected back to Maysville, and the balance of the two regiments started for Mooresville, 20 miles west, down the river. This was another lively day, and we enjoyed it very much. We felt sure this scouting was as effective to put down the rebellion as fighting, were quite certain it was less risky to life and limb, and more agreeable every way. We were not half way to Mooresville till we had a large drove of hogs and sheep, which was constantly being increased by fresh acquisitions from the sides of the road. The movements of this drove were necessarily slow and tedious. We knew if the numerous guerrilla bands that infest that country should come upon us in considerable force while our scouting squads were scattered all over the country, the guards of the herd might be overcome and the herd taken or scattered; so we sent scouts ahead to clear the guerrillas out of our way. Sergt. R. C. Clark, Co. I, who had been in command of our scouts since their organization, had been sent home to recruit, and that day the scouts were under command of Sergt. Albert Sigars, Co. A. The scouts got to Mooresville about 3 p. m., and found the place in possession of a band of guerrillas numbering about 30. There were but 10 of the scouts, but they never hesitated a moment to charge any band when the disparity in numbers was no greater than that, and dashed upon this band like furies, and soon ran them out of town. Mooresville is four miles north of the river, on Limestone Creek, quite a large stream, up which boats can come to Mooresville. At the mouth of the creek the rebels had a ferry. When our scouts drove the rebels out of town they fled down this creek towards the river. Our scouts followed, and late in the evening Corporals Kidney, I, and Sigars, A, ran on to them, in ambush, near the river, and the rebels seemed all to fire at once. Sigars fell, pierced with a half dozen bullets. Kidney opened upon them with his Spencer and scattered them; but he, well knowing that they would rally as soon as they had time to re-load their muskets, jumped down, secured Sigars' watch and money, remounted, and retreated as speedily as possible. It was sundown when we received the news of the killing of Sigars, and the Seventy-Second had not all arrived, but Capt. Thomson hastily gathered all that were present and started for the river on a run, arriving just before dark. We found no rebels on this side, but on the opposite was a force, and we immediately opened on them with our Spencers, and they promptly replied. The river was a mile wide here, and we had the very best opportunity of testing the superiority of our Spencers over the guns used by the rebels. We could hear our bullets cutting the leaves and limbs on the thither side, and see the rebels dodging, while the shots fired at us nearly all fell in the water, not one in 20 reaching our side. We secured Sigars' body and returned to Mooresville. Capt. Glaze gives an account of a skirmish, which we give in his own words:

"Company C had a fight by moonlight on the night of November 22, 1863. The regiment was camped at the town of Mooresville, Alabama. We had orders two days before to go to the Tennessee River and see if the rebels were attempting to cross, as we heard firing in that direction. All we could find out was that scouts and foragers would fire on straggling bands of guerrillas and bushwhackers. About 4 p. m. November 22d I received orders to go to the river and ascertain the cause of the firing in that locality. It was night when we got to the river, where we found about 150 rebels, who opened on us at a range of about 200 yards. We had been joined on the way by about 30 men, a portion of them belonging to the 123d Illinois, and a few scouts. We dismounted at once, formed in line, and returned the fire. It was a bright moon, and we could see them almost as plainly as in daylight while in the road, but when they took to a corn field there was no fun in it. We shot at the corn field about 10 minutes, when we charged on them. They took the road up the river, and we chased them about two miles, but could not catch them. Returning we found the dead body of one of the scouts—Al. Sigars—who had been struck by three bullets. That was our only loss. Stretching the body of our dead comrade on a board, we placed him across a mule, a man at each side to hold him on, and commenced our solemn march back to Mooresville, where we arrived at midnight. Reading the memoranda in my diary that day I find these words: 'It was a solemn scene, and one which I hope I may never witness again.' But oh, how many such scenes, and how many so much more horrible, did we witness, and how many did we see meet the fate of poor Al. Sigars! History will not tell, and the world will never know how many."

On November 20th, Col. Biggs, of the 123d Illinois, in command of the expedition, made headquarters at Mooresville, and the camp was not moved; our pack mules and captured stock were also left at that place with enough men to guard them, while the remainder of the two regiments, scattered in squads and scoured the country towards Decatur and Athens; some of Company D going as far down as Decatur, which is on the south side of the river; and when they were discovered the church bells in Decatur were rung, the rebel soldiers flew to their rifle-pits, and a piece of artillery was turned on the impudent Yankees and they were given a few shells. We were fairly overwhelmed with the vast richness and fertility of this part of northern Alabama. The crops had been good that year all over the South, and here they were simply immense. There were supplies sufficient here to subsist an army for some time.

Maysville is 32 miles from Mooresville, and we were just that far from support. It has been said that rebels, guerrillas and bushwhackers, abounded in that region, and could look down from the mountains and see all that we were doing, and count our numbers. It doubtless exasperated them beyond endurance to see us gathering up the fat of the land for the Yankee army, right under their eyes. To check this, the rebels had thrown many scouting parties across the river last night, and were still pushing them over to-day; and by the middle of the afternoon our foragers were meeting and skirmishing with these rebel bands in every direction, and the foragers began to rally at camp. At this, Col. Biggs became alarmed for his communications, and sent Capt. Thomson, with D and I, up the river towards Whitesburg, to reconnoitre. We started about two hours before sundown and moved up the river for six miles on a gallop, and seeing nothing, turned about to return to the Colonel and report. When we had gone about a mile back towards Mooresville we saw a fresh trail, which showed that a band had just come up from the river, crossed the road behind us and gone directly north a short distance and then turned towards Mooresville. We immediately gave chase. They had moved just out of sight of the road for two miles, showing themselves well acquainted with the country, and had stopped to feed their horses. We could tell, of course, just how many there were of them, and as their horses' litter was still smoking we knew we were close to them, and gave our horses spur to utmost speed through thick woods. At the end of a mile we suddenly pitched into a swamp where the oozy mud and water was as black as ink, and up to our horses' bellies. Some of the men pitched over their horses' heads into this black pool, and such another floundering and flouncing we never saw! This was our first experience in the cane brakes and black swamps of the South. This one was not more than 200 yards wide, but it took a long time to get through it, many of us having to get off and pull our horses out; and you can guess we were a muddy set. When we got out not a sign of a rebel horse track could we find At this we were surprised and puzzled, but returned and reported to Col Biggs, who immediately sent a courier to Maysville to report us surrounded, and asking that reinforcements be sent at once.

November 21st. There was some picket firing last night, and no one was allowed to leave camp this morning. Our courier got through all right, and about 11 a. m. a battalion of cavalry came to our relief, and we started back with all our stock; and oh! what a herd! and what herders we were! We started the drove straight for Huntsville; there were men in the command who had never driven a hog or sheep in their lives, and we suppose there never was such a drove or drovers. We had 500 hogs, 550 sheep, 250 cattle, and nearly 1,000 negroes, counting men women and children, and a lot of horses and mules, of which there was never any account taken. The hogs waddled along and grunted; the sheep tripped along, panted and bleated; the cattle dragged along and lowed; the mules kicked along and brayed; the negroes followed, the older ones singing and the babies crying; women carried babies on their backs and bundles on their heads; the men carried the larger children and all sorts of cabin "traps." As the motley mass moved along, to us it looked like it had been collected by a flood of waters, which sees not what it gathers and bears away. The afternoon was warm, and we made but six or eight miles. When we went into camp it was funny to see grim soldiers, used to keeping guard in front of the enemy, set as guards over hogs, sheep, cattle, mules and negroes.

On November 22d the 123d took the drove directly to Huntsville, the Seventy-Second scouting, and at night going into camp by companies, some at Huntsville and some where night overtook them; Companies I and C camped on a large plantation, four miles southwest of Huntsville, where they quartered in the barns and had stable room for 200 horses and mules, and remained there until the 26th. Company C, on the 22d, found 35 horses and mules hid in a canebrake and brought them into camp. Sergt. Magee, of I, in trying to ride one of these animals, got so badly crippled that he lay in that barn two weeks, before he was able to turn over, and was off duty six weeks an account of his injuries.

It became evident that if we kept the rebels *out* of this rich country west of Huntsville, we must move *into* it. On the 1st of November Gen. Sherman, with part of his corps, passed through Maysville on his way to the relief of Chattanooga; and on the 25th of November the battle of Missionary Ridge was fought and Bragg badly whipped. This victory of the Union armies opened the line of transportation to Chattanooga; part of Sherman's army was distributed along the Memphis railroad, towards our camp at Maysville, and the Lightning Brigade was ordered to Huntsville. The order came on the 26th, and we immediately moved and went into camp at Huntsville, on Russell Hill, one mile west of town, in a very beautiful place. Our quarters at Maysville were largely constructed of boards, and being the most comfortable we ever had, we hated to leave them. The teams had little to do, and Col. Miller learning our desires, told us to take the teams, go to Maysville and bring back with us all that we wished, and to make ourselves as comfortable as possible. One can never tell what good such little acts of kindness by officers to men like this by Col. Miller accomplish. But let one that knows assure the reader that such kindness paid more than a hundred fold. On the 27th the teams of the brigade all went back and brought everything of value from our old Maysville camp, which, with what we got at Huntsville, was sufficient to construct neat and comfortable quarters. As Company D had the chapel at Maysville, Company I determined to "go one better" here, and built what was known in the brigade as the Seventy-Second meeting house; it was 28 feet long, and the inside was well supplied with all the modern improvements. We remained in camp here a month, lacking two days, during which time Chaplain De LaMater held services in this chapel twice each week, which were participated in by many of the Seventy-Second and other regiments in the brigade. These services were earnest, edifying and elevating, and we still look back with pleasure to the humble part we were permitted to take in them.

We were in camp at Maysville 25 days, and in that time had taken four scouts of four to six days each. While at Huntsville we had a more sedentary life than ever before since entering the service. Capt. Thomson's Company, D, were provost guards, and of course had charge of prisoners captured in the department, and at intervals had to forward them to Chattanooga. We take pleasure in giving a few incidents of forwarding prisoners, furnished by Lieut. Jas. A. Mount and Sergt. A. M. Cory:

On December 1st, 1863, Capt. Thomson, Sergts. A. M. Cory and Jas. A. Mount, privates John W. H. Hill, John Ball and Noah McKinsey, started from Huntsville to Chattanooga, with some prisoners. They walked to Brownsburg, which was quite a task for men used to riding. At Brownsburg they took cars for Chattanooga; arriving at Bridgeport late in the evening they were told they could go no further on the cars, but must go the balance of the way on a steamboat, which would not start until morning; they were also ordered to cross the main channel of the river on a pontoon bridge and camp on an island. They obeyed orders. But what was their surprise and horror, in the morning, to find that during the night the bridge had been taken up, that the boat awaited them on the other side, and their only way to reach it was by walking over the half-completed railroad bridge, which had nothing but the narrow stringers laid down—no cross-ties and no friendly board for their feet, or to shut out the head-turning waters from sight which glided far below. The bridge was over a half mile long and 60 feet above the water. Cory says he regards walking over it as the most perilous feat of his life. All got over safely, took the boat and arrived at Chattanooga without further adventure.

When they had reported their prisoners to Gen. Thomas, Capt. Thomson asked him for permission to go out on the battle-field of Chicamauga and find and bury their comrades Cain, of D, and Campbell, of C, killed in that battle, on the 19th of September. Gen. Thomas told him it would be extremely hazardous to go out there with any force smaller than a brigade, as the enemy was camped not far from the battle-field. Capt. Thomson assured the General that he had six experienced soldiers, tried and true, armed with Spencer rifles, and they were able to take care of themselves in any emergency. The noble General granted the pass to these noble hearted comrades of the gallant dead, and the little squad started for the gory field on which they had fought all day September 19th, and left on the morning of September 20th. The field was reached late in the evening as the pines cast their weird gloom over the forms of decaying soldiers, many of whom lay as they had fallen, while others lay in groups where they had been gathered together as the last act of affection that could be bestowed by their comrades as they stood in "the jaws of death, in the mouth of hell," in that fearful battle. They had not been buried by the enemy, and the autumn winds had sounded through the forests, the only requiem that had been wailed over their manly forms. Capt. Thomson and men stopped for the night in the little log cabin on the ridge, so often spoken of in our account of the battle. The rebel surgeons had used it for an amputating hospital during that action, and many wounded had been carried to it, only to lie there and die; and around it at this time lay scores of dead and decaying bodies, limbs and human bones. It was a ghastly sight, over which night, in tenderness, spread her sable curtains as Capt. Thomson's party approached. They passed the night not so much in sleep as in deep meditation. How broad and deep the contrast between the stillness of this night and the night of the 19th of September, after the day of hard battle which baptized the earth with human blood! Then, as we lay in line of battle, we heard in front of us the shrieks and moans of the wounded and dying as they called for water and help, while in rear and flanks we heard the grum and gruff movements of troops, both friend and foe. Now all is deserted—and so still! How impossible a battle seems on such a night, in such a place.

After a long and cheerless night came the morning full of gloom. The little party passed over the field of battle, and found their comrades just as we had left them on the 19th—buried them and returned to Chattanooga. This was a brave and manly deed, and well illustrates the love and devotion that comrade bore for comrade in those days of blood and death.

We have remarked that our camp life at Huntsville was very quiet. We did little picketing, and only gathered what corn our horses ate, and fed, curried and kept them fat. While the guerrillas and bushwhackers bothered us considerably, it was not possible for us to follow them into the mountains on horseback, and they could look down like eagles from their lofty perches, and sweep down on us when they saw we could be taken at the most disadvantage. Any soldier who went out foraging alone, or fell behind his party, was liable to be picked up at any time. The railroad was only repaired to Brownsburg, and we had to haul our mail, sugar and coffee, from that place, and the balance of our subsistence we got off the country. About the 17th of December a party of these mountain-goat guerrillas swooped down upon our train and came very near capturing it, but were driven off. Frequent expeditions were sent up into the mountains on foot after these guerrillas, and many of them were killed.

On December 22d we got orders to be ready to move. This, on ordinary occasions, would have been hailed with delight, for as a rule we so thoroughly hated camp life that we were glad to be on the move. But here we had such a good camp, our duty had been so light, and the country and weather so delightful, that we were loth to leave the place. But on December 24th our whole command, that is, all that were camped at Huntsville under the command of Gen. Crook, moved 22 miles on the road toward Athens, and went into camp near that town. The days were delightful, but the nights cold enough to freeze the ground considerably, which, owing to our having been used to sleeping in warm, comfortable houses, made it pretty cold for us to sleep on the ground.

The 25th, Christmas, was one of the most delightful days we ever saw—warm and pleasant as the northern Indian summer. We passed through Athens and moved straight north for Pulaski. Our whole division train was along, and our regiment was rear guard. From Athens north to Elk River is a dense, flat forest, 20 miles wide, through which the roads are soft and miry. In a short time the trains had them so cut up that it was almost impossible to get through the mud. The teams soon began to stall, and wagons to upset, and in three hours the train was strung out 10 miles long. Our progress was so slow that when night came we were not more than 15 miles from Athens, when the advance had gone into camp at Elk River, 30 miles from Athens. Every half mile we had to help some wagon out of the mud. Just at night it had clouded up, and was dark as pitch. A soldier always wants light, so we set the woods on fire, and we never saw the leaves burn prettier. Just then the patience of the boys became exhausted at the slowness of the train, and a happy thought of a device to hurry the train along struck them. It was to place some of our metallic cartridges in front of the burning leaves, so when the fire burned up to them they would explode and sound like skirmishing, and thus make the teamsters in front believe that the train was being attacked in the rear. The scheme worked like a charm, and the teamsters in front got out of the way as fast as possible, for if there was anything in the world that would make a teamster get up and dust it was to know that the "Johnnies" were after him For a mile or two the train moved off lively. Throwing cartridges in the fire was so much fun for the boys that they could not quit, and finally one of the officers became so exasperated that he undertook to make them quit. This proved a "bigger job than he bargained for," and no sooner did he ride to one end of the line than "pop! pop! pop!" would go the cartridges at the other; then back he would come, swearing like a trooper. The men became so disgusted to see what a fool he made of himself that they threw a shower of cartridges in the fire all round him, which so frightened his horse that it ran away with him.

About midnight the train got out to the fields and cultivated grounds, and soon got so jammed up that it could go no further. It began to rain, and we abandoned the train and undertook to move past it and get to our brigade. We wound along through the fields at the side of the road until 1 o'clock, when we were yet four miles from camp, and it was pouring down rain; so we hitched our horses to the fence, laid down and slept till morning. When we arose we still found the train standing in the road, and worse stuck in the mud and jammed than we had ever before seen it.

On the 26th of December, as soon as we were up, we moved to Elk River, and found it so swollen that crossing was dangerous. The whole division—men, horses, artillery and wagons—were jammed up in utter confusion, none seeming to want to venture across. But finally, about noon, the Seventy-Second went into it, the water running over thebacks of the large horses; swimming the smaller ones and the mules. It was our fortune to be riding a mule, and of course we got our obverse side wet. There was a little town on the bank of the river, or had been, called Elktown, and we loitered about here till all the division got across and passed us. The head of the column took the pike to Pulaski, and two miles from the river turned up a hollow or cove. Our regiment was in the rear of the whole division, and when we turned up the cove we passed Gen. Crook's headquarters. This was about 2 or 3 p. m. It had been raining since noon. The entire division was in front of us, and we could see that as each regiment had passed headquarters it had gone into camp. The cove was narrow, and instead of the regiments going into camp at right angles with the road, as was the usual custom, they had moved out to the side of the road in line just as they had been marching, and of course were making a very long line along the side of the road; the second regiment passing the first, the third passing the second, and so on, which was precisely reversing the order of march, throwing our regiment furthest from headquarters, and making it the last to get into camp. The hills were high on both sides of the road, and it was dark almost as soon as we turned up the valley. It was two hours later before we got into camp at the top of the cove, nearly five miles from Gen. Crook's headquarters. The rain was pouring down in torrents, and as we moved slowly along in the dark we had ample time for reflection, and to serve our service in the army all over again. The burden of our reflections was the contrast of the service and the feelings of the soldiers. All sunshine, or midnight darkness; all feast, or famine; all idleness, or labor most exhausting; all joyous, exhilarating play, or all fast, fatiguing scouting. We cannot better express our own feelings than by repeating the following soliloquy of Orderly Sergt. A. W. Lane, Co. G: "A soldier's life is one of extremes—no middle ground. His endurance is taxed to the utmost, or he is idling around camp with nothing to do. He is uneasy from having eaten too much, or suffering from want of food. It is intense pleasure or despondency."

On this particular evening to say that we were wet would be drawing it mildly. We had got one end wet in the river and the other one by a deluge from above. To say we were mad at having to reverse the usual order of going into camp would be a tame expression. But go into camp we finally did, and, dark as it was, wood, water, feed and forage are all to be provided yet; and everybody puts in his positive demurrer to everything that is required of him. Men in the darkness jam against and stumble over each other. One comrade who has just pulled his saddle from his horse attempts to throw it on to a friendly stump, and slaps it on to your head and neck as you stoop to pick up your haversack; the sudden thump knocks the haversack out of your hand, turns it inside out, and as you try to free yourself from the dripping, muddy saddle, you set your foot upon your last cracker, and it "goes to Davy Jones's," or into the mud a foot deep. A thousand fruitless attempts are made to light a fire, but everything is so wet it will not burn, and you are on the point of giving it up, when you raise your head and see that some one, not far away, has been more successful than yourself, and you go for a light (for a soldier who would not let a comrade have fire would be court-martialed and hung on the spot, or as near the spot as possible.) You get just a little bit of a blaze, when the foragers begin to come in, and they, of course, come straight toward your light, calling out at the top of their voices, "Company 'G,' 'I,' 'H,' 'A,'" etc. You answer your call, "here." Your forager hears your answer and come for your little blaze, rides his horse over your saddle, throws a bundle of corn blades into your frying pan, in which another comrade is placing the sow-belly, ready to fry as soon as the fire is ready for duty; his horse steps on your canteen, and the forager jumps off his horse, landing with his muddy boots in the middle of your sleeping blanket, stumbles forward and upsets your kettle of coffee water. You raise up with curses rising in your throat like an eruption from Mount Vesuvius, and you are about to deliver yourself of a thousand concentrated d—s in one word, when the orderly stumbles over your little fire, blotting it out forever, and raves out, "Company G, saddle up and get ready for picket duty immediately." There aren't words enough in the English language to give the faintest idea of the situation at this juncture. Company G, already 36 hours without coffee, goes on picket, doomed to shiver for 12 hours more without fire. But the companies left behind on this particular night get fires started, and by the light see wood and rails in abundance close by; they find forage in a neighboring corn field, and a straw stack near our camp. Rousing fires soon begin to make our wet clothes smoke, the sow-belly to sizzle and the coffee pots to boil. Our gum blankets are spread on the ground. We stand around with a cup in one hand and a big piece of stomach-stayer between two crackers in the other. Supper is ready, and then the grace is:

"O, never mind the weather,
We've got over double trouble,
And are bound for the happy land of Canaan."

Then it is, when with lighted pipes we gather around the fire after supper, that the practical joker does his best, and to the best advantage. The King's fool in his palmiest days never did better service than these merry fellows did in the army. Next to food and sleep they smoothed the rough duty of soldier life with merriment and "drove dull cares away." Then the boss gasser (every mess has one) comes to the front, and sits with his little hatchet, all notched and gapped with muscular strokes upon harder substance than cherry trees, where the light beats full upon his brow, and tells his newest, best and biggest, with as much zest as if any one believed a word he said. The troubles of the day are forgotten in the intense enjoyment of the occasion, and the growling, snapping and cursing of a few hours ago are buried by jests, yarns, laughter and songs. The rain ceases to fall; notes on the sights and sounds of the day are made and compared; comments made on the march and its incidents; the military situation discussed, and finally we call out:

"Make down the bed, Joe."

Have you never been there? We are just about to lay our weary bones to rest, while the merriment of the last hour is passing into more serious thoughts of home and loved ones, which border on prayer to the God of Battles, and our souls are becoming as calm as an autumn sunset, when, hark! away down the valley, at headquarters, the division band strikes up:

"We'll rally round the flag, boys,
Rally once again,
Shouting the battle cry of Freedom!"

Simultaneously the regiment next to headquarters begins to cheer by companies, three cheers to each company, and such another volume of sound, cheering and music, echoed by the hills, doubled and re-echoed, comes rolling up the valley, as we never expect to hear again; in an instant every man is on his feet, and as the cheering by companies draws nearer and nearer, each company waiting its turn, the excitement is almost enough to take away our breath; but we bide our time as the sound rolls on, each echo doubled and redoubled, until it seems to us the rushing of Niagara would scarcely equal it. Our regiment is the last up the valley, and when it strikes us we give it three of our loudest and best; then our whole regiment give it one long, loud cheer, which is answered by the regiment next below us, and by the next, until it finally reaches the last one; when all at once the whole division break out in such a tremendous, overwhelming cheer, that the foundations of the hills shake! The music ceases, the cheering stops; the stillness of death creeps along the valley, and in 30 minutes every soldier is in the land of dreams.

On the 27th of December we moved four miles and went into camp at Pulaski. It continued to rain at intervals until late New Years eve, when it turned cold. While at Pulaski the usual amount of picketing, foraging and scouting was attended to, till December 31st, late in the evening, when there came an order to prepare and march immediately. Many of the boys were out foraging, others were on picket, and still others sick from the late severe changes in the weather and exposure.. Unexpected and untimely as this order was, we began with our usual promptness and cheerfulness to prepare to obey it; and rattled away in our lively style, pulling down tents, packing knapsacks, etc. By the time we got our tents down it began to rain hard; just then we got orders not to take baggage, as we were going on a four days' scout, that we were to move light and camp would remain at Pulaski. This order made it necessary for some one to stay in camp to take care of our effects, and those who didn't care to go, stayed.

We moved out on the road about 4 p. m. and turned towards Pulaski. The rain had been coming from the south-west, but just as we turned down the hill, north towards town, the wind whipped around towards the north, and the rain and hail, driven by a fierce hurricane, struck us full in the face, and we suppose that poor soldiers never faced a worse storm. When we got into Pulaski it was the fortune of the Historian to be detailed to return and help to take care of the camp. We did then, and do now, regard this as an act of Providence; and with heartfelt sympathy and pity for the poor fellows who had to go, we made our way back to camp. The 300 men and officers of the Seventy-Second who left camp that evening had untold hardships, and did not return for nearly three months. We will let them tell their own story when they get back. When the writer returned to camp he found he was the ranking officer, and we had charge of the camp until Capt. Robinson and Lieut. Geiger, of Company C, returned on the evening of January 3d, with 68 new recruits. Capt. Robinson then took command of the camp, and we were the ranking Sergeant present for duty. There were left of each company from 12 to 20 men, and 15 to 20 horses, aggregating 175 men a-

225 horses. That night proved the coldest we experienced in the service, and the next day is remembered by all soldiers in the service as the "cold New Year." Several convalescent horses froze to death right where they stood in the mud, the sudden change being more severe on them than on the men; but many soldiers throughout the armies of the United States froze to death, and numbers were greatly injured by the cold. For four or five days and nights we suffered beyond description. We had recently left most comfortable quarters where we could sleep as warm as if at home, but here we had only the bare frozen ground to lie on, and nothing to protect us from the pitiless cold and piercing wind but our shelter tents. We were camped in a dense woods which sheltered us a little, but there were no rails near; so we cut down numbers of trees, built log-heap fires and passed day and night in roasting one side while the other froze, until some of the boys said they were getting soft on the outside like a half roasted apple.

About this time there was a great stir in all the western armies about going into the "veteran service." Any regiment which had been in the service two years was offered a furlough home for 60 days, provided its members would re-enlist for three years more, or during the war. As very few of the western troops had ever had furloughs, most of those who had a chance veteranized and availed themselves of the 60 days furlough; for they really believed that the war would be over before their original term of service expired. On the 2d of January, Col. Wilder, who left us at Chicamauga, returned, and through his persuasion the 17th enlisted in the veteran service and went home, the Colonel going back with them.

Capt. Robinson, in command of the camp, had a great deal of military pride, neatness and order; by his good management everything was put into military ship-shape, and kept in good running order. We carefully gathered up all that our absent comrades left behind, so not a single knapsack or tent was lost. By the 7th of February the weather had moderated very much, but the snow on the ground was three inches deep. It was about this time we got an installment of recruits, about 150. They were distributed to the different companies. We shall never forget how we received our "fresh fish." Many of them were from our own homes, and we were glad to see them on that account, besides a dozen other good reasons we could mention. Their unsophisticated manners amused us amazingly, and no doubt they thought us a little bit rude for laughing at them so much, but we actually could not help it. As most of them served till the close of the war and made excellently good soldiers, *they* will pardon a little diversion. They had come from Nashville without rations, and were as hungry as wolves. It was late when they got to camp; our rations were out, but we did not expect to get any until morning and had none to give them. The idea of going to bed so hungry was horrible to them and they couldn't stand it at all. It was our misfortune to be acting commissary, sergeant-major, and a kind of roustabout generally, for the detachment, and they came to us in a body demanding rations. We told them they could have plenty in the morning, upon hearing which, their spokesman cried out as if smitten, "Good heavens! but we haven't had a bite since daylight." We told them we were sorry, but couldn't help it; they then begged us to see if we "couldn't find them something to eat of some kind, as they were just starving." Moved by their entreaties we went to the commissary, followed by the recruits in a body; as luck would have it he had a few rations left over from the last that were drawn, and we got three boxes of crackers. When the commissary called them to get their coffee and sugar, they began to look at each other and then at us, and finally said, "we have nothing to carry sugar and coffee in." This was fun for us, for we had not entirely fotgotten the first time we ever drew rations, and began to laugh, which made them think us a fool. After enjoying their discomfiture for a while we sent them back to get some gum blankets—something we didn't have when we first went out. The commissary poured their coffee and sugar on to the blankets, threw a couple of large sides of sow-belly on to the ground, and told them to "clear out." Well, the crackers, sugar and coffee they could carry; but how were they to get the meat to their quarters? By this time—besides having something else to do—we were getting tired of the fun, and cut a hickory withe, punched holes through the sides of meat with a picket pin, drew the withe threw the holes, and started for camp, dragging it behind us over the snow and frozen ground. One of the recruits said he was awful hungry, but he'd be d—d if he could eat any of that meat. Of course every old soldier knows that he soon got bravely over that. This was their first night at camping out; to us who were used to the service it was bad enough, but their sufferings were intense. But it was surprising to see how naturally they took to crackers; we never saw so many crackers eaten by so few men as they ate in the next two weeks; about every other day we had to make a special requisition for them.

On January 12th, our entire division, what there was left of it, started back to Huntsville. The whole of the train went, but as several regiments had gone in different directions, there were but few soldiers with the trains The roads were tolerably good; we made good time, and the trains all crossed the river at Elktown that day, and went into camp on the same ground they occupied on the night of the 25th ult., and our detachment stood picket near the same ground we lay upon on that night. On the morning of the 13th we remained at our post until the whole train passed us, and then took a road south-east, straight for Huntsville, our detachment being again rear guard. The road lay through a forest we have before spoken of, and we traveled 20 miles without seeing a house. Our rear guard duty was about as disagreeable as any we had ever done before, and we failed to get into camp that night. We reached Huntsville on the 15th, and went into camp a half mile north-east of town, in a very beautiful place. We were delighted to get back to what seemed to us home and comfort. Here Capt. Robinson had us put our bunks in regular order, police our camps, and also put *us* to drilling recruits. It was genuine pleasure to us to see the progress they made.

Few people now-a-days have any idea of the amount of mail matter that passed back and forth between the soldiers and their friends at home, and we relate an instance to give some hint of its bulk. Our camp was near a very large brick house, owned by a gentleman named Moore. This gentleman had a large India rubber tree which he kept as a house plant. It was a tropical plant, and a kind of natural curiosity. But the late cold weather had frozen it, and he had set it out of doors. Our boys took leaves from it to send home as souvenirs —Col. Miller among the rest. He was more lucky than some of us, as he has one of the leaves at his home in Lebanon, Indiana. They were large, leathery sort of leaves, and when put in a letter made it feel like it was full of greenbacks. The day after these leaves were mailed for home the mail was captured, and over a hundred of the letters containing the leaves were cut open. You may imagine that the rebs, who thought they were making a big haul of Yankee greenbacks, swore when they found each promising letter contained but a leaf. As a further illustration: The regiment was gone, as before stated, nearly three months, during which time their mail came to our camp, and when they returned there were over 400 letters for Compan I alone, making 4,000 for the regiment, besides what had come to us who did not go, during that time.

On January 16th Col. Miller came back from home, having been absent since December 19th. Gen. Crook, who had commanded the division since the Wheeler raid began, was ordered to Chattanooga, and Col. Miller, being the senior officer present for duty, was in command of the division, and also of the post. Sherman, in his

Memoirs, vol. 1, p. 395, says: "About this time we were much embarrassed by an order from the War Department promising a 30 days' furlough to all soldiers who would "veteranize"—re-enlist for the rest of the war. This secured the services of a large portion of the men who had almost completed a three years' enlistment, and were veteran soldiers in feeling and habit. But to furlough so many of our men at that instant of time was like disbanding an army in the very midst of a battle."

About this time nearly one-third of the army was at home on veteran furlough, or on other leave of absence, which the rebels of course knew as well as ourselves, and they thought it would be a good time to cross the river below us, move on to the railroads supplying the army at Chattanooga, and compel a retreat. Accordingly the enemy began to mass his cavalry along the river below us. On the 23d of January Col. Miller received the following dispatch:

"*Col. A. O. Miller:*—The word here is, through Gen. Dodge, commanding at Pulaski, Tenn., that a large force is concentrating at Tuscumbia, Ala., intending to cross at Florence, Ala., and make a raid on our line of communications with Nashville. Without delay I want to know the truth of such statements, and prevent the carrying out of such a scheme. Respectfully,

"GEORGE H. THOMAS,
"Com'd'g forces at Chattanooga, Tenn.

"COL. A. O. MILLER, Com'd'g forces, Huntsville, Ala."

This order came to Col. Miller at 10 a. m. At 12 m. he started with all the available forces then at Huntsville. The 17th was still at home on furlough; part of the 98th were in East Tennessee; most of our regiment was in Mississippi; the 123d had two days before moved down to Mooresville, which left but the 92d Illinois and a detachment of the 98th Illinois, and our detachment. The 92d had 400 men, the 98th 125, and the Seventy-Second 150—a total of 675 men. We moved rapidly down toward Athens, and went into camp near that place. Col. Miller's report to Gen. Thomas explains the balance, and we insert it entire:

"HEADQUARTERS 2D CAVALRY DIVISION, 14th A. C.,
"HUNTSVILLE, ALA., Jan. 28th, 1864.

"*General:*—I received your order of 22d at 10 a. m. of 23d, and at 12 m. started for Athens with 675 men, all that were available at that time; camped at Athens, where I learned from Col. Phillips, of the 9th Illinois Mounted Infantry, that he had been down in the region of Florence a few days before, and had been driven out of the country by a large force. At the same time he showe
d

me a letter from some one, that had been dropped at his door the night before, stating that a force would cross the Tennessee at Lamb's Ferry, near Rogersville, and would take him in on the morning of the 25th. 'But,' said he, 'the idea is ridiculous.' I left the matter with him, remarking that there might be some truth in it. On the 24th, Sunday, we marched 25 miles and encamped below Rogersville, opposite and near the upper end of Mussel Shoals. On the 25th I sent the detachment of the Seventy-Second, under Capt. Robinson, to the river, with orders to destroy all boats and water craft he could find. The main column moved on down to Shoal Creek, and just as my advance got across the bridge it met a force coming up from Bainbridge's Ferry, a mile south of the bridge across Shoal Creek, and a sharp skirmish ensued. There were about 200 of the enemy. The 92d being in front scattered them, driving a part back toward the river, the balance retreating toward Florence. Those retreating toward the river were driven behind the bluff to shelter themselves, but my men shot their horses and would have captured the whole force, but a body of the enemy on yon side, by firing across the river, kept my men from getting close enough to take them. We captured a few prisoners at the bridge, and they told us there was something in the wind, and that the fun would soon commence—they thinking all the while that we were Col. Phillips' men. We moved on toward Florence, skirmishing pretty lively all the way, till about an hour before sundown, we met a force coming up from Florence, on their way to Athens. Here those we had been driving before us made a stand, and a desperate fight took place, the rebels still thinking we were Phillips' men, whom they had so often run out of there before. The 92d was all dismounted, and also the detachment of the 98th; but still the rebels pushed on to us, being two to our one in numbers. Just at this critical juncture the Seventy-Second came up behind us on the keen run. They had heard the skirmishing when 10 miles away, and had hurried up with all speed in order to take a hand in in the fight. They dismounted and went in on the right on the run, and never stopped a moment; for when the rebels heard my men charge, they broke and run, and my men were on their heels, driving them like deer for nearly two miles. We killed 25 or 30 of them, and among the number was the commander of the forces, and from his pocket we took an order stating that he should load his wagons with corn and send them across the river, and then go on up the north side and join the force that would cross at Lamb's Ferry, and in conjunction with it move on up and capture Athens; and winding up with the injunction: 'And let there be no failure on your part.' I was certain that the enemy we had just fought would give us no further trouble, and so I determined to go back up the river with this order and information in my possession, and get in behind the forces that were to cross at Lamb's Ferry. It was now near sundown, and I told the citizens who came in after the fight to gather up the dead and wounded and care for them. We captured several prisoners, who again confirmed the story of the letter found by Phillips. We about-faced and marched till 10 o'clock at night, when we met Phillips and his regiment, who had followed us. I told him what I was sure would be the case, that Athens would be attacked the next morning at daylight. He treated the information with contempt. But he finally agreed to return to Athens and send his scouts to the crossing, learn the facts, and report. I then asked if his scouts were reliable, intending to send my own, whom I knew I could trust. He said they were perfectly reliable, and started back. I told him I would feed and follow at midnight, and would follow till I got word from him. We were on the road by the time agreed upon, and marched till 2 o'clock on the morning of the 25th, when Phillips sent word that his scouts had been to the crossing and no enemy had crossed. On this information we went into camp. Next morning we started back toward Florence, and had hardly got under way when a courier from Phillips came dashing up and stated that Athens had been attacked, and requested help. We started with all speed, hoping to get to Lamb's Ferry in time to cut off their retreat. After marching 20 miles we got to the ferry just in time to see the last of them in their boats on the opposite side of the river. Just about the time they were beginning the attack on Athens, they got the word that their comrades had been defeated at Florence, when they broke for their boats, and did not even take time to break open headquarters nor to clean out the sutlers' tents, of which there were three there; but broke for their boats, and got there as above indicated.

"General, I have been thus lengthy and particular because I feel chagrined at the result. Had I not relied upon the statement of Col. Phillips, or had no word at all from him, I am certain I could have captured the whole command; for they were scared and running as soon as they found we were in their rear. They had more men than I had, and two pieces of artillery; but I had no fear as to results in an engagement. My command arrived here this evening, in good order. I forward 50 prisoners to-morrow. A. O. MILLER,

"Com'd'g 2d Cav. Div. 14th A. C., Huntsville, Ala.

"MAJ. GEN. GEO. H. THOMAS, Com'd'g forces, Chattanooga, Tenn."

"HEADQUARTERS ARMY OF CUMBERLAND,
"CHATTANOOGA, TENN, Jan. 30, 1864.

"*Col. A. O. Miller:*—Your report received, and I thank you for your promptness, fidelity and good judgment. I think you did well under the circumstances. GEORGE H. THOMAS, Maj. Gen.,
"Com'd'g forces, Chattanooga, Tenn."

This scout was of such importance to our cause and to the army at Chattanooga, that at the risk of wearying the reader we will recapitulate a little. Our army lay at Chattanooga on the east of the Cumberland mountains. Its base of supplies was at Nashville, 136 miles distant, and for nearly 100 miles on the west of the Cumberland, the railroad, over which all our army supplies were transported, ran southwest to Cowan, and for the whole of this distance was little more than 100 miles from the Tennessee River. Hence the rebels, by throwing a large force of cavalry across the river at Whitesburg, Mooresville, Decatur, Lamb's Ferry, or even as far down as Florence, could, in a little over two days' march, reach this railroad, and in two hours so destroy it as to make it practically inadequate to supplying the army at Chattanooga. There were many natural advantages that would favor such a movement of the enemy. Along the Tennessee and Alabama line, between Huntsville and Fayetteville, and between Decatur and Pulaski, for nearly 150 miles, there is a dense forest and broken country, always full of guerrillas and bushwhackers; and a large force once in this part of the country could move with ease, and without much fear of being observed. Of course all these things were as well or better understood by the rebels as by us. But Gen. Thomas well appreciated the importance of always keeping his single line of railroad free from molestation, and for this very purpose he posted our brigade along the river to nip in the bud any movements the rebels might make against it. This scout showed the superior judgment of Gen. Thomas in the selection of his men; and on our part it demonstrated that his confidence was not misplaced; that we were not only competent to guard a hundred miles of river, but that we could whip any force—not more than three to one—that the enemy might send over.

There was another thing demonstrated by this scout. We have frequently spoken of the vast amount of forage afforded by the country, and of the desperate attempts the rebels were constantly making to get as much as possible of it across the river. We found them still at it; so on the morning of the 24th, after we left Rogersville, Col. Miller sent the detachment of the Seventy-Second, Capt. Robinson in command, to follow the river and destroy as many boats as we could find. As a matter of course, the rebels would keep most of the boats on their side of the river; but we found 20 boats in all, and at one place 10 boats of all sizes, from a large skiff up to a large flat-boat (there were three of the latter), all of which had been used in getting forage over the river. We chopped them to pieces. A short distance further down we found a lot of darkies gathering corn. They told us the corn was "for de confed'r'ts." We burned the wagons and took the mules and horses along with us. Soon after this we heard skirmishing north-west of us, and immediately left the river and struck straight for the shooting. We had a terrible time getting along through the fields and woods, over ravines and logs, and it was fully eight miles to where we came out into the road at the bridge over Shoal Creek. By this time the fighting had commenced in earnest, full two miles west of us. We now had a good road, and lit out at full speed. This was the time to try the courage of our recruits. There was little time to reason or philosophize on the situation, for on we went, and when within a half mile of the fighting it broke out with desperate fury. We had not heard such a popping of Spencers since the battle of Farmington, and we spurred our horses a little faster. Just then there came down the road toward us 500 horses running at the top of their speed, with saddles, blankets, camp-kettles and coffee-pots flying in the air like fragments from a volcano. They swept past us like a whirlwind, and with the tramp and thunder, or roar, of a vast herd of stampeding buffalo. We solemnly think we never saw anything more frightful than this charge upon us. It was enough to make old soldiers feel shaky; but now, as most of our numbers were recruits, the matter became a serious one. And right here we had a fine opportunity of seeing how the words and actions of a single brave man inspired the whole command. When some of the men seemed appalled with fright at the terrible noise and confusion, George Wakeman, private Co. I, called out, "Come on, boys; let the horses go to h—l, and we'll go for the rebs!" This assured the faltering ones, and we galloped up so close that the bullets came whistling over us. We dismounted and formed line in a field right behind the 98th Illinois, whose brave men were still working with all their might to check the rebels as they came charging upon them. As soon as our lines were formed, we started into the woods with a cheer which electrified the 98th and 92d, who had just all they could do to hold their own, and they also commenced cheering, which made the rebels think our line had been reinforced by a thousand men. The rebels halted, and we poured a galling fire into them. They broke and ran; we after them, having never halted since we started into the woods

We pursued them for a mile, when most of us were entirely given out. Wm. Harvey, private Co. I, performed some daring feats of bravery. After the enemy started to run he followed them faster and further than any other man in the regiment, and when we halted to dress up our lines he was a half mile in front, still cheering and shooting away, and it was necessary to *order* him back before he would come. This was the shortest, sharpest and quickest fight we were ever in, except the battle of Rock Springs, which stands without a parallel. How many were killed and wounded we never knew certainly, for the reason already stated in Col. Miller's report. A captured confederate captain informed Capt. Robinson that there were 28 rebels killed, including their commanding officer, and many wounded, among the latter three commissioned officers. We made no effort to gather the dead and wounded, but right in his own line of march the Historian counted five dead rebels, all lying in the yard of a little log cabin in the woods. One rebel was in the agonies of death, who had his revolver in his hand and the muzzle in his mouth. The gnashing of his teeth on the revolver, and his terrible writhing and contortions, were horrible to behold. We suppose that, finding himself mortally wounded, he had undertaken to end his misery by blowing his brains out, but failed to get the hammer drawn back. Private James Armstrong, Co. C, pulled the revolver out of the poor fellow's mouth.

At the lowest calculation we must have killed 30 of the enemy. Our loss was but one killed and seven wounded. For the timely and valuable reinforcement received from the men of the Seventy-Second under Capt. Robinson, who rode like each man was a Sheridan, and dashed into the battle at the nick of time, and with such admirable enthusiasm, saving the day, Col. Miller thanked both Capt. Robinson and his men, and complimented them highly, making special mention of the recruits, who were under fire for the first time that day, and behaved with admirable coolness.

It was sundown by the time we got straightened up and ready to mount. We must now tell about the stampeded horses before mentioned, and in doing that must do something else, which ought, perhaps, to have been done before—that is, explain our manner of fighting. Every morning, as each company first forms, it tells off in fours. Well, now, it is the duty of No. 4 to take care of his own horse, and also the horses of Nos. 1, 2, and 3, as often as they have to dismount. On approaching an enemy, when it becomes necessary to send forward skirmishers, No. 1 always dismounts and moves forward. If the enemy in front is stubborn and hard to move, Nos. 2 and 3 dismount and go to the assistance of No. 1.

Now then, with this idea of our method of fighting on foot, we go back to Shoal Creek bridge, where the 92d first struck the rebels. No. 1 was dismounted and drove the rebels toward Florence, which is four miles below Shoal Creek. After driving them two miles, the rebels made a stand, and Nos. 2 and 3 were dismounted and hurried to the front. Just then the rebels were reinforced and came on to the 92d in overwhelming numbers, and at this instant, as the 98th had not all got up yet, the Colonel dismounted No. 4 and hurried them also into the fight, thus leaving all the 92d horses massed in column without anybody holding them. In a few minutes the 98th were in line and opened on the rebels with their Spencers, which made such a tremendous popping that it so frightened these loose horses that they tried to get away from there as fast as they could, and came charging down the road as before indicated. But after getting some distance away from the sound, and somewhat tired from running, they turned into an old field, wound themselves up, and stopped. There was not a saddle lost. We have spoken of a party of rebs being driven from the bridge straight south to the river. A detachment of our men stayed there to watch them; but when the fight commenced, from some cause or other the detachment left the river and came to the front, and as soon as the rebels found the detachment gone they hurried back to the bridge and chopped holes in the floor. The bridge was about 100 feet long, and covered tight; darkness had come long before we got to it, and you better think we had ticklish times getting over those holes.

When the rebels attacked Athens, on the morning of the 25th, they found but a few pickets, who mounted their horses and got out of the way. The rebels then charged into the camp of the 9th Illinois, killed a negro boy and captured five soldiers. Just then a courier came dashing in among them with the information that their comrades had been defeated at Florence, and that the Yankees were upon them. Without stopping to clean out the sutlers' "shebangs," they took to their heels and went away faster than they came.

Capt. Robinson says: "On the 26th we marched and countermarched over that scope of country several times, to give the enemy to understand we would not permit them on this side of the Tennessee. We camped that night at Athens. Next day, January 27th, our command made the march back to the old camp at Huntsville, a distance of 40 miles, having accomplished another of those successful raids for which the History of the War for the Union gives the Lightning Brigade due credit."

CHAPTER XXVI.

From January 26th to April 3d, 1864—Move Camp from Huntsville to Lime Stone Creek—The Order Not to Forage—How Things would Come into Camp and get into Receptacles—Could Hide Just as Well as Steal—Recruits Tear Down a Water Tank to get Boards to Build Bunks—We Gather 10,000 Bushels of Corn—Rebel Attempt to Burn Corn Foiled—Big Snow which Scares the Natives—A Snow-ball Battle—Rumor that Our Absent Comrades had been in Hard Battle—Home Sick to Have Them Come Back—Delight at the News that They Were Coming—Joy and Sorrow Blended—Tears for the Unreturning Braves—History of the Mississippi Raid—Marching Through Bitter Cold—Couldn't Freeze a Gray-Back—Gen. Smith wants Us and Our Spencers to Go With Him—Maj. Carr Consents in Spite of the Protests of the Officers—Incidents of Scouts and Skirmishes—Short of Ammunition—Somebody's Great Blunder—Shooting All Night at One Horse—Bushwhackers Killing Men—Our Slow Movements—Enemy Concentrating—100 Miles Too Slow—We Retreat, the Rebels Pressing Us—A Stampede Before the Enemy—The Seventy-Second Fights Every Inch of Ground and Holds the Enemy in Check—Battle of Okolona, February 22d, 1864—Result of the Expedition—Losses, Casualties and Incidents—Sherman's Report—Gen. W. S. Smith's Letter Refuting Falsehoods and Lauding the Seventy-Second—Great Joy on Receipt of Order to Join the Old Brigade—On the Way Back—Bushwhackers Captured and Shot—Sanitary Commission at Murfreesboro Gives Us Clothing and Vegetables—We Join the Old Command—Great Rejoicing—"A Time for Memory and for Tears."

Our detachment lay at Huntsville till the 16th of February, with little of interest outside of the regular routine of camp life. On that date we were ordered to Mooresville, and as we expected to make the trip in a day, everything, blankets, etc., were put into the wagons. But the wagons had all the baggage of our men who were in Mississippi to haul, which made the loads almost too heavy for the teams as soft as the roads were, and as a consequence we failed, by four or five miles, to get to Mooresville that day, and had to sleep without tents or blankets. The contrast and exposure was so great as to give every man a severe cold, and for several days few were able for duty. We reached Mooresville on the 17th, and went into camp close to the railroad, on the banks of the Lime Stone Creek. Our camp was in a beautiful place, and under the efficient discipline of Capt. Robinson was soon in splendid order. The Memphis & Chattanooga railroad had been repaired for some distance west of Huntsville, and Gen.

Thomas had determined to secure for his army at Chattanooga some of the vast amount of corn still standing in the fields near Mooresville. We were now under the command of Col. Biggs, of the 123d Illinois, which regiment had been here for a month. It will be remembered that Col. Biggs was in command of our expedition to this region in the middle of November, when Sigars was killed; and our boys always charged him with being a little too easy and liberal with some of the rebels who, on that occasion, came to him to get their stock back; and further charged that, in some instances, he turned out more stock to them than they ever had before. We only speak of this to introduce another matter. If there ever was any weakness in a man of the Seventy-Second it was his proclivity to forage on the slightest provocation; but when we went into camp at Mooresville, Biggs issued strict orders to the Seventy-Second that foraging should entirely cease, and any soldier caught in the country foraging, or with forage in his possession, should surely be punished. Of course our boys were too good soldiers and too well drilled in dicipline not to obey; but the first thing they did after getting the order, was to dig in each bunk a subterranean receptacle for hams, chickens, pigs, flour, dried fruit, potatoes and molasses, which, somehow or other, would keep coming into camp and getting into the very places prepared to receive them. We shall describe our own, because we were more familiar with its structure than with any others, though we are aware there were others in camp more elaborate and of better construction than ours. Then our bunk was a nice little cozy house 6 by 12 feet, and four feet high, covered with our dog tents. In the end which was next to the street we had a window and a door; just by the side of the door we always kept our cracker box, having a lid with leather hinges and straps to fasten it down. Right under this we dug a hole the size of the cracker box, and put just such a box as we have described down into it, so that we had two cracker boxes, the lower one immediately below the surface. Somehow or other the lower one was always full of various articles of diet for the soldier, which, we are led to believe, grew upon some neighboring plantation. We have known the half of a hog that would weigh 200 pounds to get into that box, and a quarter of a yearling calf; or a half dozen chickens, or a bushel of sweet potatoes; or a jug of molasses that would come into camp and get into that box; and once having *come* into camp contrary to Col. Biggs' orders, why, we felt that the laws of war justified us in confiscating them. But we hadn't been in camp a week until our reputation for stealing became a little too prominent, and the boys talked of holding an indignation meeting; but finally concluded to let time (which makes all things even) vindicate our character. By the end of the week the citizens, for miles around, began to be seriously exercised over the prospect of losing the last pig and chicken they had, and began to present their pitiful claims to Col. Biggs. On each complaint the Colonel would send his Adjutant with the wronged and complaining butternut over to the camp of the "thieving Seventy-Second," as he was pleased to call it. The adjutant would come and lay his complaint before Capt. Robinson; and before the doleful tale was half told every body in camp knew he was there, and in a twinkling had everything snug. Capt. Robinson would listen patiently, and then very blandly tell them that he certainly didn't think his men would steal; but they were welcome to go through the companies, and if they found anything, why, take it along, of course. As our bunk was rather pretentious and close to the Captain's headquarters, they usually began with us. They would come to us and say, "well, men, there has been some stealing done, and by order of Col. Biggs we have come to get the articles. Have you got anything?"

"Reckon not, Captain, but you can go in and see."

In they would go and turn our bunk upside down, shake our blankets, open our cracker box, scrape the crackers from end to end; look into every nook and corner, then stop and stare each other vacantly in the face, and then come out; while all this time we were out in the street, gawking like an unsophisticated country jake, just dropped down into a large city. Each bunk in the whole detachment would undergo this searching scrutiny, and these visits were repeated about every third day as long as we stayed there. But we never heard of a single case of an article being found that had ever been on a southern plantation; and of course, we felt that the character of the regiment for truthfulness, uprightness and integrity was most thoroughly vindicated, and were very happy over the result. Soon after we went into camp the 58th Indiana pioneer regiment came to us and built a bridge over Lime Stone Creek; the bridge was a long one, and they were two weeks building it.

Here we got our second installment of recruits. As we had been in camp about two weeks, of course every board and rail within a half mile had disappeared. Some of these recruits wanted some boards to make bunks of. The enterprising Grismar, Company K, came to their relief; said he'd fix 'em up; said he knew they were coming and had saved some boards on purpose for 'em. So he took them to the railroad crossing at the creek, three-quarters of a mile from our camp and showed them the water tank, and said he had reserved that on purpose for 'em. It is needless to say that this water tank was about as essential to us as the railroad itself, yet they went to work and tore it down and carried the boards to camp; but before they had their bunks fixed up the Colonel found it out and made them carry the boards back.

Our detachment, while lying here, gathered 10,000 bushels of corn, which kept us busy. B. M. Thompson, sergeant-major of the regiment, was absent on leave, and we were the ranking sergeant, and had the detailing to do, and remember several times when there were not men enough in the detachment to fill the details. Our camp was in a delightful location, the men were all in the best of health, the weather was grand and our duty light, but we had a great deal of it. As soon as the bridge across Limestone Creek was completed we began to ship the corn to Chattanooga. An expedition was prepared at Athens to cross the river, take possession of Decatur and thus more thoroughly cover the two roads that formed a junction, just north of Decatur and four miles south of Athens. One of the roads ran east to Chattanooga, and the other north to Nashville. About the time the railroad began to near completion the rebels began to want to burn our corn, and we had to keep a strong picket at the pens all the time. On the night of March 6th our men got safely over the river at Decatur, and held the place, so that much of the vigilance of the pickets was relaxed. The rebels knew this, and on the night of March 20th, a party of them crossed the river and tried to burn the corn, and would have succeeded had it not been for the promptness of some men of Company G, and a few others. The pens were a mile and a half from camp, and these men declare to this day that they saddled up and were at the pens in 20 minutes from the time of getting the alarm. On the night of the 21st these same rebels, or others just like them, actually burned some of our wagons a mile from camp. This taught us that "eternal vigilance is the price" of corn, especially rebel corn, cribbed by Yankee soldiers; and by the Eternal we were vigilant from that time until the corn was shipped to Chattanooga.

We have again occasion to call attention to the various moods and feelings of soldiers, as a whole, as frequently exhibited by our regiment. A body of men constantly together are like children at school. Indeed, they are children grown up. It often occurred after our men had been lying in camp for a length of time, that they would take spells of melancholy, and for two or three days would be so quiet you would think there wasn't any body at home. Men would mope about or saunter around, and you could scarcely get a word out of them. And then, again, they would take spells of romping and playing, and for several hours would just turn the whole camp upside down and smash things generally.

The following passage in the history of our regiment fully demonstrates our observations. The weather through March had been most delightful, and by the 12th, peach trees were out in full bloom; our work though not hard was constant, and we had settled down to it as regularly as ever a farmer did to the gathering of his crops, or to the plowing of his corn. For 10 days there had been no gossip nor a single tale of scandal. On the night of the 21st of March it snowed seven inches deep. Hoo-oo-oo! Bully for the sunny South. A clap of thunder at noonday from a clear sky could not have alarmed the natives like this did. Some of them had never seen snow in their lives, and the wisest of them declared that the "gol-busted Yanks had turned the world on eend;" or that we really had brought the cold weather with us. This would have been a big snow for central Indiana, and we suppose the like really never did occur, before or since, in Alabama.

This, of course, stopped the corn "shucking," and during the forenoon the men lay around in their bunks as blue as defeated candidates after an election. But after dinner the sun came out clear and warm, and the men began to crawl out of their holes, and the very first impulse was to pick up some of the snow and dab it into the face of a comrade. The idea was catching and the infection spread, till pretty soon the skirmishing began in earnest. The first brush began between Companies I and C, but pretty soon nearly the whole regiment was engaged, and in a few minutes the balls were flying over a row of dog houses as thick as hail.

This fight lasted two hours and a half, and was determined and desperate in the extreme. You may talk of your prize drills, dress parades, grand reviews and sham battles; but this one would "lay over" them all till they would never see daylight again. When the fight ended there was scarcely enough snow left in camp to make a snow-ball; they had literally worn it all out. And, strangest of all, not a single man was seriously hurt, and when it ended everybody was in the best possible humor.

From the time our regiment left us, up to the 1st of March, we had not heard a single word from them, and had no more idea where they were than the man in the moon. On the 6th of March there came a *rumor* that they had been in a fight and got badly handled; but where they were we could not even guess. We had longed and wished, and wished and longed, for them to come back, ever since they went away, and this rumor added fuel to the flame of our desire to see them. As we sat around our camp-fires after night, the most constant theme of convervation was "the boys;" and the last words we said to each other as we started for our bunks to go to bed were, "I wish the boys would come home." In every company there were cases of attachment almost as sacred as between man and wife. They had been sealed by blood and danger, and nothing but death could break them. In every mess these attachments existed, and like disconsolate lovers the men waited and wondered why their absent mess-mates did not return. As for our own part there was many a day we were *never* more lonesome in our life than when thinking of our absent bunk-mates. Our case was peculiar. We believe there was not another mess in the regiment but had two or more men left behind, but in ours we alone were left. There were men in our mess we loved as we scarcely ever loved a brother, and it made us homesick to think that perhaps harm had befallen them. No family at home ever more earnestly discussed the return of absent brother, sister, father or mother, than we did the return of our bunk-mates.

On the 21st of March another installment of recruits came to us; but better still, some of our old bunk-mates. This was the first reliable information we had of the whereabouts of the regiment. They were dismounted and our regiment had come to Nashville on its way back to us, and these had come through on the cars, and told us that the regiment was on its way marching to join us. We were almost wild with delight to see them. But what pangs of sorrow shot through our inmost soul when they whispered that *some* would never come back! Bitter tears were shed for the unreturning braves as we clasped the returning ones by the hands. It was a blending of joy and sorrow in many messes, such as is rarely experienced, even in the fortunes of war. We spent most of the night in telling of all the haps and mishaps that had befallen each other since we parted; and as this was the first intimation we had received of where they had been, we will begin here and tell it all:

We have already told how they left us on the evening of the 31st of December, in that terrible storm of rain, hail, sleet and snow; and how we left them at Pulaski and turned back to camp. They turned west on the Lawrenceburg road, moved four miles and went into camp. Soon after starting the wind began to blow a hurricane. (Let us say that as this is the story of the regiment, as told by a dozen or more comrades still living, and in precisely the same words, we shall use the pronoun "we" just as if we were present.) It soon became too cold to snow, but our clothes were already as wet as water could make them. We never saw it turn cold faster in our own Northern homes than it did then and there, after we had turned into a woodland and undertook to dismount. Records, of Co. I, says: "I was literally frozen to the saddle; mud had splashed against my feet and the stirrups and frozen till I could scarcely break them loose. My coat tails were also frozen to my saddle skirts. I succeeded in breaking everything loose but my gun; this was frozen to my saddle so solidly that I was forced to let it remain till a fire was kindled. A nice fix for a surprise." And this was the condition of almost all the men. Dr. Cole says: "My saddle was frozen to my horse so tightly that I could not remove it." We built huge fires, hallooed and pitched on more rails; yelled and piled on more rails, and bade defiance to the storm; but it proved to be the worst night we had yet experienced in the service. Our camp ground was enclosed by a high rail fence, and it was evident the order to "take only the top rail" was obeyed to the letter, for when day came not a top rail was to be seen. Dr. Cole says: "A bright fire was our only comfort, for we had no shelter." Capt. Thomson says: "That night was long and sleepless; the day long coming, and when it came at last, the thermometer indicated four degrees below zero." It was too cold to move mounted; but a forced march was to be made, and the frigid atmosphere must be endured, and marching dismounted during the day, and moving the snow to obtain a bed of leaves for night, was the soldier's lot. Many in the regiment had neither overcoats nor mittens, and as a consequence numbers were frost-bitten, and some very severely. Dr. Cole froze one of his toes till it crippled him for many days. Sergt. Stewart says many had their ears frozen and also their feet.

Before going any further, it may be well to state that the expedition was under the command of Maj. H. M. Carr, Capt. Adam Pinkerton acting major, and the destination is Savannah, on the Tennessee River. But the *object* was not so *clear*, as, according to Dr. Cole, Maj. Carr lost his orders the first night out. We moved 25 miles this terrible day, and camped near Lawrenceburg for the night.

January 2d proved to be another bitter cold day. We marched 28 miles, and camped near Pointer's Furnace, about six miles from Waynesboro. We passed through such a miserably poor country that it was difficult to obtain forage for the horses. Another bitter cold night.

We have so often called attention to that "everlasting body guard," gray-back, that we beg pardon, but we find him to-night under trying circumstances, and we are moved to tears of sympathy. The "tail" of his woes is a horrible one, and if it were not for the fact that all the witnesses of his "eend" are still living and ready to substantiate by oath, affirmation, or otherwise, all we are about to say, we would forbear. The names of the parties are Sergt. W. S. Wakeman, Corpl. A. M. Stanfield, Priv. Wm. Sale, and others, of Company I. As the regiment was about going into camp, Stanfield said, "This will be another hard night on the gray-backs." Wakeman said it wouldn't freeze one. Stanfield allowed it would. Said Wakeman, "I'll bet you a dollar you may hang one up all night and it won't hurt it." The bet was taken, and Sale held the stakes. Wakeman secured a good, healthy one, about the size of a grain of wheat, tied a thread carefully around his body, and hung him to a limb. The next morning they took the poor fellow down, warmed him carefully, and he walked off with the thread, and Wakeman walked off with the stakes.

We give the following from the Journals of comrades:

January 3d. Soon after passing through Waynesboro it began to snow, and presently to rain, making marching most disagreeable. We made 25 miles and camped on Indian Creek, 16 miles from Savannah. Out of rations.

January 4th. Moved on to Savannah; considerable rain falling during the day. So far our regiment, and the scouts, under Capt. Kilborn, are all that are with us; the time we were to be out is expired and rations are exhausted, and yet it has not transpired to us in ranks what the object of this expedition is.

January 5th, Gen. W. S. Smith, Sherman's chief of cavalry, under escort of two companies of the 4th East Tennessee Union Cavalry, arrived at Savannah.

January 6th. A brigade of cavalry arrived, consisting of three Tennessee and one Kentucky regiments, under command of Col. Ray.

On the 7th, the 4th U. S. Cavalry arrived; they had belonged to Minty's brigade and had been along with us on the Wheeler raid, recognized us at once, and called us the Wilder men.

Gen. Smith has taken a notion that our battalion of "Spencers" would be a good body guard for him on a raid he contemplates making down into the heart of Mississippi. We have spoken of our regimental drunk at Glasgow, and of Company A's drunk at Rogersville, and here Company H got on a "High Lonesome" and "cut up jack generally." These spasmodic drunks occurred at rare intervals, and were always a big load of fun for the participants.

At Savannah a detail was made to forage for provisions. Among the number was Michael Batterall, private Company H, a Dutchman, a devoted Christian and decidedly opposed to stealing, in the home acceptation of the term. In due course of time a smoke-house was found and the men went for the meat, the lady of the house protesting they would be left to starve; when Michael, with a ham in each hand, accosted her thus: "Vel now, madams, I neffer did shteals noddings to home, und I neffer shteals noddings here; put now I is detailed to shteal for de government and must do as I bees ordered, und you musht excuse me."

January 8th. The troops here commenced crossing to-day in three transports, which came up last night accompanied by two gunboats. Dr. Cole says: "Without any regard to the expressed wishes of the officers to the contrary, and with no remonstrance whatever, as was his duty on being taken out of the department, Carr crossed the river with the detachment to follow the fortunes of Gen. Smith, rather than return to his brigade and regiment at Pulaski, as we conceived to be his duty. We crossed the river on the boats Bluebird and Masonic Gem, moved up the river and camped a little beyond "Crump's Landing."

January 9th. The regiment moved through Adamsville and camped a mile and a half from Corinth. The 10th was spent in camp re-shoeing horses. From the terrible cold and exposure of the last ten days many are sick, and Corpl. Joseph R. Higinbotham, of Company A, died. In commenting on this, Stewart, of Company A, says: "Let some of the feather bed patriots of the North, just for one night, go to bed on the warm side of the frozen ground, with but a single thin blanket over him, and the wind whistling Yankee Doodle, Hail Columbia, and Dixie Land, around his pillow, and we imagine that his patriotism would all leak out before morning."

January 11th. Men and horses were put on cars and shipped to Middleton, Tenn., a station on the Memphis and Chattanooga railroad.

January 12th. We took to our saddles and marched to Lavergne, where we remained one day, drawing a little clothing, four days' rations and two days' forage.

January 14th. On the move again; to-day we stopped awhile at Moscow, which is garrisoned exclusively by colored troops. They have a fort and one piece of artillery. They had recently been attacked by Forest and suffered considerable loss, but Forest withdrew, leaving the darkies to claim a victory. We arrived at Colliersville, Tenn., 30 miles east of Memphis, on the Memphis and Chattanooga railroad, having actually traveled 203 miles from Pulaski. As up to this time we have had no definite idea of what we have been brought here for, some explanations may be in order, that our subsequent movements may be more intelligible to the general reader. We quote from Gen. Sherman's Memoirs, vol. 2, pp. 388, 389.

"The rebels still maintained considerable force of infantry and cavalry in the State of Mississippi, threatening the river, whose navigation had become to us so delicate and important a matter. I was satisfied that I could check this by one or two quick moves inland. So about the 20th of January I reached Memphis, where I found Gen. Hurlburt and explained to him my purpose to collect from his garrison and those of McPherson about 20,000 men, with which, in February, to march out from Vicksburg as far as Meridian, break up the Mobile and Ohio railroad, and also one leading from Vicksburg to Selma. Also I instructed him to select two good divisions and be ready with them, at Memphis, to go along. I found Gen. W. Sooy Smith with a force of 2,500 cavalry which he had brought across from Middle Tennessee, to assist in our general purpose, as well as to punish the rebel Gen. Forest, who had been most active in harrassing our garrisons in western Tennessee and Mississippi. A *chief* part of the enterprise was to *destroy* the rebel cavalry commanded by Gen. Forest, who were a constant threat to our railway communications in Middle Tennessee; and I committed this task to Gen. W. Sooy Smith. Gen. Hurlburt had in his command about 7,500 cavalry. Out of these and the force Smith had brought with him, we proposed to make up an "effective" aggregate of 7,000 men. With this force Gen. Smith was ordered to move from Memphis straight for Meridian, Miss., *and to start by the 1st of February.* I explained to him personally the nature of Forest as a man, and of his peculiar force; told him (Smith) that in his route he was sure to encounter him, who always attacked with a vehemence for which he must be prepared, and that after he had repelled the first attack, he must in turn assume the most determined offensive, overwhelm him and utterly destroy his whole force.

"I knew that Forest could not have over 4,000 cavalry, and my own movements would give employment to every other man in the rebel army not immediately present with him, so that Smith might safely act upon the hypothesis I have stated."

Gen. Sherman completed all his preparations for the enterprise, and on the morning of the 3d of February *his* forces started from Vicksburg for Meridian, expecting, of course, that Smith would start from Memphis by the 1st, in obedience to the above instructions. But Smith did not start; so we will go back to our regiment and tell the part it took in this enterprise and then let Sherman explain the failure.

On January 19th an order was read to us transferring us from the Army of the Cumberland to the Army of the Mississippi, and assigning us to McCrillis' Brigade, Grierson's Cavalry Division, 16th Army Corps. This seemed almost like reading a death warrant to us, but as it did not appear that we had any choice in the matter, all we could do was to submit and content ourselves as best we could. Yet we longed to be again in the old Lightning Brigade – a hope we then expected never to realize. We spent hours and hours talking of the times we used to have with the old brigade, and then we would wonder where the old 17th was? and what was the old 98th doing? and what had become of the 123d? until we would become fairly home-sick.

The brigade to which we were attached was composed of the 1st and 2d East Tennessee, 5th Kentucky, 3d Illinois, and our own Seventy-Second.

On January 25th all unserviceable stock was turned over and sent to Memphis by a detail from the Seventy-Second. Sergt. McClure, Co. H, was in command of part of this detail. After turning over the horses his squad were quartered in deserted houses on the outskirts of the city, got melodiously drunk, and improved their target practice by shooting dogs by moonlight.

On the 28th of January all troops east of Colliersville were moved to Memphis, also the garrison here. January 30th, anticipating an attack, we moved inside the fortifications. Capt. Kilborn and his scouts went out 12 miles south-east, in the vicinity of Mount Pleasant, stayed over night, and on the morning of the 31st a part of his boys got into an ambush, and two were captured; and in a subsequent encounter Birch Tenery, Co. E., was wounded. The Captain sent a message back reporting the state of affairs in his field of operations, which created quite an alarm in camp. We were immediately called to arms, and remained in a state of readiness for an attack all day. It happened the rebs did not follow Kilborn after he beat off their second attack; but in this skirmish Wm. Clark, Co. H, who was with the scouts, was thrown from his horse, and the horse ran into the rebel lines, taking with it all of Clark's traps except his gun. Records gives this account of Clark's escape: "After Clark was dismounted he got into some high grass in an old field, still keeping his rifle with him. Presently he observed a rebel hunting for him, when he got in a ditch partly filled with water and lay down in the water; but for all that the rebel found him and ordered him to surrender, when Clark took a snap shot at him and killed him, and then ran to a wood near by, and by its shelter made his escape, arriving in camp about midnight, bare-headed, wet, and muddy, with his rifle and just one cartridge left."

The scouts under Capt. Kilborn were called the division scouts, and were made up of details from companies of the Seventy-Second.

February 5th. Our camp here is on the south side of Wolf River, and the country for miles around is thoroughly foraged out; but the north side is so protected by deep, unfordable streams, that it has not suffered much, and, being rich and fertile, is well supplied with provisions and forage. True to their nature and instincts, the Seventy-Second has a wonderful hankering for that side of the river, and various plans for getting over the stream have been cussed and discussed; but none adopted until this morning, when Lieut. Cravens, Co. D, took a detail and crossed the river by unsaddling their horses and swimming them over, and passing the men and saddles across in an old canoe. The Seventy-Second remained on the south side as a support for Cravens, but soon waked up to the conviction that we were about as good as no support at all; for if Cravens should get into trouble out in the country we could be of no service to him whatever. He had not been gone long when the men began to swear that it was time we were fixing some way to get over, when Major Carr asked, "How can you do it?" "Well, we will show you, if you will let us." "Go in on it," says the Major. At this the enlisted men took license and began to discuss their plans, while the officers stood around with a broad grin on their faces, not expecting anything to come of it. We had observed that a tree of ordinary height would reach across the river, though it was quite deep, with scarcely any current. We soon came to the conclusion that by cutting down two trees on the south side and letting them fall across the stream with their tops to the north side, and then crossing on these, we could fall two trees from the north side so as to lap on to the tops of the first two. Then with a little lapping down of brush we could take fence rails and complete the job. "Well," says the Major, "I don't believe your bridge will be worth a d—n, but you can go ahead and try it." Well, we did; and in a few hours had it fixed up so that cavalry and teams could cross it. On Lieut. Cravens' return he gave a very glowing account of the prospect for forage; it was truly "a land flowing with milk and honey." He backed his report with an ox-cart loaded with hams so savory that old Mars no doubt rejoiced in the sweet odor that ascended from our camp-fires that night and next morning.

So next day, February 6th, the entire regiment saddled up early and struck for the north side of Wolf River, where the companies were directed to separate and forage for their own as well as their country's good. All the companies did well, and yet we hope to be able to report just *how* well each did, but as yet have not the figures. Co I realized three wagons, four mules, one horse, five yoke of oxen, seven barrels of flour, and 2,400 pounds of hams and shoulders.

On the 7th the regiment went north of the river again. This time another party was upon the ground, and two men of Company C and one of Company F got captured by getting a little too far from the column. Company A, Capt. Andrew J. Klepser, came in contact with the rebels and repulsed them without hurt to himself or company. He reported at camp at 7 in the evening, and left again in a short time with four companies for the north side, where he lay in ambush till morning, and then surprised a rebel camp, recaptured our men and made prisoner a rebel captain. Some detachments of the regiment had not yet reported when Capt. Klepser went out in the evening, and on going out he fell in with them and they went back. But those of us who were left in camp had an anxious night of it, for by some means we got word in camp that there was a large rebel force over there, and that most if not all our comrades not reporting had been captured. We suppose it is impossible for people who have never been disturbed by the immediate presence of an armed foe to realize the terrible suspense we endured. Some of us had brothers with those reported captured, and all of us had bunk-mates with them whom we loved as brothers; and it was a wonderful relief to us when Klepser came in again on the 8th. While north of the river Klepser fell in with a detachment of the 4th Regulars, and these men at once decided to stay with him, and *they did.* They had the utmost confidence in the Seventy-Second, and always called our battle-flag "the Wilder flag," and in every case of difficulty or trouble would always rally to the "Wilder flag."

It was now found that the soldiers of our battalion were short of ammunition, and this was the beginning of all our sorrows. A supply had been ordered from Cincinnati, O., but when it came it was found that the cartridges would not fit our guns, and they were sent back. Henry Hoover, Co. B, who was captured on the expedition, says, "We started with not more than ten rounds to the man." No better evidence of mismanagement somewhere than this simple statement implies need be furnished. Take the bravest and best disciplined troops in the world, and when the last shot is fired all hope is fled. We have seen, by "Sherman's Book," that this expedition was to start by the 1st of February. And now we quote from Dr. Cole's journal of February 9th: "We are expecting every day when Gen.

Smith's expedition into Mississippi will move;" and from Corpl. Records' notes of the same date we quote: "It now stands forth in well-developed reality that a cavalry raid into the enemy's country is being organized at this place. Our brigade has been here for several days, and to-day other troops have arrived, making in all that are here and coming, seventeen regiments. To-morrow the expedition is to start, and, notwithstanding we are so poorly supplied with ammunition, we must go. We could have supplied ourselves well at our camp at Pulaski, and it doubtless would have been done, notwithstanding the hurry of our leaving, if we had had the faintest idea in the world that we should not have been back there inside of four days from the time of leaving."

We quote again from Dr. Cole's journal of February 10th: "At last we are under way toward the South; our detachment is temporarily attached to the 3d brigade, commanded by Col. McCrillis, of the 3d Illinois cavalry. Three brigades of cavalry compose the command, which starts to-day for the west center of Mississippi, to divert attention from Sherman, who is moving toward Meridian from Vicksburg, and our little band of less than 300 Spencer rifles *unfortunately* forms a part of the force moving into Mississippi. We moved across Cold Water River and camped 15 miles from Colliersville." From Records we quote: "February 10th. Set out this morning without drawing ammunition. On inspection it was found that we had what would make about 25 rounds to the man, about one-fourth of what we ought to have had. Went into camp 16 miles from Holly Springs, Company I on picket. A corporal and private of Company B, 4th East Tennessee cavalry, also on picket, were bushwhacked and killed, two wounded, and one private of 3d Illinois cavalry wounded." No wagons were used on this expedition, but pack-mules instead.

February 11. We didn't move, but buried our men killed by the bushwhackers. Scouting parties gather in several rebel officers who are at home on furlough.

On account of bushwhackers, the Tennessee cavalrymen were afraid to go on picket to-night, and the deficiency was promptly made up by the Seventy-Second. Sergt. McClure, Co. H, says that during the day these East Tennesseeans have burned large quantities of property in retaliation for murdering their comrades last night, and for that reason were afraid to go on picket. McClure thus gives his experience on picket that night: "I had charge of 20 men, and put them out after dark on a road running south from camp, and on account of what had happened received strict orders that if anything tried to approach us from that direction to shoot without halting. In the night my pickets heard what they thought to be men galloping up from the front, and you may be sure that under the circumstances they were wide awake, and opened fire at once. When the firing occurred we could hear the horses pass over a fence into an enclosed pasture on our left, which lay in an angle between the road running south and another one running east of our headquarters at the forks of the road. I had two videttes on each road and one in the pasture between them. We could hear the accoutrements rattle, as the horses, as we thought, moved around among the trees. At every movement our boys would shoot, for we were all anxious, as we thought the rebels were dismounting in that pasture to slip up on and bushwhack us. We could get no reply from them when we would shoot, and my men kept up firing so constantly that Company F saddled up and came to our support. When daylight came, behold! there stood one lone horse that belonged to an Illinois regiment. By some means he had gotten outside of our lines, and was trying to come in from the south. He had on him saddle, bridle, carbine, sabre, canteen, and all the equipments of a cavalryman, attached to the saddle, and it was the rattling of these that had fooled us. The only reason why he was not shot to pieces was that he was in a hollow, and being put on duty after dark we knew nothing of the 'lay of the land,' and had been shooting over him." We have given this incident as showing the watchfulness of the men of the Seventy-Second, who were *never surprised by the enemy during their whole term of service.*

February 12th. The bushwhackers tried it again on some parts of our lines, and got whacked themselves. They did not seem to appreciate the Seventy-Second's manner of picketing.

Dr. Cole says, February 12th: "The 4th East Tennessee cavalry were again unfortunate in having three men killed and four wounded last night on picket."

Records says, same date: "The command moved at daylight, Co. B, 4th East Tennessee, in advance. Early in the morning they were ambushed, and one sergeant and two privates killed."

We arrived at Holly Springs, Mississippi, about 11 a. m. After fooling away two or three hours in swearing old citizens to be loyal to the United States, the column moved on and got into the Tippar swamps early in the afternoon, floundered along till night, when we reached high ground and went into camp. Dr. Cole lost his headquarters tent in that swamp.

February 13th. We started early and soon came to the Tippar River, which was difficult to ford. We had to cross in single file, which prolonged the column.

During the night some bushwhackers dressed in women's clothes, came to the picket line and tried to talk like women; but our boys discovered the deception and fired into them, wounding one, which settled the question of sex beyond a doubt.

February 14th. A drizzly, disagreeable day; in the saddle early, but made very slow progress. As the command was crossing the Tallahatchie River, it was foggy and difficult to distinguish objects. Some men of the 2d and 3d brigades ran into each other and began firing, neither brigade knowing that the other was in the country. Dr. Cole says, a 3d Tennessee man was wounded; the firing was so rapid as to cause our brigade to get into line. We made six miles for the day. Head Genius of the expedition had already developed a wonderful faculty for killing time.

February 15th. A thunder-storm last night. Two regiments of our brigade went in the direction of Okolona. The balance of the division are in camp or out foraging.

February 16th. Moved eight miles and went into camp 10 miles from Pontotoc.

Dr. Cole says: "We burned a vast amount of cotton to-day. We saw a poor boy with the mark of a rope around his neck; he had been hung up for refusing to tell the whereabouts of some deserters from the rebel army, showing that the leaders of this infernal rebellion are madly determined on its success."

February 17th. Gen. Smith, commanding the expedition, ordered division scouts, Capt. Kilborn and Companies C and I, Seventy-Second, to make a reconnoissance on Okolona.

The command lay in camp till late in the afternoon. Dr. Cole says: "We seem to be taking things quite cool and rather slow; am fearful we are giving the rebels ample time to concentrate their forces and defeat our object. The only thing we seem to be in dead earnest about, is foraging, which the men seem to enjoy hugely. We are the first live Yankees ever seen in these parts, and the citizens express themselves as well satisfied with the sight, which costs them so much." After passing Pontotoc the command went into camp eight miles south of that place. The enemy is reported as concentrating his scattered forces in front of us and a few miles south.

February 18th. Cold and snowy. We moved early, taking the road to Okolona, and camped for the night near that place. The smoke of burning fences, cotton gins and presses, could now be seen ascending in every direction. Reports represent Forest moving south, not yet having received sufficient force to justify him in attacking us. The weather cold and ground frozen.

February 19th. Weather moderating a little. We moved early, making tolerably good time; encamped for the night in the edge of the Chickasaw Plains, a section of country hardly ever equaled and never surpassed in natural fertility. Immense quantities of corn and cotton were stored at the different stations along the Mobile and Ohio railroad, all of which were burned as fast as we could get access to them. A 7th Indiana cavalryman, who escaped from Forest, came in to-day and reports him in strong force at West Point.

February 20th. We moved early and went into camp near West Point. We made very little progress before noon; both brigades in front of ours, and also the advance, skirmishing with the rebels, and the rear guard with corn-cribs, cotton gins, presses and fences, all of which fall before the flames. The destruction of property was fearful to contemplate. The advance drove the rebels out of West Point, and in the fight lost a Lieutenant and five men killed. From about sundown till 11 p. m. we moved pretty rapidly, and just before going into camp, Henry Nobes, of Company C, got his thigh broken by his horse falling on him. The fracture was adjusted by Dr. Cole; but as he could not be moved he was left at a house to fall into the hands of the rebels. He and several others have furnished most graphic accounts of their capture and imprisonment, and we will let them tell it themselves in another place. The rebel Gen. Forest and his forces camped just south of West Point.

We now turn to Gen. Sherman's book, vol. 2, pages 390 and 392, to see how the land lies with Sherman and our co-operation. He says: "On the morning of February 3d, we left Vicksburg in two columns of two divisions each, preceded by a light force of cavalry. We were lightly equipped as to wagons, and marched without deployment, straight for Meridian, distant 150 miles. On the 14th we entered Meridian, the enemy retreating towards Demopolis, Ala. We stayed in Meridian five days, expecting every hour to hear from Sooy Smith, but could get no tidings of him whatever."

This brings the time up to our camp, to-night, near West Point, just 100 miles from Meridian, where Sherman expected us to be on the 14th, or by the time he got there. That is, we are more than 100 miles behind Sherman's calculation, and it will be seen, soon, that this dilatoriness cost us severely in blood and equipage.

February 21st. We quote Dr. Cole: "We countermarched rather unceremoniously at daylight, the object of our raid reported to have been accomplished; but as we afterwards learned, Sherman not having the co-operation of the cavalry as he expected, was returning from Meridian to Vicksburg, which, of course, left the enemy free to turn his entire attention to us. The expedition had been too slow in getting under way, and after starting moved at a snail's pace through the country." We went into camp two miles south of Okolona; the rear brigade have been skirmishing heavily all day.

Records says this skirmishing began at daylight. Being used to the tactics of the department of the Cumberland, with such leaders as Old Rosy, Pap Thomas and Miller, whose motto was to "go for 'em wherever you can find 'em," we had our minds made up to go for 'em as soon as we got our breakfast; but to our surprise instead of an advance a retreat was ordered. The retrograde movement began about sun-up. We moved rapidly, frequently at a gallop, passing over almost as much ground that day as we had in three days previous. This evening the inefficiency of the head of the concern manifested itself by a confusion of orders to the Seventy-Second. We were ordered to go back eight miles to reinforce Col. Warring, who was commanding 1st brigade. We had about faced and moved the length of the regiment when we got orders to halt and await further orders. We waited about an hour, when we got orders to move on to camp, but before camp was reached we got orders to await further orders. It was now night; we waited an hour and a half, when we were ordered to accompany the 4th Tennessee Cavalry and go at once and report to Col. Warring; but no sooner were we in motion than that order was countermanded and then we went into camp, with orders not to unsaddle for the night.

February 22d. This day, memorable as the birthday of Washington, proved a busy one for us. The rear (2d brigade) was hard pressed all day yesterday, and lost in killed and wounded 50 men, and it now becomes our turn to take the rear, nominally, but really the front. The column began to move about 4 a. m. It was five hours before the balance of the two brigades got out of our way so we could move; by this time the head of the rebel column was right east of us, on a road running north, and about a mile east of the one we were on, the two roads running parallel. The rebels were also in sight in our rear when we started, and it began to be rather a serious question with us whether the rebels east of us would not beat us to Okolona, two miles away. As we neared the town the roads seemed to get closer to each other, and the flankers from each column were skirmishing, and the rear guard suffered some. We reached Okolona about 10 a. m., finding some very bad roads on the way. We observed that the troops ahead of us had abandoned some ambulances and other vehicles in the mud; some were burned, and still others intact. At Okolona the enemy were in sight on several roads, and the head of the rebel column just in the edge of town. Our brigade was formed in line of battle, and we waited an hour for the rebels to come upon us, but they made no attack. Of course the time given enabled them to close up their forces in the rear. We now got orders to withdraw, and our brigade commander made a fatal blunder. The country was open and the enemy could see our every movement, and instead of withdrawing in line of battle, we began to withdraw in column. The wily Forest observed this, dashed impetuously upon us and caused a stampede. The 4th regulars were in the rear, and stood up manfully against the rebel host that were hurled against them, repulsing their charges twice in succession. Our regiment dismounted in order to support the regulars, but just then the regulars were driven back upon the 2d Tennessee, in some confusion, when the Tennessee regiment became panic stricken and broke like stampeded buffalo, and ran like wild horses, pell mell over us, trampling many a brave soldier under their feet and separating many more from their horses. The horses, on getting loose, were carried away with the herd. This stampeded force rushed into the road and forced a battery of howitzers into the cotton fields, which were full of gullies, in which the battery soon got stuck, the artillerymen became panic stricken, cut loose from their guns and joined in the general flight, leaving their guns behind. This was one of the most humiliating things we ever saw. Nothing could exceed the confusion of this stampede, and the rapid advance of the rebels allowed no time for rallying them. On the enemy pressed, riding down our men and separating them from their horses (many never saw their horses again) so that it was impossible to remount until all the cavalry had passed, and then it was done under a sharp fire of the enemy, in whose possession the field was left. From that time until late in the afternoon the Seventy-Second was without organization, when the men were collected and re-organized in an old field on the Ely farm, many miles from Okolona, although the fight we had there is called the Okolona fight. While in this scattered condition almost every member of the regiment was the hero of some startling adventure; and when we began to get together many reported who had been considered by their comrades lost. Well do we remember the cheer Corpl. Brown, Co. I, gave, when he saw Corpl. Records and Wm. Ogborn, Co. I, come up all right, whom he was sure he had seen go down in the first collision in the forenoon. But genuine joy as it was to see each other there alive once more, it was *brief, very brief*; for before that day's sun went down some of our comrades went down to death, some with wounds, and some were captured. In the first effort to get the scattered men together, Adjt. Byrnes, Capt. Thomson, Capt. Kilborn, and some others, were conspicuous. After comparative quiet was restored, an order was received for the Seventy-Second to take position across the road, where it followed along a narrow ridge, and to hold the road at all hazards. We left No. 4's with the horses, and went on foot to the position assigned us. We found the ridge cut almost in two by a deep ravine, on the bank of which was a straggling sort of rail fence. Here we formed, our left resting upon the road, flanked by timber—our right extending along the line of fence down into an old cotton field. About 700 yards in front of us was a line of cavalry, already skirmishing with the enemy. Behind us, about the same distance, was another line of cavalry.

As soon as formed, we lay down behind the fence. Presently the line in front "broke" and came back "a-tearing." The rebels were dismounted and moving right up, firing as they came, the balls dropping about us as thick as hail; but we could not fire till our cavalry got out of the way. And as our supply of ammunition was very light, our officers gave the order, and then frequently repeated it, "Save your ammunition, men;" "don't throw a single ball away;" "don't shoot until you are sure of your man." Consequently we reserved our fire until the rebels were on the opposite bank of the ravine. They did not seem to be aware that any line was there until we began firing. We were lying so flat on the ground that the old fence screened us. We never knew the Seventy-Second to do such slow, deliberate firing, before or since, as they did then. But from the tumbling constantly going on in the enemy's lines it would seem that every shot told. The range was short, and both lines lay principally in the open field, which made bloody work of it. Had it not been that the enemy had a column of fresh troops constantly moving up, we would undoubtedly have repulsed them easily; but as it was they never suffered their fire to slacken, although unable to advance on account of the terrrible work of our Spencers. It was at this place that Col. Forest, the General's brother, was killed. We thought our left in the timber was covered by cavalry, but it was not. The enemy took advantage of that blunder and moved a column through the timber and flanked us. The first thing we knew the balls were flying through our ranks from three directions. Then it was the gallant Seventy-Second showed her metal, but it was at a fearful cost. Our men began to fall all along the line. About that time we were ordered "to horse." It had been easy enough to take hold, but it was not so easy to let go. We did not obey the first order "to horse;" but immediately an officer of Gen. Smith's staff rode along our lines calling out: "Seventy-Second, Gen. Smith says to horse! to horse!" We then jumped up and started to run back to our horses. This move was more disastrous to us than the fighting had been, for as we ran the rebels peppered us from three sides, as we were in an open field; and notwithstanding the herculean efforts of the men to save themselves, one-tenth of the whole regiment was killed, wounded or captured. It would have required a most desperate effort on the part of every man of the Seventy-Second to reach his horse, on account of the rebels being so close on each side of them; but what made it in many instances ten times worse, was the fact that the rebels had got close enough to the lead horses to shoot into them, and the horses were moved away just in time to leave many a poor fellow, who thought he was almost safe, to fall into the hands of the rebels. Everything had now been moved but the last line of cavalry spoken of heretofore. This was supported by artillery, and as soon as we could get out of the way the artillery opened on the advancing rebels, which caused them to recoil. Capt. Thomson, Co. D, and quite a number of the Seventy-Second, fell in with the cavalry. The cavalry seemed to be debating the propriety of making a charge. We became aware of the fact that the rebels were murdering our wounded men, and urged the cavalry to make a charge, promising them that we would go along and help. Capt. Thomson was very solicitous, as R. W. Sims, his lieutenant, had his thigh broken, and he was anxious to save him; others were also just as anxious, and for like reasons. Finally, just at sundown, the charge was made, and proved successful, driving the rebels off the field, and securing all the wounded who had not already fallen into the hands of the enemy. We cannot stop to give incidents here, but must hasten on to a safer place. As soon as the Seventy-Second got mounted it was ordered to go to the front, or head of column, as quickly as possible, and to form across the road and stop the fugitives who were panic-stricken.

We formed single file, and moved as rapidly as we could through fields and woods by the side of the road till near midnight, when we reached the head of column and turned the fugitives into an old field near by, which was soon lit up by big fires. The commanders of regiments here collected their men and re-organized them. In a short time the whole column moved on again, before the rear had near time to catch up. Dr. Cole says the march was kept up all night. The large number of negro contrabands, 1,500 and the long train of captured stock, horses and mules, 1,500, impeded the movement considerably. The ambulances also were heavily loaded with the wounded and sick, contrasting strongly with the pleasant march southward a few days ago. The whole loss of the brigade on this day—killed, wounded and missing—was 200.

February 23. We passed through Pontotoc this morning. We crossed the Tallahatchie river at New Albany, and then destroyed the bridge and felled trees in the ford. Moving on, we arrived at Hickory Flats at midnight, where we halted, fed our horses, got supper, and lay down and slept till 4 o'clock. It had been 36 hours since we had a chance to eat and sleep. The bread we ate on that occasion tasted sweeter than any we ever had. It was made of flour mixed with dirty water on a gum blanket, without salt, and baked by placing it on the flat side of a rail before the fire. We broiled meat in the fire on a sharp stick. As soon as we had somewhat satisfied the gnawings of hunger we abandoned ourselves, with bridle reins in our hands, to sleep.

February 24th. We were aroused from our slumbers at 4 a. m. by the sound of the bugle; crossed the Tippar River at a different place from that at which we crossed it in going south, and did not find the swamp nearly so bad. Just after dinner, when we had formed to move forward, an alarm was sounded and the entire brigade was dismounted and formed to fight on foot. We lay in line of battle till 8 p. m. We encamped, as we thought for the night, but about 12 o'clock we were ordered to move forward some two miles, and upon arriving at the point designated we got a most peremptory order to go back to where we first stopped, double-quick. There we were told not to unsaddle, but to hitch our horses and lie down.

February 25th. We got in motion about daylight, passed through Hudsonville, and on arriving at Mount Pleasant a detail of 50 men from the Seventy-Second was made, to go foraging for provisions. Lieut. Cravens, Company D, was in command. We were entirely out of everything in the shape of food. The detail was to meet the command at Colliersville. We had first rate success and went to Colliersville as ordered, but the command stopped eight miles short of that point, and as a consequence went to bed supperless.

February 26th. The column came up early in the forenoon, but without stopping moved on to Germantown, where we arrived at 12 m. There the order must have been to cook, and to eat some without cooking. Thus ended what has always been termed the Mississippi raid.

As to the result of this expedition, it is proper to say that we have never seen an official report of the raid; but from numerous reports of different individuals who took part in it, we make an average about this way: Captured 1,500 slaves, 1500 horses and mules: destroyed 10,000 bales of cotton, 100,000 bushels of corn; utterly destroyed 40 miles of the Mobile and Ohio railroad, and laid waste 150 miles of country to such an extent that the enemy could not possibly live in it. The loss of the expedition in men and horses was, of course, heavy, and we shall attempt to give only that of our regiment, and we are conscious that we shall fail even in that, because there always is a loss, under such circumstances, that can never be gauged by *so* many men, or *so* many horses.

In Company A, Corpl. Frederic Landis, private W. E. Seagraves, and George Baily, private, were captured. The last two named died in Andersonville. They were noble boys and the best of soldiers. W. H. P. Dimmitt, private, was severely wounded in the right arm.

Company B—John Landers, private, wounded by a spent ball; Henry Hoover, sergeant, missing; John C. Doss, private, missing; supposed to be dead.

Company C—Oscar F. Bryant, sergeant, missing; Phillip Schnepp, private, missing; Henry Nobes, private, missing.

Company D—C. G. Thomson, captain, wounded by spent ball; Robert W. Sims, 1st lieutenant, seriously, right thigh broken; John Fenton, missing, died in Andersonville—a good soldier; Robert S. Green, missing, died in Andersonville—a good soldier.

Company E—Lewis C. Priest, 1st lieutenant, killed.

Company G—E. B. Martin, orderly sergeant, part of ear shot off; Andrew Bryan, private, wounded by spent ball; John W. Wagoner, private, wounded by spent ball.

Company H—Theodore E. Stow, corporal, wounded severely in face, and thumb, and neck; John Johnson, private, in head, seriously, and died; a number one soldier.

Company I—H. C. Cassel, 2d lieutenant, wounded in right arm severely; Levi D. Brown, corporal, in face severely; James Drummond, corporal, by spent ball, in eye, severely; Wm. E. Ogborn, missing; died in Andersonville—a good soldier.

Company K—Erasmus M. Choat, corporal, killed—a good soldier: Alfred McGraw, private, wounded by spent ball.

A total of 27, killed, wounded and missing. Hoover, for years after getting home, was a wreck in body and mind; and Nobes, if possible, suffered a thousand deaths. Both have furnished reminiscences of their prison life, which we shall condense for our readers. But the one thing, above all others, that to-day rankles in the bosoms of surviving comrades, as it did in the bosoms of those who have died, to the last day they lived, is the thought of ingloriously retreating before an enemy.

Of course, in such a stampede and melee as the one just given, there are a thousand incidents of rarest bravery, heroism, and daring, and we would like to mention all of them, as well as some of the serio-comic and ridiculous. During the stampede Corpls. Brown and Records, and others of Company I, were riding through the fields at the side of the road, when suddenly they found themselves stopped by a big hedge, and to get to the road they would have to go back some distance. On turning around they saw the rebs were nearer the end of the hedge than they were, and seeing their predicament, began to close upon them. It was a case so plain as to need no argument to show that they were in for it; so they turned their horses' heads toward the hedge and spurred them into such frenzy that they dashed through the thorny fence, leaving shreds of the boys' clothing sticking to every thorn they touched. The rebs yelled and laughed prodigiously at this feat.

It is hardly possible to conceive the love and veneration soldiers have for the battle-flag or colors they have carried through many engagements. About the middle of the afternoon Corpls. Tolby, of Company G, Records, and a few others, came across Corpl. Kent, who still had the colors, and the thought of collecting their straggling men together struck them; so they rode to a high ridge, unfurled the flag and "waved a rally there," and in a short time, both the Seventy-Second and the 4th regulars began to rally around it, and formed in line. By this time the enemy came in sight, and seeing a line and a flag, they halted and began to deploy, which, of course, delayed them and gave us more time. Just then Capt. Dalton, of Company F, came along and took command, and thought best to move on. We had not gone far till we fell in with Capt. Thomson, of Company D, who had collected a like squad. He was greatly rejoiced to see the old flag once more, for he thought Kent and flag were both gone. Thus our scattered forces were getting together, and Capt. Thomson proposed that we should give the rebels a brush; but Col. Thornburg came along and ordered us to move forward.

Lieut. A. W. Lane, of Company G, a most gallant soldier and accomplished gentleman, in speaking of the battle of Okolona, says:

"An incident comes to my mind—an act which falls but little short of the heroic. During that terrible stampede of the 2d and 3d Tennessee Cavalry, in which we were instantly carried away, and in that mighty current, during those moments of terrible excitement, when it was almost certain death to dismount, the rebels pressing us ever" step with pistol and saber, cleaving the heads of those who became dismounted by shot or fallen horses—when you could see, as I did, men shot from the saddle, their foot catching in the stirrup, dragged to death by mad hosres in their efforts to keep up with the flying column—just then we passed by the battery that had been abandoned, when Wm. G. Keese, of Company G, (known in the left wing as "Massasocker," from an incident that happened during the Decherd raid, on top of the Cumberland Mountains) deliberately dismounted and undertook to spike the guns with knife blades; but failed for want of something sufficiently heavy to drive them.

"Scenes of that stampede and fight are indellibly stamped upon my memory. For four miles it was a race for life, in which "devil take the hindmost!" was the order of march; horses stumbling and falling; riders trampled to death; rebels riding promiscuously among us and cutting men down right and left; dismounted men running on foot and imploring help from their more fortunate companions; officers powerless, abandoning sick, wounded and footmen, to the merciless foe. The retreat of the gallant 200 of the Seventy-Second, after the stand on that ridge, in the evening, and mounting under that murderous cross-fire, was by odds the tightest place ever the Seventy-Second got into. I well remember the faces of "Sooy" Smith, Grierson, and McCrillis. At night we parked in the valley, every man to his horse, not a word to be said, nor a fire to be lighted to cheer the dismal hour. Tormented by hunger and helpless pity for our famishing horses; the rebel signal fires gleaming from mountain-top to crag; the faces of our officers sad with the forebodings for the morrow."

We have already told of the fine battery of little mountain howitzers that were lost in the first stampede, early in the morning. The Captain of this battery was a fine looking fellow, of commanding figure, and a good rider; from the time he lost his battery he assumed the duty of rallying the entire retreating column. Just before Thornburg came along and ordered us to move on, this battery Captain came up, and with great flourish of sword and flow of word, began to exhort us to stand and fight to the death; and began to point out the excellency of our position, telling us we could hold it against the whole Southern confederacy. While he was talking, a rifle ball came singing close to his ear, and cutting short his discourse, and remembering duties in the rear, he gave his horse the full length of spurs and sped away with a velocity little short of that of the ball that waked him up. There is no part of this terrible day's work that deserves more prominence, and should be spoken of in more pathetic terms, than the efforts of our boys to help each other, and to get our wound ed off the field. There has been many a monument erected to heroism not half so great or deserving as this.

Just after the regiment had been ordered "to horse" the last time, and many had started back, Lieut. Sims, Co. D, started to go, but had not gone far till a musket ball went crashing through his right thigh, shattering the bone. After he fell he saw the man who did it deliberately load his gun and shoot at him again as he lay upon his back; this time the ball struck him on the side of the breast, knocking the breath out of him, tearing away part of his vest and shirt, but fortunately not wounding him severely, though at the time it was thought to have gone clear through him.

Capt. Thomson started after Sims, and accidentally stumbled upon him soon after he had been struck the second time, and stopped and bent over him just as he supposed he was gasping his last. The bullets were whistling around him from every side. Sims finally told him for God's sake to hurry on, or he would be killed or captured. The Captain, seeing he could do nothing for him, with a heart as heavy as the lead which was raining around him, hastened on, with a determination that was desperate to return at every hazard and get his lieutenant. Nothing but a special Providence could possibly have shielded him from the missiles of death filling the air everywhere around him; but he finally succeeded in getting beyond the range of the enemy's guns, when the last of his strength was exhausted, and here, a second time, he came near being left at the mercy of the enemy. The Captain's horse had been left in the hands of a faithful negro boy, and some of the flying fugitives from the wrath of the rebels thought a horse would help them faster than their legs, and were just on the point of tearing the Captain's horse away from the negro, when Priv. Joseph M. Brannan, Co. I, rushed up with Spencer at his face and drove them away. But for the timely interference of Brannan, the Captain would surely have found his way to Libby prison. Brannan seized the Captain's horse and rushed back to meet him just as the last lingering rays of hope had fled. We have already seen how he, with others, assisted in the cavalry charge to get Sims from the field. We suppose that very few men ever endured the excruciating torture Sims did for four days, and survived it. He was placed upon a horse with his leg dangling like an empty sleeve, was hurried to the rear and placed in the bottom of an ambulance. He was driven over a hundred miles, and was never taken out or had his wound dressed till arriving at Colliersville, on the 26th. There certainly never was a grander exhibition of fortitude than he displayed. He finally got well, and although badly crippled is still living, at Frankfort, Indiana, beloved and respected by all who knew him—a gentleman in every sense of the word.

Soon after the rebels opened on our men at the old fence, in the afternoon, Corpl. Brown, of Co. I, was shot in the mouth, the ball knocking out his front teeth passing under his tongue, and lodging in the back of his neck. He started for the rear, but had not gone far before he fell exhausted from the loss of blood. Among the last to leave the fence was Corpl. Records, of Co. I. He had not gone far till he run upon the prostrate form of Corpl. Brown. He did not expect to find him alive, but stopped a moment to see if life was left, when Brown's pitiful appeals not to be left alone nerved Records to the effort to rescue him. He could not carry Brown, but by getting Brown's arms around his neck he succeeded in dragging him about 600 yards. By this time the rebels were closing in on him and hallooing "halt! halt!" Sergt. Dan. Moore, of Co. C, seeing their desperate situation, rushed in and pulled Brown on to his horse behind him, and galloped away. This left Records alone, but so exhausted as to scarcely be able to raise the trot; yet he determined to go as long and as far as he could. The rebels were still shooting at him and commanding him to halt, but he pushed on, and having gone 50 yards further he came up to Buck Duddleson, of Co. G, who had Simeon Strawn's mule fast on a willow bush. Many a man under the circumstances would have abandoned the "concern," but not so with Buck. He declared his intention to save the whole outfit, and did succeed in disengaging the mule just as Records came in calling distance, and turned about in the very teeth of the enemy and dragged the exhausted Records on to the mule, and both skinned out; but not without a rapid parting salute fired by the rebels. None but a skeptic could fail to see the hand of Providence in saving them. On the first order to dismount in the morning, and in the stampede that immediately followed, James M. Starbuck, priv. Co. D, was among the number who found himself without a horse, and saw it no more for three days, losing his saddle, rations and complete outfit. After running about four miles he was picked up by Capt. Thomson, who had rallied a squad of men and was trying to hold the enemy at bay until all the dismounted men should catch up and get mounted. Later in the day Capt. Kilborn had gathered a similar squad by the side of the road and had the regimental colors unfurled to rally the stragglers to. We well remember the remark he made on looking along the line and seeing how few we were. He said: "Well, boys, they may kill us, but they can never capture us."

Our men always called this the Okolona stampede; but from different sources we have learned the rebels always called the last fight in the evening the battle of Prairie Mound. This was the time Capt. Thomson was severely stunned by a ball which struck him in the breast, and was stopped by a book in his pocket.

Dr. Cole, in speaking of the retreat, says: "Our brigade skirmished all day with the advance of the enemy, and we marched all night; and at one time, when everything seemed to be so thoroughly jammed up in front that it would be impossible to move any further. I was a little amused at Gen. Smith's chaplain, who by some unlucky chance had been caught in the retreating column, not very far from the rear, and from the terrible jam was unable to extricate himself or to get forward. He was a great, big, burly German, and a Catholic priest. Finally his patience became entirely exhausted, and he exclaimed: '*Oh! dey go zo zlow! I vonder vy zey don' drot?*'"

On February 25th he says: "Marching hard to-day. We reached and crossed Tippar river, and our brigade was attacked while crossing. The men are on short rations, and many have nothing at all to eat. I have charge of the ambulance train, and as we have no time for foraging, it is with the greatest difficulty that provisions can be obtained for the sick and wounded men. The wounded are suffering from the great distance they have been brought—some of them being seriously wounded. Lieut. R. M. Sims has a fractured thigh, but bears up manfully. Marched all night on the 26th; passed through Mount Pleasant to Colliersville. The skirmishing ceased to-day about noon, having been kept up with little cessation since our retrograde movement from West Point began, on the morning of the 21st. The horses have never been unsaddled, or scarcely fed during this time. The wounded were taken out of the ambulances, for the first time, and their wounds dressed."

Sherman, in summing up the results of the Meridian expedition, says:

"The object was to strike the roads inland, so to paralyze the rebel forces, that we could take from the defense of the Mississippi River the equivalent of a corps of 20,000 men, to be used in the next Georgia campaign, and this was actually done. At the same time I wanted to destroy Gen. Forest, who with an irregular force of cavalry was constantly threatening Memphis and the river above, as well as our routes of supply in Middle Tennessee. In this we utterly failed, because Gen. W. Sooy Smith did not fulfill his orders. Instead of starting at date ordered, February 1st, he did not leave Memphis till the 11th, and then when he did start he allowed Gen. Forest to head him off, and to defeat him with an inferior force near West Point, below Okolona, on the Mobile and Ohio Railroad. We waited at Meridian till the 20th to hear from Gen. Smith, but hearing nothing of him whatever, I ordered Gen. McPherson to move back slowly toward Canton with Hurlburt's infantry. I turned north to Marion, and thence to a place called Union, whence I dispatched the cavalry further to the north to Philadelphia, and as far as Louisville, to feel, as it were, for Gen. Smith. On the 26th we all reached Canton, but we had not heard a word from Gen. Smith. I had set so much store on his part of the project that I was disappointed, and so reported officially to Gen. Grant. Gen. Smith never regained my confidence as a soldier, though I still regard him as a most accomplished gentleman, and skillful engineer."

But for the magnificent failure, and terrible disaster attending it, we want to show that the Seventy-Second is in no way responsible. Had the balance of the command behaved one-half as gallantly as did the Seventy-Second, there would have been little to complain of, all of which is abundantly proven by the following letter to Maj. Carr:

"HEADQUARTERS CHIEF OF CAVALRY,
"MILITARY DIVISION OF MISSISSIPPI, March 19, 1864.

"H. M. Carr, Major commanding Seventy-Second Ind. Mounted Infantry:

"*Dear Sir:*—Having learned that certain false rumors regarding your gallant regiment have been circulated in the State of Indiana, for the apparent purpose of injuring the splendid reputation it has so nobly won on the bloody fields of the present war, I hasten to do your regiment justice in the matter.

"1. All reports to the effect that the Seventy-Second Indiana failed in any case to discharge their duty *faithfully* and *completely*, in battle or out of battle, on the recent expedition, are utterly, meanly and wickedly false, and were originated by none but cowardly stragglers or by persons who knew nothing of the regiment.

"2. To the Seventy-Second Indiana Mounted Infantry is justly due the glory of saving the entire expedition from rout and ruin on the afternoon of February 22d. On that occasion the Seventy-Second justly *established* the reputation it has long enjoyed of being one of the bravest, coolest, and most irresistible regiments in the U. S. Army. You were run over by four regiments of your brigade in the morning, in a perfect stampede; yet, nothing abashed, you waited to fight rather than follow those who were retreating. The enemy came upon you three brigades strong; they were flanking and overwhelming you, yet not a man moved from his post until Gen. Grierson ordered you to fall back, when you moved off as orderly as it was possible under the circumstances. Your men exhibited no signs of panic, or that excitement which is usually exhibited by the best regiments on such occasions; but every man appeared perfectly cool and self-possessed, and even appeared delighted at the prospect of cutting up the enemy when they should get him on open ground.

"In the engagement in the afternoon, when the enemy was finally checked for the day, the indomitable heroism of the Seventy-Second Indiana was gloriously conspicuous. You were assailed in front and on both flanks by not less than eight regiments of the enemy, yet you held your position, cutting the enemy down as fast as he approached, until, convinced he never could meet you on equal terms, he moved a heavy column on either flank, and actually fired two volleys in your rear; when, disdaining to see so noble a band of men struggling against such fearful odds and disadvantages, I ordered you to fall back. Your men obeyed slowly and reluctantly, taking their time to it, and still keeping up a regular fire upon the enemy until he ceased to pursue.

"I am, sir, really surprised that any one should credit such slanders on a regiment which, like the Seventy-Second Indiana, had followed the flag of Wilder through the bloodiest campaigns of American history, and which has never flinched though the enemy met it *ten* to *one*; but has earned a reputation of which its members may be proud half a century hence.

"I am, sir, very respectfully, &c.,

"W. S. SMITH,

"Chief of Cavalry, Military Division of Mississippi."

If there ever was a set of men who richly deserved rest and recreation, it was the Seventy-Second on reaching Germantown, 15 miles east of Memphis, and Gen. Smith, to show how well he appreciated their services, ordered a rousing ration of whisky, which, of course, was taken as a compliment by many of the regiment, who, in drinking to the long life and health of Gen. Smith, got a little more of the "O-be-joyful" than they could carry right steadily, and they could carry a good deal without a bicker.

Companies C and H took the lead upon this occasion, and got so supremely happy that, like two spooney lovers, they slobbered all over each other. While we were at Bowling Green, shortly after going into service, Company H, one day, had all the company rations of beef in one large camp kettle, cooking for dinner; just about the time dinner was ready and the meat all tender and sweet, Dan. Moore, of Company C, stole the kettle, meat and all. Company H had to go hungry, but they didn't mind that half so much as they did being played off on, without knowing who to pay for it, and up to this time, "who stole Company H's beef?" was a profound mystery. But here a Company C man and a Company H man got too full to walk, and so got astraddle of a log, facing each other, and began to brag, each on the other's company. Finally the Company C man said to the other, "My company and yours are bully fellows; we can do more foraging and fighting than *any body*; and then we have always got along so well together, if we did steal your beef at Bowling Green." This let the old cat out of the bag, and Company H knew who to pay, with interest, for the beef affair.

The command lay at Germantown till the 5th of March, by which time Gen. Sherman had begun to move all available troops toward Chattanooga, in order to engage in the grand, overwhelming expedition, that was to let the life right out of the rebellion.

The Seventy-Second was once more directed to join the old brigade. Our unconditional discharge from the service, just at that time, could not have been more pleasant to us.

Our route back lay along the railroad through Colliersville to Moscow.

On the 6th we camped in the vicinity of New Castle. On the 7th we passed through Middleburg and Bolivar, struck the Hatchie river at Bolivar, landing about 11 a. m. This is a navigable stream, and a bridge had to be built before we could cross. The Seventy-Second and a battalion of pioneers were set to work. We pulled down some warehouses and vacant dwelling houses, and by 4 p. m. we had the bridge done, and began to cross. After crossing we entered a large cane-brake swamp and forded some deep sloughs. We had to go eight miles before we could get forage. It was night by the time we got out of the swamp, and just then a most terrific rain storm, with thunder and lightning, burst upon us. Our road was so crooked, the night was so dark, and the woods and brush were so thick, that we could not tell which way we were going. The men will always remember it as the night nearly every man in the regiment had his hat knocked off and lost. The darkness was so intense that we could not see our file leader, or the man next in front of us, and the only way we could keep track of each other was by constantly calling to each other. We went into camp at 10 p. m.

March 8th. Marched early; crossed the south fork of Deer Creek and camped for the night near Mt. Pinson. Several prisoners were picked up during the day, and among the number a bushwhacker by the name of Bales. He was shot.

March 9th. We moved and camped 10 miles south-west of Lexington. Two more bushwhackers were captured, one a Lieutenant by the name of Dodds. It was proven that these men belonged to a band of guerrillas who had captured a squad of the 19th Pennsylvania Cavalry and murdered them one at a time, as they seemed to require some special and devilish amusement. Both of them were shot.

March 11th. Captured a rebel mail to-day and many of the letters were directed to Gen. Forest and staff, written by ladies in this vicinity, confirming all that we had surmised in the above cases. We were always careful never to do violence to a confederate soldier, and we never punished a miserable bushwhacker without conclusive evidence that he had murdered a Union soldier. These wretches were simply murderers and robbers of the bloodiest kind. No one must infer from the statements about the shooting of such bloody outlaws that the Seventy-Second acted wantonly and without orders.

On the 12th we passed through Clarksburg and Huntington, and camped within 15 miles of Ft. Henry. We started this morning at 2 a. m., and charged into Paris at daylight, expecting to surprise and capture a rebel band A Captain, Lieutenant and two privates, comprised the number captured.

13th. This morning we moved by the mouth of Big Sandy, on the Tennessee River, then directed our course to Ft. Hymen, opposite Ft. Henry, but missed the road and got involved in swamps and thickets. While passing through this out-of-the-way place, we captured a lot of prisoners, and among the number was Simeon Gerrard, who had been recruited by R. C. Clark, Company I, and had been started to the company. The joke was that no one knew he had ever enlisted at all, as the regiment had left Pulaski before it knew anything about any recruits being sent to it; but most of the men knew him, and questioned him so closely about what he was doing down there, that he finally confessed the whole thing. When Maj. Carr heard of it he told the boys just to shoot him and throw his carcass into the river, and the boys had their own fun with him for a while, nearly scaring him to death by pretending that they were getting ready to do it. In the evening he was put on a gunboat, along with the rest of the prisoners, and started up the river for Nashville; but the boys had so worked upon his fears that he determined never to go to Nashville, and that night jumped overboard and swam ashore. He kept himself shady till the war was over, after which he became a kind of freebooter, or land pirate, and in October, 1881, was in Warren County, Ind., a terror to every one who thought himself near him. A great many unsuccessful attempts had been made to capture him, and we think to-day, (February 1882) he is still at large.

We crossed the river on the transport Bluebird, the same one that took us over the river at Savannah in the early part of January. Our quarters were in cabins deserted by rebels.

On the 14th of March we lay in camp, drew from the transports five days' rations and two of forage.

March 15th. We reached Fort Donelson by noon, passed through Dover, and camped six miles from that place.

March 16th. Marched to Cumberland Furnace, 43 miles from Nashville. On the 17th we crossed Harpeth River and camped 12 miles from Nashville. On the 18th we went into camp just outside of the city, and stayed there till the 20th, when we went to Lavergne. For some reason we had not brought forage, and our poor horses had to go hungry. We got to Murfreesboro on the 21st, drew forage and got horse-shoeing done. We were in a terribly bad fix for underclothing, and the Indiana Sanitary Commission (*God bless them!*) just threw open their doors and told the old Seventy-Second to help themselves. We got shirts, drawers, socks, and mittens, as well as a good supply of vegetables.

March 22d. We camped near Shelbyville, on the same ground we camped the night before the battle of Farmington.

From here on to Mooresville there was but little to note except that Johnny Greensbury, the regimental bugler, got sick near Fayetteville, and was left at a house, but the next day a detail with one ambulance were sent back for him. He was a universal favorite in the regiment.

On the 26th Dr. Cole says: "We joined our old command to-day, and thus ended our almost three months' scout."

And now, comrades and readers, we beg pardon for quoting from Records, as follows: "We joined that part of the regiment we had left behind at Pulaski on December 31, 1863, with a lot of recruits added, making quite a respectable regiment for numbers. Indeed, this part of the regiment was now larger than our own. Here we found our mail, which had been accumulating for three months; and here we found all our baggage that we had left behind—thanks to Sergeant Magee; for notwithstanding the regiment had been dragged about a great deal, he had looked so carefully after the baggage of each absent one that not a piece was lost. But how sad to see the knapsacks, with their names upon them, of the brave boys we had left behind!"

Reader, a word of indulgence. It has often been said that tears, like talk, are cheap, and that women and children weep often, and often from trivial causes. But when the large-hearted, brave warrior, who is inured to scenes of blood and death, and all hardship, weeps, it is from a cause far greater than the ordinary cares of the world; a cause that reaches and stirs his inmost soul. Brave men wept at that meeting—the first reunion of the Seventy-Second—as they looked upon the relics of their brave, dead comrades. The name on that knapsack suggests the noble comrade who has shared with you the bunk and picket-post, forage and mess, march and battle; who has been the brave, generous comrade in all things, from the giving of a cup of cold water to your fever-parched lips, to touching the elbow on the field of battle and facing the foe to the last. In the loss of such men there is a grief which no generous heart can ever bear without tears. And at this reunion, at the recitations of these losses, and the viewing of the property of the fallen heroes, there was weeping —it was truly "a time for memory and for tears." By the light of the camp-fires sat circles of mess-mates who did go out on the expedition, reciting to those who did not go, all the particulars; and when the story of how a mess-mate met death, gallantly doing his duty, was reached, the narrator's voice became choked with emotion, and a pause followed. All tne circle sympathized in tears.

Until this day, when you visit the various reunions, and see the old soldiers run to meet and grasp their comrades by the hand, you can hardly realize the warmth and strength of the friendships which have been cemented by hardship and blood. At such reunions there are other long camp-fire talks over the past; talks of camp, of march, of battle, of comrades wounded and killed in action; of comrades who fell by the wayside, smitten by sickness; of comrades captured and taken to the prison hells of the Southern confederacy, and who never returned; of comrades who survived the service and have yielded to the power of disease or wounds since, and of comrades living who could not be present. If the affection of old soldiers for old soldiers seems a weakness to any who were not soldiers, let such reflect that we knew each other for years in the heart and heat of war; that we saw test after test of the true manhood of each other, not only for deeds of courage, but also for deeds of generosity and tenderness which would test the heart of mother or wife; and that it is natural for men to love and revere each other for such qualities when thus brought out. Remember, too, that we had to be to each other, for love and devotion, Mother, Wife, and Child. Those tender and kind deeds which every comrade would have conferred on the beloved ones of his family, we had, in a measure, for the very lack of the presence of these, to confer on our comrades. Hence our love then, and our love now, for each other.

While encamped at Mooresville, Capt. Robinson, of Co. C, became bedfast from the effects of injuries received on the Wheeler raid, and was taken to the home of a planter near camp, where he remained for some time under treatment of our surgeons. During the raid, and when rapidly pursuing Wheeler's command through the streets of Pulaski, just after dusk on the evening of October 8th, his horse stumbled over a high stone street crossing, and plunging forward fell to the ground, and, while struggling to get up, rolled over upon its prostrate rider, inflicting internal bodily injuries on the Captain, from which he had been ever since suffering. Our surgeons decided that Capt. Robinson was unfitted for further field service owing to these injuries, when he resigned, but shortly afterward re-entered the army in the invalid corps, when he was commissioned by President Lincoln as captain and commissary of subsistence, "for meritorious service in the field." He served in that position at Fort Scott, Kas., on the Plains, and at Denver, Col., till September, 1866, when he was mustered out with the rank of brevet lieutenant colonel by a War Department order mustering out all volunteer officers, "their services being no longer required." Capt. R. was soon afterward commissioned by President Grant as second lieutenant in the 9th U. S. Cavalry, but was compelled to decline the honor because of his inability to perform horseback service, he not having recovered from the effects of the injuries received by his horse falling upon him. Lieut. John Glaze succeeded to the captaincy of company C.

CHAPTER XXVII.

From April 3d to June 9th, 1864—Move to Columbia—Drilling and Inspecting the Recruits—Orders to Move without Extras—Extra Clothing Sent Home—Sherman Running the Machine, and Allows No Foolishness—No Trotting of Horses—Orders to Move with 30 Days' Rations—Constitution of the Division—We Move to the Front on April 30th—A Bad Start through Rain and Mud—Passing Over the Old Farmington Battle-field—Through Decherd and Over the Mountains—Pine Knots—Hear Artillery Firing 60 Miles Away—Cross Lookout Mountain—We are Put into McPherson's Corps—Johnston has 60,000 and Sherman has 120,000—Line of the Summer's Campaign—Flanking Movements of Sherman—He Flanks Johnston out of Buzzard Roost—A Rebel Woman's Opinion of We'uns—Hush! Those are Wilder's Men—On the Battlefield of Resaca—Completely Surrounded near Rome—15th Corps Comes to Our Relief—The Enemy Bagged—The Bag Open at the Wrong End—Terrible Fighting to get on to Powder Springs Road—Horses Dying of Starvation—Hard Fighting of May 28th and 29th—Rebels Thought We were "Niggers," and didn't Know We were Each Loaded Seven Times, but Found Out when They Charged Us, and were Repulsed with Great Loss—Terrible Fighting and Charging in the Night—Company C Gallantly Holds the Line All Night—Killing Beeves that may Die Before Next Killing—Using Wheat for Horse Feed—Guarding the Etowah Bridge Description of Pontoons—Sherman on the Move Again—Sherman's Prejudice Against Cavalry—We give one of His Aid's Proof of Our Pluck by Taking Him in Sight of Johnston's Army.

We remained in camp at Mooresville until April 3d, 1864, when our regiment, 123d Illinois, and Board of Trade Battery, left there, by the way of Huntsville, Fayetteville, Louisburg and Hurricane for Columbia. Our whole division train was along, the roads were muddy and we did not get to Columbia till the 8th. We went into camp on the north side of Duck River, and on the 11th moved back and went into camp west of Columbia, near the Polk and Pillow farms. The only incidents of note during this march were, that Brig. Gen. Kenar Gerrard took command of the division just before leaving Mooresville; and the day we left Mooresville (April 3d) Capt. Alex A. Rice, A. A. G. for the brigade, left it with many regrets from the men of the Seventy-Second. He resigned and went home. After we got to Columbia, all those who had gone home to recruit had returned, and also all the recruits we got that spring had reported for duty, and once more we had a splendid, large regiment. It was necessary to make soldiers out of those recruits as fast as possible; so the first thing was to put them on camp guard, then on picket, then give them squad drill, then company drill, skirmish drill, fatigue duty, etc. Notwithstanding the country, the weather, the duty and everything, was just as lovely as it could be, many of the recruits thought we were putting on a "heap of style." We were also inspected by Gen. Elliot, Sherman's chief of cavalry, and Gen. Gerrard, our division commander. All this, of course, was necessary for the recruits, and also to let our commanders see what condition we were in for the summer campaign.

On the 27th of April, 1864, at 8 p. m., we received orders to get ready to move, and with these orders we also got orders that no soldier would be allowed to take any extra baggage whatever, either of blankets nor clothing. This struck our men *hard*. We had always done about as we pleased about carrying extra blankets and clothes. The fact is, as we had always done extra duty, we were allowed extra indulgences, and now almost every man had two sleeping blankets and two dog tents, and all had their overcoats. But now Gen. Sherman was "running the machine," and he would allow no "foolishness." The men were recommended to box their goods and store them, but they thought that would be equivalent to throwing them away, as they had boxed and stored effects last spring, on leaving Murfreesboro, and had never heard of them since, some of the men losing $30 or $40 worth of clothes, our regiment being unfortunate in this respect, for most of the regiments which stored their extras, got them again. Hence our boys boxed their extras and overcoats and sent them home, most of which, we believe, finally got through all right.

Among the specifications of our order to move, was that we should start with 30 days' rations, which was 18 days more than we had ever started with before. Another specification was, that any soldier, who, from any cause whatever should become dismounted, should be sent back permanently to do guard duty in the rear; that is, he should be transferred to dismounted infantry and never be allowed a horse again. It is proper to remark that all *good* soldiers of our regiment paid especial attention to this order, and kept themselves mounted just as long as possible.

Our division was now composed of three brigades, the 1st commanded by Col. Long, the 2d by Col. Minty, and the 3d by Col. Wilder. Minty's brigade was composed of the 4th Michigan, 7th Pennsylvania, 3d Ohio and 4th United States Regulars, all cavalry. Our brigade was composed of the 17th and Seventy-Second Indiana, and the 98th and 123d Illinois, all mounted infantry. Long's brigade was not yet fully mounted and was left behind to follow as soon as mounted. Attached to our division was the Chicago Board of Trade Battery.

On the morning of April 30th, 1864, our division moved from Columbia for some point at the "front." We got an early start and passed through Columbia and took the road south-east for Farmington. We made 26 miles and went into camp on a large stream near that place. We had 30 days' rations and five days' forage in our wagons. We were to draw two day's rations at a time, and they were to last us three days. Our regiment had more men mounted, and they were mounted on better horses, than ever before, and our officers were more particular about how we took care of our horses than ever before. In no case were we to ride them out of ranks; and if by any chance a soldier should ride his horse faster than a walk he was promptly dismounted and compelled to lead his horse the balance of the day. This was the unkindest cut of all, and we noticed *very many* leading their horses as they went into camp at night.

It had been most beautiful weather while we lay at Columbia, but shortly after we left there it began to rain, and toward evening poured down in torrents, and continued all night. The consequence was that nine miles out from Columbia quite a lot of forage was thrown out of the wagons to lighten the loads, and notwithstanding all this, the trains failed to reach camp by six miles, and as a consequence our horses had to stand all night without a bite to eat. This was making a bad start.

May 1st. The bugle called us up at 3 a. m., with orders to move at daylight. But daylight came, then sun-up, then six o'clock, and no move. Then a detail was made to go back to the teams for forage; and still later another heavy detail was ordered to go clear back after the sacks that were thrown out of the wagons yesterday. About 4 p. m. the trains began to come in; but it was long after night before the boys got in with the sacks. They had a miserable time of it, too, and wore some of their horses entirely out. A bad start. Col. Miller says, "our General (Garrard) does not seem to understand this western country, having just come from the East."

May 2d. We started this morning at sun-up; the weather was warm and beautiful, but we had not gone three miles till there came a regular "nor'-wester" upon us, with rain, disagreeably cold wind, and some spitty snow. We passed through Farmington and took the pike east for Shelbyville; and as it was right here, and 12 miles right east on this road, that our brigade fought Wheeler on the 7th of last October. We noted with deep interest nearly every foot of the way; and as the woods were so well marked with bullets and shells, and grape and canister, each soldier could tell exactly the friendly stump, tree, or log, behind which he stood or lay and took deadly aim at a reb, just so many yards away. Everything looked very familiar, but we were passing over the road in the opposite direction to the course we traveled then, and in quite a different manner. Then we fought nearly every step of the way, but to-day we move very quietly, and each man has plenty of time to verify or disprove the many ideas he had formed of the great battle of Farmington. We camped at Shelbyville.

May 3d. We started this morning at sun-up. From Shelbyville we took the road south-east for Tullahoma, 18 miles. We had bad roads all day—parts of them mountainous and rocky, other parts of them very swampy. When the campaign opened in June last, Bragg was driven from Shelbyville and the line of Duck River, and fell back to Tullahoma, and there determined to "die in the last ditch" But when our brigade struck and entered upon the work of destroying the railroad in his rear at Decherd, his courage "leaked out," he started for Dixie, and never stopped till he had crossed the river at Bridgeport, 100 miles away. We camped to-night seven miles south of Tullahoma. Our train did not get up till midnight. It always seemed to us that teamsters had a hard time of it, and that no one would be a teamster unless he was afraid he "couldn't stand the racket."

May 4th. Left camp early and passed through Decherd long before noon. Here we lay in the boiling sun for two hours. (The boys said for the officers to "licker" up; this was slander, of course.) It was a terrible bore to lie in the sun. We got dinner, and when the trains caught up we started up the mountain, and after an hour and a half hard climbing, leading our horses, went in camp just over the ridge, close by a mountain spring, and just at the mouth of the railroad tunnel on the east side of the ridge. Our camp was picturesque in the extreme. The spring was so close to the top of the mountain we wondered whence the water in it came. It formed a large brook, which went rolling down the mountain side at a fearful rate, and a half mile distant was a thousand feet below the fountain head, and forms the source of Crow Creek, which empties into the Tennessee River 30 miles straight south, and is there a very large stream. While we were admiring this grand panorama three long trains, one after the other, came out of the east end of the tunnel, precisely like they had sprung out of the ground, full of life and animation, and went winding along down the mountain side like huge serpents, at a fearful height above the stream. Our rations had been out for 24 hours, and no chance to draw till our trains came up. It was 10 o'clock before we got our coffee and were ready for bed.

May 5th. Started this morning long before we could see the sun. We pushed down the narrow defile through which the stream and railroad made their way, and in three or four miles came to where it opened into a little valley. During the day we must have crossed the stream nearly a hundred times. At night we went into camp a mile and a half from Stevenson, where the creek was three or four rods wide, and in some places very deep. After going into camp seven long trains, all loaded with soldiers, passed us. All were going to the front. This looked like business, as soldiers had been passing us for two days.

May 6th. We lay in camp till 11 a. m. for the empty wagons to fill up with "grub" and forage, and then moved east up the river to Bridgeport, 12 miles. We then crossed the river and moved up on the east side eight miles, and did not get into camp until three hours after night, and our train did not get in at all; so our horses had to stand all night again without a bite to eat.

May 7th. Bugle call before sun-up, as usual, but no train till 10 a. m. While we were waiting there was a collision on the railroad close to camp, smashing two engines and killing two men. As soon as the train came up we drew three days' rations and loaded 25 teams with forage for our brigade. By 11 a. m. our brigade started southeast up a long cove in the Sand mountain; Minty's brigade and the battery going up toward Chattanooga in order to get around the north end of Lookout mountain, it being too steep for the trains to climb over—they intending to meet us on the east side of Lookout and south of Chattanooga. We kept on up the cove and by 10 p. m. reached the top of the mountain, where we had the most beautiful roads in the world, through a forest of red oak, chestnut, and pine trees. We went into camp 25 miles from Shell Moun. Here we had our first experience in burning pine knots, and are indebted to their light for a part of these notes. These knots are a curiosity, and we are satisfied that many of our readers do not know, nor ever will know, much about them; therefore we will describe them. They are in shape like a very large and long sweet potato, and in many places lying around over the ground in greatest abundance. They are all that is left of an ancient forest, which from their abundance must have been a large one. Every vestige of the forest has disappeared except the knots, which, from their resinous nature, would never decay. You could not find even a piece of an old log of the former forest, while the present forest standing there seemed to be 150 to 200 years old and in the best of health and vigor. These knots were simply the limbs which had started from the heart of the tree and grown with the tree till two or three inches in diameter, then died and broken off; the tree would grow over the end of the limb which remained upon it; then finally the tree would die, fall down, and all rot away except these butts of limbs, which would never decay. When set on fire they burn rapidly like tar. They made splendid torches, and we used them for candles, lighting one end and sticking the other in the ground. After supper we went out beyond the line of camp and could hear artillery firing away to the east of us. This we afterward learned was at Buzzard's Roost, in front of Dalton, and more than 60 miles away.

May 8th. We got a good start, and in two hours passed down off the mountain into Lookout valley, at a little town called Trenton, 30 miles south-west of Chattanooga. Here the teams that came along with us unloaded and started for Chattanooga, and each fellow had to take three days' forage for his horse, in addition to the loads we already had to carry, which was rough on the horse, although we were never allowed to ride either up or down a hill. We always had to dismount and walk. Our camp last night was four miles from Trenton, and after getting our forage we moved right across Lookout valley and immediately started up Lookout mountain, which we found the highest, steepest, and most rugged, of any we had yet climbed. After getting on top we found the mountain only seven miles wide and as level as a floor. The descent was very difficult. The place at which we crossed is called Johnson's Crook. After getting down off the mountain we moved six miles east and camped on the Chicamauga, making 23 miles for the day, and by odds the hardest marching we had yet done—up one mountain and down two. Company I moved two miles further, and stood on picket in what last summer we called Pigeon Gap, but what the citizens called Dug Gap, in the Pigeon mountains. Right on this road is where the centre of Rosecrans' army first ran on to the rebels after they had evacuated Chattanooga, and in this gap, too, is where Negley's division was repulsed several days before the battle of Chicamauga, which was fought 15 to 25 miles north of this.

May 9th. It was long after night when the videttes were stationed, and our headquarters were in the cove. As the rebels were supposed to occupy the top of the cove, little sleeping was done on picket. About 3 o'clock in the morning Company I and one company of the 123d Illinois were sent forward to take possession of the gap and secure the pass. The hill was not so very high, long, or steep, but was well fortified, and from the tortuous direction of the road an assaulting column could have been raked from both sides, front and rear, before reaching the top. We never saw a position naturally so strong as this one, and the rebels had fortified it so well that an assaulting party would have had rough work getting up. When we got to the top we found that the Johnnies had gone away; our troops coming down from the north on the east side of the ridge had rendered this position useless, and we tell you *we* were glad. By 8 a. m. we had reached LaFayette, the county seat of Walker County, and went into camp. This is a good-sized town, and before the battle of Chicamauga was Bragg's headquarters. It is eight miles from Rock Springs, where Capt. McMurtry was killed; 20 miles from Ringgold, and 40 from Chattanooga. We spent the day foraging and scouting on all the roads leading south from LaFayette.

May 10th. We lay in camp all day; rations out yesterday, and little or nothing to eat in the country. Trains came up late in the evening, but we did not draw rations till the evening of the 11th.

We have now come to a point where a few explanations of the purposes of the campaign, and the part we took in it, are pertinent, and which given here may save the necessity of repeating at different times and places.

After the battle of Chicamauga Rosecrans was superseded by Thomas, and the Union army was besieged in Chattanooga. Four corps came to Thomas' relief: the 11th, Howard's, and the 12th, Hooker's, from the Army of the Potomac; and the 15th, Logan's, and the 16th, Blair's, from the Army of the Tennessee.

The battle of Mission Ridge was fought, and Bragg defeated and driven off. He was then superseded by Gen. Joseph E. Johnston, who took a strong position behind Taylor's Ridge, with his headquarters at Dalton, and at the opening of this campaign, May 5th, had an army of 65,000 men. Gen. Sherman moved against him with an aggregate force of 120,000 men (see Sherman's Memoirs, vol. 2, p. 15 and p. 24,) and 254 guns. Sherman's army was composed of three departments combined into one grand army, viz: The Army of the Ohio, commanded by Gen. J. M. Schofield, which constituted the left wing. The Army of the Cumberland, commanded by Maj-Gen. George H. Thomas, which constituted the center of the army; and the Army of the Tennessee, commanded by Maj.-Gen. J. B. McPherson, which constituted the right wing of the army; and to this wing of the army, the 2d cavalry division, our brigade was attached. And notwithstanding we were often shifted from one wing to the other, to front and to rear, our proper place was with McPherson's corps, and here the 10th of May finds us at LaFayette, on the extreme right of his corps.

Early on the morning of May 11th our division took the road east toward Resaca, our regiment being rear guard for the train. By noon our train reached Taylor's Ridge, where we also found a part of McPherson's train and a lot of beef cattle, and for the first time on the march, saw some infantry, who apprised us that we were somewhere in the neighborhood of the main army. We could hear heavy connonading north-east of us. We crossed the ridge at Ship's Gap, and had great difficulty in getting our trains over. We moved six miles and went into camp at Vilanan, in the west end of Snake Creek Gap, and were thoroughly incorporated into the grand army of invasion, having traveled 200 miles in 12 days. The Memphis and Charleston Railroad runs south-east from Chattanooga through Ringgold, Dalton, Kingston and Marietta, to Atlanta; and it was right along this railroad that the whole summer's campaign was fought. In this connection we explain the flanking movements for which Sherman was pre-eminently celebrated, as our division *alwiys* had a very prominent part to perform in them. A single description will illustrate all of them.

On the 5th of May we have Johnston and his army at Dalton, just behind Rocky Face Ridge; and the only direct road to get from Ringgold to Dalton is through a gap called Buzzard Roost. This gap had been so strongly fortified that perhaps no army in the world could ever have gotten through it if properly defended. Here, of course, Sherman stalled. But 15 miles south of Buzzard Roost, in the same impassable mountain, was Snake Creek Gap, through which, if Sherman could pass his army, he would strike the railroad in the rear of Dalton and compel Johnston to evacuate Buzzard Roost and retreat, or fight on ground of Sherman's own choosing. As the art of war consists largely in one side deceiving the other, Sherman kept up a bold front at Buzzard Roost and kept hammering away with his artillery at that point, as though he intended to knock the whole mountain to pieces and blow it away, while he was at the same time quietly moving his army by the right flank through Snake Creek Gap, and was actually astride the railroad at Resaca, in the rear of Dalton, before Johnston knew what he was about. A desperate battle was fought, in which Johnston succeeded in getting across the Oostenaula River with small loss to himself; but it shows how he was compelled to run away from his best fortified positions without getting any benefit of them. It was during these operations that we joined the army, and we lay in camp at Vilanan all day the 12th, while Thomas' corps passed through the gap. However, we were not idle during the day, as scouting parties were sent south and south-west, and Company I even went clear back to the foot of Lookout Mountain, to see that no meddling cavalry force should pounce upon our trains from the direction of Rome. While on our scout we run on to a strange individual who said he was Gen. Thomas' spy. It would be impossible to describe this strange medley of horse, alligator and monkey. His clothes were of various cloth and hues, blue, brown, grey, etc. He had a pass signed by Gen. Thomas, all right; but to this day we believe he was a rebel, because we never could tell why he should be just in that place just at that time if he wasn't.

On the 13th we were still in camp; we spent the day in grazing our horses. Last night our old friends, the 10th Indiana, camped with us.

On the 14th most of the army had got through the gap, and in the afternoon at 2 p. m. we started south for Rome, about 36 miles distant. Our brigade in the advance made half the distance and went into camp at 10 p. m. Sherman, in his Memoirs, vol. 2, page 35, says: "At the same time I dispatched Garrard with his cavalry division down the Oostenaula, by the Rome road, with orders to cross over, if possible, and to attack or threaten the railroad at any point below Calhoun and above Kingston." Garrard's division was the one we were in.

May 15th. We moved slowly in the direction of Rome, Minty's brigade in the advance, the cavalry skirmishing in front, killing a rebel captain, wounding four or five privates and taking a few prisoners. When we reached the Arimurchee River we found the chances for a fight first rate, the cavalry having been repulsed. This was about four miles from Rome; the enemy were in force on the south side of the river, and our skirmishers were already engaged. In the afternoon we were withdrawn and moved back six or eight miles toward Resaca and went into camp. Minty's loss for the day was four men wounded.

This was the day the great battle of Resaca was fought, and the cannonading continued very heavy till late in the night.

May 16th. We lay in camp grazing our horses, some of the companies scouting. Hornaday relates the following incident, which transpired with Company F: "Stopping by a farm house, the lady and her daughter came out to see the soldiers, and, on being told we were Yankees, they opened their eyes with astonishment. After looking awhile, the mother exclaimed: 'I say, Cap'n, our folks has not told us the truth about you'uns; they told us you'uns was painted savages, and that you all had horns; but you'ns is just like our folks, but I believe you'uns is the best lookin.'" This lady was of more than ordinary intelligence, which shows the horrid lies the leaders of this infernal rebellion had told to deceive the masses.

Late in the evening we started north-east toward Resacca, and away in the night met Davis' division of infantry (See Sherman) marching as rapidly as they could toward Rome. As foot soldiers always have the road in preference to mounted ones, and as the roads were swampy and flanked by thick brush, we had a very rough time getting past this division. Cavalry and infantry are never on the most amicable terms. In this division were part of Sheridan's troops who ran so at Chicamauga, and as we were toiling through the underbrush at the side of the road it was impossible for us to help crowding them a little, when they began to pay us the compliments usually paid cavalrymen. The fact is, in the first part of the war our cavalry were in bad repute, and infantry thought they wouldn't fight at all, and were always making scurrilous remarks regarding their bravery. So when these fellows met us they began: "Johnnies ahead, eh? that's right, skin out for the rear; that's the safest place," &c. And, in defense, we began to halloo: "Make way for Sheridan! make way for Sheridan!" when we could hear them say: "Hush! hush! that's Wilder's brigade." Thenceforth we had no difficulty getting past the division.

It was near midnight when we got to Lay's Ferry, four miles south of Resacca, where we crossed to Oostenaula on a pontoon. This took us to where much of the hardest fighting had been done on the 15th. Our army lost on that field 600 men killed and 3,300 wounded. It was 2 o'clock in the morning before we got across. We went into camp near our hospitals, and amputated limbs were in piles by the hundred.

May 17th. We saddled up early and were ready to move, but as we did not move till 4 p. m. we had ample time to look over the battle-field, and see some of the horrid work of war.

At 4 p. m. our division moved down the river on the east side, toward Rome. We took a direct course through the woods and fields regardless of roads, going through many swamps and sloughs. Bivouacked at 9 p. m., 12 miles from Rome.

We moved on the morning of May 18th till within eight miles of Rome, and then changed direction to the south-east toward Kingston, and eight miles further came to a most beautiful valley, surrounded on three sides by high hills. In this valley lived an English gentleman by the name of Blanchford. His house was a mansion, and his plantation embraced the whole valley. This delightful situation was six miles from Kingston. When we approached this place Minty's brigade, in the advance, encountered the rebels, a skirmish ensued, and the pickets were driven in. Most of the Seventy-Second was thrown out on different roads as pickets, and the balance of the brigade dismounted and moved forward in line of battle. As this movement was simply a precautionary one, not at all unusual, and everything in front perfectly quiet, nothing was thought of it till presently a sharp volley was heard, followed by a rattling of rifles that waked up the echoes of the hills. Immediately our cavalry came hurrying back in confusion, a regiment of rebel cavalry at their heels, yelling like demons; the cavalry passed through our brigade and the Johnnies came on like a whirlwind, and when within range of our Spencers we opened on them. If ever cavalry came suddenly to a halt, it was then and there. The colonel leading the charge fell dead from his horse within 10 feet of our lines. The 4th Michigan, of Minty's brigade, had several killed and wounded in this charge. By the time the charge was repulsed there was picket firing on every road leading to our position. This place was called Woodlawn, and was seven miles from Adairsville, on the railroad north-east of us. Gen. Garrard undertook to send a dispatch over to McPherson, at that place, but the squad of six men who started with it were driven back five minutes after passing our picket post. Company F was sharply attacked on another road and driven in, and firing was heard in every direction from our position. The sun was not more than an hour high, and it began to be a serious question whether we could hold our position till dark. Garrard now started a battalion of cavalry with orders to carry the dispatch to McPherson, and to cut their way through at all hazards. Company I was farthest north-east toward the infantry, and we waited with a good deal of suspense after the battalion passed out. In a few moments we could hear them begin to shoot and charge, and felt relieved that they did not come back, as the others had done. At dark the 15th corps came to our relief, and we lay in line all night. Just how many rebels were opposed to us we never knew, but there never was a time during the whole service when we were more completely surrounded.

This being in the middle of a dense forest, the movements of the enemy were concealed. When the fight began the Englishman raised his English flag, hoping thereby to save his bacon and beans. Wilder's adjutant general was so drunk that he rode right into the rebel lines and was captured.

On May 19th reveille sounded at daylight, and at sun-up the 15th corps, east of us, began to move, and shelling and skirmishing began. We moved right back towards Rome till within eight miles of there, then turned south and about eight miles from our camp struck the

Rome and Kingston road, and turned east about 10 miles from Kingston and moved toward that place, and when within two miles of it our whole brigade charged into and through the town, and five miles south-east, to a bridge across the Etowah. This was a long as well as a lively chase. We were told that the enemy had been driven into a bend of the river and that this bridge was their only chance of escape, and that we were to hold it at all hazards, and against all comers. For our part we didn't believe a word of it, but most of the men did; they said we had the rebels completely bagged this time, and no mistake; so we went to work with a will and before night had a line of works thrown up from which it would have cost a good many lives to have driven us. By reference to Sherman's book, you will see that he really expected a decisive battle to be fought right here. We lay all night in our trenches and had ample time to discuss the situation. Although private soldiers are supposed to know nothing of general movements, it is a little surprising how well posted the most intelligent were on the situation on that night. Indeed, we could tell nearly about the exact situation of the two armies just by the artillery firing we heard during the evening. The subject of bagging rebels was largely discussed by the whole regiment. The truth is we *did* have them bagged just like we had at Dalton, Resaca and other places; but unfortunately for us the mouth of the bag was the wrong way, and when the Johnnies got ready they simply went out and took the bag along with them. It was so this time, and before the morning of the 20th, Johnston's whole army was across the Etowah, and he had taken position in the Alatoona Mountains. But to keep up the deception as long as possible, we were compelled to lay in the trenches all day on the 20th, when we knew as well as we knew anything that there was not a rebel north of the river, because we had not heard a single gun fired the whole day.

May 21st. We are lying in a beautiful camp, in a most productive country, close to a large spring, in the best of health and spirits. We have made 100 miles of hard driving and fighting in 15 days, and are now catching our breath. This country has never felt the effects of war before, and there is an abundance of food and forage in the country, especially south of the river, and we have sent over numerous scouting parties to-day, which all came back heavily loaded; and also report Johnston as being reinforced. His position south of the river, near Alatoona Pass, is a strong one, and may require flanking to get him out of it.

May 22d. Still in camp with orders to be ready for a 20 days' march to-morrow morning. Sure enough Sherman has determined to cut loose from the railroad and his base of supplies, take 20 days' rations and forage, to move around the Alatoona Mountains and compel Johnston to fight somewhere else. We got orders to shoe up all the horses, to wash our clothes, to have inspection and get everything in good shape for to-morrow. Had inspection early in the morning, washed up all our clothes, and had glorious fun bathing. In the evening we had preaching by our Chaplain, and were never better fixed for moving.

May 23d. Early this morning we crossed the river from our camp at Big Spring bridge, our division in advance, and were immediately followed by the 15th corps; this corps took straight south-west for Vanwert, county seat of Polk County, while our division moved straight south, up the west side of the Enhartee River. As our division was moved on purpose to mask or cover the movement of the infantry, we will explain: As fast as our head of column would strike a road running east a company would move on that road and dash up boldly toward the rebel pickets that were strung along up the Enhartee River, attack them and drive them in. If the Johnnies showed fight we were to fall back quickly as though we were few in numbers and did not want to fight. These movements were kept up till the middle of the afternoon, and the 15th corps had got away off to the south, near Vanwert, when we moved off rapidly and camped near that place. We encountered the rebels on every road running east and some skirmishing occurred on each occasion, but we were careful not to aggravate them too much. We passed over the most delightful country we had seen since crossing the Tennessee River, and we do not recollect to have seen so much growing wheat in any 10 days of our life. Corn was a foot high, and a great deal of it.

May 24th. Our division moved early, Minty's brigade in the advance, taking the direct road to Atlanta. As our regiment was in advance yesterday, we were in rear to-day, and did not get started till 9 a. m., and then the infantry followed close after us. After passing through Vanwert we turned south-east and began to climb the Alatoona Mountains. These mountains are not very high nor steep, but the most rugged, rocky and barren of any we have yet seen. The country is desolate beyond description. We moved along slowly till the middle of the afternoon, when we came down off the mountains to quite a large stream, called Pumpkinvine Creek. Here Minty's brigade ran into the rebels, capturing about 20 of them; several of Minty's men were wounded. He moved two miles forward to Dallas, or near there, when he met a rebel force coming in from the north, which Johnston had sent there on a scout. These rebels pitched into

Minty, and a sharp fight ensued. We suppose this was the first intimation that Johnston had of the real state of the flanking movement. Minty's cavalry soon gave way, and our brigade was hurried up, dismounted, and immediately made a spirited attack; our battery was brought up and began to shell them. We soon found the rebels were in strong force and position, and as the sun was nearly down we concluded not to press them much; but we kept up a sharp skirmish till dark, when the rebels and our division fell back a distance. Our division left a strong picket right where we had the fight. We think Company C was on this post. The adjutant of the 17th was mortally wounded in the engagement. We moved back west of the Pumpkin vine and bivouacked. McPherson's command camped four miles back on the mountain, and when Garrard reported to him that the rebels were in front, he would not believe it.

May 25th. Our men who were on picket last night, where we fought last evening, had a lively time; firing was kept up all night. Immediately after breakfast details of 10 men from each company were sent for forage, all under command of Lieut. Cravens. They went across the creek and east to our picket post, then turned south, wandered around over the hills for several miles, finding nothing but a few blades. Here Lieut. Cravens got discouraged and turned back toward camp, and Sergt. Magee took a part of the squad and went further; along with this squad was Capt. Vance's negro. We hadn't gone far till we ran right into the advance guard of a rebel brigade, and before we knew it were nearly surrounded; we are prepared to say the rebels did some good shooting too. We had urgent business toward camp just then, and started accordingly, the Johnnies after us, hollooing "halt! halt!" but we didn't halt, and were soon lost to the sight of the pursuing rebs, and our hats lost from our sight, too, as the brush was very thick. At the first fire the "nigger" was close beside us, riding an old convalescent mare that had been abandoned; he was barefooted, but wore spurs that would weigh a pound apiece, the rowels of which were more than an inch long. He seemed just to pick his old mare up on his spurs and shake her a few times, and she went bounding over the brush like a big straw hat over the prairie on a windy day, or like the fabled Pegasus.

About the time the rebels came upon us, they also charged on our pickets in front of Dallas, and drove them clear back across the creek and thus were between us and camp. The whole brigade was ordered into line and held the rebs at bay till the 15th corps came up and relieved the brigade. But how to get to camp was bothering us; the rebs were between us and camp, and we were between two bodies of rebs. The "nigger" got to camp; how we never could tell, neither could he; perhaps he and the old mare flew. He told the Colonel we were all captured, and Capt. Thomson was sent out with a battalion to look after us, and you better believe we were glad when we accidentally stumbled on to him. We got back to camp about 10 a. m., and just then the infantry came up.

Gen. McPherson, still thinking there was no force of importance in front, ordered our division to Powder Springs, 12 miles south-east of Dallas. We saddled and started, but from the terrible fighting we heard soon after starting, we incline to think McPherson found somebody in his front; and the truth is, it was mote than a week before McPherson's army got as close to Dallas as we had been. We were stopped about six miles from camp, and Sergt. Magee got his hat. We lay around all day without unsaddling, picketing heavily to the east and south.

May 26th. Laying in camp all day, ready for any emergency, we learned more about the terrible fighting McPherson had yesterday. Col Miller says we are out of corn. Stock suffering, and horses dying every day.

May 27th. We were up and saddled early, and lay in camp till 8 o'clock. Col. Miller says in his notes: "I took my regiment (Seventy-Second) to support Col. Minty in an effort to put the infantry on the Powder Springs road. This will be remembered by all who participated as one of the terrible fighting days of the war for this army, and for our regiment especially. Fighting in Minty's brigade had begun before we left camp. We had nearly four miles to go to get to Minty's position, and though we were not long getting there, yet the rebels had swung around on Minty's right and fired into the lead horses of the 7th Pennsylvania, and had driven in the skirmishers. We rushed straight into the midst of the fray, and skirmishing began before we got dismounted. We assure you we were not long in getting into line behind a fence and in pushing our skirmishers forward. We had no time to get our line of works strengthened by logs till the enemy began to shell us furiously, and for two hours they warmed us up lively by dropping their shells much too close for comfort. Indeed they had our range and distance so accurately that they could gauge their shells to burst within four feet of us nearly every shot. Providentially none burst in front of our line, and none of us were hurt. It is surprising how close to the ground a fellow can lie on such an occasion. Our battery took a position to our right rear, and for two hours the music was lively, if not so cheerful. About 11 a. m. one of our guns was having a caisson moved along in the rear of our line and about 100 yards behind us, when a shell went directly through the two wheel-horses, just behind the fore legs, cutting off both the stirrup straps of the driver. About two minutes later they dropped a shell right down in the middle of our lead horses, three-fourths of a mile in our rear, scattering them in every direction. About 1 o'clock the skirmishing in front of our regiment was severe. Alferd Birt, private of Co. I, had his right arm shattered to pieces by a sharp-shooter, the same ball going through his arm twice. He died of exhaustion. He was a recruit, and an excellent soldier. We lay in line of battle till dark, but of course did not succeed in getting the infantry on to the Dallas and Powder Springs road; indeed, we didn't get within two miles of it. At dark we went back to our old camp.

May 28th. We quote Dr. Cole: "Moved out again to-day, and went into line on the right of the infantry; our left closed up to McPherson's army. Temporary works were erected, and every precaution taken for suitable defense. The enemy occupied a strong position in our front. The engagement opened with severe artillery practice, which after a while slackened, and we could then hear their savage yells as they charged McPherson on our left.

Failing to move the veterans of the Tennessee, our line was tried in the same manner, the demons yelling like bloodhounds as they approached our works, where they were met with leaden hail from 1,500 Spencers, which handsomely repulsed them. Our loss was slight—one man killed and two wounded. The rebel loss was heavy, as they had no shelter. A rebel, whose wound I dressed, said that just before they made the charge on our brigade they were told that the line was held by colored troops, who would be easily driven back."

This night will long be remembered by all who held horses. The lead horses of the whole brigade were parked a half mile in rear of our lines, and all under command of Maj. Carr. By some means the rebs found where our horses were, and late in the evening began to shell them, and they had to be moved; but still the shells kept dropping among them till after midnight, when Carr moved them back nearly two miles to get them out of danger. The horses had been four days without anything to eat, and there was scarcely a vestige of herbbage of any kind for miles around; and it makes one's shoulders ache to think of the terrible pulling and jerking the men had to endure to keep the whole outfit from getting away from them. We always preferred taking the skirmish line to such work as this.

On the morning of the 29th Dr. Cole says: "The musketry and artillery practice continued all night, and my position was made peculiarly unpleasant by the occasional dropping of a leaden messenger in the immediate vicinity of my humble couch of three rails laid together on the ground."

Sunday, May 29th. All day our brigade lay in line just where we fought yesterday, and we spent much of the day throwing up dirt to strengthen our works, the artillery and skirmishing going on constantly night and day. The rebels treated our line with a little more respect than yesterday, having found out that we were not "niggers." Soon after night our brigade quietly withdrew from the works, and it was the intention of McPherson's army to do likewise; but just after we fell back the rebels became aware that some change was being made in the lines and immediately charged the infantry on our left. We suppose the infernal regions can furnish nothing so horrible as these night attacks were, and shall attempt no description of this one, (See Sherman, vol. 2, pp. 43-46,) but close with the words of Dr. Cole, who says, "they make sad work for surgeons and grave diggers." Company C had been on the skirmish line for two days and a night, and when the brigade was about to fall back Col. Miller told Capt. Glaze that the brigade was ready to move, and said: "Keep up constant firing, if you can, till the brigade is well out of the way." They kept it up till near midnight, by which time the rebels were getting nearer and nearer. Sergt. Dan. Moore was left with a squad to hold the skirmish line till the company should get mounted. The company waited for him till capture was imminent, and left without him, taking to the woods to get away, and supposed he was certainly captured; but Dan. turned up all right the next day, to the joy of his comrades.

As soon as our brigade was relieved it moved back, but as the horses were so far away, it was 10 o'clock before we reached them and got mounted. We moved back four miles, to where we struck the Pumpkinvine on the 24th; crossed it, and then turned north and moved four miles, then east four miles, and were still but six miles from where we started; yet it took us nearly the whole night to make it. Our horses had not had any grain for five days, and scores of them fell dead in the road that night. The men were so overcome from exhaustion and want of sleep as to remember this night's march as one of the most miserable of their lives. About 3 o'clock on the morning of the 30th we laid down and had an hour and a half of good sleep—the first we had taken for nearly 72 hours.

May 30th. Up at sun-up and ordered to saddle, but at 10 a. m. we were ordered to unsaddle and send out foragers; by noon most of them had come back with nothing but a few small bunches of green wheat in the bloom, which, in the exhausted state of our horses, was little better than nothing. These old Alatoona Mountains are the most God-forsaken country we ever saw; two whippoorwills could scarcely get a living on a mile square, and if a third one should come on a visit, he would have to bring his rations or all three would starve to death.

Our butcher, Johny Spies, Company F, here killed some beef, which was the first we had had for a long time. We speak of it because it was the last he killed for us, for in two days the Johnnies got him and took him to Andersonville. He was a very clever man, and is still living at Boswell. Ind, Jordan B. Roberts, private Company I, who was detailed to drive and herd the beef cattle allotted to our division, tells in a few words the terrible time the cattle had eating the scrubby white-oak brush to keep life in them a few days. He says their orders were to look over the herd carefully, and to pick out the ones to kill that were sure to die before the next killing; yet in spite of their best endeavors to fulfill the orders, they would sometimes make mistakes, and the next morning the old bull would be dead, which was not only a clear loss to the government, but the soldiers got that much the less beef.

May 30th. Saddled up at 5 p. m., and ordered to go to the west of our train. Moved two or three miles and camped.

May 31st. Lay in camp all day; got a few handfulls of corn for our horses, the first since the 24th.

June 1st. We moved north eight miles toward Etowah River and camped near Burnt Hickory. John Spies, private Company F, the butcher, was captured.

June 2d. We moved 16 miles north and camped on the Etowah River, neat Cartersville. Our camp was beside a large field of wheat, 15 acres, perhaps; the wheat was ripe, just ready to cut, and would have made 40 bushels to the acre and as nice as we ever saw. In three days there was scarcely a stubble of it left three inches long. This campaign was short but terribly severe. We had lost one-third of our horses and the men suffered very severely, an idea of which can be given by stating that we lost 25 pounds in weight, and all our comrades suffered quite as severely. The object in coming back to this camp was, 1st, to recruit our horses, 2d, to guard the pioneers who were building a bridge there, over the Etowah River. The bridge here which was quite a structure was burned by the retreating rebels; it was over 100 feet high and 100 yards long. After crossing the river the railroad runs through the Alatoona Pass, or gap, and it was this gap Johnston occupied when we began the flank movement on Dallas. We are picketing pretty strong here as the cars run right down to this place, and are piling up rations and forage rapidly. Vast trains are in the neighborhood, and should a division of rebel cavalry dash in here, they could make bad work for us.

Our men have already put a wagon bridge and two pontoon bridges across the river here. These pontoons are curious things and deserve description. They are simply a light, stout frame of what would make a boat 14 feet long and four wide; but instead of boards being used to cover the frames, stout duck canvas is used. Two men can easily carry one, and they can be put together and laid down on the water in five minutes, and taken up as quickly. These boats are anchored a proper distance apart in the stream and used the same as bents of a bridge, stringers reaching from one boat to the other, which are covered with plank for a floor, which completes the bridge. Very heavily loaded trains can cross on them. They were extensively used in the army, and those who handled them were organized as a special branch of the service, called pontoon corps.

We lay in this place, picketing and resting our horses, till June 7th, during which time Sherman had tried to let go his hold near Dallas, where we found the rebels so well fortified in the hills round about that they could not be moved. On the 1st of June Sherman began to push forward the left wing of his army and tried to withdraw his right, but the rebels watched every movement so closely that every motion was the signal for a fight Dallas is 18 miles from the railroad at Big Shanty, and Sherman had been trying to push his left wing eastward far enough to get back on to the railroad again, but up to the 7th it was still five or six miles from Big Shanty. On the morning of the 8th we crossed the pontoons and took a south-east direction over the Alatoona Mountains, leaving Alatoona station to our right. We made 12 miles for that day, and camped two miles east of Ackworth. As before stated about one-third of our brigade had lost their horses, and these were left behind to-day, all under command of Col. Kirkpatrick, and sent back to Columbia, Tenn., to do guard duty there. Col. Long, with the 2d brigade, was left at that place when we started to the front, and brought his brigade up yesterday; so our division is about the same in numbers as it was before the dismounted men were sent back.

June 9th. Up early and were ordered to leave our pack mules in camp and be ready to move at the sound of the bugle. As before intimated, Sherman never seemed very friendly toward cavalry in general, and our division in particular; and while he was continually depending on us to do some daring and dangerous service, he never seemed willing to give us credit for what we did. While, to our mind, there never was any good reason for the rule, yet we always had to go ahead and make reconnoissances and find out for the infantry where the enemy were. It often occurred that we were nearly marched to death running from one wing of the army to the other, hunting the whereabouts of the rebels, while the infantry would be getting fat lying behind their works, snug as a bug in a rug. While we were in no sense cavalry, except that we had horses to ride, we always had to bear the odium attached to that branch of the service. Sherman had frequently said he never saw a dead cavalryman; and it is not surprising that inferior officers and privates should get to believe that it was so because we never got close enough to the enemy to be killed. This, however, did not worry us so much, because we were willing our fighting qualities should go before the world as proven by the number of rebels we had killed and captured; what galled us worse than all else, was to be sent on an important expedition, to learn some important fact, and after we had got all that had been sought, and more, to be treated as though the information wasn't of much importance, or that it wasn't reliable. Take, for instance, the battle of Chicamauga, when Rosecrans actually refused to believe the rebels were crossing the creek till 10,000 of them were across. Then at Pumpkinvine, on the 24th of May, when we had a fight in the evening and McPherson said it was only a picket post. So this morning, as usual, we were ordered to make a reconnoissance toward Marietta and find the enemy. Sherman, with his usual distrust, sent one of his staff officers over to go along with us, and to see that we found something.

As we moved out, Wilder was in an ambulance by the side of the road, and the men began passing the word along the line, "Wilder has the diarrhœa, to-day, and Miller the brigade; there is something up for us to-day." We speak of this because it was the last we ever saw of Wilder, and further, as a coincidence that whenever the brigade got into a fight Col. Miller was always with it. When about two miles from Big Shanty we struck the rebel pickets and drove them in; but just before getting to the village we saw a long line of rail works reaching clear across the fields between us and the town. We dismounted, and at this juncture it was found the Seventy-Second was without a field officer; Col. Kirkpatrick had gone back and Maj. Carr had become very suddenly indisposed. Capt. Thomson, Company D, senior officer present for duty, took command and moved the regiment to its place in line. The brigade moved forward, and at a single charge cleared the works at a bound, and sent the rebels flying through the town, This charge was made without much loss to us. We had killed a few rebels, wounded more, and captured some, which were duly taken to Sherman's staff officer for inspection. That officer simply remarked, "a cavalry picket." Our lines were straightened up in the farther edge of the town, and just down in the edge of the woods another line of works was visible. Our orders on this occasion were to advance to a certain point, fire four rounds and lie down. When all was ready we started. This time the rebels were in numbers equal to two to one of us, but when we got to the point where we were to lie down, the rebels opened on us such a volley that we felt it worse to stop than to go ahead. They peppered us like hail, but in a minute we were on to them, and as they went flying down through the woods we poured volley after volley into their backs, and followed them to an open space where we could see fresh earth thrown up beyond. We lost several men in the brigade this time, and captured 30 prisoners; these, too, were duly paraded before the doubting staff officer, and Col. Miller told Gen. Garrard that it would hardly be possible to go farther without having to fight the whole of Johnston's army, directing his attention to the long line of smoke and camps not two miles away, at the foot of the Kenesaw. We could also see a fort to our left, not a mile off. The General asked the staff officer if he was satisfied; he said he was himself, but as all the prisoners as well as the dead seemed to be cavalry, Sherman would say he had not gone far enough to know anything certain. Col. Miller then showed him the long line of breastworks, just across an open space, in the edge of the woods, behind which with his glass he could see the men throwing up dirt to complete their works—all of which he admitted; it would certainly have satisfied Sherman if he had been there to see, that the whole of Johnston's army was in his front. Gen. Garrard said to the officer, "Col. Miller can bring you in some infantry the next drive he makes, if that is what you want, for you can certainly see that the Johnnies behind the works are infantry."

After getting the brigade in good line, and letting the men understand that we had to produce some infantry prisoners before Sherman would believe there were any there, we started for their works across the field. The men knew as well as the officers that this advance meant business and bloody work, as they could plainly see the Johnnies waiting for them. The whole brigade moved forward as one man, without firing a shot, until within short range, and then, with a cheer, set forward, determined to give the rebels a chance for as few shots as possible. At this point the flag-bearer was disabled, when the brave Capt. Thomson, of Co. D, sprung to his rescue, caught the flag in one hand, and, with sword in the other, he led the advance of his regiment. He triumphantly bore the banner and led the regiment until the third line of defense had been carried, and the enemy driven back. Though the Captain, in his noble daring, escaped the missiles of death, the flag of the regiment he so heroically bore was riddled with balls. The clash of this charge was terrific, but lasted only a minute. Our men went over the earthworks, killed a captain and several of his men, and captured a company, officers and all. We did not attempt to hold this line of works, and upon bringing off the prisoners they were marched up to the staff officer with their guns and accoutrements all on. "Well," said he, "if that does not convince Sherman where Johnston's army is, he will find out when he occupies the ground we are now on with his infantry." Garrard then said to Col. Miller: "What do you say to the way the sharp-shooters are sending their compliments, and the looks of those movements on our left?" Col. Miller replied: "I think the best for our good will be to get out of here." Sherman's staff officer said: "Yes, and that soon, or *I* will. Those balls make more noise in the brush than I am used to at headquarters." The brigade soon got to their horses and made good time getting back from under the fire of the sharp-shooters, feeling we had done a good day's work. Col. Jordan, of the 17th Indiana, tells of an incident that day, when he obeyed orders the most cheerfully he ever did in his life. It was the habit of Maj. Vail, of that regiment, to always go into action on horseback, and, said Jordan, "of course I also had to, or the men would say I was a coward. After the last charge, although we had taken their works, the sharp-shooters kept up a constant buzzing of bullets around our ears. We rode up to brigade headquarters on the road, when Col. Miller said: 'Get down off your horses; no sense in sitting there just to be shot at.' Then's when I obeyed orders promptly."

We moved back to our camp, two miles from Ackworth, at 9 p. m. It is proper here to state that McPherson's army was five full days fighting its way up to the point we reached on the 9th. Company A was not in the engagement, through no fault of the men, as they would have much preferred to have taken part in battle than to have been on picket; but some one had to do picket duty, and the lot fell to them. Just after starting out of camp, and while the column was in motion, a detail was made from the regiment and placed under command of Sergt. Magee to go and hunt beef cattle. This detail fell into an ambush down on North Noonday Creek, near Little River, and had one horse killed and Private William H. Clark, of Co. I, captured. He was a good soldier, and died in Andersonville. In the engagement for the day, Patrick Lellis, of Company H, was severely wounded in the shoulder, and as he was being taken to the rear he hallooed to Sergt. McClure to take care of his horse until he got well enough to come back. His horse was a great favorite with him, but he never got able for duty afterward, and was discharged in November following. He was a good soldier. Andrew Fiddler, of Co. C, was seriously wounded in the right fore-arm. James Schoonover, of Co. F, thigh and left leg, severely. James McCann, of Co. C, right arm and elbow, severely. Thomas Haywood, Co. E, while on the skirmish line, and when holding his gun at a "ready," had a musket ball pass through the breech of his gun and knock the wind out of him, but soon recovered, and was able to return with the command in the evening. Loss in the brigade was 14 wounded—five in our regiment.

CHAPTER XXVIII.

From June 10th to July 4th, 1864—*Rain, rain*—50,000 *Soldiers Cheer a Locomotive Whistle—Col. Wilder Retires from Service—Out of the Wilderness—Great Guns Bristling Horribly from the Mountains—Very Close to the Rebels, and Can Hear Them Talk—Grand Artillery Practice—Terrible Fighting on the* 19*th—The Seventy-Second in a Close Place in the Rain—Close Call for Capt. Kilborn—Artillery of Heaven and Earth in Full Play—Casualties—Sherman Peremptorily Orders Garrard Across Noonday Creek—Minty's Brigade Crosses and is Roughly Handled—The Seventy-Second Comes to the Rescue—A Rebel Letter, with About a Lie to the Word—Andrew Bryant Captures a Rebel with a Stick—A Rebel Chases Capt. Vance Around an Old Oak Tree—Description of Kenesaw Mountain—Assault on Kenesaw, and* 100,000 *Men in Mortal Combat—Camp at Buzzard's Paradise—Filth Concentrated—Flies Blow Our Clothing and Everything Else—Sherman Flanks Kenesaw—Kenesaw Taken—Rebel Caricature of Gen. Sherman—Where's Gar'd? where's Gar'd?—Skirmish at Rottenwood Creek—John Barnard Lies in the Creek all Night—The Fourth of July in Camp.*

June 10th. We lay in camp till near noon, and then moved northeast three miles, when we struck a road running south-east toward Marietta. We followed this road six or eight miles, and went into camp six six miles north of Big Shanty. We found plenty of rebels on the road in front of us. On our march we passed through a comparatively level country, densely wooded. We also passed over quite a scope of country that had once been worked for gold, the long deep trenches being still open just as the miners had left them, being very dangerou pits to fall into. Heavy rain and thunderstorm this afternoon.

June 11th. Up and saddled early, ready to move by daylight, but it began to rain soon and rained all day hard, and we did not move at all, remaining in camp saddled, expecting every minute to mount, as Minty's brigade was on the road in front of us, and his pickets kept firing occasionally all day, and just before night the rebs charged them, and killed and wounded several. This made quite a racket, and in less than three minutes our regiment was mounted and on the gallop toward the firing; but before we got to the posts the rebels had fallen back and all was quiet, and we went back to camp.

June 12th. It rained all day again, and most of the men put up their tents, for the first time, we believe, since leaving Columbia, Tennessee!

June 13th. Still raining, and the armies are doing nothing. Our regiment sent out a strong foraging squad under command of Capt. Thomson. They went north to Noonday Creek, and found plenty of corn. The country gets better as we gradually get down off the Alatoona mountains, eastward.

June 14th. We lay in camp all day, and the only thing to note is the coming up of our train with forage and rations. There is one thing connected with this campaign that excites our profoundest admiration, and that is, the way Sherman keeps up his railroad and our rations. On the 11th the High Tower bridge was completed, and an engine crossed immediately, put on right down to Big Shanty, and as it came up to the station and gave its loudest whistle and said, "How do you do, Gen. Sherman?" the sound was greeted with loud and prolonged cheers from more than 50,000 soldiers, and a corresponding growl of displeasure from the rebs. As the engine went screaming on down the road six miles further, to a water-tank, and got water the Johnnies greeted it with artillery from their batteries on the Kenesaw mountain, dropping their shells all around the engine. Nothing daunted, the brave engineer got his water, and came back amid the deafening applause of all the army who were near enough to hear, and we voted him a hero. The coming of this friendly iron horse, with its shouts which made the mountains and valleys echo and re-echo in thrilling tones, "Make way for Liberty!" caused more genuine heart-rejoicings throughout that host of loyal heroes than even though they had been reinforced by a corps of 20,000 men. Right away the rations began to pile up at Ackworth, which made every soldier think he had come to stay, and that our provisions were assured. The sun came out to-day, the first time for several days. We speak of the weather, because it has so much to do with army movements.

On June 15th Col. Wilder retired from the service, and Col. Miller took permanent command of the brigade. Dr. Cole became our brigade surgeon, and Dr. G. W. Kirkpatick, brother of Lieut.-Col. Kirkpatrick, became regimental surgeon, and Maj. Carr had command of the regiment. That day our brigade moved to the right of Long's brigade, near Big Shanty, to fill a gap between his brigade and the infantry. Our movement provoked the rebels to make an attack on Long, resulting in a sharp skirmish and the killing and wounding of 18 of his men. Company C, of the Seventy-Second, while scouting, got on the road in front of Long, and came very near getting into battle with the entire rebel force. Col. Long came up behind them, and expressed great displeasure that they should get in his front. Capt. Glaze suggested to the Colonel that his brigade would get whipped if it went much further; but the Colonel, Braddock-like, didn't thank the Captain for his advice, proceeded, and was whipped, with the loss above stated. Our brigade was fortunate that day, and suffered no loss. The movement spoken of brought us out of the forest wilderness in which we had been ever since we left the Etowah, into an open and tolerably well cultivated country.

On emerging from this forest we could see, for the first time during our service, nearly the entire field of strife. The panorama was terribly grand and awe-inspiring. Had we the time, and the power of Homer, we should like to describe it. What was most repugnant to our feelings, and made us shrink back a little on emerging from the dark woods, was to see on the north end of Kenesaw an eight-gun battery, of largest calibre, which seemed within a stone's throw of us, and ready to drop death and destruction amongst us. The battery was really four miles away, but so clear was the air that the grim guns seemed very near. The truth is, as we swept our eyes over the scene, horrible with devices and enginery of death, the prospect for a speedy termination of the conflict was not at all encouraging. Every mountain and hill, in front and away to the right, fairly bristled with artillery and swarmed with rebels. Never before had we seen so many rebels at one time.

We immediately threw up a line of works and joined them to the works occupied by the infantry. The rebels were in heavy force just in our front, and Noonday Creek, another Chickamauga, winds along between us and the north end of Kenesaw, and we were exactly north of that mountain. We occupied this position till the 19th, doing nothing but keeping up a strong skirmish line in front. Our pickets and those of the enemy were so close together that after night, when it happened to be still, we could hear every word the rebels said when talking in loud conversation. But during the night, as a rule, we had more noise than in the day-time, for it seemed that the rebels took special delight in keeping us awake, and it often appeared to us that every hill and mountain had suddenly become a volcano, and from 500 craters were pouring down upon us streams of fire and death. These artillery duels after night were the most thrillingly grand exhibitions we ever witnessed. Dr. Cole says, June 18th: "The earth, as far as eye can reach to the south-west of us, is one vast sea of breast-works and rifle-pits." Col. Miller says: "Both sides are wasting a heap of powder, and the story is circulating in camp that some one told Sherman he never could take Kenesaw mountain. He replied that he *would* 'take it, or shoot it d—d full of old iron.'"

June 19th will long be remembered as one of the great battles of Kenesaw. It is true that some part of our lines had been fighting every day, and almost every hour, day and night too. But to-day the *whole* army was engaged and the fighting terrible. During the night of the 18th the rebel army fell back on both its flanks and shortened up its lines so that Sherman thought they had retreated, and ordered an assault along the whole line. Our division was ordered to cross the Noonday Creek. We were up and saddled by sun-up. About 8 a. m. we mounted and moved straight to our skirmish line, then dismounted and formed line facing south-east, and moved forward about a half mile, where we struck the Marietta road, on which we had picketed so many days. Our brigade swung around to the right across this road, which here runs due south. The two cavalry brigades were on our right and left rear to protect our flanks. We had hardly straightened our line when the rebels opened on us with a three-gun battery, away across to our left front, from a lunette fort, and skirmishing began in front. We moved forward about a half mile, driving the rebels before us, when suddenly we came upon a large, deep stream, which we could not cross, while just on the opposite bank was a heavy line of works composed of rocks and earth, and beind these works lay a heavy line of infantry ready to slaughter us. Before we got to the stream it began to rain in torrents, which prevented us from seeing clearly what was before us, and we were not aware of our proximity to the creek nor to the rebels on the other side till we ran fully up to the creek. The bluff on the opposite side was higher than on ours, and as soon as we reached the creek, and were thrown into some confusion to know just what to do, the Johnnies opened on us but fortunately overshot us. As muddy and raining as it was we dropped upon our bellies, and opened fire on them. This stream was not at any place more than three rods wide and at some places not half that width; but it was very deep and the banks very steep. This was the first time our brigade had ever met with an obstacle it could not go through or over. But here we were really checked. We could not go forward. We never retreated; and so were "in a fix." The rain was still pouring down in a deluge and proved a Godsend to us, for once, for in two minutes the smoke was so thick we could not see across the creek. The rebel lines and ours at the right of the regiment were not six rods apart, and at the first volley or two the rebels had wounded a half dozen men. After the smoke got so thick neither side could see we had the advantage of them, as we kept firing at the flash of each other's guns and we could give them about 20 shots for every one they sent us. We soon made them keep their heads behind their works. For a short time we thought they had got the range remarkably close. Capt. Glaze says of this affair, "Company C had been on the skirmish line all the night before, and when the command moved to engage the enemy, left C in the rear. Not wishing to remain there, the hazardous attempt was made to join from the rear the regiment, which was then under fire as spoken of above. We were soon aware of our mistake, but having started, determined to go on. Any one who has never gone to front under fire can form no idea of the danger. The rebels were across the creek, upon a high bluff, too steep to ascend, and the regiment were lying on their faces in the wood. Firing down, as the enemy did, most all of their shots went overhead, and the "high" ones were what made it so hot for Company C. By jumping from tree to tree, and from one log to another, we all managed to escape unhurt, but it was a miracle. Capt. Kilborn had a narrow escape that day. While sitting with a number of us in a fence corner, a bullet barely missed his head and buried itself in a rail behind him. It was impossible to protect ourselves, and it was a wonder our loss was not a heavy one, and we owe it to poor shooting or good luck that any of us are alive to tell of it."

We have spoken of a lunette fort on the south side of the creek; when our line got to the creek we were about even with this fort, and the enemy opened on us from it with shells, which went whizzing and sputtering right over our lines from end to end, but luckily for us they had again cut their fuses too long and the shells went tearing through the trees and exploded to our right. But we assure you they made us flatten out on the ground wonderfully. This continued half an hour, when our Board of Trade Battery got into position and opened on the fort. The rebs then let us alone and went to throwing shell at the battery. About the first one they threw went away over the battery and exploded in Dr. Cole's ambulance train, scattering them in every direction. It was still raining as steadily as ever; the excitement had all worn off, and everything had settled down to business. In about an hour our battery had disabled the guns in the fort and they quit firing. Our battery then moved around on to a ridge to the right rear of our regiment in order to get a position from which to rake the rebel line of works. From the excessive rains of the past few days their ammunition was bad, and for a time we were in much more danger from our own battery than from the rebs, the shells dropping in our rear and exploding behind us. It was some time before we could get our batterymen to understand what was the matter, and when a shower of grape and canister came pouring down over us, the most of the right wing of the regiment wanted to get out of there.

We can think of nothing so terribly awful as this battle, except that Chicamauga approximated it, but was on a smaller scale. Bear in mind that it was pouring down rain in torrents, the lightning flashing a constant sea of fire from above, and the guns a sea of fire beneath; peal after peal of deafening thunder, and volley after volley of more deafening artillery, rolled on earth and in heaven, which made the ground tremble and shake, and the reverberations and re-echoes through the mountains made a constant roar more terrific than that of a thousand Niagaras. All this time, with thunderbolts, shot and shell, crashing and shrieking above and around us, we were lying flat on our bellies in the mud. By two o'clock the infantry away up the creek to our right had succeeded in getting across the stream, pushed the rebel line back till their position at the creek became untenable and they let go their hold and retired, leaving but a skirmish line in their works in our front, which kept up a desultory firing. The rain had raised the creek to a flood and we did not attempt to cross, but about an hour by sun fell back a short distance to the rear, threw up a line of works and lay behind them all night.

After the rain ceased it turned cold and we lay in the mud and slush all night without fire.

The casualties were as follows: Capt. John Glaze, C, wound in left leg; Capt. John C. Scott, H, wound in foot; private John I. Williams, K, compound fracture left arm, severe; private Thomas Hughes, K, left fore arm; private Sandford Bowen, K, contusion of right hip; private H. S. Kreshere, K, Shoulder; private Michael McCain, C, forearm.

Sherman, as usual, seemed displeased because we had not succeeded in getting the whole division across Noonday Creek, (see Sherman, 2, 56). And on the morning of the 10th, peremptorily* ordered

Garrard to cross the creek. We all well knew that the entire force of rebel cavalry was just across the creek in front of us, and Garrard mildly suggested that in the present condition of the roads it would be impossible to move his artillery, and was extremely hazardous to cross without it. But Sherman's partial failure all along his lines seemed to exasperate him, and he ordered Garrard to go across at all hazards. So Gen. Garrard, not even hoping to make a permanent lodgment on the east side of the creek, concluded to send but a single brigade across at first, to make a reconnoissance. Col. Miller told him that it was rather a doubtful move, the force being too large to run, and too small to fight much, and proposed to take our whole brigade across, prepared to fight all that might come against it. At this time there were four companies of the Seventy-Second on picket. Garrard sent Col. Minty, with the 1st brigade, across, about 1 or 2 p. m., nearly two miles below where we fought yesterday, and at the same time detachments from the other two brigades went scouting to the north and rear of us. Minty had crossed north-east of our camp and turned straight south, and when just east of us very suddenly and unexpectedly found himself attacked on three sides; he was effectually cut off from retreating by the way he had advanced, and his only chance was to fight the best he could. Sergt. Remley, Co. E, in his notes, says: "From our picket-post, the whole of the battle was in plain view, and was the hardest cavalry fight I ever saw." This was about 3 p. m., and it began to rain and never ceased till midnight. Minty could do nothing but fight, which he did with courage and discretion, his regiments charging the rebs furiously to check them till he could send for help. Part of our brigade was hurried down to the creek to help Minty "to let go," as he had such a hold that he couldn't without help. The pioneers were hurried down to the creek to make a bridge across the nasty stream for our men to cross on, but before any of our brigade got to the creek the rebels had closed in on Minty from north, east and south, and with charge after charge were driving him into the creek, and on the north had taken possession of the road and actually compelled some of them to jump their horses into the creek, where they became mired down and the men had to abandon them. It seemed but a question of a few moments when the whole brigade should be swept into the creek. Everything was in a hurry and roar. Our battery was got into position and began to shell the woods. Our men dismounted, bravely charged across the creek with cheers, and drove the rebels back; they rallied, came on thicker and thicker, driving Minty's brigade before them, till they came in range of the Spencer rifles, when they promptly checked up, and

Minty's cavalry crossed on a bridge that had been hastily built by the pioneers. During the progress of the fight those of the Seventy Second who were in camp were lying quietly, but we could plainly hear the terrible conflict going on over the creek, and when the rebels set up their devilish yells we began to get ready for a fight, and Capt Pinkerton and Capt. Thomson began to form the companies. The infernal yells still coming louder and closer, we started on quick time for the creek, but as we neared the stream it seemed to us, from the terrible noise and yells, that the rebels were just gobbling up everything before them, and every man of the Seventy-Second was excited to the highest pitch. Just then a most terrific thunder storm burst upon us, and as the lightning's blaze would illumine the heavens with oceans of fire, and in an instant midnight darkness would follow, we set up such a cheer, and went down to the creek with such a rush, that the rebels must have thought a whole division was upon them. They ceased firing and retired as a hungry lion when armed men rush upon it, and our cavalry got back over the creek without further molestation, barely escaping the red fangs of death or the fate of capture.

Dr. Cole, in his report of this battle, says: "Col. Minty was ordered out with the 1st brigade, but had scarcely crossed his command over the boggy bottom, when he was attacked by a large force and thrown into confusion, his regiments falling back in disorder. At this time the 3d brigade (ours) was ordered over to his relief, and finally succeeded in checking the enemy and holding that side till nightfall, when the troops were all withdrawn. This situation was a desperate one, and we considered ourselves fortunate to get out of it." Col. Miller, in his notes, says: "My brigade had three killed and seven wounded. Minty had 11 killed, 40 wounded and several captured."

The rebels left 30 killed on the field, but carried off all their wounded. Of the two brigades—Minty's and our own—there were about 2,200 men engaged. Now, this is our side of the story—a plain, unvarnished statement of facts—and to show you that one chivalrous Southerner was hardly equal to their oft-boasted task of whipping three Yankees, we give their side of the story, as published in the Atlanta *Appeal*, a paper which we captured on the 3d of July, just east of Marietta:

"Correspondence of Atlanta Appeal.

"SUCCESSFUL CAVALRY EXPEDITION OF WILLIAMS' KY. CAVALRY BRIGADE.

"*Five Miles North of Marietta, Ga., June* 21.

"EDITORS APPEAL:—A brief account of a little expedition, made on yesterday by a portion of Wheeler's cavalry, on the flank of the enemy, may prove interesting to the readers of your highly appreciated and popular paper, and also gratifying to Kentuckians, to learn the gallant part this little brigade acted in a fight that reflects great credit on our arm of the service. About 12 m. yesterday Gen. Wheeler learned that the enemy was advancing on the Bell's Ferry road, in the direction of Marietta, and also that he had a force occupying the Noonday church. He at once decided to move and attack the enemy and drive him from the road, and, if possible, to cut him off. Therefore orders were given and the command moved at 2 p. m., this brigade in advance, commanded by Gen. Williams, and followed by the divisions of Gens. Kelly and Martin, (two divisions and one brigade.) We moved up by a circuitous route on a road little traveled, which led into Bell's Ferry road at Noonday church. Upon arriving within 600 yards of the church, Gen. Williams directed Lieut.-Col. Griffith, commanding the 1st Kentucky regiment, to scour the woods to the left of the road on which we were moving, and drive the enemy's videttes and pickets, while Major Lewis, commanding the 2d Kentucky regiment, was ordered to drive the enemy on the north of the road, and, if possible, gain possession of the Bell's Ferry road north of the church, in order to prevent the enemy from moving on us from Woodstock or Dr. McAfee's. While these orders were being promptly and gallantly executed, the 9th Kentucky and 7th Kentucky battery, and Allison's squadron, were moved to the rear of a hill about 300 yards from the church, and formed in full view and under the fire of the enemy, which came from the church and dwelling house, and an old cotton gin behind which the enemy was strongly posted. Two companies of the 2d battalion, under the command of Capts. Harris and Humber, were dismounted, and ordered to drive the enemy from and take possession of the houses, which they succeeded in doing after about 15 minutes' hard fighting against a greatly superior force. The 9th Kentucky regiment was formed to charge the enemy in case he was driven from the houses, and the moment the Yankees began to show their backs, with a yell, and led by the gallant Col. Breckinridge, the 9th was upon them, and soon began to club them with their guns. Noonday Creek runs near the church, is a very muddy stream, and almost impassable except where it is crossed by a ford. About 100 of the Yankees being unable to gain the ford, were cut off and attempted to cross below, when so many of their horses became mired down as to almost completely bridge the stream. The frightened Yankees, taking advantage of their misfortune, abandoned their mired horses and crossed on the backs of those in their front. Col. Breckinridge, with the quickness of perception, dismounted his men and charged the fleeing Yankees on foot, crossing many of his men over the same pontoon horse bridge made of Yankee horses, while the remainder of his men waded the stream, waist deep, capturing over 20 prisoners. About this time were seen large columns of the enemy on the opposite hill, preparing in turn to charge the two dismounted companies of the 2d battalion and the 9th Kentucky regiment, which had already gained the opposite side of the stream. A battery was also brought in position, and began to open on us with but little effect.

"All was now excitement, as the enemy adjusted his lines preparatory to the charge. But it was soon over, as but a few moments elapsed before on he came to meet the same fate as before. A few well-directed shells from the 9th Kentucky battery completely checked and routed the column moving on it, while the column moving on the two companies of the 2d battalion was met by the 3d confederate regiment, supported by the 5th Georgia regiment. Here for a few minutes a hand-to-hand fight ensued, but Gen. Kelley having gotten his command into position on our left, and Gen. Martin his division on Kelley's left, our whole line was ordered to advance, when we drove the enemy for over a mile, completely routing him from every position, and driving him pell-mell through the wood. A heavy rain and night coming on prevented further pursuit. The enemy left a large number of his killed and wounded upon the field, being so hotly pursued as to not be able to get them off. The forces we fought were Gen. Wilder's troops, under command of Gen. Garrard, and were greatly superior to ours, besides having every advantage of position, but notwithstanding all this he could not resist the impetuosity of our men. His loss was not less than 200, while ours was not more than 40. The loss in this brigade was 17 killed and wounded Our whole cavalry was managed with great skill by Gen. Wheeler."

This, of course, does not quite average a lie to the line, but the most casual reader will not fail to note the disparity of numbers between two whole divisions and a full brigade on the part of the rebels, to much less than two brigades on the part of the Yankees. We have given our exact loss, as the records will show, and also the number of the rebel dead actually counted on the field, to say nothing of others not found, or mortally wounded and carried off by their friends.

Night and total darkness came on so suddenly, as before indicatdd, that rebels and Yankees were all mixed up on the east side of the creek, and there were many thrilling adventures took place. A great many of our men stayed all night east of the creek. We only have time and space for a single incident. Andrew Bryant, private Co. G, by some means found himself in the rear of the rebel lines without horse or gun. After night set in, the first thing he knew he ran into a long line of cavalry, and wasn't long in finding out they were Johnnies, but was too close to retreat. Supposing, as a matter of course, they were facing toward the Yankees, he started through, and when asked where he was going told them he was going to his regiment. When asked what regiment, he told them the 5th Georgia, or some other rebel regiment. Fortune favored him, for they told him that regiment was on the skirmish line, and he passed on through, but when away from the main line made up his mind to avoid the skirmishers if he could. He wandered around for some time, when he ran suddenly upon a reb leaning against a tree, and he quietly picked up a stick, slipped up to the Johnny and gave him a slight punch with it, and told him to throw down his gun, which he did. Bryant picked it up and stood guard over the Johnny till morning, when he marched him into our camp. One of our men, belonging to the 98th Illinois, had his thigh broken, and lay out in the rain all night, and was brought in next morning. He said several times during the night the rebs came very near him, as they were hunting up our dead and stripping the clothes off of them. The poor fellow had to have his leg taken off, and never rallied after the operation.

June 21st. In camp. Raining all day; we did nothing but care for the dead and wounded.

June 22d. Still raining. For six days our clothes have never been dry; everything seems to be stuck in mud, but the everlasting roar of artillery goes on all the same. We send out strong scouting parties every day to our left rear, to see if the Johnnies are not trying to get around on our hard-tack line.

June 23d. Our camps are just where they have been since the battle of the 19th, and are simply detestable; the mud is deep enough to swamp a horse. To-day we moved south-west, up the creek, to more comfortable quarters. Just after noon our brigade moved across the creek in a south-east direction, to help the infantry make a drive, as we called it; that is, we protected their left flank while they advanced their lines. These advances always brought on a fight, and our brigade had some fighting but had no loss.

We had advanced toward the rebel lines and were throwing up temporary works, but before we had got them completed a regiment of cavalry charged upon us. They came in an oblique direction from the way we were facing, and struck our right in the flank, some of them coming in behind our line. One fellow, more venturesome than the rest, got nearly to the centre of the rear of the regiment before any one saw him; the others had disappeared about as suddenly as they came, but this fellow seeing Capt. Vance, Company I, standing there doing nothing, went for him, cheese-knife (sabre) in hand and death in his looks. Vance just then made the best time on record around an old oak tree, yelling at the top of his voice for some one to "shoot the d—d rascal." This was a sight of fun for the boys, but Vance failed to see any in it, as he had nothing but his old frog-sticker and was no match for a well mounted trooper with revolver, carbine and sabre. Corpls. Samuel, K, and Huntsinger, A, shot and wounded the rebel, but his horse carried him out of reach of our lines. Long's brigade had two men wounded to-day. As soon as the infantry got their lines established we went back to camp north of the creek.

On June 24th there was nothing but scouting and picketing. On the 25th we had the opportunity of passing over the battle-field after the battle, which is of great value in getting at the facts as to the topography, directions, distances and points at which the hardest fighting had been done. On that day Company I went on picket at the ford where we had the fight on the 19th, (other pickets had been there before us) and we had a good opportunity to verify or correct all our impressions of the fight. We occupied the rebel works on the south side of the creek, one-half of the company in the lunette fort and the other half further south. On the morning of the 26th it was very foggy and smoky, and the rebels undertook to capture the squad in the fort by crawling up from the south-east between the two posts, and were actually within 25 yards of the fort when discovered. Our boys opened on them, but the Johnnies charged into the fort so quickly that we hardly knew what we were about. Our boys jumped over on the outside of the fort and opened fire on them, and our post further south poured in an oblique fire on the rebels and they left very suddenly; the fog and smoke permitted them to get away. Near noon they tried it again, but were handled more roughly as this time we could see them before they got so close. The sun came out that day for the first time in several days, and was hot enough to roast eggs.

June 26th. This afternoon we moved camp a mile south of the creek, which brought us close to and just in the rear of the left wing of the infantry, and also on ground that had long been occupied as a camp by the rebel cavalry, and certainly the most filthy and detestable place we ever saw; but we propose to pay our respects to it another day. When we went to bed we had orders to be ready to move at six o'clock.

On June 27th the hardest fighting since the siege of the Kenesaw commenced. We were called up early and saddled before daylight, but at 6 a. m. were ordered to fall in on foot, leaving our horses in camp. Our brigade moved with a day's rations in haversacks south-east about two miles and closed up on the infantry; but before we had our lines straightened the rebs commenced to shell us, the shells exploding high in front of us and the pieces passing over us thick and fast, whistling "Wher-r-r-are-re you, wher-r-r-r are-re you?" which made us flatten out for a while, and Dr. Cole says it was fortunate for us that we were worse scared than hurt. Somehow or other, they failed to get our range, so we straightened up our lines and threw up a strong line of works and held our position, with our skirmish lines 300 yards in front all day. Nothing special occurred; the shells kept coming over us all day, at times in showers, but were very high and beyond scaring us badly did no harm.

Hitherto we have purposely let the other part of the army take care of themselves, but we are sure that a little explanation here will be of interest to the general reader. Since the 9th of June the rebel army has occupied Kenesaw Mountain and the approaches thereto. Kenesaw itself is a narrow, high and very steep ridge, breaking off very abruptly at the north end; very steep and rocky on its north-western face and tapering off into a long, low ridge, at the north-east and south-west; it is three miles long, but the ridge extends south much further. Sherman's army had gradually driven the rebels from one strong position to another till now they occupied only the mountain itself and the ridge extending south.

The rebels had a strong line of works extending from the northern end of Kenesaw nearly east, and to-day our brigade is facing that line and about 1,000 yards from it. Sherman had worked his army plump up against the northern end of Kenesaw and all along the north-western face, and along the ridge south. It seems impossible to go farther. The rebels are so strong at every point that they cannot be moved. There are but two alternatives; either to assault and go through them, or pull up and go around them, as had been done at Snake Creek Gap. This time Sherman chose to assault; a very sad mistake as the event proved. So this morning he ordered a strong feint at our end of the line and also at the other end of the line 20 miles away, in hope that Johnston might thin out the center till our troops could break through.

By 8 o'clock the fight began along the whole line and was terrible beyond description. Never before in the history of our war had so many men been engaged in mortal combat at the same time. It is a safe calculation that on our side there were at least 60,000 men engaged, and of the rebels at least 40,000, making 100,000 men bent and determined upon each others' destruction. We have no words to describe this awful day. To us who had but little to do but listen to the roar of artillery, the hissing of shot, the bursting and shrieking of shells, the terrific crashing of small arms, the shouts and groans of the combatants, and see the work of death, the sight was sickening and might well make one ashamed of his race. The infantry next to us made a splendid charge and partially took a strong line of works, but were driven back with terrible slaughter. So the battle raged all along the west side of the mountain, and so it rolls away down to the right 10 miles along a line of flame, and smoke, and blood. But on the extreme right of the army our men are more successful and drive the rebels back till the extreme right of the army is just about south of us, while Marietta is between us and them, and Kenesaw is a mile to our right Our men on the south have taken three lines of the enemy's works and hold two miles of them, but are driven from the third with fearful slaughter. This has all occurred before 10 a. m., and it has become apparent, even to Sherman, that the assault is a failure and that it is worse than folly to try further to drive the rebels from their works. Our men from this hour only aim to hold all they have gained; but the rebs are not satisfied with this ground already taken from them on their right, and make three desperate attempts to recover it, but are unsuccessful and lose heavily, which in the game of war *partially* compensates for *our* terrible loss. Near sundown we are relieved and go back to camp.

June 28th. It has quit raining so steadily, and the weather is so intolerably hot at midday that we are glad to lay in the shade. While we lay here we shall pay our respects to our camp, as we promised to do nearly a year ago. We introduced you to Maggot Hill, on Duck River, and then thought we had seen all the stinks in the universe so compounded, concentrated, and intensified, that there could not be anything beyond, above or beneath it; but we just confess we had never smelled the "boss" stink till we came here, nor saw filth till we saw it here. The truth is, the whole of Gen. Wheeler's corps, about 10,000 men, had been in camp right on this ground from the 8th of June till the 19th, and it looks like they tried to see how much filth and nastiness they could leave behind. We have said before that we never saw a rebel sink. Now, if you can tell how 10,000 men could void all their excrements for 10 days on a few acres of ground, without literally covering the whole surface, you beat us. This of itself would be sufficient reason for the man in the moon holding his nose while passing over our camp; but added to this were the rotten carcasses of hundreds of dead horses and mules, and the offal of all the beeves they had killed in that time. But all this is not what we want to call your attention most particularly to at present. We spoke of maggots before, and all we said was true, but here we are struck just in a way we never were before. We told you several days ago that our clothes had not been dry for a week. Well, they are more or less wet all the time yet, and the tormenting flies not only deposit their eggs on the filth spoken of, but on our clothes, and blankets, and bread, and sugar; and there isn't anything in this country that we know of but what they do blow. We have come in off picket or scout with our horses and sleeping blankets wet, unsaddled our horses and thrown our blankets in the sun, and in two minutes thousands of flies would swarm around them and deposit their eggs on the blankets, and in a few minutes more maggots would be crawling all over them; and as we lay down to sleep these pestiferous wigglers would get in our shirts and squirm and twist all over us. We can compare their plowing and sucking to nothing but a mole trying to bore a hole in the middle of a hard road. Of course what we are telling must be repugnant to the refined and elegant, but we could not be a true Historian unless we told the facts just as they were. It was our misfortune to have a large hole in our arm, eaten there by poisonous vaccination, and in spite of our every effort to keep clean, the worms would get into that sore and from that would crawl all over us, and it makes every fibre of our flesh creep yet as we think how they wiggled and squirmed, and sucked and plowed their beaks into our creeping skin. We boiled our clothes every day of the world when we had time to do it, but so long as we lay in this camp it did but little good. Just why green flies should blow clean sugar, and blackberries fresh from the bushes, we never could tell; but they did do it. The only way we could manage to keep our bread was to leave it in the boxes, break open a box just at meal-time, and eat all there was in it at a single meal. The only way we could get any good of our beef was to kill it in the night and cook and eat it before morning. Of course "body-guards," in a general way, were the soldiers' torment; but we had rather have a thousand "body-guards" than a hundred maggots. We dedicated our camp on Duck River "Maggot Hill." We call this "Buzzards' Paradise."

July 1st and 2d were as hot days as we ever saw, and it rained in showers both days, and the maggots literally moved us out of camp. We moved back south-west, on higher ground, where we had a pleasant camp. As we had nothing to do but to picket and scout, we could have enjoyed ourselves hugely but for the intolerable heat. About this time it began to be whispered that Sherman contemplated soon to begin another one of his flank movements, and compel Johnston by strategy to do what he had failed to make him do by fighting. His plans were to move his whole army by the right flank and abandon the siege of the Kenesaw, and were completed by the evening of the 2d, at which time our division was ordered back nearly to Big Shanty, and three companies of each regiment in our brigade were ordered to relieve all the skirmishers along the north and west of the mountain. This was a good plan, as one company of our regiment could do as much shooting with our Spencers as a whole regiment could with single shooting guns. As soon as it was dark three of our companies, D, I, and C, took their places, and the whole army, except our division and the 15th corps, with muffled artillery, moved off to the right, and long before daylight were miles away. The entire absence of skirmishing and artillery firing during the night was ominous for the rebs, and they started off for Dixie, too. As soon as it began to get a little light, our boys in front of Kenesaw began to feel their way forward, and by the time it was fairly daylight our men had reached the top of the mountain, and we could see them running along the ridge. Then burst forth one long, loud and continued cheer, announcing to the rest of the Union army that at last Kenesaw was ours. Sherman immediately ordered our division and the 15th corps to pursue with all possible speed, and by 8 o'clock our signal flag was waving from the top of Kenesaw, and the 15th corps had got started. But our companies had to come back to the division, after which the whole division had to draw rations, which took up considerable time, and it was near 10 a. m. before we got started. We took the road from Big Shanty to Marietta, which led us around the north end of Kenesaw mountain. The 15th corps had got started an hour sooner, and went around the south end. As soon as we got beyond our camp of yesterday, we began to pass line after line of the most substantial earthworks, which the enemy must have hated very much to leave, because he was comparatively safe behind them as long as we persisted in fighting in front of them. But no sooner did Sherman move his army past them on the flank than these works became useless to the rebels. This made the mistake of Sherman, in ordering the assault on the 19th, and again on the 27th, the more glaringly apparent. The most stupid soldier we had would remark: "Why didn't Billy do that long ago, and save the 5,000 men he lost in the two assaults?"

To-day the Seventy-Second is in the advance, and Companies A,

F, D, and I, advance guard. As we passed the north end of Kenesaw we encountered a most substantial line of earthworks running straight east, and had to follow along it some distance before we could find a place to get through. After getting through it and within a mile of Marietta we saw a large board nailed up to a tree, and painted on it were characters representing "Billy Sherman Hugging a Nigger Wench," and underneath the pictures were the words: "*Come on, and we'll give you a warm reception on the 4th.*"

This convinced us that the rebels had not hurried away, but had done it deliberately and on purpose, and the real history of the case has proven that both armies began to move at the same hour of the night—Sherman by the right flank, and Johnston to retreat. But the fact still remained, all the same, that Johnston's constant falling back from such strong positions was most discouraging and demoralizing to his army, and cause of great joy and encouragement to our own.

The siege of Kenesaw had virtually lasted from June 10th to July 2d, and was a remarkable one in many respects. Thousands of brave men lost their lives; its lessons were learned at tremendous cost, but were *well* learned, and had an important bearing upon all the subsequent movements of this army; and, in estimating simply the factors of war, were worth all they cost.

It was about noon on July 3d, 1864, when the Seventy-Second entered Marietta from the north, and a few minutes after we got on to Main street the advance of the 15th corps came in from the west, and a few minutes later Gen. Sherman came up with his staff, and was as full of wrath as a steam-chest, and swearing worse than the army in Flanders. Garrard, our division commander, was back with the head of column, which was just then coming in from the north. As soon as Sherman got up to us he began to let off steam about this way: "Where's Gar'd? where's Gar'd?" (as he called Garrard.) "Where'n the h—l's Gar'd?" Pretty soon Garrard came up, when a perfect storm of abuse broke forth from Sherman, mingled with cursing, because Garrard hadn't got into Marietta three hours sooner. Garrard very mildly and meekly tried to explain to him that his men had to come down off the mountain, walk nearly four miles to get to their regiments, and then to draw rations before he could start at all, all of which took time; but Sherman got madder and madder, and finally railed out: "Git out of here, quick!" Garrard asked him which way we should go. "Don't make a d—d bit of difference, so you get out of here and go for the rebels." So we lit out of there ively, but during the "parley" the infantry had passed right on through town, taking the road straight east to Roswell, and as this was the only road we saw that would likely give us our proper place on the left, we took it, too, and in our hurry to get past them got terribly mixed up, and some cursing was done; but a half mile east Sherman turned the infantry south and a mile further sent a staff officer ahead to turn us south-east. In less than two miles from Marietta we ran on to Wheeler's cavalry, covering the retreating army as rear guard. From the time we got inside the rebel works we had been picking up many stragglers, who were entirely worn out with the terrible fatigue of the protracted siege, and were glad to quit fighting, Skirmishing began immediately, and we began to push them back. The woods were full of roads leading in almost every direction except in the direction we wanted to go. The roads had been prepared by the rebels in anticipation of this retreat, and we had not gone more than four miles from Marietta till we found our four companies all deployed on as many different roads, and all skirmishing lively. The rebels seemed to be moving more to the south than we were. During the skirmishing Company D captured a couple of Johnnies, who were taken back by one of the men, and as the woods were very thick, they both started to run in different directions. Our man soon brought one of them "to" with his Spencer, but the other one would have gotten away entirely if he had not run into another company and got captured again. About 3 o'clock in the afternoon our regiment got concentrated on a road leading toward Atlanta, while Minty's and Long's brigades picketed the roads to the left of us. This road was a mile east of the infantry, that is, we were both moving in the same direction, but there was a gap of a mile between us. We commenced to move forward, and the rebels began to thicken in front of us. Sergt. W. R. Stewart, Co. A, was in charge of the advance videttes, and after receiving the fire of the enemy immediately charged upon them and chased them across Rottenwood Creek. Here the videttes halted till the balance of Company A and the other four companies came up; then Orderly Sergt. R. W. Pilling was ordered to take a part of Company A and move across the creek. There was a piece of open ground on this side of the creek, and a high bluff thickly covered with brush on yon side. Company A rode into the creek and let their horses drink; all was still as death beyond, but just as they got out of the creek on yon side a volley was poured into them. John Hughes, private, was killed; Stephen Gard, private, was shot through the lower jaw, shattering the bone; George Staley, private, was captured; and as the company turned to get out of there Sergt. Samuel T. Stewart's horse pitched him down the bank into the creek, injuring his back so he could not stand up. John

Barnard got dismounted and would have been captured had he not jumped into a drift pile in the creek. Sergt. Barnes' horse was shot through the jaw, and absolutely refused to go further, and Barnes had to run across the field on foot, getting many a close call from the rebels as he did so. The balance of Company A got safely back out of range of the rebel fire.

John Hughes was a Georgian by birth, and had joined Company A but a few days before the battle of Chicamauga, and in that battle fired 54 rounds at the enemy. He was on the Mississippi raid, and always ready for duty. George Staley, who was captured, was a good soldier, always cheerful and ready for duty. The poor fellow died in Andersonville.

As soon as the firing commenced on A, the other Companies, F, D, I, E, and some others, were hurried up under command of Capt. Thomson, dismounted and moved up to the support of Company A. This was about 4 p. m., and from that till sundown the skirmishing was kept up, at times quite lively and severe. The balance of the brigade did not come to our help, and we found the rebels so strongly posted and in such numbers on the opposite side of the creek that we could not move them, and made no further attempt to cross the creek. Samuel Stewart, who had been pitched down a bank eight feet high, and badly injured, dragged himself along down the creek, and when the firing slackened up a little managed to get close enough to our lines to be heard by our men, and was rescued, but for many weeks was a terrible sufferer in the hospital. John Barnard, who got dismounted and jumped into the creek, thought he would just wait there till the command came up; but the command did not come, and as he could not get out without exposing himself to the rebels, he lay there till dark, expecting to get out then; but just as soon as we fell back the rebels placed their pickets along the creek so close to him that he could hear every word they said, although they only talked in very low tones. John said he was afraid they would hear his heart beating, for to save his life he couldn't keep it still. He had not laid in his uncomfortable position long till he got so chilled and so thoroughly miserable that many times during the night he was upon the point of calling to the rebels to come and get him; but then he would think of Andersonville and hold on a little longer. This fully illustrates the terrible dread we had for that fearful hell for Yankee prisoners. Towards morning the pickets were withdrawn, and John crawled out, but was so benumbed as not to be able to stand; finally he got into camp, all covered with mud, and in the most deplorable plight you ever saw a man. John was "six feet six" high, and when he got to his company and finally assured himself he was really not a candidate for Andersonville, he straightened himself up, and in his peculiar style and brogue said: "Well, boys, that was pretty rough, wasn't it?"

After we rescued Stewart we quietly withdrew and fell back a mile and a half, where we found the balance of the brigade had gone into camp. Our regiment captured 20 prisoners for the day. Loss, one killed, one captured, and two wounded.

July 4th, 1864. Bugle call this morning at 2 o'clock, and orders to be ready to move at daylight. The division moved out at sun-up, and as the rebels were still in force about where we left them yesterday, we left our horses in camp and went on foot. Our brigade formed line nearly where we lay yesterday evening, and our battery was got into position and shelled the woods across the creek; but we found we were a mile in advance of the infantry on our right, and still further to the right the infantry were meeting with strong resistance, and heavy fighting was in progress. We did not try to advance, but the heavy firing we heard to our right reminded us of the "finger-board" we saw north of Marietta, yesterday, which said "come along and we'll give you a warm reception on the 4th." About 10 a. m. the infantry to our right rear began to advance and shell the woods, their shells dropping right into our lines. An orderly was sent to tell the infantry to quit shelling in our direction, but no attention was paid to him and the shells still kept coming. A staff officer was sent who told them they were throwing their shells right into our rear. The commander of the infantry brigade said he knew that could not possibly be, as he was very sure no part of the army had advanced farther than his brigade. Our staff officer told him he was certainly mistaken, and if he didn't quit throwing his shells into us we would be compelled to fall back; yet he would not believe we were in front until he sent one of his own staff officers over to see. This is simply another exhibition of the contempt the infantry had for the service rendered by mounted soldiers. It was the middle of the afternoon before the infantry got their lines up even with us.

Of the vast pile of manuscript now before us, we find that *every one* speaks of the manner in which we spent the 4th of July. Col. Miller says: "We made a heap of noise for the benefit of the enemy." Dr. Cole says: "Had hoped to celebrate this day in Atlanta, but may yet see several long days before reaching that city." Records says: "Out of rations and o-rations." Hall, Co. D, "Big dinner, parched corn and coffee." McClure says: "Short of hard-tack." While Sergt. Stewart has a reminder of it nearly this way: Capt. Thomson and Stewart were pointing out to a member of Gen. Garrard's staff the position of the enemy, when a sharp-shooter sent them his compliments in the shape of a Minie ball, which went through the back of Stewart's coat, also cutting four holes in his shirt and blistering a road across his back an inch wide and four inches long. Of course Stewart jumped about a rod; the ball then went through a pine sapling and lodged in a horse's foot. In the evening our division went back to camp, simply leaving a strong picket to keep up our part of the line of battle. Sergt. Remley says: "Our company was on picket and we were so close to the rebels that we could hear the officers giving command, and toward morning could hear the rumbling of artillery as they commenced to fall back."

CHAPTER XXIX.

From July 5th to August 16th, 1864—Feeling for the Chattahoochie River—Very Hot Weather—Blackberries Abundant—Burning Factories in Roswell—Hunting for Fords on the Chattahoochie—Thrilling Description of Wading the Chattahoochie in Front of the Enemy, and Driving the Rebels from Their Position—"Bully Boys! Whisky in the Morning!"—Some Duckings and the Whisky in the Morning—Preaching in Roswell—Pork Found in a Graveyard—Corn Starch and Blackberries—"You'uns Will 'Flink' Around We'uns"—Take McAffee's Bridge—Ignorance of the Natives—Destroying the Railroad—Destruction of Stores at Stone Mountain Station—Closing in on Atlanta—Heavy Fighting—Burn Bridges Across Yellow River—Capture and Burn Trains—Capture Prisoners—Burn Mills and Stores at Covington and Other Places—Loading Down with Tobacco—A Scorpion in our Coffee—"Gim-me a Chaw Tobbakker"—Gen. McPherson Killed, and Great Sorrow Over His Death—Lightning Brigade Surrounded—Cutting Our Way Through the Rebel Lines—Running Rebels—Sherman's Explanation—Stoneman's Capture—We are Put in the Trenches Before Atlanta—Facts About the Siege of Atlanta—Hard Battles—Approaching the Enemy's Works by Parallels—"Wherever You See a Head Shoot at It"—Scenes Among the Rebel Dead—A Dead Rebel Chases a Live Yankee—We Leave the Trenches and Go to Decatur—Fight with the Rebels Near Decatur—End of Our Second Year's Service—Celebrate the Day Washing and Patching.

July 5th, 1864. This morning early our division was relieved entirely from the front, and we went back four miles toward Marietta, and when within two miles of it turned east on the Roswell road, moved four miles and turned into the shade, while scouting parties were sent south and east to the Chattahoochie River. It was too fearfully hot to do anything. Late in the evening we moved on and went into camp four miles from Roswell, in a dense wood. Here we had three days' rest, and never was rest more needed, or more enjoyed. The dense shade shielded the burning rays of the sun from our heads, and the woods were so full of blackberries—such large and nice ones—that a man in a few minutes could pick as many as he would want to eat through the day. They were so conducive to health we almost lived upon them. Our custom was to pick for a mess of eight a gallon of blackberries, cover with a gallon of water and bring to a boil, and then stir in three pounds of broken crackers and a pound of sugar, and the gods never ate a better dish. We have it down in our notes that these were among the happiest days of our soldiering; but it must not be inferred that our brigade was entirely idle during these three days. Col. Miller, in his notes on the 6th, says: "Visited Roswell to-day. The cotton factory here is the largest in the South. Five hundred employes are engaged manufacturing goods for the Southern confederacy. After allowing the employes to take away all they could carry, it was burned." In his notes of the 7th he says: "All the enemy are across the Chattahoochie except Hardee's corps."

The Chattahoochie was a wide, and in many places a deep, stream. Where shallow the bottom was of soapstone, and plowed with thousands of deep narrow trenches, pits and holes, which made it an ugly stream to cross at any place. Where shallow the water ran as swiftly as a mill race, and where deep was full of dangerous eddies. To cross this in the face of a determined enemy was perilous in the extreme. It was our business to find as many crossing places as possible, and at the proper time to cross, no matter what opposition might be brought to bear. Citizens seldom undertook to cross this river except where bridged, and knew nothing of any fords or places where it could be forded. Our cavalry drove a party of rebel pickets out of Roswell on the 5th, and they, after retreating across the only bridge near here, set fire to it before our men could prevent it. So for the next few days our scouts were kept constantly busy hunting for fords and places to cross, and by the 7th had succeeded in finding several places that in an ordinary stage of water could be forded but for the numerous trenches, pits and holes, previously referred to. The rains that had continuously poured down all through and up to the very last days of June, had flooded all the streams in the country, and the Chattahoochie was still swollen. Besides, on the opposite banks were steep bluffs, densely wooded, and for miles and miles were strongly fortified where the rebels had the least idea that the Yanks would undertake to cross. This gives you, kind reader, an idea of the perilous work before us, of which *we* poor soldiers were purposely kept in the most profound ignorance. And now, after having nearly 18 years to think over and study about the matter, we can think of no better reason for keeping our brigade camped in that dense woods, so far away from the river all this time, than that we might know nothing of the dangers of the work before us.

On the 6th of July, Gen. Sherman reported to Gen. Halleck, at Washington, as follows: "I propose to study the crossings of the Chattahoochie, and when all is ready to move quickly. As a beginning, I will keep the troops and wagons well back from the river, and only display to the enemy our picket line, with a few field batteries along at random. At present the waters are turbid and swollen from recent rains, but if the present hot weather lasts, the water will run down very fast. All the regular crossing places are covered by forts apparently of long standing, but we shall cross in due time. This is a delicate movement, and must be done with caution. Our army is in good condition, and full of confidence, but the weather is intensely hot, and a good many have fallen with sun-stroke. Of course, I expect every resistance in crossing the Chattahoochie River, and have made up my mind to feign on the right, but actually to cross by the left."

Of the places found by scouting parties deemed practicable for crossing, one was near Roswell, and in regard to the practicability of this crossing, we quote from Col. Miller's notes, July 8th: "Came down to the river to-day to look at the ford where I am to cross the men of my brigade, under the fire of the enemy, whom I can see behind the works on the opposite side of the river. I moved the brigade down to Roswell after dark, and was up all night." From Dr. Cole we quote: "By a reconnoisance of the ford a mile from Roswell, to-day, it was found that the rebels were guarding it in force, and as we design crossing it, if possible, early to-morrow morning, at this point, we may have some work to do. Consequently I have taken charge of the Presbyterian church, placed the sick in it, and am prepared for the contest."

Now you have the preliminaries before you, all of which had been kept profoundly secret from us. Our division began to move immediately after dark, and just before midnight our brigade bivouacked in the edge of the village of Roswell, a mile from the river, and were ordered to keep as quiet as possible, and not build any fires. We lay down and slept till 3 a. m., when we were very quietly called up and immediately fell into ranks and moved down to the river on foot. There was no moon; it was dark, and along the river very foggy, which entirely concealed our movements. Our brigade was formed in line of battle up and down the river, though some distance from it, while two companies of the 17th, and two companies (D and I) of our regiment, were deployed as skirmishers right along the edge of the water, and secreted in the brush. These four companies were under command of Capt. Thomson, Co. D, Seventy-Second. While these movements were going on, our Board of Trade battery was quietly got into position on the high hill overlooking the river. Capt. Thomson, who was in command of the skirmishers, was ordered to report to Col. Miller as soon as he got the men deployed. After this work was done, and the Captain was passing along the line, he heard the men wondering what in the world they were going to do there. The river was four hundred yards wide, and the fog so heavy upon the water that the men could not see across, and it seemed so deep that scarcely a man dreamed they were expected to cross. Capt. Thomson says he really expected that they had been deployed for the purpose of protecting the pioneers while they should lay a pontoon across the river, never suspecting the real work that was before him.

The Captain, on his way to report to Col. Miller, and when half way up the hill, turned to view the situation. It was then getting a little light, and he could see a big white house on yon side of the river, and a lot of soldiers sleeping on the porch, and the sentinels at regular intervals along the line of the river, and others passing up and down the hill in numbers sufficient to convince him that it would be hazardous to undertake to cross, if, indeed, they were *expected* to cross. The rebels seemed all unconscious of an enemy near them. The Captain reported to Col. Miller, and said his men were deployed and in position. "Well," said the Colonel, "as soon as the artillery opens, move your men right across." The Captain for a moment was struck with astonishment, but immediately replied: "You don't mean to say that we are expected to wade that river?" "Yes, that is what we have been sent here for, and we expect to do it." The Captain says he never realized anything in his life that looked so extremely perilous as that did, and he ventured to suggest as much to Col. Miller, but said: "If you order it, we will try it." Col. Miller says that just at this time he overheard some men in the main line of battle debating the propriety of crossing, when one of the men said: "By G—d, I'll not believe it till Miller says so!" When Capt. Thomson got back to his men all of them seemed to have been discussing the matter, and the first words he heard were: "We'll never cross it;" and the next were: "If they order us to, we'll do it; but I don't believe Col. Miller will ever order us to."

Here we wish to record our idea of true bravery. The man who never sees or never realizes danger is not brave, though he may perform never so many foolhardy adventures; but the man who feels and realizes what danger is, and then goes forward in the discharge of duty, *is* brave. Here were men of intelligence, and with two years' experience in every conceivable phase of war, and none knew better than they of the danger they were about to face. The water may be 10 or even 50 feet deep just before them, for aught they know. The rebels on the opposite side may be ten to one, or even more. But they have no time for further reflection; for just then the artillery belches forth a volley of shells, which burst among the sleeping sentinels with the sound of mighty thunder. Capt. Thomson gives the command "forward!" and without a moment's hesitancy the men plunge into the water up to their arm-pits. Not a faltering one; not a laggard! But with a cheer they rush into the water and charge for the other shore. Gen. Garrard now rides to the water's edge and cheers them on, shouting, "Bully boys! bully boys! *Whisky in the morning!*" The whole brigade now rises up, and with cheer after cheer urges them forward, while the battery men work away at their guns, determined that the expedition shall not fail for want of energy on their part. However, it is not all smooth sailing with our brave men in the water. As the shells burst among the sleeping rebels on the opposite bank, they start up in the wildest flight, and realize for the first time that the Yankees are upon them. They seize their guns and rush to the water's edge and open upon our men in the river, but, as frightened men usually do, they shoot clear over their heads, but the men are having a rough time of it; the water is so deep and the current so swift that they can scarcely stand on their feet, let alone make any advancement, and as they attempt to move forward step into the numerous trenches and holes, and go under. Still on they rush; the rebels firing volley after volley at them; and if you could divest your mind for a moment of all thought of danger, the motion of the line would appear laughably comical and ridiculous. As the line moves forward a comrade suddenly steps into a hole or trench, and under he goes, as if dodging the rebel bullets. By this time our men are half way across the stream, and open fire on the rebels in the brush along the shore.

As our men rush up out of the water and immediately open fire with their Spencers, the river is all ablaze, the rebels think that pandemonium has broken loose, and all the imps of the lower regions are now coming for their lawful prey, and they break and run up the hill. our men shooting them in the back. Now there is a race who of our brave men shall reach the shore first. The water has gradually become shallower, and now is scarcely to their hips, and such another running, shooting. cheering and splashing. was never witnessed before. Sergt. James A. Mount, Co. D, ever anxious to excel, was perhaps the first to reach the shore, and David Frazier, Co. I, was but little behind him. But where every man of those four companies did his noble, clean best, and each and every one got there just as quick as he could, we will not be invidious with further distinctions. As our men reach the shore they rush for the top of the hill and capture three or four prisoners as they ascend, who are blanched and trembling with fright, declaring that our men had just raised up out of the water and commenced to shoot at them From these prisoners we learn that Martin's whole brigade of cavalry is camped near by as support for the pickets, and we immediately take to trees, and stumps, and logs, for defense. The whole brigade now moves across in column, and our skirmishers are peering into the woods and brush ahead, momentarily expecting Martin's brigade to move upon them; but the frightened fugitives had told the General that Wilder's whole brigade was already across, and he thought discretion was the better part of valor, and contented himself with simply watching our movements. The whole brigade got across in a few minutes, moved out to a good position and went to work throwing up defensive works, and in half an hour could not have been driven from them by all Johnston's army. Our brigade were the first troops to cross the Chattahoochie, and although it was effected without the loss of a man, we cannot help shuddering when we think of the fearful peril we were in when first ordered to pitch into the water.

We remained in position all day till late in the evening, when Newton's division of the 4th corps came up from further down the river, waded across and relieved us, and we waded back and went into camp where our horses had been all day. The contrast between our feelings on wading back with what they were on going over, was great as it was agreeable. Many of the men sought to get back to camp with dry clothes by pulling them off and carrying them on top of their heads. Capt. Thomson was among the number, and being a very tall man the plan promised success; but he had not reached the middle of the river till he stepped into a luckless hole and fell sprawling in the water, going clear to the bottom, and came near losing his clothes in the bargain. This was more fun than the boys had seen for many a day, and the whole regiment joined in a hearty laugh at the Captain's expense.

As soon as our men had secured a lodgment on the east side of the river, the doctors, chaplain, and non-combatants generally, came back. I quote from Dr. Cole of July 9th: "I have about 20 of the brigade on hand sick. Chaplain De LaMatyr, of the Seventy-Second, preached in the hospital to-day. The pastor of this church, Rev. Mr. King, was not at all pleased at our polluting his house with sick and wounded Yankee soldiers, notwithstanding the land of wooden nutmegs was his early home." From our own notes we make this extract: "This morning at 10 o'clock the bugle blew for preaching, the first time we had heard it for many a day. Every unemployed soldier about camp went to church, and notwithstanding the house was very large it was well filled. Our whole brigade was composed of men who were in the habit of going to church when at home, and the bugle-call for preaching was never unheeded in the army. Our Chaplain was universally loved and respected by every one. The services were unusually impressive, and by contrast with present surroundings brought to mind other scenes far away; and could the *common people* of the South have been permitted to look in upon our devotions, they must have been convinced that we Yankees were not the vandals their leaders had pictured us to be."

Sunday, July 10th. This is the first time our brigade was ever camped right in a town; and this is a most beautiful place of about 2,000 inhabitants, a manufacturing town of vast importance to the Southern confederacy. In addition to the cotton factory before spoken of, there was a woolen mill and paper mill, all in the employ of the confederate government. The town is most beautifully situated at the mouth of Victory's Creek, which furnished the power for running all the machinery. The employes were all women, and there were more of them than we had seen since leaving Nashville, and as they were all from the north, were really good looking; most all the women we have seen for the past year have been fearfully homely. When our men first came here, on the 5th, one of the mills hung out the French flag, and the other one the English colors. The proprietors belonging respectively to those two governments, and they were in hopes thereby to save their property; but as they had cast their lots with the enemy of course we treated them as enemies. According to promise, Gen. Garrard, right away after breakfast this morning, sent around the whisky. This was the second time we ever had drawn, or ever had, whisky issued to us since we entered the service. and we think *this* was a mistake, as the men never needed it, or asked for it, and always got along just as well without it. The whisky ration was about a gill, and not enough to hurt any one, provided each one just drank his own ration; but there were always in each company some who would never draw their rations at all, which would just leave that much more for somebody else, while among those who did draw their rations there were some who were not content to drink them alone, but had a way of gambling "drink for drink" till some would get a pint, or even a quart, and of course got foolishly drunk. Upon this occasion their delirium took the form of making love to the women, and before night Col. Miller found it necessary to move the brigade a mile north of the town.

The 16th army corps, Gen. Dodge commanding, came up from the south, put a pontoon across the river and relieved Newton's division, which went back to its proper place in the line.

Before leaving town—which, by the way, is a very high toned place, possessing a most beautiful cemetery, in which were some splendid family vaults of solid masonry, some of Company G were sauntering around through the grave yard, and as they were short of sow-belly had a very sharp scent for meat. One of the boys declared that he knew there must be meat somewhere close, as he could smell it. Upon a close examination of the premises a flat rock was found upon which a piece of meat had evidently been laid. This was near a large and elaborately constructed vault, and our "scenter" declared he knew there was meat in there, because he could smell it. A hole was soon made in the wall, and sure enough, they found a lot of bacon, hams and molasses, to all of which our boys, without praying the lief of the dead, began to help themselves; but before they got away with their booty the old woman pounced upon them and broke out about this way: "I've allus hearn tell o' you'uns robbin' the cradle and the grave to fight we'uns, and now I know you'uns will rob the grave." Dr. Cole had his headquarters in the church and kept his horses in some stables near by, and he says, on the 11th, "our darkies found a large lot of hidden stores in the stable to-day."

Our camp north of Roswell was a most beautiful one. Long years ago it had been cultivated till naturally worn out and then abandoned. The ridges and furrows were still plainly visible, and along the ridges had grown numerous pine trees that were now six to eight inches in diameter and 30 to 40 feet high, making the most delightful shade imaginable, which we were needing very much during the heat of the day, as we never felt the sun pour down his rays with such penetrating power before.

On the 11th, Company I was sent over the river to picket in front of the infantry, and to scout toward Atlanta. In our rounds we ran on to a small building full of medical stores, among which were 1,000 pounds of the nicest corn starch we ever saw. It was all done up nicely in four-pound packages, all of which we strapped to our saddles. There were bushels of blackberries everywhere, and so long as our corn starch lasted no Roman emperor ever fared more sumptuously than we did. A gallon of well cooked blackberries thickened with a few ounces of corn starch made the most delicate pudding we have ever tasted.

On the 10th, Gen. Johnston succeeded in getting his whole army across the river and burned all the bridges in his rear.

On July 12th Company H was sent about six miles north to a place called Alpharetta for a load of charcoal for blacksmithing purposes. While out on picket at that place, private Joseph Price was shot at by a bushwhacker. He didn't hit Price, but his mare, which was standing by his side was struck in the stifle joint; and although they scoured the woods and brush over and over, they failed to find the rascal who did the shooting, and lucky for him that they didn't find him. Price was very much chagrined at having to leave his mare, as he had been riding her ever since we were mounted at Murfreesboro, Tenn., in 1863.

July 13th. We lay in camp all day without anything of note, and we have time to tell a story which we heard several days ago, but have just been reminded of it again, and we vouch for its truthfulness.

Several days ago some of our boys were passing by a house and saw a woman out in the yard, who seemed to be in a terrible rage. She was blustering around at a fearful rate. When some one asked her what was the matter, she roared out: "You ole Yankees are the meanest folks I ever seed; you'uns don't fight we'uns fair; we'll throw up breastworks and fix a place to fight you'uns behind, and we'uns expect you'uns to fight us all before it; instead of that you'uns 'flink' around and pitch into we'uns' eend. We fixed a place at Buzzard Roost for you'uns to fight us, and you'uns flinked us, and you flinked us at Carterville, and flinked us at Dallas, and you flinked us at Big Shanty, and you flinked us at Kenesaw; and it 'peers like you'uns are 'allus' pitchin' into we'uns' eend. And 'tother day Capt. Hooker flinked around here with his critter company and throwed cannonades as big as my wash-kittle and jist knocked my ash-hopper all to pieces"—which was a "joak" on the ash-hopper, surely.

It does begin to look like "Billy" allows to "flink around" this way and pitch into "we'uns' eend" from this end of the line, as McPherson is moving up this way with the balance of his army, the 15th and 17th corps.

July 14th, our division moved about eight miles north-east up the river and took possession of what is known as McAfee's bridge. There was a company of rebels on picket there. It was a covered bridge and they had it stuffed with cotton ready to fire it quickly if the Yanks should come near it and undertake to cross. Our men slipped up and drove them away so quickly that they didn't have time to fire it. We left a strong picket at the bridge and then moved back four miles due west of the bridge and went into camp at a village not down on the maps, which was called Newton, and consisted of a house and cross roads. Our line of battle is now over 40 miles long, extending from this bridge clear down to Campbelltown, below Sandtown, which leaves the line "thin" in places. Our object here is to secure the bridge and then to cover all the approaches to Marietta so as to keep the rebel cavalry from getting back into our rear and breaking our hard-tack line. There has been less fighting done in the last 10 days than took place on any single day for two months previous; but the army is not idle. The infantry are constantly throwing up works in front and strengthening their defences in the rear, so that the whole Southern confederacy could not drive them from ground once captured; while the cavalry are just as busy scouting in the rear to see that no force of meddlesome cavalry or lawless guerrillas tear up the railroad; and also moving out to the front and hanging on the flanks of the enemy to ascertain their exact position and strength.

July 15th. This morning at five o'clock our regiment and the 123d Illinois, all under command of Lieut.-Col. Biggs, 123d Illinois, left camp and moved straight for the river at McAfee's Bridge, crossed it and turned directly south for Atlanta. After going 12 miles we struck the rebels in force at Crosskeys, formed line of battle and skirmished with them for two or three hours, capturing a few prisoners without loss to ourselves. Near here we saw marks of ignorance that, up to this time, we had supposed were hardly possible in a free country. On our way we passed a log cabin; standing at the fence was a man whose looks indicated him to be four score years old. We asked how far it was to Atlanta. He said he had never been there but guessed it was about 16 miles. "How long have you lived here?" he was asked, "Ever sense I kin rie'leck," he replied. "How far is it to Crosskeys?" "I don't know," he replied; and yet this man was not a fool. Soon after passing his house we saw by the side of the road a large chestnut tree. It had been peeled on the side next to the road and two large crossed keys cut in the wood, and under them were cut three notches; all of which we rightly interpreted, three miles to Crosskeys. Near the place we saw a large guide board with the letters Roswell painted upon it, and on the post under it were eight deeply cut notches, which, of course, meant eight miles to Roswell. We saw many such signs afterwards. Crosskeys is 13 miles from Atlanta, and our reconnoissance was a bold and risky one, as there was a large cavalry force of the enemy above McAfee's Bridge on the east side of the river, which might have easily cut off our return. We got back to camp just at sundown. Wheat and oats were ripe and in abundance on the east side of the river; apples were ripe and plenty.

July 16th. Squads of deserters coming in every day; we suppose our position on the flanks enables us to see most of these.

July 17th. Our division crossed the river at the bridge and moved two miles north-west of Crosskeys, where we struck the left wing of our army, which is now all east of the river. McPherson, with the 15th, 16th and 17th corps, is on the left, and we took our place in line of battle and went into camp. Crosskeys is 13 miles north of Atlanta and 14 miles north-west of Stone Mountain.

July 18th. As soon as we could, our brigade and Minty's started for Stone Mountain, a brigade of infantry following us. We moved north-east four or five miles, so as to avoid the enemy at Crosskeys, and then turned south-east and moved straight for Stone Mountain. Just before we turned south-east our regiment halted by a large plantation where there were scores of negroes, all of whom very naturally came out "to see dem Yankees." Among the number was the funniest creature of the human species we ever saw. She was just about as thick as she was high, and the laughing surface of her face was simply extensive. She would weigh 300 pounds, and came waddling right out into the road, frightening our horses, and began immediately to talk and chatter like a parrot: "Where all you'uns gwine to?" We told her we were going down here to tear up the railroad. "What yu'uns want to tar up de railroad fo'?" "To keep the rebels from using it." This puzzled her, and for a second she was silent, when some one told her we were Yankees. She was the very picture of astonishment, and said, "No!" We told her we were, for a fact; when she raised her hands and said, "Dey dun tole us you all had horns!"

When within about four miles of Stone Mountain our scouts struck the rebel pickets and commenced to skirmish with them; but as there was no heavy force of rebels in our front we moved right on till within two miles of the railroad, when we dismounted, took a bee line across the woods and fields straight for it, on the double quick. When we got to the road we were told that a heavy force of the enemy were near and that we should destroy as much as possible before they came upon us. This was new business to us, and we did not know just how to go at it. Gen. Garrard told us to build fires on the ends of the rails. We could not see just what good or harm that would do, but we went to work. There was a good board fence on each side of the track, and in an incredibly short time there were a hundred fires burning along a mile of the track, and we were curious to see what effect it would have. In a few minutes the rails were red-hot and quivering like leaves in the wind, and we could see they were expanding; in a few minutes more there would be a sudden lurch, and the ties would fly up, or spring out sidewise, and the rails would be bent in almost every conceivable shape, some of them in nearly the exact shape of a letter S. Notwithstanding the great heat of the fires was added to the great heat of the sun, it was fun for us, and we worked nearly hard enough to kill ourselves. We struck the railroad about half way between Stone Mountain and Decatur, at noon, and our brigade worked east toward Stone Mountain. In about an hour later a brigade of infantry came up and began to destroy the road toward Decatur. They pursued a different method from what we did. They would march up by the side of the track in single file, front face, lay down their guns, take hold of the rail next to them the whole length of the regiment, and just turn the track, ties and all, up side down; then tear the ties loose from the iron, pile them in huge heaps, then pile the iron rails across the tops of the ties and set fire to the ties—everything was dry as powder—soon the rails would be almost melting hot and were taken off and bent in every conceivable shape. We considered *our method* just as effectual, as none of the rails could be used till re-rolled, and it was vastly easier and so much more speedy. We destroyed about three miles of the track, and in the evening fell back about three miles and went into camp, the whole of McPherson's army camping near us.

July 19th. This forenoon most of our brigade were scouting to the north of us, while several companies of our regiment were on picket, but at noon all had got in, and the brigade mounted and moved out on the same road we were on yesterday, and at the same place as yesterday struck the rebels—this time in vastly increased numbers. Our regiment dismounted and drove them back, but by the time we had driven them to the point up to which we had burned the railroad yesterday, they were in such numbers that the whole brigade was dismounted and moved forward, and the artillery brought up—our regiment stil in the advance—and we drove the rebels to the edge of the town of Gibraltar, or Stone Mountain Station. Here the rebels took refuge in the houses, and behind them, and annoyed us considerably. Especially was there a sharp fire poured upon us from a two-story house. Col. Miller had a piece of artillery brought up, and opened on the house. The first shell struck six inches above the first floor, and passed clear through the house without bursting, knocking the chair from under the proprietor without injuring him. He was, however, fully awakened to a sense of his condition, and the rebels got out of that house quick. We then charged the rebels, driving them through the town; not, however, until they had set fire to the depot. Col. Miller, in his notes of this affair, says: "With my brigade I drove two brigades of rebels out of Stone Mountain Station. They burned the depot and 200 bales of cotton. My boys did some splendid skirmishing." We captured one car, a lot of corn and tobacco, killed a few rebels, made prisoners of several, and burned the railroad as far as we went. The citizens took refuge upon Stone Mountain, which is one of the grandest natural curiosities we have ever seen. It is simply a huge bowlder, which Dr. Cole says is 600 feet high, and Sergt. McClure says is 2,200 feet above the level of the sea. It is of the same species of granite that we have here on the Grand Prairie, and call gray-stone, or "nigger-heads." It is nearly black in color, and may be seen for 60 miles, the country for nearly that distance in every direction being flat and level. The only eminence near it is Kenesaw, 30 miles north-west. It is entirely destitute of vegetation of any kind, except a few stunted laurels and cedars in the crevices near its base; but what is most remarkable about it is a fissure from top to bottom, running clear through it from north to south. This crack may be seen a distance of 15 or 20 miles. What a thunder-bolt was that which split this monster in twain! Do you grasp the idea?

July 19. Gen. Sherman sent general orders to all parts of the army that Gen. Joseph E. Johnston had relinquished command of the rebel army, and that Gen. J. B Hood had succeeded him, and that Gen. Johnston's retreating policy was distasteful to the confederate government, and that the change meant *fight*, and that renewed caution and watchfulness should be exercised by every branch of the service.

During the fight to-day Lieut.-Col. Kirkpatrick came to the front from Columbia, Tenn., where he had been in command of the dismounted men of the brigade; but when Maj. Carr resigned and went home Kirkpatrick was ordered "front." During the interval Capt. Adam

Pinkerton had been in command of the regiment. Col. Kirkpatrick came up just when we were in the thickest of the fight, and we cheered him loud and long and went for the rebels bold and strong.

July 20th. The whole army to-day is closing in on Atlanta. Hooker, with the 20th corps, is on the extreme right, moving down the river, and near where the railroad crosses the Chattahoochie The 14th corps is next, also facing south, and its left reached to Buckhead, on the Roswell and Atlanta road, and six miles from the river. The 4th corps, Gen. O. O. Howard, is still east of the 14th. corps, facing a little to the south-west. Gen. Schofield, with the 23d corps, has his left wing near Decatur, and facing south-west toward Atlanta, while McPherson is at Decatur, seven miles north-east of Atlanta. At daylight all these armies begin to move toward Atlanta. The morning is bright, beautiful, calm and still, and we can plainly hear a rifle shot five miles away, and a six-pound cannon shot 20 miles away. Skirmishing begins at daylight, and we can tell by the firing that our whole army is driving the rebels before it. All of McPherson's trains are on the road between our camp and Decatur, and our division is deployed on the east side of the road so as to cover the trains, and our regiment is rear guard for the trains. About 9 o'clock cannonading begins all along the lines, and toward noon increases in volume. Shortly after noon the continuous roar of artillery, away over to the south-west from us, and fully 20 miles away, warns us that a terrible battle is being fought in that direction. The trains in front of us have not all got strung out on the road, and our regiment is still in camp, expecting every minute to move. It is these hours of suspense, when the soldier is conscious of some desperate conflict near him, that wear him out faster than all the activities of his life. About 2 p. m. all the trains get to moving and we mount and move on slowly after them. After following them five or six miles we ride past them to Decatur, getting there late in the evening and go into camp where we found the balance of our brigade, a half mile south of the town, which is a most beautiful place, seven miles north-east of Atlanta, the county seat of DeKalb County. The town is situated on high, rolling ground, well shaded (an item of vast importance in southern cities) and has 1,000 inhabitants. The advance of McPherson's army reached this place late yesterday evening, causing the rebels to burn a train of their own wagons and ambulances, and also the depot. The whole army to-night is within three miles of Atlanta, and on the east, north and north-west, lapping around it in a semi-circle. Notwithstanding that the length of the line of battle of this great army averages 20 miles all the time, news travels from one end to the other in a very short time, and to-night we learn that a terrible battle has been fought about six miles north-west of Atlanta, along the Peach-tree Creek. The rebels under Gen. Hood moved out of their works and attacked our men. This, for the second day Hood has been in command, does pretty well, and shows that a change has come over the spirit of their dreams. About the time the war broke out there was an expression very glibly used, and oft repeated by the Southern leaders, that they would "die in the last ditch" before they would submit to the "Lincoln Government." On this campaign we were first told that the last ditch was at Buzzard Roost; but at that place few of them felt like "shuffling off this mortal coil," and "ran away that they might live to fight another day." At Resaca, at Cartersville, at Dallas, at Kenesaw, and at Chattahoochie, they said they would be "blowed" if they ran another step further. Yet every time when *we* thought the supreme, opportune moment had come, for them to do their dying *then* and *there*, *they* seemed to have urgent business somewhere else. But to-day's work begins to look like they mean business, and makes us begin to think the "last ditch" is somewhere not far from this place.

We have spoken of the rapidity with which news traveled from one end of the line to the other; and we may as well here as any where tell the reader that as soon as Gen. Sherman establishes his headquarters for the night, there is immediately run from his headquarters to each corps headquarters telegraph wires, and these are put up and taken down so rapidly that communication between the army commanders is very rapid and certain; but they do not care to let the private soldiers know anything at all if they can help it, never communicating anything themselves nor suffering their inferior officers to do so. Yet in spite of every precaution we would get the news somehow, not always correctly nor reliable, but by the time we were ready to go to bed each night we had a pretty correct statement of the day's doings and would go to bed discussing our chances for to-morrow.

July 21st. Late this evening, our pack mules, which we left in camp on the morning of the 18th, came into camp, and we had orders to be ready to move immediately with four days' rations in our haversacks, and all the salt we had. We had lain quietly in camp all day, picketing to the south and east of Decatur, while the fighting around Atlanta had been severe. About 4 p. m. our whole division, Gen. Garrard commanding, moved north on the road we came in on yesterday. We quote from Miller's notes: "We start off on a raid of some days. We have orders to destroy the Augusta railroad up as far as Yellow

River, and the depot at Covington, county seat of Newton County and 45 miles east of Atlanta."

After passing the camp we occupied while tearing up the railroad at Stone Mountain, we turned north-east, leaving the mountain several miles to our right, giving it a wide berth for fear of observation by sentries on its summit. We moved seven or eight miles and then turned south-east and traveled steadily till midnight, having made 25 miles, and bivouacked on Yellow River; turning into the thick pine woods we were ordered to lay down without building fires.

July 22d. This morning at 3 o'clock we were quietly called up by our officers, and by daylight were mounted and on the road. Up to this time we had not been told what we were going to do, but it now leaked out that we were going to a large town called Covington, 25 miles away, and that we were to destroy as much railroad and other property as possible. As soon as we got across the river, two companies of the 98th Illinois were started down the river for the railroad five or six miles to our right. When they got to the railroad they found a very long wooden bridge across the river, a magnificent structure, guarded by a company of rebels. Our men drove them away, killing a soldier whose hair was white as snow; he must have been 80 years old. We set fire to the bridge, and while it was burning heard a train of cars coming from the west, and went back down the road toward Stone Mountain some distance and secreted ourselves and let the train run up near the burning bridge, and then closed in behind and captured it. There was a Colonel, a Captain and 15 private soldiers on the train, which consisted of an engine and 15 cars, all heavily laden with cotton, molasses, and other valuable property, all of which was burned. There was another train still behind, which, of course, was cut off and could not get away. A heavy column of rebels coming from toward Atlanta admonished us to be going, and our column moved rapidly forward on a road parallel with the railroad, and five or six miles from it. There were a great many streams crossing our road, all running south, and of course must cross the railroad also, and at every stream of considerable size a detail would be sent down to burn the bridge.

On our march this forenoon we overtook numerous refugees from the vicinity of Atlanta. The men seemed to have no mercy on this class of people, and made free with horses, mules, and everything else that seemed to strike their fancy; and it was sometimes distressing to see their blank, vacant stare, as they would be left with their wagons in the road minus horses or mules, when they hadn't thought there was a Yankee nearer them than Decatur. We made good time, and by 11 o'clock the division was halted to close up. This was five miles from Covington. Here the division was divided, Long's brigade taking a road that led to the east of Covington, where he burned two bridges, one across Crawfish Creek, and another across the Ulcofauhatchee River, eight miles east of Covington. Our brigade and Minty's moved directly on the city, striking a little town two miles north of Covington called Oxford at 12 m. Here the Seventy-Second was turned to the right, striking the railroad two miles west of Covington. We immediately began to burn the railroad culverts, bridges and track, getting to the city at 2 p. m. Here we set fire to a very large mill containing 8,000 bushels of corn and a large quantity of flour; also a very large warehouse filled with various articles of supplies for the confederate government. This made the largest single fire we ever saw; we are satisfied the blaze reached 100 feet high. We next burned a train of cars. It was now 3 p. m. and our regiment had not been in the city, the railroad only running through the suburbs. But the other regiments began to come in from the east, having destroyed the railroad for seven miles out. We mounted our horses and rode slowly through the city, going north to Oxford, which we found still intact. Here we burned three large warehouses and at least 2,000 bales of cotton; we broke open another large warehouse that we did not burn. It was full of shoes and tobacco. You ought to have seen our boys go for the tobacco. We had not seen our sutler for more than a month, and we suppose there had not been a chew of tobacco in the regiment for weeks, and all who used it felt that they were nearly dead for tobacco. Here it was, more than our whole division could carry off, and oh! what a chew the boys did take; and then you would have smiled to see them load themselves down with it; every pocket, and haversack, and saddle-bags, crammed to their utmost capacity, and yet some of them not satisfied, would, after mounting, have their comrades to hand them up "another box." Though there were shoes enough to supply the whole division, it was only after they found they could not possibly carry any more tobacco that they thought of taking the shoes; and then we saw men take a box of shoes on before them and hand them out to the men after we began to move. The cotton we burned was all in one pile and made the hottest fire we ever saw; as we urged our horses along the street past it, it was so hot as to scorch our clothes and singe the hair on our horses.

This wound up the work for the day, so far as our regiment was concerned, and we shall speak of a few personal incidents. When we struck Oxford the rebels were taken completely by surprise, and many of the officers and soldiers secreted themselves in the houses. A detail from company D, Sergt. J. A. Mount in command, went to a stately mansion and told the ladies they had orders to search the house. "What for?" said the ladies. "For rebel soldiers," was the prompt reply. "Do you suppose we would harbor rebel soldiers in our private parlors?" was the indignant rejoinder. The sergeant responded, "Rebel soldiers are not so unpopular in Georgia as to be deprived of the privacy of your parlors in which to harbor when Union soldiers are in town." "You must not enter our house." "My order is imperative." "There are no rebels in our house." "Ladies, without further controversy, I shall soon settle the question." The sergeant says: "I entered the house and passed rapidly up stairs, and my attention was attracted by the closing of a door; I immediately opened it, and Maj. Vaughn, of the 5th Tennessee, and a brother of Gen. Vaughn, and a rebel captain, immediately surrendered to me." As our scouts dashed into Covington there were 75 mounted men in the place, who fled very precipitately; but shortly afterward two of the scouts were shot by citizens and died within two hours. Neither of the citizens lived long after their treachery, but were shot to pieces in a minute. These two men were our only loss on the entire expedition. Dr. Cole says: * * * "We captured large quantities of tobacco. The last named article was very acceptable to our men, and they supplied themselves well, not forgetting their infantry brethren behind the works near Atlanta. * * * When the work of destruction on the railroad commenced Gen. Garrard sent me to examine patients in the hospital, and select such as would be able to travel. I had 40 "play offs" marched out who were soon in company with 350 other prisoners marching toward Atlanta." There were three large hospitals full of sick and wounded soldiers, all of whom (150) were paroled. In addition to the burning our regiment had done, the rest of our division had burned another train of cars, 30 stand of arms, several kegs of powder, besides getting all the bacon and salt they wanted to carry; and also burned the depot and several manufacturing establishments.

It was near sundown when all the division gathered at Oxford, when we moved out straight north, and as long as it was light enough for us to see the road was strewed full of plunder, principally tobacco and shoes. There must have been thousands of dollars' worth of each scattered along the road. First tobacco, then shoes; next shoes and then tobacco; then tobacco and shoes mixed. We either missed the road we wished to go, or else our officers anticipated we should be followed, or something was the matter, as we doubled on our track, and once in the night went square across a road we had traveled on an hour before, and it was near midnight when we went into camp, Dr. Cole says, eight miles from Covington. This day was one long to be remembered by us as being full of peculiar and lively interest. We still had a very vivid recollection of the Wheeler raid, and how we had kept his rear closed upon him in his hurried march of 400 miles across the state of Tennessee, and we thought it possible *we* might have our rear closed upon us just as promptly. Besides, about 11 a. m. we could distinctly hear heavy and prolonged artillery firing in the direction of Atlanta, and we well knew another terrible battle was being fought. The ominous sounds increased in force and frequency as the day advanced; larger guns were being used, and at times the earth would tremble as if shaken by an earthquake. Although we were well pleased with our day's work, and entered into it with a spirit and zeal never excelled, those fearful sounds promptly checked any demonstration of delight or applause, and we never knew our regiment to move so noiselessly as it did to-night. The men scarcely spoke at all, and when they did it was in subdued tones. There was no moon, but the burning fires behind us made it as light as a full moon would have done. Of course we were tired and hungry, and sadly needed our coffee, as that above every thing else was a panacea for all our ills; but we had to lie down without it, not even unsaddling our horses, and were soon sleeping the sleep of the innocent.

July 23d. We were called up very quietly at 3 o'clock, and without breakfast or feeding, mounted immediately and moved nearly north, passing through a little place called Walnut Hill, where we burned a lot more cotton; from here we turned north-west and stopped for feeding and dinner at Lawrenceville, 20 miles from where we started this morning. In the afternoon we moved steadily south-west, picking up a great many horses. Late in the afternoon we struck Yellow River several miles higher up than where we crossed it yesterday, at a place called Rock Bridge. Three miles south of this we struck the road we were on yesterday and found that a large force of rebels had passed along this morning going after us toward Covington. They had burned the bridge in their rear across Yellow River in hopes of cutting us off; but Yankee like we had moved too far north and come around behind them, very neatly. Three miles further west we went into camp, and unsaddled for the first time since leaving Decatur, having made 40 miles for the day. Here Sergt. Magee and his mess had an odd experience. This was the first time he had made coffee, and we enjoyed it hugely. Knowing that we would be likely to move at daylight, we determined, if possible, to have coffee for breakfast; so the last thing before going to bed we filled up our large tin coffee pot with water and set it where it would be ready to put on the fire by the first one who should get up. We were camped in a thick woods where the leaves were four inches deep, and among these leaves were numerous scorpions, reptiles which were not so terribly dangerous, but for which we had no very pleasant feelings. We went to bed with orders to move at daylight, but officers and privates, horses and mules, were so overcome with fatigue that the sun was up before *anybody* woke up, and when the men began to stir we jumped up, and seeing how late it was, thought our chances for coffee were slim, slapped our pot on the fire and then fed and began to saddle. By the time we were saddled the water was boiling and we slapped our coffee in. In two minutes more we were eating our breakfast, but somehow the coffee didn't taste just right, and we tried to make up in quantity what the coffee lacked in quality. We drained the pot of the last drop, which of course would make the grounds hard to throw out. Just then we were ordered to mount, and in our efforts to get the grounds out of the pot found a large scorpion which had crawled into it during the night and had been boiled with the coffee. No serious results followed, but you may well believe there was a deal of spitting done during the day.

We were now thought to be out of reach of the enemy, and some details were sent out for forage towards noon, and among them private Simon Y. E. Dixon, of Company H. The details had got some miles from the column, and Simon far enough ahead of his comrades to be entirely out of sight, when he came to a cabin near which stood a rebel. He brought his Spencer to bear on Mr. Reb. and called for him to surrender, which he did, and came to the road and stood near Dixon's horse. But Simon forgot one important matter, and that was to search his man for arms. Simon took down his gun and turned in his saddle to look for his comrades, but lo! when Simon took the next look at his man the tables had turned, for Mr. Reb. had a revolver pointed in his face and demanded his gun, which he very reluctantly gave up, and as the rest of the squad was now in hearing the rebel took to the woods and made his escape, leaving Dixon minus a gun. We reached Decatur shortly after noon of the 24th of July. We had left our pack train here and nearly the whole of McPherson's wagon train; but what was our surprise on approaching the town to find it occupied by rebels. This called to mind the terrible fighting we heard two days before, and we began to surmise that may be the rebels had found the "last ditch" for a fact.

There were evidences of a terrible battle having been fought here, and for aught we knew our army had been driven back across the Chattahoochie. There was not a single Union soldier, team or mule, to be seen, and in the direction of Atlanta everything was quiet. Our scouts drove the pickets in and our brigade dismounted and moved in line of battle to the center of the town, where we halted and sent forward skirmishers, who soon developed the fact that the rebels were in force not far away. While lying there in line of battle, close to the Court-house, Gen Garrard and his staff, and Col. Miller, came and sat down on the Court-house steps, and the General made out his report of our expedition; and as it was our fortune to be close enough to hear every word of it, we will repeat a part of it for the benefit of our readers: "We destroyed 3,000 bales of cotton, 14,000 pounds of bacon, 8,000 bushels of corn, two locomotives and three trains of cars, a depot and 10 miles of track; burned three long bridges, numerous mills, warehouses, and other manufacturing establishments; captured 450 prisoners, 300 of whom we brought in, paroling the balance, and captured 2,000 horses and mules. Our entire loss was two killed " Late in the evening we got orders to abandon Decatur, which we did, going into camp two miles north-west of the place, where our pack train joined us. Our position brought us in the rear of the left wing of the army, and by some means it soon became known to the infantry that Wilder's brigade had been on a raid and had got back, and between that and morning it seemed like nearly half of the army visited us. Every hour of the night could be heard some one calling out: "Is this Wilder's brigade?" "Give me a chew of tobacco."

July 25th. We lay in camp till late in the evening, and as we have nothing special to do, we will write up *some* of the events that have taken place while we were gone, simply because all our pack train, and the boys with it, are especially interested in the facts. On the morning of the 22d, after we had left Decatur, Hood, with nearly his whole army, had moved out of Atlanta to the south-east three or four miles, and then turned straight north and attacked McPherson's army in the left flank. A fearful battle was fought, in which McPherson was killed. This was one of the most desperate battles of the war, and lasted nearly the entire day. In the morning the whole of McPherson's trains were parked at Decatur, and so also was our pack train. I quote from Sherman's book, vol. 2, page 79: "At the same time Hood had sent Wheeler's division of cavalry against the trains parked at Decatur. Unluckily for us, I had sent away the whole of Garrard's division of cavalry during the night of the 21st, with orders to proceed to Covington, 40 miles east, to burn two important bridges across Ulcofauhatchee and Yellow Rivers, to tear up the railroad and to damage it as much as possible from Stone Mountain eastward, and to be gone four days; so that McPherson had no cavalry in hand to guard that flank. The trains at Decatur were guarded by a brigade of infantry commanded by Col. Sprague, of the 63d Ohio." About 10 a. m., Wheeler charged into Decatur, drove the brigade of infantry back through the town and captured several wagons. Our boys with the pack mules were used to moving quick, and so gathered up and got out of the way without loss, but they were terribly scared, and said they did wish our brigade had been there. The infantry rallied, and as soon as our boys got the pack mules out of the way, all that could be spared rushed to the rescue, and by their help the infantry were enabled to drive the rebels back through the town; but they were in turn reinforced by such numbers as to drive our men back again; but they fell back slowly, and by this time the trains were all hitched up and moved rapidly to the west. This fight, for the numbers engaged, was just as desperate as on any part of the lines, and there is not the least bit of doubt that but for the boys of our brigade the rebels would have gobbled the whole outfit. Sergt. Stewart, of Company A, speaks thus of Henry Heiney, private of the same company, which simply illustrates what was done by numbers of others: "He went through the whole of the engagement, firing nearly 100 rounds of ammunition. His Spencer rifle was a great curiosity to the infantry regiment he fell in with; he knew they were hard pressed and needed his help, and as he had plenty of ammunition and there were plenty of rebels to shoot, he entirely satisfied their curiosity." We have more than once had occasion to speak of the distrust with which Gen. Sherman treated our division; but the fight at Decatur fully demonstrated that he thought we were of some account after all.

We want now to drop a tear of sorrow and regret for the death of McPherson. On more than one occasion when Sherman had been harsh with us had McPherson interposed in our behalf, and we honored and loved him. We are very sure there never was a General killed in any war who was so sincerely mourned by so many soldiers. Strong men wept like children when they heard of his death. Late at night our division, which had been saddled up all day, moved south and joined on to the left of the infantry, going into camp at midnight.

July 26th was spent in shoeing up and getting ready for a fight or hard marching. The pack train was sent west to the rear of the center of the army.

July 27th. Our division moved at 4 o'clock, going east, and got to Decatur just after sun-up. Here we halted and Gen. Stoneman's division of cavalry filed past us, taking the dirt road for Covington. Our division followed, and we learned that our destination was the Macon Railroad. We moved off briskly for 12 or 15 miles, nearly south-east, till we came to a place called Lattimers, when we turned due south-west, Stoneman still going straight on the road toward Covington. Up to this time we had not seen any rebels, but our advance had captured six or eight teams and two or three ambulances, besides a drove of sheep, goats and cattle, 100 in all. We moved on this road south six or eight miles, which brought us to South River, at a place called Flat Rock, or South River Shoals. This was between 1 and 2 o'clock, and we bivouacked without unsaddling. Col. Miller, in his notes of July 27th, says: "Started this morning on a raid. Stoneman is on our left; we are to do the fighting and he is to do the raiding and tear up the railroad." Late in the evening it began to rain, and rained till after dark. About the time it quit raining we unsaddled, and just as we had our suppers over and dog-tents stretched ready for bed, the rebels attacked our pickets in our rear, on the road on which we had been moving. We saddled up as quickly as we could and reinforcements were sent to the pickets. This was at 10 p. m.; the rebels still kept crowding on the pickets, and by 11 p. m. our whole brigade was in line of battle stretched across the road to support the pickets. It turned cold and we suffered from that till morning. Our camp was within 13 miles of the Macon Railroad, and as this was the hard-tack line for the rebel army in Atlanta, they felt a little sensitive about our getting so close to it, and were making every preparation to capture us. Atlanta, 12 or 15 miles away, was nearly between us and our army, and the whole of the rebel army might reach us in three or four hours, so that the gravity of the situation becomes apparent.

At daylight on the 28th, we found the rebels had placed a camp guard clear around us, and before sun-up all our videttes and pickets on the north and west had been driven in and two of our men severely wounded. Soon after Long's brigade on the east received similar attention, and the rebel bullets from both north and south were cutting through the trees over our heads. A pretty fix for the bold raiders; right in the rear of the rebel army and entirely surrounded. A flag of truce now brings in a demand for our immediate surrender, and as if to make the demand more impressive a few shells from rebel batteries came tearing through our camp. Gen. Garrard sends back word, "If they want us to come and get us." Our brigade now hastily throw up a line of defensive rail works to the west and north, and we settle ourselves for the conflict. It is 8 o'clock and we can see the rebel lines are being constantly augmented by fresh troops from Atlanta; their skirmishers are still crawling up closer and closer; the lowering clouds of war are growing darker and darker, the bullets are now whistling over our heads in chorus, and the bursting shells roar above us more frequently. It leaked out among the soldiers that Stoneman had ordered Garrard to hold this crossing till noon at all hazards, and thus cover his rear till he should get so far away that the rebel cavalry could not overtake him. But can we do it? It is now 10 o'clock and yet the rebels do not attack; they are still strengthening their lines. A prisoner just captured tells us they already have seven brigades in position, while of us there are but three. We now begin to discuss the chances of the rebel infantry coming from Atlanta before we get out of here. Dr. Cole says: "A council of our General and his chief officers determined that every additional moment spent here increased our danger materially; it would therefore be prudent to move out." After this decision it was determined that our brigade should make the effort to clear the way. Prepartaory to this, two pieces of artillery (Board of Trade) were run down to Long's position on the river and opened on the rebels vigorously on the east and south. They replied, and for a time the music was lively. Col. Miller came along our lines and told us frankly, and in his usual friendly way, that we were surrounded by a greatly superior force; that it was determined that we should cut our way out, and that he had selected our regiment to break the lines first; that he had selected us because he knew just what sort of stuff we were made of, that he had confidence in us, and that he knew we could go right through anything the rebels could bring against us. After giving us particular instructions just what he wanted us to do, he left us to see about the lead horses and artillery. The lead horses were now brought close up to our rear with orders to follow as soon as the rebels should give way. The balance of the artillery was brought up and two pieces unlimbered and put in position, and when everything was ready the artillery opened out. We jumped over our works and without uttering a word started on a keen run. We struck the rebel skirmish line 200 yards out before they knew we were coming. We opened on them with our Spencers, killed a few and captured others. They were taken so completely by surprise that many of them never even fired a single round, but skinned out for Atlanta as fast as their legs could carry them. We now raised the cheer and charged right into the main line along with their own skirmishers. Never was surprise more complete. We are sure that not half of the main line ever fired a shot, and those who did were so badly scared that scarcely a shot took effect. The last mother's son of them ran away with such earnestness that you would have thought the "last ditch" was far away from there; we never saw men make better time. Had our cavalry been there mounted and ready to follow us we could have captured the whole force of rebels in front of us; but the cavalry were engaged in the rear, and by the time we had run 600 yards we were all given out, and were still 600 yards from the rebel lead horses; the best we could do was for our battery to throw shells into them as they were mounting. This, we suppose, materially aided them to mount, for in less than 20 minutes from the time we jumped over our works the last rebel horseman was sailing away in the direction of Atlanta "flying light" We never saw such a dust kicked up before. Our lead horses had kept well closed up behind us, and we mounted and moved off slowly, the balance of the division following in good order. The rebels, contenting themselves with skirmishing with the rear guard, followed us a few miles. We moved back to the Covington road and then turned east and went four miles and went into camp at Lithonia, on the Augusta railroad. Our only loss in the engagement was private John Boyd, of Company A, who was accidentally shot by one of Company F's boys, and died the next day. He was a noble boy, a good soldier, and sadly missed by his comrades. Peace to his ashes. Capt. Hart, of the 123d Illinois, was wounded, and two men of the same regiment mortally wounded in the fight, who with the two men wounded last night comprised our loss. What the rebel loss was we never stopped to find out; we think it was not heavy, but we saw two dead rebels in our line of march just after we struck the skirmishers, and about the same time we saw a most ridiculous incident. The rebel skirmish line in front of us was near a house, where there were a lot of bees; and just before we struck the skirmish line a rebel soldier had turned a stand over and was helping himself to the honey. The bees lit all over him and began to sting him furiously and without mercy; about the time we began to shoot at him he began to slap himself, jump up and down, lie down and roll over, and was going through the wildest contortions when we came upon him. For a time we thought he was trying to dodge our bullets, but we soon got close enough to see what was the matter with him, and left him still fighting the bees. After he got the bees off of him he was taken in charge by the men with the lead horses.

Just before we made the charge, when we had come to the conclusion that our chances for Andersonville were at least favorable, Adjutant Byrns came along and as usual was the butt of jest and remark. You see the boys had been discussing the order that we were to tear up the Macon railroad, and had finally come to the conclusion that may be we wouldn't do much of it this time; so some one asked Byrns how far it was to the Macon River, and another how far it was to Macon road, when Corpl. James Daugherty, Company B, seriously asked him how far it was to Macon our escape. We have no idea where Stoneman expects to strike the Macon Railroad.

July 29th. Lay in camp all day at Lithonia, and as it is said the object of our keeping the rebels back has been accomplished, we seem to be taking things very coolly. We wonder why the rebels do not pay us their respects to-day, as we are only 10 miles from where they surrounded us yesterday. Scouting parties were sent out in various directions toward Covington; among these was a squad under command of Sergt. Plunkett, Company E. Passing by a house they saw a little boy on the fence and Plunkett said: "Bub, where does this road go to?" He replied like the Arkansas Traveler, "It don't go anywhere, and never has went anywhere since I've been here." There was a laugh at Plunkett's expense. We cannot better explain our movement yesterday than to quote from Sherman, vol. 2, pages 85, 88, 92, who says: "About this time I was advised by Gen. Grant, then investing Richmond, that the rebel government at Richmond had become aroused to the critical condition of things about Atlanta, and that I must look out for Hood being greatly reinforced. I therefore resolved to push matters, and at once ordered all the cavalry to be ready to pass around Atlanta on both flanks, to break up the Macon road so as to cut off all supplies to the rebel army inside, and thus to force it to evacuate or come out and fight us on equal terms. The cavalry was assembled in two strong divisions. That of McCook numbered about 3,500 effective cavalry, and was posted to our right rear at Turner's Ferry; and to our left rear at and about Decatur were the two cavalry divisions of Stoneman 2,500 and Garrard 4,000, united for the time and occasion under the command of Maj.-Gen. George Stoneman, a cavalry officer of high repute. My plan of action was to move the Army of the Tennessee to the right rapidly and boldly against the railroad below Atlanta, and at the same time to send all the cavalry around by the right and left to make a lodgment on the Macon road about Jonesboro. All orders were given, and the morning of the 27th was fixed for commencing the movement. On the 26th I received a note from Gen. Stoneman asking permission (after having accomplished his orders to break up the railroad at Jonesboro) to go on to Macon to rescue our prisoners of war known to be held there, and then to push on to Andersonville, where was the great depot of Union prisoners, in which were penned at one time as many as 23,000 of our men, badly fed and harshly treated. I wrote him an answer substantially consenting to his proposition, only modifying it by requiring him to send back Gen. Garrard's division to its position on our left flank after he had broken up the railroad at Jonesboro. Promptly on time all got off." We shall now get our division back to Atlanta and quote again from Sherman to show some of the results.

July 30th. Although we knew nothing of the co-operating forces with us, or of the real service we had performed in helping *them*, we felt that *our* expedition was rather a failure. We hadheard nothing of Stoneman, and so this morning early our division moved north through Lithonia and made a wide circuit around Stone Mountain and went into camp near Crosskeys, 14 miles west of Stone Mountain, having marched 40 miles. Out of forage and rations.

July 31st. Moved straight south toward Atlanta and bivouacked just after crossing Peach-tree Creek, five miles north of Atlanta and close to Gen. Sherman's headquarters. No word from Stoneman. Gen. Sherman says: "Gen. Garrard's division returned to-day and reported that Gen. Stoneman had posted him at Flat Rock, while Stoneman went on to Macon. * * * On the 3d of August Gen. McCook came in and reported the actual results of his cavalry expedition. He had crossed the Chattahoochie below Campbellton, had then marched rapidly across to the Macon Railroad at Lovejoy's Station, where he had reason to expect Gen. Stoneman, but not hearing of him he set to work, tore up two miles of the track, burned two trains of cars, and cut away five miles of telegraph wire. He also found the wagon train belonging to the rebel army in Atlanta, burned 500 wagons, killed 800 mules, and captured 72 officers and 350 men. Finding his progress eastward, toward McDonough, barred by a superior force, he turned back to Newnan, where he found himself completely surrounded by infantry and cavalry. He had to drop his prisoners and fight his way out, losing 600 men killed and captured. In the meantime rumors came that Stoneman was down about Macon, on the east bank of the Ocmulgee.

"On the 4th of August Col. Adams got to Marietta with his small brigade of 900 belonging to Stoneman's cavalry, reporting, as usual, all the rest lost, and this was partially confirmed by a report which came to me all the way around by Gen. Grant's headquarters before Richmond. A few days later Col. Capron also got in with another small brigade, perfectly demoralized, and confirmed the report that Gen. Stoneman had covered the escape of these two brigades, himself standing with a reserve of 700 men, with which he surrendered. Thus another of my cavalry divisions was badly damaged. Stoneman had not obeyed his orders to attack the railroad *first* before going to Macon and Andersonville, but had crossed the Ocmulgee River high up at Covington, and gone down that river on the east bank. He reached Clinton and sent out detachments, which struck the railroad leading from Macon to Savannah at Griswold Station, where they destroyed 17 locomotives, and over 100 cars, and burned the bridge across the Oconee, and re-united the division before Macon. Stoneman shelled the town across the river but could not cross over, and returned to Clinton, where he found his retreat obstructed, as he supposed, by a superior force, became bewildered and sacrificed himself for the safety of his command. Of course I was disturbed by the losses in these two divisions (Stoneman's and McCook's) of cavalry, and made all possible preparations to strengthen our guards along the railroad to the rear, upon the theory that the force of cavalry that defeated McCook would at once be upon the railroad about Marietta. I now became satisfied that cavalry could not or would not make sufficient lodgment upon the railroad below Atlanta, and that nothing would suffice but for us to reach it with the main army, and to Schofield (23d) corps was committed the charge of this special object. At the same time Garrard was ordered to occupy the trenches on our left, while Schofield's whole army moved to the extreme right."

Now, gentle reader, you have a much better idea of the situation than we had when on the 1st of August, 1864, we moved camp to within three miles north of Atlanta, dismounted and left all our horses, pack mules, camp and garrison equipage, except what we could carry, and late in the evening marched two miles south-east till we struck the lines of the 23d army corps, which we relieved, and took their places in the trenches, Minty's brigade joining on to the left of the 20th corps, which occupied the line right north of the city; and, the position occupied by Minty's brigade extended nearly due east for half a mile, while our brigade took up the line to the left of Minty, and running around in a semi-circle nearly a mile to the east and north-east. These two brigades were dismounted, while Long's brigade kept up a chain of outposts or pickets on horseback from our left clear around to the Chattahoochie, a distance of 12 or 15 miles. Up to this time we had not staid two days in a place since crossing the Chattahoochie River, but we staid here just two weeks to a day, and had plenty of time to write up several things of interest to the general reader.

It was midnight before the 23d corps all got moved out of the trenches and our brigade took their places. Our whole regiment went on to the skirmish line. The movement was so well conducted that the rebels never noticed the change and our pickets were able to do enough shooting on the skirmish line to answer for the whole corps that had just left.

August 2d. This morning, for the first time, we beheld the spires in Atlanta, being just a mile from the city. Last night to our right there was heavy shelling from both sides, while this morning there is nothing but the usual lively skirmishing from the rifle-pits.

A *regimental* history is supposed to simply narrate what the *regiment did* in the war of the rebellion; but our children want to know some of the grand results we helped to attain; and we think every comrade of the regiment will be pleased to see left upon record some of the grand achievements of the war in which our regiment took so honorable and conspicuous a part. We have passed over the siege of Kenesaw Mountain and told exactly the part that was taken by our regiment in that memorable siege, and yet upon reading it over we are conscious that the general reader will form a very meagre idea of the meaning of the word. We propose therefore to use a few pages in describing the siege of Atlanta, as we took part in it, and in doing this we shall tell many things which it has never been our fortune to read or see in any book. We have already spoken of the great battle that occurred along the line of the Peach-tree Creek, five miles north-west of Atlanta, on July 20th. This took place just after Hood took command of the rebel army, and outside the outer defensive works surrounding the city. Sherman's army was then scattered and Hood expected to whip each portion of it in detail. In this first attempt he failed. The battle was terrible and losses about equal on both sides. On the 21st of July Sherman's entire army moved forward toward Atlanta, thus bringing its parts closer together. On the 22d the investment or siege really began, and we have the whole army in the positions as follows:

1, Beginning on the extreme left, the 16th corps strung along the railroad and between Atlanta and Decatur, and facing south.

2, The 17th corps three miles east of Atlanta, its right wing resting on the railroad, and the corps facing west.

3, The 15th corps a little nearer Atlanta, its left wing resting on the railroad, and facing nearly west.

4, The 23d corps north-east of the city, and facing south-west.

5, The 20th corps north of the city, and facing south.

6, The 4th corps north-west of the city and facing south-east.

7, The 14th corps west of the city and facing east.

Thus the Union army lay in the shape of a reaping hook and invested about one-half of the city.

On the morning of July 22d, Hood made a second attempt to whip a part of Sherman's army, by moving out of Atlanta, south-east, and attacking McPherson's army in the left rear; and had not the 16th corps been just in the position it was, Hood, no doubt, would have been successful. This was the most desperate battle, in open field, without works, of the whole campaign, and as before stated, McPherson was killed.

On the night of July 27th the 15th, 16th and 17th corps, under command of Maj.-Gen. O. O. Howard, moved from the extreme left of the army around in the rear of the other corps and took position on the right of the 14th corps and south-west of Atlanta. Hood detected this movement, and on the morning of July 28th attacked these three corps before they had got in position. Another dreadful battle ensued. Both sides lost heavily, but the loss of the rebels was simply fearful to contemplate, as our men, after repulsing the first charge of the enemy, hastily threw up breastworks behind which they fought the balance of the day; and to show you of how much importance this simple precaution was we quote from Dr. Killen, of the 10th Indiana, who was over the battle-field early next morning: "In front of one of our regiments I counted 58 dead rebels all in line just as they had been killed by a single volley. This of course threw the rebels into confusion and they fell back, re-formed and came on the second time; but this time our men did not wait so long and a second volley killed 52 of them, all in line, just as the others were. The next day after this battle we captured a rebel, and of course asked him a great many questions, among the rest, how many men Hood had. He replied, 'Well, about enough for two more killings if you don't make them too large.'"

On the 29th Howard's army moved forward on a general left wheel, hoping to lap around far enough on the south side of the city to get on to the Macon Railroad. But after getting his lines all dressed up facing east he found he was still a mile from the railroad; so the next move was to relieve the 23d corps and send it to the right to protect the right flank of Howard's army. This brings us up to the time of our going into the trenches vacated by the 23d corps. Sherman now made an effort to get on to the railroad by regular siege, parallel after parallel. You ask what this means and how it is done. Well, we have never seen any description of the process in any book, and of course cannot give a scientific explanation, and shall only attempt to tell it just as we saw it done, and that, too, in our own homely way. When our army was approaching a heavy line of rebel works we sometimes sent forward our skirmishers in the day time and sometimes in the night. In the day time it almost always brought on a fight, and sometimes a heavy battle. After getting our main line of battle in a position we thought we would be able to hold, and then wishing to establish a line close up to and parallel with the rebel line, a skirmish line would be started forward with gun and spade in hand. A soldier would crawl flat of his belly as close to the enemy's lines as he dare go, lay his gun beside him and with his spade begin to make a hole in front of him, throwing the dirt forward. Of course if the rebel pickets are vigilant they soon see this and begin to send him their compliments. He has no time to pay any attention to this, but must dig for life. In a few moments he has enough dirt thrown up in front of him to protect his head, but must be careful to keep it very low and his legs straight behind him. In a few moments more he has a hole big enough to sit down in, when he works his feet around to the front and puts them in the hole, but does not yet dare to raise his head. His feet now aid him in thrusting in his spade, and in a few minutes more he can raise upon his knees, and of course works faster, as he is less cramped. Directly he stands on his feet, but never raises his head until the dirt in front of him is high enough to entirely hide him from the rebels. All this has been done perhaps inside of 20 minutes. He now breathes freer and commences to enlarge the hole and to shape it up, and in one hour from the time he began to dig he is ready to lay down his spade and take up his gun. But even then his feelings cannot always be the most pleasant. He well knows he cannot get out of that hole till night; six or eight rods from him on either side is a comrade in just the same fix, and as they lay aside their spades and begin to shoot it brings down upon the fresh piles of earth all the concentrated wrath of the rebels in their front; the sharpshooters begin on them and the grape and canister are rained all over them. As they lie there in the broiling sun, perhaps wounded and dying, they may wish in vain for a friendly voice to cheer them. It would simply be sacrificing another life to go to their relief. Night comes and the poor fellows are each relieved by two others who spend most of their time digging toward their comrades on the right and left, well knowing that when the day dawns the rebels may be so exasperated by the increased size of the piles of dirt as to charge on them and kill or capture them. This frequently occurred, as the rebels well knew that they would never be able to drive our men out of their pits after the third night's work. Another anxious day is passed, and at night these two are relieved by four or six, and during the third night the trenches are dug into one continuous line, and on the third day, or fourth at farthest, the whole line of battle is ready to move up, and the works are made so strong that no army could drive our men from behind them, and we are ready for another advance. Both armies used the same kind of skirmish pits and the same kind of earthworks, but the rebels always had theirs prepared in advance and just fell back from one position to another, while our men always had to prepare theirs under fire, and that, too, just as hot as the rebels could make it. From the experience of our men in front of Kenesaw and Atlanta I suppose they became the most expert skirmishers and diggers in the world. After we had lain in the trenches a few days the everlasting skirmishing and incessant roar of artillery became monotonous, and we began to look about for amusement. Some of the boys nailed cleats to a large pine tree, clear up to the top, and used it for an observatory. It afforded a view of a grand panorama, especially after night, when both lines were putting in their best licks shelling each other; but the position was not so pleasant when the rebels threw their 64-pound shells at the tree. A few of us one day took a stroll down along the works to the right as far as the right of the 4th corps. Some places the rebel sharpshooters had got the range of our works so accurately that our men dare not stick their heads above the works at all. For the benefit of those who might grow careless, or who might not know where these places were, large guide boards were stuck up with something like this: "*Keep down here.*" "*Do not stand on the works.*" At other places we were cautioned not to "bunch up," two or three men in a place, or we would be promptly scattered by a shell. Many places we could get a tolerable view of the city through the openings of the trees, while at one particular point we got a splendid view of the rebel works and our own rifle pits for nearly a mile down the line. For half an hour we watched our sharpshooters in the skirmish pits shooting at the rebels. We observed that the rebels didn't shoot very much. But whenever there would be a puff of smoke curl up from the rebel pits we could see a like puff from a dozen of our skirmish pits, sometimes for nearly a half mile up and down our lines, and then we could see the dirt fly up around the luckless Johnny's head as the bullets came at it from so many directions. There were times when our skirmishers had orders to fire their 80 rounds every 24 hours, and from two weeks' constant practice like this, our soldiers became the best marksmen in the world. Their orders were in no case to let a rebel stick his head above their works.

We have spoken of the 23d corps going to the right to help get on to the railroad south of Macon. After it got in position it was found that the rebels still had heavy works between them and the railroad, and Sherman found he would still need more men to enable him to get on to the road. His next move was to take his whole army south, much like a fish worm crawls on the ground; that is by the "stretching process." This was accomplished by working the 20th and 4th corps as close up to the rebel works as they could be got, thus very materially shortening their lines, and then making their works so strong that they could be held by fewer men; then these two corps were stretched out so as to relieve three divisions of the 14th corps, which were moved to the right of the 23d corps. But Hood was equal to the emergency, and it was found that he could stretch as fast as Sherman could, and at whatever place our men would come up toward the railroad they would still find a heavy line of works between them and the road. Sherman telegraphed to Gen. Halleck, at Washington, August 7th: "We keep hammering away all the time, and there is no peace inside or outside of Atlanta. Gen. Schofield yesterday drove the enemy behind his main breastworks, which cover the railroad from Atlanta to Macon at East Point, and captured a good many of the skirmishers, who are his best troops, for the militia hug the breastworks close. I do not deem it prudent to extend any more to the right, but will push forward daily by parallels and make the inside of Atlanta too hot to be endured. I have sent back to Chattanooga for two 32-pound Parrotts, with which we can pick out almost any house in town. I am too impatient for a siege, and don't know but this is as good a place to fight it out on as further inland. One thing is certain, whether we get into Atlanta or not, it will be a used-up community when we are done with it."

Our every move was vigilantly watched and resisted to the death, consequently heavy and severe fighting was going on all the time, day in and day out, from morn till night and from night till morn; from one week's end till the next the constant roar of musketry and artillery was kept up. Indeed, the roar was so incessant that a lull of a single minute was noticed and remarked; and if a silence of 20 or 30 minutes came at any time we all began to wonder, for these instances were ominous, so often being the precursors of a terrible storm; they almost always occurred just before one side or the other would make a charge. We got so accustomed to these things that whenever there would be a lull in the firing we would ask each other, "which side is going to try it this time?" We could always tell which side was making the charge by the hearty cheering of *our* men, or by the devilish yells of the rebels. The rebels did not fire regularly all along their works, but would break out now and then at different points on the line. On the night of the 5th they gave *us* a pretty thorough shaking up. From our lines the firing was regular and systematic. We suppose that Sherman had over 100 guns in position bearing on the city, and there were many days at a time when every gun had orders to fire a shell every five minutes. Day and night the incessant roar goes on. The line of our works reaches fully 10 miles, and it often happens that the firing will commence on the extreme left and run clear around to the extreme right, very much like dragging a log chain regularly over a rail; by the time the sound dies away on the right it begins again on the left, and round after round wears the night away.

This is becoming monotonous, but do not get the idea that we are idle spectators. Our pickets were attacked almost every day and the rebels shelled us almost every night, and on the night of the 13th gave us a terrible round, killing a number of horses, and shot off the leg of a 7th Pennsylvania cavalryman right in our quarters. We have time for but a few incidents. Our horses were left in camp three miles west of our position in line, and close to the battlefield of Peachtree Creek, and we had ample opportunity of rambling over it. Near our camp was a trench in which 75 of our men were buried, and buried we suppose as well as could be done under the circumstances; but we noticed a horrid stench rising from the ground, and the flies and worms working in the loose earth. Further down to the west, in the woods, we saw a hundred or more rebels that had only been partially buried, just as they had been shot down, some of them with but a few shovelfulls of dirt thrown over them. Of course our own dead were buried first, and it was two days before our men came on to the ground where these rebels lay, and then the weather was so hot and they had so far decayed that it was impossible to bury them. Joab Moffit, private Company I, was with us, and as we passed around among the dead his remarks were anything but complimentary to the Johnnies. One fellow's haversack lay close to his head, as if he needed his rations on his journey to the happy hunting grounds. The haversack had a piece of pork in it. The meat was all sound but the Johnny wasn't. Finally we came to one that had but a few shovelfulls of dirt thrown over his body, while his head, arms and legs, were without any dirt over them at all. Joab accidentally stumbled over one of his feet, and the body was so far decayed that the foot came off and rolled away. "There," says Joab, "Just as I expected—sock and all."

Such scenes as these, and many that were worse, were so common as to breed contempt. While we were in the trenches the surgeon of the 98th got leave of absence and went home, and wanted to take a rebel skull with him in the interests of science, and also as a sort of reminder of what he had seen; and he agreed to give Grismar, of Company K, Seventy-Second, $5.00 if he would bring him a skull. We suppose Grismar did not care to be seen carrying the skull in broad daylight, so he reported to the Doctor's quarters about sundown, and the Doctor gave him an old dull spade and told him he should not fail. Grismar had about a mile to go to get to where the rebels were unburied, and it was getting dark when he got there. He wasn't long in finding what he supposed was a proper subject, but from some cause or other it proved to be not so much decayed as some of the others. He stepped astride the body and raised the spade to chop the head off. After a lick or two he thought to look down and see how he was getting along; but not timing his motions right he looked just as he brought the spade down upon the man's neck, when to his horror the Johnny opened his mouth and his teeth gleamed in the fading light; he lifted the spade and the man's mouth went to with a snap. Grismar threw the spade as far as he could send it and started for camp, and as he started he thought he could see the Johnny start up behind him. Fear lent wings to his feet, and as he ran he was sure he could feel the Johnny clutching at his coat-tails. He flew over the distance from there to camp with the speed of the wind. He arrived at his quarters out of breath and speechless. Fortunately for him his comrades had gone to bed, and he never told of the circumstance till the war was over.

All through July the weather had been extremely hot, but dry, and our constant movements kept us in good health. After going into the trenches it turned wet and just as hot as ever, and the health of the brigade failed wonderfully in the two weeks we were there. The constant watchfulness of our skirmishers was wearing on us. We were covering such an extended line that it kept us on duty six days out of seven; at least that was the case with your humble servant. We have a story furnished by Remley, showing the constant watchfulness of our men. Calvin E. Swindler, private Company E, entered the service when but a boy, but made a No. 1 soldier, a good shot and remarkably cool in time of danger. One night while on picket to the north-east of Atlanta he heard something coming up the by-road on which he was standing, and sang out "Halt! Who comes there?" No response, and the sound comes moving rapidly towards him. In an instant "whang!" goes his trusty Spencer. The sergeant of the guard hastens out to see what is the matter. He found Cal. at his post, and pointing to a dark object just in front of him said "there it is." A mule had come running up the road toward him, and not being light enough for him to see whether there was any one on it, he had fired, and the mule came stumbling on and fell dead at his feet. There was no fun in standing the long lonely two hours alone. Besides, no one was sure when he went out to his post that he would ever get back alive. We here insert a rebel letter written to a man's wife just at this time, as showing the terrible straits to which the rebels were reduced and the sore privations which they must have endured. Our condition was bad enough, but we would hardly be willing to exchange with them. This letter was picked up by Sergt. A. W. Lane, of Company G, a few days after written:

"IN THE TRENCHES BEFORE ATLANTA, August 15th, 1864.

MY DEAR WIFE:

Your war-worn husband takes his pen in hand, in a strange land, on a foreign strand. My ink is pale, I have no ale. My paper is poor; so is my grub. Our quarters in camp are passable, but quarters in my pocket are not. Last night I had a wagon bolster for a "piller," while I was covered with a sheet of water. I long for more biscuits and less bullets. How I wish you were here. The farther I get from you the better I like you. So that you may know how we work in spite of the cussed Yanks, I send you a diary of daily labor. 5 o'clock, called up by a roll of the drum, from a roll in the mud; no rolls of bread. 6 to 7, shoulder spades. Throw up the earth, also my yesterday's rations. 7:30, another roll of the drum, and we roll logs. Filing off into line, as well as defiling my breeches with the sacred soil of Georgia; drawing ramrods but no pay; no shelling out by the government, but a cussed sight by the Yanks. 9 a. m. More drilling, but not of the cotton kind, wherewith to increase my present supply of one shirt. 10:00 More spadular researches into the geological formation of the earth. 11:00 Corps takes a chew of tobacco. 12:00 See signs of dinner. Skippers throwing up works on a hog's jowl to resist the attack of the captain's cook. My eyes are sunk so far into my head that I can look down my windpipe into my restaurant department. I would make a first class telescope, I have three glasses"

Here a Spencer ball put a quietus to his further soliloquizing. But the reader would like to get away from Atlanta, and so would we; yet the siege is scarcely half over, and we hear that Wheeler has got on to our railroad away up about Dalton and Tunnel Hill.

August 14th. We quote from Dr. Cole: "Late this evening we were relieved and moved back to our horses very well satisfied to be out of the ditches. The health of the command became poor while confined to the trenches." Col. Miller says: "Shelled the enemy all night from our whole lines. The word is that Wheeler is in our rear; I was ordered to be ready to move at daylight for Dalton." We got a good night's rest and were up long before daylight on August 15th, and ready to move out by sun-up, supposing that we would go back to the rear to see about Wheeler. But instead of that we moved out at 8 a. m., going to Decatur, 10 miles from our camp. This place was abandoned by us more than two weeks ago since, which time it has been in the hands of the rebels. When our advance got there they found it occupied by the rebels and our scouts captured two of their videttes. After getting to the town the brigade was sent out in detachments on different roads, the Seventy-Second taking a road running south, which we followed a mile and a half, ran out to the rebel picket-posts and drove them back a mile further, where we stirred up the whole nest, and they came on to us by the thousand. As there were none of our brigade near us we concluded discretion was the better part of valor, and fell back, the rebels closing up on our rear guard lively; some members of Company D showing great coolness and courage in keeping back the rebels. The rebels were not only following us but pushing ahead on another road trying to cut us off from Decatur. After getting back past the intersection of the roads we stopped and formed line of battle on a high ridge, half a mile south of town, and dared the rebels to come on. It began to rain just as we commenced to fall back, and by the time we got our line of battle formed it poured down in torrents, and continued so till night. We had a good position, with an open field for a mile in front of us, sloping from our line nearly two-thirds of the way across it. The rebels were saucy and formed their line of battle in the open field in front of us and in plain view, and sent forward their skirmishers, who began to fire upon us when about half way across the field, their shots falling short 50 to 100 yards. Then we began to laugh at them and tell them to come closer; that their guns were no account; to come and get a piece of corn bread; and a hundred like expressions. They raised their accustomed yell and started, but a volley from our Spencers flattened them out on the ground in a minute. Then we had the laugh on them again and kept hallooing at them to get up out of the mud. This exasperated them so they made a second attempt, but a few shots from our lines sent them to grass again. The railroad from Decatur to Atlanta ran from the right of our position in the woods through a deep cut for more than a half mile to the south-west, and by some means we were made aware of the rebels coming up through that cut to our right rear, and Company G, with some skirmishers from Company D, was sent over on the railroad. This move was none too soon, as they had scarcely gone a quarter of a mile till the rebels opened on them, wounding George Passale, private Company G, severely in the chest, but our men had the advantage of the timber and the railroad bank and held the rebels at bay. Just as the firing began on our right the rebels made another attempt to advance in our front, and although it was still raining as hard as it could pour we could see them so plainly and our men opened on them with such deliberation that they scarcely got a dozen rods till they were all flat on their bellies again. They then tried shooting at us from their positions on the ground. A few shots went over our heads, and a few struck the fence in front of us, but most of them dropped far short of their mark; no rebel dare stick up his head for a second but he was glad to get it down again. All this time we were keeping up a lively conversation with the rebels, doing most of the talking ourselves, however. We held our position till it began to get dark, when we fell back slowly to town, mounted our horses and moved slowly to camp, getting in just at midnight.

August 16, 1864. Two years ago to-day we were mustered into the service, and whether we had any orders on the subject or not we never could tell, but somehow or other, by intuition, instinct, or some other method, we got the idea that we would have a day's rest, an article we were sadly in need of, as we had not had one since crossing the Chattahoochee. By common consent we all improved the time bathing in the Peach-tree Creek, washing and mending our clothes—a very much needed exercise. By evening we had cleaned up and mended up till we had things in tolerable "ship shape," and at night had a general jollification and some speech making by the officers. We feel wonderfully inclined right here to let ourselves out on "Patriotism," but forbear.

CHAPTER XXX.

From August 17th to September 18th.—Hungry Children—Minty's and Long's Brigades Roughly Handled—Sherman Raises the Siege and Moves South of Atlanta—Sleeping in the Saddle—The Trains at Sand Town—A Mad Dutch Sutler—Sherman Slipped Off and the Rebels did not Find it Out until Morning—The Rebels think Sherman is in Full Retreat and Rejoice—How the Trains of a Great Army Move—Hood finds out what Sherman is up to after Sherman Cuts the Rebel Railroads—Thomas and Schofield Cut the Rebel Army in two—Rebels Whipped and Lose 3,000 Prisoners—This Finishes the Atlanta Campaign—Getting Honey and Whipping Rebels—Scooping in Videttes—Montgomery's Strategy—Gen. Slocum Marches into Atlanta—Sherman Announces that "Atlanta is Ours, and Fairly Won"—100,000 Soldiers Wild with Joy over the Victorious Ending of the Campaign—Congratulations from the Patriotic North, from Gens. Sherman and Grant and President Lincoln—A Season of Rest—Pay Promised—Woods Full of Rebel Stragglers—Rest, Service, Sanitary Supplies and Getting Well—In Camp near Cross Keys—Get the Papers and Read up—The Presidential Contest—Col. Miller Tells us to Vote—We Organize and Vote 352 Majority for Uncle Abe, 400 Majority for O. P. Morton, and Hail the Result with Cheers—Speeches which Scorch Copper Heads—Viewing the Siege Guns and Fortifications at Atlanta—City and Fortifications Described—Sherman and Hood Exchange 2,000 Prisoners—Sherman Orders All Citizens to Evacuate Atlanta, and the Rebels Howl with Indignation—Sketch of Major Adam Pinkerton.

August 17th. Spent the day lying around loose, expecting every minute to get orders to move, but got no orders till nearly night, when our brigade was ordered to relieve Long's brigade, which for more than two weeks had been picketing from the left of the infantry clear around back to the river close to Roswell. When relieved, Minty's and Long's brigades moved down to Sandtown to assist Kilpatrick's division to make another attempt on the Macon Railroad.

August 18th. Our regiment was on picket till late in the evening, and from Miller's notes we have this: "The word is that the enemy are moving on our left. We have no forage and half the brigade is on picket." It appears that Wheeler did really get on to the railroad by making a wide circuit around our left, and struck the railroad away up above Resaca, tore up a few miles of the track and captured 1,000 head of our beef cattle. See Sherman, vol. 2, p. 103. On the 16th another detachment passing around our right flank struck the railroad about the Etowa, and tore up the road there, and for several days our horses were without forage. When we got to camp we had orders to be ready to move at 2 a. m. to-morrow morning.

August 19th. Moved this morning promptly at 2 o'clock, taking the road to Decatur, and got there by the time the sun was an hour high, killing two rebel videttes and capturing two others. We remained in town all day foraging on all the roads in every direction for two miles and a half from it. Just at noon most of our brigade were in town feeding their horses on roasting-ears brought in from the country. A part of our regiment fed their horses on the north side of the square next the side-walk; as the men began to scatter and move off we noticed three little children come out on the side-walk who were the very picture of distress. After looking at our horses in astonishment for a while, the little boy, about three years old, happened to see the cobs where our horses had eaten, and immediately ran and picked up one of the cobs and began to gnaw and suck it as if his life depended upon it. The little girl noticed him and begged him to let her have some, but he could not be persuaded to part with it. She then asked him where he got it. Without stopping he motioned his head to the edge of the side-walk. She ran to the gutter and immediately uttered an exclamation of surprise, jumped down among the cobs and began to gather up her hands full, but seeing one with about half the corn left on she grabbed it up and exclaimed: "Oh bubby! bubby! Lookey here what a great big nice one!" Bubby threw down his cob and made a desperate effort to take the corn away from her, and perhaps would have succeeded but she threw him off his guard by saying: "Oh bubby, less give it to the baby, and we'll get more." The little fellow's wrath was appeased in a moment. They gave the corn to the baby a year and a half old, and set about hunting among the cobs for any chance one that might have a few grains upon it. Just a month ago our advance entered this town, killing a few rebel soldiers, and among the number was the father of these children. He had fallen, fighting as he supposed for his country, and now for more than three weeks this place had been inside the rebel lines. Yet his comrades were so base that they could see this wretched woman and her children starve, without making a single effort to help them. We acquainted our Colonel, who was one of the kindest hearted men in the world, with the circumstances, and he immediately sent for an ambulance and had the widow and her children sent north, where it is to be hoped the children have grown up to love their country. Such little touches of human nature as this make the world akin

Late in the evening our brigade moved two miles north-west of Decatur and went into camp. Just as we left camp this morning, and two hours before daylight, a ferocious cannonading began all along the lines, and in a short time we could see vast volumes of smoke and flame rise from Atlanta, showing that our shells were making it warm for the good people inside.

August 20th. This morning we were up and back to Decatur by

daylight. Foraged all the forenoon for our horses, without seeing any rebels. After dinner we went back to our old camp on Peach-tree, reached it by the middle of the afternoon and got a good night's sleep and rest which we were needing badly.

August 21st. We begin to realize that it is not much fun to have our railroad cut, as in this wooded country forage is scarce at best, and after our army has swept over a strip of it 50 miles wide we find it quite a task to find forage enough to keep our horses from starving. It is 12 miles from our camp to the edge of this strip, and we cannot carry enough on our horses to last any time; and to-day we have sent out our wagons for forage. Company H went along as guards for this train. They went away up near McAfee's Bridge and were very successful, getting all the wagons full of corn and blades.

August 22d. On picket again, and we quote from Dr. Cole's journal: "This evening the Kilpatrick raiders returned. The two brigades, Minty's and Long's, belonging to our division, have been roughly handled. The loss in killed and wounded in 1st brigade is 113, and in the 2d 90. The surgeons and assistants of my brigade rendered every assistance to the wounded. The two brigades from our division suffered comparatively more than any other part of Kilpatrick's command, from the fact that when surrounded they led the charge out through the enemy's lines. They tore up the railroad at Jonesboro and burned some government property, and on returning made the entire circuit of Atlanta; but the work accomplished failed to pay the cost."

August 23d. Sherman says: "We saw trains coming in from the south to-day, showing that the cavalry could not or would not work hard enough to disable a railroad properly, and I therefore resolved at once to proceed to put into execution my original plan of raising the siege and moving boldly to some point on the Macon Railroad below East Point." So, on the morning of August 24th, our brigade mounted at daylight and as usual moved out to Decatur. There were yet about four miles of the Augusta Railroad, between Decatur and Stone Mountain, that had not been torn up, and we worked hard all day, destroying it entirely. There were heavy fires in Atlanta all day, and it seems to us there will be little of it left to fight about in a week longer.

August 25th. Our brigade in camp all day anxiously expecting something to turn up. Just at night the Seventy-Second mounted and rode up as close to the rear of the 20th corps as we dare go without attracting the attention of the rebels, and then dismounted and took our places along in the trenches of that corps, and just after dark, with artillery all muffled, the corps left the trenches and very quietly moved back across the Chattahoochie. About 10 at night we quietly called in our skirmishers and pickets and followed the infantry, getting across the river at Vining's Station about 1 o'clock a. m. of the 26th. During our march in the night our regiment was in the rear of the brigade, and it seems after we got started the brigade moved off pretty lively and got into camp by midnight, but we noticed after we had moved two or three miles that our regiment kept going slower and slower and finally stopped still. We sent a man forward to see what was the matter, not wishing to make much noise. When our man reached the head of column he found the captain, who was at its head, sitting there on his horse sound asleep; and in fact nearly every man in the whole regiment was sound asleep. We had moved so much after night, and had become so accustomed to sleeping on horseback, that we could sleep about as well that way as any other, and our horses would keep their places all the same whether we were asleep or awake. But somehow the captain's horse got stopped, and if somebody had not waked the captain we might have remained there till morning. When the captain was waked up he was so confused he did not know which end of the road to take, and had it not been for the men he would have gone right straight back to Atlanta, and it took a good deal of parleying to get him to move forward. We got across the river an hour after the balance of the regiment and brigade had been in camp, and a half mile from the river met Col. Miller, who had put the rest in camp, got impatient and had started to look for us. When we met him he was about as mad a man as you ever saw He pitched into the captain, and for once used language more forcible than elegant. By this time the men began to jeer and make remarks which partially explained the situation, so that the longer Miller talked the madder he got, and finally, telling the captain he might get into camp the best way he could, turned off and left him. This and our laughing so exasperated the captain that he told us *we* might get into camp the best way *we* could. Of course one place suited us quite as well as another, and every fellow went for the nearest tree, hitched his horse, and in five minutes was sleeping the sleep of the just.

August 26th. When we woke up this morning the sun was up, and we found our brigade was camped a half mile away and our whole division train near us. We drew rations and the train began to move early, taking the road to Sand Town, 20 miles south-west, down the river. After they all got strung out on the road we mounted and moved on slowly after them all day without stopping, and near sundown went into camp four miles north of Sand Town. The move last night was a perfect success. At the same time the 20th corps moved out of the trenches the 4th corps also left and moved down toward Sand Town, on the east side of the river, and all so quietly that the rebels never missed them till morning, and then they thought our whole army had begun to retreat. A dispatch from Gen. Sherman to Gen. Halleck explains the present move: "August 24th. Heavy fires in Atlanta all day caused by our artillery. I will be all ready and commence the movement around Atlanta by the south to-morrow night, and for some time you will hear little of us. I will keep open a courier line back to the Chattahoochie bridge by way of Sand Town. The 20th corps will hold the railroad bridge, and I will move with the balance of the army provisioned for 20 days."

August 27th. We started this morning at sun-up and moved on past the trains and got to the river by 8 or 9 o'clock, crossed over on a good wagon bridge, and when we got into Sand Town we found the whole army had abandoned the siege and moved south, and all the trains of the army were coming into Sand Town, in obedience to orders as fast as they could. It had been a long time since we had seen such a rush and jam of trains. It is no small job to manage three or four thousand trains under the most favorable circumstances, and in the present instance the confusion was simply fearful. Sand Town is 15 miles south-west of Atlanta. All the trains belonging to the army were scattered along in the rear of the brigades to which they belonged, and covered an extent of country several miles long. All were coming in on different roads and had got here about the same time, and it took more than the remainder of the day to get them all started out on different roads to the south-east. The fact is, all the trains did not get into Sand Town to-day; but about noon our division moved out on the road they were coming in on from toward Atlanta; and late in the afternoon found the rear of them six or seven miles from Sand Town, and then we went into camp near Eutaw Post-office. After getting our coffee and dinner Companies D and I were sent on picket, going toward Atlanta two miles further. On our way out we met a Dutch sutler coming in bare-headed and bare-footed, and without any coat. He was as mad as wrath, and had a terrible tale of woe to tell. As a rule wagon masters do not care much to be bothered with sutlers, and do not take much pains to give them orders when and where to move. So the trains had moved off in the night and left the Dutch sutler in entire ignorance of when and where they were going. This morning when he woke up he found the Johnnies all around him, and it didn't take them long to clean him out. They took every thing he had—a good mule team and wagon, a large wall tent well filled with goods, his hat, coat and boots, and then kicked him because he hadn't more. As he was not a soldier they kicked and cuffed him around a while and then let him go. He was the maddest man we ever saw. They had taken $5,000 worth of stuff from him, and he was so Dutchy that it would make the oldest man in the world laugh to hear him tell it. About sundown the rear guard (about 200 infantry) passed and told us to look sharp, as the rebs would be on to us before morning. The night passed off quietly, but just at daylight our videttes commenced shooting and we thought the Johnnies were on to us sure enough. But when it got light enough, we could see they were our own men who had straggled from their commands and got lost. We never could have any patience with such vagabonds as these, and should not have cared had some of them got killed.

August 28th. We were called in at 9 o'clock this morning, went to where the brigade had camped and then took a road running south, went three miles and caught up with the trains, which during the night had all got started out in a south-east direction, and now our business for several days is to guard these trains. This is a bold venture, and Sherman has but 20 days' rations in his wagons and cannot afford to lose one of them; hence we are required to exercise the utmost caution and vigilance. Of all the duty we ever did this is the most tedious.

The movement thus far has been a grand success. Up to the present time there have only been a half dozen wagons lost, and, as above indicated, more than half of them belonged to suttlers. We moved on slowly after the trains all the afternoon, and at 7 p. m. went into camp near Mt. Gilead Church, having made but six miles for the day. We have already given the movement of the 20th and 4th corps and our division on the night of the 25th, and have spoken of its success. On the night of the 26th Sherman moved the balance of his army back south-west toward Sand Town, so that the Johnnies really thought he was retreating and intended to cross at that place. The news was telegraphed all over the South that the Yanks were in full retreat, and there was great joy in Atlanta. Yesterday morning there were several trains of cars came up from Macon loaded with ladies and the elite of the South to help celebrate Hood's great victory; but to-day we think they are beginning to find out their mistake, for they have been feeling out in this direction with all the cavalry they have, to find out our exact whereabouts, and picket firing is going on all the time.

August 29th. We did not unsaddle at all last night, and were ready to move early, but did not move till 10 o'clock, and then only three miles during the day, camping on the south side of Camp Creek; that is to say, our camp is only three miles from where it was last night, but some portion of the division are constantly moving back and forth all the time, the object being to keep up as big a show of troops between our trains and Atlanta as possible.

As we have nowhere given the reader an idea of how the trains of a vast army move across the country, we will, in a few words, describe the method. In the first place, then, there are now in this vast train 3,000 army wagons, besides the artillery caissons, forges, ambulances, sutler wagons, &c., and not less than 20,000 horses and mules (see Sherman's book), and were they all strung out on one road, closed up as closely as possible, the column would be 50 miles long. As the object is to keep the trains belonging to each brigade or division as near as possible to the rear of the infantry to which they belong, you can see it is impossible for all the trains to move upon one road, or even a dozen, because if they did the infantry would not get to see their trains from one week's end to another, and some of them would never get to see them at all. As our army sweeps across the country in a line of battle from 10 to 40 miles long, and from time to time wheeling upon the right or left flank like a huge and ponderous gate swinging upon its hinges, this vast train of wagons sweeps over the country after it; and notwithstanding this is a heavily wooded country, thinly inhabited, and in a manner no roads at all, this train of wagons sweeps over the country like a vast herd of buffalo, always heading after their respective commands. You would be surprised to see with what ease and how noiselessly they slip along through the woods. Of course where the woods are too thick for them to get through they have to be cut away, but there is no noise or fuss made about it; slowly and steadily they move forward in the direction indicated. As all the wagons are provided with bows and canvas covers, it would be a novel and interesting sight to be up high enough to see them all moving at once. This grand sight the members of the signal corps often witnessed from their elevations upon hill-tops, tree-tops or mountain peaks, with their glasses that swept the country for many miles in all directions. This the more excites our wonder and admiration, as it is something entirely new in the history of military tactics for a very large army to cut loose from a base of supplies and push boldly out into an enemy's country, with only 20 days' rations in wagons; and there is a heated controversy going on all the time among the men about the propriety of the move; about half of the men shaking their heads and declaring—to say the least of it—that it is very risky, while the other half declare that in 20 days Sherman can move this army clear around Atlanta and back to the place he started from; and if Hood wants to come out of his works and attack us, let him do it, for we can whip him in an open field fight so quick he will never want to try it but once.

From the time we crossed the river at Sand Town up to the evening of September 2d, our duties day after day were just the same, always keeping between our trains and Atlanta, while the army had swept around over the country on a general left wheel from Sand Town on the south-west to Jonesboro on the south-east, and for the work performed each day we refer you to Sherman's book, only noting just so much of it as will make our own work as plain and conspicuous as it should be.

On the 28th the whole army was on the Montgomery railroad, from East Point to Red Oak and Fairburn, a distance of 20 miles south-west, thoroughly destroying it. On the 31st the entire army was on the Macon railroad from Rough-and-Ready to below Jonesboro, south-east, a distance of 20 miles. It was not till the 28th that Hood found out that Sherman had not retreated but was going for his railroad, and on the 29th and 30th Hood sent two of his veteran corps, his own old corps and Hardee's, to Jonesboro to meet Howard's army, which was now moving straight for that place. On the evening of the 30th Hood attacked Howard and a severe battle was fought, Hood being driven back into his works. On the evening of the 31st Schofield and Thomas had pushed across the Macon railroad far enough to cut the rebel army in two, two divisions—conscripts and state militia—still being in Atlanta. On the 1st of September Schofield and Thomas pushed down along the railroad to Jonesboro, and in the evening lapped around to the north and north-east, and another battle ensued, in which the rebels lost 3,000 prisoners, two batteries of ten guns, and had not night come on so soon would have lost nearly the whole of those two corps. What was left retreated during the night to Lovejoy's station, six miles south of Jonesboro. This was really the finishing stroke of the campaign. On the 1st of September our division crossed the Macon railroad and went into camp seven miles from Jonesboro, Company D on picket near Rough-and-Ready. A squad went to a neighboring house where there were lots of bees, secured a large wash-pan, and went for the honey, but just about the time they had the pan full a party of rebs charged upon them. They set the pan down and went to work on the rebs with their

Spencers, and soon drove them away and carried off the honey in triumph.

September 1st. Last night Company E was on picket east of Jonesboro, near the rebel lines, and this morning made preparations to take in the rebel videttes on the same road close to them. There was a dense wood between the two outposts which favored the movement. Captain Kilborn had doubled the outposts, and preparations were made for them to charge the rebels just as it beg n to get light. This was done in a most gallant style and was entirely successful, bringing in the entire squad without making any fuss about it. The rebels soon found out their videttes had been captured and at once put out others in their places, who were immediately taken in in the same way. On this charge private George W. Montgomery bore down upon the rebel vidette and fired, and when he attempted to re-load found the cartridge shell was fast in his gun. He was so close that retreat was out of the question, so he just charged right up to the rebel and presented his empty gun; the rebel was so frightened that he gave up *his* gun, which was loaded. Montgomery marched him back to headquarters, then took out his knife and picked out the shell, the rebel watching him, and when he had got it out he said, "Now she's all right," and threw another load in. The rebel said, "Well that beats h—l." "What beats h—l?" said Sergt. Wilhite. "Why, I surrendered to a man with an empty gun, and mine was loaded." He was a Mississippian, and had once before been a prisoner at Indianapolis; and he said, "I don't mind being beat fair, but d—n a man that will surrender to another with an empty gun; but I thought you fellows could just shoot all the time, and his first shot came so close to me I was afraid to let him shoot again." These two charges had been so successful that Sergt. Plunkett and some more of the boys thought they would try it again. A member of the 123d Illinois volunteered to go along with them, but by this time the rebels had got the hang of it, and as our boys charged down upon the rebel videttes they ran right into a pocket formed by the rebels on each side of the road. They discovered their misfortune in time for all of them to get out but the 123d man, who was captured.

September 2d. Went into camp two miles eastof Jonesboro. We quote from Dr. Cole: "The 14th corps gained a complete and decisive victory over the rebels at Jonesboro yesterday evening. * * * The wounded fell into our hands to be provided for. Our loss was also severe, as the rebels were entrenched and our men were compelled to drive them out at the point of the bayonet. The woods are full of wounded rebels, and I have had my ambulance engaged in picking them up and bringing them to hospital." Our regiment went on a scout north-east of the railroad for several miles till we came near the Atlanta and McDonough road. Here we found the rebel army that had been left in Atlanta. It was making good time to catch up with Hood. We skirmished with them awhile and then went into camp with the brigade near Jonesboro. Last night about midnight continued and heavy reports of fire-arms came from the direction of Atlanta, and we supposed a battle was going on. We were 15 miles from Atlanta, but could hear the firing distinctly. The 20th corps, Gen. Slocum in command, which had been left at the Chattahoochie, had orders to watch the rebels in Atlanta very closely and attack them on the slightest appearance of their giving way. Gen. Slocum had heard these reports the same as we had, and this morning had moved forward to Atlanta and found the city entirely deserted and entered it unobstructed. About 9 or 10 o'clock rumors began to come to us that the rebels had retreated from Atlanta, and the column we saw later in the day confirmed the reports. As Slocum entered Atlanta an engine followed him into the city, and he sent the engine on down the Macon Railroad with a despatch to Sherman. The engine came on down to Rough and Ready till it struck the place torn up by our army. From there the courier made his way down the railroad on foot till he reached our division, and then the dispatch was sent on down to Sherman, who, with most of the army, was away below Jonesboro.

September 3d. Lying in camp to-day. As soon as Sherman got the dispatch yesterday, he called a halt of all the army and went into camp, and to-day sent circulars to all parts of the army announcing that "Atlanta is ours and fairly won," and further that he had accomplished all he had in view, and declared the campaign ended. We suppose there never were 100,000 soldiers in the history of the world who, all at the same time, enjoyed this stupendous victory as we did. There never were before such cheering and joyful exclamations as now came from the throats of these 100,000 soldiers simultaneously and continuously through the whole day. For four months this army had not known rest, and although we had not suffered defeat, there were many times whan success seemed doubtful. It was all over now, and oh! how good we felt. No people could realize this great victory just as we could. We knew just what it had cost us. From the beginning of the war up to the present there had been many more dark days than bright ones, but now we felt assured that a new and brighter day had dawned upon us, and that the beams of peace would soon brighten the whole land; for we all regarded the fall of Atlanta as the death knell of the Southern confederacy. The day has been a miserable, wet, drizzly one; just such a day as, upon ordinary occasions, we would like to lie in onr dog-tents, feel grum and scold. Our feelings have been in broad contrast with the weather, and we have not even thought of putting up our tents, but have spent the day moving about, visiting, talking and laughing, and having a regular holiday jollification. From early dawn till late at night the congratulations of the whole North have poured upon us, and the cheering still goes on. Late in the evening we were called up in line to hear read Gen. Sherman's order of congratulation on our success in capturing Atlanta, and also the thanks of the President, Abraham Lincoln, and Gen. Grant. The order also stated that the army would now gradually fall back to East Point, Atlanta and Decatur, and enjoy a season of rest and recuperation.

In the afternoon we visited one of the rebel hospitals near our camp. It had been established here several days ago and there were 250 wounded soldiers in it, and we should say that one-half of them had a hand, arm, foot, or leg, taken off—a pretty hard sight. Outside of the building was a huge pile of hands, feet, arms and legs, that had been taken off and thrown out to rot, or be devoured by dogs or crows. There had been no supplies of any kind left by the rebels for this hospital, and for two days the wounded soldiers had been without anything to eat.

September 4th. The whole army started for Atlanta, and as our division was camped upon the road the infantry would use, we moved north-east four miles, to get out of their way;- the trains in this case reversing the usual order of march and going before, while we were left in the rear of the infantiy to keep the rebels off of them. Still raining.

On the 5th and 6th, we did not move more than two or three miles, but changed camp every day, just as we have done ever since we crossed the river at Sand Town. This was done to mask the movements of the infantry and to cover the trains. We have spoken of the rebels retreating from Atlanta to McDonough. These were conscripts and State militia, and just as soon as they got out of the trenches and into the woods they began to scatter in every direction. We quote from Miller's notes, September 5th: "The woods are full of stragglers, and my brigade has captured over 100 prisoners in the last three days." By the 6th most of the infantry had got past us, and the rebels began to feel of our lines to see if there was any chance of cutting off any of our trains, and our pickets were attacked frequently through the day. Company E had a very lively time of it, and had one of their videttes captured, and in turn charged the rebels and captured five prisoners. It rained both the 5th and 6th, and the ground is getting so soft that a few trains passing over the roads render them almost impassable.

On the 7th of September we began to fall back slowly toward Decatur, going right north, our division train being immediately in front of us, and the last of the 23d corps just ahead of the train. We passed a little place to-day called Shakerag, which reminded us very much of a little town we passed through in Kentucky called Dogwalk. We went into camp on the McDonough road about the middle of the afternoon. The rebels followed us closely all day, capturing two men of Company K, Albert Weeks and Wm. M. Spencer. Weeks was shot through the body and was exchanged. Spencer suffered many hardships and finally made his escape, and has furnished a narrative of his prison life, which we shall take great pleasure in publishing.

September 8th. It rained again to-day, and we moved slowly back to Decatur and went into camp south of the town and in front of the infantry, the whole of the 23d corps being camped in regular order at that place. We lay in camp all day the 9th, without anything of note transpiring except a kind of general lassitude or laziness pervaded the division, the result of relaxation after great mental strain, anxious watching, and care.

September 10th. Moved 10 miles back north-west from Decatur and went into camp on a high, sandy ridge, near Crosskeys, in a most beautiful place for a cavalry camp. It was heavily timbered and the location dry and healthy. The waters of the Peach-tree Creek ran on three sides of our camp and were comparatively pure. We got to this place about noon and went into camp in regular order, and before night had our quarters cleaned up and everything as nice as a pin. This was the first time we had gone into regular camp since leaving Columbia, Tenn., the last of April, and our officers told us we should stay here long enough to get a good rest, to fix up our papers and be paid off. So we began right away to fix up our quarters and make them as home-like as possible, and by the end of three days had everything in splendid order, including a swing, gymnasium, tight rope, cross-beams, etc.

On the 13th we built a large and splendid bower by setting posts in the ground and putting poles across and covering it thickly with evergreens. We tore down a log house and made very comfortable seats. This was a most delightful place for reading and reflection. On the 14th this bower was dedicated to the worship of Almighty God, our Chaplain, Rev. De La Matyr, officiating; and as long as we remained at this camp, regular social and preaching services were kept up, and it is still the source of profound gratification to know that in the Seventy-Second the ratio of staunch, loyal Christian men, of stamina and fixed determination in the service of God, was just as large, if not larger, than in the best and most orderly communities of to-day. During the Jonesboro campaign we were in the rain almost constantly, and our duty required us much of the time to be in the black gum swamps of the head waters of the Cotton River, where the water was never clearer than muddy coffee, and often black as the Styx; and fully one-third of the regiment contracted chills, which stuck to us like burrs to a sheep. When we got to camp scurvy in mild form was manifesting itself in numerous cases. Your humble servant was one of the victims. Just at this time we met with a God-send in the shape of a lot of sanitary stores, sent to us by the Christian Commission. God bless them. This was the first favor of the kind we had ever received. Somehow or other we had gotten the idea that the people up North in God's country didn't think the Army of the Cumberland amounted to much, and we often felt that we were neglected. But the capture of Atlanta, the Gate City of the South, had waked up the people of the North to the fact that we were at least doing our share of the hard work, for here we were, now, right in the heart of the Southern confederacy, and had fought every step of the way to get here; and of course had inflicted incalculable loss upon the enemy. So they began to appreciate us and sent us a good supply of sanitary stores, which, to say the least, we were sadly in need of. Among these stores were a lot of dry onions, and a large barrel of pickled onions to each company. To say they were appreciated would be rather mild. They seemed to be life itself to us. As long as blackberries lasted we managed to keep in good health, but they were gone now, and as before intimated dyspepsia and scurvy had manifested themselves. But in three days these onions set us up all right again. We cannot better illustrate the general feeling of thankfulness in the regiment for the onions than to relate an incident. About the third day after we got the onions we were enjoying a good dinner, when our bunk mate, Bestana Munson, seemed rapt in profound meditation. We always called him "Yank;" he had been suffering with chills and scurvy. Finally "Yank" raised up and very deliberately remarked: "Well, when I get home I'm going to pray twice for the man who sent us the onions." "Hadn't you better do some of your praying now, Yank?" "Well, I am not so sure that I'll ever get home, and in that case the onions won't do me so much good after all." This was bad philosophy, but it shows that with many there was always an uncertainty of feeling in regard to their living to get home. We never had such a feeling, but can easily imagine that to be constantly haunted with it would be anything but pleasant.

We never before had such good rations, and had lighter duty to do, and were resting in the fullest sense of the word. Who says we had not earned the right to rest? For four months we had not known rest, and almost every single day of that time we heard the strife of deadly conflict going on, and were frequently in battle. Now for a whole week we had not heard a single artillery report, and oh, how quiet everything seemed.

On the 13th we got mail, the first we had received for three weeks: we also had a chance to read the papers and to inform ourselves as to how things were going on in the other armies, and also at home. No part of a soldier's life is more prized than the privilege of writing and reading, and we can yet recall to mind that upon more than one occasion orders came around, "two hours for writing letters," or "the mail will go out in an hour and a half." The thousands of letters, all over the North, that are yet preserved as sacred mementoes, attest how well those few moments were improved. Next to this privilege of writing was the privilege of reading; and soldiers read everything they could get hold of, good, bad and indifferent And here we read that about the time we started on this campaign, Gen. Grant had, with a most powerful army, started from Culpepper for Richmond; that soon after starting he had some terrible battles with Gen. Lee, and had finally run up against the defensive works around Petersburg, near Richmond, and had been hammering away there all summer; and that along the sea coast we had not been very successful, and with the exception of Mobile we had not captured a single place of importance; which, by contrast, made our work the more conspicuous. We also found the most exciting political campaign that our country had ever experienced was now going on, and at its hight. One party in this contest was headed by Gen. George B. McClellan, as a candidate for the Presidency, who in the beginning of the war was thought to be loyal, was tolerably successful as a General, and was given the command of the Army of the Potomac, but with that grand and noble army made such a failure that he was superseded, which "soured" him. The party that nominated him was composed principally of old line Democrats, and the principal plank in their platform was the one declaring that "after years of failure by the experiment of war, * * * hat timmediate efforts be made for a cessation of hostilities, with a view to the ultimate convention of the States, or other peaceable means, to the end that, at the earliest practicable moment, peace may be restored, on the basis of the federal union of the States." Some of the advocates of this platform and of Gen. McClellan's election, who were Congressmen, had gone to the extreme of declaring that they were opposed to voting another man or another dollar for putting down the rebellion. The soldiers regarded such men as at heart rebels, and we had a great deal more respect for the rebels who were bold enough and honest enough to meet us, arms in hand, on the battle-field, and fight us in front, than for those in our rear who were stabbing us in the back, prolonging the war, and giving aid and comfort to the enemies of the country. The proposition for a cessation of hostilities and a conference of States was particularly unpopular with the soldiers:

1. Because they believed that the rebellion was almost crushed, and a few more blows would finish the work.

2. Because they knew the time of the armistice would be spent by the rebels in strengthening their works and recruiting their wasted strength.

3. That inactivity would destroy as many of the Union troops as war.

4. And most powerful, because to ask and accept such an armistice would be saying to the rebels, and to the world, "We can't whip them; we must beg them to come to terms; we stack our arms after many splendid victories, and give up the effort."

Every noble soldier felt certain in his heart that we could whip them, could crush the rebellion, disperse the rebel government, and force the rebel armies to an unconditional surrender, and by the help of God, and to our own glory and honor, WE DID.

Opposed to McClellan stood Abraham Lincoln, at the head of all the loyal, country-loving citizens of the North, and of ALL the soldiers of the Union armies in the South; and it was with the most painful feelings of solicitude that we regarded the contest as doubtful. Soldiers were not allowed to vote—not being citizens—and nearly one-half of all the men who voted for Lincoln the first time he ran for the presidency were now in the army, which made us tremble for the results of the election. To avoid this fearful calamity many of the loyal Republican States of the North had passed laws that would enable their soldiers to vote in the field. The legislature of Indiana was democratic and refused to pass such a law, and thus 100,000 of her best citizens were disfranchised. Of course our regiment was very indignant, and indignation meetings in all Indiana regiments and batteries were in order. We determined to speak so loud on the subject as to be heard at home. So on the evening of the 18th, about an hour before sundown, our Colonel came around and told each company to proceed, without fear, favor, or affection, to cast our votes for President of the United States and for Governor of the State of Indiana, and to hand our votes in at tattoo roll call. As there was but one hour to do all in, of course there was no time for electioneering; but nobody *wanted* to electioneer. Our minds were already made up, and we proceeded at once to organize a board of judges in each company, and proceeded to vote, and just as we were finishing up the count a big siege gun, a rebel gun in a rebel fort, in Atlanta, belched forth a volume of sound that went rolling over hill and plain and mountain. This was the first gun we had heard since the fight at Jonesboro, on the 2d, and it told us the hour for evening roll call had come. We had not had a single roll call since leaving Columbia. Our camp was 10 miles from Decatur, 14 from Atlanta, and 25 from the extreme right of the army at East Point; but the evening was still, and no sooner had the report of the gun rolled away in the distance than there came rolling up the valley of the Peach-tree such a volume of sound, and cheering, the like of which we had heard but twice before in our life. It was such incidents as these that made this army one grand unit, moved and actuated by the same impulses, and all governed by the same master spirit. Inside the next 10 minutes the roll of 75,000 soldiers was called and it requires no stretch of imagination to *think* we hear them every one answer "HERE!" But what vivid recollections the sound of those evening guns calls up!! A joyful supper and political gossip ensues. When the bugle blows "tattoo," with cheering and joyful "hurrahs for Lincoln" the regiment *en masse* makes its way to the Colonel's headquarters, and amid almost breathless silence the vote is canvassed and the result announced:

For President—Abraham Lincoln, 380; George B. McClellan, 27; John C. Fremont, 1. Majority for Lincoln, 352.

Three cheers *a la militaire* were given, and with a will, too, and a "tiger" to boot.

For Governor—O. P. Morton, 404; Joseph E. McDonald, 4. Majority for Morton, 400.

This time, three times three were given, and we almost imagined we were at home and really voting for President. We then had a half dozen really good speeches, in which copperheads and peace sneaks were handled without gloves. We guess if our Democratic legislature could have heard us they would have thought we had *some* rights they were bound to respect.

Right away, as soon as we went into camp here, there was an

official permit of three from each company, each day, to go to the city to see the fortifications, big siege guns, &c. The men gladly availed themselves of this opportunity, and we make a few extracts from the various manuscripts before us. Dr. Cole says: "I found many of the buildings knocked to pieces by our shells. I also learned that many of the citizens were killed. A 'bomb-proof' in every yard gave evidence of the terror the inhabitants must have felt during those many long days of our bombardment. The long wreck of cars on the Augusta railroad attracted my attention. Seven locomotives and over 80 cars loaded with shot and shell were blown up on that dreadful night of the evacuation." From our own notes we make this: "We passed by a house that stood a half mile outside the rebel works, that was just literally honeycombed by bullets It had been used by both sides alternately as a skirmish post. The east and south sides of the city were in good preservation, but the north and west were all knocked to pieces, and in many places south and east of the city were houses that had been knocked to pieces by our shells, which could not have been less than four miles from our batteries. In the rebel works there were yet 11 big 64-pounder siege guns in position, ready for use. On the north side of the city we found the works much more formidable than on the east, and they certainly could never have been taken by assault. Just inside the rebel skirmish pits all the timber had been cut down and the tops turned toward our lines, all the limbs carefully trimmed and pointed sharp.

These trees lay so closely together, and the limbs stuck up so thickly that on looking at them from the outside nothing could be seen but the countless sharp stakes sticking right towards us. We don't see how men could possibly ever get through them. The name of this kind of works is abattis. Inside of this abattis were two lines of *chevaux de frise* (shevo de freeze) a curious defense which we used to call "sheep-racks." They were made by taking the trunks of small trees, and as long ones as could be got, and boring two rows of holes through them at right angles and 10 or 12 inches apart. The stakes, four to six feet long, with points sharpened, were put through the holes, half of each stake sticking out on either side; when completed they look as much like sheep racks as anything we can thing of. They were an ugly thing for a person to climb over, as they would keep rolling and keep the sharp points of the stakes sticking right up in one's face, and the more one would climb the farther one would get away. The only way we could get through them at all was to take hold of them and swing them around like a gate. We noticed many horses that were riddled with bullets that were a full mile from our skirmish pits, which showed that our army was armed with the very best shooting guns.

When we went into camp here we expected to be paid off inside of a week, and I make this extract from Dr. Cole's journal: "September 19th. Anniversary of the battle of Chicamauga, and will ever be remembered by us; it is also the anniversary of the battle of Contreras, in Mexico, in which I was a participant."

Now for some items to keep up connections. When Sherman fell back from Jonesboro to Atlanta, Hood again occupied Jonesboro, and a correspondence sprung up between the two generals about an exchange of prisoners, and about the removal of the entire civil population from Atlanta. Hood proposed an exchange of prisoners, and 2,000 were exchanged, but when it came to moving the citizens out of Atlanta, *we tell you* there was a howl from Hood, from the citizens themselves, and from the whole Southern confederacy generally. But Sherman was inexorable and told them they had to "git;" that he had captured the place by a fair fight, that he needed all the houses that were left standing for purely military purposes, that he expected to convert the whole place into a military fortress for stores, and that it would be no suitable place for women and children, and the very best thing they could do would be to go at once.

SKETCH OF MAJOR ADAM PINKERTON.

We very much desired to give a sketch of Maj. Adam Pinkerton at the time he began to discharge the duties of Major, but being in the midst of the stirring Atlanta campaign the column could not be halted. It is proper to state that he had been discharging the duties of the office for some time previous to his muster in on September 15th, 1864. From the following sketch by Capt. John Nivin, President of the First National Bank, Thorntown, Ind., who sailed with him on the high seas as a fellow officer, one can learn much of the sterling character of Maj. Pinkerton. Capt. Nivin says:

"In the month of July, 1841, I was then chief officer of the ship Ramsay, moored off the Chandpool Ghaut, in the Hooghly River, at Calcutta; and while in the harbor we learned that a junior officer belonging to our owners was detained at the port as witness in the case of a Bengali carpenter who was drowned from the ship in which he was second officer. We requested him to make his home with us until the sailing of our ship; and then for the first time I became personally acquainted with Adam Pinkerton, whose record I am about to make. He was then a fine, muscular fellow, ruddy cheeked, and seemed as if nothing terrestrial ever gave him the slightest concern. Being about the same age, and temperaments alike, during the few days he was aboard our ship he endeared himself much, not only to myself, but all the officers on board; and our Captain was extremely anxious that he should become one of the crew. We stated to him that we were on a trading voyage, and on our passage to Maalmain *via* the Mauritius, so that he could make his arrangements after the trial was over to join us. We parted; and to me it was a genuine sorrow; but sailor-like, once more sailing over the ocean, other matters occupied my attention, and our good ship anchored in the delightful haven of Port Louis, after a tempestuous passage, on the 1st of October, 1841. Our passengers, Dr. A. Judson, wife and children, disembarked, and we commenced unloading our cargo of teak timber. After unloading we took in a promiscuous cargo for Maalmain.

"On the last Sunday of October I received a little note purporting to come from the ship Barbara, a little Irish Barque lying in the harbor, just arrived from Calcutta, stating that Adam Pinkerton was on board and was some degrees from happiness. Our Captain, at my request, repaired on board to see, and learned whilst there that he was barbarously used, that he desired to leave the ship, but his commander valued him too much as a sailor to permit him either to leave or be exchanged. When the facts were communicated, I determined upon a course of action; and sent a message to Pinkerton to have his cable clear, and tunnage stowed, for it might be possible before cock-crow the next morning an angel of deliverance would come to his relief.

That night, about the witching hour, any one in that little sheet of water might have discovered a tiny craft, propelled by six stout Lascars with muffled oars; and as no noise was emitted, only the phosphorescent wake could have revealed that anything was moving on the face of the waters. In due time we dropped our boat under the bows of the Barbara, and had the satisfaction of conveying our persecuted friend to the "Ramsay;" and whilst he was stowing himself in the sail locker, I asked him why he had not communicated with us earlier. He soon set my mind at rest by telling me that his officer had used the brief authority with which he was clothed to insult him; and knowing that no arrests would be made on Sunday, and that the Captain and crew would be ashore, he made it a Sunday's exercise to give the miserable rascal a tremendous hammering, which the same he was capable of doing, being active as a cat. I don't believe Pinkerton ever knew fear. However, to proceed. Having Pinkerton stowed away, we awaited further developments. The next morning a bevy of officers, armed with a warrant, came on board of our ship. I received them very graciously and led them aft, to where he was snugly tucked under the sails, they the while expressing doubts of finding him near the officers' quarters. Suffice it to say they did not find him, and the next morning, with all sails set, we bade adieu to Port Louis; and calling the crew to the quarter deck announced to them that from that time they were to acknowledge and treat Adam Pinkerton as boatswain of the ship, and to obey him as such. As we had no longer any interest in the Barbara we thought no more of her, as her hull disappeared from our sight. With a spanking breeze we steered for our port of Maalmain. In his position as the direct medium between the quarter-deck and forecastle, Pinkerton was every inch an officer, always reliable and at his post. When we arrived at our port, my Captain, in a discussion with me as to his capabilities, came to the conclusion that he was wasting his energies in the subordinate position he held, and jointly we procured him a berth as chief officer in a ship employed as a transport during the Chinese war. We parted and did not meet again until 1846, when I found him exercising his talents as chief officer of a large ship bound for Calcutta. Again we diverged and sailed on traverse courses until 1852, when we spoke on the streets of LaFayette, Indiana, he in the role of a pedagogue in a district school; and his record, is it not faithfully held in the hearts and minds of many distinguished citizens of all the regions watered by the fierce Wild Cat and undulating Wea Creeks?

"At the commencement of the unpleasant fraternal relations between ourselves and the Southern denizens, true to his loyal instinct he left his home and family, and as a high private in the gallant Seventy-Second he went to the front. Of his conduct there I will let others speak, as I am of the genus shellback and class marine, and know little of soldiering. My next meeting with Adam Pinkerton was in Wisconsin, where, in the dual position of granger and preacher, he won much favor and affection as a citizen, foremost in aiding the weak and the struggling. Whilst in the pulpit a perfect Boanerges, yet he was gentle as a child. I never shall forget the kaleidoscopic fancies that rushed through my mind as I sat in the humble kirk in a village of Wisconsin. 'Can it be this man who is entreating these humble villagers to flee from the wrath to come is the same man whom I have seen, with persuasive eloquence aided by a stalwart arm and rugged fist, demonstrate to a wayward mariner that the way of the transgressor is hard?' Yes, he whom I had heard, with clarion voice, singing out, 'all hands save ship! Jump up!' rendered almost imperative by sundry epithets strictly nautical, minus piety—there he was; and in an humble and contrite voice he meekly addressed his congregation: 'Let us unite in prayer to the all seeing, wise God, and our blessed Father.' Had I space, and I thought it would be interesting, I could fill a big tome describing this admirable character of the sundown of the nineteenth century. But a care for other folks' feelings who are not so much interested in the man leads me to desist."

Adam Pinkerton, born in Berwickshire, Scotland, educated at the Edinburgh High School and University; designed by his parents to be a Presbyterian minister; but before finishing his regular collegiate course left home and went to sea, and for some 13 years, in various capacities, and on almost every sea, lived a sailor's life.

In 1851, being about 30 years of age, he came west, not with the intention of remaining in this country; but being taken sick in LaFayette, Indiana, he concluded to remain in America. In the fall of the same year he taught school on Wild Cat Prairie, and continued to live in that neighborhood, farming a little and teaching school, until the breaking out of the war of the rebellion. In the summer of 1861 he assisted in organizing a volunteer military company, which met in Dayton for weekly drills. A majority of that company enlisted in the fall, and became Company A, of the 40th Indiana, but owing to the severe sickness of his wife he was compelled to remain at home. For the next nine or ten months he taught the Dayton High School, and on the 15th of July, 1862, enlisted in LaFayette. Receiving from Col. Chris. Miller authority to enlist men for the Seventy-Second Indiana, in connection with Col. S. C. Kirkpatrick he raised a full company, which on the organization of the regiment became Company G. By a vote of the company he was elected Captain, and continued to serve as such until after the fall of Atlanta, when, on September 15th, 1864, "for faithful service in the field," he was promoted to Major. He resigned November 28th, 1864, on account of a serious injury in the left hip and groin, received by a fall, while in the line of duty near Hartsville, Tenn., December 7th, 1862, full particulars of which have been given, from which he had at times suffered severely. He acted as major during the Mississippi raid, and after the resignation of Maj. Carr, and in the absence of Lieut.-Col. Kirkpatrick, commanded the regiment during a part of the Atlanta campaign.

He has been thrice married, has seven living children and *two grandchildren*, has lived in Wisconsin since November, 1865, engaged in preaching, and is at present Pastor of the Arena Congregational Church.

Major Pinkerton is held in high esteem by his church and people as an exponent of the gospel, and a faithful, laborious pastor.

In a recent letter to the editor he says: "I shall never march again." We confess that, like My Uncle Toby, when Trim told him LaFever should never march again, we felt very much like insisting that he should march, while our heart swelled with emotion and tears filled our eyes.

March again in this life or not, Major Adam Pinkerton has the sort of soul that will forever "go marching on."

CHAPTER XXXI.

From July 1st to October 8th, 1864.—Hood's Attempt to Flank Sherman—Crossing the Chattahoochie on Horseback—Crossing on Pontoons—Sherman Finds Out Hood's Real Design—He is "Going For our Grub"—Fighting at Kenesaw Again—Rebels in Our Old Works and We in Their old Works—Capt. Glaze in a Tight Place—Sherman's Alarm—Alatoona Surrounded and Gen. Corse Demanded to Surrender in Five Minutes—Gen. Corse's Bold Reply—Sherman Watches from the Mountain Top the Fight Raging at Alatoona—"Hold the Fort, for I am Coming"—"Minus a Cheek Bone and an Ear, but Able to Whip all Hell Yet"—The Rebels Defeated and Beaten—Repairing the Railroad—Particulars of the Bloody Battle of Alatoona—We Stick in the Mud and the Rebels Escape—Capture the Rebel Gen. Young—Gen. Sherman Congratulates Gen. Corse and His Command.

On the 21st of September, Hood moved his army from Jonesboro over to Palmetto Station, on the Montgomery railroad, 35 miles west and south of Atlanta. This move was effected very quietly, and we think took Sherman by surprise, although it proved to be just what Sherman wanted, as he had already *thought* of marching to the sea, and Hood had now simply stepped out of his way. The fact still remained that Hood and his army had to be disposed of in some way, before Sherman could carry out any such a scheme. As no one in our division knew at the time anything of Sherman's plans, we shall speak of every transaction just as it seemed to us at the time. Hood's move was preceded by all the cavalry then with him, which on the 20th began to cross the Chattahoochie, and rumors began to come to us that they were swinging around on both our flanks and making for our hard-tack line. This news broke in on our quietude sadly, for there were as yet no signs of our being paid off, and we well knew if these rumors were true we would soon have to get out of this. We had been over 10 months without pay and were needing money badly; but such are the uncertain chances of war.

September 20th. Rained hard all day, and on the morning of the 21st the bugle blowed very early, and at roll call we got orders to move at daylight. This was a bitter pill. It was raining hard and it is always harder getting started after lying in camp a short time than when we move every day. We got off tolerably early, but moved slowly, taking the road to Atlanta, and after getting there the column moved in such a way as to give the men a chance to see the fortifications and siege guns. We went into camp just outside the rebel works. It rained hard all day and all night, and we had a miserable night of it.

September 22d. It rained the whole day; we moved slowly and steadily till we got to Sand Town, where we bivouacked. This town is rather an oddity in its way, having neither streets nor stores. There were some good houses in it, but they were scattered about at random, and what the people ever did for a living we never could tell, as there were no evidences of business of any kind in the place. The country around it seemed to be a wilderness, sandy and poor.

September 23d. We crossed the river and went down 10 miles on a reconnoissance. The rain drenched us in showers most of the day. We found the rebel infantry had already begun to cross the river, and that three brigades of mounted troops were already across and had gone north toward Marietta. We came back and went into camp opposite Sand Town. On the 24th we started after the mounted force that had gone for our railroad; we took the road toward Dallas, made 22 miles and camped near Powder Springs; still raining. Here we learned from the citizens that the rebels passed here yesterday and that they had got on to our railroad and played smash generally.

September 25th. We moved early, passing through Powder Springs. We saw some mounted rebels off to our left, apparently watching us: we turned north and passed over Lost Mountain and Pine Mountain, places of much interest the middle of last June, and had some splendid views of the battle-fields west of Kenesaw. We got to Ackworth just at night and bivouacked, having made 30 miles for the day, and for a wonder it did not rain. We found the rebels had struck the railroad at this place the evening before, just as there were five trains going down to Atlanta, and succeeded in capturing the hindmost one, 60 prisoners, and five of the guard who were on guard duty at the station. They then tore up three or four hundred yards of the track, burned the train, and "lit out," going in the direction of Dallas. This was about all the damage they did. On the next day the damage was all repaired and trains running as usual.

On the 26th our regiment lay in camp while some of the other regiments went on a scout toward Dallas, but found no rebels.

September 27th. We moved north-east toward Canton and crossed Noonday Creek at the point where Sergt. Magee and his squad were bushwhacked on the 9th of June, and private W. H. Clark, Company I, was captured. The skeleton of Clark's horse was still lying there. Thus in our rambling around over the country we pass over sections often enough to get thoroughly acquainted. From this place we kept on north-east across Little River and bivouacked near Hickory Flats, making 25 miles for the day. This was 10 miles north-east of where any Yankees had ever been. We found the country rich and forage abundant. Citizens report a brigade at Hickory Flats, and during the night our pickets were bushwhacked, but the whackers got the worst of it as we certainly killed one man, because we saw him afterwards, and think we killed or crippled others. Company I was on picke .

September 28th. We turned our heads south-east toward Roswell, passing north of Sweat's Mountain; we found the woods full of bushwhackers and guerrillas, and our scouts had some lively chases after them during the day, but the woods were so thick that they did not succeed in catching any of them. At one time during the day we began to think we were going to get into a fight as there were rebels firing on us from every side. Since the Atlanta campaign a part of Minty's brigade had been stationed at Roswell as garrison, and yesterday afternoon a party of rebs charged in on them and drove them clear out of town; but soon put off north-west, and we suppose it was these same fellows that had been bothering us. It rained on us this afternoon, and when we got to Roswell we found the Chattahoochie River swollen, but we put into it. The water ran so very swiftly and the bottom was so slick and full of holes that our horses could scarcely keep their feet. Several men in the brigade came near being lost, but we shall give but the experience of one man in our own company, as illustrating the peril of all. When about half way across a horse belonging to a man in Company I stepped into a hole and fell; his rider went under and the horse went rolling over and over like a log, the water running so swiftly that he could not get on to his feet; but after rolling down for 15 or 20 rods he managed to strike some obstruction and regained his standing, and was so frightened that it would have made you laugh to see him take a step at a time and then study a while before taking the next one. He finally got out. The man was being washed down just as rapidly, and certainly must have been lost had he not managed to catch another horse by the tail, and was dragged to shore. This was the third time we had crossed this river at this place, but we thought this time was about the most ticklish business we ever did. We went into camp just as soon as we got across, as wet as rats, and had neither forage nor rations. A miserable night for man and beast.

September 29th. Were up early, and as we had no feeding to do or breakfast to get we soon got off, moving straight for our old camp near Crosskeys, a distance of nine miles, arriving at 9 o'clock; and when we got to camp Col. Miller told us now we *would* get to rest and be paid off. So we set to work getting our breakfast and putting up our dog-tents; but had not got our tents up till there came an order to be ready to move to-morrow morning at 6 o'clock. After a nine days' march and traveling 150 miles, nearly the whole of it in the rain, we are not to have a single day's rest. Such is war. The rumor now is that Hood, with his whole army, has crossed the river below Sand Town and is now going for the railroad with all speed. If this is so we will not get to rest for a month.

The last day of September and the 1st of October we were still in camp, but all the time in a most aggravating state of suspense. Every morning snd every night, and several times through the day, we would get orders to be ready to move in a few minutes. It seemed to us that Hood's movements were bothering Sherman; for being conducted very quietly it was very difficult for him to find out what Hood really intended to do. He first supposed that Hood only intended to move his army over on the Montgomery Railroad in order to get his supplies from the south-west; but he soon found Hood was not stopping at the railroad but pushed on square across it and immediately began to cross the Chattahoochie below Campbellton. Sherman says: (vol. 2, p. 144.) "There was great difficulty in obtaining correct information about Hood's movements from Palmetto Station. I could not get spies to penetrate his camps; but on the 1st of October I was satisfied that the bulk of his infantry was at and across the Chattahoochie River, near Campbellton, and that his cavalry was on the west side of Powder Springs." Had he believed *us* he might have known this a week sooner. Sherman now begins to send back troops to be distributed along the railroad at the most vital points; one division to Rome, and another to Chattanooga. On the 29th he sent Gen. Thomas back to Chattanooga, supposing that if Hood attempted to get on to the railroad at all it would be somewhere away up there; but we shall see. It continued to rain right straight along on the 29th, 30th, 1st and 2d, and it seemed impossible for an army to move at all while it was so wet and muddy. Especially on the night of the 30th was there a terrible rain storm, flooding the tents till the men had to abandon them.

On the morning of October 2d, 1864, our whole division, trains and all, pulled out from Crosskeys, and we have it in our journal: "We do hope we will never come back to this place again;" and we never did. We took the road toward Atlanta after crossing the Peach-tree and our old camp there, turned to the right and passed over most of the battle-field of July 20th, and kept on south-west for three or four miles, as if we were going to Sand Town. We think we got different orders, as we turned north toward the railroad bridge across the Chattahoochie, and when we got there found the river at its highest and the bridge washed away. We then turned up the river, crossed the creek again, and when we got to the main road leading from Atlanta to Marietta found it full of troops and trains, and it was with difficulty we made our way past them. When we got to the river we found the hills for miles around were covered with trains. There was a single pontoon bridge across the river, and it required all the skill at the command of the pontoon brigade to keep it in its place. We never saw anything more fearful than crossing this bridge; the water was so high and ran so swiftly, and it was so full of drift-wood. Whenever there would come down a big log on to the bridge it would go right through it, knocking boats stringers and boards into the water for a rod or more, and they would be gone in a minute. No matter if horses, mules, or men happened to be on it, they went into the water, and the chances were ten to one against their getting out. We went into camp near one of the large rebel forts that was built here to keep our men from crossing the river. We moved 22 miles to-day and are now only 10 miles from Crosskeys.

October 3d. This morning early our division secured the right of way across the bridge, but it was 10 o'clock before we all got over. As soon as we had all crossed we moved south-west toward Sand Town for six miles, and then turned north west toward Powder Springs. We found that the 3d cavalry division, Kilpatrick's, had been skirmishing all day yesterday with the rebels, and had been driven back, and this morning we could hear an occasional cannon-shot, which told us they were still at it. Gen. Elliott is chief of cavalry for this army, but has never taken the field in person till to-day, when he came up to us; his staff are all with him, which makes us think there is considerable importance attached to this move. Minty's brigade was ahead of us to-day, and about the middle of the afternoon ran on to the rebels. Kilpatrick was still to our left and front skirmishing with the rebels, and Minty kept crowding them to the west. We moved on straight north-west till within four miles of Powder Springs, where we bivouacked on the same ground occupied by us on the night of the 24th of September. Gen. Elliott is still with us, and we have just heard a good joke on him. We have before spoken of the fact that we had never seen him before, and that he had never taken the field in person to command a single expedition, and to us he always seemed a kind of figure head on Gen. Sherman's staff. The weather always seemed to have a great effect on Gen. Sherman, and just at this time he seemed out of humor and out of patience with everybody, and this morning he pitched into Elliott about this way: "Elliott, why in the h—l don't you do something? D—n it, get out and do something. If you can't do nothing else, get out and hunt up an old wagon that is stuck in the mud; get *that* and bring *it* in." We know this story to be true. This, of course, made Elliott mad, and for the balance of the campaign he stuck right to us.

Just before we went into camp this evening Gen. Elliott sent back a dispatch to Gen. Sherman, by one of his Lieutenants and two orderlies, and they had not got out of gun shot from our regiment till they were bushwhacked and the Lieutenant killed and one of the orderlies wounded. Both the orderlies succeeded in getting back to our column. We only moved 18 miles for the day; the main column of rebels is at Dallas, 15 miles north-west of us. It rained again in the afternoon and the night was wet.

October 4th. This morning we were up early, and moved north-east to Marietta, passing over the ground occupied by the rebels during the siege of Kenesaw, and when we got due south of Marietta, and at least two miles in the rear of the rebel works, we saw a solid shot sticking in a tree, about thirty feet from the ground, that had been fired by one of our Parrott guns, at least three miles away to the west. These shots were 10 inches long and three inches in diameter, and this one had passed clear through a tree two feet in diameter, and full eight inches of it was sticking out on the other side. It looked just like a dead limb sticking out of the tree, and was remarked by the whole regiment. When we got to Marietta we found there had been a tremendous scare the evening before among the citizens and what few troops there were stationed there, as it was reported that two corps of rebels were moving on that place. This was about the first intimation Sherman seemed to have of Hood's *real* intentions, as on the 1st of October he telegraphed to Gen. Grant: "Hood is evidently across the Chattahoochee below Sweetwater. If he attempts to get on our road this side the Etowa I will attack him; but if he goes to the Selma and Talladega road, why will it not do to leave Tennessee to the forces with Thomas, and for me to destroy Atlanta and march across Georgia to Savannah or Charleston?" We see from this that Sherman just now very much wants Hood out of his way, that he may march to the sea, and this wish was perhaps father to the thought that Hood would move over on to the Talladega railroad. This morning our signal station from the top of Kenesaw reported the whole country west of Kenesaw and toward Dallas full of rebels moving north toward our railroad, and on the 3d Sherman writes: "My first impressions were that Hood would go for the Talladega railroad, but the indications now are that he will strike our road near us, viz: about Kingston or Marietta. Orders were at once given for the 20th corps, Gen. Slocum commanding, to hold Atlanta and the bridges of the Chattahoochee, and the other corps, 4th, 14th, 15th, 17th and 23d, were put in motion for Marietta. The army had undergone many changes since the capture of Atlanta. Gen. Schofield had gone to Knoxville, from the 23d corps. Gen. Thomas had gone to Chattanooga, and taken one division from the 4th corps, and one from the 14th. Gen. Dodge, of the 16th corps, had been wounded, and his corps been divided up and put into the 15th and 17th corps, and these corps had been reduced very much in strength by detachments and discharges; so that for the purpose of fighting Hood I had only about 60,000 infantry and artillery and two small divisions (Kilpatrick's and Garrard's) of cavalry. * * * I had little fear of the enemy's cavalry damaging our roads seriously, for they rarely made a break that we could not repair in a few days But it was absolutely necessary to keep Hood's infantry off our main route of communication and supplies."

But here were the rebels already in a manner on the railroad, and Sherman and his army stuck in the mud on the banks of the Chattahoochee. We shall now quote from Miller's notes, for three days in succession, to show the real situation and the real feeling of our whole brigade on this move:

"October 3d. Moved to near Powder Springs. The enemy are moving for the railroad in force. At least two corps are over the Chattahoochee and camped at Lost Mountain last night. They are going for us, certain. Our hard-tack will be cut off for a fact. October 4th—Marched to Kenesaw Mountain. The enemy are in force on the railroad at Big Shanty. Took prisoners from both Lee's and Stewart's corps to-day. They are going for our grub. October 5th—Moved out near Lost Mountain. We had some skirmishing with the enemy, who occupy a line from Powder Springs to Allatoona Mountain. The scene looks dark."

When we got to Marietta this morning, our brigade took the road running west to Dallas, passing over the south end of Kenesaw Mountain. By the time we got on to the ridge we heard cannonading at the north end of Kenesaw, where the railroad passes between

Kenesaw and Bald Ridge, or Bald Knob. Our regiment was in advance, and just as we had passed the line of works occupied by the 10th Indiana, on the 23d of June last, the firing up north was resumed, and Gen. Elliott, who was still with us, called a halt, and a council with Miller and Garrard was held, and it was determined to send scouting parties up in that direction to see what was the matter. Accordingly, A, F, and D, of our regiment, were sent on different roads, and we awaited the result. In about an hour they sent back word that, sure enough, the rebels were in heavy force all along our railroad between Kenesaw and Big Shanty, and some of the garrison from Marietta had taken possession of the old rebel works on the north end of Kenesaw and were shelling the rebels who were occupying our old works in front of Kenesaw. Was there ever such a change as this? You have heard of the great general who marched his men up the hill and then marched them down again, but in this case we had driven the rebels down the hill and were now trying to drive them up. As soon as Gen. Elliott found the real state of affairs, he ordered our division up on the west of Kenesaw, to connect with the infantry on the north, and to stretch out west toward Lost Mountain. In doing this we occupied the old line of rebel works, occupied by them on the 9th of June. While this was being done, Companies I and C, of our regiment, were ordered on a reconnoissance further to the west toward Lost Mountain. We had not gone a mile till we ran on to a strong force of rebels. Capt. Glaze, Company C, being the ranking officer present, was riding at the head of Company I, and we here insert an incident just as he has furnished it:

He says: "I think the greatest danger I was ever in, and the only time I was really afraid, was when I was ordered to take my company and Company I and follow a slough to which I was directed, and find a place where the division could cross. (This was the head waters of Olley's Creek, and very swampy.) As soon as the slough was reached I joined the advance guard, and as we rode along the bank would direct the men to ride in, now and then, to test the bottom. We had been engaged this way for half an hour, and were so occupied in the work in hand that the fact of our being alone and in the vicinity of the enemy entirely escaped our minds. I was sitting on my horse, so near a large tree that my knee touched it, when I was brought to a sense of my danger by a sharp report and the spat of a bullet into the tree along side of my head. On turning to the left I saw a long row of heads over a line of our old works, not 10 rods away. I turned to go, and as I did so I leaned over to the side of my horse as much as I could. My efforts to get away were seconded by another shot which fortunately missed. In leaning over, my gold braid band slid off my hat. It had been sent to me by my wife and I was determined to have it. I slipped off my horse and stooped to pick it up, when a third shot whisked through the grass under my hand, and that's the last I ever saw of the hat-band. I was soon down the bank and running for life. I was badly scared and mad besides. In a few minutes our companies were making it lively for that row of heads. We had all dismounted and were occupying an old line of rebel works about 200 yards away, and in a few minutes not a head was to be seen, and for some time all was quiet on their side. We interpreted this as a show of weakness on their part in order to get us to charge them, and some of our boys were really in favor of doing it; but we were too old to be caught that way. We were close enough to hear them talk; besides, at the first onset we had seen a great many more of them than there were of us. So a couple of our boys crawled up to a strip of woods to our left and got into a position to see behind the works occupied by the rebels, and on returning reported the rebels still there as thick as thieves, and we made up our minds just to stay right there with them. Just then the General sent his orderly to tell us not to fight, as they were not prepared for an engagement. In a few minutes we were ordered to draw off, and we mounted and went on a scout to the south-west, and found the rebels on all the roads in that direction. Late in the evening we returned and found the division going into camp not far from where we had left it. So this movement of Hood has demonstrated the fact that the lesson in flank movements which Sherman has been teaching him has been well learned, and also that what is sauce for the goose may possibly be eaten by the gander. This movement "bangs" anything we ever heard of, as our army now occupies almost the exact position the rebels did three months ago, and they exactly occupy ours; and they are making just as thorough work destroying our railroad as we ever did in destroying theirs. Our hard-tack line is broken, for a fact, and we may have to go hungry; but there is one consolation about the matter which is being thoroughly discussed by our men, and that is, Hood has now *no base* of supplies *at all* for *his* army, and he cannot possibly haul more than six days' supplies with him, and we have come to the conclusion that we can stand it about as well as he can.

October 5th. Early this morning Gen. Sherman sent to our brigade for a regiment to report to him. Capt. Thomson, Company D, being the ranking officer of the Seventy-Second present for duty, reported. When Capt. Thomson reported, and after making himself known, the General said to him: "Take your regiment and go out there and see what the rebels are doing, and be gone all day. Find out all you can and come back to-morrow morning. May-be I'll want you and your regiment to-morrow." This was rather curious, and the orders rather indefinite, and left the Captain in rather a doubtful state of mind. He wanted very much for Mr. Sherman to be a little more explicit and was too bashful to say so. But he came back and immediately we moved west from camp four or five miles and found the rebels in strong force, dismounted, threw up a line of works and lay in line of battle all day, with heavy picket firing and skirmishing at times. This was close to Lost Mountain. During the greater part of the day we could hear heavy artillery firing away to the north of us, and we supposed that our infantry had followed up the railroad from Marietta and overtaken the rebels, and that a battle ensued.

We have left Sherman and his Army stuck in the mud on the banks of the Chattahoochie, and have now arrived at a point where the excitement and interest of every soldier in both armies were at their highest pitch, and we are satisfied that everybody will be pleased to have the situation made plain. We have already intimated that Hood's move had taken Sherman by surprise. That is, Sherman expected Hood to move his army over on to the Talladega railroad, or if he attempted to get on to our railroad at all it would be away up about Resaca, Dalton or Tunnel Hill. As evidence of this we have seen that Sherman had sent Thomas and two or three divisions back to Rome and Chattanooga. As a further evidence of the surprise we point to the fact that Sherman could have very easily prevented Hood's getting on to the railroad at all if he had suspected he was going to make the attempt. In moving his army from Jonesboro to Big Shanty Hood had to move in a circle of 100 miles, and it took him two weeks to do it; whereas, from Atlanta, where Sherman laid, to Big Shanty, was not more than twenty-five miles, and Sherman could have made the distance in two days' easy marching. But Hood got clear past Atlanta and as near to Big Shanty as Sherman was before Sherman began to move at all, and then it began to rain so intolerably that he could scarcely move his artillery and trains at all, and as Hood had but few trains to bother him of course he beat Sherman in the race more than half way, and we certainly think Sherman never realized his danger till the morning of the 4th, when the signal officer on the top of Kenesaw signaled to Sherman, then at Vining's Station, that north of the Chattahoochie the whole country west of Kenesaw was full of rebels, and that they were moving rapidly north and would be on the railroad in a few hours. We imagine we can hear Sherman exclaim, "Good heavens, and so close as that!" He mounts his horse and immediately starts for Kenesaw, but we will let him tell it: "We crossed the Chattahoochee during the 3d and 4th of October, rendezvoused at the old battle-field of Smyrnia camp. The telegraph wires had been cut above Marietta, and learning that heavy masses of infantry, artillery and cavalry, had been seen from Kenesaw (marching north) I inferred that Allatoona was their objective point, and on the 4th of October I signaled from Vining's Station to Kenesaw and from Kenesaw to Allatoona, over the heads of the enemy, a message for Gen. Corse at Rome, to hurry back to the assistance of the garrison at Allatoona. Allatoona was held by a small brigade commanded by Lieut. Col. Tourtellotte. He had two small redoubts on either side of the railroad, overlooking the village of Allatoona and the warehouses in which were stored over a million rations of bread." Here was Hood in a manner already on the railroad at Big Shanty and Sherman two days' march behind him—present roads considered—and he well knew he could never catch him, and he also knew that for anything he or his army could do the vast store-houses of rations at Allatoona would be gobbled by the enemy. And he further knew that just at this time Hood's army was sadly needing those very rations, and would surely make a most desperate effort to get them; and unless the garrison at Allatoona was speedily reinforced from the north all was hopelessly lost, as nothing in the world could hinder Hood from tearing the railroad up clear to the Etowa and burning the high tower bridge, and Sherman would of course be compelled to begin a disastrous retreat.

The interest of the whole army now centers in Allatoona, and the night of the 4th was one of dreadful suspense to the garrison at that place, as well as to Sherman himself. The garrison consisted of 890 men, all told, and from their elevated position they could see the railroad clear to Kenesaw, and as the rebels advanced, burning the railroad, it looked to them like a huge serpent of fire gradually crawling up to swallow them, and they knew unless they were reinforced they would be swallowed at a gulp. They had got Gen. Sherman's order to send for Gen. Corse all right, and had sent the dispatch to Rome by telegraph. But could Corse get there in time to do any good? He was 35 miles away, and unless he could get cars, and everything should favor him, they felt that their case was hopeless. What terrible suspense! We can think of no suspense so fearful as the certainty of meeting death just a little way ahead, and yet not to know just how soon. The huge serpent of fire still crawls nearer and nearer. This night to them was one of the longest of their lives, and to many—yes, to very many of them —it was the last. Gallant Corse has got the word, and is doing all that mortal can do to get to their relief. He sends immediately to Kingston, 18 miles distant, for cars, and a train of 30 is started for Rome. One-third of them get off the track and cause delay, and only 20 of them finally reach Rome, arriving at 7 o'clock P. M. In one hour he has 1,000 men on board, and starts for Allatoona. The track is in a wretched condition, and it is 1 o'clock A. M. of the 5th before these few men arrive. By this time the serpent has reached the place, and is opening wide his jaws to swallow them. Favored by the darkness, the serpent gradually crawls around on either side, and by daylight has this devoted little band entirely within its folds, and demands its surrender in these words:

"AROUND ALLATOONA, October 5th, 1864.

"Commanding Officer United States Forces, Allatoona:

"I have placed the forces under my command in such position that you are surrounded, and to avoid a needless effusion of blood, I call on you to surrender your forces at once, and unconditionally. Five minutes will be allowed you to decide. Should you accede to this you will be treated in the most honorable manner as prisoners of war. I have the honor to be, very respectfully, yours,

S. G. FRENCH,

Major General Commanding Forces Confederate States.

General Corse answered immediately:

HEADQUARTERS 4TH DIVISION 15TH ARMY CORPS,
Allatoona, Georgia, 8:30 a.m., October 5th, 1864.

Major General S. G. French, Confederate States, etc.:

Your communication demanding surrender of my command I acknowledge receipt of, and respectfully reply that we are prepared for the "needless effusion of blood" whenever it is agreeable to you.

I am, very respectfully, your obedient servant,

JOHN M. CORSE,

Brigadier General Commanding forces United States.

Of course the attack immediately began.

We now go back to Sherman and his army at Vining's Station. The night of the 4th was a sleepless one for Sherman, and at first peep of dawn he starts his army for Marietta, mounts his horse and as soon as possible rides to Kenesaw. We suppose he got there about the time we did. He immediately goes to the top of Kenesaw and inquires of his signal officer, "What from Allatoona?" The officer shakes his head and says, "Nothing." The morning is bright and beautiful, and with his glass he can see the whole country for 50 miles to the south; and the whole range of the Allatoona mountains from Dallas clear up to Allatoona, and the intervening space seems immediately under his feet, although 18 miles wide. The panorama is one of grandeur rarely excelled in the world, but to Sherman's practiced eye the scene is not one of brightest prospect. He realizes that this is a critical moment, and that at this stage of the game of war the chances are against him. The heavy smoke of camp-fires off to the south-west, just in front of our position and toward Dallas, tells him the bulk of Hood's army is there, while the line of fire up to the north-west tells him his railroad is entirely destroyed. But see! the smoke that is so rapidly curling up about Allatoona is not that of camp-fires, nor yet of the burning railroad. And hark! The heavy reverberations of musketry and artillery as they come rolling over the plain, also tell him that a fearful battle is raging there. As yet he knew not that Corse had got his orders to come to the relief of Allatoona; but he well knew that if Corse *had not* come, from what he could hear and see, the garrison there could not possibly hold out till relieved by forces from his army, then toiling along through the mud and swamps below Marietta, in the head-waters of Soaps creek and Rottenwood.

Again he inquires of the signal officer, who is still peering with his glass in the direction of Allatoona, "Is there any word from Allatoona?" The officer answers, "There is nothing." Then what can be done to make up for this terrible loss—loss that may never be repaired? Sherman sees that his only chance of taking any advantage of this desperate state of affairs is to push a strong head of column in between Hood's main army at Dallas and the force on his railroad, and capture the assaulting column at Allatoona before a junction could be made with Hood; hence he immediately ordered the 23d corps to move due west from Marietta on the Burnt Hickory road, and to burn houses or piles of brush, or anything that would make a smoke, as it progressed, to indicate to him the position of the head of the column, and our regiment was sent out as an advance guard to feel the way, while our brigade followed as a support, while the balance of the army was ordered to march straight on Allatoona. On moving out, as we have before said, for four or five miles we found the rebels had anticipated just such a move as this, and had purposely put a whole division of infantry on the Burnt Hickory road to prevent it. Of course we could not attack this division without bringing on a fight, and we thought it not best to do that with the 23d corps still 10 miles away; we accordingly lay in line of battle all day, only skirmishing. Sherman now divides his time between watching the progress of the battle and the smoke made by head of column of the 23d corps. He says: "I watched, with painful suspense, the indications of the battle raging there, and was dreadfully impatient at the slow progress of the relieving column, whose advance was marked by the smokes which were made according to order." The smoke of the burning railroad and of the battle raging at Allatoona so obscured the vision that Sherman's signal officer for many hours fails to catch a sight of the flag at that place. The general's patience is exhausted and his anxiety at its highest pitch, when a gentle breeze from the south-west sweeps over the plain and bends the smoke out of the way, and the officer once more catches a glimpse of the tell-tale flag, and slowly begins to read:

"C. R. S. E. H. E. R.—CORSE IS HERE—WHERE IN THE HELL IS SHERMAN?"

A loud, long cheer, goes up from the group of officers gathered around the signal station, and Sherman immediately sends back word:

"HOLD ON, I'M COMING!" and again the smoke curls up and stops all communication. From these memorable words has been written he popular song, "Hold the Fort, for I am Coming." This is the first intimation Sherman has had that Allatoona is adequately garrisoned, and he now bends all his energies toward capturing the assaulting column, and urges the 23d corps forward with all speed. Yet it seemed to him a snail might move as fast; indeed, it only made 12 miles that day and went into camp when it reached the rear of our brigade, and was still four miles from the road leading from Allatoona to Dallas. Sherman is still on top of Kenesaw, and still keeps his glass turned in the direction of Allatoona, and by 3 o'clock he observes that the smoke of battle is growing less, and he knows that one side or the other is almost exhausted; which side he does not know, and his anxiety again increases. About 4 p. m. the smoke begins to lift, and Sherman and his officers once more eagerly gather around the signal officer and wait in breathless silence as he slowly catches a glimpse of the flag once more and reads this characteristic dispatch from Gen. Corse: "*Minus a cheek bone and an ear, but able to whip all hell yet.*"

Another prolonged and deafening cheer is given, and Sherman turns the army he had sent up the railroad to the south-west, towards Dallas, still in hopes of cutting off the rebels that had made such dreadful havoc with his railroad, and had well nigh made the glory of the great Atlanta campaign a hiss and a by-word. We think he might have succeeded in capturing these, but at 2 o'clock on the morning of the 6th it began to rain, and rained as it only does rain in the South, one sheet of water after another, till 2 o'clock in the afternoon, when the face of the country was one vast flood of water and the whole army swamped in the mud.

October 6th, 1864. Our rations and forage are out and our train still away back near the Chattahoochee, and we know it will be utterly impossible for them to get here through the mud; we also know it will be quite as impossible for the army to move, as the artillery would be all swamped the first 100 yards after starting. So early this morning our division was ordered to send the pack mules back to Marietta, eight miles, for rations, and Capt. Thomson again reported to Gen. Sherman with the Seventy-Second, who ordered us to go over on to the railroad and follow it up as far as the rebels had gone and see how much damage they had done. We moved north-east from our camp six miles and struck the railroad at a point just where the rebels had, half-way between Kenesaw and Big Shanty and three miles below that place. Here the rebels had captured a train loaded with hardtack and coffee, and we suppose for once in their lives they had a good square meal. There were bushels of coffee scattered over the ground in every direction. The train consisted of 12 or 15 cars, which they had burned, together with the rations they could not carry with them. Here we found 500 hands already on the road fixing it up. We moved on up the road to Ackworth, eight miles above Big Shanty, and found the rebels had done a splendid job, burning nearly every tie and bending and twisting all the rails. When we got to Ackworth we saw where the rebels had burned three or four of our cars that were full of beef cattle; they had set fire to the cars without killing the cattle and burned them alive. An eye witness to this horrible deed says that the terrible writhing, bellowing and contortions of the cattle was the most distressing sight he ever saw. We also learned the full particulars of the terrible battle that was fought yesterday, and as it was one of such vast importance to Sherman's army and the country, and was one of the most bloody of the war; and as Gen. Sherman made it the subject of a general order, which was read to every company in the whole army, we shall make a brief review.

Allatoona is a small village at a pass in the mountains through which the railroad runs, and is six or seven miles south of the Etowa, or Hightower bridge. It was defended by 1,890 men all told. It was attacked at daylight by a full division of rebels 5,000 strong, under command of Gen. French. The battle lasted till 4 p. m., and was never excelled by earnestness and perseverence of attack nor by dogged stubborness of resistance, and finally resulted in the most signal and disastrous repulse of the rebels with a loss of 2,000 men, or two-fifths of the attacking division. While the Union loss was, killed, wounded and missing 707, which is also nearly two-fifths of the whole number of Union soldiers engaged. Our men also captured 411 prisoners, three regimental colors and 800 muskets.

We found that the rebels immediately after abandoning the attack began to retreat towards Dallas. They had struck our railroad a heavy blow, burning every tie and bending the rails for eight miles. So that the estimate for repairs called for 35,000 new ties and six miles of iron; 10,000 men were distributed along the break to replace the ties and to repair the road bed, while the regular repair party under Col. W. W. Wright, came down from Chattanooga with iron, spikes etc. Within seven days the whole break was repaired and the road all right again. It was by such acts of extraordinary energy as these that the rebels were discouraged. They felt it was a waste of time and labor for them to march hurriedly on wide circuits day and night to burn a bridge or tear up a mile or so of track when they knew we could replace them so quickly. They supposed we always kept on hand distributed along the road duplicates of every bridge and culvert of any importance, and we have a good story illustrating this. During our advance on Kenesaw, before the middle of June, a group of rebels, one hot day, were laying in the shade on top of Kenesaw, overlooking our camps at Big Shanty. One soldier remarked to his fellows: "Well, the Yanks will have to get up and get now, for I heard Gen. Johnston himself say that Gen. Wheeler had blown up the tunnel near Dalton, and that the Yanks would have to retreat because they could get no more rations." "Oh, hell!" said a listener, "Don't you know that Gen. Sherman carries a duplicate tunnel along?" And while we are at it we will relate another, as related by Gen. Johnston himself. He says: "that our feats at bridge building and repairs of roads had excited his profoundest admiration. Along in June while we were on Kenesaw, an officer of Wheeler's cavalry had reported to me in person, that he had come from Gen. Wheeler who had made a bad break in Sherman's road, about Tilton Station, which he said would take at least a fortnight to repair; and while we were talking, a train was seen coming down the road which had passed that very break, and had reached us at Big Shanty, as soon as the fleet horseman had reached me at Kenesaw."

After learning all we could about Ackworth, Allatoona, etc., we turned about and went back to Big Shanty and started southwest to go to our camp, near Lost Mountain. As before stated, it had rained until 2 o'clock in the afternoon, and it was night when we left Big Shanty. Our road led us through the head waters and swamps of the Noonday Creek. The night was dark and there was water most of the way, in many places belly deep to our horses, and we had a miserable time getting back to camp. It was 10 o'clock before we got in. We found our pack mules had got back from Marietta with three days' rations and forage, and we did our best to put one-third of them where the rain would not spoil them. We traveled 28 miles that day, and found that the whole army had got into position in line of battle west of our camp, and still three miles east of the Allatoona road, and was so completely mud-bound that it could do nothing but stand there and see the best troops of Hood's army march unmolested in front of them, without even being able to give them a passing salute. We had heard a wonderful sight all along, during the war, about bagging rebels, and yesterday we were really in hopes that we surely would catch the two divisions that had been on our railroad, but now our hopes are vanishing.

October 7th. We were up early, and shortly after 6 o'clock we moved out. The 4th, 14th, 15th, and 17th corps moved southwest toward Dallas, but our brigade moved west, went about four miles and struck the Dallas and Allatoona road running south. Here we found a division of the 23d corps, which we have already stated moved west from Kenesaw on the 5th and struck this road last night soon after the rebels had passed south from Allatoona, and that's the way we bagged the rebels this time. Our division here turned south, and went about four miles toward Dallas, when we ran into the Company of the rear guard of the retreating rebels. A fight ensued in which we captured Brigadier General Young, a Lieutenant-Colonel, an ambulance and four privates. This rebel general had been wounded at Allatoona. He formerly belonged to the United States service, and was a quartermaster of the 4th regulars belonging to Minty's brigade of our division, and was at once recognized by them. He had deserted the service of the government, cast his lot with the rebels, and deserved a rebel fate. Gen. Sherman, in his "Memoirs," page 150, Vol. II, gives the credit of capturing this famous general to the forces at Allatoona, but we all know he is mistaken, because we were right here to-day and saw it done two days after that battle. In this fight our brigade drove the rebels fully two miles, which brought us to New Hope church. This church is the place where there was such desperate fighting from the 25th to the 30th of May last, and our infantry always called it "Hell Hole," on account of the terrible fighting here. We have never seen any place where the trees are so shot to pieces with bullets as here. Our division went into camp a half mile back, and Company I was left on picket.

We had our headquarters by the church, and slept in the house at night, putting out our videttes toward Dallas. Here the rebel works and our own are not more than 50 yards apart, and the church stands right between them. We do not now remember of ever seeing any place where the two opposing lines of works were so close together as these. They are so close together that neither side could, or did, use artillerv, but the trees are just literally shot to pieces with bullets.

October 8th. Our division lay in camp to-day. Sherman has abandoned the pursuit of Hood in this direction. The 98th Illinois, of our brigade, went on a scout to learn the whereabouts of the rebels. They went out past us at the church and about a mile this side of Dallas came up to the rebel videttes and charged them pell-mell right through headquarters of the pickets, but owing to an unfortunate blunder only captured four of them. They then went on through Dallas and ascertained that the two brigades which composed Hood's rear guard camped last night on Pumpkinvine, four miles west of Dallas, at the place where we camped on the night of the 24th of May last. They also learned that Hood was shoving for Rome as fast as possible, nearly to days' march ahead of Sherman. We have no means of knowing how many troops there are at Rome, but if Hood should capture that place the whole valley of Oostenaula would be open before him and nothing in the world to hinder him from getting on to the railroad again, and burning it from Resaca up to Tunnel Hill. Early this morning we went on a reconnoitering scout down the Sand Town road. Hood's army came up to this place on this road and we wanted to see if any luckless wagon or ambulance was left sticking in the mud. We found that Hood had but few trains with him, but what few he had must have had a terrible time getting through the mud as the deep ruts all over the country plainly indicated. The whole train had been parked in a field just south-east of the church, and we could come very near telling how many trains he had. We think his artillery and ambulances amounted to half of the whole. Late in the evening the 98th came back and reported Hood's rations entirely exhausted and the men living on cane stalks. We don't know how true this is, but we do know that every road they have traveled upon, we have found strewn full of the "cuds" of chewed cane stalks. When we were relieved and went back to camp we had this congratulatory order read to us:

"The General commanding avails himself of the opportunity, in the handsome defense of Allatoona, to illustrate the most important principle in war, that fortified posts should be defended to the last regardless of the relative numbers of the attacking and attacked.

The thanks of this army are due and are hereby accorded to Gen. Corse, Col. Tourtellotte, Col. Rowette, officers and men for their determined and gallant defense of Allatoona, and it is made an example to illustrate the importance of preparing in time, and meeting the danger when present, boldly, manfully and well.

Commanders and garrisons of the posts along our railroad are hereby instructed that they must hold their posts to the last minute, sure that the time gained is valuable and necessary to their comrades at the front.

By order of MAJ.-GEN. W. T. SHERMAN.

L. M. DAYTON, Aide de-camp.

And thus this terrible battle and heroic defense, and splendid victory passed into history. It quit raining on the 6th and the last two nights have been very cold, the wind coming down off the Allatoona Mountains cold enough to freeze.

CHAPTER XXXII.

From October 9th to October 27th, 1864.—Hood Across the Allatoona Mountains—Rebels Making Shoes of Beef Hides and Eating Corn Stalks—We Follow the Rebels—Marching to Rome—Expecting Hood to Attack the Place—Sherman Puzzled About the "Whole Batch of Devils Turned Loose Without Home"—Telegraphs to Grant and Gen. Thomas—Rebels Attack us near Rome—The Lightning Brigade's Bold and Successful Charge and Chase of the Rebels—Charging Through the Forest—Shell Dodging Drill, "Down" 'Up and Forward'—A Splendid Charge, Capturing a Battery—Pretty Fighting—Compliments from Gen. Cox to the Seventy-Second Regiment—Casualties of the Battle—Sherman Gives the Credit to Gen. Corse, when it Justly Belongs to Gen. Garrard and Col. Miller—Gathering the Old Englishman's Onions and Potatoes—Carrying Bee Hives from under the General's Nose—We Start Back Towards Rome—Skirmishing with and Driving the Rebels—Battle of Blue Pond Gen. Garrard Don't Want to Fight on Sunday—The Rebel Trap Set for Us—Gen. Beauregard Takes Command of the Rebels—Rebel Army Moving North—Heavy Rains—Gen. Wilson Takes Command of the Cavalry—Why We Don't Go to Jacksonville—Lost from Camp.

October 9th. Sunday, and our division is lying in camp, and all quiet. We have sent out heavy details scouting, and they have taken two days' rations. We suppose the object is to find the exact whereabouts of Hood, for as yet Sherman seems in doubt as to Hood's real intentions, and so long as Hood stays in the neighborhood of Dallas, Sherman can do nothing but stay where he is and watch him, as from this point he can threaten either Rome, Kingston or Atlanta.

October 10th. Last night, after dark, the scouts we sent out yesterday morning returned and reported the whole of Hood's army across the Allatoona mountains beyond Vanwert. This morning our division was up long before daylight and moved at sun-up, going due west and leaving Dallas three miles to our left, we passed over the road that a part of Hood's army had passed over, and observed that the road still was strewn full of chewed canestalks, and when we came to their camps on the Pumpkinvine, we were led to believe the rebel soldiers were sadly in need of shoes, as we saw where there had been at least a hundred beef cattle killed and their hides taken to make moccasins of, and worn out shoes of the same kind were left scattered about their camps. After crossing the Pumpkinvine creek we struck the Cartersville road near Burnt Hickory, where we were in camp the last of May after the Pumpkinvine campaign; there we turned north and went to the Etowa and then turned down the river four miles and bivouacked near Stilesborough, having made 24 miles for the day. We quote from Col. Miller's notes, Monday, October 10th: "Marched all day. Passed over the Allatoona range and down the Etowa valley towards Rome. The news is that the enemy are on the west side of the Coosa river and we are ordered to be there by daylight; have 26 miles to march to-night." Soon after we had gone into camp Gen. Garrard got orders to report to Rome by daylight, as the rebels had already made their appearance south of Rome. The distance from our camp to Rome, the shortest route was 20 miles, and we were ordered to feed and curry our horses as good as we could, and get ready to move by 8 p. m.; but from some cause or other we did not get off till just midnight. We still kept on down the river till we passed through a village called Snydersville, and then took a road running due west which led us away from the river several miles, the river running to the north-west. We had made 20 miles, and just as it began to get daylight our scouts run on to the rebel pickets, captured one of the videttes and drove in the pickets. Here our regiment and the 123d dismounted and a sharp fight ensued, in which private D. W. Laverty, of Co. D, Seventy-Second, was killed. He was a noble comrade and faithful soldier. This lasted about an hour, when we charged them and drove them about a mile, capturing a lot of guns, saddles, saddle-bags, haversacks, hats and camp equipments. We do not know whether we killed any of them or not, but the amount of blood we saw, indicated that a great many were severely wounded. This was our second attempt to get to Rome. We had tried it from the north on the 14th and 15th of May last, and got within five miles of the place and had to back out; and here we were again, 10 miles right south of Rome with Armstead's division and another mounted brigade of rebels between us and that place. During the fight the balance of our division had come up and gone into camp at the place where we ran on to the rebel pickets. After we had driven the rebels about as far as we could without bringing on a general engagement, we left six companies, the left of our regiment, on the skirmish line, fell back to our division and got breakfast. While we were eating, the commanders, Gens. Garrard, Miller and others, were in consultation about the situation. They were close enough for us to hear what was said. The General was determined to go through at all hazards. Said he, "I could go through right on the road we are on, but it would cost me the lives of 15 or 20 men; besides there is another road leading to Rome and there is no necessity for fighting now, as we would gain nothing by it." You may hardly realize how much such expressions as these endeared that man, Gen. Garrard, to us The fight took place near Cave Springs. So after breakfast, about 10 o'clock a. m. of the 11th of October, we turned square east and moved about a mile and then turned north again, thus leaving the rebels two miles to the west of us, and leaving our pickets in front of them until the column had gotten well out of the way, thus masking our movements completely. Companies D and I were advance guards, and we moved very slowly and cautiously, picketing all the roads leading to the west, until the column had moved five or six miles. We expected the rebels would attack us, but they did not. Along in the afternoon we passed several miles through one of the most beautiful pine forests in the world. The pine was of the long leaved species, and was used as a turpentine orchard—*Pinus Sylvestris*. The trees were all large, 18 inches to four feet in diameter, and towering a hundred feet high. There was scarcely a shrub or bush to be seen. The ground was sandy, and without a spear of grass upon it, but it was covered with the leaves that had accumulated from year to year, till now there was the softest carpet, three to four inches deep, imaginable. As we were moving along in perfect silence, and having slept none the night before, we longed to tumble off our horses and go to sleep; but on we went, slowly and silently, till about 4 o'clock p. m., when we came out into an open country, and more than two miles away, north to the front of us, we caught sight of a sentry. He was on one of the many high knobs surrounding Rome, and was so far that we could not make out whether he was friend or foe. We had our flag with us and unfurled it to the breeze. In an instant he knew that we were friends, he seeing the old, familiar stars and stripes, and did not long leave us in doubt, but caught the inspiration, and at once gathered up a flag and unfurled the stars and stripes also, and waived us a hearty welcome. This was the signal for a long and hearty cheer from our column. We had emerged suddenly into a valley, and our cheering called others to the scene, and in a minute we could see the whole company hastily forming on the hill, as if falling in for a fight; but the next minute we could see their hats flying high in the air, and three cheers and a tiger came rolling down the valley toward us. We had heard during the day that the rebels had got possession of Rome, and you may guess that these cheering tokens of the falsehood sent the blood galloping through our veins. We quickened our pace and in half an hour came up to the outposts. There was a high knob to our right from which we had observed the signal, and another high ridge to our left, with a valley between them, leading due north to Rome, two miles distant. Just as we got to the pickets we heard rapid firing over the ridge, to the northwest of us. Our scouts immediately struck out around the north end of the ridge and down on the west side, and we followed in hot haste. We have before spoken of the 9th Illinois mounted infantry, and they were here on picket, and a squad of rebel cavalry had charged them, and might have damaged them considerably but for our coming on to the field just in time. The rebels were feeling of the position of our forces at Rome with a view of attacking the place from the south. Our scouts charged them and drove them for several miles down the valley of the Coosa river, killing two of them and capturing two others; but our two companies, D and I, only went out as far as the picket post and stopped, while the division had moved quietly in and went into camp a mile south-west of Rome. We waited until our scouts came back and reported that the rebels were not likely to bother us any more on that road during the night, and then went into camp at the north end of the ridge, while the six companies we left on picket in the morning were coming in.

On the morning of the 10th the advance of Hood's army began to cross the Coosa river at Cedar Bluffs, 12 miles below Rome, and all day to-day the country west of Rome has been full of rebels, and the troops stationed here were expecting every minute to be attacked, and they knew, too, that Sherman's army was still away about Allatoona and could do them no good; and they also knew that if Hood would attack them with his whole army it would go hard with them, as there was but one division, Gen. Corse's, here that had come back immediately after the battle of Allatoona. No doubt it was a great relief to the sentinel on the hill when he first saw our column coming in from the south, and it was just as great a relief to us to see him, because, ever since the 7th, we have been too far from the rest of the army for them to do us any good in case we should get into a fight; and we never expected to get to Rome without a fight. The prisoners we had captured told us Hood said he would take Rome or sacrifice his whole army, and the citizens we saw this morning told us he had already taken the place. We tell you it did us good when we got to the picket line and saw the steeples of the town and our old flag still waiving over them. But the fact still remained that just across the river, not a mile from us, was a large part of Hood's army, seemingly making preparations for an attack on Rome in the morning, and we went to bed thinking on the morrow.

October 12th, 1864. The first thing we have to do this morning is to give you a short description of Rome and surroundings, that you may have a clear idea of our subsequent movements. Rome stands, or sits, right on a high point of land, formed by the junction of the Oostenaula and Etowa Rivers. The Oostenaula comes down from a little east of north, and the Etowa comes from a little south of east, and the two form the Coosa, which runs south-west from here. The whole country is mountainous and extremely rough, covered with dense forests, so that it is impossible to tell anything about the movements of an army, except by the smoke of the camp-fires as seen from the hills. There are numerous very high knobs and hills around Rome which were well fortified by the rebels last winter, and these have been strengthened by our own forces during the summer. Yesterday morning, on looking out from these forts, our men discovered the whole valley opposite Rome full of rebels. The smoke from the numerous camp-fires indicating that all of Hood's army was there. They were close enough for our men to have dropped shells right down among them, but they were afraid of bringing on a general engagement, and so laid still all day, as did also the rebels, or moved on up the valley, toward our railroad so quietly that the forces still in Rome did not detect their movements, and still believe they are there. There is certainly nothing to hinder Hood from getting on to the railroad again if he wanted to. This was another surprise for Sherman, and as our hard-tack line was of such vast importance to us, we shall again quote a few paragraphs from his book, to keep the reader posted on the general movements of both armies, and to illustrate some points of "strategy." Sherman says: "In person I reached Allatoona on the 9th of October, still in doubt as to Hood's immediate intentions. Our cavalry could do little against his infantry in the rough and wooded country about Dallas, which masked the enemies movements. But Gen. Corse, at Rome, with Spencer's 1st Alabama

Cavalry and a mounted regiment of (9th) Illinois mounted infantry, could feel the country south of Rome, about Cedartown and Villa Rica, and reported the enemy to be in force at both places; and on the same day I telegraphed to Gen. Grant: 'It will be impossible to protect the roads now that Hood, Forest, Wheeler and the whole batch of Devils are turned loose without home or habitation. I think Hood's movements indicate a diversion to the end of the Selma and Talledago road at Blue Mountain, about 60 miles south-west of Rome, from which he will threaten Kingston, Bridgeport, and Decatur, Alabama. By attempting to hold the roads we will lose a thousand men each month and will gain no results.' On the 10th of October the enemy appeared south of the Etowa River, at Rome, when I ordered all the armies to march to Kingston and telegraphed to Gen. Thomas: 'It looks to me as though Hood was bound for Tuscumbia. He is now crossing the Coosa River below Rome, looking west.' On the 11th I rode to Kingston and learned by telegraph from Gen. Corse, at Rome, that Hood's army had disappeared but in what direction he was still in doubt." We are of the opinion he will not be left in doubt long. But we return to our own narrative.

We were up early this morning, and immediately sent our pack mules ahead into Rome to draw rations, and Long's brigade followed, crossing the Etowa on a pontoon bridge just at the mouth of the river. Minty's brigade followed closely, and by the time the sun was two hours high, our brigade was closing up on to the rear of Minty's, at the river. Our regiment was advance guard yesterday and of course we were in the rear to-day, and just about the time Long's and Minty's brigades were all across the river, and while we were moving out on to the road and yet a mile back on the bluffs, we heard picket-firing off to the west of town, and could plainly see the rebels forming their lines behind a ridge that ran parallel with the river. They were out of sight from the town but in full view from our elevated position. We were hurried forward with all speed and the 1st brigade (Long's) immediately began to cross the Oostenaula on a pontoon bridge, a half mile above its mouth. By this time we could plainly see the rebels driving our infantry pickets back on to the ridge toward town. We could see nearly a mile of our skirmish line, and on some parts of it they were falling back in some confusion, while on other parts they were falling back more deliberately, and were fighting manfully. There was no mistaking the fact that the whole line was being driven back, which told to us as plainly as anything could tell us, that the rebel line was a long one, By the time we got across the Etowa, Long's brigade had got across the Oostenaula and advanced skirmishers on horseback on the road leading west from town, while most of his brigade was massed in column to the left of the road, and just at the foot of the ridge. Minty began to mass his brigade as fast as they got across the river, just at the right of the road. Long now formed line of battle on horseback, to the left of the road and tried to advance his skirmishers, and we think it was intended that Minty should do the same thing on the right of the road, but just as soon as Eong's skirmishers reached the brow of the ridge they were driven back in haste, and the infantry to the right of the road, and still further north up the river, came fa'ling back in confusion. During this time our brigade had got across the Etowa, and as we had about three-fourths of a mile to go around through town to get to the pontoon on the Oostenaula, we found our pack mules with our rations along the sides of the streets, and the orderly sergeants were there ready to issue our rations to us. The column was not allowed to halt a moment but kept moving right along as fast as the advance could cross the pontoon, and we had to issue the rations to the men while the column was moving. We suppose there was about a half hour during this time that the houses concealed from our view what was going on west of the river; by the time we got to where we could see again, the infantry, on the extreme right, had been driven clear back into the Oostenaula and they came pouring down along the river under cover of the bank like frightened deer, and some of them never stopped till they ran across the pontoon and got into the town; it became necessary to place a guard at the farther end of the pontoon to stop them. By the time we got to the river things began to look desperate, and we wondered why the rebels did not immediately take Long's and Minty's brigades. From the river to the foot of the ridge was three-fourths of a mile, bare of trees, and the rebels didn't seem to want to leave the timber just yet; but we could see them still thickening upon the brow of the hill, as if getting ready for a charge. Long's and Minty's brigades did not seem to be doing anything but standing there, waiting for us. We had to dismount to lead our horses across the bridge, and as fast as we got over, the horses of our brigade were massed in column behind Minty's, and the men prepared to fight on foot. Without ever stopping at all we marched past Minty's in column, and then formed line of battle with two regiments on the right of the road and two on the left, facing west; our regiment was on the extreme right, and as soon as we got our lines straightened we moved forward till near the foot of the hill where the rebel skirmishers were, and charged them, never stopping till we got nearly to the brow of the hill, making a mile the first drive. This

brought us within range of the main line of rebels and they opened on us heavy, using artillery. Indeed, some of our men got clear to the top of the ridge and had to fall back. We lay down here and rested half an hour, the shells passing right over us all the time, and bursting as close as 20 feet behind us. During this time the other two brigades were formed in line to our right and left rear, and preparations made to have them follow up our movement and take advantage of a stampede of the rebels, if we should be so fortunate as to move them again. After we had got a good rest and supposed everything was ready in the rear, we straightened our lines and went for them again. We struck the main line about 300 yards from where we started, and we tell you our Spencers made some lively music for five or ten minutes, when the rebels broke and run like sheep. The artillery never fired but one round after we started, but limbered up and skipped out, taking a road that run south-west. The infantry also fell back in that direction. Our brigade, on a general left wheel, charged on after them. We drove them a mile this time, when we found our brigade in wheeling to the left had become so scattered, that there was hardly any two men of the same company near each other, but every fellow had struck out for himself in the direction he had seen the last rebel, and had run as fast and as long as he could. We never saw our brigade so mixed up before. It took nearly an hour to get our lines straightened up again. How many rebels we killed in this charge we never went back to see, but suppose 50 would be a fair estimate, as we counted five dead rebels in our own line of march. Had the other two brigades come up promptly after we got the rebels to running, we might have captured their artillery and most of their lead horses; but as it was they were half an hour too late, and then Long's brigade charged over the hill to our left, and came out into the road in front of our line of battle, after the rebels had all got mounted and out of the way, while Minty charged straight west from where he started, and never got near the rebels we were fighting. We were now two miles from Rome, south-west. Here we rested three or four hours, while Long straighted his brigade, and scouted to our front and found the rebels were still in force a mile in front of us. Company D was left on picket, and here we fell back and went into camp a mile west of Rome. It seems now that Hood's army, except Armstead's division of Texas rangers, which we have been fighting to-day, have moved up the Oostenaula toward Resaca, to destroy our railroad. We suppose this division was left here on purpose to threaten Rome in such a way as to deceive Sherman. Our move to-day has cut this division off from Hood. Sherman says: "On October 12th I went to Rome, where the news came that Hood had made his appearance at Resaca, and had demanded the surrender of the place. He had evidently marched with rapidity up the Chattanooga valley by Summerville, Lafayette, Ships Gap and Snake Creek, and had with him his whole army except a small force left behind to watch Rome." So that Sherman was undeceived now as to Hood's intentions, but not in time to save his railroad. He further says: "I turned all the heads of columns for Resaca, where they got during the night of the 12th, and on the morning of the 13th I learned that Hood's whole army had passed up the valley toward Dalton, burning the railroad and doing all the damage possible, destroying the railroad clear up to Tunnel Hill, 20 miles, and capturing a regiment of colored troops at Dalton."

October 13th. On going to bed last night, we had orders to be ready to move at 6 o'clock. We had heavy picket firing all night. Company D was close enough to hear the rebel pickets talking. We were up before daylight and moved at sun up, taking the road we were on yesterday. This road runs down the valley of the Coosa south-west, two or three miles from the river.

Two miles from camp we came to the picket post of Company D, who had most effectually barricaded the road, and told us the rebels were just across the field Our brigade was dismounted and prepared to fight on foot. By this time the rebels had begun to advance on us, and before we got our lines formed, they were so close that their bullets were whistling over our heads. We formed our lines the same as on yesterday, two regiments on either side of the road, ours being on the extreme right. We had hardly got our lines straightened, when the rebels opened on us with a piece of artillery, and the shells went tearing through the trees to our left, near the road. Our line was on the north side of a field 200 yards wide, while in the woods on the south side, the rebels were pretty thick, and their skirmishers were along the fence, peppering us the best they could. In less time than it has taken to write it, we had our line formed and our skirmishers started. They went across that field with a yell, and in two minutes reached the opposite side, and a sharp fight ensued at the fence. We followed our skirmishers closely and by the time we got half way across the field, we opened on the woods, and the rebels broke and ran, we after them. The artillery limbered up and put out for the rear. A half hour ago they were advancing to attack us—now they think they have urgent business somewhere else. The road we were on ran right along the west side of the ridge we spoke of yesterday. This ridge ran parallel with the river, while from a half mile to a mile west of the river ran quite a large stream, and it also ran nearly south, parallel with the road. The whole country was densely wooded on both sides of the road, except in a few places where the valley, or bottom land, reached out to the road. This bottom land was cultivated all along the stream, and of course was bare of trees, except a few dead ones. In the timber there was the densest undergrowth of little pine trees we ever saw anywhere. In many places they were so thick it was impossible to get through them at all. The fact is, they grew so close together you could scarcely stick your finger between them. We never saw hazel-brush grow half as close to-gether. There were also hundreds of old pine trees blown down among the brush in every conceivable direction, which made marching in line of battle out of the question; yet we did our best to push through the woods, and had not gone a hundred yards till we found ourselves completely swamped in the brush. Here our line quite broke up, and each fellow for himself, pushed ahead as fast as possible. We are free to confess that we never went into a fight with such feelings of dread, as we did into this one. We had not gone far till we forgot all about it, and were wonderfully amused at seeing the men trying to hurry through the brush. Many times we absolutely stuck fast and had to back out and go around. It was a common thing to see 20 or 30 men march square up to a big log so high, and in the brush so thick, that they could not get over it, and then to see them file to the right or left and run around the end of it like a gang of turkeys. It was funny. All this time we were pushing ahead as fast as possible, and the Johnnies kept banging away at us just enough to let us know which way to go. We pushed ahead in this manner for full a mile and a half, while our scouts, at the commencement of the action, had moved over west to the creek and were driving a squad of rebels down before them, and at several points had some sharp firing, killing some rebel horses and capturing several others. At the end of a mile and a half the valley and the road come so near together, that it threw our regiment into the open field, and we were done with the pine brush for awhile. Here we stopped and rested a half hour. During this march the rebels had continued to throw shells, but most of them went tearing through the trees, along the road, and through the center of the brigade. They would fire a few shots, then limber up, fall back a short distance, and then open on us again. When we came out into the valley and rested, everything was quiet in front, and we didn't know but the rebels were gone, but directly they opened on us again. . This time we could see them plainly. About two miles ahead of us, the stream and valley turned squarely to the left across the road, and beyond the creek the bluff was high and steep. The rebels had fallen back to this position and formed a line of battle along on the bluff, where they could see our every movement; and the fact that we could just as plainly see that battery no doubt saved many of our lives, as we shall presently explain. While we were lying here resting, our skirmishers kept on working their way down the creek toward the battery, and the rebs gave them a few rounds. This whole valley had been in wheat, and after harvest, rag weeds had grown up about two feet high, and as thick as they could grow. The rebels soon found they could do nothing with the skirmishers, and turned their attention to us. Just then we had no thanks for special favors. The first shell they threw, went whizzing over our heads fully 300 feet high, and must have gone a mile to our rear. Just then the word "Forward!" came to us, and we started again. This time we had nothing to bother us, and we moved off lively, and in the prettiest line we ever saw. We were in single rank, four to six feet apart. In less than ten minutes, Col. Miller, who was on the road behind the center of the brigade, sent his orderly over to halt us; he could not get through the brush to come to us on horseback, and had to come afoot, and by this time we were nearly a half mile ahead of the other three regiments, which were struggling along through the pine brush. We halted and lay down again. We could now see plainly that there were but two pieces of artillery firing. One of them kept throwing shells along the road through the wood to the left of us, the other one kept working away at us, and we could tell by every shot that went over us, that they were trying to lower their pieces, and to get the range; yet the shells still went as high as the tree-tops.

As we had never seen the road since crossing the little field on starting, we had to guess at the distance and keep closed up to the regiment on our left, by feeling for it; and when we got out into the open field, we found many places where the strips of woods between the road and the field were wider than the length of the regiment next to us, and the Colonel would keep commanding "close up to the left;" but we had had enough of the brush in ours and preferred to stay out in the open field, even if it did give the Johnnies a better chance at us. It took 15 or 20 minutes for the balance of the brigade to get even with us, and we began to move forward again as soon as they came up; this time they tried to get us to move as slowly as the other regiments, but it was no use. When those shells came screaming over us the boys wanted to be going ahead and did go ahead in spite of all the efforts of the officers to keep them from it. We would move up one or two hundred yards and then lie down and wait. During all this time the battery was playing away on us as fast as they could load and shoot, and by the time we had gone a mile they had lowered their guns, till a shell struck a large dead tree about 30 feet from the ground, cutting the tree right in two and exploding 100 yards behind us, while the whole top of the tree came down with a thundering crash a few feet from us. This waked us up, and we confess frightened us terribly, and from that on the game became quite interesting. We started forward again, and both pieces opened on our regiment and as they would fire alternately we hadn't much time for gawking about. Besides they lowered their pieces till the shells would nip the weeds as they would pass over us.

Now came the grandest sight the military man or drill master ever beheld. It more than realized all that we had ever imagined in regard to the skirmish drill, or evolutions of the battalion under fire. Nothing we had ever witnessed on the drill ground would begin to compare with this, and we went through it all with scarcely a word of command. We were about a mile from the battery and could see them plainly. Every time the smoke would spirt up from the touch-hole some one would call out "Down!" and in a twinkling every man in the regiment was flat on the ground; not a man to be seen. No one needed to be told the second time to get down, for in an instant the shell would come over, nipping the weeds, hissing and whizzing and saying wher-r-r-are-you, wher-r-r-are-you? and then with a deafen-pop, burst behind us. Lucky too, that every one of them *did* burst just behind us. No sooner had the shell burst than the word "forward!" rang out, and every man was up again moving on. But now the shells come so thick and fast, that we are on the ground half the time, and as we get closer to the guns they give us less time from the time the smoke spirts up from the touch-hole till the shell is upon us, so that we have to mind our "P's" and "Q's." But we still keep our line perfectly straight, and can compare our ups and downs to nothing more like a revolving hay rake. We are now about a half mile from the guns and rest a few minutes for the other three regiments to catch up; by this time our skirmishers have got within 400 yards of the main line of rebels, and for the first we can hear the skirmishers from the other three regiments, begin to fire. They have just got to the edge of the woods, along the bottom, where it turned square to the left across the road. Those from our regiment have been engaged constantly from the start; this increased firing from the left front adds very materially to the interest of the occasion, for we have scarcely heard a single gun on our left from the time we struck the open field, and we had about come to the conclusion that all the rebels were in our immediate front; but this firing seemed to arouse the other regiments, for when we start again they move off more lively, and with our very many "downs" and "ups" we had to move on quick time to keep even with them. This time we move on without halting, and are within 600 yards of the guns when we hear the boys begin to say, "we'll have 'em," "we'll have 'em." But just now there comes such a screaming, and whistling, and whizzing, and tearing through the air as we never heard. They had opened on us with grape and canister. Good heavens! the air seems fairly blue and thick with the devilish missiles. We are laying flat, and most of them go over us. Again we start; this time on the double-quick, determined to give them time for as few such kind regards as possible. We have made 200 yards and see the smoke spirt up again from both guns at once. Heavens and earth! Of all the lively screaming we ever heard this is the liveliest. By this time we have got so close to the guns that they cannot depress them enough to touch us, and without a word of command from anyone we raise the yell and go for the guns like a tornado. Just then the other three regiments get out of the brush into the bottom and do their best to beat us running and hallooing. The main line of rebels now open on us with musketry and it seems to us the seven thunders have all broke loose at once. On we go, and in less time than it takes to tell it, we are across the bottom and strike the creek, which is in many places more than waist deep; but right through it we go. A short desperate fight and the guns are ours! We raised the yell, the artillerymen limber up and start off on the gallop, but we go over the 400 yards in time to save them, by shooting a horse belonging to each gun after they get started. Now comes the crowing act of the day. Minty, at the head of his brigade, has followed our line closely, and his whole brigade closes up in column of "4's," and just as we are getting on top of the hill we hear another tremendous cheer to our left, and here comes the cavalry on the full run. The next minute they are charging across an open field in front of us, and the next minute have disappeared down the road and through the woods, and the rapid firing tells us plainly that they mean business. We still charge on across the open field, but by the time we reach the woods the firing begins to die away in the distance, and we halt, dress up our lines, and rest.

If there is anything pretty in war, this was one of the prettiest fights in the world. In a short time we went to the road and moved down it in column for about three miles, when we began to meet squads of cavalry coming back. Here we halted and rested about an hour, when Gen. Cox, then commanding the 23d corps, came up to our regiment and made us a speech. Said he had come out from Rome this morning with two divisions of infantry, to help us clean the rebels out of the valley, and that he had got up to the rear of our line just in time to witness the whole of our movements, and during the whole war he had not seen such a splendid charge. That no troops in the world could have beaten it. We gave him three cheers. We were now 10 miles from Rome. Most of the cavalry had came back, the infantry had come up to our rear and were eating their dinner. At this time a cavalryman came up with a battle flag that he had captured five or six miles down the road. We think it belonged to Terrell's "Texas Rangers." Our cavalry followed the rebels eight or nine miles down the valley, keeping after them as long as they could keep in sight of any of them.

Now for results: The two guns we captured (and the credit for this belongs to our regiment because *we* shot the horses so they could not get away), were a part of a six-gun battery that the rebs had captured from our men at Murfreesboro in the fall of 1862, when Buell fell back from Tennessee to Louisville; the other four having been captured back before this. We had killed and wounded 150 and captured as many more, and broken up the whole division, for this is the last we ever heard of Armstead's division. And strange as it may seem we only had two men killed and 10 wounded in the whole division. So much for generalship, discipline, drill, and Spencer rifles; and this battle was a fair representation of the superiority of Spencer rifles over single shooting guns. In our description of this battle we have only related just what *our* regiment did, but it must not be supposed this is all there was of it. Indeed the heaviest firing that was done after the charge began was, done by the other three regiments, and the line of rebels on the hill in front of them seemed to be the strongest, and they had woods behind them and held their position longest, after those in front of us began to run; and had those in front of us had heavy woods to fall back upon, it might have gone worse with us. On the top of the hill close by the guns there was a log cabin and four or five acres of cleared land to the south-west of it; when we got the rebels started from the brow of the hill they had to fall back over this field, and here is where we killed the most of them. There were many points during the progress of the battle that were as grand as ever we saw. It will be remembered that on the 14th of last May, while the army was passing through Snake Creek Gap,

Sherman sent our division down the Chattannoga valley toward Rome with orders to cross the Oostenaula, take the place and threaten the railroad at Adairsville, &c. Well, when we got to the Armurchee we found it so strongly defended, and Minty's brigade was so badly handled while trying to cross, that we gave it up. This seemed to irritate Sherman wonderfully, and from that on it always seemed to us that he was never willing to give us credit for what we really did do; and in his book he makes no effort to conceal the fact that he did not like Garrard, our division commander, while our whole division just revered him. And now Sherman, with his usual partiality, in his "memoirs," gives all the credit of capturing these two guns, and in fact the success of the whole affair, to Gen. Corse, commanding a division of the 15th Corps, when the fact is, that Gen. Corse, nor a man of the 15th Corps, was not within eight miles of the battle-field. Neither Gen. Corse nor any part of the 15th Corps had a thing to do with it. As before stated, Gen. Cox and two divisions of the 23d Corps did come down to help us, but the men never fired a gun, and were not within a half mile of the battle-field till it was all over. So the credit of the whole thing, so far as generalship is concerned, belongs to Gen. Garrard, and the credit of doing the work all belongs to Col. Miller and his trusty regiments, and two regiments of Minty's cavalry.

As already stated this morning, as soon as we got to our picket-post, we dismounted and prepared to fight on foot, and our lead horses were taken back to camp; so here we were at least nine miles from our horses, and as we had not marched any for 18 months, the thoughts of having to walk back went smartly against the grain; but our grand success made us cheerful, and we gathered our command together and moved slowly back, getting to camp by 4 p. m.

October 14th. Moved early this morning and went back through Rome, where we passed our wagon train. This is the first time we have seen our train since leaving Crosskeys, on the 2d. Here we got some mail, which was a great treat, as we observed that since Hood & Co. had been operating our railroads, the postal department had been rather irregular. From Rome we took the road east for Kingston. We found all the army had passed up north toward Resaca, and the whole army train and beef cattle were massed in the rear, and moving up in that direction too; it was the business of our division to form a chain picket or guard in the rear of the train. We moved seven miles toward Kingston and turned north toward Adairsville, keeping a mile or two in the rear of the train. Just after noon we come to a place that looked very familiar; it was Woodlawn or Blanchfield's plantation, the place where our division was surrounded on the 18th of May, and where the adjutant of the brigade was captured. It seemed to us that we had always been acquainted with the place, and as we were now simply guarding the train we had ample time to look around. During the fight here last spring, the old gentleman who is an Englishman, raised the British flag in hopes thereby of saving his bacon and beans, and we observed that his property had not been molested much; but to-day, while most of the officers of our brigade were in the house enjoying the old gentleman's hospitality, *we* were in his garden digging his potatoes and pulling his onions. We lay here two hours, and when we pulled out our haversacks were all well filled. We went into camp early, half way between Woodlawn and Adairsville, having made 20 miles for the day. Soon after going into camp, Sergeant Willhide, Company E, went to a house to get some water, and saw Gen. Garrard and his adjutant standing in front of a wagon, and the wagon in front of the smoke-house, as a kind of safe-guard for the smoke-house; as it was thought soldiers would hardly try to take anything out when "headquarters" were so close. Willhide saw three stands of bees by the smoke-house, and unobserved by the general and his staff, picked up the heaviest one and made off through the orchard with it. In a short time he had returned to camp with his bucket full of honey instead of water. This excited the envy of his comrades, and they determined to have some honey too. So quite a number of them started for it, but when they got there they found they were too late. The General had missed the honey, and had placed a guard over the other two stands, and he was amused at the chagrin the boys manifested at their failure. A few days after this some rebel sharpshooters were annoying our column. They were in and around a house; the General turned to Company E, and said, "Now, boys, you wanted honey the other day; there's just dead loads of honey up at that house, and you can go and get all you want of it." The boys got the honey.

October 15th. Moved at sun up, going directly to Adairsville. This is a small station on the railroad, and has 50 or 75 houses. We didn't see any white folks about the place, but plenty of negroes. When our army passed through here last May, the white folks "gone and runned away," leaving the negroes in undisputed posession. As we passed through they swarmed out to see us. We noticed one little fellow about four years old, who didn't seem to care whether school kept or not; he was lying on a long, hewn log, sunning himself, and was as naked as when he was born. He reminded us of an alligator we saw down on the Ocmulgee, that had crawled out of the water to sun itself. The "nigger" didn't seem to notice us at all, although the whole regiment was passing within two rods of him. He looked so very "cute" that our whole regiment involuntarily got to laughing and yelling at him, but still he paid no attention to it. Finally one of our boys turned his horse out as though he intended to ride over him, and yelled out, "you little rascal, get out out of this!" This roused the little fellow up, and he slid off the log in a twinkling, and he took to his heels, with the fellow after him, yelling every jump like an Indian. We never saw anything run like that negro did, and in less than a minute he had disappeared around a corner of a square. This caused more merriment than anything we had seen for a fortnight, and served to keep us all in a good humor the balance of the day. After we got through Adairsville we turned east and moved three or four miles, till we struck the main road from Carterville to Resacca; this road runs nearly north and parallel with the railroad, while west of the railroad was ancther road on which our trains were moving. Our regiment was farthest to the east, while other portions of our division were on the railroad, and still further to the west, in the rear of the train, companies I and D, advance guard. We were moving slowly along east of where any of our troops had been, and found an abundance of forage for man and beast. We bivouacked late in the evening, four miles south-east of Resacca, having made 25 miles for the day.

October 16th. Moved this morning at sun up, going straight to Resacca, and when we got there, found the army train, beef-cattle and all. We crossed the Oostenaula on a pontoon, and lay in town three or four hours, for the trains to get across, and then we drew five days' rations and moved out, down the river, without any road, and had almost the worst time we ever experienced, getting across a miserable little quick-sand stream. When across, we turned northwest again, and went into camp two miles from Resacca.

October 17th. It took the trains all day yesterday and all of last night to get out of Resacca. They took the road through Snake Creek gap, and this morning, an hour by sun, we moved after them five or six miles, which took us well up into Snake Creek gap. Hood, by this time, had completely destroyed the railroad up to Tunnel Hill, and then turned south, going down on the east side of Taylor's Ridge, crossed the ridge at Ship Gap, and was now near Lafayette. Sherman was at Valanan. The valley of the Chattooga was open before Hood, and nothing to hinder him from going directly back down to Rome, if he wanted to. When we got the train safe into Snake Creek gap, we turned back and went down toward Rome, on the east side of the Chattooga Mountain, passed its southern end, and went into camp, having made 30 miles for the day. The mountain scenery is superbly grand. The valleys ar immensely rich, and forage in abundance.

October 18th. Moved early this morning, going directly west across John's Creek. We struck the road that leads from Valanan to Rome, near Floyd's Springs, where we camped on the 15th of May last, when we tried to get to Rome, but didn't. It adds wonderfully to the interest of our tramping around, to so frequently come upon places we are familiar with. At this point we turned south, went about four miles, and struck the road leading north-west from Rome to Summerville. This was 11 miles from Rome. Here we found a battallion of the 1st Alabama (Union) cavalry. They had just come out from Rome, and had a sharp skirmish with the rebs at this point, which looked like the rebels were really feeling their way back toward Rome. The rebels fell back toward Summerville, and we followed after them, crossing the Big Armurchee Creek and a little further on crossed the Little Armurchee, and turned up this stream, going nearly north. We moved on steadily but slowly, as the rebels had obstructed the roads in numerous places, and in some places entirely blockaded it, so that our advance had to use axes to get the logs and trees out of the way. We passed two large mills on the creek, and bivouacked at sun down in the mouth of White's Gap, near a place called Dirt Town. Dirt Town consists of two large, fine houses, and a mill, and White's Gap is in Taylor's Ridge, which extends from here up to Ringgold. Have made 30 miles to-day.

October 19th. We moved this morning at sun up, turning west into the mouth of White's Gap, and after going up gradually for two miles we passed a division of the 23d corps in camp. Four miles from camp we got on top of the ridge and found a heavy line of earthworks which the rebels had thrown up on the night of the 17th. After starting down the ridge, in about two miles we passed another division of the 23d corps, and shortly afterward crossed quite a large stream called Chattooga River, and soon after we got to Summerville, where we found Gen. Sherman's headquarters and also most of the army. The Chattooga River heads away up about LaFayette and runs straight south to the Coosa River at Cedar Bluffs, 30 miles below Rome. We turned south down this river—Long's brigade just ahead of ours. We had gone 10 miles from Summerville when he ran into the rebels, and a running fight was kept up for three or four miles; this brought us into the State of Alabama by night, but not finding a good place to camp we fell back and camped in Georgia. Made 25 miles for the day.

October 20th. Moved this morning promptly at sun-up, and found the rebels had stood picket right where we left them yesterday evening, which shows they are determined to dispute every foot of ground and delay us as much as possible. We moved slowly and steadily till near noon, when we ran on to their rear guard again. This was at a little town called Galesville; at this point the river runs very close to a mountain. The rebels had cut down trees and rolled the road full of logs and made some resistance; but a few shots from our advance frightened them away and we drove them like sheep through Galesville. They took a road leading south-west to Blue Pond, and we still pushed on after them till we got near another large stream called Little River, or Little Chattooga; here the rebels made another stand Their cavalry was drawn up across the road with infantry behind them, but our men charged them so furiously that they drove the cavalry right through the infantry and scattered them in every direction, capturing quite a number of the infantry. This was about the middle of the afternoon, and most of the rebels managed to get across the river. This was a deep and difficult stream to cross, and the rebels had obstructed all the fords by felling trees into them. Just on the opposite bank was a strong line of earthworks, and the whole of Hardee's corps there ready to slaughter us if we should attempt to cross. This brought us promptly to a halt. We skirmished with them across the river till dark and then went into camp near the river. The prisoners we captured say Hood intends to make a stand and fight at Blue Pond, three miles from here. This is at the southern end of Missionary Ridge, or rather where the ridge breaks off into numerous very high knobs, and one of these, just across the river, is occupied by the rebels, who can look right down into our camp and tell exactly how many there are of us.

October 21st It has been a month to-day since Hood crossed the Chattahoochee at Campbelltown, below Atlanta, and the month has been one of deep interest to both armies, and a busy one for our division. Some time during the night the rebels fell back from the river, and this morning there are none to be seen. We were up early, and shortly after sun-up our division and one brigade of Kilpatrick's division were sent across Little river on a reconnoissance; while the 15th corps, which had come down the valley of the Little river on our right, moved up to the river and began to fortify, as though Sherman expected Hood would fight. Our division took the road south-west for Blue Pond, and about two miles from the river came on to a heavy line of earthworks nearly a mile long, which must have been thrown up yesterday, which shows that Hood either intended to fight here, or that he has a tremendous heavy rear guard, as it would have taken 10,000 men five or six hours to build such a line of works; but the rebels had abandoned them and we pushed on after them. Minty's brigade was in the advance, and a half mile beyond this line of works we passed through a straggling little village of a few houses; this was Blue Pond. Here the main road ran straight west to a place called Collinsville, 15 or 20 miles distant, on the west side of Lookout mountain. A half mile west of Blue Pond our advance ran into the rear of the rebs and skirmishing began. The rebels soon gave way, but instead of going west on the main road, they turned south-west on a road leading down the Coosa valley to Double Springs, at the south end of Lookout mountain. Our division turned off after them, and a mile from this came to a good-sized stream of water running between two of those high knobs spoken of before. Here the rebels were so strongly posted and in such numbers that Minty's brigade could not move them. Our brigade was dismounted and moved around one of those knobs to the right, and when we got even with the rebels they let go their hold at the creek and fell back, and our men pushed on after them, and here Sergt. Stewart says: "We captured a train of 30 wagons which the rebels had just set on fire to keep them from falling into our hands." As Minty followed the rebels they kept thickening up and falling back slowly until they greatly outnumbered his brigade. About five miles south-west of Blue Pond we found the rebels in good position behind strong works, waiting for us. As usual our brigade was hurried forward and dismounted, and formed line of battle in the usual order; and as usual we went for them on the charge. Davis, of Company D, says there were two divisions of them, and we could plainly see the "gray buggers" and their muskets lying on their works in front of them. "Drive them from their works," called out Capt. Thomson, in command of the Seventy-Second; but the rebels were so strongly posted and there were so many of them that they didn't want to drive. The rebels held their fire as we came upon them, and when within a few rods of their works Capt. Thomson sang out, "Lie down." A sheet of flame burst over us and the thunder of that volley made the earth tremble! We sprang to our feet and went over their works in a twinkling, a desperate fight ensued, and for a moment it seemed the force of superior numbers would crush us. It was but for a moment. They broke and ran, and we at their heels. At this juncture Col. Miller rides up and calls out, "Halt! Halt!" It was no trouble to get us started, but not so easy to get us stopped. Over on our right we saw our cavalry falling back before superior numbers of the enemy in great confusion. After strenuous efforts on the part of the officers our brigade was stopped and re-formed at the works, and as heavy masses of infantry were still just in front of us we thought best not to push them further. So we gathered up our dead and wounded and fell back. This was always called the battle of Blue Pond, though it took place five miles south-west of that place. We never knew what damage we inflicted on the rebels, but as they fought behind works and we did not pursue them (on account of the cavalry giving way), their loss could not have been so terribly severe as it might have been had we pursued them further.

The loss of our brigade was 12 men killed and wounded. There was but one man killed in our regiment, and as usual that man belonged to Company D. Granville Edwards, private, of D, was also wounded. It was now nearly four o'clock in the afternoon. Loading our dead and wounded into ambulances we moved slowly back to our old camp at Little river, and buried our dead on the banks of the stream. Captain Thomson says of private Milton Millikan, Company D: "Sadly, in that far off land, did we bury our noble and beloved comrade. But the ground was consecrated ground, and his death, with that of others, gained the victories that preserved a Nation that will ever mourn the memory of its fallen heroes.

It seems a little strange that we do so much fighting and use so little artillery. But the fact is our brigade hardly ever gives our own battery time to get up to the front before we have the rebels running like sheep, and ever since the battle of Rome the rebels are a little careful about leaving *their* artillery anywhere near the rear for fear it might accidentally get gobbled. There is not another brigade in the whole army so well known all over the Southern Confederacy as our Lightning Brigade; and whenever we open on the rebels with our Spencers they know who we are in a minute, and unless they are more than twice our number, and very strongly posted, they soon start "on for Dixie," and this very fact, no doubt, has saved many of our lives.

October 22d. Yesterday, while we were gone, the 15th corps came up to the river and went into camp; a regiment went across and dug a line of rifle-pits, covering the ford, and this morning, soon after sun-up, we moved across the river, and our brigade massed in column by companies, right in the very thickest pine brush, just beyond the line of rifle-pits, and lay there till 8 or 9 o'clock, when the whole of the 15th corps came across the river, and formed a line of battle immediately outside of our position. At 10 a. m. an order came around that we should have an hour for letter writing. As it had been a month and a day since we had such an opportunity, we improved it to the fullest extent. It wasn't 10 minutes before nearly every man in the regiment had out his writing material, and with his paper on his knee, was scribbling away. The vast consequences of that one hour will never be known this side of eternity. Very many of the important points in this history were noted down in that hour, and it was many a day before we had such another opportunity. A hasty dinner, and we moved at 2 p. m. over the same road we were on yesterday, going into camp on the battlefield, just at the last line of works from which we drove the rebels. We are close to Lookout Mountain, and 10 miles south of here the Coosa river runs very close to its southern end. Our whole division is here, and one brigade of Kilpatrick's division. Gen. Elliott is also with us.

October 23d. Moved this morning at sun-up, taking the road south-west; our brigade and our regiment in advance, A, F. D, and I, advance guard. We had not gone a half mile outside of our pickets till we ran on to the rebel videttes. Skirmishing began immediately, and at times grew pretty warm, as we drove them back. The Seventy-Second scouts were ahead of us, and dismounted as soon as we struck the rebels, and as the firing would grow rapid in front, the men of our companies would jump off their horses and run forward to take a hand, and would keep driving ahead till they would get quite tired, and then fall back to their horses, and others would take their places. We never before saw men so keen to go on to the skirmish line. Thus we drove them slowly but steadily back for two miles and a half, when Col. Watkins' brigade of Kilpatrick's division came in on a road to our left, and ahead of us, and relieved us. This was a cross road, and called King's Hill; here the rebels had another line of works, but Watkins' cavalry charged right over it, scattering the rebels in every direction. From this point, one road ran straight west over Lookout Mountain, and the 123d Illinois moved out on this, while we kept on south after Watkins' brigade, which continued to drive the rebels on down the valley, charging them twice and driving them three miles from King's Hill, which brought them to the narrow pass we have spoken of between the Coosa and Lookout. This pass is very narrow and easily defended. Here we found a heavy body of the enemy behind a line of works that extended clear across the valley, from the river to the mountain, and they had artillery in position, but masked so as to deceive us.

The rebels tried various plans to get the cavalry to charge on to these works in order to ambush them and take them in, but the cavalry failed to go in, and our three regiments were dismounted and moved to the front. Just then the rebels found they could not get the cavalry within their grasp, and so opened on them with their artillery, and the shells did some damage, wounding several and driving the rest back in confusion. We now sent forward *our* skirmishers and waited their developments. The rebels still kept up their shelling. To the left of the road was an open field for half a mile, and beyond the field dense woods, and the rebels were so concealed in these we could not tell their number; but while the cavalry were skirmishing some of our boys (as before remarked) were so very keen to get into a fight that they had jumped off their horses and actually crawled up to the line of rebel works and saw just how the matter stood, and came back and reported to Gen. Garrard, and to Miller.

During all this time Elliott was near us watching the skirmishers, and Garrard and Miller were close enough for us to hear them talk. Finally Elliott said he did not believe it would be hard to drive them out of that, and asked Miller and Garrard what they thought about it. They told him they wanted to see further before putting their men into it. So together they rode out east on to one of the numerous high knobs, and with their field-glasses examined the rebel works for an hour. During this time our line of battle broke up completely, and officers and men set about reconnoitering; many more of our boys crawled up close to the works, and every one who did so would come back and shake his head. One of them remarked, "We'll get hell if we try it." By this time the rebels had quit shelling and there were no signs of life in front; but Garrard and Miller had ascertained that there were more of the enemy than of us; they had a dozen pieces of artillery and every advantage which a good position well fortified could give them. When they came back to the road Miller said to Elliott: "You may do just as you please, but I don't want to take my men in there and have them slaughtered." Gen. Garrard then said to Elliott: "I believe I could move them out of that if it was necessary, but I don't believe in fighting for fight's sake; we have enough of it to do when it is necessary. Besides this is Sunday, and I do not want to fight *to-day*; and *further* if we let them alone they will be gone by to-morrow anyhow." With a full knowledge that we have such commanders as these over us, we always feel perfectly willing to undertake anything they ask us to do. Gen. Elliott then ordered us to go into camp. We called in our skirmishers and rode back to King's Hill and have to wait quite a while for the 123d to return, and while we wait we will give some further details of what seemed to be the general plan of the rebels to capture our division. It must be borne in mind that the rebs possess at least a hundred advantages to our one in knowing exactly our every movement, number and position, while we had all the time to be guessing at theirs. They were thoroughly acquainted with the country, and had their spies and sentries on every hill, while we were always in the valleys. When the 123d left King's Hill they went about five miles and met a column of rebels marching east to get into our rear. Thus, you see, they had a complete trap set for us. Had we become engaged with those in front we certainly would have had all we could attend to, and had this force then attacked us in the rear, owing to the extreme narrowness of the valley our escape would have been difficult. But the 123d attacked this column so vigorously that the enemy thought the regiment was our whole division, and fell back promptly. The 123d followed briskly, and when they got on top of the mountain they could look over to the south and west and see nearly the whole of Hood's army with nothing but the mountain, five or six miles wide, between us. They also captured a circular which announced that Gen. Beauregard had assumed command of the rebel army in this department. They further learned that the rebel army was heading for Decatur, on the Tennessee River. We went into camp where we were last night.

October 24th. The sun was an hour high when we mounted and rode back to Little river and went into camp a mile above the ford, on the west side of the river, just after noon. As we went into camp our trains came up to us. We were very glad to see them, for many reasons. In the first place, we always considered that when we would go into camp and our trains were with us we were at home. In the next place our rations had been out for two days; and in the third place we had not had a change of clothes, or a chance to change, for 22 days, and they were getting entirely "*too many of us.*" We hoped we might now have a chance to wash ourselves and put on a clean shirt. We got dinner, drew rations, and immediately got orders to be ready to move at five p. m., but the whole brigade made a break for the river. We were determined to have a wash and a clean shirt at all hazards, and we think we saw more men swimming than we ever saw at any time in our lives. Almost everybody washed their clothes and spent a good part of the night drying them. We did not move that night, but were called up at two o'clock in the morning of October 25th, and moved in one hour. We got back to our old camp of the 23d just at sun-up, and found that the 15th corps had camped there and had moved on down the valley at daylight. We followed them, and when we got to King's Hill we heard heavy skirmishing, with some artillery firing, down at the place where we were checked yesterday. The firing did not last long, and when we came to where we were day before yesterday we found, sure enough, that the rebels had evacuated their works, just as Gen. Garrard said they would, simply leaving a small rear guard with which the infantry had been skirmishing. It was now found, too, that we did well not to attack the rebels at this place, as all of Hardee's corps were lying behind the works, and had their artillery so planted as to rake nearly every foot of the whole valley in front of their works. The 15th corps went into camp at the works, and sent one division on around the southern end of the mountain to see which direction the rebels had taken. Our division bivouacked and spent the day foraging, Company I on picket at King's Hill. Plenty of forage for man and beast.

October 26th. Moved back to Little River at daylight, taking a road to the right of one we had run back and forth on so often. This road led us past quite extensive iron works, and a little village called Round Mountain Town; both the works and the village had been burned. Everything indicated that a large business had been done there. We got back to camp at noon and found the mail had come in, making only four days' mail in six weeks. After dinner we sent out strong foraging parties. We supposed we would now get to rest, as it was generally well understood that all further pursuit of Hood was abandoned for the present It began to rain in the evening and rained hard and steadily all night.

October 27th. We were called up this morning at 3 o'clock. We had had 20 days without a drop of rain, and the nicest of weather; but when it rains in the South it rains, and now it seemed to be trying to make up for lost time, and we had the worst time getting our coffee boiled we had had for many a day. We forgot to state, in its proper place, that Minty's brigade had run so nearly out of horses that they turned all they had over to our brigade and started on foot for Chattanooga yesterday. It was a bitter pill getting started this morning, but we got off long before daylight; we crossed the Little River to the east, or north side, and went right down it seven miles till we struck the Chattooga, which we found so swollen by the rain last night that we could not cross it, hence we turned north up the stream four miles, to where the 23d corps had a pontoon, crossed, and went six miles to Cedar Bluffs, where we found the 23d corps camped on both sides of the Coosa river, and a good pontoon, over which we crossed. This is said to be the point at which Gen. Jackson once crossed this river on one of his expeditions against the Indians.

Here Maj.-Gen. Wilson came to us. He had been sent out here from the Army of the Potomac by Gen. Grant, to take command of all the cavalry in the West. He is said to be the best cavalry general in the army and has just relieved Gen. Elliott. Garrard and Wilson are both with us. None of our division are on this expedition except our brigade and the 3d Ohio, of Long's brigade, which is temporarily attached to our brigade, the balance of Long's brigade having turned over their horses and gone to the rear to re-mount. After crossing the Coosa we went nearly due south 11 miles, which brought us to a large, deep stream, called Terrapin Creek; we crossed it about the middle of the afternoon, and the 3d Ohio, 98th and 123d Illinois, bivouacked, or at least got dinner, but the 17th was ordered to go to Leediga, while Capt. Thomson, Co. D, Seventy-Second, was ordered to take our regiment and go to Jacksonville, 20 miles distant, nearly south from where we then were. Gen. Wilson told him it was reported that there were some rebels out there and to go out and see. This was rather indefinite instructions, but we started. Three miles south-east of where we left the command we passed through a little town called Coloma, where there was quite a large flouring mill. From here we took straight south, up one branch of Terrapin Creek, and went three miles further, when the advance guard, one-half mile ahead, on the top of a hill, were seen to come suddenly to a halt. Capt. Thomson halted the column and sent forward to see what was the matter. From the top of the hill where the advance guard were could be seen a long line of works and an army of men behind them, a little more than a mile away. This was at a little town called Goshen, and here were two divisions of rebels. Capt Thomson sent back a courier to Gen. Wilson to tell him he thought we had better not go to Jacksonville. But pretty soon skirmishing began, and it was soon found that we had got such a good hold we could not let go, and, to say the least of it, we felt a little bit cheap, as we were at least eight miles from any support, and the rebels were pressing our skirmishers pretty closely, trying to find out how many of us there were. We were well satisfied, from the number already seen, that if we should undertake to fall back, or show any signs of weakness at all, they would capture us. So we firmly held our ground and kept up the boldest kind of a front till after sundown. This made the Johnnies think we had come to stay. The courier from Gen. Wilson returned and told us he didn't think we had better go to Jacksonville; but how to get away from there had been botherings us for two hours. Company C, Capt. Glaze, was put on rear guard, and we mounted as quietly as we could and "lit out" lively, though very quietly. We got back to Colmoa just as it began to grow a little dark. Here we got all the flour we needed, and had orders to get forage between that and camp. About a mile from the mill a squad from Company I turned off to the left after forage. We had gone but a little way and were moving on quietly, when a mounted rebel dashed up to us and was within 20 feet of us before we had time to halt him; when halted he wheeled his horse and was lost in the darkness in a minute. We at once concluded he was on his way to burn the bridge and thus cut off our retreat. A mile from the road we found plenty of corn, and while some were filling the forage sacks others killed a hog that weighed 200 pounds, and in a few minutes we were mounted and started for camp. It was now dark as pitch.

We must get Company C away from the rebels, and shall do it in Capt. Glaze's own words: "The rebels pursued us closely. How to keep them off and get our forage (which *must* be had) was the problem. The balance of the regiment was soon out of sight, and if we were to have any forage we must fight for it. The company was divided into three squads; one was rear guard, one was kept in readiness to fight when the rear was pursued too closely, and the remainder got the grub. It was a hard afternoon (or night, rather) on the boys of Company C, but we got to camp safe and sound, although followed inside the picket line. It was long after dark when we got to camp."

When the squad from company I started for camp they had already ridden 38 miles during the day, and they and their horses had been 16 hours without a bite to eat. Their horses were now so heavily laden with forage, and they were so jaded already, that they could scarcely raise the trot. We were yet three miles from where we left the command at the bridge, and our regiment had broken up in squads of from four to a dozen each, and gone for forage. We were sure the rebels were following us, and wasted no time in getting back to the bridge. It was 9 o'clock when we got there, and to our surprise and disgust not a man was to be found. While we were gone, the command had gone back over the bridge, and camped four miles up the creek, and, so far as we could then see, had left no trace of their ever having been there, and we could only guess at the direction they had gone. We thought of camping at once, but we knew the rebels would be on us in a few minutes, and that our comrades were needing the provisions we had with us; hence we concluded to make an effort to find camp. But everything was so still! Not even the braying of a hungry mule to indicate that camp was within 10 miles of us, and we mark down that night as being the worst experience of our lives in finding camp. It was midnight when we got in.

The 17th Indiana had a lively scout, as well as our regiment. They took a road up the creek two or three miles to the east of the one we were on, and went about nine miles. The road they were on led to a little town called Leediga, three miles east of Goshen. They were more fortunate and successful than we were. They encountered a squad of rebels, captured 13 of them, and 20 of their horses, besides picking up 10 or 12 horses on the road; had one man wounded, and got back to camp in good time.

CHAPTER XXXIII.

From October 28th to December 1st, 1864.—We Find as Many Rebels as Gen. Wilson Wants to See—How we Let Go—Gen. Thomas to Take Care of Hood and Sherman Turns Back Towards Atlanta—All Go Foraging and Come Back in Haste and Save a Train from Capture—Shooting Hogs and Scaring the Darkies—Excitement About Being Dismounted—Order to Turn Over Horses, Saddles and Bridles—The Order Not Received with Applause—Incidents of Turning Over the Horses—Big Bundles and Hard Marching—Rations of Whisky and a Rainy Night—Severe Marching in the Rain and Wind—Trying to Go North on the Trains—Capt. Thomson Prevents an Explosion—Get to Chattanooga—Taking Wood from the Provost Guard—Going to Clean the Guards Out—Sickness in the Chattanooga Mud Hole—Going to Nashville—A Narrow Escape Back to Louisville—Camp at Oakland—Looking over Into God's Land—Suffering for Wood—"I Want My Money"—Making Out Pay Rolls—Gov. Morton Sets About Relieving our Sufferings—Our Indiana Friends Flock In—We Get One Year's Pay—Thanksgiving Dinner—Soldiers Going Home—Exchanging Clothing with Citizen Friends—Presenting a Sword to Col. Miller—Addresses.

October 28th. We were up by 4 o'clock this morning and moved at daylight; taking the road the 17th were on yesterday we went up one branch of Terrapin creek, in a south-east direction, for eight miles, and then crossed to the south side of the creek by a very large grist-mill. After going up the creek a short distance, the column was halted and the 17th and 123d sent forward to feel for the rebels. They had not gone a mile till they were very successful in finding them. Two companies of the 17th were advance guard, and the first thing they knew were entirely surrounded, had two men killed and two wounded, and five captured, and had they not fought manfully, and the balance of the regiment charged promptly, the whole of the two companies would have been gobbled beyond a peradventure. But they charged right into the thickest of them, and thus saved the two companies. The whole regiment now found itself in just the same fix the two companies had been. The rebels were shooting into them from every side, front and rear. The 123d Illinois and 3d Ohio hurried up and cleared the way in the rear of the 17th, but they soon found there were at least four brigades of Gen. Jackson's cavalry against the three regiments. They were posted for a fight and prepared for it, and had our men given back the least bit, or shown any weakness, the rebels no doubt would have charged upon them; but our men stood their ground manfully, and began to fall back slowly. It began to be a serious question how we were going to let go our hold, or get away from there. Gen. Wilson's orders to the 17th were to capture a prisoner if they had to take him out of the column. It was a plain case now that he was getting to see all the rebels he wanted to. We did not go there for a fight, were not expecting it, nor were we prepared for it. But something had to be done, and that quickly, too. So the Seventy-Second and 98th were hastily dismounted and *all* the lead horses sent back across the creek, and the two regiments formed a line of battle just behind the other three, and let them fall back slowly through our ranks, and we held the rebels in check till they in turn had re-formed their line in *our* rear, when we all began to fall back slowly, skirmishing all the way. Our horses were now brought back and so arranged that the men could mount without delay, and after much difficulty all got safely across the creek, burning the mill as we fell back. Col. Miller, in his notes of this affair, says: "Near Leediga had an engagement with the rebel Gen. Jackson's cavalry. Lost 10 men killed and wounded." We moved back 10 miles toward Cedar Bluff, the rebels following us for six miles, closing up the rear guard on to the main column, at times quite lively, and skirmishing all the time. As we moved north-west the whole country south of us seemed to be full of rebels, and several times they came into the road between our rear guard and the main column. Company E, of our regiment, was rear guard, and Sergeant Wilhite in his manuscript, says: "The rebels followed and pressed us all the afternoon. We took the advantage of every field and opening by riding fast as we could across them, and then would halt behind the fence and await the rebels and fire on them as they would attempt to cross the open space; but the rebels would soon move around on both sides and flank us, and we would have to skin out for the next position." There is no disguising the fact that we made pretty good time, and went into camp seven miles from Cedar Bluffs. The whole of the 23d corps were in camp close to us. The main part of Hood's army had appeared at Decatur, a hundred miles from where we skirmished with them on the 23d. Hood had left all the cavalry he then had with him, under the command of Gen. Jackson, at Gadsen, on the Coosa river, 10 miles south of where we last met them, and when Sherman abandoned the pursuit of Hood and began to move his army towards

Atlanta, the cavalry had moved straight east to Goshen and Leediga, and we were sent out to feel of these fellows, and in turn got felt of ourselves.

October 29th. Gen. Sherman has now sent back to Chattanooga the 4th corps to aid Gen. Thomas to keep Hood out of Tennessee, while he (Sherman) is now moving back to Atlanta with the balance of the army. The 23d corps moved early this morning, going south to a road leading toward Atlanta, called the old Alabama road, three miles south of our camp. They moved on the road leading to Leediga; at the crossing of these two roads is the Spring Creek post office, and about 11 a. m. we mounted and moved out to this cross roads, as a guard for the train, and bivouacked north of the old Alabama road, our regiment on the east side of the Leediga road, and the balance of the brigade on the west side. In the north-east angle of the cross roads stood a house (post office), and north-east of the house a field of eight or ten acres, and our regiment was camped at the north-east corner of this field, a quarter of a mile from the cross roads. Just on going into camp we got orders to send out foragers. As the order was given in such a general way, nearly every man in the brigade thought that meant him, and in less than 20 minutes there was not one-third of the different regiments, including lead-horses, pack-mules, niggers, and all, left in camp. All the balance had struck out south, toward Leediga and the valley of the Terrapin Creek, for forage, and of course, just literally swarmed all over the whole country, two to ten men in a squad. In less than an hour some of them had got five or six miles from camp, and some of them soon ran foul of the rebels, and four or five got captured, and many others terribly frightened, and in a short time came rushing into camp, scattering the alarm, like fire, in every direction, stating that our foragers were being all gobbled up, and that the rebels would be on us in a few minutes. The rapid firing we heard away over south of us, gave a rich, glowing color to the story. There wasn't a commissioned officer of the Seventy-Second present in camp, but Sergeant Magee gathered his gun and hallooed: "Come on, every man of you!" and started as hard as he could run for the cross roads. We got there just as Capt. Thomson did, with four others from other regiments. There was a long train of wagons passing along the road to the east, and we hastened to the south side of the road; by this time the foragers were coming in from the south like a whirlwind, the forage flying in every direction, the firing a mile out, lively, and coming closer. There had been no orders given, because there had been no officers present to give orders.

But in less than five minutes from the time the alarm was given, every fellow in camp had instinctively gathered his gun and struck out for the point of danger. In less than ten minutes more, about 200 out of the brigade had formed a line of battle on the south side of the road, and up to this time there were not half a dozen officers present from the whole brigade, but every fellow felt the importance of being on time, and the men had fallen in line just as fast as they had come up, regardless of regiment or company. By this time Col. Miller was on hand, and his presence encouraged us. We had a strong picket out on the road south, and Col. Miller sent his orderly out to see if they were all at their posts. The foragers were still pouring in, and the firing still coming closer, and we were getting ready to move forward, when the orderly returned and said the pickets were all right, had a strong line of works thrown up across the road, and enough foragers had stopped there to whip a whole brigade.

By this time the rebels had got up to the picket post, and were soon driven off, which was quite a relief to us. The wagon train had also got past, and the rear guard, a regiment of infantry, came along, and the colonel, seeing us there in line of battle, asked what was the matter. It was explained to him that if it had not been for us, the rebels, in all probability, would have got his train. He thanked us very kindly, and turned to a full brigade band and said: "Give 'em a tune." They played us some splendid music, and we gave them three cheers, and Col. Miller dismissed us.

There were about 100 of the Seventy-Second present, and we all started in a bunch, just east of the house, north-east towards our camp, when one of the most ridiculous scenes occurred we had yet seen. Just then a party of foragers that belonged to the infantry with the train, drove a bunch of 20 or 30 nice hogs into the field, at the north-west corner, for the purpose of catching them. The hogs started to run right along in front of us toward the south-east corner. Our regiment deliberately deployed in single rank and made a grand charge on those hogs, and such another hallooing and shooting we never heard. In less than two minutes we simply cleaned that bunch of hogs out. We don't think one of them escaped; and furthermore we do not think the infantry got a single hog. But the fun of it is still to come. The center of the field was higher than where we were, so that every shot we fired struck the ground and glanced (ricocheted) up and went whistling through the trees right over our camp. Most of the foragers had got in, and while unsaddling their horses were telling the negroes how near the Johnnies came to getting them. The pack mules were unsaddled and the negroes were getting dinner; when we raised the yell and began to shoot, and the bullets to whistle through the trees, and as they could not see us they supposed the Johnnies were right on to them. It scared the negroes, and some of the men too, nearly to death, and such another saddling up and getting out of that you never did see. Some of the niggers took to the woods and didn't get back for an hour; but we were into camp before the men had time to think what they were about; and then to see them jerk off their saddles and pretend they weren't scared, was the most ridiculous thing we ever saw; but it was no use It was too plain a case, and we think we never heard such laughing as we had at their expense.

October 30th. Last night five or six hundred wagons parked in the little field south of our camp, and about midnight those that came in first began to pull out east toward Atlanta, and by sun-up about half of them had got out on to the road. At this time we mounted and put out on the road. We found the teams were kept well closed up, and as the roads were good they were moving fast. There was a line of infantry in single file and eight or ten paces apart marching right along on the south side of the road. We moved as fast as we could, also on the south side of the road, over logs and through the brush, and as fast as we would come to a road leading south would leave a half company to picket it, for a half mile to the south, as we anticipated the rebels would attack the train. These pickets would stay out until the train and rear guard had passed them, and then fall in behind. It was 20 miles from Spring Creek Postoffice to Cave Springs, and at night, when Capt. Thomson got through, he had but one company and the half of another; the balance of the regiment had been put on picket on the various roads leading south, and it wasn't much of a country for roads either. The rebels did not molest us through the day (reason: we were prepared) and the train got through all right, which was a big drive for so large a train. The rebs were still watching every movement and were on all the roads south of us. Before going into camp, a squad from Co. E bethought themselves that they needed some fresh pork to help them forget hunger; but not a hog had they seen during the day. Over south of them they saw a house that indicated plenty. There were *plenty* Johnnies there, too, but the demands of the occasion seemed to be imperative. So Sergt. Wilhite, Thos. Haywood, Mason, and three others, charged up to the house, shooting, yelling and making as much noise as a young brigade. The Johnnies "lit" out, and Haywood "lit" in to the hog-pen. The old lady rushed out and said: "Don't you take that hog." Haywood told her they *had to have some pork*. The old lady said: "Never mind, the confedrits will be back here directly and give you h—l!" The boys didn't stop to argue the case, but took the hog, all the same. They were also fortunate in finding a patch of potatoes that had been planted under straw, and they had nothing to do but to kick the straw away and pick up the potatoes. John B. Davis, Co. D, was also fortunate late in the evening in laying in a good supply of meat for his company. We had marched all day through dense woods and a poor country, but to-night we were camped in a most beautiful place called Grand Valley, and there is here, or has been, a most delightful little village called Lordstown. It is here where the rebels were camped when we ran on to their rear guard on the morning of the 11th, and had a man in Co. D killed, three miles east of this. We do not wonder now that Hood could get along very well without any base of supplies, since we have seen the many immensely rich valleys through which he has passed. This valley has afforded an abundance of supplies for the confederate army, but "woe is war," the Yanks will leave but little for the rebels to boast or be proud of. The most of the army are camped here to-night, and to-morrow this beautiful land will be a desolate waste.

October 31st. Bugle-call this morning at 3, and we moved at 5, taking the road north for Rome, the 23d corps and all *its* trains moving just as we moved yesterday, and the 29th Illinois picketing the roads to the east as we did to the south. They were fired on some during the day, but no damage done. The 23d corps is going back to Chattanooga to help "Pap" Thomas manage Hood. We got to our old camp of the 11th, a mile and a half south-west of Rome, by the middle of the afternoon. We found our wagon train and pack mules here; they had come straight across from Galesville and had been here for a couple of days. The only thing of interest that transpired was the long discussion, participated in by most of the regiment, about Sherman going on a 60 days' raid, and about our turning over horses. As these were mere rumors, and nobody knew anything about it, we did not get the matter fixed up in any definite shape.

November 1st, 1864. For the first time since we can remember we had no bugle call this morning, but the idea was so prevalent in the brigade that some very radical change in our 'status" was going to take place, that most of the men were up early. Nearly every one by this time had made up his mind that we were going to be dismounted, and it was bothering the men wonderfully to know what would become of us if we should be. It must not be forgotten that we were sworn into the service as foot infantry, and it struck us as probable, if we should turn over our horses, that we might never get any more, and the idea of having to march and carry a knapsack was not pleasant, to say the least of it. Breakfast was not over until the wildest excitement prevailed in all our camps, and rumors were flying thick and fast We had never seen the whole brigade so excited before. About the first thing the men began to do after breakfast was to overhaul their knapsacks and see what things they could best afford to throw away in case they *should* be dismounted. Not more than one-third of the men had knapsacks at all, and most of these had been cut to pieces and remodeled so as to strap them on the saddle, and were entirely unfitted to carry on the back. Besides, since we were mounted we had carried everything we wanted, "general orders" and "punishments," to the contrary notwithstanding, and every man of us had twice as much clothing and blankets as foot-infantry ever carried, and *what should we do with them?* The fact is, we had so long been used to so many luxuries that we were entirely spoiled and unfitted for foot-infantry, and so the question was answered by each fellow for himself determining to take all he had along with him, cost what it would. The excitement still increased until about 9 a. m., when commanders of companies came into the men's quarters and told them to get their horses, saddles and bridles, ready to turn over immediately The order was not received with any demonstrations of applause, nor yet with cursing, as we had seen orders received many times before. But the men were not in a hurry to obey. A moment's reflection took all the excitement out of them, and for the first time some of them seemed to realize that they were about to part with something that was dear to them, and a sullen indifference seemed to settle down over them, and the order had to be repeated several times before any attempt was made to obey. During these few minutes of comparative silence a thousand reflections rushed through their minds. It was the parting of old friends; the assuming of new relations; and the ponderous thought of "how in the world will I carry all my clothes and blankets?" But we must quit generalizing, and give our own individual experience, and venture the assertion that it will answer for nine out of every ten private soldiers in the brigade. Since we had left the hospital in July, 16 months ago, we had not had our knapsack strapped to our back, and had never carried it. We had cut it to pieces and remodeled it so as to fit closely and compactly to the cannel of our saddle; our haversack we had never carried, and it was fastened to the near side of the pommel; our canteen was hung to the other side of the pommel, as was also a good hatchet. When on a march our cartridge box was swung loosely to the pommel, and if we had five days' rations, it hung on the right side, and if our rations were out it hung on the left, but was never fast, so that any moment we could dismount and sling it over our shoulder. The muzzle of our gun, up to the first band, was stuck into a boot at the right side, by the saddle girth, and a strap around our shoulder held it up by our side when riding, and this was the only article strapped or fastened to us. Under our saddle we carried two good sleeping blankets, a "dog-tent," and a gum blanket. In our cartridge box we carried 40 rounds of metallic cartridges, and in our saddle pockets 40 to 60 rounds more, an extra horse shoe, some nails, etc. In our knapsack were a shirt, pair of socks, pair of drawers, a portfolio (our children will some day be proud of that old portfolio, as this history owes all its value to that,) paper, envelopes, thread, buttons, and a Bible (we have it yet,) and other useful articles. Bear in mind that a cavalry man and his horse live together, and we never slept a night, except when laying in camp, but our saddle was under our head, or near it; and day or night we could just lay our hand on any single article we wanted. But what should we do with all these things now? We had been so long together that each piece seemed a part of ourself. At the pommel of our saddles were three stout leather straps, with buckles, and at the stern were three more, with which we could strap anything fast, from a spring chicken to a yearling calf.

Well, after repeated orders, the men reluctantly went to their saddles and stripped everything off that belonged to the "soldier," knapsacks, tents, blankets, &c., rolled them up, and then deliberately took off the straps and buckled around them. This was against positive orders, as the straps belonged to the saddles, and the saddles *didn't* belong to the men. But the men sat down on their things and said, "Now, if you want these straps, come and get them." But now (to us) came the most painful part of the whole business, and we doubt not very many others felt it as keenly as we did. We were ordered to lead out our horses. We are a man of most powerful attachments. *Anything* that we do love, we love as life itself, and no *friend* ever had occasion to reproach us with a want of attachment. The reflection is a happy one with us, that we had not an enemy in the regiment. *All* had treated us with the most profound respect, and to many we were more strongly attached than to a brother, because our attachment had been sealed by blood and danger. To none were we more firmly attached than to our horse, "Stumbler." Upon more than one occasion, by his sagacity, had he saved our life, and how *could* we part with him? There is only one step from the sublime to the ridiculous, and just now we have witnessed that step. The horses of our brigade are to go to Kilpatrick's division, and his Inspector General stands on a high stump with a long whip in his hand, and as the horses are led past him a motion of the whip to the right or left indicates whether the horse is received or rejected. Well, we have the order that all horses that are rejected are to be ridden through to Chattanooga, along with our wagon train, and the officers' horses, which belong to them, and the dismounted men, are to go through on the cars; and it is funny to see the stratagems used by the men to get the horses to pass muster. Company H has just had three horses rejected, and yet the men keep whipping around and fall in line and try it again, and finally succeed in getting them off their hands. While there was scarcely a horse in the whole brigade (or but few at least) that had started from Columbia, Tennessee, with us, ours was yet strong, hearty, and in good condition, and we believe we could have used him till the end of the war. But we were ordered to lead him out, and he had to go. You may call us a fool, but we felt just like we were parting with our best friend. We had eaten together and slept together till he seemed a part of ourself. Each company led out their horses and turned them over to another company, drawn up in line to receive them, and as our horse was about the best in the company, he fell to the lot of an orderly sergeant. We gave him a short history of the horse, told him he had saved our life, that he was good, faithful and kind, and begged him to take good care of him, and sorrowfully hastened away. We went back to where we had left our things, but what desolation! Horses, saddles and bridles, all gone. It didn't look like camp at all, and it wasn't camp, either. All discipline was gone, and nothing but a perfect mob was left. But let the curtain fall—the campaign is ended.

By noon everything but our guns and accoutrements and our individual "traps" was turned over to Kilpatrick's division, and we now know that Sherman is going on a 60 days' raid, and that we are going back somewhere in the rear to be re-mounted. But just where we are going to, or how we are going to get there, we cannot tell. The fact is, we hardly know how to get our dinners. The men are now trying to arrange their enormous loads so as to carry them, and we think that David dressed up in Saul's armor could not have felt more awkward than we do. As our wagons are going back we don't see why they might not haul our extra cartridges, at least—but no! Red tape says we shall carry them. This may do for discipline, but it is hard on the poor soldier. From the time we began to write this book we have dreaded this chapter. From the time we turned over our horses till we were re-mounted "woe betide us." It is a tale of suffering and hardship. But we must begin. So about 4 p. m. we were all called up into line, old infantry style, ready for a march of 24 miles, nearly north, to Calhoun, on the railroad, and 10 or 12 miles south of Resaca. And we'll bet you a quart of soap you never saw such bundles for men to undertake to carry, in your life. Our bundles on first going into the service, at Indianapolis, were nowhere in comparison. We used to say we could tell a recruit or a *new* regiment just by the loads they carried, but we now discounted any set of recruits we ever saw. We think Col. Miller fully comprehended the situation. and he came around to each of the regiments and in his usual good natured way explained to us just what he wanted us to do. He told us that we were expected to make the trip to Calhoun by to-morrow night; that he well knew we were in no condition to march, and the trip would be a hard one, but the more we made of it this evening the less we would have to do to-morrow, and that if we all should do our best and behave as well as we always had, he would give us a dram of whisky. These little speeches always did us a great deal of good; we gave him three cheers and started—our hearts a great deal lighter than our loads. We crossed the Etowa on a pontoon, passed through Rome, and we never saw such marching but once before, and that was our run from Salt River to Louisville, two years ago. With whoop and halloo, we were on the run nearly half of the time. but we kept together and well closed up, and went into camp old infantry style, in an old corn field, just at dark, six miles from Rome, Company E on picket. The march was not long, but oh! it was terrible. Sure enough the whisky was forthcoming by the time we had supper over, and each man got over half a pint—more than twice the usual ration. We have written what would make over four pages of this book, trying to describe what followed, but just give it up. We can't do the subject justice and so shall leave out the whole of it, and confine ourselves to a few common-place remarks. Suffice it to say that those who, by experience, had a right to know, said it was good whisky; but every one was so very tired, and the terrible excitement of the last two days had worn so heavily upon the nervous system, that what nearly every man needed more than anything else was to lie down and sleep, and almost every one did so as soon as he got his supper. But there are always some fools in every crowd, and our regiment was no exception to the rule. Well, some of these fellows commenced to drink as soon as they got their whisky, and by midnight were melodiously drunk. Webb Reed, of Co. F, fell in the fire and would have burned up if Kendall had not pulled him out, and he has never been known to drink a drop since. But hold on, we'll not tell on any more. There had been no tents put up; the men just tumbled down in the corn furrows, and in a few minutes were sleeping as only a tired soldier can sleep. Just about 9 o'clock it began to rain, an easy, good natured rain, without any bluster or fuss about it, and kept it up so steadily that by 1 o'clock the corn furrows were full of water. About that time some "cuss" stumbled over us and waked us up. As long as we lay still the water warmed up about as fast as it fell and we didn't feel it, but when the fellow put his foot right where we put our last night's rations, of course we moved a little. "Thunder and Blixun!" We were in water four inches deep, and to say we "yelled," hardly conveys the idea. We made noise enough to wake up somebody else, and of course he yelled too, being just as deep in the water as we were; and like a hundred mules feeding at the same trough, the "kick" went round, and in less than 10 minutes every man in the regiment was up, yelling like an Indian. We never heard just such hallooing but once before. Every man in the regiment was wet as he could be, and for the next half hour kept up the yelling as if his life depended upon it. You must mind it was November and the water was cold enough to make a fellow halloo whether he wanted to or not, and by common consent it was agreed that there would be no more sleeping that night. Those who had not drank their whisky before going to bed, thought a little would be good now, but we promised not to tell it. The next hard work was to build fires, and notwithstanding the rain was now pouring down in torrents, in a short time there were a hundred piles of rails "blazing high."

November 2d. As already stated, we were up at one o'clock, not from choice, but because some drunken vagabond happened to set his foot—well, I'll say from the force of circumstances. While we were standing around our fire trying to dry one side as fast as the other got wet, we got our breakfast, and were all ready to move an hour before daylight. It kept on raining harder and harder, and our officers didn't like to move. Just as it began to get a little light we fell in and moved out on the road. Col. Miller came around again and told us he would not ask us to march in ranks or to keep closed up. Every man might take his time to it and march as he pleased, so he made the trip to-day; that we would take the cars as soon as we got to Calhoun. One thing we must not do, we must not get off the road or straggle off through the country, nor even stop at the houses, as the country was full of bushwhackers and he would be sorry to lose a single man of us. Nothing but the profoundest love and respect for an officer would prompt men to obey such an order as that; yet, sir, every fellow did his very best to get to Calhoun in the shortest possible time, and it took some of them three days to make it. This beat all the marching we ever saw a soldier do. After Col. Miller made us his little speech we cheered him and struck out. The rain had raised all the little streams till many we had to wade were knee-deep. The mud was two inches deep and very sticky and heavy. We hadn't marched more than a half mile till some of them began to think we were going too fast and others thought we were going too slow, and from that we broke ranks and began to scatter. At the end of three miles we sat down on a fence and looked ahead and behind to see how we were getting along. We never saw such a mob in our life. Some were two miles ahead of us and some about that far behind; some were just about drunk enough to lie down and go to sleep, and others had taken just enough to make them feel as strong as Samson and lively as crickets; some were mad as hares and cursing till everything was fairly blue; others were singing like nightingales. For our own part we felt it was going to take all our strength, all our energies and utmost exertions, to make the "riffle," so we started on at a slower pace and rested every three miles, and at the end of 12 miles had plenty of company; but from that time did most of our marching alone, and for two hours at a time there was no one close enough to speak to. Some of the men got through the 18 miles by noon, but the sun was not an hour high when we got there, a perfectly used-up man. We think we never suffered more from marching, and this is saying a good deal. We could not step over a rail three inches high. Not one-third of the regiment had got in yet. It had rained on us nearly all day. We went to bed at dark and never got up until the sun was an hour high, and some did not get up till noon, and had we been required to move the next day not one in ten would have been able to move at all. Men came staggering into camp every hour of the night, and when morning came a hundred men were still missing. Col. Miller says, in his notes, "The men are suffering from cold and wet."

November 3d. Our camp last night was on a hill half a mile north of the railroad depot and the village, and at 9 a. m. we moved down to the railroad ready to take the cars for Chattanooga. A few trains came along going north, but the train-men declared their trains were so heavily laden they could not haul us, and refused to let us on them, and we had to lie there by the railroad in the sun till noon, when we deliberately took possession of the abandoned houses, and declared we would stay there a dry month before we would put ourselves to any further trouble to get to the rear. If we were needed at any given point let those in authority make a way for us to get there. In this we reckoned a little bit without our host, as we had started from Rome with but five days' rations, and two days were already out, and there was no depot of rations near us. We had the most comfortable quarters, and weren't in a hurry to leave them. There were about a hundred houses in the town, and but three or four families, including the negroes. The balance had all "started on for Dixie" when Gen. Johnson abandoned Resaca last spring. Of course all who had gone were rebels and we felt we had a right to all the benefits and privileges of the place, and felt perfectly at home. The 23d corps had left Rome the day before we did, marched back to Resaca and there taken the cars and gone to the rear; their camp and garrison equipage was now going back on the cars. While there were a score of trains going south all empty, those going back were all heavy. We think one regiment did get away by climbing on top of a train, 15 or 20 to the car. We had ridden on top of cars before and it wasn't a bit funny, and so waited. But we did have some fun during the day nevertheless. We have already intimated that yesterday morning, about the time we left camp, some of the men got a little too much "tanglefoot" and had finally laid down and gone to sleep. Many others got crippled in the will, while others actually couldn't make the trip. All these had just naturally lain down and gone to sleep one or two in a place, just where they happened to be. To-day by 9 or 10 o'clock they began to come in one at a time, then two, three, six or ten, and at every fresh arrival the regiment would fall out and cheer them. Many of the stragglers had not forgotten their predilection for picking up things, had wandered around over the country till they found an old convalescent horse or mule, made halters out of withes and strings, strapped all their "traps," guns and accoutrements on to them, and came moving into camp with all the dignity of a market-gardner peddling "truck." Some of the cases were provokingly amusing. Late in the evening, about the last to come in were four fellows who had pressed in an old cow, that looked as though she might have been one that Daniel Boone had lost on his way from North Carolina up into Kentucky. Citizens say he passed right by here. They had strapped all their things on to her, which made a bundle about as big as a hay cock. One had her by the horns, another by the tail, and one on each side, just to keep her straight, you know. The whole regiment fell into line and gave them three and a tiger. It rained in the evening and almost all night.

November 4th. We had a good night's rest, sleeping on the floor, and we enjoyed it hugely, and this morning began to feel like fighting-cocks again. Another regiment got off by climbing on top the cars. Still we waited. Col. Miller began to get afraid we would get out of rations, and also took the cars and went ahead to see if he could make any arrangements for us. His train got as far as Dalton, ran off the track, had to lie over night, and the next day, the 5th, went clear around by Cleveland and got to Chattanooga after night. While we are waiting, we will tell a little story of Davis, company D, and some of his comrades. From our present prospect of getting transportation, they began to think a "shortage" of rations probable, and as both armies had passed over this country, there was little left that could crow or squeal. But after considerable reconnoissance they found a nice hog in a close pen, and a Springfield rifle in the hands of a soldier belonging to an Illinois regiment standing beside it. The night was dark; a charge was made on the sentry, his gun taken away from him, the hog killed and carried in triumph to camp, and the fellow's gun left to guard the pen. It may be proper here to say that Sherman, in making preparations for his march to the sea, had 3,000 car loads of military stores he did not want to take along with him. This would require 200 trains to move back as soon as he wanted it done, and just now these 200 trains were on their way to Atlanta, all going down, but none coming up. There are no telegraph stations along the road now, and of course the trains all have to go one way at a time, or else there would be innumerable collisions. It was getting late in the evening, and we were getting a little shaky, our rations were nearly out, and we knew we would have to go one way or the other, or starve. So we determined to climb on the next train going north, at a venture. For about an hour, late in the evening, the trains ceased going south, and then just one came up from that direction, and we went for it. The train men didn't want to let us on, but we told them it was no use, we were going. The train was so short that we did not have two cars to the company. They were all box cars, and all as full as they could be crammed; hence we had to take the top, or stay. We thought this might be our last chance, and climbed on. We got to Resaca just after dark; here we met some more trains, and as trains going to the front had the right of way, ours had to turn out. It would take a long chapter to tell of the concentrated miseries we endured as we lay on that train of cars during that long, cold night. The trains kept coming all night, not in a regular stream, but by fits and starts, sometimes two and then a half dozen in quick succession; sometimes 10 minutes between trains, sometimes an hour. There was no telegraph, and our train men were afraid to start. We were afraid to get off and build fires lest the train might pull out and leave us, and so we piled up on top the cars, more like hogs than men, and wore our hip bones and the night out. This was one of the longest nights we ever put through. Morning came at last, but with it no hope. More trains kept coming, and we noticed our train men were getting about as anxious as we were, and they began to halloo at the men going down and ask them how many trains were behind. As there was but little time for compliments, they would answer by holding up a finger, meaning one train, or two fingers, meaning two trains. The train men coming down seemed to realize our situation and to sympathize with us, and always answered correctly, sometimes ho'ding up one hand, all the fingers and thumb spread out, and one finger on the other, and sure enough, along would come the six trains. Late in the afternoon there came along a train that had a brakeman on the rear car who must have been considerable of a wag, for when our men asked him the usual question, he seemed to take in the whole situation in a minute, and immediately held up both hands with thumbs stuck out, and then stuck up both feet. Then our train men began to offer some damns, and sure enough, there were a dozen came right along in a string, as close together as they dare run. After they got by, our train men had grown so desperate that they concluded to risk it, and pulled out. It was now sundown, and we made good time till we got within a mile of Dalton, when all at once our engine began to whistle, and scream, and squeal vociferously, and came very suddenly to a stop. Here transpired an incident showing that presence of mind is one of the most valuable qualities. One of the cars, on which Capt. Thomson and his men were riding, was loaded with fixed ammunition, powder, shot, and immense shells used by the siege guns in bombarding Atlanta. The additional weight of the men to the already heavy load of ammunition had so heated up a box as to cause it to blaze up and set fire to the car. The fire soon would reach the ammunition, when an explosion that can be contemplated but with horror must take place. Men who had been calm in the face of an enemy with musketry and artillery, were now pale with fear. Their trusty Spencers were of no avail now. Brave men were almost panic-stricken. There was necessity of *presence of mind* in a commanding officer, as well as *courage*, and Capt. Thomson rushed to the tender of the engine, and with pails carried water and subdued the flames that in a moment's delay would have been so surely disastrous. This was about 9 p. m. Just then we could hear the most terrific whistling and screaming ahead of us we had ever heard. It seemed like a hundred engines all at once were trying to scare something off the track; while our own engine kept squealing out three short toots at a time every minute for nearly an hour.

We had met another batch of 15 or 20 trains, and several of them had already got past Dalton when they met our train, and they didn't want to back out, but insisted on our train backing out. The difficulty was a serious one, and had there not been another road at this place branching off to Knoxville, we do not see but we would have had to back out. After whistling and squalling and cursing for nearly an hour, the trains just in front of us backed up the Knoxville road and we pulled slowly into Dalton, "side tracked," and waited for the balance of the trains to pull out. We never heard so much noise of the kind before; 20 engines all ringing their bells and whistling at once can make a "heap" of noise. Finally they all got off for Atlanta and we got started again. It was now 11 p. m. Our train was short but much too heavily loaded for the engine. The country was mountainous, and the road in a wretched condition, and we stalled many times, and while going down the grades the train would go so fast as to make the men's hair whistle, and many of them lost their knapsacks, blankets and hats. Altogether it was the most miserable night's ride we ever took. We reached Chattanooga shortly after sun-up on the morning of November 6th, having made 54 miles from Resaca.

Ever since the war commenced Chattanooga had been a military post of some importance to either army, and at times had been occupied by as many as 100,000 troops, and immense quantities of ammunition, quartermasters' and commissary stores, were stored here. The ground was rich and loose, and every vestige of sod or grass had long since disappeared, and when it was wet the whole place soon became a perfect quagmire. The place was under the most strict military discipline and police regulations; of these by actual experience we knew nothing, having always been at the front and *never* where we were under such regulations; had always been where we could go and come when we wanted to. So when we got to the city and got off the cars some officious, pompous fellow, belonging to the provost guard, told us we might go into camp "there." The spot indicated was a vacant spot of about an acre near the railroad, was very low and flat and looked as though subject to repeated overflows. There had been no rain for two or three days, yet the ground was still muddy. We never had camped in such a place, and the men declared they never would. The mutinous spirit was spreading and would soon have caused trouble, but just then Col. Miller came around and made us one of his little speeches. He told us we were only going to stay there tilll there would be a train going back to Nashville; that he wanted us close to the railroad so there would be no trouble in getting on to the first train that should go north; that we only wanted to stop and draw rations and then go on. Well, whatever Miller said, that we'd do, no matter what it was; so our officers tried to get us into something like a regiment camp, in columns by companies, but it wasn't any use. Just as soon as they left us we picked up our traps and moved to the highest ground on the lot, and fixed up our dog-tents just as our fancy or convenience dictated No one company was all camped together, but the companies were all mixed through each other promiscuously. Since the morning of the 3d we had not a chance to get a regular meal; that is, we hadn't made coffee, and we never called it a meal without coffee; so as soon as we got our bunks up we determined to have some coffee, and as there was a long pile of wood corded up close at hand, the men just took what they wanted. Some of the officers of the provost guard observed this and pretty soon there was a guard standing by the wood, watching it.

Along in the afternoon we drew some rations, and when supper-time came we wanted more wood, and very naturally went for it, but the guard tried to prevent us from taking it. Our men paid no attention to him, except to curse him a little, and continued to carry off the wood. The guard then hallooed for the "Corporal of the guard," and pretty soon he came with a squad of men and undertook to arrest some of the boys, but they wouldn't arrest worth a cent, but broke for their quarters, got their Spencers, and swore they would just naturally clean the whole d—d provost guard right out, saying they needed the wood and were going to have it. They would certainly have made their words good, but just in the nick of time Col. Miller came on to the ground, and by a half dozen words made everything quiet. He told them they should have all the wood they needed, but so long as we were compelled to stay in this nasty hole we would have to obey orders; that we would get out of here just as soon as we could; and further, that our orderly sergeant should draw our wood, just as he drew our rations, and if we didn't get as much as we needed, let him know and he would make it all right. With this our men were perfectly satisfied and came back and put up their guns; but before doing so they took occasion to inform the guards that they should never cross our path, and as long as we stayed there we just went all over that town and did as we pleased. And we pleased to do a great many things we ought not to have done.

As soon as the guards would find out where we belonged they

would let us pass. We have already spoken of the vast number of trains required to haul back from Atlanta the surplus stores there that Sherman did not want to take with him. There are just 200 engines now engaged in this business, and until all that stuff is brought back to this point there will be no trains go north of this. It took till the 10th to get all the trains ready to start back, and on that day some trains started for Nashville, but they were loaded with sick and wounded soldiers and hospital stores. On the 11th some more trains went north, but still loaded with hospital stores, sick, wounded, &c. It began to rain the day we got to Chattanooga, and rained almost constantly all the time we were there; our camp was a most horrible mud hole, and we suffered intensely, men taking sick and dying in a few days of diarrhœa who had not been sick at all during their service. About 4 p. m. of November 12th, there were three trains started for Nashville; the first one was loaded with hospital stores, sick, wounded, &c., and our division and brigade officers were in the hindmost coach of this train. The next one was of box cars, and the Seventy-Second was put on top of this one, and we were more crowded than we were on the trip from Calhoun. The road before us was the most tortuous, over a country the most mountainous, and the scenery the grandest; but we weren't in a humor to appreciate the scenery. We had ridden over all the country, and over some of it two or three times, and were familiar with it, and weren't caring a fig for high mountains, deep valleys or grand scenery. We had scarcely ever ridden a mile in the service without suffering and torture, and the trip before us wasn't very pleasant to contemplate. We made pretty good time till about sundown, when our train very unceremoniously came to a halt. Twenty-six miles from Chattanooga there is a stream cutting through the Sand mountains to the northwest, called Whiteside creek. There is a bridge 126 feet high over it. This bridge is not a straight one, but semi-circular in shape. Just as the train ahead of us was approaching this bridge, and about 100 yards from the bridge, the hindmost car flew the track. The train kept right ahead, and at the end of 50 yards the trucks were knocked from under the car, at least the hindmost ones were, while the forward trucks had been driven right up through the bottom of the car at the front end, piling the officers rather promiscuously up in the rear of the car. Still the train pulled on, dragging the car along on the rails to the middle of the bridge, and as the bridge was all the time bending to the right, so all the time was the car being dragged nearer and nearer the edge of the bridge, and by the time the cars reached the middle it was so nearly tumbling over that it looked like twenty pounds on the outside corner would tip it off. Just then the coupling broke and the car stopped. We went down into that creek and looked up at that car, and never saw anything look so fearful. It seemed to us the car would surely tumble over on us; it made us shiver to look up. For a moment after the car broke loose all inside was still. The officers had been so bumped and jammed together at the rear that for a time they could not get the door open. They raised the windows and looked out, but drew back in terror. Finally they got the door open and began to crawl out on their hands and knees, one at a time, and strange to say, not a single one of them was hurt. Our old General was about the last to get out, and after he had got out on the bridge it was so high he was scared worse than he had yet been; but he finally succeeded in crawling to the end of the bridge. When he got on to his feet once more he turned around and looked a while at the bridge, then at the car, then away down into the abyss, and as he turned around said, "Those who ride must pay the driver." We passed another miserable night, part of the time on the ground and a part of the time on the cars, not getting to sleep any either place. The night was cold and our sufferings intense. There were several trains in our gang, but all lay still till morning, when it was found necessary to send back to Chattanooga for a wrecking train before the car could be got off the bridge and out of the way. All this took time, and it was noon before an effort was made to get the car off the bridge, and the middle of the afternoon before we got started on again. Thus we had been 24 hours making 26 miles. After passing through the tunnel at the top of the Cumberland mountains, it is three or four miles down to Cowan and we weren't long in going that distance; but half way down the train broke in two and the front end ran clear on to Decherd, 10 miles, before the engineer missed us, and then he had to come back, and it was 11 o'clock before he got hitched on to us again. Our part of the train ran two miles past Cowan before stopping. You see we were having another miserable night of it, as it rained on us almost all night. We will not weary you with further details of our misfortunes. We got to Nashville on the 14th by 9 or 10 o'clock, and were told we could not get horses there, but would have to go back to Louisville. We moved on, getting to Louisville on the evening of the 15th of November, having been five days and nights on top of the cars from the time we left Calhoun till we got to Louisville. We were the worst used up set of fellows you ever saw. We quote from Miller's notes: "Arrived at Louisville and went into camp once more; I am tired of moving on the railroad; I would much rather be at the front and on a campaign than go to the rear." So say we all, as the five days have been the most disagreeable ones we have ever passed in succession. Our brigade moved back on the railroad and went into camp at the Oakland house, on the opposite side of the railroad from our first camp on Southern soil, on August 18th, 1862.

We had a beautiful place for a camp, a rolling, grassy common, large enough to accommodate the whole brigade without crowding. As we well understood we were to stay here till we got horses, we felt the importance of putting our dog tents up in regular order, and in such a way as to keep us as warm as possible, because we were nearly 500 miles north of where we had been at Jonesboro, on the 1st of September, and winter was upon us. We were sure we would suffer with cold, do the very best we could. In undertaking to do this we found ourselves very much embarrassed right in the start. We had always been at the front; always occupied ground from which we had driven the rebels, and always felt that we had a perfect right to appropriate to our own use anything we needed for our comfort or convenience. On going into winter quarters, we would collect boards to make the walls of our houses, and cover them with our dog tents or gum blankets, thus making ourselves very comfortable so far as quarters were concerned. Here were plenty of board fences, and old abandoned houses, all around us, and we could have made ourselves comfortable in half a day, but we were now told we were in the LOYAL STATE OF KENTUCKY, and we mustn't touch a thing except what belonged to the government. So here we were, perfectly helpless, because we hadn't a thing to do with. We could not put up our tents, nor even get our supper. We lay in camp here just six weeks, and during that whole time suffered more from cold and other inconveniences than ever before. The great distance in latitude over which we had traveled was sufficient to make a vast difference in the weather, and besides, on the third day after going into camp it rained and then turned severely cold, even for this country, freezing solid ice, three inches thick. In the next place we had not had a chance to draw clothes for five months, and were all of us nearly naked. In the next place we had no straw to sleep on, and no more wood than would barely cook our meals. This seemed to us "the unkindest cut of all." We had many times before seen the weather so cold we could not sleep, but under such circumstances could build huge fires and keep ourselves warm; but here we had nothing to keep ourselves comfortable any way, no straw! no wood! no clothes. It doesn't take long, under such circumstances, for discontent to manifest itself among the best disciplined troops in the world. Illustrative of this feeling we have a story from Hornada, of Company F: A Dutchman came along one of those cold days and stopped at the guard line with a load of wood which he proposed to sell to Company F. As we had not been paid for 13 months we thought that was adding insult to injury; besides we were not furnishing wood. "Grand Pap," (well known in the regiment) went out and was going to take a few sticks, but the Dutchman objected. Grand Pap just stretched out one of his arms in the direction of the Dutchman's head and he went to sleep for a few minutes, and by the time he woke up his wood was all gone, and he didn't think he had any business further down town, but went back home for more wood. But he didn't come to Company F to sell it.

A better one from Davis, of Company D, is this: "The weather being cold we had need of considerable wood, and the amount daily issued to us would last only till 10 a. m., thus leaving us to shiver the balance of the day. We laid our complaint before the proper officer and were politely told it was all we could get, and that we would certainly be punished if we 'cabbaged' any, Wood was what we wanted and were going to have. We sent to each company in the regiment and told them Co. D's resolution. A certain rail fence was grinning at us across the guard line. We proposed to walk it over into camp. 'All right,' said they, 'We'll share in the fun.' The regiment fell into line, and swinging our hats in the air, and with a yell that would cause even LOYAL KENTUCKY to tremble, we charged upon the rail fence and marched it into camp." To show that none of our own officers were responsible for our suffering we quote from Col. Miller's notes: "November 16th. Tried hard all day to get things for the brigade. * * * Hope to get the men fixed up soon. November 18th. Still raining; have a great deal of trouble in getting the command in living order. November 20th. Clear for once. The men feel better over the weather, for which I feel grateful. November 21st. Very cold. The men are suffering much; got new clothes for most of them. November 22d. Still cold and freezing. I don't care how soon we start for the front where we can get wood." There was a combination of circumstances that heightened and intensified our feelings of discontent. In the first place we had not been paid since the 12th of November last year at Maysville, and that payment was up to October 31st, 1863. In the next place our camp was on ground sufficiently high to enable us to see clear over the city and our own Indiana hills for miles and miles beyond. This was God's country, and after being so far away made us feel like we were almost at home; so near that the thoughts of home constantly haunted us, while at the front these thoughts never brought longing or anxiety with them; but now those hills were a constant invitation to "come over," an invitation which many of our boys found it impossible to resist. We had been promised a furlough of 30 days for each year's service (which is according to the regulations), and as yet but four or five out of each company had ever got furloughs at all, and these only for 20 days apiece, and we had but nine months of our three years yet to serve, and every man of us well knew that when we left this place for the front again we would not see Indiana till the war was over or our time out. We were well satisfied we would stay here a month at least. Then why not let us go home; we could certainly get back long before we would be ready for the front again. But one thing checked the thought in the start, and no doubt saved many from the disgrace of "*Absent without leave*"—that was, the *means* of getting home. It is true there was a strong provost guard in the city, at the river and upon the ferry-boats, to prevent just what a great many worst of all wanted to do, and no soldier was allowed to go to the city or to cross the river without being armed with the necessary pass. This of itself would not have kept our men from going, as was afterwards fully demonstrated. Our men could(and afterwards did)procure citizens' clothes and pass by the guards with impunity. So it was soon found necessary to stop all crossing at the river unless persons had passes signed by the Provost Marshal. This order was promulgated on purpose to keep the men of our brigade from going home without leave. While this was hard on the citizens, it didn't amount to a snap with our soldiers. Our men were too old for that. No provost guard, no camp guard, nor any other kind of a guard, could keep them from going just where they pleased whenever they took a notion. Many times during our service had there been the most positive orders issued by Major Generals for our officers to keep their men in camp, and that, too, under threats of cashiering and dismissal upon their failure to do it, and our officers, in obedience to these orders, had tried every plan they could think of to keep us in, yet to no purpose, and finally gave it up in disgust; for the last 18 months they had never attempted to keep on guards of any kind unless ordered to by their superior officers, and then the thing was so well understood between officers and men—so well understood all around—that guard duty was not kept up as a restraint of any kind, but simply to keep up appearances. Col. Miller soon learned to trust to our honesty and intelligence for anything he wanted done, and he never failed to get us to do anything by appealing to our reason, and we in turn felt that *his* slightest wish was our strongest command, because he had always been honest and straightforward with us, and had never asked us to do anything unreasonable; and on going into camp at Louisville had he told his men they might all go home provided they would come back at the end of three weeks, we verily believe 49 out of 50 would have done it. But we commenced to tell why our whole regiment didn't make a general stampede for the north side of the river the third day after going into camp, for we had never seen such wide-spread dissatisfaction in our regiment. The great desideratum was money. More than a whole year without pay, and we doubt if there was ten dollars in the whole regiment, and we were sure that if we did not get our pay while we were here we would not get it till the war was over; so we could do nothing but sit down and wait and growl, and growl and wait. Not because we wanted the money so badly, because we still had faith in Uncle Sam's ability to pay, and we were sure we would get it some time; but then we wanted to go home so badly and could not go without the money. While at the front such thoughts never haunted us, and a thousand times we had reason to curse the day we started to the rear, and a thousand times we wished we were at the front again. Just now money was what we wanted, and we insert here an actual occurrence in the regiment, as showing the intensity of feeling sometimes manifested by our regiment. During the long and bitter cold nights just after we went into camp, when it was too cold to sleep, when we had no fire, or wood to make a fire with, we would be standing and shivering over a few smoking embers, and the men cursing (not very loud, but very deep) their ill luck, and thinking over their hard service and poor pay, some poor fellow, with feelings overcome, would at the top of his voice, and in doleful refrain, yell out: "*I want my money!*" The sound would be taken up and run from man to man, "*I want my money!*" and from company to company still roll on, "*I want my money!!*" And from regiment to regiment the echo would roll across the city and be reverberated back by the hills beyond, "*I want my money!!!*" For a week there was not a single hour, day or night, but what the doleful sound might be heard, "*I want my money.*" These were no uncertain sounds, either, uttered for pastime or amusement. Sometimes during our service we had been without rations, and then, when tired and hungry, and our patience exhausted, our cry was "*Sowbelly!*" "*Sowbelly!*" "*Sowbelly!*" and it is no fancy sketch to think we see our commissary going to bed after listening to this most euphonious expression for 24 hours, and as he sleeps he sees a thousand demons, with blood-red eyes, fleshless limbs, bristling hair, grinning teeth and forked tongues, spitting fire, rush upon him, hurl him into the bottomless pit, and with forks toss huge chunks of meat after him, and yell in his ears, "*Sowbelly!*" "*Sowbelly!*" "*Sowbelly!*" We tell you, if rations could be got for love or money, they would be got the next morning. Again, when we had served till the middle of December—the first year we went out—with scant clothing, and less than half enough blankets to the regiment, the ground was frozen and covered with snow, (we were then marching from Frankfort, Ky., to the Cumberland River) and when we thought we could stand it no longer, we commenced, every time we would see our quartermaster, to halloo "Overcoats," "Overcoats" He didn't stand it long till he hurried to Nashville and got them. We are very sure that our officers now got but very little undisturbed sleep for listening to the doleful sound "*I want my money!*" But from the quotations already made from Col. Miller's notes we are very sure our own officers were responsible for the long delay in our getting our money, but they began right away to make out pay rolls. This always took three days, always having to be made out in duplicate. And there were not more than three men in each company (on an average) that could make them out at all—our education and habits at home were altogether on a different line. In this case our officers had not made out pay-rolls for so long that they had forgotten how, or else they did their work too hurriedly, or the paymaster was more particular than common, for after they had been made out in the whole brigade they were handed to the paymaster for inspection, and that *august* personage sent every one of them back and said there was not a single pay-roll in the whole brigade made out right. So there was nothing left to do but to go to work and make them out over again. And while they are doing it we will write up *other parts* of this wonderful machine.

When we came here the 1st division was already here, and Minty's and Long's brigades of our division also, so that there were at least 20 regiments here waiting for horses; and strange as it may seem, so far as our observation went, there was no regular depot of supplies; and as already stated, we had no wood, no straw, no clothes, and suffered sevêrely with cold, and had scarcely ever been so meagerly supplied. In a few days Gov. Morton found out we were here, and immediately our State Sanitary Commission set about relieving our wants. They first brought us a lot of onions, potatoes and dried fruit, and in a few days we had nothing to complain of as to rations. Then after some very vigorous expostulations, in which a great deal of bad language was used, they began to issue more wood to us, so that we could have a little more fire and thus keep ourselves more comfortable. Then as soon as a requisition could be made for clothing, and they could be shipped from Cincinnati, New York, Washington, or somewhere else, we drew all the clothes we wanted, overcoats included. Then the weather moderated a little, so that all around we began to feel in a little better humor. What, above everything else, made us forget our hardships, was the fact that within four or five days all the friends of the Seventy-Second knew we were here, and they began to come down in squads and droves, and by the end of ten days there were nearly as many citizens in our camp as there were soldiers. Next to *going* right home is the pleasure of seeing your best friend right *from* home; and every fresh arrival was greeted with the wildest demonstrations of delight and cheering. Of course the greetings were mutual. A separation of nearly two years and a half adds wonderfully to our appreciation of friends and friendships. Among the numerous arrivals were many soldiers' wives and their children. This was the happiest sight of all. To see a lot of nice, pretty, well-dressed women and children come into camp and hunt their husbands and fathers, would make most *anybody* feel a peculiar sensation in the throat and a little moist about the eyes. Many of them came, too, before our new clothes got to us, while we were ragged and dirty, and it was sometimes amusing to see a great big, burly, stout soldier, who had never flinched in the hour of battle, become so timid and shaky in the presence of ladies. For our own part, we felt so awkward we did not know what to do; we had no thought of dirt and rags before, and heartily wished ourself back to the front again, as rags and dirt were at no discount there. Among the "recruits," as we called them, were a number of preachers come to see us, and several of them preached for us just as though they thought we were heathen, had been away from religious ministrations for over two years, and of course were bad fellows. Among the number was a very noted character at home, and also in Kentucky, Rev. Evan Stevenson, who had a son, Hiram, in Company I. He preached a time or two for us, and we shall never forget an anecdote he told to us, privately, of course. He went out as a chaplain of the 15th Ind., and while in Western Virginia, he was one day preaching to his regiment. It may not generally be known that just as the war broke out the word "bully" began to be used, in the sense of very good or very great, and like all other slang words, was used by everybody upon every conceivable occasion, and of course often in a most ridiculous sense. He said that with all his power and eloquence he was doing his best to exalt the character of Jesus Christ in the minds of his hearers. He noticed a great big, burly Irishman standing two feet in front of them all, absorbed in the subject and all attention. As he warmed up with the subject, the old man took occasion to refer to Gen. Sherman, Gen. Burnside, Gen. Meade, Gen. Grant, and others, remarking that they were all the greatest Generals the world ever saw; but, said he, Jesus Christ, as the great captain of the plan of our salvation, was a greater General than them all. The big Irishman looked up in his face, and with all the simplicity of his soul said, "Bully for Jesus!" The preacher said he had nothing further to add, but just dismissed the regiment.

November 23d. At last our pay rolls were all fixed up in such shape that red tape could find no fault with them, and to-day we got one year's pay. How many young men now in the country would engage to work for Uncle Sam, or any body else, for a whole year, at $13 a month, and not get a cent of it till a month after all the service had been rendered?

November 24th was Thanksgiving, and the Sanitary Commission and the citizens of Louisville made us a Thanksgiving dinner. Hornaday, of company F, says he will remember this dinner as long as he lives, as while carving the turkey he cut his finger, and took erysipelas in it right away, which came very near putting an end to his further soldiering. Now we want to show you that soldiers are subject to greater extremes of feeling than any other class of people in the world. We have spoken of our extreme suffering after going into camp, and how we grumbled. But more wood made us feel better; potatoes and onions made us feel better; new clothes made us feel better still. When Uncle Samuel's paymaster doled out to us a year's rations of "Lincoln Skins," (greenbacks,) we thought the climax of feeling was about reached. That thanksgiving dinner, however, made us feel "*awful* GOOD." We blessed the Sanitary Commission, Governor Morton, Old Abe, everybody else, and his wife, too.

Some how or other, we have always had the idea that pandemonium was a kind of a noisy place, but for a few days after our regiment was paid off we think it could just discount anything in the universe for noise, and we have an idea that the council chamber of imps would be comparatively quiet by the side of our camp. Everybody who was in the habit of taking "suthin," took it; then "friendly set-tos" in the regiment were numerous, and many old scores were settled on the *square* after numerous *rounds*. We have spoken of the universal desire of the soldiers to go home, and we are hazarding nothing when we say that Col. Miller, Capt. Thomson, and others in the command, would have been willing to take each man's individual promise to be back on a certain day, and told them to go home, if they dared to do it. But they were subject to military law, just the same as we were, and of course could neither give or take any such promises. But it often happened this way: Capt. Thomson says to John B. Davis: "Now John, if you are here when the regiment moves, I will stand between you and all danger." Well, as soon as the men were paid off, they began to skin out for home. No one could get a furlough to go home, and of course, all who did so were deserters in the eyes of the law, and of envious officers also; but many of them went, nevertheless, and this was called taking a "French furlough," or going on an "India rubber pass." Very few of the men sneaked off, or slipped off unknown to the company officers; they just told the officers plainly that they were going, and that they would be back on a certain day, and we think *all* who did this made their words good—came back when they agreed to, and nothing was ever said about it; while many others had friends come down, just for the fun of the thing, and to gratify the soldiers, changed clothes with them, and answered to their names till they came back.

We have spoken of Provost Marshal's papers. Our men had seen a great many of them, and it didn't take long to make one, and we hazard nothing in saying that many went home and came back without their company officers knowing anything about it.

We have a hundred times before this had occasion to speak of the love and respect that all of the regiment had for our Colonel, A. O. Miller, and as this confidence between us and him seemed to be mutual, we determined, after we got our pay, to give him some substantial evidence of our esteem. So the matter was talked over privately among the "non-commish" and privates and a plan soon matured. The result was the appointment of a committee of one from each company to solicit subscriptions for the purpose of buying a sword, sash and belt, to be presented to the Colonel. Subscriptions were limited to one dollar for each soldier, and no one was to be urged to contribute. In less than twenty-four hours after the thing was first mooted $400 was secured, and the sword, sash and belt bought. They were all enclosed in the finest rosewood case we ever saw, and every article was much the finest of the kind we had ever seen. They were simply splendid. After the articles were brought to camp arrangements were privately made for a public presentation. The other three regiments were privately notified, and the companies and regiments all fell in quietly and marched up to the Colonel's headquarters and formed in solid column by regiments doubled on the centre, right in front of the Colonel's "marquee." A table was then placed before the tent and the articles laid upon it. All this was done so quietly the Colonel seemed to know nothing at all about it. Just then he came out of his tent as if going on some business, and we shall never forget his look of bewilderment and surprise on beholding his whole brigade right in front of him. He uttered an exclamation of surprise which brought his wife to the door, who had just come down to see him. She looked like she was really frightened, but on seeing we had no guns soon became re-assured. But the Colonel seemed dumbfounded and began to inquire "What does all this mean?" A sergeant from each company, headed by the Sergeant-Major, B. M. Thompson, advanced to the table, and the Sergeant-Major spoke as follows: "Fellow-soldiers of the Seventy-Second Indiana volunteers: You are met to present to Col. A. O. Miller a sword in appreciation of his gallant conduct on so many fields of slaughter. In this there can be no mistake, for he won your unwavering confidence in the battle of Hoover's Gap, and his unprecedented coolness and skill at Chickamauga, Chattanooga, McMinnville, Shelbyville, Farmington, Sweetwater, Dallas, Big Shanty, Kenesaw Mountain, Noonday Creek, Chattahoochee, Stone Mountain, Decatur, Flat Shoals, Atlanta, Rome, Blue Pond, and in many other engagements, gave you a confidence in his courage, abilities and patriotism, that can never be shaken. The old 17th Indiana veteran volunteers, the 123d Illinois and 98th Illinois, together with our regiment, have under his leadership always gone just where they pleased in the face and in spite of the enemy." Here Colonel Miller stepped forward, and two orderly sergeants, Perry Toms, Company H, and Aisel Derby, Company C, arranged the sash and belt on him, saluted the Colonel and retired. Thompson continued: "Colonel, your regiment—brave boys as ever lived, or fought, or died, and who have never faltered in the execution of your commands, however perilous—are met to present you a sword in appreciation of your courage, your skill and your kindness. They, with you, have passed through the perils of nearly three years, during which time your tears over their dying comrades on the battle-field, and your words and deeds of kindness to the sick and wounded, together with the respect you have shown them on every occasion, have won for you a very enviable place in their affections, while three years replete with successful engagements with the enemy, under your leadership, have won their full confidence. Here, then Colonel, is the sword. It is a testimonial of their respect. Please receive it as such. Of itself it is inadequate; but coming as it does from your own brave boys, from your own dear regiment, upon whose tattered flag no stigma shall ever rest, may they not hope, Colonel, that you will very highly appreciate it?"

To which Col. Miller responded:

"Members of the Seventy-Second Indiana volunteers: I thank you for this magnificent sword. It is a costly present, and in appreciation of it I shall never forget from whose hands it came. You have been toiling and fighting nearly three years. The enemy has never been able to present a line of battle but what you have repulsed. No privations, however great, have ever caused you to murmur. You have always been ready to cheerfully execute the most difficult and hazardous commands. Many of your comrades have fallen. They fell by your sides in battle doing their duty as true patriots to their country. The colors under which they fell shall never be disgraced; you have done your whole duty most nobly and skillfully. I have always been proud of you. I am proud of this magnificent sword, and I will again tender you my thanks for it. But in this happy hour of my life, I cannot forget that man may to-day be wafted by the kind breezes of fortune, and to-morrow sink into oblivion. Not so with the regiment; that is to live in history."

Before the Colonel got through with his speech the tears began to come, and the sleeve of many a "round-about" was drawn across the faces of the men before him. His wife came to his side and took the sword and seemed the happiest woman we ever saw; although she never said a word she turned to the men with such a sweet look of thankfulness that the men interpreted it as thanks more eloquent than words could have spoken. The whole brigade now gave the Colonel three cheers, and oh, such hearty cheers, too, and then as quietly went to their quarters as they had come, feeling that a most proper thing had been done in a most proper way. This was on the 1st day of December.

CHAPTER XXXIV.

From December 1st, 1864, to January 9th, 1865—Charles Town Accidentally Shot—Resignation of Major Pinkerton—Promotion of Capt. Thomson to the Lieutenant-Colonelcy, and Capt. Kilborn to the Majority of the Regiment—Col. Thomson's first attempt at Dress Parade—Sketches of Lieutenant-Colonel Thomson and Major Kilborn—Duties of Dismounted Men—Rebels Destroying our Communication—Adventures of Sergt. Records, and others—Records Captures Two Men with his empty Gun—Capturing Rebel Pickets—Orders to Press Horses in the City of Louisville—Sherman Marches for the Sea and Hood for Nashville—The Bloody Battle of Franklin—Hood Loses 6,000 Men—Hood Advances to Nashville—Thomas Preparing to attack Hood—Bitter Complaint of Thomas, and Logan sent to Relieve Him—Thomas attacks Hood, Whips Him in a Two Days' Fight, and Utterly Annihilates Hood's Army—Drawing Horses, and Difficulties of Distributing Them—First Drill with the new Horses—Trying to get them into Review—Rain, and Fearful Mud—Getting Ready to Move in the Bitter Cold—Wild Horses Rant and Rear, and Wild Pack Mules Run Away with the Camp Kettles—Twenty Miles the First Day Toward the Front—Plenty of "Loyal" Kentucky Rails Again—Dr. Sherk and Capt. McCormick Murdered by Guerrillas—Incidents of the March Southward to the Front, through Bitter Cold, Mud and Snow—Five Foragers Brutally Murdered—We go out and Capture and Kill 14 of the Bushwhackers—The whole Division once more Together—Sketches of Lieut-Col. Kirkpatrick, Lieut.-Col. Thomson, and Maj. Kilborn.

We think it was on November 22d that a most melancholy accident occurred in Company H. Private Charles Town, a good soldier, who had been with the regiment from its organization, received a gun-shot wound in the head which resulted in his death a few days afterward. The gun was in the hands of private James A. Halstead, of the same company, a recruit who had only been in service about a month. It was supposed that the accident occurred on account of his inexperience with the fixed ammunition of our Spencer rifles.

On the 28th of November, Maj. Adam Pinkerton, the old Scotch war-horse, whose sterling integrity and moral worth as well as bravery and good sense were the admiration of all who knew him, resigned on account of the injury received on the race to Hartsville, December 7th, 1862, which has been stated, from which for two years he had suffered very seriously, but still stuck to the service, while many a man would have thought himself unable to walk. But the gallant Major never complained, and let the duty be never so hard he was always ready for it. Finally he found his injury was fast dragging him down to the grave, and he was compelled to resign. He was a man of powerful religious convictions, and went into the war from a sense of justice and right. The men of the regiment will long remember his wise counsels and faithful admonitions. He was universally liked in the regiment, and his resignation left us without a field officer, Col. Miller being in command of the brigade.

On December 6th, Capt. Chester G. Thomson, of Co. D, was mustered as Lieutenant-Colonel of the regiment, and Capt. Lawson S. Kilborn, of Co. E, was mustered Major of the regiment. These officers, by their many acts of bravery, faithfulness, good judgment and integrity, had well won their promotion, which was looked upon by the whole regiment as a matter of course. We have so frequently referred to the many acts of gallantry by Col. Thomson that it is not necessary to further specify them here, except to say that the privates all liked him very much and always treated him with profound respect, except once, and then the circumstances were peculiar. When the Colonel got the silver leaf on his shoulder for the first time, and his "bran new clothes" on, he no doubt felt a little elated, as he had a perfect right to, not because he had new clothes, nor yet because he had a silver leaf on his shoulder, but because it was fairly merited. Well, the Colonel's friends were down to see him, and he was feeling so comfortable that of course he thought everybody else felt so. So the next Sunday afternoon, the 11th of December, after he was mustered as Lieutenant-Colonel of the regiment, it was warm and bright, and everything was lovely, and the Colonel proposed to show his friends that he was Colonel, and that he commanded one of the best regiments in the service; and as dress parade afforded the best opportunity of anything else at hand (they could have done much better on the skirmish line) he concluded to have that. Somehow or other the men of the Seventy-Second always did despise everything that was done for mere show. As long as they considered any duty necessary, or thought it would add to their efficiency as soldiers, they would do it cheerfully and to the best of their ability; but whenever anything was attempted for "style," or for mere show, they went through with it just for the sake of obeying orders, and cared little or nothing about the *manner* in which that duty was done. It was upon this occasion the men, as soon as they got the orders for dress parade, began to remark to each other in undertones that the Colonel wanted to put on some "style;" so they weren't in much of a hurry getting ready, and after they were ready they presented the most "devil-may-care" appearance imaginable. The truth is, we had then about 250 recruits who had scarcely ever seen a dress parade, and none of them knew *much* about the manual of arms, and many of them nothing; and as we had not had dress parade for nine months, and in fact but very few times while we were in the service, many of the old soldiers had forgotten all about the *modus operandi* of the affair. All of this the Colonel must have forgotten or didn't think of; consequently when we got out into line, it was the worst one we had ever seen, and when we came to going through the manual of arms it was such a complete failure that we think the Colonel was so thoroughly disgusted with it that he resolved never to attempt it again; and he never did. According to our best recollection we never had dress parade afterwards. Our regiment was the best exemplification in the world of the fact that men *might* become most excellent soldiers and not know anything at all about a great many things that were *called*, and went to make up, the soldier's drill. Put us on the skirmish line and we could crawl up to an enemy as quickly, and do as much execution, as any regiment in the service. Put us in front of artillery and we would march up to it as boldly, and with as little loss, as any zouave regiment in the world: and we would defy the world to beat us on a charge. Native good sense is about as good drill in actual combat as can be laid down in the books. We do not despise drill by any means; we believe the more of it the better, if of the right kind, but we should never spend an hour in teaching soldiers anything but what would be of actual use to them in front of an enemy.

We spoke about the order we got at Columbia, Tenn., on the last of April, on leaving that place for the front, in regard to all soldiers who for any cause should become dismounted. The order stated that all who should become dismounted should be sent to the rear to do guard duty, and that they should serve as foot-infantry. The object of this order was two-fold: 1st. To induce the men to take good care of their horses; they had been mounted long enough to know that riding was often preferable to walking, and if anything would induce them to take care of their horses, it would be the certainty of having to walk the balance of their time out. 2d, To secure the services of every man in the army. Two years of war, with all its cost of life and treasure, with so little accomplished, had more than demonstrated the necessity of using every available means of putting down the rebellion, and of bringing every power to bear for the accomplishment of the work in hand. There must be no more foolishness in the matter. Every man in the service must either skin or hold a leg while others skinned. Hitherto, dismounted cavalrymen, to say the least of it, were unprofitable servants; the custom always had been to send all dismounted cavalrymen to the train to which they belonged, where they spent their time in idleness and consuming the rations of those who were doing the fighting; but now new hands had taken command; men who were terribly in earnest in putting down the rebellion. The order worked well; men who had been in the habit of playing out a good horse in three days after being furnished with one, now took care of them, and the trains were not burthened by a lot of vagabonds ready to filch everything they could lay their hands upon. Yet notwithstanding the best efforts of the best soldiers to take care of their horses, many of them literally starved to death, and many more were being killed almost every day, and at the end of the first month of Sherman's Atlanta campaign one-fourth of all his mounted troops found themselves without horses. As Sherman's army advanced further into the heart of the Southern confederacy, of course his line of communications with his base of supplies at Nashville became longer and required more guards for its protection, and these dismounted men could profitably be used as such guards. As the line grew longer of course the temptation for the rebels to destroy it became stronger, and it was absolutely necessary to use every precaution against it. As before stated, after the Dallas campaign, it was determined to send all the dismounted men of our division back to Columbia, Tenn., to do guard-duty at that point, because, as we have frequently shown, our railroad in middle Tennessee was our weak point and most likely to be attacked. On the 6th of June, while we were in camp on the Etowa river, near Cartersville, Ga., Col. Sipes, of the 7th Pennsylvania cavalry, was detailed to take command of all dismounted men of the 2d cavalry division, Lieut. Col. S. C. Kirkpatrick, of the Seventy-Second Indiana, second in command, and Lieut. R. C. Clark, Company D, Seventy-Second, in command of those from the Seventy-Second Indiana, and Surgeon Elias B. Sterling, of the Seventy-Second, to accompany the detachment as surgeon. On June 8th the detachment rendezvoused at Cartersville for a short time, until transportation could be supplied, when they were transported by railroad to Columbia, Tenn., and were organized into companies and battalions.

After the battles around Atlanta, in which Hood got worsted every time, and when he found Sherman had got such a hold that he could not shake him off, he determined to try the method of cutting off his supplies, and thus compel him to let go that way. Accordingly, nearly the whole of the cavalry force then with him was turned loose upon the railroads in our rear; besides, all the cavalry in the department of the Mississippi, under Gen. Forrest, were ordered into the same field, which made lively work for the guards all along the railroads, in all of which the detachment from our division bore a very conspicuous part. We have before spoken of Wheeler getting on to our railroad at Tilton Station, above Resaca, the first part of August, and capturing 1,000 head of our beef cattle. From there he moved north via Cleveland, crossed the Tennessee River above Chattanooga, and made for our railroads about Shelbyville and Columbia, Tennessee. We have been furnished with a few most thrilling adventures, in which members of the Seventy-Second bore a prominent part, and we give them as specimens of the work performed by the detachment. On getting back to Columbia they were given some horses, and a portion of the command, including the scouts, were mounted. By Col. Sipes' orders, E. S. Records, private of Company I, Seventy-Second Indiana, was made acting sergeant, and placed in command of six privates of the Seventy-Second, to act as scouts. A like number of the 17th Indiana were commanded by Corporal Brown, a veteran of the 15th Indiana, and the whole commanded by Sergeant McDonald, also a veteran of the 15th. It is proper to state that all the soldiers of the 15th who went into the veteran service were transferred to the 17th Indiana. On the 26th of August the above command, together with five men of the 3d Ohio cavalry, and five from the 4th Ohio cavalry, (all of our division,) were ordered from Columbia to scout to Farmington, and then from there to Fayetteville, Tennessee, and thence return. The sergeants were each armed with a Spencer rifle and two navy revolvers; the men were armed with a Burnside carbine, two revolvers, and a sabre each, and were warriors who were tried and true. They left camp about 2 o'clock in the afternoon of the 27th. They were marching two abreast, the sergeants in front with their rifles in readiness to fire at the first note of alarm. They were drawing near to Ball's blacksmith shop, which is at the intersection of the Columbia and Farmington and Lewisburg and Farmington roads. The angle between the Columbia and Lewisburg roads is covered with a dense growth of cedars, which prevents a view of one road from the other. Just as they were turning the angle they met the advance of a rebel column. It would seem that the Union scouts were the first to take in the situation, for they were the first to fire, sending a withering charge into the very face of the foe. The rebels proved to be no novices at the business, but stood their ground, and in the twinkling of an eye was flash answered by flash, and the rifles' sharp crash by muskets' louder report. "Men advance carbine!" the Federal sergeant cried. "Stand your ground!" the rebel captain replied. The Federals rushed up to the front beside their leaders, emptying their rifles and carbines into the enemy's ranks, when the half of their horses fell wounded, dying and dead. Perceiving that the enemy were only armed with a single shooting gun, a musket, the sergeant then ordered, "close in on them!" and, dropping their guns, they drew their revolvers and went in upon them, some on horseback, some on foot. The rebels had mostly emptied their guns, and had not had time to reload, yet they clubbed our men with their guns, and actually stood at bay until as many of them were dead and dying as there were in the entire squad of Federals, before they gave way. But when they started they all seemed to go at once, and left the Federals victors. The first thing was to ascertain our own loss, which proved to be two men slightly wounded and five horses killed or disabled. On looking to see what evidence of loss the enemy sustained, they found nine dead and five wounded, some of them dying. They got nine good horses, out of which enough were selected to remount the dismounted. From the wounded rebels it was ascertained that their force consisted of a company of 100 picked men. A brief consultation was held, deciding they had not seen enough of the enemy, and that they would proceed to Fayetteville. Stopping at night, they arrived at Fayetteville about 2 o'clock in the afternoon of the 28th. Fayetteville is situated on the north side of Elk River. The stream is spanned by a stone bridge. There is a very large hill on the north side of town. Soon after entering the town the sergeant sent one of the men to the bridge, and almost simultaneously with his arrival at the bridge he saw a force of rebels approaching from the south side. He took shelter behind the wall of the bridge and began to operate on them with his Spencer. Although he emptied some of their saddles, they came on, getting so near that if he did not run he would be killed—so he preferred to run. The firing had attracted the rest of the squad, and on his retreat he met them coming. Knowing that with such a large force in pursuit they would stand no show on the main road, they went at once to the hill and scrambled up that as fast as possible. On arriving at its summit they formed and began to fire. The enemy flanked them, which compelled them to retreat in haste, and in doing so Records' horse fell and caught him underneath the back of the saddle, which scraped the skin off his back and bedded itself in his hip. The rebs were pressing hard, and no time was to be spared; but in the face of all this McDonald turned about, and calling to his men, said, "For God's sake, let us not leave Records," and they actually fought the rebels off till they got his horse up and put him on it. For miles in the direction of Columbia the country is very rough and covered with cedars. At every hill-top they reached they formed and gave battle, and as many times did the enemy flank them out of their position, until a road was reached that went through a pass in some cliffs of rocks, where a successful stand was made and the enemy retired, leaving eight of their number dead. Concluding by that time they had seen enough of the enemy, they took a straight course for Columbia, where they arrived at 3 o'clock on the morning of the 30th of August.

We here make an extract from a letter by Corpl. J. Frank Tolby, of Co. G, and a color-guard for the regiment. It was written to Sergt. A. W. Lane, of the same company, then at the front, and is dated just after Wheeler had made a break in the railroad:

"FRIEND GUS.: As the railroad was completed yesterday, and all breaks made in it by 'Mr. Wheeler' made good, I suppose you have all the news. We are all well and having a gay and festive time. Money, and newspapers, and clothing, tobacco, whisky, &c., &c., &c., plentiful, and good news every day. But my purpose is not to tantalize you boys at the front in regard to the enjoyments of life, for I assure you I had rather be with you than to be here. Gen. Wheeler has come and gone, and at Columbia nobody is hurt. He intended to attack us, but quietly marched by us on the right. The reason is obvious—we were too well prepared. However, at Culldoka, 11 miles south of here, less than 100 of us had a trial of strength with him which resulted favorably for us. After Columbia had been deemed safe, about 100 of the detachment from our brigade, commanded by Capt. Henley, of the 17th Indiana, were ordered to Culldoka for the security of the long trestle bridge at that place. We reached there on the afternoon of the 3d of August, and everything remaining quiet until next morning about 7 o'clock, we had just mounted the train to return to this place, when information reached us that the enemy were approaching. We immediately dismounted from the train, when I was sent out in command of a small party to check the advance of the enemy on the main road, while the command sought an advantageous position. I was soon attacked by the rebel 3d Alabama, but held our position 'at all hazards.' I had formed my line in the rear of the crest of a hill, so that the Johnnies shot over us, while we tumbled them right briskly. Finally they came upon us in such numbers, and seeing that if they ever got my small party from under cover they would riddle us at a single volley, I ordered the line to the rear of a fence 100 yards further back, which we had gained by the time the Johnnies gained the crest of the hill. Here finding ourselves under the fire of the main line of our force, we fell back to the line formed by Capt. Henley. Here the conflict commenced earnestly and lasted with varying success until 3 p. m., when the enemy withdrew. The party attacking us were the 3d and 4th Alabama regiments of cavalry. During a lull in the engagement Jack Yeoman, of the 17th Indiana, and myself, were sent out to ascertain the enemy's position and strength. We went around their left flank and came up in their rear—ascertained their numbers, &c., and had a conversation with an old man and his darkies, within a few rods of their line of battle—and returned without observation, except by one of our own men, who fired on us, thinking we were rebels. Everything went off well till next morning, when Aaron Patton accidentally shot himself and died instantly. We brought him to this place and buried him with the honors of war. We have a great deal of duty to do here, but not more than we are able for. I have been acting as sergeant while at this post. I do not wish to remain idle here while everybody else is so busy at the front. Joe. Vance is still orderly for Col. Sipes, commanding post; Robert Bull orderly at brigade headquarters, and Corpl. Riddle is acting as hospital steward, and fills his responsible position with much dignity. Sergt. Stearns, of Co. F, is in the provost marshal's office, and the truth is most every position of trust and profit is filled by somebody belonging to the Seventy-Second.

Yours truly, J. FRANK TOLBY."

E. S. Records, as before stated, had been detailed as sergeant in command of six men of the Seventy-Second, to act as scouts, and furnishes this account of his adventure:

"On the morning of September 4th, 1874, Capt. Garrett, of the 7th Pennsylvania cavalry, and 45 men, and Capt. Lamson, of the 17th Indiana, and Lieut. Clark, of the Seventy-Second Indiana, and the scouts, were ordered out on a scouting expedition. Fifteen of the 45 men were members of the Seventy-Second. They arrived at Mt. Pleasant at 11 a. m., where a force of about 150 rebel cavalry appeared to be mightily interested in getting something to eat, and did not observe our approach. Capt. Garrett ordered us to charge, which we did, and sent them flying from the place by every route it was possible for them to take. I, with my squad, took after about 40 that were running away on the Screamerville road. Governed in the order in which we pursued only by the speed and power of our horses, sometimes one was ahead, and sometimes another. Finally in the long run my horse outstripped them all, took the lead and kept it. I soon caught one fellow, and leaving him in charge of one of my men, I rushed on. After running them about three miles, three of them made a stand. As I came up I demanded a surrender, but as it was not promptly obeyed, I fired upon the one nearest, and he fell, crying, "Oh! I'm killed! I'm a dead man! I ought to have surrendered." I threw down the lever of my Spencer rifle to re-load, when, to my horror, I found I had used the last cartridge. But I did not lose my wits. I instantly cocked and aimed the empty gun at them, and again ordered them to surrender, which they did at once. After they had thrown down their arms, I forced one of them, at the muzzle of my empty gun, to hand me, 'stock foremost,' a Smith & Wesson six-shooter. As soon as I got it in my hands I dropped my empty gun and presented the pistol, for it was loaded all around. Then, as one of them afterward expressed it, 'they realized that they had given themselves away.' This occurred in the timber, entirely out of sight of my squad, and the work was done, and I had started toward the command with my prisoners, before any one came up. That made three prisoners and one killed for my part of that day's job. Capt. Lamson and Lieut. Clark complimented me. I got three pairs of revolvers. The man killed was a Capt. Steele, A. A. G. of Gen. Wheeler's staff. One of the prisoners was a 1st lieutenant of the 9th Georgia. We remained at Mt. Pleasant that night, and did not return to Columbia until the 6th. We put in the time scouting and picking up stragglers from the rebel cavalry. Soon after the affair at Mt. Pleasant, rebel cavalry again made their appearance in the vicinity of Columbia."

On the 11th of September, 1864, Capt. Lamson with 40 men, set out in pursuit of a small force of rebels. They marched until midnight, when they came to Swan creek, at a point about five miles from Newburgh, Hickman county, Tenn. E. S. Records, Company I, Seventy-Second, was in the advance. We will now let him relate the balance of the story. He says: "I think I was about one hundred yards ahead of the column, with Corpl. Brown, of the 17th, about twenty yards behind me, with Hooten and James Ross, of the Seventy-Second, about fifty yards behind him. Just as my horse stepped into the stream I stopped him to let him drink, when a voice from the opposite side called out, 'Halt! who comes thar?' 'A friend to Wheeler,' I answered. Said he, 'if you are a friend to Wheeler you are all right.' I then challenged him by saying, 'Who are you?' Answer: 'A friend to Marl.' I replied by saying, 'If you are a friend to Marl you are all right.' While this was going on, Corpl. Brown came up. The rebel then said, 'Did you fetch our horses?' Said I, 'No, they are where you left them; one of you had better go and get them.' After a moment's talk among themselves, one of them started and came towards us, which suggested to me the probability that we were between them and their camp, which proved to be the fact, and accounted for the easy manner in which they were duped. Brown and I managed to let him pass between us, then thrusting our revolvers suddenly into his face, we whispered the word, 'SURRENDER!' Then whispering the order, 'Keep still, or you are a dead man,' we moved on to the other two men that remained. Instantly covering them with our pistols we ordered them to surrender. But so certain were they that we were some of their own command that they thought it was all a joke; but Ross and Hooten came up, and Ross said, 'Records, what have you got there?' 'Rebs,' I answered, when they instantly realized the situation, and surrendered at once. By that time the captain with his command was up. After complimenting us for the neat and quiet manner in which we had secured the pickets, he proceeded to invest the camp. We found it in the creek valley, at the base of an inaccessible cliff. The captain deployed us upon three sides, leaving the cliff to hold the fourth side. We then waited until daylight, when we opened fire upon them. Never were men more completely taken by surprise. They sprang from their beds and began to make frantic efforts to escape. But turn what way they would they would meet a Spencer rifle. After a few moments' peppering with rifle balls they surrendered. We took 42 prisoners and 45 horses. Our line was so close to them that when they began to waken we could hear their conversation. I heard a couple discussing the breakfast question. As soon as this job was accomplished we set out for Columbia, where we arrived late in the evening of September 12th, without the loss of a single man. About one-third of the expedition were members of the Seventy-Second.

When Sherman abandoned the pursuit of Hood at Galesville, on the 21st of October, he began to make selections of the forces he intended to take with him on his march to the sea; and, as before stated, his cavalry had become so reduced by being dismounted that he ordered McCook's division and Minty and Long's brigades of our division to turn over their horses to Kilpatrick's division, and at that time intended to take our brigade along with him; but after we got to Rome he changed his notion, as a great many men of Kilpatrick's division were still without horses, and we had to go to the rear. At the above date, when he thought he would take us along, all of the dismounted men of our brigade, then at Columbia, were ordered to the front. On the 19th of September our brigade surgeon, Dr. Cole, got leave of absence and went home, and on his return got to Chattanooga in time to find Hood's army between him and our division. We will let him tell how the dismounted men got to the command. While lying in Chattanooga he became very impatient at the prospect of getting to the front, and says: "I took a train going north, but at Bridgeport meeting our dismounted detachment under charge of Col. Biggs, of the 123d Illinois, coming south, I returned with them. On the 27th we left Chattanooga for Rome, in search of the command. We got to Rome on the evening of the 29th, where we expected our division to meet us. We found them there, and they have been with us ever since." Sergeant McClure says: "Louisville, November 16th. Our companies are now nearly all together once more, and we are in fine spirits."

On November 25th Brig. Gen. Garrard—Old Pap Garrard, as we called him—was relieved, and the division reorganized. Our brigade is now the first brigade; Brig. Gen. Eli Long, of Long's brigade, now commands the division, and Col. Miller still commands our brigade, which is not changed in its formation. We quote from Dr. Cole's journal of November 24th: "The men are getting tired of camp life, and long to go on the war path again." We have spoken of there being 20 regiments here waiting for horses, and it began to look to us as though we might wait till our time was out. So on December 9th the Government issued orders for our men to press horses in the City of Louisville. This was no new business for our men, and they went at it in a very systematic way. Men were stationed all over the city, and just when business was at its highest and the streets full of horses, at a given signal they brought everything to a stand-still by taking every horse that would at all do for the cavalry service. The famous army of Flanders never did half of the swearing that was done in Louisville that day. Of course there were many amusing incidents occurred. A very common occurrence was to see a lot of fashionable ladies in a carriage drawn by a spanking team, driven by a son of Ham dark as the ace of spades, brought very suddenly to a halt, and in a twinkling the horses would be stripped from the carriage and the women left sitting there as helpless as infants. Long before night the streets were full of vehicles of all kinds, with no horses to be seen near them.

All through this last summer's campaign Gen. Sherman has been such a central figure, and the operations of ourselves and our division so mixed up and mingled with the grand achievements of his powerful army, that we now propose to occupy a page in taking our final leave of Sherman and his army. When the pursuit of Hood ended at the south end of Lookout Mountain, near Gadsden, on the Coosa River, Sherman was at Galesville with his army, on Little River, west of Rome.

We have told how the 4th and 23d corps came back to Chattanooga while Sherman, with the 14th, 15th and 17th corps, moved leisurely back to Atlanta, where the 20th corps had remained all the time we were after Hood. On the 16th of November Sherman, with these four corps, started for Savannah, and accomplished his glorious march to the sea, which will live in history as one of the grandest military achievements which perhaps the world has ever witnessed.

Immediately after we left Hood, at Gadsden, on the Coosa River, he moved directly north to Decatur, on the Tennessee River. Here we had a small division of negro troops, commanded by Gen. R. S. Granger; but as they were tolerably well fortified Hood only besieged the place for a few days and then moved his army on down the river, west, to Florence and Tuscumbia, and drew his supplies from Corinth and Selma. Gen. Sherman sent Gen. Thomas back from Atlanta to Chattanooga and Nashville, anticipating that Hood would try to go into Tennessee. As Hood had an army of at least 45,000 men, and Thomas but the 4th and 23d corps, that he could depend upon, to meet him, it looked like Sherman had left a big job on Thomas' hands. These two corps numbered about 20,000 fighting men. Besides Thomas had raked and scraped together about 10,000 good cavalry, under the command of Gen. Wilson; making altogether 30,000 men, which he immediately placed north of the Tennessee River, opposite Florence, the cavalry being near Florence, and the infantry at Pulaski, Tenn. The day after Sherman started for Savannah, Hood crossed the river and started immediately for Nashville. He moved to Waynesboro, west of Pulaski, thus flanking Gen. Schofield, in command at Pulaski. Schofield fell back to Columbia, Hood following him closely. Hood only aimed to hold him at that place while he immediately commenced crossing the Duck River below and west of the town. Thus Schofield was again compelled to fall back to Franklin, on the south side of Harpeth River, and 18 miles right south of Nashville, which he reached on the 30th of November On the same day Hood attacked him in position, and the battle of Franklin was fought, which was one of the most fearful slaughters of the war, in which Hood lost 6,000 men; our loss was also heavy. The rebels were so severely punished that they let Schofield fall back the next day to the defenses of Nashville without molesting him. On the 2d day of December Hood moved on to Nashville, immediately invested the place, began to fortify and to advance by regular approaches. Ever since Thomas had come back to Nashville he had been busily engaged organizing the quartermaster employees and dismounted cavalrymen into a division, and putting them into the forts and defenses of Nashville. He had raked and scraped up about 10,000 of these; yet, all told, he had but about 40,000 men, and a part of them indifferent troops, to cope with Hood's army of veterans, and he still had to act on the defensive. During the first 10 days of

December the weather was bitter cold and both armies suffered severely, especially the rebels, as they were so poorly supplied with clothes, shoes and blankets, and not at all used to such cold weather. At this crisis there was the most terrible howl raised all over the North against Gen. Thomas, because he did not, with his indfferent troops, immediately attack Hood's veterans. So bitter became the complaint against him that Gen. Grant actually dispatched Gen. Logan to supersede Gen. Thomas. But Thomas knew his business, and kept steadily at work, paying no attention to the howling. He knew he was not yet strong enough to fight Hood on ground of Hood's own choosing. He also knew there were two divisions of the 16th corps which had been ordered to report to him from Missouri, and they were on their way, but had not yet reported, but reached Nashville just the day before Logan got there, were already in position, and Thomas was ready to fight, and attacked Hood without hesitation. On the 15th and 16th of December, 1864, was fought the great battle of Nashville, in which Hood's whole army was annihilated, broken up and demoralized, and it was never heard of afterwards. There never was a more complete victory than the grand old Rock of Chicamauga achieved in that battle.

Our trains, officers, horses and convalescent stock, left Rome when we did, and came all the way by land to Nashville, and got there on the 20th of November, went into camp at Edgefield, on the north side of the river, and the men did picket duty. True to their instincts, to always take a hand in every fight near them, they deserted their post, put across the river and pitched into the thickest of the fight, and helped to achieve the grand result by "lifting a little." We could mention some names, but where *all* did so nobly it would be mean to speak of the *few*.

We had now been at Louisville just a month, and everything was becoming irksome and monotonous in the extreme. The great battle of Nashville had been fought, Hood's army had been defeated and broken up, all his artillery captured, and we all regretted that we had not been there to help achieve the glorious result. We were still waiting for horses, and as we had but eight months to serve, we wanted to be somewhere where time would fly faster than it was now doing. It would take about 10,000 horses and mules to re-mount our division, and we wondered where they were to come from. On the 17th the other two brigades began to draw their horses, which gave us some encouragement, the 1st division having already drawn their horses and started for the front. On the 18th our brigade drew horses. The order was for each company to draw as many horses as there were men in the company, and an extra horse for each commissioned officer, and four pack mules for the company. The horses were in tolerably good condition as regards flesh. Some of them were really good ones, and some were just as bad as they well could be. It used to be a custom among farmers at the North if they had a horse they could do nothing at all with, to sell him to the government for the army. Of course every one was anxious to get a good horse, and those who had to take a bad one felt that they were imposed upon, and the feeling among some of the men amounted almost to mutiny. As this "draw" struck us in an entirely new place, it may be interesting to note some of the methods adopted by the company officers to get the horses *off* their hands without getting a fuss *on*. Hitherto we had got our horses in rather an irregular way, often a few at a time, and never before had the whole companies a chance to draw horses at once; and had all the horses been equally good, there would have been no trouble about it; but the difference was so great that the difficulty of making an honest distribution was a serious one. In some cases commanders of companies took upon themselves the privilege of giving to each soldier just such a horse as he thought the soldier deserved, and of course gave a good horse to a good soldier and a bad one to a bad soldier. This worked badly, and showed favoritism so plainly that no commander could stand the storm that such a course brought upon him. In all such cases the captains were obliged to take the horses all back and adopt some other method of distribution. In some cases companies had three different trials of it, and then, after all, there was the most serious dissatisfaction. Of all the articles we had ever drawn from the government before there had been such a slight difference in quality that the men just took things as they were given them, without saying a word about it; but now it was a month before they became reconciled to the situation. The mules we drew were large enough, but were only two years old, were not broke to lead, and were wild as deers. As soon as we got our horses we began actively to make preparations to get "off to the war again;" however, we had so much to do that it took more than a week to get ready. We had to draw new saddles, bridles, halters, blankets, spurs, picket-ropes and pins, and also a new set of cooking utensils, tents and garrison equipage. And as all these things were drawn separately, and separate rolls made out for each article which all had to be signed by the men as they were distributed, it took up much time and kept all the men busy signing rolls and the officers very busy making them out. By the 25th (Christmas) we were nearly ready to move; the weather had got warmer and it set in wet. On the 26th everything had been fixed up, and we were ordered to get ready for review by to-morrow morning at 9 o'clock. The weather was still wet, and all night it continued to rain, and the ground, which had been hard frozen, had now got as soft as mush.

December 27th. Still raining; but in anticipation of our grand review we were up early. We had seen all the *infantry* drill, from squad drill up to company, battalion, brigade and division drill, and were familiar with them all; we had studied them theoretically and practically, and had also seen all the "reviews," from company inspection every Sunday morning up to the regimental, brigade and division, so far as the infantry were concerned; but had never seen a division on horseback reviewed, and we were all anxious to see the display; but when we got up and saw it still raining, and how deep the mud was, our hopes for the success of the review were considerably dampened. Yet we cheerfully set about getting ready, and when at 8 o'clock the bugle at headquarters blowed "boots and saddles" we greeted it with loud and prolonged cheers. It was the first time we had heard it for two months, and it sounded like the voice of a familiar friend. We had often heard it when it meant far different work to what it did now. We had always observed that somehow or other the "saddle call" was always obeyed more promptly than any other of the many we had to obey, and our camp just now presented a scene of the liveliest confusion imaginable. Everything was new, the horses were wild and unbroken, and we have often thought if the rebels had been right on to us, as they were at Chicamauga, how easily they could have taken us in. We had observed that as a rule the horses would learn the drill much quicker than the men. A thousand times we had thought of Job's description of the war-horse, and had verified it, but just now, unpoetic as we were, we thought as applied to this particular set of horses that the picture was a little overdrawn. After saddling the first thing was to get the horses all in a line side by side with a soldier at the right side of each horse's head, and left hand hold of the bridle close to the bits; next number the men by "2's;" next "prepare to mount," at which number "1" was to lead forward four paces. Here is where the fun began. None of them were used to the military curb-bit, and many of them wouldn't lead any way but backward, and in less than a minute the horses were in every conceivable shape except in two ranks as they ought to have been. So after trying several times and failing to get all the horses in the notion of doing the same thing at the same time, it was given up, and the men told to mount the best they could. We began to think it would be a funny review. The next move was to get the horses in column by twos, faced to the right; we were a little more successful in this, but some of the horses could not be kept in ranks at all, but persisted in going about where they pleased, and finally had to be left in camp. Even after we got the regiment formed and started to move down in to the city, some of the men had to be dismissed and sent back to camp, for fear their horses would be so unmanageable as to spoil the review.

The review took place on Broadway, which is said to be one of the finest streets in the world. Most of the streets in Louisville are narrow and unattractive, but this one is seven miles long, and people who have seen both say this one is a finer street than Broadway, New York. It afforded plenty of room for the review. It must have been 10 o'clock when we got to our position on the street and got our lines dressed up ready to be looked at, yet our brigade was an hour ahead of time, or else the other two brigades were an hour behind, and we had to sit there that long in the rain, and wait for them. They came at last, and took up their position on our left, as we faced to the south, and when all was ready and we opened ranks, we presented one of the finest views we had ever beheld. There were two lines of blue overcoats reaching as far as we could see. There were at least a third more men in each of the brigades than has been in the ranks at one time since we had been mounted, and this was the first time that we had ever seen more than two-thirds of our division at one view. The fact is, during the whole of our service there had been but few occasions where a person could get to see more than a brigade and a half at one view; but here we were all mounted and strung out in two ranks, and reaching more than two miles. It was about noon when Gens. Boyle and Long, and Cols. Miller and Minty started at the right of our lines and rode along in front of us to the extreme left, and then rode back in the rear of us to the extreme right, and the review proper was over. The regiments now closed ranks and faced to the right, and countermarched by the left, just in front of the other regiments, and just in the same manner as the reviewing officers had done, until the head of column had passed the extreme left of column, and then countermarched by the left again. Thus the soldiers all passed each other twice, giving us a fair chance to see each other and exchange friendly salutations. Had the weather been warm and bright this would have been a most pleasant and enjoyable affair, but it rained hard the whole day, and being the 27th of December of course the rain was very cold; and as we had to wait an hour in the rain before the review began, we all got mad; our horses got mad, too, and very restless, and the wonder to us was that the whole thing was not entirely spoiled. When we began to move and to recognize old familiar faces, and talk to each other, and of the happy prospect of getting back to the front once more, much of our discontent was forgotten. It was 2 o'clock and still raining when we got back to camp, wet, hungry as wolves and cross as bears. Our fires were all out, and mud in our camps a foot deep. By the time we got our fires built and dinner over it was dark, and a miserable night it proved to be. Late in the evening we received orders to move at daylight to-morrow morning. When we came in from review our horses sank to their knees in the mud almost anywhere in our camp. We never saw horses suffer so in our lives as ours did that night. Each company had a long picket rope stretched close to its quarters. and all the horses and pack-mules belonging to the company were tied to this rope very closely side by side. In a short time they would have the ground tramped into thin mortar a foot deep, and there was no chance to feed them or get them out of the mud. From cold and hunger they soon became very restless, and kept rearing, kicking and stamping about, which only made the mud deeper, and still added more to their misery. It kept four men constanly on duty in each company, the whole night through, guarding the horses, lest some of them should get down in the mud and get trampled clear under and perish, or perhaps some might get loose and wander off and get lost, and to add to the horrors of the situation, about midnight the wind whipped around to the north-west, and the weather, from being tolerably warm, got as cold as Greenland; so cold, indeed, that by daylight the ground was frozen hard enough to bear the horses up. Now if you can imagine what our horses must have suffered during this sudden transition, you can beat us. By morning they were all nearly chilled to death. The mud was frozen all over their bellies and legs, and their tails were sclid frozen rolls of mud five or six inches in diameter, and of enormous weight. The only redeeming feature about the situation was that we now had a chance to feed them.

It is always, and under any circumstances, a difficult job to get ready to move after laying in camp for a time, and a worse time cannot be imagined than this one. We had been here six weeks. All our camp and garrison equipage was entirely new. Our horses and pack-mules were wild and unbroken, and everything about our camps in the worst possible shape to move at all. Our pack-saddles had never been fitted to our mules, and our personal traps had never been fitted to our saddles. Nevertheless, at 4 o'clock on the morning of December 28th, the bugle blowed reveille, and we rolled out of our dog-tents immediately. No sooner had we stuck our noses out than we began to smell frost, a very bitter pill. The wind seemed to blow right through us, and to freeze the very marrow of our bones. Indeed, the wind blew so hard that it was difficult to get our fires to burn sufficiently to get our breakfast, and we were not half through when the bugle warned us to "strike tents." We thought this was crowding the season a little, yet when a few minutes later it sounded for "boots and saddles," the men began to swear. The scene of confusion that ensued can hardly be imagined, much less described. Everything had been wet, and was now frozen stiff and hard. Our dog-tents were frozen stiff enough to break when we attempted to bend them, and had to be thawed and dried before we could put them on our horses All our saddles and bridles were new, wet, and frozen so stiff that we could not move a buckle, and they had to be thawed, too. It was just beginning to get daylight when the bugle blowed to "fall in." Not one-third of the men were ready yet, and we are safe in saying, headquarters excepted, not an officer in the brigade was ready. But Col. Miller wasn't anything if he wasn't *prompt*, and when he got orders to move his brigade at a certain hour, the brigade had to *move* precisely at that hour, or a good reason be given for it. There are in every body of men always some who have a chronic disposition to be *not quite ready*, and we have observed that these same men were always in trouble, no matter how easy it might have been for them to fill the requirements of the order. But on this occasion, where it required all the efforts, and pluck and perseverance of the most determined and energetic to get ready in time, it is not surprising that when the bugle blowed for the companies to "fall in," there were some tents still standing; nor that there was a deal of most horrid cursing from those who were behind. It was just sun-up when we saw Col. Miller mount his horse and order his bugler to blow "mount." Aside from Col. Thomson, scarcely an officer was ready, and the men were still running about in the wildest confusion. All the confusion, and cursing and swearing, that had taken place up to this time, was Sabbath stillness and quiet in comparison with what now followed. Wild and unbroken as the horses were, when the men would mount them they might be seen rearing, plunging and charging about in any direction but the one desired. The pack-mules were as wild as deer, having never had a pack-saddle or anything else on them, and when the saddles were strapped upon their backs, and then a lot of camp-kettles and cooking utensils fastened on to them, they invariably tried to get away from there as fast as they could. On an average, there were about four men to each mule, to keep it in the right direction, but in spite of all their efforts many of the mules broke entirely away, and, as they ran, the way the camp-kettles and pack-saddles went flying in every direction was more than ridiculous.

We had seen pack mules (a few of them at a time) run with camp kettles tied to them before this, and it was always fun for us, and we enjoyed it hugely. Here was the most fun we ever saw in so small a space. Every sweet has its bitter and every rose its thorn, and our unbounded delight was a little bit spoiled by the fact that we were the head of Mess No. 3, and that Mess No. 3 had a pack mule too, and that said mule was by no means as gentle as a lamb, nor as steady as a well broken plow-horse. True, it was hardly as lively as a cricket, nor did its feelings seem to get the better of it and break out in the wild exuberance of joy that characterized others which broke loose and ran with all their might, just for the fun of hearing the camp kettles rattle. But its disease took on the mild form of fixed determination not to leave camp at all. As we were the head of the mess, and the mule had all our cooking utensils on it, and as we felt a little bit concerned for the proper preparation of our sowbelly and coffee for the future, of course we were interested in seeing that mule walk out of camp with dignity and propriety. So we got two men before it to pull and two behind to whip, and with these mild and gentle persuasions and coaxing we got the thing started. By this time the whole brigade, from a set of cursing troopers had settled down to a well developed and thoroughly organized mob, organized in this, that no two men wanted to do the same thing in the same way and at the same time.

Col. Miller had moved out on the Bardstown pike, but instead of the brigade moving out after him by companies and regiments, as orderly soldiers should do, every fellow considered himself a committee of one to look after his own business, and as fast as he got mounted made a rush for the Bardstown pike. All this noise and confusion came to an end at last, not at once, but gradually, as squad after squad would get ready to move off. It was the middle of the afternoon before the column settled down to the usual order of marching, and even then there were several refractory horses and mules to each company which made trouble all day. There was a horse in Company I which kept up his rearing and charging during the whole day. He seemed determined to die game, and he did, too, for next morning he was too stiff to get up and never got up again.

We moved very slowly and steadily all day, and just at sundown went into camp near a place called Mount Washington, 20 miles from Louisville. It was a miserable cold and hard march on us, and when we saw the head of column turn off the road to go into camp we greeted it with cheers. We bivouacked on a high ridge in a wood-lawn that was well fenced. As we turned into camp Col. Thomson stationed himself by the side of the road and reminded us that we were still in the "*loyal State of Kentucky*," and there must be no foraging or destruction of property of any kind; but as it was very cold and we were likely to suffer, we might take the "top" rail off the fence. We have stated that our camp was well fenced. This conveys a poor idea of the facts in the case. A well fenced farm in Kentucky is quite a different thing from a well fenced farm in Indiana or Illinois. The farm we went into camp upon was cut up into five to 20 acre fields, and all the fences 10 big rails high and staked and ridered, so that there was a vast amount of rails on a small farm. But the next morning there wasn't a rail within a quarter of a mile of our camp.

We have spoken of "*loyal Kentucky*," and as no history gives the facts just as they are, it may be of some benefit to our children to tell what we mean by "loyal Kentucky." When the war broke out all the "slave States" except Kentucky, and a few others, seceded from the Union, and formed what they called a Southern confederacy. At that time Magoffin was Governor of Kentucky, a bitter traitor at heart, and tried to get his State to secede from the Union too; but a majority of the State Legislature was loyal to the Union and refused to pass an "ordinance" of secession. The people of the State were very nearly evenly divided; that is, in some parts of the State nearly all were for the Union, and in other parts nearly all "secesh." When Magoffin found he could not get his State to secede he tried the next best thing to help the rebel cause, and that was to declare the State neutral in the war, and by some means got the General Government to pay some respect to the neutrality of Kentucky in the war, and for a time few Union soldiers were allowed to enter Kentucky. During all this time Magoffin had been doing all he could to help the confederate cause. He had appointed Simon B. Buckner Major General of all the Kentucky militia, and that gentleman had been hard at work organizing and arming them as fast as he could, and thus had got possession of all the arms in the State, and the very first opportunity turned the whole outfit, arms, troops and all, over to the Southern confederacy. This, and the fact that every part of the State that we had operated in had been most thoroughly rebel, had bred within us the most thorough contempt for the loyalty of any part of Kentucky. Indeed, if there was any State we thoroughly hated, that State was Kentucky, and if you could have seen the enormous piles of rails in our quarters that night, and the rousing fires by which we ate our suppers and lay down to sleep, you would have thought our hatred was taking a practical shape. It was cold and the wind whistled over that ridge in furious blasts; but we didn't suffer much from cold; we always thought that big poplar Kentucky rails made a nice fire.

December 29th. Bugle call before daylight, and by sun-up we were out on the road; the weather was still very cold and we had not gone far till we struck a region of country covered with three inches of snow. We made 20 miles and went into camp near Bardstown, an hour by sun. As the night promised to be a cold one the rail question was one of importance. They were not so plenty as they were last night, and just as soon as the head of column began to go into camp it began to gather in rails, and by the time our regiment—which was in the rear—got to camp, there were few rails left, and a quarrel sprung up between Co. C and Co. I about the rails, which had to be settled by the Colonel.

Minty's brigade was in the advance to-day, and went into camp at Bardstown by the middle of the afternoon, and soon after it had gone into camp, Dr. Sherk, of the 7th Pennsylvania, and Capt. McClamrock, brigade inspector, went out to a Union house where they were acquainted, and were murdered by guerrillas.

December 30th. Up at daylight, as usual. As we had fewer rails last night than night before we felt the cold more keenly. We pulled out at sun-up, going through Bardstown for the third time, and traveled the same road we did over two years ago, took the road to New Haven, and soon got out of the region of snow and it began to get much warmer, thawed a little, and about the middle of the afternoon began to rain. Went into camp two miles south of New Haven and it immediately began to snow. Our camp was in a flat beech woods, where the leaves were four inches deep, and had they been dry would have made as good a bed as a soldier wants. We raked them in piles and slept on them anyhow.

December 31st. Bugle call at 4 a. m., and when we rolled out found the snow four inches deep and the weather turning cold rapidly had a serious time getting fires. To shake the snow off our tents and dry them consumed all the time we had, and all our patience, too. When it came daylight we found the air was full of frost, and as the day advanced the wind increased in fury, and at times during the day the frost was flying so thickly we could scarcely see. We pulled out a little before sun-up, and we tell you there were a great many "ah's" and "oh's," from those who did not swear, and a great many damns and oaths from those who did. We took the road for Elizabethtown, distant, the way we went, 35 miles. The ground was hard frozen and the roughest we had traveled. As we made the distance by a little after sundown, we had to keep moving very steadily all day. It was so desperately cold we could not stand to ride over a mile or two till we would have to jump off and run to keep warm. This was by all odds the hardest day's marching we had done since we were mounted. Our horses were yet unbroken and would not keep their places like our old horses would, so that one-half had to walk at a time and the others take care of the horses. It finally got so cold and we got so tired and hungry and so completely chilled through that we could not stand it to ride but a few minutes at a time. We had to walk and lead our horses, and there were many times during the day when there would be but two or three men riding in the regiment. This is the only day we can now call to mind that we moved steadily all day long without stopping a single moment. It was so desperately cold we had to keep moving to keep from freezing. From Miller's notes, December 31st: "Cold as Greenland to-day; froze one of my feet." We went into camp a little north of Elizabethtown in a dense woods, which kepts ome of the wind off of us. We managed to find a little straw, and by scraping away the snow, and staking our tents very close to the ground, and sleeping six in a bunk, managed to get through the night without freezing. This was by far the coldest night we passed while in the service.

January 1st, 1865. The coldest morning we saw while in the service. Dr. Cole says: "Ground covered with snow and very cold; some of the men were frosted and one man's hands and feet badly frozen." On going 400 yards to water our horse we frosted one foot and one ear badly, and we went as quickly as we could. No bugle call this morning, but as it was too cold to sleep the men were up early. It was so intolerably cold we just supposed we would not try to move at all, but about 8 o'clock the bugle blowed "strike tents," and we pulled out at 9, going directly south. It was still very cold, but the wind did not blow so hard. We passed through Nolan and bivouacked near a little place called Sonora, in the thickest brush we had ever camped in, which aided materially in keeping us warm. We fared tolerably well, as we were beginning to get a little used to the cold and settling down to a regular campaign life again. We observe that things which used to interest us wonderfully on first entering the service are but little noticed now.

January 2d. Moved at sun-up, 20 miles straight south, which brought us to Green river, by noon at Mumfordsville. By this time it had got warm enough to rain, which it immediately commenced to do. When we got to the river we found it at flood tide, and no means of crossing it except a small flat-boat that would not hold more than 10 horses at a time, and not a single thing to propel it across back and forth. The water was too deep to use poles to push it, and ran too swiftly to use oars to paddle it aeross, so the prospect looked favorable for us to have to stay there till the water ran down, and as it was now raining as hard as it could, it looked as though we might get hungry before the water got much lower. At the end of two hours we got a picket rope stretched across the river and tied to trees on either side. A half-dozen soldiers placing themselves in the upper side of the boat and taking hold of the rope could pull the boat across and back in about five minutes, thus crossing two companies in about an hour. Our regiment was in the advance, and the first to cross, and it was long after dark before we all got across. We went into camp about two miles south of the river, while the balance of the division went into camp on the north side.

January 3d. The men in our regiment slept this morning till they got hungry. The fore part of the day was foggy and miserable, the frost coming out of the ground. We did but little except to sit around the fire and try to dry our clothes and keep warm; we were glad to have a day's rest. It took nearly the whole day for the balance of the division to get across the river.

January 4th. Bugle call at daylight, as usual, and our march was resumed at sun-up. The weather had got comfortably warm, and for two days was dry and pleasant, and our march, though very monotonous, was much pleasanter than laying in camp. We had already passed over this part of the road three times, and felt very little interest in it. We made 25 miles and camped at Rocky Hill station.

January 5th. Moved at sun-up, and another slow but steady march of 30 miles brought us to our old camping ground west of Bowling Green, where we camped the fall of '62.

January 6th. Up at daylight, and in one hour out on the road ready to move; but the time is so short that almost invariably there are some from every company in the division who are not just ready to move for an hour after the division starts, if there was no one to hurry them up, because when the company officers go off and leave a fellow in camp, he thinks there is no one to bother him, and he will take his time to it. So the division commander has found it necessary to detail a company for rear guard each day, and it is the business of this company to hunt up all stragglers and get them out to the road and start them on after the command. When we got up this morning it was raining, and continued to rain hard all day. This was the most monotonous and lonesome day's march we ever made. For hours together scarcely a single word was uttered by any one, the steady pattering rain keeping time to our horses' feet on the hard pike. Passed through Franklin and bore to the right a little, and left the railroad and main road to Gallatin to our left, or east of us. Late in the evening it began to snow, and by the time we got into camp was snowing for all that was out. We went into camp right in thick woods, a long ways from a house or fence, and four miles west of Mitchellsville, the prospect for a miserable night certainly most flattering. Scraping away the snow we laid down on the mud to sleep.

January 7th. Called up this morning as usual before daylight. We found it very cold and the snow four inches deep. There was not a fire in the whole camp and no possible chance of building one, and for the first and only time during our service we began the day's march without coffee, that is, when we had the coffee to make and the time to make it. We thought it would be impossible for us to move at all. Our tents were covered with snow, which had frozen to them so tightly we could not shake it off, and the tents were so stiff as to break when bent. Our horses' tails were full of snow and mud, and frozen in rolls four or five inches thick. Our bridles and saddles were covered with ice and frozen fast to anything they might be touching. As our forage was nearly out and our rations ditto, and we were two full days' march yet from Nashville, or any place else to get supplies, it was absolutely necessary we should move. But how to get started was the question bothering us above all others. It was hard to start from Louisville, but there we had fire; it was harder to start from New Haven, but there we had fire. But here we were in a worse fix than at either of those places, and no fire at all. If we had been disgusted and bewildered then, how much greater was our astonishment when just a few minutes after getting up the bugle blowed "strike tents." We have been studying over the matter for 18 years trying to find some words or way to describe what followed, but we give it up. In just 10 minutes more the bugle blowed the "saddle call," and a few minutes later to "mount." Scarcely a tent was down yet, nor a horse saddled. If the infernal regions can get up a scene that would beat the noise and confusion we had there, we never want to hear it. When the bugle blowed "forward," the head of the regiment began to move, that is, Col. Thomson did, and a captain or two, and a few straggling soldiers. It was the middle of the forenoon before the majority of them got to their places in the column, and we know of some who never caught up during the whole day, and as long as a soldier of the Seventy-Second lives he will always remember our camp on the night of the 6th of January. The division moved rapidly and without stopping, 20 miles, and went into camp by the middle of the afternoon, near Tyree Springs; camp in a very pleasant place on an old abandoned plantation. The sun came out bright and warm and the men had a chance to rest and dry their things, and recuperate generally; all of which was very highly appreciated by the poor soldiers, especially the sensible ones. There are always some fools in every crowd of men, and some of these, not satisfied with getting a good rest and a good supper, must indulge their old propensity for foraging. So they saddled up and put out into the country, and six of them, belonging to the 17th Indiana, were gobbled up by a lot of bushwhackers and deliberately murdered—that is, five of them were, and the other one shot through the shoulder and feigned to be dead, but afterwards showed signs of life, and they came back to him, struck him over the head and kicked him several times, and piled all his dead companions across him and left him. He was gritty, and finally crawled out and made his way to our camp near Nashville on the evening of next day. It seems there had been a company of bushwhackers following us and hovering around our flanks ever since we left Louisville. At Bardstown they got two officers, as already indicated. As soon as the poor fellow reported to camp 150 of our men went out right away and succeeded in putting a quietus to 14 of the bushwhackers, and their further uncivilized warfare.

January 8th. We had a good night's rest and resumed our march, but not quite so early as usual. Forage and rations both out. We had a beautiful, nice warm day, for marching; by noon the snow had all disappeared, and as we got down on to the limestone regions north of Nashville, the roads were tolerably good; we made good time and went into camp three miles north-east of Nashville, near Edgefield, an hour by sun. We quote from Dr. Cole's journal: "This evening a soldier of the 17th Indiana came in, wounded severely in the shoulder. He and five other soldiers of our brigade were captured last evening near Tyree Springs, while out foraging, by guerrillas, taken several miles from camp, tied two and two, then seated on a log side by side and fired into, killing all but this man, who by feigning death escaped after the desperadoes had robbed the bodies and left." When we got to Edgefield we found our division train, which had marched all the way from Rome and had been here since the 20th of November, and thus our whole command was together once more. Our long march for the present was ended, and we had got back to our old fighting ground. We had been in Tennessee so long and all over it so often, it seemed like we had just got back home. We had made 30 miles for the day, and 240 for the trip. While it is only 185 miles from Louisville to Nashville, we had come very much out of a direct line and increased the distance considerably.

January 9th. All our trains, ambulances, artillery and men, reported to their respective commands this morning, bringing us forage and rations. As they drove into camp we cheered them lustily. It was like the meeting of long-separated members of the same family. We had been separated two months, which had been full of hardship and adventure to all of us, and it took a great many log-heap chats to tell each other all that had happened. It rained all night last night and kept it up more or less while we remained at Nashville. We were now told we could have a few days rest, which we were in a condition to appreciate, if the weather had been favorable.

SKETCH OF LIEUT. COL. SAMUEL C. KIRKPATRICK.

A man among men, a patriot of the truest type and unflagging energy, was Col. Kirkpatrick. We feel humiliated that we have not at our command more data from which to compile a sketch of this sterling man and brave soldier. From all we can learn he kept no notes of his field service, and such facts as we desired could not be had. Perhaps they are not needed, as every soldier who served with him will bear record to the fact that there was no man braver on the field, no officer in the service more generous and attentive to all the wants of the soldier in all the vicissitudes of the service. No soldier was ever more resolute and determined to conquer in every action, and no soldier was ever more considerate and even tender to a fallen foe. His name was the synonym of bravery, honor and generosity.

The following from the La Fayette Daily *Journal*, of May 4th, 1874, is so replete with fact, and so just to the character of our beloved dead comrade, that we give it in full:

"DEATH OF COLONEL SAMUEL C. KIRKPATRICK.—It is with feelings of sorrow that we announce this morning the death of Col. S. C. Kirkpatrick, which sad event took place at 3 o'clock yesterday afternoon, at his residence near Culver's station, in this county. He had long been a sufferer from that fell disease, consumption, and his death was not unlooked for. Indeed, it seemed almost a wonder that he lived as long as he did, and had it not been for his indomitable will and iron-like constitution, he would have gone several weeks ago. He retained his mental faculties to the last, and an hour before death bade his friends good-bye, saying that he was going the way all must go, and that it was but a question of time. Deceased was born in Picka-

Col. Kirkpatrick, as a neighbor and as a soldier. We remember how deep and constant was his sympathy for all in distress. He sat up with every man who was sick enough to need nursing for miles around his home. His motto as a neighbor was: "I'll lend everything on my farm but my wife." His motto as a man was: "Be honorable." His motto as a soldier was: "Go for 'em!"

He is the only field officer of the Seventy-Second who has paid the great debt. He was not stout when he entered the service. The death of his brother James, lieutenant-colonel of the 40th Indiana, who was drowned in the service, fell upon him with crushing weight, and other sorrows by death added their sting. He left his wife and four sons, most of them small when he entered the service, and despite all his efforts his affectionate heart ached for care of them all the time while gone. He was not rich—such a man cannot be rich—and the care for those he so fondly loved weighed heavily upon him. He left the service with health utterly shattered, and a speedy death certain.

The name of Col. Kirkpatrick will always be precious to every surviving comrade, and his memory honorable and green.

SKETCH OF LIEUT.-COL. C. G THOMSON.

We have been commanded by Col. Thomson to say little or nothing about himself, as he prefers the pages of the book shall be devoted to the history of the regiment. We cannot quite comply, but will be as brief as possible:

C. G. Thomson was born near the present site of Shannondale, Montgomery County, Indiana, May 8th, 1833. His father, James A. Thomson, emigrated from Nicholas County, Kentucky, in 1830, and settled in the then wilderness of Indiana. Born in poverty, brought up to industry and frugality, as was necessary for the hardy pioneers of early times, he was well prepared for the hardships of army life. He inherited from both parents a patriotic love of country, and hatred for the institution of slavery, which was the cause of the war. His service in the army was conscientious service, an important auxiliary to true courage. The primitive log school house afforded a very limited opportunity for an education, but the three months' winter school was highly appreciated when it could be obtained. When twenty-one years old, he spent one year at Wabash College, and subsequently took a course in Bacon's Mercantile College, Cincinnati.

He went west in 1856 to Omaha, Nebraska, but the panic of 1857 made it impossible to find remunerative employment in that new country. In the fall of 1858 he went to Brunswick, Missouri, and

C. G. Thomson

engaged successfully in teaching until the beginning of the war, where he had an opportunity of knowing what it was to be a true Union man among Southern chivalry. Returning to Crawfordsville, young Thomson was among the first to enlist for the Seventy-Second Regiment, and, on going to Thorntown, was urged strongly to make up a company and accept the command of it; but not desiring so responsible a position, consented to assist in organizing a company if Capt. LaFollette would take the command. The company was very soon organized, and LaFollette elected captain and Thomson first lieutenant. LaFollette's health failed him in a few months, and Thomson succeeded to the command of the company, and the future of his service is well known. The object was faithful service rather than the seeking of promotion, and the promotions that followed were evidences that faithful service was appreciated. After having been in command of the regiment for almost a year, on reporting to Gov. Morton with the regiment for discharge, the Governor complimented him with having obtained the several commissions without personal solicitation or the influence of civilian friends; something very unusual in the volunteer service, and a compliment received with great satisfaction. During the three years of service of unprecedented activity, the regiment never made a *march*, or *engaged in a battle or skirmish*, that Col. Thomson was not with it.

He had chosen the law for a profession, and was studying with that in view when interrupted by the war. The loss of four years' time, and injury to health, made it necessary to give up a professional life and engage in other business.

After the capture of Jeff. Davis, Capt. Henri Wirz, and others who had perpetrated diabolical cruelties upon Union prisoners of war while in the prison pens of the South, Gen. Wilson appointed a court martial to try these prisoners, so distinguished for their high position, brutality, and zeal for the rebel cause. Col. Thomson was not only made a member of the court martial, but its president, which mark of confidence showed that he was held in highest esteem by his General officer and fellow officers, not only as a soldier, but also as a man of ability and justice. However, before Col. Thomson's court martial had an opportunity to try the cruel traitors, the prisoners were ordered to Washington. It is hardly probable that this court would have passed sentence of death on Wirz, the miserable tool of Jeff. Davis, and permitted the author and arch traitor to escape the same fate; it would not have given him life and liberty that he might live to boast of his deeds, and be lionized by traitors for years to come. We must express sorrow that the court martial was not permitted to dispose of the whole group; the duty would have been well discharged.

After Col. Thomson left the service he went into the business of pork and beef packing, and the firm of "Thomson & Horn, LaFayette, Ind., curers of choice sugar cured hams, breakfast bacon, dried beef, etc." is known all over the country as one of the most reliable.

Col. Thomson is quietly but firmly religious; he took his christianity into the army with him and it never failed him. No comrade can say that on any occasion he ever heard a word, or knew of a deed, by Col. Thomson, that in the least degree trenched upon his Christian profession. He was a most staunch support to the Chaplain, and a very strong stay to the religious sentiment and steadfastness of the regiment. All this, too, without a whit of officiousness or parade.

He has a fine, commanding physique, a large head, and a broad, open countenance, indicating at once kindness, frankness, purpose and invincible resolution. He is cordial in his manners, but neither loquacious nor demonstrative; slow and exact in his speech, and cautious in his statements, never exaggerating or using florid expressions. By all who know him he is esteemed a model man, loved, honored and trusted. His heart is very warm, his sympathies very keen, and his efforts to relieve the sufferings of others have never ceased.

We have told of his bravery on many a field, and his bravery was no more conspicuous than his kindness to his men as Captain and Colonel. Their needs were always looked after first, his own afterwards. The best that could be had he would have for them. He followed them to the hospital, and looked after their wants when sick or wounded, as long as they were in his reach. He knew every man in the regiment, and could call most of them by name.

Were we selecting a model regimental officer for powers of endurance, persoanl appearance, presence, ability to command, quiet dignity, bravery, constant presence of mind and prudence in action, kindness to his men, orderliness in camp and on the march, elevation of character and evenness of temper, we would select Col. C. G. Thomson, of the Seventy-Second Indiana.

We can say the above because it is true, and because he is at this date (August 3d, 1882) away in the wheat fields of Dakota, reaping the golden grain, and cannot see, and erase, what we say. May long life be his lot. His comrades love him, and he knows it. He is worthy of their love, and they know it. One of God's noblemen is Lieut.-Col. C. G. Thomson.

CHAPTER XXXV.

From January 12th to March 20th, 1865—Getting Started Again—Viewing Hood's old Works about Nashville—The Colored Troops Fought Bravely—Dead Men and Severed Limbs in Our Quarters—How Hood's Army Fought and Retreated—Battle Field at Franklin—Felling a Tree on Horses—Reach Columbia—Bishop Polk's House—March to Gravelly Springs through Mud, Snow, and Wilderness, to Join Gen. Wilson—We Report to Him 29 Days after leaving Louisville—Camp at Gravelly Springs—Gen. Wilson's Kindness to the Horses and Cruelty to the Men—Did Some One Else Get Our Rations?—Almost Starved—We Eat Horse Feed—Hungry to Starvation—The Historidn's Experience—Stealing Corn from the Horses—A little Pickled Pork Issued—Adventure of Stealing a Box of Hard Tack—Scaring Cavalry uutil they Drop their Meal Sacks—What Oar Comrades Say, and How they Got Something to Eat—Gen. Wilson's Numerous Orders—Bugle Calls—Building Stables—6.000,000 Clapboards—New Drill—"Hooking" the Sutler's Money with a Tarred Ramrod—Grand Review by Gen. Wilson—Splendid Results of Drill—We Move without Regret—Crossing the Tennessee—Forage Spoiled by High Water—Stealing a Barrel of Meat, which turns out to be Coal Tar—Exchanging Ariicles on Our Own Motion

When we began the sketches of the field officers, we left the command resting a day or two at Edgefield, three miles north-east of Nashville. We now return and resume the thread of the History of the Seventy-Second. On January 12th we started for Eastport Landing, on the Tennessee river, just below the Alabama line and in the edge of Mississippi. About 9 o'clock we saddled and began to pull out in the direction of Nashville; the steady rains had flooded the country with water and the roads were so intolerably muddy that it was noon by the time we crossed the river into the city, and by 2 o'clock we had only got to Hood's line of breastworks with which he invested the city. These were very substantial works, well built of wood, logs and stone, with earth thrown up in front of them, and were about three miles from the heart of the city, in easy shelling distance of most of the town. We went into camp at these works. In coming out we crossed the ridge over which Gen. Steadman's brigade of negro troops charged so lustily. When the question of making soldiers out of the negroes was first discussed there were thousands in the North opposed to it, as it would be inhuman to array the negroes against their former masters. The friends of the measure argued that the negro could stop a rebel bullet just as well as a white man, and do it just as effectually; and that it would be quite as well to have them do it and save that many white soldiers. But the strongest argument was that it would be folly to arm the negroes, as they wouldn't fight. The ground we passed over to-day more than demonstrated that they *would* fight. The marks of the terrible conflict were plain and plenty. Hundreds of rebel graves attested the valor and efficiency of the negro troops. Soon after going into camp the sun, which we had not seen for four days, came out bright and beautiful, and we had ample time to look over the battlefield. As usual, where men are buried very hurriedly, many of the graves were quite shallow. There were some rebels even in our quarters whose arms and legs were not covered at all. There was a man's leg lying there just as it had been cut off by a shell. The trees were torn to pieces by shot and shell, and everything indicated that the rebels had not been *scared* away from their works, but had stuck to them till the last moment. However, from here to Columbia every foot of the way showed plainly the great haste and confusion in which the rebels had retreated, as the entire way was lined with dead horses, dead mules, dead cattle, and dead men too, as we passed numerous graves. The way was strewn full of every kind of plunder belonging to an army; broken wagons, caissons, ambulances, artillery wagons, &c. We never saw such evidences of defeat and disaster. It had now been three months since our division trains and all had moved together, and it took all the first day for us to get straightened out rightly on the road. Our brigade was in the advance and we went into camp not long after noon, but it was night before all the trains got in. From here on to Columbia our march was slow and very irregular. Although the weather was cold it was dry and pleasant. We always moved early, made 10 or 14 miles and then went into camp. This made it pleasant for us and enabled the teams to keep up with us all the time, and as long as the weather kept dry we enjoyed ourselves very well, a thousand times better than lying in camp. Both armies had passed over this part of the country a half dozen times, and there was not a single rail, or any wood, scarcely a house or anything else, left within a half mile of the main road. Everything that would burn had been burned, and had we been in just the same fix for marching as when we left Louisville we might have fared badly; but our trains were now with us, besides we carried plenty of axes with with we cut down trees and built huge log heaps that served to keep us warm during the long, cold nights. After supper each evening we had unbounded fun sitting around those same heaps playing our tricks and spinning our long yarns. When the weather was good we certainly had more fun than any set of men in the world.

January 13th. Our brigade laid in camp while Minty's brigade moved on.

January 14th. Passed through Brentwood and camped south of Franklin, near the famous battle-ground at that place. Nearly the whole brigade took a stroll over the field. A desire seemed to possess every one to see the ground on which one of the most desperate conflicts of the war took place.

January 15th. Marched through Thompson's station and camped three miles south of Spring Hill, getting into camp a little after noon. The first thing on going into camp is to stretch a long two-inch rope, which we called a picket-rope; to this the horses were tied, and then the next thing would be to chop down trees to build a fire. Well, to-day, when all the ropes had been stretched and all the horses tied in their places, one of the companies commenced to chop down a tree to make their accustomed log-heap. The tree was hickory and much taller than the men calculated it to be, and when it fell it just reached to the centre of one of the picket-ropes, and although there wasn't a limb thicker than your thumb that struck any of the horses, five of the horses were knocked down and three of them never kicked; the other two got up after a while and didn't seem to be much hurt. This caused a terrible quarrel and hard feeling between the two companies, which we think was finally settled by paying for the horses. Last night, at Franklin, another man belonging to our brigade was killed by bushwhackers.

January 16th. We got to Duck River, opposite Columbia, and went into camp three miles from that place. Minty's brigade had been here for two days. All bridges had been destroyed by the retreating rebels, and no way to cross until one could be made, which took all day the 17th. During these two days we were without rations.

January 18th. We got across the river this morning and passed through Columbia, took the road south-west, passed our old camp of last April, and bivouacked five miles from Columbia, on the Polk & Pillow farm. Our camp was in a most beautiful place, and notwithstanding so many soldiers of both armies had been through here, we found some forage, and rations, too. The country along the Duck River is very rich.

January 19th. We lay in camp waiting on the commissary. At Columbia we drew six days' rations, which were to last us until we got to the Tennessee River.

January 20th. Early this morning we moved on the Mount Pleasant road, and soon after passed the large mansion of the Right Rev. Maj.-Gen. Bishop Polk, a rebel general who was killed in front of Kenesaw, the 14th of June last. This was the grandest country residence we had yet seen. A half mile to the left we saw quite an extensive village, which proved to be the negro quarters of the Southern divine. A few steps south a church, and opposite the church the residence of the Bishop's negro driver. We marched through Mount Pleasant, crossed Buffalo Creek, through Henryville, and camped a few miles south of that place. The roads after leaving the pike were simply horrible.

January 21st. The rain poured down in torrents all day, and the roads were so miserable that we only made 12 miles.

January 22d. Dr. Cole says: "Passed through Waynesboro and camped three miles south of that place; made 15 miles. The ambulances are fast filling up with sick and disabled soldiers." We were now just 10 miles from the Tennessee River at Clifton. We had started for Eastport, and up to this time our direction from Columbia had been straight south-west. Here we got orders to report to Gravelly Springs, 50 miles distant and east of south. So on the 23d we changed our course and traveled a whole day through the woods in an easterly direction, without seeing any houses or signs of life. It snowed last night and we had a bad job getting started, and a lonesome day's march. Made 20 miles and camped in the woods late at night, and far away from anybody or any place that had a name. The small stream we were on was the head waters of Cyprus Creek, which empties into the Tennessee River not far from Florence. The day was very cold.

January 24th. Minty's brigade moved toward Gravelly Springs, and all the division train, except brigade ambulances and headquarters wagons, went on with him, while our brigade lay in camp—just what for will forever remain the most profound mystery to the private soldiers, as both rations and forage were out, and we were full 25 miles from any supplies, and in this God-forsaken country there wasn't enough food to make a square meal for a whippoorwill. It was another cold day and about as cheerless as could be imagined. We sent out strong foraging parties from each company, but as the whole country was a vast wilderness of course they got nothing. The ground was frozen hard, and this lying over proved to be very unfortunate, especially to our horses, as they still had a hard day's march before them and had to do it after fasting all day.

January 25th. Moved bright and early for Gravelly Springs. Snow on the ground and the ground frozen just hard enough not to bear. We had 25 miles to go and it took till sundown to make it. At the battle of Nashville Gen. Wilson was in command of all the cavalry in this department, and he followed the retreating rebels until they crossed the Tennessee River, and then camped near Gravelly Springs and had his headquarters two or three miles east of that place. We reported to him about sundown and he sent us to camp five or six miles west of where he was. It took us long after night to get there, and it was after 9 o'clock when we went into camp, on a bleak, cold hill, and very tired and hungry.

We had been just 29 days making the trip from Louisville to Gravelly Springs, and had traveled over 400 miles. This trip had been harder on us than our whole campaign last summer, when we had to fight nearly every day. During this march there were many things took place that once would have possessed a deep interest, but such events as are constantly being repeated, and will be the same while the war lasts, and have long since ceased to attract attention. It must be a very startling event if we think of it 10 minutes after it occurs.

Of the dozen manuscripts now before us, we find that none of them have a daily record of events for our camp at Gravelly Springs. The reason is obvious. Unless some very extraordinary event occurs, one day in camp is just like another. It is the same old story of "wash, iron, scrub, bake—wash, iron, scrub, bake." So we shall just proceed to write up the camp, without exact dates—naming, of course, the day particular events took place, when the date is known.

The first question, then, from the *general* reader, is, why we came here at all? There are now about 35,000 troops near here, mostly cavalry, and the wonder is, what for? Do not become frightened, now; we are not going to write the history of the rebellion, but going to give you, in few words, an intelligent idea why the Seventy-Second Indiana has marched over 400 miles and gone into camp in this vast region of desolation.

Then, at the risk of repetition, we say again that just at the time Hood began his raid on our railroad at Big Shanty, Gen. Grant, then in command of all the armies, had become dissatisfied with the management of the cavalry in this department, and sent one of his cavalry officers from the Army of the Potomac to take command of all the cavalry in the West, to organize them into one grand army of invasion to march triumphantly through the Southern confederacy and destroy everything that would be of any value to the rebel cause. This officer was Maj. Gen. James H. Wilson, who had achieved a very enviable reputation by his raids around Richmond. We have before explained when and where he came to us. When the first and second divisions went back to Louisville to re-mount, Gen. Wilson went to Nashville to assist Gen. Thomas in the defense of that place. He began immediately to organize all the cavalry in the Department of the Cumberland for that purpose, and at the great battle fought there our cavalry played a very important part, actually capturing from the rebels some of their strongest forts and earthworks, and more artillery in proportion to numbers than any other branch of the service. When the rebels began to retreat, the cavalry followed them up with such impetuosity as to entirely break up Hood's army, so that we never heard of Hood's army afterwards. Much of the credit for all this is due to the energy and perseverance of Gen. Wilson. Had the first and second divisions been re-mounted in time to take a part in the pursuit, we have no doubt but that the whole army might have been captured. After Wilson had chased all the scattered rebels across the Tennessee, he camped his army along the river from Florence to Eastport, so as to cover all the approaches into Tennessee, and then ordered his army to go into winter quarters.

Now comes the question of supplies, pre-eminently the most important one of all others. Where were the supplies to come from? They must come by way of the rivers from Nashville, Louisville, or St. Louis, a trip consuming 10 days. Now, suppose that he started after Hood with 10 days' rations, and in five days reached the river, and that within 24 hours after he reaches the river rationd were started to him,—his men must be without rations for five days before they get there. Which was just exactly the case, causing great suffering. There was one trait of Gen. Wilson's character that, as long as we lay in camp, made the whole army despise him. He swore that the *horses* had to be well taken care of, if the men starved; and to prove and enforce just what he said, from the very first arrival of the transports full rations of oats were issued to the horses, but the poor soldiers had to eke out a miserable existence on scant half rations for full five days more. All this took place with Wilson and his army before we joined him, and as the boats had been running regularly for three weeks, and the horses were getting fat on full rations of oats, it might reasonably be supposed that by the time we got here there would have been rations enough ahead to let us have a little, at least. But, no; not a bit of rations did we get for full five days after we got here. We will tell you all about it after awhile. The next morning after we arrived, and from that date, our horses had all the oats they could eat. This was a little too much for frail humanity to endure quietly. While it was food for reflection, it didn't fill our empty stomachs a bit. We did not object to having the horses well fed, but we did object to doing without ourselves. Of course, when an intelligent man enlists in the army and becomes a soldier, he loses his identity and becomes a horse, or a mere machine; but we have known horses that we thought could reason a little, and dumb as private soldiers are supposed to be we could not help reasoning that the same line of transports which brought such an *abundance* of forage could just as well have brought us a *little* rations. Besides, Uncle Sam had a plentiful supply of rations for us, and we were most sure that *somebody* got those five days' rations which were intended for us. Now, suppose that there were 30,000 troops here after our division arrived, and that the whole of them were full five days without any rations at all, and five more with scant half rations, and we have seven-and a-half days. Now count each ration at 35 cents a day, and we have 225,000 rations, worth $78,750. Quite a respectable fortune for somebody; and it would take a great deal of most profound reasoning to make *us* believe the Government did not pay for that many rations which were intended for us, and which we never got, but which somebody else did *get*.

As before stated, we got into camp about 9 o'clock at night, on the 25th of January, 1865, five miles below Gravelly Springs, Alabama. We don't know how much gravel there is at or near the springs in order to give them their name, but we do know that the ridge or knob on which we were camped that night seemed to be composed almost entirely of gravel stones from the size of hick'ory-nuts and walnuts to goose-eggs. It was entirely bare of herbage of any kind, and the trees were low and stunted. The day had been tolerably pleasant, but the night set in cold and the wind came whistling over that ridge in gusts that pierced us to the very bones; but we had got somewhat used to the cold, and under ordinary circumstances should not have cared a whit. The weather was dry, and if we could only have had our suppers, and plenty of strong coffee, we should have forgotten all our troubles in less than two hours; but hungry as we were the wind seemed to blow right through us.. Wood was so scarce we could not keep our fires burning all night, and the sleep we got did us no good, and in the morning we were the most haggard and woe-begone set of looking fellows you ever saw.

January 26th. No bugle call this morning, but the men were up by daylight and began to hunt around for wood and built huge fires, crowded around them, and spent the time growling and cursing, and wondering why we did not draw rations. We drew feed for our horses, and everybody expected we would draw rations soon, but the morning wore slowly away, and about 9 o'clock we were ordered to saddle up, which we very slowly and complainingly did. About 11 a. m. we mounted and moved about a mile north on the same ridge, had orders to go into camp in regular order and to put our bunks up so as to make ourselves comfortable as possible. It was after noon before we got our camp staked off, our picket-ropes stretched and our horses tied. The sun came out bright and warm, and if we could have had plenty of sowbelly, crackers and coffee, we would have been a jolly set of fellows. As it was we were cross as bears, and never jostled each other without growling, and finally, when we got our horses tied and fed, we threw our saddles, guns and accoutrements, dog-tents and camp equipage, into piles, and just "lolled" around in sullen silence, not making a single effort to clean up our quarters or to put up our bunks, while ordinarily we would have had our quarters cleaned up before night and our camp in good condition.

January 27th. No bugle call this morning, but the men were up early and went moping about as though they were looking for something, they hardly knew what. As there was nothing to cook, there were no fires built. When the men came to feed the horses they broke out into the most bitter cursing, damning Gen. Wilson, the Commissary General, the transports, and everybody and everything that had anything to do with our rations, swearing if they could just eat oats the horses would get damned little of *that* feed. The men spent the day straggling around over the country, and from regiment to regiment, in hopes of finding something to eat, but all in vain. We found a mill about a mile and a half from our camp, but not a grain of corn or wheat in it. Indeed, there were no plantations near it, and we wondered what use there could be for a mill in this wooden country. There were no efforts made toward putting up our bunks or cleaning our quarters. In the evening, when the companies drew their horse-feed, it was found there was about one-fifth corn mixed with the oats, but the corn was badly damaged, not more than one grain in three being sound, the balance being quite rotten. However, the men picked out the sound grains, parched and ate them, making a small handful for each man. This was the first we had eaten for three days, and instead of allaying our hunger, only aggravated it. Again we went to bed in a mood the farthest from amiable. Although we were not bothered with nightmare, our dreams were not pleasant. Huge piles of hard-tack and sowbelly were almost within our reach, but a chasm a thousand fathoms deep separated us from it.

January 28th. The men were up early as usual; this was the fourth day without rations, and the case had become so desperate that they gathered around in knots, and were engaged in the most earnest discussions in regard to procuring food at all hazards. Many desperate remedies were proposed but immediately abandoned, because there was no food within 50 miles of the place, and it was no use laying plans to get food when there was none to get. Many expedients were tried to find food; some going away back into the forest through which we had come on moving down here, to hunt, and some few deer were killed, but most of these enterprises were entire failures. Some tried hunting for forage in different directions, and in rare cases were successful; we shall speak of the successful ones presently. No efforts had yet been made to put up our bunks or police the quarters. About 8 o'clock the sergeant-major came around with orders from the Colonel to put up bunks and police the quarters. Some of the men swore they would not do it. If they *had to starve* they could do it without bunks or quarters either, and that they did not intend to do a thing till they got something to eat. As above intimated some few were successful in finding something, but nine out of every 10 were starving. Before us now are piles of manuscript corroborating every word we say, and we would like to publish all, but not one of them tells the whole story all the way through; and as there are so many of them it would consume pages so fast to undertake to write them all up, that we have, after much hesitancy, concluded to give our own experience, well knowing that it will answer for nine-tenths of the regiment; and we further feel satisfied that our comrades will pardon the egotism in just this once dropping the plural "we," and using the singular "I." There is only one thing that prompts me to this course, and that is I can tell my own experience in fewer words than I can tell a dozen others. At the time the sergeant-major came aronnd with orders to put up bunks, half of the regiment were out in the country hunting food. As I had always tried to obey every legitimate order I and a few bunk-mates set about building a bunk. There was plenty of timber close at hand, and we cut poles 16 feet long and intended to build a bunk of that length, six feet wide, and cover it with our dog-tents. Six or eight of us went to work, and by resting each other every few minutes succeeded in cutting enough by the middle of the afternoon, and lest some of the other companies should steal them during the night we concluded to try and carry them to camp. They were six to 10 inches in diameter, and had I been eating plenty I could have carried one of them myself; but when we undertook to carry one of them we found it was all that six of us could do to lift it by getting hand-spikes under it, and before we got it half way to the place I "stubbed" my toe, staggered and fell; this threw more weight on the others and they all went down together. There was neither laughing nor cursing, but a hollow look of despair depicted in each one's countenance, and we lay there some minutes without saying a word, when I told the boys I should neve do another lick of work till I got something to eat. Just then the sergeant-major came into our company quarters for a detail of a sergeant and eight men to go as guards for a train that was going to the landing for rations. Every soldier who heard this announcement greeted it with cheers, and the orderly found no difficulty in finding men willing to go. It happened to be my turn in regular order, and the orderly told me I would have to go, but I felt so weak I could hardly walk without staggering and did not see how I possibly could go. My bunk-mates all urged me to go, in hopes that I might get something a little sooner than we would get in the regular way. It was about an hour by sun when we got the detail, and we were to report on horseback to brigade headquarters, a mile from our camp. It was nearly sundown when we got there, and when I reported to the quartermaster, behold! he had entirely forgotten that he had ever sent for the detail at all. This is a fair exhibition of the care some officers have for their men. He finally told us he guessed he would send for the rations any how, but we would have to wait till he sent for the teams. Well, by the time the detail was made, the teams hitched up, and reported to headquarters, it was getting dark. As the sun had shone very warm during the day the weather was warm and pleasant, and as we knew the landing was only two miles from our camp we expected to get back in two hours, and none of us had thought of taking our overcoats along; but as soon as the sun went down it got bitter cold. About dark we got started, and instead of going to the landing nearest to our camp we went away up the river to another landing fully nine miles, and it was after 9 o'clock before we got there. We were too weak to walk or to climb on and off our horses without great effort, and so suffered terribly with the cold before we reached the landing. When we got to the river everything was still as death. There was a steamboat anchored in the middle of the river 400 yards from the shore, from which our loudest hallooing failed to elicit any response. The commissary sergeant was along with the teams, and he now rode off in the direction of Gen. Wilson's headquarters, to see if he could find any one who could tell us anything about our rations. While he was gone we built a fire and tried to warm ourselves. Up to this time we had been groping around in the dark. When we got the fire built we found there was an old building not very far from us, and we went for it in hopes of finding something to eat, or that we might carry back to camp We had all brought our haversacks along, determined to break open the first box of crackers we got our hands on; but what was our wrath when we got to the building to find nothing but a few barrels of pickled pork. This seemed like mockery to us. Had it been sowbelly (smoked side meat) we could have eaten it without cooking, or further ceremony. We looked upon this salt meat as an aggravation that would not pay for bursting the barrels. In about an hour the commissary came back and the teamsters rolled the barrels into the wagons and we started back. It was long after midnight when we got back to camp. I was so stiff with cold and so thoroughly exhausted that I could not carry my saddle, but just jerked it off and let it lay. The men in my company were awake, anxiously awaiting our return in hopes we would have our haversacks well filled with hard-tack. Blasted hopes! We knew that in the course of time we would get some of the salt pork, but that was not the kind of food we needed; besides, the amount would be so small that it would do us but little good.

January 29th. This was our fifth day without rations, and this morning, for the first time, we drew shelled corn for our horses instead of oats, under threats of dire punishment from the officers if we should appropriate a grain of it to our own use. We managed to get about one-third of our horses' rations into our pockets while feeding them. Many of the boys had managed to steal some corn from the quartermaster the night before in hopes of getting to grind it at the mill already spoken of, but the quartermaster had already taken possession of the mill, and would permit no grinding for private soldiers. It could only grind about as fast as all the officers in the brigade could eat, and shoulder-straps had to be served first. Then what to do with the corn was the question. Various methods of fixing it up to make it palatable were resorted to. Some parched and ate it at once, while others boiled it in ashes, washed the hull off and cooked it till a little soft. By any method it was a slow process of relieving hunger. The truth is, it was simply an aggravation. Late in the afternoon the pickled pork was issued to the companies, and on dividing it among the men each one got a piece not larger than two by three inches square, and that is the first bite we had for five full days, except the little bit of corn just referred to. During the 30th the men managed to steal more corn and put in the day trying to appease hunger on it. You ask why, when men were starving, it was necessary to steal it? Just because, as I have before told you, "General Starvation," as we called Gen. Wilson, had issued the most positive orders that the horses should have all they could eat if the men starved, and there was only a feed at a time issued to us, so that we were compelled to steal it if we got it. During all this time we heard but little complaint from the officers. We knew the quartermaster had taken possession of the mill, and that the officers would get th benefit of that, so far as it went; but we began to very strongly suspect that they were getting rations from some source or other that we knew not of. So in the afternoon I determined to make a tour of inspection over the various camps near us to see what discoveries I could make. Two others went with me, and late in the afternoon we strolled around by the brigade commissary's quarters, and sure enough, there was a pile of about 50 boxes of hard tack right in front of his tent, and piled up so closely that there was barely room for a guard to pass between the boxes and the tent door. We observed, too, a guard pacing his beat there. As all the officers had to buy their rations from the government, we knew they would be served first from any supplies that might come to our camps, and that all the brigade headquarters, including the Colonel, Quartermaster and Commissary, with all their orderlies, teamsters, blacksmiths, surgeons, stewards, and all the different regimental headquarters, including the Colonel's quartermaster, commissary, ordnance sergeants, sergeant-majors, adjutants, majors, surgeons, captains and lieutenants of companies, had to be supplied out of that pile before the private soldier could get a bite. We do not want you to infer that just now these officers were faring sumptuously; they were not, but they always got the first cut at everything, and we knew that in the regular round of red-tape it would be twenty-four hours before those crackers would be distributed to the companies; and as there were but about 50 boxes altogether, or about a day's rations for the private soldiers of the brigade, and that after all the commissioned officers were supplied our chances would be slim indeed, we resolvedto take time by the forelock and have some of those crackers along with the commissioned officers, or before, if we could get them. We went back to camp and said nothing about our discovery, but lounged around till after the bugle blowed for lights out, and the camp had settled down to stillness; then we started. There were some camps between ours and the commissary, which was a mile away, but we avoided the camps by taking down the hollow which ran down on the west side of the ridge on which we were camped. All the lights were out in the camp till we came to the commissary's. There we found the lights burning, and we saw by the shadows as we passed by the tent that there were several persons in there, that the guard in pacing his beat would frequently stop and look into the tent door. We moved past the tent without attracting attention, and a short distance down the ridge held a council of war, and made, as we thought, provision for every possible contingency, From the bottom of the hollow to the top of the ridge where the tent stood was 200 yards, and very steep. Our plan was for "Yank" to go up and stop the guard at the tent door behind the pile of crackers from us, and engage him there in conversation till E. S. Records should slip up behind the pile, get a box and make off down the hill with it, in a south-west direction. The rest of us were to station ourselves along the proposed line of retreat, about 50 yards apart, in order to relieve each other of the load, as in our present famished condition we were a little doubtful of our ability to carry a 50-pound box of crackers; and in case the guard should detect us and halt us, after getting started with the crackers, we were to pay no attention to him, but just keep right on and run the risk of getting hit if he should shoot, but in no case to let go of the crackers.

Everything being arranged, Yank and Records went up behind the pile; Yank walked boldly up to the tent door and asked the guard what those fellows were doing in there. He told him they were gambling. Yank says, "Let's go and see them." So they both went to the door and looked in. There a half dozen officers and orderlies were very deeply engaged in a game of "draw poker." Records now got a box on his shoulder, and thus far our plans had worked well; but the box was so heavy for him that he almost had to run to carry it at all, and I suppose there was something hurrying him, too. At any rate he started down the hill at a pretty lively gait, and had not gone more than 25 yards when he stubbed his toe and pitched 10 feet, headlong down the hill. The box flew out of his grasp and went bounding down the hill at a fearful rate, making as much noise as an empty wagon. Records regained his feet in an instant and pitched on down the hill after the box, and at the end of 10 rods caught up with it and threw himself upon it in hopes of stopping it, or at least stopping the thundering noise. But the two together by this time had gained such momentum that stopping was out of the question, and they both went bounding down the hill with the velocity of a whirlwind, Records holding on to it manfully, and like the Irishman and the sawlog, was a full match for it, being on top half the time. Instead of going down the line we intended, it took straight down the hill square to the west, and we all made a rush for it. "Billygoat" being nearest, caught up first, and as he ran jerked off his overcoat and threw it over the fast revolving bodies, hoping at least to deaden the sound. This proved to be the happiest stroke of policy, as it not only deadened the sound but acted as a brake, and when near the bottom we all pitched in a pile together on the box. Divest this exploit of the danger there was in it, and it was the funniest thing I ever saw. As long as the war lasted it served us for a good laugh as often as we thought of it. The serious part of it is yet to relate. When the box started down the hill with such a thundering noise "Yank" said he thought the "jig was up." He realized the situation in a moment. The guard turned quickly to listen, but "Yank" caught him by the arm and called his attention to some particular phase of the game that just then happened to transpire, and said, "Let's step in here where we can see better," at which he parted the curtains a little and they both stepped in, unobserved by the players, and stood there till the noise died away, and he knew we were safe. He then slipped out and followed, leaving the guard in the most blissful ignorance of what had taken place. I thought Records would have been pounded to a jelly, yet I didn't stop to inquire about it much then, but gathered up the box and ran up the hollow 50 yards with it, when I was completely exhausted. This took us out of danger, and we gathered up our forces and moved slowly back to camp, getting there about 11 o'clock. You who have never been hungry in your lives, can never tell how good those crackers tasted. We ate what we wanted, divided the rest out among our friends, burned the box, and went to bed in the best humor we had been for a week.

January 31st. On the 18th of this month, at Columbia, Tenn., we drew six days' rations; and about the middle of this afternoon a few boxes of crackers were distributed to the companies and we got just three crackers apiece. From this date for the next five days we drew only a few crackers each day—just enough to keep us fearful hungry the whole time. When our soldiers who were prisoners in Andersonville speak of their terrible, gnawing, distressed hunger, we believe every word they say, and more too. Now these are the facts in regard to our five whole days without food, as far as the regiment was concerned, as a whole. We have numerous stories before us of those who fared better, and shall make extracts from them just to show they were exceptional cases. The first is from A. W. Lane, Co. G: "You remember how distressingly short of grub we were at Gravelly Springs. Two or three of our boys undertook a foraging expedition in spite of strict orders and the extreme destitution of the country. After going 20 miles on foot and finding absolutely nothing they were returning to camp, in no very enviable frame of mind, when a small squad of cavalrymen were seen at a distance, approaching. On close examination they proved to be pretty well loaded with sowbelly and meal. Our boys quickly deployed as skirmishers in the dense woods, and when they came up began firing at them, and calling on them to halt; taking care to keep themselves concealed in the brush. The cavalry began drawing their pistols, and in their endeavors to control their horses lost their grip on the meal-sacks. By this time our boys made such a noise that the cavalry thought the woods were full of rebels and lit out, throwing away the meat. Our boys gathered up their plunder and skipped out for camp, happy at the success of their harmless ruse.

We now make an extract from the journal of S. B. Johnson, sergeant Co. D.:

"Friday, January 27th. Still very cold and no grub and no prospect of any. Saturday, January 28th. Still cold and nothing to eat. Sunday, January 29th. Drew a pint of meal and a very small piece of meat to each man, for two days' rations. Monday, January 30th. Weather more pleasant, but no hard-tack yet.

"Here we had more bad weather and less to eat than during any other portion of our service. Sometimes we had hard-tack, but oftener none, and scarcely ever saw meat. Semi-occasionally we drew something called fish, which had about as much substance in them as saw-dust. We called them sand-sharks. Perhaps among a better class of people than we were they would be called cod-fish. There were six days in this camp in which we had nothing in the world to eat but a little corn. Steamboats landed almost every day, loaded with hay, corn and oats, for the horses, but no rations. Who was to blame for this state of things? I do not know. Surely some one was. We had to take extra care of our horses and were forbidden to take one out of camp. But getting desperate hungry some six or seven of us fed early and hitched our horses out until after roll-call, when we mounted and away we went in quest of something to appease hunger. We returned that evening with what would have been two hogs, had they been confined in a corn-field for two months with plenty of water; but the meat was just as good to us as the best steak would be now, if not more so. For this disobedience of orders these brave boys were given five days' extra duty in carrying stone off the parade ground."

The next is from John B. Davis, also of Co. D: "Thousands of bushels of oats were piled up for our horses, but nothing for us. Scant three days' rations were issued to us to do five days, and for nearly two weeks after this we were forced to live on parched corn. Bunk No. 2, of Co. D, however, fared a little better. A special friend of mine, David Sands, Co. B, was running a country mill close by. We resolved on some desperate effort to get some meal. After dark A. B. Tucker and myself paid a flying visit to a neighboring corn pile, and unnoticed by the guards carried off two sacks of corn. Early the following morning I slipped my horse past the horse guards and down the hill-side into the valley, and returned to camp to await day-break. At early dawn, with a bushel and a half of corn astride my horse, I wended my way to the mill, where I arrived before sun-up. "Dave" was at work. "Well," says he, "John, a man was just turned off by the Quartermaster because he had ground for a soldier, but *you* shall have it," and sooner than you could say "Jack Robinson" he had dumped my corn out and filled up my sack with meal, and I was off for camp. But no salt, nor grease, nor soda! We put our wits to work to see if there was any remedy. I went to the brigade commissary and saw a few barrels of meat, one of them some distance from the others. I said to myself, "Mister barrel, if you're there to-night I'll dump you down the hill." After dark, with others, I went to the place, but the lone barrel, with the others, had been rolled up near the tent door, and two guards were sitting on the barrels. Foiled in this, we went to our regimental quartermaster's tent. Two candles were burning in the tent and two darkies lying asleep. We noticed a suspicious-looking box in the back part of the tent. Lifting the tent and raising the lid of the box, lo, the object of our search! About sixty pounds. Result: Fat pickled pork and greasy corn-cakes for breakfast."

The next is an extract from the experience of Basil Lamb, Company B: "We had not been in camp long till we found there was something wrong in the commissary department. We had nothing to eat and no chance to forage for anything. Our command always lived well when the country afforded anything. If the citizens were loyal they could afford to give. If they were not, they *ought* to give. After being in camp three or four days, our company held an indignation meeting to decide what was best to be done. We knew of a grist-mill about 20 miles from camp, that we had passed on the road down to this place, and there were some wheat, corn and hogs there. but it was also true that there was a band of 90 bushwhackers in the vicinity, and that it was dangerous to go there. However, necessity knows no law, and with starvation staring us in the face, we thought what we could not do by force we might do by strategy. So Hugh Myers, Jacob Ristine, Joseph Narlock, James Doherty, James Sellers, Solomon Sellers, John Weeks, myself and Thornton Van Buskirk, who was a miller by trade, and a few others, concluded we would take the chances and go to that mill. We arrived there about noon the first day, and took possession of the mill and what stuff there was in it. On our arrival the man who was tending the mill began to knock out the wedges so as to render the mill useless, but we soon stopped that part of the job and dismissed him. We sent out squads into the country to get sweet potatoes and molasses, and in a short time we had a feast that a king might desire. At this point a woman came to the mill whose husband was in the Union army, and told us that every man in the country around was a rebel and a bushwhacker, and that they were making arrangements to take us by surprise. We told her we were prepared for this, that there were more men close by, and the impudence with which we foraged around over the country lent some assurance to our words. They sent in a spy in the evening and we told him we had taken possession of the mill to run it a hundred days, and that there were plenty of men close by. We kept up a bold front for two nights and a day, and then concluded we had better get out of that, which we did, taking all the meal, flour and molasses, we could carry.

Gen. Wilson came to us from the Army of the Potomac, and brought with him much of the "grand review" style of that army; that of itself was sufficient to prejudice all Western soldiers against him; for if there was anything Western troops did hate, it was anything that was done for mere style, without a corresponding benefit. But added to this love of show, he seemed to study just how to keep every soldier in his whole army on duty every day. We hadn't drawn a single ration yet till we had general orders read to us from Gen. Wilson every morning, and upon almost every conceivable subject. Telling us first just how we should take care of our horses, he said the *horses must be taken care of first*, and then if there was anything left the soldier might have it. Next he told us how to put up our bunks and police our quarters, just as though we had been in the service almost three years and yet did not know how to make ourselves comfortable and keep clean. He next told us how to conduct ourselves in order to be *good* soldiers. In this order was a command to keep on camp guard constantly, day and night. This was the most detestable order of the batch, for we well knew camp guard was only intended for appearance, and never did one bit of good, and was never obeyed only in obedience to orders from headquarters, and then only in the day time; for just as soon as the lights were blown out every camp guard would deliberately go to his quarters and go to bed. But the idea of keeping 60 to 100 men on camp guard even in the day time was very repugnant to us. He also issued an order about digging sinks, just as though we naturally loved filth and were in the habit of stabling our horses in our bunks. We had not all got our bunks up till he ordered us to build stables for our horses. We were not through with this till he ordered us to drill so many hours each day. For two or three weeks every man was on duty every day, and it frequently happened that there were not men enough in the companies to fill the details. All this might have served to keep lazy soldiers in good health, yet all *we* asked on that score was just to get enough to eat. But after all was said and done, when we broke camp in the spring we were no better prepared for the campaign than when we went into camp. Extravagant use of authority always reverts on the author. As we did everything by the bugle call, we will enumerate them, so you may know how much we had to learn and to obey each day, and to show you that this bugling was no small matter we state that at each division headquarters there was a chief bugler, whose call governed all buglers in the division. At each brigade headquarters there was a bugler, and his call governed all the regimental buglers in the brigade. Then at each regimental headquarters there was a bugler, and his call governed all the company buglers, and each company had a bugler, whose business it was to repeat every call blown by the regimental bugler. The order of blowing was this way: first, the division bugler would blow a call, which was repeated in concert by all the brigade buglers; next by the regimental buglers in concert, and lastly by each company bugler in concert. In our army of 30,000 men there would be about 300 buglers blowing all at the same time, which would make about as much noise as you would care to listen to. The order of the calls was about in this way: first, in the morning, about 5 o'clock in winter and 4 in summer, was the musicians', or buglers' call, at which every bugler in the army had to turn out and get ready to blow; second, the "orderly's call," at which every orderly sergeant had to turn out and get ready to call the roll: third, "roll call," at which every soldier in the army had to turn out and be ready to answer to his name by the time the bugle was done sounding. This opened the duties of the day. The fourth was feed call; fifth, breakfast call; sixth, curry horses; seventh, police quarters; eighth, sick call; ninth, guard mount; tenth, fatigue duty; eleventh, water horses; twelfth, squad drill; thirteenth, dinner call; fourteenth, company drill; fifteenth, battalion drill; sixteenth, water call; seventeenth, feed your horses; eighteenth, supper; nineteenth, evening roll call—this always blew just at sundown; twentieth, tattoo roll call; 21st, taps, or lights out, at 9 p. m.; when all the lights had to be put out and all go to bed. Besides all these, our every movement in squad, company, or battalion drill, were all governed by the bugle, making 20 or 30 more calls. Our horses would learn these quicker than the men. We once had a little nigger in Company D, of our regiment, who made a rhyme for almost all of the calls, so that the words would just apply to the notes, and he would sing them just as the buglers would play. We remember only his rhyme for the feed call, which was, "Come all you that are able, and go to the stable, and feed your horses hay, oats and corn. Or if you don't, de colonel will know it, and put you in de guard house, sure as you are born."

We have spoken of building stables for our horses, and you may want to know how we did it. Well, there was certainly plenty of timber handy to do it with, as we were camped in a forest that extended from the river 20 to 50 miles north of us, with very few inhabitants. There were no saw mills, however, to cut the trees up into lumber, or the work would have been easy. We had to do all the work with the ax, the cross-cut saw, and the froe. Our first work was to set three rows of posts in the ground, 12 feet apart, and the rows just as long as we wanted our stables to be. Now, suppose the horses stood in two rows, with their heads together in the middle, and that four feet were allowed to each horse, and that there were 80 horses and pack-mules in the company, and we must have a stable 160 feet long to accommodate them, which was just the length of the one in Company I. It took 10,000 clapboards to cover the stable of each company of the regiment. Multiply this by 600, about the number of companies in this army, and we have the enormous sum of 6,000,000 clapboards, which we made in about two weeks. You see what a vast amount of work we did. When done, the stables were just as comfortable as any horse need stand in.

There had been some change made in the drill and movements for the cavalry, and before we were done with the stables we were ordered to go to drilling on horseback in order to learn the new tactics. So we had squad and company drill every day, battalion drill twice a week, and brigade and division drill once a week. Hence we never saw an idle day as long as we lay in camp. About the second day after we went into camp, two deer came running along on the ridge on which we were camped, passing through the 17th, then through our regiment, then through the 123d, and then on south through other regiments. There were a thousand shots fired at them, and one of them was killed about two miles south of us, while the other one kept on south, and finally got to the river, swam across, and thus saved his hide. There were numbers of them killed in the forest north of us afterwards, and in our starving condition deer meat was considered quite a treat. This brings us to one of the thousands of jokes that were played off while here. Lieut. Clark, of Company I, was acting quartermaster of the regiment, and about a week after we went into camp he distributed a lot of shoes. Nearly all the men of Company C wore 7's. The supply of 7's was soon exhausted, and yet Company C was not half supplied. After the distribution was made, Clark found he had left on his hands a pair of number 14's, which nobody wanted. So he sent for "Aise" Derby, orderly sergeant of Company C, stating that he had two 7s left, and to come down and get them. Derby started off in a great hurry, for fear somebody would be ahead of him, supposing, of course, that there were two pairs of 7's. When he got there he wanted to know where those two pairs of shoes were. Clark then threw down the pair of 14's, which looked like young gunboats. Derby said his men were not in the habit of going with both feet in one shoe, and he guessed he wouldn't take them. The laugh was on Derby. A day or two after this, Derby went down to Clark's tent, and in a very unconcerned way got to talking about the boys going hunting, and remarked that one of them had killed a deer. Clark became interested at once, and said he'd like to have some. Derby said he had no doubt he could get some if he would go before it was all gone. Clark hurried off to Company C's quarters to find the man who killed the deer. After inquiring at every bunk in the vain attempt, he stopped and began to think there must have been some mistake, when Derby stuck his head out of the captain's tent and shouted, "Here's your two 7's!" Clark put back to his quarters, feeling like he had let a bird go.

There is so very little that is pleasant to contemplate about our camp at Gravelly Springs, that we shall purposely skip over numerous incidents of deep interest to all who participated in them, in order to get away from the place as soon as possible. In the first place, this seemed to be the most God-forsaken country we had ever been in—poor beyond description. In the next place, the idea of *winter quarters* was repulsive. We wanted to be going, and to think we would have to stay there so long detracted very much from any sport or pleasure we usually enjoyed. We had always been where we could get mail at intervals, and knew what was going on at home, and in the different departments of the army, and so felt we were still a part and parcel of God's creation; but here we only got mail two or three times, and then always nearly a month behind the times On looking back over the whole period of our service, we can think of no place where we lay in camp any length of time but we had some special arrangements for amusement and pleasure of some kind. Sometimes we would have one thing and sometimes another, but always something. Here, however, we were so constantly kept on duty of one kind or another, that a general plan of amusement was out of the question, and one had to look out for his own amusement. We give you the method adopted upon one occasion by Company K's "forager," to amuse himself, and also to get even with the sutler. Everybody remembers the crowds of soldiers that would gather around the sutler's "chebang" just after getting on a fresh load of "truck." At just such a time, when the boys were about six or eight deep, all struggling around the front of the tent to get a chance to buy something, the sutler very busy *handing out* pickled pig's-feet, canned peaches, and a two inch square plug of tobacco for a dollar, and just as busy *taking in* the shinplasters, (fractional currency), the box containing said shinplasters was of course left where it would be handy to make change, our "forager" was quietly standing by. He had the ramrod of an old "Springfield," the hollow end of which was filled with tar, and whenever the sutler's back was turned he would give his ramrod a "job" in his box of "fractional," and with easy dexterity take up such denominations as he wished and pass them out to the boys, who could well afford to keep still.

It was a common occurrence for the officers to lie down on their bunks or cots and go to sleep in the day time. This was always fun for the privates. We had picket-ropes 30 feet long, and used to tie or picket our horses out to grass; we had also iron pins 18 inches long, with a ring in the end, and by sticking the pin in the ground we could tie our horses out anywhere. Well, the boys would take one of these ropes and tie the officer to his bunk in such a way that he could neither get up nor untie himself, and go off and leave him. We would almost always hear from the fellow shortly after he would wake up. At other times they would tie the officer's legs together and then torment him till he would jump up and start after them, and of course get a good fall. We saw a lieutenant come down to the company quarters one day and loll around a while, and finally lie down on one of the boys' beds and go to sleep. This was too good a chance for fun to be lost. The fellow took his picket-rope, tied one end around his leg and the other to a stump; he then got a long, slender stick or switch and tied a long thread to the little end; then he caught a large bug and tied the thread to it and placed himself out of sight and let the bug drop heavily in the lieutenant's face. This roused him up, and seeing the bug he began to strike at it violently, but the fellow kept the bug out of his reach, yet kept "dabbing" him in the face. You never saw a fellow fight bumble-bees harder than the lieutenant fought that bug. Finally, becoming alarmed, he started up in the wildest fright, fighting the bug for dear life. This was too much for the boys to see and not laugh. This assured the lieutenant he had been given away, and also directed his attention to the fellow who was holding the pole. With hades in his thoughts and blood in his eye he bounded to his feet and took after the fellow with the pole. The fellow took down hill with the lieutenant clutching at his coat-tails. He was a big, long-legged fellow, and half a dozen strides brought him to the end of the picket-rope, and he pitched headlong down the hill, with a crash that shook the ground like a young earthquake. It nearly jolted the life out of him, and for a few minutes he could not tell whether he had been shot out of a cannon or dropped down from the moon. At any rate he was almost sure he had heard something "drap." He finally gathered himself up, untied the rope and put off to his quarters, and was never known to go to sleep in the company quarters afterwards.

We guess almost everybody is good for something, but it has bothered us wonderfully sometimes to tell just what some people are good for. We are acquainted with a fellow, whom we shall call Bob, for two reasons—first, because it is handy, and second, because that isn't his name. Bob was just the poorest stick for a soldier we ever knew; he was just too "ornery" to keep the lice off of him, but he was a good forager. During all the time we were so starving hungry Bob always had plenty to eat. This, too, he found somewhere in this God-forsaken country. We never could tell how nor where, but *he got it*, and was so supremely selfish with everything he would capture that if his mess or bunkmates ever got anything from him they had to steal it, which was hard to do, because he always carried his haversack with him. One day he came in with his haversack plumb full of meat, bread, and even coffee—enough for his whole mess—but not a bite would he give them. Well, some of the other boys of his mess had been out in the country and found a house where there were a couple of hogs in a pen close by the house, but there was a soldier stationed there to guard the hogs. They reported to Bob and he said he could get the hogs, guard or no guard. So three or four of the boys went along with him. The pig-pen was close by the porch, and there happened to a girl about the house that the guard seemed to very much interested in, and the girl seemed to be just as sweet on him; the two sat there on the porch till the boys' patience was exhausted and they had to give it up. While they were gone the boys unloaded Bob's haversack, (which, for a wonder, he had not taken with him), and as he was not a very early riser, the boys had everything cleaned up before he was up. After a while Bob came around smelling of the fire-places and chimneys to see if he could get a scent of meat. He was too late; the scent had all passed off, but it was fearful the way he did cuss.

On the 11th of March Gen. Wilson reviewed our division. This was the grandest display we ever saw, and left a lasting impression on our minds. Along in the first part of the war Gen. McClellan, in command of the Army of the Potomac, indulged in so many of these grand reviews and so little fighting that the loyal people of the North became disgusted with it, and finally caused McClellan to be superseded, and western troops were prejudiced against them. You may know that these grand reviews were not very common, as while we were at Murfreesboro our division (Gen. Reynolds,) was reviewed once; and our division (2d cavalry) was reviewed at Louisville. These are all the division reviews we had ever seen. Western troops were not much for display, but a great deal for business. We began to tell you about our grand review. It took place on an old plantation near Gen. Wilson's headquarters, about four miles from our camp. The ground was a plain of three or four hundred acres in extent, and so nearly level that we could see the whole division at once, which had only occurred twice before during our service; this time very much plainer than the others. The review was to take place at 1 o'clock; our regiment left camp at 11, and the movements of all the regiments in the division were so well timed that all arrived on the ground at the same time and took up the positions assigned them, without waiting or delay. As there was not room for the whole division to be formed in one single straight line, we were formed in two lines 100 yards apart, facing to the east, and each line was a mile and a half long—the Colonels 50 yards in front of the front line, opposite the center of their respective regiments; each brigade commander 100 yards in front of the center of his brigade; while Gen. Long, our division commander, was 50 yards in front of the line of brigade commanders, and opposite the center of the division, making him 250 yards in front of the rear line of soldiers. Our regiment was in the rear line, which gave us the better chance to see all the movements, as we were not allowed to "gawk" about or change our position. Gen. Wilson's headquarters were at a big white house, on an eminence, a half mile in front of us, and we could see every movement very plainly. There were quite a lot of ladies there to witness the spectacle, and also two or three hundred officers belonging to the other divisions. The day was one of the most beautiful we ever saw and contrasted very strongly with the day of our review at Louisville. When we had all taken our places and straightened our lines they were so straight that a person in the ranks on looking either way could only see the man next to him, and on bending backward or forward he could just see one continued line of blue, but not a single man in the whole line. We never saw any regiment on dress parade make a better line—we had drilled so much that our horses were completely broken and understood every movement as well as the soldiers themselves. When Gen. Wilson, from his headquarters, saw that our lines were formed, he and his staff mounted and rode directly to Gen. Long, saluted him and passed the time of day; then ordered him to have his division to open ranks. Gen. Long then turned his horse and gave command:

"ATTENTION BATTALIONS! OPEN RANKS. TEN PACES FORWARD. MARCH!"

Every company, *always*, on falling in to march or move any where, is numbered off by "4's," and in opening ranks numbers 1 and 3 always move forward, numbers 2 and 4 standing fast; and in this case the odd numbers moved out so promptly and kept so well dressed that when they halted the line was as well dressed and just as straight as when they started. We never saw a single battalion execute this movement better in our lives. When this movement was executed Gen. Wilson, with Gen. Long to his right, wheeled their horses to the right and on a quick gallop started around the entire division, and in passing clear around made a circuit of four miles, which completely played out many of the staff officers' horses, some of them before getting half way around. Every regiment had all its flags, banners and guidons flying, and when the officers would reach the heads of regiments the regiment would "dip" its colors and present arms, and remain perfectly motionless till they were past, then come to a shoulder again. As the officers would reach the head of each brigade the brigade commander would take his place by the side of Gen. Wilson, and as they galloped along would give him the name and number of each regiment, and answer such questions about the efficiency, equipment and drill, as might be asked him, and after passing the brigade take his place again. The programme of this review would have required the General to pass both in the front and in the rear of each line, which would have made a heat of eight miles; but he found the horses would not stand it, so they only passed in the front of our line and in the rear of the other. But every thing passed off so well and the General was so well pleased with our appearance, that when he reached the "front and center," where they started from, he ordered Gen. Long to hold his division in readiness to move at a minute's notice. Gen. Long now turned to the division and gave command, "*Attention Battalions! Close order, March!*" When we closed up he drew his sword, and with it saluted the divisions, and our colors again went down. He then gave command, "*Parade is dismissed.*" Brigade commanders then turned to their brigades and gave command: "*Attention battalions! By fours, Right turn, Forward, Left turn, March!*" and we started to our camps, perfectly delighted with the grand success of our review. There had not been a single blunder or mistake, and had we gone through these movements every day for a month we could not possibly have executed them better. That evening at roll call we had orders read to us from Gen. Wilson to be ready to move right away, at a minute's notice.

It rarely happens that an event of such magnitude as this passes off without some ridiculous thing happening, and William Grismar, private Co. K, tells this: "I had made up my mind to go foraging that day, and when the captain came around in the morning and told us to get ready to go on review, I told him I didn't want to go. Said he, "You *have* to go." Well, just before we started I took out my knife and ripped my coat from the tail to the collar, and when my belt was on it gaped open like the back of a young locust. I went on the review and happened to be in the rear line, and when the General was just opposite me he stopped very suddenly and hallooed out, "Captain, send that man to his quarters." You bet I went, and as soon as I was out of sight struck out foraging. The only thing I could find was a little bit of a pig which I cooked in the coffee pot, so you can bet I was hungry."

We believe the Tennessee River is larger than the Ohio. Some time after we had gone into camp here the river rose to its highest notch, and as we were not so very far below the Muscle shoals, and numerous rapids, the water came rushing down in the most fearful commotion we ever witnessed. The river was four miles wide and perfectly frightful to look upon. The waves seemed to roll 20 feet high. While it was at its highest some transports came up and landed in an old field not far from our camp, but more than a mile from the landing at an ordinary stage of water. These were the spring floods. The rise was very rapid and caused a loss of fully $250,000 worth of forage and material belonging to this army.

March 13th, 1865. Last night at midnight the second (Minty's) brigade of our division began to move. They took the road down the river for Waterloo, 12 miles below us, getting there at daylight, and immediately began to cross the river, the fifth cavalry division having crossed a few days before, and went into camp at Eastport, Mississippi.

We were ordered last night to be ready this morning to move at sun-up. This order was received with pleasure. There was much less discussion and speculation as to where we were going than common. The men didn't seem to care much where we went so we got out of this miserable country. All along through our service we had scarcely ever moved camp but what the men had fixed up in their minds just where we were going to, but this time we heard very little of that. We now had but five months to serve, and we believe nine out of every ten would rather put the whole of that time in active campaigning than to lie in camp; especially if we had to pass the time as we had spent it here. This morning we were up bright and early, and in a good humor—in broad contrast with our condition on going into camp here. We began right away cheerfully to pack our traps ready to move. There was no hurrying, fussing, or confusion; but when the bugle blowed "strike tents" everybody was ready. We pulled out about 7 o'clock, taking a last look at our stables, and the vast amount of work we had done, without regret. The river is at flood-tide again, and before we get to Waterloo we strike a large bayou, and have to make a circuit of five miles to get around it. It was noon when we got to Waterloo, unsaddled, fed and got dinner, and from that till midnight had nothing to do but lie down and sleep, or stroll around over the country. The whole country for miles around looked just like the place we had left; that is, large bodies of troops had been camped here, their stables and winter quarters still standing, but the troops were gone. They had been crossing here for the last three days and nights. Minty's brigade began to cross early this morning, and the last of it did not get over till after sundown. They crossed on two large transports, or steamboats, and each transport had a flat-bottomed boat lashed to it, which would hold about 60 or 100 horses. The boats had to go down the river two miles to get to the landing on yonder side, and it took two full hours to make the trip across and back. About 11 o'clock at night we were ordered to saddle up, and just at midnight we got on board "The Swallow" and the barge, holding about one-third of our regiment. It was half-past 1 o'clock when we landed at Chickasaw. This is simply a little village of a few houses, nearly on the line between Mississippi and Alabama. We went out about three-fourths of a mile south-east and went into camp between a large bayou, or swamp, and the bluff. Owing to the darkness and thick brush, we had a terrible time getting into camp.

March 14th. It took the whole night for our brigade to get across. We had no bugle call, but as usual when going into a new place, the men were up early, looking around to see where we were.

and what the chances were to get something fresh. We found the country out from the river very much like the country we left at Gravelly Springs—very rough, hilly, and miserably poor—and aside from the few houses right at the landing, uninhabited. The only place of interest any where for miles around was at the river, and aside from the vast military preparations, there was nothing else there. Our teams were got across to-day. We have not spoken of what troops have been camped along the river. When our division reached Gravelly Springs there were the first, second, fourth, fifth and seventh cavalry, and at Waterloo were two divisions of the sixteenth corps, A. J. Smith commanding. On the 11th of February the seventh division and the infantry embarked for New Orleans.

A person who has never seen any military preparations at all can form no idea of the vast amount of everything that it takes to keep up an army even as small as 30,000 cavalry. We will mention the simple item of forage, to help you to guess at other things. We suppose from the time Wilson's great raid was determined upon, that this point was selected as the most practicable from which the expedition could start, and as soon as he got forage and rations enough up to keep us going, he commenced to pile up forage here, and just before the first flood of the river, three or four weeks ago, he had 500,000 bushels of oats here all in one pile, and as he supposed clear above high water mark. This was about 60 days' rations for all the horses in our armies here, and the pile was larger than any warehouse we ever saw. When the river got up to its highest, it ran several feet over the top of the pile, and spoiled every bushel. The weather was warm after the water ran down, and the oats heated up so hot as to nearly burn them to ashes. They were all in sacks, and of course swelled so as to burst all the sacks, and yet when we got there they were so hot as to be uncomfortable to walk over. We heard a camp follower say he would give five cents a bushel for the privilege of emptying the sacks. We don't know what he really did pay, but a day or two afterwards we saw him emptying the sacks and baling them up. He said he allowed to take them to Cincinnati, where they would bring him 20 cents each.

March 15th. Gen. Wilson and staff came across to-day. During the time we laid here the landing was a busy place. We frequently counted as high as 14 transports and five gunboats in one day. As there were numerous bands of guerrillas and bushwhackers all along the river all the boats had to go in fleets, and the gun-boats had to go along with them for protection. Just below the landing and inside the Mississippi line was a redoubt—a strong earth work—that was said to have been built by Andrew Jackson, on one of his expeditions against the Indians. It looked old enough, but we should guess it was built by the rebels about the time of the Fort Donelson campaign, the first year of the war. Eastport was two miles below this, on the south side of the river.

March 16th. The 4th division got across to-day. While we stayed at the landing the hour of our departure was often fixed and as often postponed on account of not being ready. Of course we had the stereotyped and usual orders in regard to leaving behind us all surplus clothing, blankets, overcoats, dog-tents, camp and garrison equipage, and all officers' tents of every description; but this order further indicated that we were to move much lighter than ever before

We had seen so little meat of any kind since we came to Gravelly Springs that the men have finally concluded that the supply left over from the Mexican war is about exhausted, and that henceforth they will have to depend upon their own resources for all the meat they get. With this understanding of the case we insert an expedition of Co. D, as related by John B. Davis: "We now had plenty of hard-tack but no meat. When any of our brigade was on picket or patrol duty we could pass by them apparently unnoticed. To remedy this matter Gen. Wilson put none but his cavalry on out-post duty; but we were so ravenously hungry for meat that we determined to run all risks and have some meat if there was any in rebeldom. Six or eight of us, guns in hands, left camp at an early hour; our journey lay over the hills and hollows for full 10 miles before finding what we wanted. After securing it we pressed in an old "hoss" to carry it, but he refused to do duty in the Union cause, and broke away from us and came near taking our meat with him; so we had to carry it ourselves. We pulled slowly for camp, and when we came near the pickets took around through the woods to avoid them; but when nearly past them they spied us and tried to arrest us. Luckily for us we had put a very deep hollow between us and them and so we laughed at their threats to shoot. When near our camp Dr. Kirkpatrick kindly warned us to be careful or we would be caught, and for a long ways we had to crawl on our bellies to get past headquarters unobserved; but the meat tasted all the sweeter when we got to camp." John M. Riddle, corporal of Co. G, tells this in regard to their efforts to get meat: "In our meanderings along the landing we passed by the commissary department; and lo! to the delight of our astonished eyes we beheld some barrels of pickled pork once more. As our chances of drawing any of that delectable article in the 'regular way' were very slim, we concluded to try the *irregular* way. So after the bugle blowed for lights out, myself, John Yeager and Dennis P. Howland sallied forth. Arriving at the commissary's I walked boldly up to the guard and engaged him in conversation; Howland and Yeager slipped a barrel out from under the back side of the tent and quietly rolled it away. When about 400 yards from the tent I joined them. From here to a place of safety we had several deep ravines and numerous logs to cross, and any amount of low hazel brush and briars to go through, and it required our utmost strength to get it out of sight of headquarters; but finally, near midnight, we succeeded in getting it to a place where we thought we would be safe. Howland took up a big rock and said, 'now for some meat.' Down went the rock with a crash, in went the head, and so did our hands up to the elbows—when, oh! horror! It was coal tar, and we spent the balance of the night trying to wash it off.

On the 19th our division trains and pontoon train pulled out from the landing, taking the road southward, and we expected to follow on the morrow, but when the 20th came we were seemingly no nearer ready than we were the day after we crossed the river. There were yet six or seven transports at the river laden with forage and commissary stores, and they all had to be unloaded and the stuff put into the train wagons.

On the 21st Minty's brigade moved out, taking the same road southward as the trains had done. We have spoken about all extra stuff of all kinds ordered to be left behind, and we spent much of the day at the landing watching all this stuff come in from the camps. It was all thrown into one pile, and that pile was huge and heterogeneous, composed of everything that an army has any use for, and as we very well knew the men would not part with anything they really needed, we wondered where all the stuff came from. While viewing this huge pile a happy thought struck us. Here, now, was a chance for a little sharp practice for the privates—the only chance we had ever had, and we determined to avail ourselves of it. You see private soldiers had to receipt for everything they drew, and if we lost anything belonging to the Government we had to pay for it. Receipting for any article of camp or garrison equigage did not make it ours; it still belonged to the Government, and the only way we could get rid of paying for an article that might be lost, was to have the brigade inspector inspect it, and when worn out, or out of repair, he would condemn it, and then we might lose it without paying for it. But here was a chance to "draw" without giving the customary receipt. So we went back to camp and turned over our dog-tents, &c., pretending that we allowed to move without them; but we afterwards went down to the pile and picked out just such things as we wanted. Our excuse for this was that we could get a better article of the same kind than we had, and, as a fair exchange was no robbery, we argued that Uncle Sam would lose nothing by the transaction.

CHAPTER XXXVI.

From March 21st to April 2d, 1865.—We Finally Move—Order of March—Going to Tuscumbia—To Subsist of the Country and Destroy All that may be of Use to the Enemy—Lightning Brigade in its Glory Again—Capturing Prisoners—Soon Strike a Better Country and Find Abundance of Forage and Provisions—Crossing Great Swamps—Crossing the Black Warrior River—Many Thrilling Incidents—Crossing Five-Mile Creek—Burning the Red Mountain Iron Works—Rebels Try to Cut our Army in Two—We Lead our Horses Over a Railroad Bridge on the Ties—A Fearful Bridge 100 Feet High—Over Safe—Scouting, Foraging and Burning—The Whole Country a Sheet of Flame or Cloud of Smoke—We Reach Montevallo—Forest, at Selma, Hears of Our Advance—We Begin to Skirmish with Forest's Troops—The Rebels Running as if the De'il were After Them—Gen. Forest Just in Front of Us—Skirmish Line Driving Back a Whole Rebel Column—Gen. Dick Taylor Almost Captured and His Forage Train Taken in—Capt. Taylor Wounds Gen. Forest in the Arm with his Saber and Forest Shoots Him—Forest Defeated and Demoralized at the Battle of Ebenezer Church—Bravery of Sergeant Murphy and His Squad.

On the 21st we got orders to move to-morrow morning, and as usual we were down to the river and heard the commander go around to each boat and give the order to clean up immediately, and to take on the loads assigned them right away, as every boat had to move out of the river before to-morrow night—and we knew that the time of our departure was at hand. We were ordered to take five days' rations in haversacks, and five days' forage on horses, and the train was to haul five days' rations of hard-tack, and 45 of salt, sugar and coffee, and each man was to take 100 rounds of cartridges.

March 22d, 1865. This morning, just at sun-up, we pulled out from the river, taking the road for Tuscumbia, which for eight miles led us over a miserable, rough, hilly and poor country, in a south-east direction. It was hills and ravines the whole way. We then came to a most beautiful plain of several miles in extent, which contained several thousand acres of the finest land in the world, and at one day it must have been the garden spot of Alabama, but now all is desolate. The deserted mansion, the old and decrepit, white and black, and those too young or too old for war, are all that are left. Buell's army passed over this ground in 1862, Sherman's in 1863, and the rebel army two or three times, and all together had stripped this beautiful plain of everything that would render living in it possible.

Here we turned straight south, and at the end of eight miles struck the Memphis & Charleston Railroad at Cherokee Station. Here we passed the First Division, McCook's; nine miles south of this we went into camp in a gorge or deep hollow, on Rock Creek, a stream that comes down off the lower end of the Sand Mountains. About an hour by sun we passed the pontoon train, and after we had gone into camp we found our train was just two miles ahead of us. They had been three days making 27 miles. The recent rains had made the roads soft clear down, and the last nine miles we traveled seemed to have no bottom at all. We made 25 miles for the day, which we regarded as a good beginning. During the day, by a general order, it was made known to us how many troops there were going along with us, and also the order of march. There had been five divisions camped on the river and all of them had moved; two of them had taken different directions in order to mask our movement and our real object. So there were, then, after all of our winter's preparation, but three divisions of us, less than 15,000 men all told. They were the 1st division, commanded by Gen. McCook, the 2d (our own), commanded by Gen. Long, and the 4th, commanded by Gen. Upton. The order of march was Gen. McCook on the right, Gen. Long in the center, and Gen. Upton on the left, the pontoon train moving with the centre. Detachments were to be sent out each day on all tne roads so as to distract the enemy. Dr. Cole says: "The men are expected to subsist off the country through which we pass. The hospital department transport nothing but tent flies and one wall tent to a division. Two wagons for brigade headquarters and the ambulance train comprise the brigade train."

But not a word or hint did we get as to the objective point or aim of our expedition. Our instructions were to get our living and forage off the country, and to take with us or destroy everything that would be of any service to the rebel cause. This looks like business, and we went to bed with happy hearts, because we knew the end could not be far off. Our regiment and brigade was in its glory again and felt once more at home.

March 23d. Bugle call at 2 a. m. and moved at daylight, passing our train at sun-up. It has now got on high ground. After we had gone five miles we stopped for three hours for the pontoon train to catch up. Bivouacked soon after noon at a little village called Frankfort, the county seat of Franklin county, 15 miles south of Tuscumbia, making only 15 miles for the day. Roads good and trains all well closed up. Our regiment in advance. Captured some prisoners to-day, including a rebel major and some of Rhoddy's scouts.

March 24th. Our division moved out early, but as our regiment was in the advance yesterday we had to take the rear to-day; so we lay in camp to let our own train and the pontoon train pass us. It took them till near noon. Owing to the negligence of our officers or some other cause we lay in camp too long, let the train all pass by and the 1st division, being right behind it, about half of it got past us when we began to move, and then we had to ride fast and file past it. This is always quite a job even when the roads are good and the country open, but to-day our roads were but by-paths, miserably bad. and the brush very thick, and we thought sometimes we would not make it, as we would always lose a little every time we would come to where the brush was very thick. Nine miles from camp we came to Russellville, the 1st division halted and we got past them without further trouble. Here the 4th division had come in from the north by the way of Tuscumbia. This was the first we had seen of them since leaving the landing at Cherokee. They took a road leading due east and we saw them no more for five or six days.

To this place our road had led over a succession of ridges and ravines, and a miserable poor country, in a north-east direction, and we began to think that if all the country we had to pass over was like this our "living off of the country" would be rather slim. It was the middle of the afternoon when we got to Russellville, where we turned straight south, still keeping behind the pontoon train till we went into camp. The country became level and withal very rich, and for the first time in many long months the whole command got some fresh provisions. Evidences of wealth were numerous, and just before sundown we passed Gen. Wilson's headquarters at a big white house, (the rebels called him "Dandy Wilson,") and this was the first we had seen of him since our grand review. We went into camp long after night on Cedar Creek, six miles south of Russellville, making 15 miles for the day. Our division and the balance of the brigade got to camp by noon, but we were so late, and it got so dark, we really did not get into camp at all, but just stopped in a lane as we were marching along, hitched our horses in the fence corners on one side of the road and used the fence on the other side for fires. It had been so long since we had eaten anything fresh that our appetite for chicken and pig was simply marvelous, and it is not surprising that a great many over-did the thing and paid the penalty by a lively tussle with the "Tennessee quick step."

March 25th. On stopping last night we had orders to send out foragers at daylight to get forage for our horses and meat to last us two days, as there was supposed to be some more barren country just ahead of us. This detail consisted of about 20 from each company, (no trouble to get men to go in this detail,) or 200 from the regiment, all under command of Lieut. Clark, Co. I, acting quartermaster for the regiment. We found an abundance of everything we needed for man and beast, and had a lively skirmish with some rebels, capturing a horse and a full rig, including gun and accoutrements, a Johnny and his hat—all but the Johnny. The first division began to move past us just as we started, but the sun was two hours high before it all got past, when we moved right after it, rapidly, and about the middle of the forenoon passed through a little place called Mountain Spring. About the middle of the afternoon we crossed Big Bear Creek, at Allen's Factory. This stream runs north-west and empties into the Tennessee River at Eastport, close to where we started. We moved five miles after crossing Bear Creek and bivouacked near a place called Thornhill, on a little mountain stream that runs south into the Buttahachee River. After leaving the Big Bear Creek our road lay over a mountain ridge and was very good, but the country was uninhabited and entirely too poor for any body to live in. Made 20 miles to-day.

March 26th. Since leaving Russellville we have been on a road leading straight south to Tuscaloosa, and this morning the 1st division kept straight on that road, and we saw no more of it for several days. Our division turned square east, the pontoon and all the other division trains along with us. Our road almost all day lay along the top of a mountain ridge, very sandy and covered with a species of "bitter oak" entirely new to us, chestnut and sassafras, some of the latter two feet in diameter, much the largest we had ever seen; roads most excellent and the trains all keeping well closed up. Our division is now by itself; Upton's away off to the north-east of us, and McCook's to the south-west. Late in the afternoon we came to the edge of the mountainous country or high table-lands, and could look for many miles to the east and south of us, and could see what appeared to be a large water course or huge swamp. Just at this time our brigade got on the wrong road and traveled three or four miles out of the way, and by the time we got back into the road we found the trains, which had kept straight ahead, had got down off the table-lands and the advanced trains had stuck fast in a huge swamp. Minty's brigade was ahead of us, and just at sundown began to try to flounder through it, while the train commenced parking on this side and our brigade massed in column by regiments. A detail of 10 men from each company in the brigade, 400 in all, was made to bridge the swamp. As the swamp was nearly a mile wide, this was no small job. This was the Sipsey's fork of the Black Warrior. The men went to work earnestly and cheerfully, while the rest of us fooled around till 9 o'clock at night, and then got orders to feed and get supper, and by the time this was over the bridge was completed and our regiment began to cross. We assure you this was a fearful job, full of danger and startling incidents; yet 17 years afterwards it makes us shiver to think of it. The night was very dark and the swamp itself just like all other swamps on the low lands of the South, a vast sea of mud, growing full of trees, vines and thick underbrush, with a large quantity of water sluggishly making its way through; a paradise for miasma, bull-frogs, serpents, and alligators. We got across without serious mishaps, went a mile and a half and came to another swamp just like the one we had crossed. This was Warrior creek. Here we were compelled to go into camp. It was just midnight, and before the column turned off the road to go into camp another detail of 10 men from each company in the brigade was made to bridge this swamp. It was our fortune to be in command of the detail from Company I, while the whole detail was under the command of Major Kilborn, of our regiment, who before this had been in command of a company of pioneers, and had abundant experience in this sort of work. We pitched into the swamp, which was full three-fourths of a mile wide, and the water in many places three feet deep. There is many a slip between cup and lip, and so there was many a slip from tussock and root that night, and we doubt if there was a man of the whole 400 who did not go under, many of them several times. But the many tricks we played on each other and the many ridiculous incidents constantly occurring, kept us in good humor, and by 2 o'clock in the morning we had our bridge done. You may be a little curious to know how we could build so long a bridge in so short a time. There was not much water except in a few places, and we just cut poles 10 feet long, laid them side by side and piled fine brush on them to keep the horses' feet from going through, and laid long poles on the ends of the brush to hold it down, leaving a way six feet wide in the middle for the horses to pass. Where the water was sufficiently deep to float our poles we had to cut down long trees and lay them lengthwise of the road and then lay our poles on top of them. There was one place like this just at the further side of the swamp, 75 yards wide. Here most of the water in the swamp seemed to be running and was deep, and had we been obliged to cut poles it would have taken us till daylight to build it; but just across the swamp was a well fenced plantation, and we went for the rails. By each taking two or three rails we could carry a thousand rails at a load, and we should guess we put near 10,000 rails into that swamp. When we got back across the swamp another trouble met us—where was our camp? After we left the command it had turned out of the road into the dense woods. The men had eaten their suppers, and as there was no occasion for building fires, had just tumbled off of their horses and gone to sleep. Had the pack mules been hungry their braying would have guided us with unerring certainty; but they had been fed, were very tired and were now sleeping the sleep of the innocent. Every thing save the hooting of the owls and the whistle of the whippoorwills was still as the grave. Even the frogs had gone to sleep. If we had our blankets we could lie down anywhere and go to sleep; but wet and cold as we were, we needed our blankets, and must find camp. After stumbling around through the dense woods for near an hour we ran upon it, and never before or afterwards did we see the whole camp, man and beast, so sound asleep. We had made 25 miles for the day. Dr. Cole says of the 26th: "Moved out early this morning and traveled hard all day; did not get into camp till late at night. Crossed one branch of Black Warrior. The fording was difficult and dangerous. The pontoon train moves with great difficulty."

March 27th. Bugle blowed this morning at 4 o'clock, and the bridge-builders got very little sleep. We moved this morning at sun-up, and immediately plunged into the swamp, and found that notwithstanding the darkness of last night, and the many disadvantages under which we had labored, we had made a tolerably passable bridge, and we got across the swamp without much difficulty. Here we found Minty's brigade just eating breakfast; the last of it managed to get through the swamp about midnight. After waiting an hour for Minty's brigade to move and our own to get across the swamp, we moved on south over a low, sandy ridge of table-land, for 12 miles, and the roads just splendid, except that they were the crookedest things in the world. This ridge was entirely uninhabited, and we did not pass a house. This had one day been a dense forest, but about two years before this a most fearful tornado had swept over and felled nearly every tree. It would be impossible to compute the vast destruction of timber. About every hundred yards we had to turn out of the road to pass around the butt or top of a fallen tree, thus doubling the distance. About noon we came to a stream of considerable size called Lost Creek, and like most of the streams of the South it was lined on either side by fearful swamps Here we found Minty's brigade massed in column, and we rested an hour and started on, but soon after starting we struck a road running straight east to

Jasper, and about the time our brigade got to it the head of the 1st Division came in from the west and cut us off, thus cutting our division in two. This was another blunder, and shows that smart men will sometimes do some very foolish things. We want to remark here that any two different commands undertaking to move on the same narrow road through the woods, in the same direction and at the same time, are bound to get into difficulty, and in this case it came very near resulting in a fight. The *right of way* certainly belonged to us, as more than half of our division was in the road before the 1st Division came up and cut it off. We tried for a long time to get to our places in the division, and were getting just about mad enough to clean the cavalry out, and there certainly would have been a fight, for McCook of the 1st out-ranked Long of the 2d Division, and it looked to us that McCook, in a very arbitrary and insulting manner, was trying to crowd us out of the road just to show his authority, and we felt bound to resent the insult, as we felt quite sure if the Johnnies had been in force in front we could have had the road without any trouble. Just then we got orders from Gen. Wilson to halt and wait till the whole train had pulled past us and then to come in behind it. This was shortly after noon, and it took the 1st Division an hour to file past us ; then came the division trains, all of them, and then the pontoon train. While we were waiting for the trains to pass we sent out foragers About the middle of the afternoon it began to rain and rained for three or four days without stopping. This struck us in just the worst time possible. Had it rained on us while in the mountains it would not have been so bad, but to commence just as we had fairly got into the swamps made fearful nasty work. It was getting dark when the rear of the train passed us and we pulled in after it. We had not gone far till we came to a large stream with steep and high banks, which had been piled full of rails, and might have been fair crossing at noon, but the rain had swollen the stream till the rails were all floating, and had there not been considerable timber just below the crossing they would have floated off. Our brigade had to cross this stream on the floating rails, which was about as difficult business as we ever did. We were now going down Lost Creek, and had not gone a mile until we found the whole train hopelessly stuck in the swamp. It seemed that every team had stuck fast in the mud at once. We dallied along till after 10 o'clock in a vain attempt to close up the train, and then went into camp not more than two miles from where we struck the Jasper road. We had made but 15 miles for the day, and it was now dark as Egypt and raining in torrents. It was midnight before we got to lie down, which we thought a little rough on the poor soldiers, especially those that built bridges the night before. Sergeant Stewart, Company A, says of the foragers who were sent out after noon: "Owing to a scarcity of forage the party got so far away from the road they got lost in the darkness and lay out all night."

March 28th. Bugle call this morning at 4 o'clock, as usual. We moved out just as it was getting light. Still raining hard. For six miles we had a fearful time passing the train. Every wagon was stuck in the mud, and it looked as though they might stay there till next August. Our regiment was in the advance, and just as we got past the trains we met Gen. Long coming back to see about the train. We have intimated before that Gen. Wilson, from the start, held our division responsible for the train. We have also stated that the train had started from the landing with five days' rations of hard-tack for the command, and that we also started with five days' rations in our haversacks. These would have been out on the 26th, but when we passed through Russellville and the rich country on Big Bear Creek we filled up till we still had plenty of rations. Gen. Long ordered us to send back details and draw the five days' rations of crackers out of the wagons, and thus, by shifting the loads, so lighten them that the teams might possibly be able to pull them out of the swamp. This we did and moved on to Jasper, county seat of Walker county. We had heard of this place for several days and expected to find a smart little village, at least, but were never so disappointed in our lives, as it was the poorest excuse for a town we ever did see. It once had a log jail and was surrounded by a half dozen log cabins, but a short time before this the jail had been burned down by Union citizens, which left the cabins alone in their glory. Dr. Cole says: "The woods through which we have passed to-day are horrible in the extreme, and the country poor beyond conjecture. It has been raining hard for the last 12 hours." When we got to Jasper we found the 1st division in camp south-west of the town, and the 4th division had just come in from the north, by way of Mount Hope, Cedar Falls, &c., and the whole command was together once more. Our division moved out nearly east for five miles and went into camp. The other divisions drew their rations, the whole train was got out of the swamp, and all went into camp three to five miles from Sanders' Ferry, on the Black Warrior River. We made 15 miles for the day.

March 29th. Reveille this morning, at 2 a. m., and we moved at 4, going directly to the river, and found the first and fourth divisions already across, and the whole train all parked close to it, ready to cross. We were surprised on seeing such a river as the Black

Warrior. All the streams that we had yet passed, since coming down off the table lands, had been vast swamps, with the water making its way slowly through them; but here was a river over 100 yards wide, with high and steep bluffs, and the water running as swift as a mill-race. Strangest of all, it had a solid rock bottom, and would be extremely dangerous to ford when the water was low. It had rained all night last night, and was yet raining, and the river was up. The fourth division had four men drowned while crossing here. Their horses would stumble, or slip, and fall—and the water ran so swiftly as to keep them rolling over and over, till drowned; and, as no man could stand in the current, of course the men were also drowned. A half mile below the crossing we saw a horse belonging to the fourth division, standing in the middle of the river, where he had been some time. He had been washed up against a large pile of rocks, and had thus been enabled to get on to his feet, but feared to move, as the water would take him down. He had a good new saddle and bridle on him, and under any ordinary circumstances would have been brought out, but it was worth a man's life to undertake it. The horse was groaning most piteously, but we had to leave him to his fate. The water was of a dark blue color, and looked extremely fearful.. We always had a peculiar feeling in going into battle—more of dread than fear. Here the two were pretty evenly divided, and an abundance of both. We confess our courage was barely up to the sticking point, but we put into it. The water was two to four feet deep, and we had a fearful time of it. In Co. H three horses went down, and the riders would certainly have made food for the fishes, had not each one managed to catch hold of a horse's tail, and been dragged to shore. In Co. I three horses also went down, but two of them were caught by the bridle, by some one who happened to be below them, and helped to regain their feet, and their riders helped on to them. The third one went rolling over and over like a log, for 200 yards down the stream, and we all said, "Good-bye, Davy," and we were sure his rider was going to follow him; but luckily he too caught a horse by the tail and was dragged out. Strangest of all, the horse finally washed out to where the water was only about two feet deep, and managed to get on his feet. It wasn't funny to the horse, but it was amusing to us to see that horse walk out of there. He seemed to be frightened nearly to death and trembled like a leaf; he would take a short step and then stop and study about it awhile before taking another, but he finally made the riffle and returned genuine horse thanks in a loud neigh. George Eaton, of Company K, was riding a small mule, and just when he came to where the water was the deepest the mule very suddenly disappeared and so did George. The mule went to Davy Jones's, and George wasn't far behind him, when he very suddenly found himself thrown upon a huge boulder. The river at this point was full of them, and George undertook the very perilous feat of jumping from one to another, but soon found himself in the water again being whirled and dashed about most fearfully. A second time he managed to climb on to a rock about 40 feet from the shore, where Capt. G. W. Brown, Company K, succeeded in getting a grape-vine to him and dragged him in to shore. Our regiment was the last of our division to cross, and although there were numerous hair breadth escapes we all got out without loss, and if there ever was a time in our lives when we felt real well it was just when we got out of that stream. We moved on straight east 10 miles and came to Locust fork of the Black Warrior. This stream was not more than half so wide or swift as the other, yet deeper, but had good gravelly bottom. Dr. Cole says: "A member of the 17th Indiana was unfortunately drowned while crossing this stream, and I also came very near losing our ambulance loaded with sick men. It floated down the river quite a distance, but we finally succeeded in getting all out safely." Here we turned south and moved five miles and went into camp, making 20 miles for the day; still raining. One of the men who got into the water to-day was Michael Batterall, of Company H, whom we have before spoken of as being "detailed" to steal, (or shteal would be better) on the Mississippi raid. Michael was a Dutchman, a good soldier and a very devoted Christian, but to-day he got his testament wet; this grieved Michael very much; he thought he was ruined and went on at a terrible rate. This reminds us of another occasion when Company H was on picket, and at daylight the videttes were fired upon. At headquarters the horses were saddled up ready for an emergency, but when the firing began Lieut. H. H. Stafford ordered the company to fall in on foot to support the videttes. All complied in haste except Michael, who was engaged in trying to tie his skillet and other traps on his saddle, The lieutenant soon gave Michael to understand that he was in earnest, when Mike sang out, "Vell, now lieutenant, schust you vait till I ties my, shkillet on and den I's cum."

March 30th. We had a bad night of it last night, and were called up at 3 o'clock, and owing to the extreme wet had a serious time getting breakfast and getting started. We pulled out just as it was getting light. Seven miles from camp we came to a narrow, deep stream, called Five-mile River. Here the rebels had made extensive preparations to receive us by obstructing the ford, building a stockade fort on the further side, and digging nearly a mile of rifle-pits along the bluff, but as usual ran away and left them, and nobody was hurt. We had to go down the river a half mile before we could get across, and the water was so deep as to run over the backs of the horses and swim the mules. After we got across, the bluff was the steepest we had ever undertaken to climb, and just on top of it were the rifle-pits, which were fearfully ugly to cross, and there was many a slip and tumble before we were all over them. We moved on briskly for 13 miles straight south, where we came to a most beautiful valley with quite a large stream running to the north-west; the stream was nameless. This was the first fertile spot we had seen since leaving the vicinity of Russellville, on the 24th, and this was not very rich, but most beautiful. Here we passed the 1st division and turned east, and about 2 p. m. came to a miserable little town called Elyton. We had heard of this place for the last four days and expected to see a town that *was* a town, but alas! for human hopes. The country was pretty, dry and sandy, and the roads most excellent, but the country was not rich. Elyton is 100 miles south of Decatur, Ala., and 90 miles north of Selma. Here the 1st division took the road south-west for Tuscaloosa, and we took a road south-east and five miles from Elyton. We passed by the smouldering ruins of what two days ago were the most extensive iron furnaces in the State, called the Red Mountain Iron Works. The out-buildings were still burning. They were set on fire by our scouts. The Southern confederacy had 450 negroes employed at these furnaces, about half of which they succeeded in running off just in advance of our scouts. The rest were still loitering around the burning buildings utterly lost and dumbfounded. Like bees without a hive they did not know where to go or what to do. We moved on five miles further and camped on Shades Creek, making 37 miles for the day; a hard day's work, but full of interest. We started in the morning before it was light, and it was getting dark when we went into camp; but the sky was red for miles around, caused by fires burning cotton-gins, mills, factories, &c., by our scouts and the 4th division, which were just ahead of us.

March 31st. We were called up at 3 a. m. and moved before it was light, and moved three miles by sun-up and struck the Cahawba. This river is 75 yards wide and very deep; the bluffs are very high and steep, and the rebels supposed they had cut our army in two by slipping in behind the 4th Division and burning the wagon bridge after it had got across and before our division reached it; but they forgot we were Yankees. You see there is a railroad laid out from

Selma to Elyton and graded all the way, and a wooden track laid down as far as the iron works which we passed yesterday evening, and over this track the iron made in this vicinity was hauled to Selma and worked up into war material. Of course this railroad had to get across the river, which necessitated a bridge, but poor deluded Johnny Reb never once dreamed that the Yankees could get across on the railroad bridge. However, we just led our horses over on the ties! Of course you smile, but that is just what we did. We tore the track up on our side of the river and carried the ties on to the bridge and laid them down as closely together as we could, and we assure you it was a fearful bridge after it was done. It was 300 feet long and 100 feet high; a trestle, with plates 10 feet long on top of each bent, and stringers two feet thick reaching from one bent to the other, and so on clear across the river. These stringers were laid six feet apart, so that when the bridge was completed and you stood upon it and looked down you could see nothing but the water a hundred feet below. To stand at the end and look across, it appeared to be suspended in the air, as you could not see that there was a thing supporting it. The ties were 8 feet long, 10 to 12 inches in diameter, and flattened just a little on two sides. As they were not very straight there were numerous cracks where a horse's foot would drop through. Now, if we have been sufficiently clear in our description, you begin to realize what a fearful thing it was, yet you can never realize it just as we did. Indeed, it was so fearful that our horses started back from it in the wildest fright, and it was with the utmost difficulty that we got them started across it. Col. Miller comprehended this and ordered the brigade to dismount and close the horses up in two ranks just as closely as they could be jammed, the riders to free themselves from all incumbrances, and to keep close to the side of their horses' heads, and in no case to let the horses stop for a moment, nor let a vacant space occur between them, lest there should be a balk and the whole column tumbled off into the river. All fully realized the importance of these precautions, as we had some experience of this kind in getting our horses on the transports at Waterloo, where it was necessary to blind-fold the lead korses and keep the rest closed up so closely they could not see where they were going nor have time to realize the danger. This by all odds was the most dangerous feat we had ever undertaken, or that we ever heard of. Allow three feet for the width occupied by each horse, and you see the men had to walk on the ends of the ties and also on the outside of the stringers under them. Now suppose the column had got started across all right and was being kept closed up just as well as it could be, and then suppose a horse should drop a leg through a crack and stick fast. In his efforts to free himself he would either tumble off himself and carry his rider with him, or push the horse by his side off the other way, make a balk in the column and play smash generally. Or suppose that both horses should at the same time "shy" a little, how easy it would be to push a man off! We want to tell you there were times while crossing that bridge when we drew our breath very short, and thanked God when we were over. We got across without loss or accident, and immediately afterwards there were heavy details made from all the companies to scour the country in search of forage, rations, horses, and mules, and to burn everything that might be of any use to the rebels. In three hours the whole country for miles around was covered with dense black smoke from burning factories, foundries, furnaces, forage, mills and commissary stores. The country was tolerably rich and seemed to be full of factories of one kind or another, and all busily at work for the confederate government. The day was beautifully bright and perfectly still, and the smoke from a burning factory or mill would rise straight into the air 500 feet high, and as the country was comparatively level we could see all of these from the column, and 20 of these vast domes of smoke might have been counted at a single view, some of them 20 miles away. This, to us, looked like business, and made us feel that the end could not be far away. Had this policy been pursued from the very first year of the war the rebellion would not have lasted 18 months.

We crossed the Cahawba at Bridgetown, where large quantities of coal were set on fire. We traveled east two miles and came to a large stream called Buck creek, where we burned Davis' grist mill, the Central Iron Works, and a large rolling mill. We now turned a little west of south and passed over a most beautiful valley, perfectly level, sandy, but not very rich; roads most excellent. About the middle of the afternoon we came to a very respectable town called Montevallo, where we ran on to the rear of the 4th Division. The advance of this division entered this place yesterday evening, more than 24 hours ahead of us, had a severe skirmish in which several of Rhoddy's men were killed and others captured; they had been skirmishing all day with the rebels and only succeeded in driving them a few miles. This is the first time we have met any rebels to amount to anything. We moved on slowly south after the 4th Division and camped three miles from Montevallo, at sundown, on quite a large stream called the Little Cahawba, not far from King's iron works, which we burned; we also burned the depot buildings, shops and two cars. Notwithstanding the country does not seem to be very rich, the plantations we pass indicate that the planters are *very rich.* Many of the houses are stately and most elegant. Tuscaloosa lies 40 miles west of this and Talladega the same distance north-east, and there is a railroad coming down from Rome through Talladega to this place, which runs straight south to Selma, 50 miles distant. The rebel Gen. Dick Taylor is in command of this department and has his headquarters at Selma; Gen. Forest is in command of all the cavalry in this department and is also at Selma. The first intimation that Forest had that Wilson was heading toward Selma was last night when Upton's advance came to this place. Forest immediately set out with all the forces he could scrape up to meet Wilson, sending one division by way of Tuscaloosa with orders to burn our train, which had gone in that direction along with the 1st Division. We shall speak of this division of rebels when we get to Selma. So to-night the situation is thus: Our division three miles south of Montevallo, the 4th Division a few miles south of us, the 1st Division off to the west of us in the direction of Tuscaloosa, and Forest's advance at Randolph, 14 miles south of us. With the exception of the division he sent toward Tuscaloosa, Forest is now concentrating his forces immediately in front of us, and to-morrow we are likely to have a fight, and may not have time to tell about our foragers of to-day, and had better do it now. With the exception of the detail from Company A, we believe every one of them were eminently successful, and the recording angel alone may be able to tell the amount of property destroyed, horses, mules and forage captured, and the extent of damage done to the southern confederacy. Sergeant Stewart says that "Company A was singularly unfortunate, not even getting a single mule." Sergeant Wilhite reports abundance of success for Companies E and B, and tells a pleasant story besides, which we are sorry space forbids inserting. Corporal Riddell, Company G, also relates an amusing incident where Companies C and G, at a mill, mistook each other for rebels, and it is hard telling which was the worst scared. Among the many animals captured by Company I, was one by Captain Vance, supposed to be the finest stable-horse in the South. The foragers did not all get in till long after midnight.

April 1st, 1865. Up to this time we have not been called upon to take the advance. Our brigade has been treated as though it was ornamental rather than useful, except we seemed to come very handy to bridge swamps and pull the trains out of the mud. But where there was no obstruction in front, what forage was left in the country after the balance of the army had passed over it was considered plenty good for us. To-day, however, we were offered the advance as soon as we could reach it. We moved just at daylight, our regiment in the advance. We had not gone far till we began to pass dead horses and dead rebels lying by the side of the road, indicating that the skirmishing yesterday evening had been pretty severe, and we learned that the 4th division had three men killed and 10 wounded. The rebels loss, of course, was much greater, as we had seen that many by the road side. We moved off briskly and by 10 a. m. had made 14 miles. This brought us to the little town of Randolph, a small station on the railroad. Here we ran on to the rear of the 4th division again. They had been skirmishing with the reebels all morning, and had finally succeeded in driving them out of the town; but in retreating the rebels had fallen back on two different roads, part of them taking the road to Maplesville, 10 miles south of Randolph, and the larger part of them taking the road directly south toward Plantersville. These two roads came together 12 miles south of Randolph. The 4th division took the left hand road and our brigade took the right. A, F, D and I, of our regiment, were sent forward as advance guard. We had not gone a mile till we ran on to the rebels and skirmishing began immediately. Here Company A dismounted and advanced as skirmishers, with Lieut. Barnes in command, Gen. Wilson telling him to march right ahead, as the rebels were not worth minding, and to march right over them; and running fights immediately commenced. Company A drove them about as fast as they could walk for about a mile, and by this time most of the men were nearly exhausted. The other three companies were keeping close up to the skirmish line. Company A fell back to their horses and company F dismounted and pushed on after the rebels, who would take advantage of every fence corner and turn in the road, fire a volley at us and retreat to the next corner and turn, thus giving us a volley about every five minutes, while our shooting at them was more constant and regular, as we kept them moving so constantly that we could see some of them nearly all the time. During this drive the rebels kept about 300 yards ahead of us, and if our shooting at them was as wild as theirs was at us we did not hurt them much ; yet we certainly frightened them terribly, as they never stopped to fire a second shot, but each time would fire and then "skin out" for the rear as fast as their horses could carry them. They were afraid to dismount or we would have gobbled them sure. About this time James Riggs, private of Company F, was wounded. In the morning before leaving camp he said he was afraid the war would soon be over and he would have to go home without a scratch. Although pretty badly hurt, he was as happy as a "big sunflower." At this point Company C was thrown forward as flankers on the left, toward the railroad, which runs from Randolph toward Selma. Sergt. Dan. Moore, Company C, says: "Our orders were to stay out there till ordered or driven in. We soon had all the fun we wanted; mile after mile we drove the rebels before us, occasionally charging them, till near Plantersville, when we were ordered to join the regiment." At the end of two miles Company F were quite exhausted and fell back to their horses. Our orders were to push them, but we found it was no use trying to keep up with them on foot; so Company F mounted and we closed up ready for a charge on horseback. This was new to us as a regiment or brigade; companies had frequently charged the enemy; but we were simply infantry mounted, and had always done our fighting on foot, and we had neither sabres nor revolvers, and up to this time had not thought of such a thing as a whole battalion charging on horseback, yet we knew just how to do it on foot. We had not been more than a half hour driving them two miles, and the order was to keep them moving. So we tightened up our saddles and made everything snug, and started. All this preparation had taken up as much as 15 minutes. This gave the rebels time to fall back a half mile, gather up their scattered forces and to form in stronger force and position than we had yet met them. As we lit out we raised our accustomed cheering and in three minutes came upon the rebels. Some of them fired, some of them didn't, but broke through the woods like the devil was after them. Up to the time we struck the rebels our four companies had kept closed up in good order; we were moving at a quick gallop and the noise of our horses' feet and our cheering swept through the woods like a tornado, and we haven't the least doubt but some of the Johnnies thought their time was about up, for they just threw away their guns, blankets, shot-pouches, haversacks, and everything they could, to lighten their loads, and made a last desperate effort to get away. As soon as we got in sight of them every fellow spurred his horse to its utmost speed, and in two minutes more there were scarcely two of us together. We think this was the most ridiculous thingwe ever saw, and we laughed till we could scarcely sit on our horse. Col. Thomson and Maj. Kilborn were both with us, had good horses and no loads to carry in comparison with the privates, and kept at the head of the column. At the end of a mile they both checked up a little and found they had but five or six men with them. Our horse was a good one and we pushed ahead and passed them in a second. They both hallooed with all their might, "Close up." The rattling of the horses' feet and the cheering of the men assured them that every fellow was doing his clean best, so they "lit out" again. At the end of another mile we came to a long lane, and the rebels were just going out at the farther end of it, and in a moment disappeared over a ridge. Here we got the word to halt. There were but four men ahead of us—our horses were out of wind and nearly exhausted. We dismounted, and for a few minutes had not time to think of the danger we might be in. for laughing at the many funny incidents we had seen. One poor fellow especially tickled us nearly to death. As he was going through the lane his saddle-girth broke and let him off, but he managed to hold on to the rein, checked up his horse and mounted again; then to see him lay his head down behind his horse's neck and dig his heels into its flanks would have made the oldest man in the world laugh. The whole way had been strewn full of everything a rebel soldier used, even to the everlasting Johnny-cake and corn dodger. It was several minutes before our four companies got closed up. We were highly elated over our grand charge. We rested a few minutes and moved on again; but had not gone a half mile till we ran on to the rebels once more, and could tell in a minute they had been reinforced. Company D now dismounted and began to push them, but they gave back more slowly and resisted every step of the way. The firing now became pretty severe and more regular, and many of the boys in Company D received very close calls, and at the end of a mile were exhausted and fell back to their horses. Just as they had mounted Capt. Cravens, of D, was struck square on the belt-buckle, and as his heels flew up and he went over backwards he exclaimed, "I'm killed." He was quite sick for a short time, but fortunately not seriously hurt. This same ball, with three others, had been fired at John B. Davis, who had charged upon three rebels who were behind a tree. We were now passing through thick woods and the rebels had every advantage and seemed determined to make the most of it. As Company D stopped to mount the rebels were emboldened to make a more determined stand. Here Company I was dismounted, one-half on each side of the road. We moved out 100 yards from the road and deployed forward as skirmishers. This enabled us to flank the rebels and they gave way, and we pushed on after them in double-quick time, but had not gone a half mile till they made another stand. Here Gen. Long caught up with the skirmish line—we had not seen him for several days. He told us to push them, and again we spread out on their flanks and poured in a cross-fire on to them, and again they started "on for Dixie." Our company drove them over a mile in this way, when we came to a cleared place with a house on one side of the road, a stable on the other, and a lane between them, a cleared field beyond them, and then thick woods again. This was a strong position for the rebels, and we now found they had been doing their best to retard our movements till they should make it still stronger by throwing up logs and rails on the further side of the field, next to the woods. For the last half mile our road had run east, the writer on the north side of the road; this brought the house between us and the rebel position. We could not see just as well as we thought we might on the south side of the road, and so started across. Just then we heard a volley, and more than a dozen bullets came tearing down the road, and we lost no time in getting out of that, and as we ran felt a heavy lick, and a sharp stinging pain just above the right knee. A ball had torn through our pants and cut a crease three inches long. We crawled up behind the house, stable, fence, tree, log and stump as closely as we could to the rebel position, and went to work on them. For 15 or 20 minutes the firing on both sides was lively, but we soon found it would be foolish for our company alone to try to move them further. Here Company C was ordered in from the left front to report to the regiment, and on coming up got between the two fires, and Dan. Moore says, "It was warm about them times and we hunted corners like ducks taking to water." During the firing two or three of us were just north of the stable behind a stump, and a half dozen were in the stable shooting out at the cracks. Presently we heard a bullet strike one of the logs "thud," and Wm. Sale, private, Company I, began to halloo till you might have heard him a mile away. The bullet had glanced through a crack, struck him in the abdomen, and doubled him up quicker than you could snap your finger, but had so flattened out on striking the log that it did not go through his clothes, and at the end of three days he was all right again. We were now watching each other like hawks, and every move on either side was the signal for a shot, and every shot was meant to kill. It was about noon when the rebels halted us. We were eight miles from Randolph, and had made that distance in a little over two hours, had skirmished the whole way, and had got so far ahead of the balance of the division that it took them till nearly 2 o'clock to all get closed up as closely as they dared to come. During this time our regiment had dismounted and formed along with the skirmish line, and four companies of the 17th had formed in our rear ready to make a charge on horseback. When we were re-mounted at Louisville a battalion of this regiment drew sabres. Up to this time they had had no use for them, and seemed very anxious to try them. Before these preparations were completed the rebel firing had ceased, and we soon afterward found they had fallen back a half mile through the thick woods and formed a new line, had planted three pieces of artillery, one of them right in the road, and had their lines all straightened up to receive us, Gen. Forest being right there in person directing movements. The balance of our brigade, except the four companies, had also dismounted and got in line, and we were ordered to move forward. We went across the open field in steady time, and when near the woods we looked back and saw the four companies coming, but the rebels falling back from the edge of the woods had deceived our officers, and the 17th had charged too soon, for just as we struck the woods the four companies raised the cheer, put down the road in column of 4's and were out of sight in a minute. We pushed on through the woods after them, and in another minute heard the artillery belch forth, and the grape and cannister came tearing up the road through our regiment. We pushed on, and in a few minutes more were even with the artillery, and the rebs were flying through the woods in every direction, completely demoralized. Just then we heard a tremendous cheer and very rapid musketry firing over east of us; this was the first we knew of Upton's division coming up in the rear of the rebels. We now changed our direction to the right and pushed on through the woods as rapidly as we could, in hopes of intercepting some of the fleeing rebels, but it was no use, they were all gone and the 4th Division sailing after them.

We must now stop to tell you that next day, at Selma, we captured nearly all these fellows who were fighting us to-day, and they told us that this morning when our four companies began to drive the rebels so fast from Randolph, Gen. Forest telegraphed to Gen. Dick Taylor, at Selma, to send 5,000 reinforcements right away. Said he: "It's no use to fight them with what men I have, as their skirmish line is just driving back my whole column." Taylor sent back word to fight, and he would come immediately with all the troops he had. So he loaded up a lot of corn for Forest's horses, and started it ahead, and followed himself on another train, and got up just in time to see Forest's troops flying past him like birds, the fourth division at their heels. We heard the engine whistle just after the 17th made the charge, and, without getting off the cars, Taylor hurried back to Selma; but the train load of corn was not so fortunate, and for once we got plenty of corn without having to run all over the country to get it.

We have no official report of this battle, but quote from some of the manuscript before us. Sergt. Dan. Moore, Co. C., says: "The official report of this action says, 'We fought Forest, who had about

4,000 men, defeated him, killing and wounding about 100 men, and captured 300 prisoners and three pieces of artillery.'" Dr. Cole says: "Our loss was 9 killed and 20 wounded, mostly of the 17th Indiana." Terrell's report says of the 17th Indiana: "Losing eight killed, 11 wounded, and five missing." This first sabre charge was unfortunate for the 17th Indiana. As before stated, it charged too soon. The plan was for us to charge first, and get the rebels started, and then for them to follow; but the rebels having fallen back from the edge of the woods deceived the four companies, and they, supposing the rebels were retreating, charged, and had got within a few yards of the artillery when the rebels discharged it, killing six or eight horses all in a pile, dismounting the men right among the rebels, who of course were captured. The balance of the men charged on through the lines and killed quite a number of rebels. Capt. James D. M. Taylor, at the head of our troops, dashed up to Gen. Forest and staff, and with his sabre wounded the General in the arm, and Forest drew his revolver, shot and killed Taylor. Those of our men who were killed were immediately stripped of everything but their shirts and drawers, and by the time we got up to them the woods were on fire all around them. Whether the rebels had set the woods on fire to cover up their meanness, or they had taken fire from the artillery, we could never tell; but you can scarcely imagine the feelings of indignation in our brigade at this barbarity. The men swore they would have revenge. The fight did not last more than 20 minutes after the lines were straightened up, but it decided the future of the whole campaign. Forest's army was the only army in this department that amounted to anything, and we had met and defeated it, and we now felt that we could just go where we pleased, and do anything Uncle Sam wanted us to do. On the other hand, it so demoralized the rebels that they felt it was useless to try to oppose us. At the point where the road Upton's division was on, and the road we were on, came together, there was a church. This was on Bogue's Creek, and the church was called Ebenezer, and the battle was always called the battle of Ebenezer church. To this church our surgeons carried our wounded, and used it for a hospital. Our dead were also gathered together and buried near it. It was 4 o'clock by the time our lead horses caught up with us, when we mounted and moved on after the fourth division. We moved four miles and camped at Plantersville, 25 miles from Selma, having made 30 miles for the day, which, all things considered, was a terrible hard day's work, and we were very tired.

April 2d, 1865. Dr. Cole says: "In the charge of the 1st Brigade yesterday, four companies of the 17th Indiana, armed with sabres, led the charge and engaged the rebel artillerymen in a hand-to-hand conflict. Capt. Taylor sabered Gen. Forest in the shoulder and was shot with a pistol ball by Gen. Forest. I accompanied these four companies on the charge, and dismounting under fire devoted my attention to the wounded, among whom was Len. Edwards, one of our best scouts. . Leaving our wounded of yesterday at Plantersville in charge of Dr. Dome, of the 17th Indiana, and nurses detailed from our own regiment, we moved at daylight." There was also a detail of 10 men from Company A, Seventy-Second, to accompany S. G. Pilling, hospital steward, back to the wagon train, for the purpose of getting medical stores for the men wounded yesterday. This detail consisted of Sergt. F. M. Murphy, Corpl. W. H. P. Dimmett, privates Samuel Foughty, Samuel Foust, John Foust, George Foust, John Montgomery, John Nyce, Daniel Sinks, Ira Creps, Daniel O'Rader, all of Company A. They proceeded back as far as Randolph and stopped to feed their horses; about the time the horses were done eating and they were getting ready to start on, Pilling and three others had gone to a different part of the town, when suddenly 61 rebels charged upon Murphy and the seven men that were with him. Pilling, before this, had been surprised and quietly captured by a lieutenant and another rebel. When the three men heard the firing they started to go to Murphy's assistance, but were also surprised and captured by the two rebels that had Pilling. Here, now, were two rebels who had four Yankees. Murphy was brave, and so were his men, and when he saw the rebels coming, formed his men across the street and they went to work on the rebels with their invincible Spencers, killing one, wounding two others, and put the rest to flight. When the two rebels with the four Yankees saw their comrades retreating, they also began to fall back, the lieutenant leading the horse on which Pilling was riding. While the lieutenant was watching the fight Pilling clinched him, and they both came off their horses together, Pilling on top, making a desperate effort to take the lieutenant's revolver away from him; but the lieutenant was too strong for him, and succeeded in shooting Pilling in the right side, but did not entirely disable him, and he started to run. The lieutenant's comrade ordered him to halt, and not obeying, he fired and shot Pilling in the left thigh; but nothing daunted he continued on his way to liberty, and succeeded in reaching Murphy's squad just as they were beginning to retreat. A running fight now began. John Montgomery was soon captured, shot after he had surrendered, and left for dead, but fortunately our wagon train came up the next day and picked him up. He is still living to tell the adventure better than any one else. Sergt. Murphy was wounded in the leg and captured, Pilling and all but four others were captured again and taken to Talledaga. Here Murphy and Pilling, being wounded, were left, and fell into the hands of Gen. Croxton's brigade of the 1st Division, and finally got with the regiment at Macon after the war was over. The rest of the squad that were captured were taken to Jacksonville, Florida, and got home about the time we were mustered out. Corporal Dimmett killed the major in command of the rebels, and he and Daniel Sinks and Daniel Rader succeeded in getting away from the rebels. John F. Nyce lost his horse and his gun, and was making his way back to the command, traveling by night and lying by in the day time. One night, while quite hungry, he started to go to a light he saw in the distance. Approaching it cautiously, he found a squad of rebels quartered in an old hay-stack, and stole quietly away. At another time he saw a rebel coming and secreted himself by the roadside till the rebel came near, and then halted him and ordered him to surrender. The rebel, not knowing how many were near, threw down his gun; Nyce then ordered him to skin out for home and stay there, and proceeded to destroy the old musket. In a few days he got in to Selma all right, and is still living.

CHAPTER XXXVII.

From April 2d to April 8th, 1865.—Approaching Selma—The Strong Works Must be Stormed—Gen. Wilson Selects the Lightning Brigade to do this Fearful Work—The Gallant Col. Miller says We Can go into the City—A Look into Selma and its Defenses Before the Battle—Its Powerful Works—Determination of Rebel Soldiers and Citizens to Defend Their Last Stronghold to the Bitter End—It is Sunday, the Church Bells Ring, the People Crowd the Churches, and the Rebel Preachers Exhort them to Fight to the Death Against the Lincoln Hirelings—Mayor and Preachers, Young and Old, Take Muskets and go into the Trenches—Preparing for the Attack—A Heavy Force of Rebels Rrported Approaching, and Nine Companies of the Seventy-Second Sent to Look After Them—Thrilling Details of Skirmishers—"Come Over and Take Our Artillery"—We Prepare to do So—Col. Miller's Advice—The Gallant Little Band Advances Against those Formidable Works—The Rebels Open a Terrible Fire—Gen. Long Falls Badly Wounded—Col. Miller is Also Severely Wounded and Disabled—Col. Biggs Also Falls in the Furious Storm of Battle—Gen. Wilson in the Thickest of the Fight—Col. Vail's Gallant Conduct—Selma is Soon Ours, with 3,000 Prisoners and All its Rich Stores—Wild Cheers and Sincere Thanks—Sergt. Mount's Graphic Account—The Lightning Brigade, Again Victorious, Carry Both Lines of Defences and Plant Their Colors Over Selma—The Rebels Flee in Consternation—3,000 Prisoners, 97 Pieces of Artillery, Machine Shops, Etc., Etc.—Gens. Forest, Taylor and Some Rebels Escape—Operations of Seventy-Second in Holding Gen. Chalmers—Historian's Description of the Battle—Gen. Wilson's Charge—Gen. Wilson to the Lightning Brigade: "Men! I Now See How it is You have got such a Hell of a Name"—Great Fire from the Burning of Saltpeter Works—Dr. Cole on Casualties—Chalmers Held at Bay by the Seventy-Second—We go Inside the Works and Sleep Among Dead Men—A Close Inspection of the Strong Works—How Could Our Men Get Through—Rebel Loss Heavier than Our Own, and Their Wounds Worse—A, F, D and I on Provost Duty in the City—Special Enumeration of the vast numbers of Guns, Wagons, Amounts of Ammunition, Machine Shops, Machinery, Locomotives, Engines, Etc., Etc.—All of which we Proceed to Smash up, Blow up and Burn—Chalmers Retreats—Releasing Union Prisoners at Cahaba—How the Rebels Made Cannon—Burying the Dead with Honors of War—Forest Robbing and Killing Prisoners—Burning of the Great Arsenal—Forming a Negro Regiment—The Citizens Greet the Negro Parade with Hisses—Putting a Negro Woman into a Barrel of Molasses—The Yankee Cavalier Newspaper—Congratulatory Order of Gen. Wilson—Farewell Order of Gen. Long.

April 2d. We were not done eating our breakfast when the advance of Minty's brigade began to pass us, and our bugle blew the saddle call. As our regiment was in the advance yesterday, we had to "go foot" to-day. We pulled out just at daylight, and moved off steadily till near noon, when we were ordered to send out foragers. These foragers were ordered to report back to the column just as soon as they should get what food and forage they needed for a day's rations. To-day we are passing over a country more level and open than any we have yet seen, and often during the day could see for miles over what appeared to be extensive plains. Although once heavily wooded, this country has been in cultivation so long that the forests have almost entirely disappeared, and the gin-houses, 30 feet high, standing on every plantation, and waiting for the crop already planted, or about to be planted, and the smoke-stacks of the sugar-furnaces, factories and mills, pointing high toward heaven, may be seen for miles around. After our foragers had been out an hour, vast domes of smoke, reaching a hundred times higher, could also be seen in every direction, marking the place where fire was devouring and licking up these same gins, furnaces, mills and factories, and also vast piles of cotton, commissary and quartermaster's stores—showing that the other branch of the work of putting down the rebellion was also going on. We had now got down on to the lowlands of the south, and as we passed down along a stream by which our road led us, there were numerous places where we could see the century plant 10 to 15 feet high. Col. Miller, in his report of the day's work, says: "About noon Gen. Wilson sent for me to come to him at the rear of our brigade. He stated what he wanted done: that my brigade would have to make the assault on the works at Selma; that they were very strong, but that he had confidence I could take my brigade over them. He further stated that Gen. Upton would make an attack on another road at the same time, but he had no hope of Upton carrying his point. The matter was left to me whether I would make the attempt across an open field, or try and pass through an open place where a small stream and the railroad passed through the works. I told him the open ground would be my preference, as it would enable us to move more rapidly. The General now made the statement that if we would take the place it would be among the big things of the war—that Sherman had started twice for that place and failed. Sturgiss lost all his forces in a similar effort. Forest had cleaned him out, horse, foot and dragoon; and that in less than six hours from now his (Wilson's) fate would be decided, whether his long preparation would be a success or failure." By 3 o'clock most of our foragers had got in, and the head of our division had reached a large deep stream, two and a half miles north-west of Selma. We had been moving right south down this stream all day, on the west side, while Upton's division had moved on the east side. About three miles north of Selma the stream broke square off to the west, and ran in a circle on three sides of the city, and emptied into the Alabama River a mile below it. The road we were on led into the city from the north-west. As soon as our division got across the bridge it began to mass in column by regiments behind a ridge that entirely hid our movements from the rebels.

Gentle reader, before we further enter upon a brief description of one of the most desperate battles and most gallant charges of the war, will you go with us into one of the strongest fortified cities of the South and there learn something of the spirit and animus of the people who are hourly expecting the Yankee hordes from the North to sweep down upon them? They have learned of the defeat of Forest yesterday. It is now the hour of 10 a. m., and already Forest's defeated army has begun to enter the city, and when once inside those impregnable defences their courage revives. The citizens turn out *en masse* and cheer them as they enter, and a firm and fixed determination now seizes every soldier and citizen to defend this stronghold to the bitter end. The church bells ring out merrily upon the stillness of the quiet Sabbath morning. Hundreds who, in a common way, cared little for the sanctuary, now flocked to the churches, as if impelled by some irresistible impulse. Everybody was all alive to the gravity of the situation, and as we learned next day from the best citizens of the place, none were more fully aroused to the vast importance of the work before them than the ministers of the various churches, who spent the hour in haranguing their hearers upon the dearest rights of the South, upon the bravery and chivalry of her soldiers, upon the cruelty and tyranny of the North, upon the cowardice of the Lincoln hirelings, winding up their fiascos by saying, "The Yankee vandals are upon you, and it is your duty, every mother's son of you, to go out and fight them to the death," and to enforce their words and to encourage every one to fight, each of the ministers, and the mayor too, buckled on a cartridge box, shouldered a musket, and went into the trenches alongside of their parishioners. And so the whole population, men and boys, young and old, turned out to fight the hated Yankees, and we shall hear from some of them again.

It was 3 p. m. by the time the head of column of our division began to cross the large stream above referred to. A half mile south of the creek was a high sandy ridge concealing all our movements from the enemy, and behind this ridge our division massed in column by regiments as fast as they came up and dismounted. It was 4 p. m. before the whole division and the Board of Trade battery were across the bridge. As before remarked, the Seventy-Second was in the rear, and the left wing of the regiment was rear-guard for the train, and about the time the advance of our regiment got across the bridge it was ascertained that a heavy force of rebels were coming in from the north-west on the Marion or Summerfield road. Company A had been detailed to support the battery in front of the works, and the other companies of the right wing of the regiment, as fast as they came up, were started scouting and picketing in the direction of the rebels approaching from the north-west. Company A was soon relieved and also sent to picket in the rear, and Company D took the place of A, and was the only full company of our regiment in the battle. During this time Gen. Long and Cols. Miller and Minty were on the ridge with their glasses examining the works and selecting a place to make a charge upon them, and we shall give Col. Miller's report of the operations of the brigade further on, but just now the rebels in our rear are claiming our undivided attention. Companies A, F and I, and part of Company C, were dismounted and sent back across the creek to where the road we came in on from the north-east was intersected by one coming in from the north-west. The road led to Marion, and we moved out on it about a quarter of a mile from the bridge, when we came to a ridge reaching across the road from north to south. Our orders were to "*hold this road at all hazards.*" While we were all talking about the position and debating the propriety of forming a line of battle along on the ridge, a party of rebels fired on us, and their bullets whistled over our heads just a little too close to be amusing, and we lost no time in stringing out on the lee side of that ridge without any regard to the order of companies. Col. Thomson was with us, and his presence encouraged and inspired us. Every one present seemed to fully understand the gravity of the situation. We sent forward skirmishers and began to pile rails for all that was out. Our skirmishers soon encountered the rebels in force, and Corporal Records, Company I, who was out there in charge of those from Company I, says, "The rebels dismounted their men and went to work on us with an energy rather unusual for confederate cavalry." Our pack train had just then reached the bridge, and we sent word for it to hurry across the bridge with all speed, and for a short time the darkies, pack mules and camp kettles, went rolling over the bridge with the noise of a tornado. At this juncture, Records says: "A company of about 50 rebels made a mounted charge on us. They came with drawn sabers, which glistening in the setting sun made a formidable appearance." From our position where we were piling rails we could now see that our skirmishers, some of them, had advanced so far on the left that they were likely to be cut off, and Corporal Stanfield and two men of Company I, on horseback, were sent to order them back. Records further says: "Just then a rattling fusilade of musketry and Spencer rifles struck up to our right rear, and we began to pile up a lunette of fence rails, when who should we see but Stanfield and two men of Company I coming to us on foot. He brought orders for us to fall back at once. Brave man! He had been sent out to us on horseback, but finding it impossible to get to us that way, had dismounted and forced his way to us and thus saved the whole of us from capture."

We were not a minute too soon in getting our line of rails piled along on the ridge, for just then the rebels opened on us and the bullets rattled on our rails like hail. Half of the train was now across the bridge and the rear closed up promptly without further orders. We opened on the now advancing rebels with our Spencers, and in two minutes sent them flying back much faster than they came on. Just then Gen. Wilson and his staff came to the bridge; he had been on the east side of the creek with Gen. Upton's division, and after seeing the lines of that division well formed for an attack, had started to come across to our division, but had to go back a mile or two before he could get across the creek. When he came up to us he inquired what was the matter out there. We told him we had just been attacked sharply by a heavy force of rebels, and that they were still out there. "All right," said he, "just keep them there." He seemed to be wonderfully pleased, and just at that time we could not tell why. He socked his spurs into his horse and galloped across the bridge. We now sent across the bridge for some of our horses, and a mounted picket was sent out on to a ridge north of us, and between the two roads, for fear the rebels might send a force across on to the road we came in on and capture a part of our trains and some of our foragers who had not yet got in. This also proved to be a stitch just in time, because when our mounted men got out on to the ridge they found the rebels already preparing to do just what we supposed they would do, and so we blocked their little game again. By this time our ambulance and pack train had got across the creek, and as fast as the companies of the left wing of the regiment came up they were deployed along the creek to the south of the bridge. We now began to feel a little easy and to think that we were able to hold at bay any force the rebels might bring against us.

During this time all the preparations for the assault on the formidable defences of the city had been completed. Col. Miller says: "On our arrival in front of the works the rebels commenced shelling us, waving their flags at us, and calling at us to come over and take their artillery as we did yesterday. After Gens. Wilson and Long, Col. Minty and myself, had selected the place where the charge was to be made, I asked Gens. Wilson and Long who were to relieve the Seventy-Second—who were then in our rear and right holding a bridge the enemy were trying to get control of—I wanted all of the brigade to make the charge. Wilson said no one would; I might have Minty's brigade of cavalry, but he *must have a force in our rear and right that would fight and hold the ground.* He said that Forest had a much larger force than ours, and as soon as we made the assault he would have Chalmers attack and stampede our rear, just as he had served Smith and Sturgis on similar occasions, which was one of Forest's old games. I tried to reason him out of keeping one of my regiments out of the charge. I told him if I succeeded in carrying the works and should have a desperate struggle to hold them I could not depend on the cavalry sticking right to us. But the General would not consent to a change, and said that a stampede in our rear would be as fatal as a repulse in front, and that I should have all needed help after getting inside the works. Said he, 'The 4th Regulars with me at their head can follow wherever you go, and I will *make* the balance do the same.' He kept his word. About an hour before the setting of the sun we commenced forming the line, under cover of the ridge before referred to, the 17th Indiana on the extreme right, the 123d Illinois next, Company D, of the Seventy-Second Indiana, with all the balance of the other companies that had left the regiment in the rear and who had come up to see the fun, next, and the 98th Illinois on the left of our brigade. Minty was to form his brigade on our left. In doing this he got the 4th Ohio in our front and caused some delay in getting them out, and on our left in line. After the lines were formed I went to each regimental commander, Col. Vail, of the 17th, Col. Biggs, of the 123d, and Col. Kitchel, of the 98th, and showed them the works and told them it was expected of us to carry them. They all remarked, 'they are certainly very strong.' I admitted it, but told them we had never made a charge that had not been attended with success. At this Col. Biggs said, 'I will go in or die.' Vail and Kitchel both said, 'Good for Biggs! We can keep up our ends of the line with our regiments.' With the advice that each one of them should see their line officers I left them, and the arrangements were completed."

Before this devoted little band start on that fearful road of death, let us tell you just what they are expected to do. Our description is no hearsay, but from actual observation and measurement. The defenses of Selma were the most formidable we had ever seen, consisting of three lines of works as strong as engineering skill could make them. The outer line was an abattis 200 yards wide, and the outer edge 400 yards from the main line of works. This consisted of trees dragged in as closely together as they could be laid side by side, limbs all left on and sharpened at the point—the butts of trees on the inside, and the sharpened ends sticking out toward our line like the bristling quills of thousands of huge porcupines. We have nowhere else seen any abattis anything near as formidable as these, except right in front of Atlanta. Inside this abattis, and 200 yards from the main line, was a row of *chevaux de frise* (sheep-racks, we called them,) which have before been described. Inside of this were several rows of low stakes driven in the ground, and wires stretched across from stake to stake, at a proper height to trip our men as they ran. Inside this wire, and 75 yards from the main line, was a row of fence rails planted in the ground close together, the tops sharpened and set at an angle to strike our men about the belt. Fifty yards outside the main line was a row of pickets or stockade, made of little pine trees, 6 to 10 inches in diameter, cut 10 feet long, and set in the ground two feet deep, and very closely together, making a solid wall six to eight feet high, and all sharpened at the tops.

Now comes the main line of earthworks. A ditch eight feet wide and eight feet deep, with a row of sharpened rails as before described planted in the bottom of the ditch at the opposite or inner side. The outer slope of the earthworks or embankment was 16 feet, and so steep that to climb it was almost impossible, even if not opposed. This embankment was eight feet high on the inside, and built with a berme on the inside of a proper height for the men to stand upon. About every 300 yards along this line of works were lunette forts, containing three gun batteries. These lines of works extended from the Alabama River, a mile below the city on the south, clear around on the west, north and north-east, to the river again, and were over six miles in length.

And these are the works our men are expected to charge and capture; and these works are defended by 32 guns and 7,000 veteran soldiers, under the daring, wily, and intrepid, Gen. Forest, all burning to avenge the defeat of yesterday, and citizens filled with malignant hate for the despised Yankees.

We wish to say, by way of parenthesis, that we have been very kindly furnished with a diagram of Selma and its fortifications, published by the War Department, giving directions, roads, distances, &c., which enables us to give full and reliable details, and for which we are under obligations.

Our little band of 1,550 officers and men are ready to charge these formidable works, and we again quote from Col. Miller: "A short time before the sun went down, the advance was made over an open plain. When we were about a half mile from the works the enemy opened out on the line with increased firing of both large and small arms. Gen. Long was soon cut down by a musket ball, receiving a dangerous wound in the head. I was shot and disabled within 100 yards of the works. Col. Biggs fell at the entrance of the road leading through the works. Gen. Wilson, as promised, was on hand with his 4th Regulars. Col. Vail now had charge of the brigade, and soon arranged for the further advance, and in a short time Selma was ours, with 3,000 prisoners."

We have now given you the official and authentic account of the battle of Selma, but we have been furnished with a very graphic description of the battle, by Sergt. Jas. A. Mount, Company D, which, with corrections to correspond with official data, we insert as giving the reader a better idea of the terrible conflict than anything yet published.

Sergt. Mount says: "The divisions of Gens. Long and Upton, of Gen. Wilson's cavalry corps, arrived in front of the defences of Selma, Ala., April 2d, 1865, at 4 p. m. Gen. Upton's division was formed on the range line road, his line being confronted by swamps and marshes, rendering his cavalry ineffective. Gen. Wilson directed Upton to dismount a regiment of his picked men, penetrate the swamps, and if possible turn the right of the confederate line. A single gun from Rodney's battery was to announce the result and be the signal for Gen. Long's assault on the main line. Gen. Long's men had defeated Forest the day before and were anxious to renew their achievements before Selma." We have already given the disposition of the division, except that the 4th U. S. Cavalry, and the 7th Pennsylvania cavalry, of Minty's brigade, were in reserve, mounted. When Gen. Long heard the battle open up between a part of the Seventy-Second Indiana and Gen. Chalmers' division, he at once realized his perilous position, attacked as he was by a heavy force in rear, and confronted by a greatly superior force in strong fortifications lined with citizens and soldiers who waved the confederate flag and beckoned us to come over. At this critical moment Gen. Long decided not to await the development of Gen. Upton, but to move at once upon the works. The brave Col. Miller rode hastily along the famous Lightning Brigade, before whose valor and Spencer rifles, no confederate line had yet been able to stand, and thus addressed the boys: "If any of you are afraid to face the cannon in those forts, or the bayonets behind the parapets, let him go to the rear." Cheer after cheer went up, but no man went to the rear. The command to advance was given. The line, led by Gen. Long,

Cols. Miller and Minty, swept forward with the swiftness of horses eager for the conflict. From the forts the cannon pealed forth in thunder tones their volleys of fire and death. From the entire line of defense flashed the musketry till all was shrouded in the smoke of battle, and only the red blaze of musketry and artillery could be seen. Under this murderous fire of musketry, shot and shell, swiftly moved the assaulting line, until in quick succession the Spencer rifles sent their missiles of death in reply to rebel musketry and artillery. Though the gallant leaders, Long and Miller, had fallen wounded, and many other brave officers and men were swept down by the storm of leaden hail, yet with undaunted courage and unswerving rapidity the line swept on, leaping a barricade six feet high, through a ditch six feet deep, up the steep side of a parapet eight feet high, and hand to hand in mortal conflict Northern valor and Southern chivalry engaged. The wonderful rapidity with which the Lightning Brigade poured in volley after volley from the Spencer rifles, and the fearful havoc produced, sent terror and consternation through the confederate ranks. Hundreds surrendered, while many fled to the next line of defense. This was quickly carried by a second assault, and the victory was complete. The confederate loss in killed and wounded was heavy. Captain Cravens, of the confederate army, told the writer that almost his entire company were killed or wounded in half a minute after our line had scaled the fortifications. A man in citizen's dress, gun in hand, called out to Captain Herron, Company B, (acting major of the Seventy-Second), saying, "I am a minister, don't kill me." Captain Herron replied, "Do you preach with that gun?" Before he could reply or throw down his gun, he fell, pierced with Spencer balls. Lieut. Gen. Dick Taylor, Gens. Forest, Armstrong, Rhoddy and Adams, escaped with remnants of their commands. Among the fruits of victory were 3,000 prisoners, and 32 pieces of artillery mounted in the works The capture of Selma was of vast importance, and the defences considered very strong by the chief officers of our government, as we are led to infer from the communications of Gen. Thomas to Gen. Wilson. Under date of March 6th, 1865, Gen. Thomas communicated to Gen. Wilson that Gen. Grant had ordered Gen. Canby, with a heavy force of infantry from Mobile, to co-operate with him in the capture of Selma. Again, under date of March 14th, he says: "Gen. Canby will move from Mobile with over 40,000 infantry to co-operate with you; this will insure success in the capture of Selma." Gen. Canby failed to reach Selma, and Gen. Long with his division carried the works that were expected to require such a large force of infantry to capture.

In conclusion, it may be safely asserted that in the annals of war there are to be found on record but few instances of such daring intrepidity, crowned with such grand results, as the battle of Selma—an assaulting line of 1,550 strong, exposed to the enemy's fire while charging 600 yards, through open field, carrying formidable fortifications defended by more than four times their number, and more than two pieces of artillery to every 100 of the assaulting column. The battle of Selma stands in the front rank among the brilliant achievements of loyal valor, and each regiment participating in the engagement is worthy of unfading laurels and lasting honor.

There are many things connected with the battle of Selma yet untold, and we again turn to the Seventy-Second, as it is now deployed along the creek watching Gen. Chalmers' division as a hawk watches its prey, while the terrible conflict still goes on in our rear. After the first determined assault of the rebels had been repulsed by the right wing of our regiment they made no further attack, but still lay in line of battle anxiously waiting for us to leave some point unguarded, or manifest some show of weakness that they might pounce upon us. We fully realized that should our assaulting column fail to gain the works, the rebels inside the works, emboldened by their success, in all probability would sally forth, and our division would be crushed between those in the works and those in the rear as grain is ground between the upper and nether millstone. While we felt competent to hold in check the whole division of Gen. Chalmers, we were by no means so sure that our men would ever live to get inside of the rebel stronghold, and while we steadily kept our eyes to the front our ears were turned to the ominous sounds of the rear. We still kept shooting at the rebels in our front as long as we could see, and manifested every possible show of strength. We cannot forbear recording our feelings just as they occurred that momentous evening. We have before given you a description of the abattis 200 yards wide, circling the defenses of the city. This was a horrid ugly thing for a line of battle to get through. But after our skirmishers once got to it, it afforded them some protection, as they could crawl into it and secrete themselves under the logs and limbs. This they did, and for an hour made it lively for the gunners in the forts, picking them off whenever they attempted to fire their pieces; and during all this time we were engaged repelling the attack of Chalmers' division. The rattle of these skirmishers was constant and lively.

After Gen. Wilson left us at the bridge he rode on to the ridge, where he could see most of his own lines, and nearly the whole line of rebel works, and waited there till he was sure everything was ready. Just as the sun is going down, his staff officers ride up to him from every part of the field and tell him everything is ready. He takes off his hat, and from where we are, north of the creek, we plainly hear him sing out, "All right!" The bugles blow "Forward!" and simultaneously our whole lines move toward the rebel works on quick time. We, across the creek, almost hold our breath. In five minutes our lines reach the outer edge of the abattis, and the batteries from all the forts open on them. Here our men lie down for a few minutes, to get their breath; for two or three minutes an ominous silence follows. Except an occasional shot from our skirmishers, all is still. You cannot conceive with what suspense we listened, but we had not long to wait. Again the bugles sound—this time a charge. Again we hold our breath, as our men raise the accustomed cheer, and start through the abattis. Now is the moment of triumph or defeat for the rebels. Every gun from their forts and batteries belches forth volumes of grape and canister. Seven thousand fiends rise up from behind their works and pour into our ranks volley after volley of leaden hail. We tremble! Is it possible that any line of battle on earth can stand such a hell as this? But see! Gen. Long goes down, shot in the head. Col. Miller goes next, shot through the thigh. Heavens and earth! can our men ever get through that abattis? Again we hear our men cheering, as one by one, and in squads, they emerge from the abattis, seize hold of the *chevaux de frise*, swing them around like gates, and rush on for the main works. They stumble and tumble over the wires stretched across their way, but are up again in an instant, and our Spencers begin to rattle. We catch our breath as the men catch hold of the stakes and twist them out of the way; they go through them, and again our Spencers play such a tune as makes our blood gallop through our veins. We raise the cheer—but stop! Another lull. Col. Edgerton, of the 4th Ohio, is killed. Our men have reached the stockade, and again the rebel musketry and artillery belch forth volumes of death. The sun goes down and hides his face from the scene. Good heavens! and must our men all be murdered there, and so close to the works, too? No! No! They seize hold of the pickets, and with giant strength break them off, twist them out of the way, or pull them out of the ground; while at other points they hoist each other over them, or bend down and let their comrades mount upon their backs, and thus leap over them. Another volley of death from the rebels! It is their last. But in that volley, at a single point an officer and four men of the 17th are killed, almost in a heap, as they try to tear out the stockade, and all along the line our men

have fallen by scores. Undaunted our men leap over the stockade in numbers, and rush through the gaps in squads, and again open out with their Spencers; and again our blood rushes through our veins. Our men again raise the cheer and rush for the ditch, and the rebels begin to fly!

During all this time Gen. Wilson has intently watched his whole line; his two regiments of mounted men are ready and eager for the fray. His body-guard and staff officers are by his side; his two blood-red battle-flags are flying at either side of him. He sees this is the supreme moment of triumph. He and his officers raise the "cheer!" The bugles from every side sound the "charge!" and with the swiftness of the wind he and his flying squadrons rush for the city—and we again catch our breath. We know that the victory *will be ours!* One by one our men reach the top of the parapet, and the flag of the 17th is already waving over the works; but many of them are shot down and roll back into the ditch, or fall forward among the rebels. Col. Biggs is shot down as he attempts to pass where the road goes through the works; and our brigade is nearly without officers. But still our men rush up the slope, gain the top in numbers, and the rebels fly for the city, a mile away, and are shot in the back as they run. Our men, remembering the charge of the 17th yesterday, and the mutilation and robbing of the dead, now make no effort to capture any prisoners.

Just where the 17th strike the main line of works is a fort that must be manned by veterans, as here the struggle is long and fearful in the extreme. Here five of our men were killed after they got inside the fort. The gunners stuck to their guns to the very last, and from the piles of dead laying under the wheels of the guns and behind the limbers we should judge that few of them made their escape, or even cared to. Gen. Wilson, with his blood red battle flags still flying at the head of his column of 4th Regulars and 7th Pennsylvania cavalry, now rushes through the works, and the victory is complete. As the men of the Lightning Brigade begin to form inside of the works he rides up to them, takes off his hat, and says: "Men, I now see how it is you have gotten such a hell of a name!" This rough compliment was properly appreciated by the men, and they greeted it with rounds of applause. It is now dark, but see!! A tongue of flame shoots 2,000 feet into the sky and lights up the country for miles around. Just on the outskirts of the city, at the north-west, were saltpeter works covering five acres of ground. These the rebels set on fire; what for we never could tell, unless it was to make a light for them to see to run away by. The burning was the most terribly grand of anything we had ever seen. We were full two miles away, but it made it as litght as if there had been a full moon shining, and the most terrific explosions followed each other in quick succession, shaking the ground like an earthquake, hurling blaze and brands hundreds of feet high. After our lines had been re-formed our division closed in on the city, and as there was but a small gap along up the Alabama River to the north-east of the city for the rebs to escape through, most of them were captured.

Dr. Cole, in speaking of this battle, says: "The 4th division took position on the north side of the city, but at the signal for the assault was not ready to move, and to the unsurpassed charge of the 2d cavalry division belongs the honor of capturing this rebel stronghold of Selma, at the terrible cost of 29 killed and 140 wounded in Miller's brigade; 15 killed and 85 wounded in Minty's brigade, of our division; and 3 killed and 10 wounded in the 4th division, which did not get up till after the works were carried. Making a total loss in the whole command engaged at Selma, of 282."

We now want to pay our parting respects to Chalmers' division, and then our regiment is also ready to move down into the city. We have told you that at Elyton, on the 30th of March, the 1st division, or a part of it, turned off to the south-west toward Tuscaloosa, and our pontoon train, by way of diversion, went along with this command. About the same time Gen. Forest matured his plans for meeting us, and sent Chalmers' division *via* Tuscaloosa, with orders to get into our rear and burn our train if possible. This division met the 1st division somewhere north-west of this place, yesterday, got defeated and put back for Selma, and had our division been two hours later getting to Selma, our men would then have had this division to fight in addition to those already inside of the works; and we suppose that it was this fact that so pleased Gen. Wilson when he found we had cut them off, and although our regiment had not been in the charge upon the works in front of Selma, we felt well pleased and satisfied with our share of the work. Our regiment and four companies of the 17th had done all the fighting which was done by our division yesterday, in the battle of Ebenezer church, and to day nine companies of our regiment had kept at bay a whole division of rebels, and thus assured the success of our whole army at Selma. The fact is, our regiment had made success possible, because there was a time when it seemed our men *must fail* or all be killed, and had there been an additional division of rebels inside of the works, who can tell but the assault might have been a failure.

About two hours after night our trains all got across the bridge, and the right wing of the regiment was relieved, and the left wing left on picket. We moved inside the works and went into camp just north of where the Summerfield or Marion road passes through, and laid down in the woods close to the works, at the point where the left of our brigade struck them.

Lieut. Barnes, of Company A, says: "We camped just inside the works, and were surrounded by the dead on all sides. The city mayor, who with many other citizens had been taking an active part in defending the city, lay within a few feet of Company A's headquarters. For superstitious men our proximity to the dead would not have been very enviable. We had very few such men in the regiment." All our men held the doctrine of Nasby, "a dead rebel makes a sweet corpse," and weren't at all afraid of them.

April 3, 1865. The writer was up shortly before daylight, and without taking time to eat, or feed our horse, started to look over the battle-field. Close to where we slept was one of the biggest men we ever saw, a rebel, shot square in the forehead. We climbed up on top of the works, and moved along south on the top of them, where we could plainly see every foot of the ground over which our division had advanced. The dead were all lying just as they had fallen. As we looked over the ground we were filled with wonder and astonishment. How in the world did our men succeed in reaching the main line at all? It seemed to us that if a single line of our brigade had been behind this embankment we could have literally annihilated any army in the world that had attempted to storm the works as our men had done. We went down south to the farthest point, where there were many dead on either side, and then got down into the ditch, climbed out on the outside, and went to the pickets, or stockades, and tried to climb over them, and found it required all our strength and skill to do so. We then went on out to the *chevaux de frise* and abattis, and wondered, again and again, how could our men get through? We then went back to the pickets, and noted with what superhuman efforts our men had torn them them out or hoisted each other over them. We went to the ditch and tried to jump across it, and to climb up the slope. This again we found required our utmost exertions, without a single thing to impede or encumber us. As we move north again, along on top of the works to the farthest point, where the works bent to the east, and as far as there were any dead, we began to estimate the number of dead, and to our utter astonishment found them about equal on both sides of the works. The sun was an hour high when we got back to our horses, and as there had been no bugle call most of the men were still asleep. After feeding, and eating our breakfast, we again extended our observations, and found we were a mile from the city, and that west and north of the city were dense woods, while outside of the works, and entirely around them, the land was bare of trees from a half mile to a mile out. We have seen Louisville, Nashville, Murfreesboro, Chattanooga, Atlanta, Macon, and nearly all the fortified places in the South, but we pronounce Selma the strongest of them all Murfreesboro had more well built forts, but no field works at all. Dr. Cole says: "I had our wounded all taken to the city, and appropriated the most aristocratic and best ventilated mansions for their use; glad that I could do anything for the comfort of such brave fellows as they have proven themselves to be. All last night the ambulances were kept running, and by daylight the wounded were all under shelter. The rebel loss in killed and wounded is heavier than our own, and their wounds also much more serious. Have spent all day with the wounded, who are receiving every possible attention."

About the middle of the forenoon, A, F, D and I, were ordered to report to Gen. Wilson, in the city, for provost guard duty. We had a terrible time getting our men to get ready to move. There was scarcely a man in camp, and there was so much to be seen that it took us two hours to get even a majority of them together, and it was noon when we got into town and got our orders. A and F went into churches, D into the Masonic hall, and I into a large school building. We hitched our horses to the fence inside the yard. We found the city one of the most beautiful places we had ever seen, and our quarters everything we could ask or expect; and we were a very well pleased set of fellows. The balance of the regiment went into camp in the north-eastern part of the town, close to the river. Immediately after dinner Companies D and I were ordered to press in all the darkies they could, and proceed at once to the machine shops and foundries and break up everything that would not burn. This gave us a chance to learn something of the vastness of our conquest. We supposed last night that the capture of this place was the grandest achievement of the war; but to-day, as we move about over the city, and trophy after trophy presents itself to us, we are lost in astonishment. Our first thought of all this greatness was nothing in comparison with the reality. In addition to the guns captured in the works, and already spoken of, we found 65 others at the foundries, completed and in course of construction, besides a vast number of old abandoned and bursted ones that had been sent here to be remoulded and remounted.

We counted 250 bran new wagons, that had never been used, besides scores of old ones that had been brought in for repairs. There were hundreds of caissons, limbers, blacksmith forges, and ambulances.

The arsenal covered six acres of ground, the largest in the South, and was plump-full of every article that an army could have any use for, from a percussion cap to the 700-pound shell, and from a pack-saddle to the heaviest gun-carriage. At the foundries we found everything in full blast, just as the men had left them yesterday and hurried out to the works to fight the hated Yankees. Here was everything that could be melted or moulded, from the smallest howitzer up to the 700-pounder siege gun. In the machine shops we found all these things in the course of finishing, from the boring of a 6-pounder to the turning of trunnions for guns of the largest calibre. Talk about the resources of the South being exhausted! The truth is, they were just getting ready for war, and, so far as resources are concerned, were never in a better fix than just now. The foundries were simply stupendous; we shall speak of them again. We found two locomotive engines and numerous stationary ones, six or seven railroad cars, and extensive shops for making others. We found the fire from the saltpetre works had spread to the city and was still burning. We went back to our quarters for supper, wondering what next?

An expedition was sent out this morning to look after Chalmers, whose force attacked us on picket yesterday evening. It was ascertained that as soon as he found he could not get into the city, nor attack us with any reasonable show of success, he retreated toward Meridian, Mississippi. The expedition went down to Cahawba, at the mouth of Cahawba River, 10 miles below here, and released some of our starving prisoners who were kept there. We saw some of the poor fellows, who looked like living skeletons. Quite a number of our regiment nad passed through that rebel prison. Just north of the city is a large stockade fort, covering three or four acres of ground. This the rebels used to keep the Yankee prisoners in, but to-night we have it so full of rebels that they can scarcely get around each other. This makes us feel pretty well, because we know that in that very bull-pen they have treated our men with untold cruelty, and we love to twit them about getting into their own trap. Citizens now tell us that Gen. Forest, with a few of his men, made his escape last night by going north-east, up the river, through a small gap between Upton's left and the river, and that Gen. Dick Taylor jumped his horse into the river and swam across. It seems that almost every house in the town is full of some kind of ammunition, because as the fire still keeps burning explosions are constantly going on. Our quarters are in a school for young ladies, and up stairs there are four pianos and organs, and as we lie down to sleep on the desks some of the boys are pounding away on them, and we go to sleep amid a medley of discordant sounds, above all of which come the report of explosions from the fire still burning.

April 4th. No bugle call this morning, and we slept till we got ready to get up, and found desks were harder to sleep upon than the ground. After breakfast we again went to our work of breaking up the foundries and machine shops and rolling ammunition into the river. We now had 400 negroes at the work, and it surprised us a little to see how cheerfully they went at it. At the arsenal they fixed up a spout on an inclined plane that led down to the river; 15 or 20 feet below the spout they fixed a platform, and when the shells would roll down the spout they would gain such velocity that on striking the platform they would bounce 50 feet out into the river. This tickled the darkies wonderfully, and for two days they just kept the river boiling.

It was our fortune to superintend the destruction of the foundry, locomotives and machine shops. We went to the shops and got a lot of hammers and set a gang of street boys to knocking the locomotives to pieces. Just then came along a fellow who had worked in the shops. He was a rebel, and we wondered afterward why he was not in the bull-pen. He ordered the boys to stop. The boys referred him to us and kept on hammering away. He came up in a whining but insolent way, and told us to make those boys quit, or, said he, "They will spoil it." "That is exactly what we want," said we; "we intend to make you people of the South feel the effects of war." "That will do no good; we can build other locomotives," replied he. "Very good; we are going to fix you so you can't build them," we said. "You can never whip us, and it's no use trying," he whined. "Very good," said we again; "You think one confederate can whip three Yankees, but we've got the three Yankees, and more besides, and are going to wear you out if we can't whip you, and the sooner your people understand this the better." He left us a sadder if not a wiser man, and in a few minutes the locomotive was knocked out of time; even the steam whistle was so mashed that it would never whistle again.

We now went into the foundry, but here we were puzzled. Everything was of such vast dimensions and strength that breaking was out of the question with any means that we had at our command.

Think of huge iron cranes of sufficient strength to lift thousands of tons. and of chains the links of which were made of round bars of iron over two inches in diameter. Not much breaking there. However, we could knock the furnaces to pieces, and the engines that moved these ponderous levers, but it took us two days to do it. Up to this time we had been ignorant of the method of making artillery guns; but here every kind of artillery was in process of manufacture, and we had plenty of time to study the methods. It may be interesting to our children to know how big guns are made, as well as how used, and we will try to tell what we saw. Almost all of the guns made at this foundry were of the Rodman and Parrott patterns, and were made of cast iron with huge hoops of steel driven on to the breech. The way they were cast was to dig a hole in the ground two to four and somtimes six feet in diameter, and three times as deep as the desired length of the gun, so that a gun four feet long would require a hole twelve feet deep; and one we saw finished 17 feet long must have taken a hole over 50 feet deep and seven feet in diameter. These holes were dug inside the foundry building, and then filled up with a clay mold in the centre, as near the desired shape of the gun as possible. These molds were now filled up with melted iron and let stand until cool, the largest size taking three weeks to cool. The clay mold was then dug from around them, the huge cranes swung around over the hole, and the ponderous chains made fast to them. Then, if you can tell how much power it would take to lift a mass of iron five feet in diameter and 50 feet long out of one of those holes, you can beat us; *we* couldn't give an intelligent guess. The object of making them so long was this: The butt of the gun being cast downwards, the immense weight on top would make them more dense and harder to burst. After these huge masses were lifted out of the holes they were placed on trucks and rolled into the machine shops, where they were placed in lathes, cut off the proper length, turned smoothly on the outside, and lastly bored out to the proper calibre. In the shops were guns undergoing all these processes, the chisels and drills all just in the positions they happened to be when the machinery was stopped and the men hurried out to the defense of the city against the Yankee hordes.

We were astonished at the apparent ease with which all this seemed to be done. We saw one chisel that had been cutting a shaving one-half inch thick, three fourths inch wide and over 20 feet long off the outside of a gun. We saw other shavings as thin as knife blades, and still others as fine as the finest wire. One thing more and we are done. The huge steel hoops that are placed around the heaviest siege guns are often four inches thick and six inches wide, and we always wondered how they were made and put on. Here we saw the whole process. They were first welded together as nearly as possible of the proper diameter, and then were put in lathes and turned to the exact size desired, both inside and out, then heated and driven on to the guns.

After breaking everything we could break on the inside of the building we went on the outside, and there lay a brand-new gun, just finished and ready to mount—a monster in size and splendid in workmanship. As it lay flat on the ground the butt just came up even with the writer's eyes, it being over five feet in diameter. The trimmings were eight inches in diameter, and we had nothing heavy enough to knock them off. It was over 17 feet long, and as we stuck our head into the muzzle we found we could easily crawl into it. We wear a No. 40 dress coat, and you can guess at the rest as well as we can tell it. Competent persons say it would throw a conical shot of 700 pounds weight, and was made for the forts at Mobile, but was too late ready, as the Yankees had taken the place before it was done. In the afternoon the 4th Ohio cavalry buried their colonel, a captain, a sergeant, a corporal, and four privates, with the honors of war. This was truly a most solemn service. The 4th regulars also buried their dead with honors; among the dead were a lieutenant and a sergeant. The general-in-chief and his staff joined in the procession. This was one of the most solemnly grand funerals we ever saw, the bands playing the most solemn chants we ever heard. Brave men were they, fallen in one of the most daring and successful charges ever made by troops. Of the sorrow and honor of their comrades they were worthy.

April 5th. Large working gangs of negroes are very busy to-day gathering up wagons, ambulances, caissons, limber-chests, blacksmith's forges, and artillery wagons, and piling them into the arsenal, preparatory to burning them. That part of the regiment not on duty in town, a part of our brigade, and a part of Minty's, went on a scout up the Alabama River for the purpose of picking up horses, mules, negroes, &c. Sergt. Stephen Aiken, Company K, says of this expedition: "Col. Minty was in command of this expedition, and we went after some horses supposed to be secreted on an island; traveled all night. April 6th, stopped at daylight and fed and made coffee, and then moved on across swamps and through thickets to where the plunder was supposed to be. On arriving at the place, Minty's brigade went across to the island and got the horses and mules, and our brigade picketed." It rained furiously, and Aiken, McClure, Remley and others, speak of this as a' most miserable trip, in which almost every body got lost in the swamps, darkness and rain.

April 6th. Hundreds of negroes still at work rolling shells out of the arsenal and piling rebel property, generally in the arsenal. This is now the fourth day they have been at that one thing. About 10 o'clock a part of the 1st division, and the pontoon train, and also our division train, got in. We were glad to see them, especially those of our own company and regiment. The train got in all right without loss, but from Elyton clear on down was constantly harassed by small roving bands of guerrillas and bushwhackers, who near Montevallo had barricaded the road, and for two or three hours stopped the train; but there happened to be a few Spencer rifles along with the train, and Peter P. Johnson, of Company I, a brave man who used to belong to the scouts, and a few other blacksmiths and teamsters, soon cleared the road. From them we learned that Forest, with a few of his men, after he made his escape on the night of the 2d, went right back up the road that we had come down on, to Plantersville, and parolled our wounded men and the nurses left with them, and also robbed them, taking Dr. Dome's horse, and also killed some of the 17th Indiana. Late this evening the negroes got through with their work of rolling shells out, and piling government plunder of all kinds into the arsenal, and just at sundown it began to rain and rained all night. Just at dark Gen. Wilson ordered the arsenal set on fire. As before stated it covered six acres of ground, and all the woodwork was of pitch pine and burned fiercely. It was set in 50 different places at once, and in 20 minutes afterwards, the rattle of exploding rifle and musket cartridges was deafening; we have not heard such a constant roar since the battle of Chicamauga. The negroes had been cautioned to get all the artillery shells out, but in half an hour they began to explode, throwing fire and old iron 1,000 feet high. This made every fellow hunt his hole and crawl into it, too. The scene was hideous and unearthly beyond anything we had ever imagined. The explosions continued for three hours, much louder than any we had ever heard, and of sufficient violence to shake the earth for miles around, making the whole city a perfect pandemonium. Had it not been for the constant and heavy rain nothing could have prevented the whole city from burning up. This frightened the citizens nearly to death. What must have been the humiliation of Gens. Forest and Taylor as they heard these tell-tale explosions and saw the firey serpent of flame writhing in the sky over Selma, the mighty, strong and rich city!

April 7th. The excessive rain last night prevented the destruction of a lot of wagons, ambulances, caissons, artillery wagons, &c., but the destruction of the building proper was complete, and this morning nothing but ashes is left of what five days ago was said to be the largest establishment of the kind in the world. For two or three days parties have been engaged in gathering up all the able bodied negroes in the country for the purpose of forming them into a negro regiment, and this evening the darkies paraded the streets 900 strong. We have never been in any place where the whole populace seemed to have such a bitter hatred for the Union as they do here. The negro procession made the natives open their eyes. They greeted it with scowls and hisses, but it made them think the Yanks had come to stay. The pontoon men commenced laying their bridge across the river to-day. This was a most difficult and dangerous job, owing to the great length of the bridge, 870 feet, the swiftness of the stream, and the smooth, solid rock bottom, entirely forbidding the use of anchors.

April 8th. This morning a heavy detail from our division was sent out south-west into the country for forage, and we have this story of Sergt. Dan. Moore, Company C. He was an inveterate forager, and never missed an opportunity to gratify his propensity if half a chance presented itself. Last night he heard of this train going out, and before daylight this morning he and three of his comrades were up and saddled. They moved out with the train till, passing the picket line, they turned into a by-road and lit out. About four miles out they came to a large plantation where there were lots of negro quarters, and everything betokened wealth and plenty. Dan. and his comrades made a dive for the smoke-house. Among the many articles they saw there that makes a soldier's mouth water to contemplate, was a large barrel, or rather open hogshead, of molasses. They proceeded at once to fill their canteens; but just then in came a negro wench about three feet and a half high and about as thick as she was high. She held in her hands a large oak paddle three feet long, used in the South as a kind of washing machine for beating clothes. With this she began belaboring the boys most unmercifully, yelling vociferously, "Git out o' dar, dees our lasses! Git out o' dar, dees our lasses!" Every time she'd halloo down would come the paddle, and it was all the boys could do to keep her from seriously hurting them while they filled their canteens. However, they paid no attention to her further than to keep her from hurting them; but she still kept whacking away and yelling at the top of her voice, "Git out o' dar, dees our lasses." Just as they had got their canteens full she managed to deal Dan.

over the head such a blow as to almost floor him. This so enraged Dan. that he roared out, "Boys, let's put the old thing into that molasses." It was no sooner said than the four strong men seized her and in a twinkling up she went and down she came "slap!" feet foremost into the barrel of molasses. The molasses flew to the rafters. They seized her again, and up she went and down she came onto the floor, in much less time than it takes you to read this. Out of the door she darted and made a straight shoot for the negro quarters, the molasses streaming out behind as she ran. She was the sweetest nigger you ever saw. After the boys had got all the hams, etc., they wanted, they started out. Just then the advance guard of the forage train (which happened to be the 98th Illinois) came in sight, and the boys beckened them to come there. About 20 of them came on a full gallop, and as the boys mounted their horses they carelessly remarked that there was some molasses in there, and to this day each one of the four solemnly declare the 98th boys drained the barrel to the last drop.

The river at this point is 300 yards wide, and the citizens say 50 feet deep, and most difficult to lay a bridge across. Owing to the smooth rock bottom the pontooniers cannot anchor a boat so as to hold the bridge steady; the current is very swift and a vast number of logs are floating in it, supposed to be thrown in by the rebels.

The following paper explains itself:

THE YANKEE CAVALIER.

VOL. I. SELMA, APRIL 8TH, 1865. NO. I.

CAPT. W. W. VAN ANTWERP AND THEO. T. SCRIBNER, EDITORS.

SALUTATORY:—The American Eagle having soared above the rattlesnake and pelican, and planted himself firmly upon the inside of the fortifications of Selma, the votaries of that noble bird have concluded to present their compliments to the citizens in the form of the Yankee Cavalier; and in the true Yankee vernacular they say, "How are ye, secesh?"

It must be a source of gratification to those Union men who have been pressed into the arsenal and other public service of the confederacy, to know their friends have arrived, scaled the fortifications of Selma, and planted the old flag once more above their heads. Those who have been so long held in the hot embrace of his satanic majesty, and submitted willingly to the menial service he has required of them, we have only to remind of the biblical injunction, that "the wages of sin is death," and "the way of the transgressor is hard." Apropos of *those clerical* gentlemen who were *found in the trenches*, one of whom said he hoped in his heart that God would permit Lee to annihilate Grant and Sherman with their armies.

We would inform the people of this benighted region that the Union still exists, and that unless they "repent and believe" very soon they will forever be damned. Subjugation is as sure to follow the track of Uncle Samuel's victorious armies as daylight is sure to follow the course of "Old Sol," unless in fact the people throw down their arms and fling themselves into the arms of "Old Uncle Abe," who takes repentant sinners to his bosom as Abraham of old did the poor, despised Lazarus.

The people of Selma, as well as the denizens of other nooks and corners of the confederacy, should understand that the old humbug of making the soldiers believe that "Yanks won't fight," is played out, *vide* the recent fight at Selma, where 1,500 Yankees took your breastworks, defended by 7,000 men, under one of your best generals, viz: N. B. Forest. Don't fool yourselves into the belief that Lee is to whip Sherman or Grant, or the confederacy has a single hope of recognition. In supporting the war you are simply supporting a few pothouse politicians in offices of luxury, while you, the simple dupes of their machinations, suffer the consequences and rot in the stockades erected for *our* soldiers. We look upon you with compassion, and we feel deep pity in our hearts when we see you blindly rushing on to destruction; for you are as sure of death as was Cæsar when he entered the fatal senate chamber of Rome, if you hold out in your blind fanaticism.

The Union is what we are fighting for, and what we *will* fight for until you are subjugated, unless you surrender.

Having said this much to rebels, we now propose to congratulate our soldiers upon their valor and perseverance. Soldiers of the Union army: God is on your side, and although your brothers are killed upon every battle-field, you have the consolation of knowing that they died in a glorious cause. May their souls rest in peace! Soldiers, the day is not far distant when the Union will be restored, and then we will all go home to our fathers, relatives, and friends, and enjoy the happy blessings of peace, with the glorious consciousness that our strong arms helped to achieve the brilliant victory that led to the munificent consummation. Take our paper, "free gratis," read, ponder, and reflect. May it lead many erring ones back to their allegiance, and inspire our soldiers to fight on as they have fought, until the achievement of the final victory."

Here follows General Wilson's congratulatory order, No. 16:

HEADQUARTERS CAVALRY CORPS, M. D. M,
Selma, Ala., April 7th, 1865.

Special Field Orders, No. 16.

The Brevet Major General commanding congratulates the officers and men of the Cavalry Corps upon their late signal victory. After a march of nearly 300 miles, over bad roads, through a sterile and mountainous country, crossing wide and rapid rivers. you, in 12 days, found yourselves in front of Selma, with its arsenals, foundries and workshops, the most important city in the south-west. The enemy attempted to delay your march at Ebenezer Church and paid the penalty of his temerity by leaving three guns and 200 prisoners in your hands. Selma lay befone you surrounded by two lines of intrenchments, the outer one continuous, flanked by impenetrable swamps, covered by stockades and defended by 7,000 troops under the command of Lieut. Gen. Forest. Like an avalanche the intrepid soldiers of the Second Cavalry Division swept over the defences on the Summerfield road, while the 4th carried those on the Plantersville road. The enemy, astonished and disheartened, broke from their strong works, and Selma was fairly won. The enemy under Chalmers attempted to drive in the 2d division's picket line during the battle, and go to the rescue of the rebel garrison, but their efforts were futile, and they were compelled to retreat rapidly beyond the Cahawba. The 1st division, in the meantime, was making hard marches, harrassing in front and rear the bewildered rebels under Jackson. The wagon train had been left behind that your march might not be impeded, but has arrived in safety, its guards having frustrated all attempts of the enemy to delay its progress.

Soldiers, you have been called upon to perform long marches, and endure many privations, but your General relied upon and believed in your capacity and courage to undergo every task imposed upon you. Trusting in your valor, discipline, and armament, he did not hesitate to attack entrenchments believed by the rebel leaders to be impregnable, and which might well have caused double your number of veteran infantry to hesitate. You have fully justified his opinions and may justly regard yourselves invincible. Your achievements will be considered among the most remarkable in the annals of cavalry. The fruits of your victory are numerous and important; 31 field pieces and one 30 pound Parrot captured on the field of battle, and over 70 pieces of heavy ordnance in the arsenal and foundry, 3,000 prisoners, and a number of battle flags. the naval foundry and machine shops, the extensive arsenal filled with every variety of military munitions, and large quantities of commissary and quartermaster stores in depots.

During your march you have destroyed seven iron works and foundries, several factories and colleries, many railroad bridges and trestle works, and large quantities of cotton.

While you exult in the success which has crowned your arms, do not forget the memory of those who died that you might conquer.

By command of BREVET MAJOR-GEN. J. H. WILSON.

E. B. BEAUMONT, Major and A. A. General.

CAPTURE OF THE CHATTANOOGA REBEL.—The type upon which the CAVALIER is printed is a portion of the material of the office of the Chattanooga *Rebel*, which paper was originally printed in Chattanooga, Tenn. From there the office was removed to Marietta, Ga., and when our army approached that place it was taken to Atlanta, where a few numbers were issued. At the evacuation of that city by the rebel army, the office was removed to Griffin, Ga. But when Gen. Sherman moved around Atlanta to Jonesboro, the *Rebel* again pulled up stakes and came to this city, where it has since been published unmolested until the arrival of Wilson's Cavalry, which was so unexpected that the indomitable proprietors did not have time to remove their material, and it fell into the hands of the Yankee vandals.

DESTROYED BY FIRE.—The offices of the Daily *Dispatch* and Daily *Reporter* were destroyed by fire on Sunday night, the 2d instant, the building which contained them having been set on fire by drunken (rebel) soldiers.

GENERAL LONG'S FAREWELL ADDRESS.

HEADQUARTERS SECOND CAVALRY DIVISION. M. D. M.
Macon, Ga., April 25th, 1865.

General Orders No. 15.

Officers and soldiers of the 2d division, cavalry corps, Military Division of the Mississippi: According to the advice of the surgeon I leave you for a time—how long I am not able to say. I do not feel like separating myself from you, possibly forever, without in a few parting words expressing my entire and heartfelt gratification at your gallant and soldierly conduct since I have had the honor and good fortune to command you; but particularly so in the present campaign. During the first portion of the march unfortunate circumstances placed you in the rear of the corps, thus rendering your labors extremely arduous, by having to travel roads originally bad but rendered miserably bad by the passage of other troops in your advance. By your untiring energy and hard work you have ever overcome these difficulties, and arrived in front of Selma, garrisoned by a strong force under command of Gen. Forest, in time to administer to him and to his command, behind almost impregnable works.

one of the most complete and severe castigations received by any command during the war. Of the circumstances and details of this fight, with which you are all familiar, it is unnecessary for me to speak. It was, however, the turning point, the decisive fight, of the campaign. The nature of the works, and the numbers, which, according to the admission of their commander, Gen. Forest himself, under flag of truce, far exceeded your own; and the number of pieces of artillery in position, are facts which show beyond controversy that this feat has been equaled by none accomplished by cavalry during this war, and excelled but in a few instances by infantry. Having naturally no love for war, and if it should be my fortune, as I hope it may be, never again to hear the fire of a gun in battle, I shall consider that it is honor enough to last me the remainder of my life to have had the honor to command you on that occasion. Whether or not all, or any portion of us, may meet again, I shall watch your career with interest, and my prayer shall be for your welfare and happiness. To all and each of you, for the time at least, I bid an affectionate farewell. ELI LONG,

Brigadier General U. S. Vols. Com'd'g.

The command of our division now devolved upon R. G. Minty, Colonel of the 4th Michigan cavalry, he being the ranking officer of the division, and Col. Vail, of the 17th Indiana, is the ranking officer in our brigade and takes command. Our division began to cross the river to-day at 3 p. m., but had not all crossed until the bridge broke in the middle, and one of Gen. McCook's staff officers and a soldier were drowned. For several days there has been a set of officers busily engaged paroling the rebel soldiers now in the stockade. Since the fight there have been numbers of rebel soldiers found secreted in cellars, smoke-houses, and other places, and taken to the bull pen, as we call it. We quote from Dr. Cole: "The sick and wounded who are in a condition to be taken along, will be moved out at 6 a. m. to-morrow. Some of the citizens, now that we are preparing to leave, begin to show ill feeling, and I fear for our poor fellows who are to be left behind."

CHAPTER XXXVIII.

From April 9th to April 29th, 1865.—Leaving Selma—The Historian at a Negro Dance Helping a Colored Lady "Cut de Pigin's Wing"—He Finds Out all About the Peculiar Odor—Leave Most of Our Prisoners—Col. Miller and Gen. Long with Column in Very Fine Carriages—Swamps, Poor Country and Hard Tackout—News that Gen. Grant has Taken Richmond Reaches Us and We Become Uproarous—We also Learn that the Rebels have Evacuated Montgomery and Surrendered Without a Fight—The Confederacy Falling to Pieces—Negroes Coming to Us by Hundreds Wanting to be Soldiers—We Pass Through Montgomery—Col. Miller Left Behind at Montgomery on Account of His Wounds—Order to Organize and Arm all Negroes with Us—Not a Wagon in the Brigade—Burning Bridges, Tearing Down Telegraph Wire, Tearing Up Railroad Track, and Tearing up Rebeldom in General—A Negro Camp—Capture of Columbus and Burning of Forts and Arsenals, Steamboats, Locomotives, Cars, Cotton, etc., etc.—The Capture of Columbus a Grand Victory—Vast Amounts of War Material—So Many Prisoners we Don't Know What to do With Them—We March Through Columbus to the Tune of "Hail Columbia"—A Little Drunk Again—We Make a Swift March for Macon—Pass 400 Demoralized Rebels, but Pay no Attention to Them—A Rebel Officer Captured says Reports of Lee's Surrender are Current—Capture of Rebel Mail and Papers at Thomaston, which Say that Lee has Surrendered to Grant—Approaching Macon.—A Rebel General's Armistice Proposition "Too Thin"—We go Into Macon with a Dash and a Whoop—Were We in a Trap?—Doubts of Lee's Surrender and the Situation—Wake up in the Midst of Heavy Forts and Grinning Guns—Meeting a Johnny at the Well who Knew Nothing of what had Occurred—An Armistice between Sherman and Johnston—Our Soldiers say "D——n the Armistice"—Gen. Cobb Surprised and Indignant at Gen. Wilson, and Wilson ready to Thrash Cobb in any Manner the Gruff Rebel Might Suggest—Conditions of Surrender—Works Around the City—All the Rebels Surrender—Suspense and Uncertainty—Exploding the Ammunition—Blowing up a Little Darkey—Peace is Dawning—Gen. Wilson's Peace Order—Thanks to Almighty God for Peace—The Shocking News of the Assassination of President Lincoln—Profound Grief and Indignation—Our Last Inspection.

Sunday, April 9th, 1865. A week ago to-day we entered Selma, and the purpose is to get away to-day. It took till the middle of the forenoon to get the pontoon joined again, when the 4th division began to cross very rapidly, and at noon the provost guards, A, F, D and I, were ordered to saddle, but about the middle of the afternoon the bridge gave way again, and we unsaddled, fed and got supper, expecting to stay over night. Just at dark the bridge was fixed once more, and we saddled again and bade good bye to our commodious quarters. Just then it began to rain, and by the time we reached the bridge it was as dark as Egypt. As soldiers always like to see what they are doing, the foundry and machine shops were set on fire, and we could not help remarking the coincidence of our coming in and going out of this place. Exactly one week ago to-night, we came in by the light of the burning saltpetre works, and the same hour of the night we go out by the light of other burning buildings. What a change in one short week has taken place in this beautiful city! There is very little of its greatness left. The people have treated us with snarls and contempt, and while we have not set fire to or destroyed any private property, we had very little heart to put out what the rebels had set. It was 9 o'clock when we got across the river, and immediately started to go to our regiment, which was camped six miles out; owing to extreme darkness, bad roads, and swamps, we did not get to the regiment at all, but went into camp at midnight four miles from Selma. Dr. Cole says: "I did not get Col. Miller across until midnight, and it was near daylight when we reached camp six miles from the river." Not more than half the prisoners have been paroled, and they, too, are being moved along.

April 10th. As soon as it was light we went to the regiment and went into camp to wait for all the trains to cross and close up. After dinner the writer was scouting around and ran on to some negro quarters where they were having a regular plantation dance. This amused us wonderfully. We had seen a great many negro dances, but they had been what we called stag dances; that is, they had all been of the male persuasion. Here they were male and female about equally divided—50 of them in a log cabin about 16 feet square—all jumping up and down, clapping their hands (patting juber), puffing and blowing like steam engines, and sweating like race horses. There were so many of them that you could hardly stick your finger between them. They had a fiddle, tambourine, banjo, and a man rattling the bones. There was a bed in the room, and we never could tell how many there were under it, but all the musicians were on it. We had heard a great deal before the war about the peculiar aroma of the "nigger," and we determined to see if there really was anything in it. So we squeezed ourself into the middle of the room, where we found our further progress cut square off by the buxom form of a wench that would weigh 200 pounds. She was "cutting the pigeon wing" in a most lively manner. We never could dance, but jammed up against her, as we were compelled to keep time whether we wanted to or not. From this fact alone, we suppose, she wasn't long in getting to think we were paying special attention to her, and thinking, no doubt, it was quite an honor to dance with a Yankee soldier, she faced about, began to jump up and down on our toes, scrape our shins, blow her slobbers and perspiration into our face, and throw her arms about in the wildest ecstasy, every now and then giving a "yoop" that satisfied us she was feeling first rate. There was but one door, and it was kept constantly shut in order to have more room. There was but one window. two feet square, and low down, and we are well prepared to say there was a peculiar odor; but whether they all smell just that way we don't know, and presume we never will; furthermore, our curiosity is entirely satisfied.

About 3 o'clock in the afternoon, Companies H and E, and two companies of the 17th Ind., under command of a staff officer, started for Pleasant Hill, 20 miles south, to see if there were any rebels in that vicinity. They reached it at midnight and then moved to Benton, getting there just at daylight, to find the command on the move, and so got no supper, neither sleep nor breakfast. By 3 p. m. of the 10th the whole command was across the Alabama river, the pontoon taken up and the train well closed. We had to leave most of our wounded behind. There are more than a thousand negroes going along with us. The Johnnys came into Selma before the pontoon was taken up, but fortunately did not fire on our men. It was found necessary to burn some of the pontoons and destroy some of the wagons in order to lighten our train, as we are now so far away from our friends and God's country that everything must be kept constantly closed up snug and ready for battle at any time. At 3 p. m. we moved on, taking the road east for Montgomery, our regiment in advance of our division. We bivouacked at 11 p. m. near Benton, 20 miles from Selma, but part of our division did not get in till daylight. Gen. Long and Col. Miller are being brought along in very fine carriages.

April 11th. We pulled out this morning about an hour by sun, so that a part of our division did not get to sleep a wink. After going five or six miles we ran into a vast swamp with a large ugly stream running through it, which Dr. Cole says was called Letahachee, but we always called it Swamp Creek. Here we stalled; the 1st and 4th divisions had so cut it up that it was impossible for us and the trains to get through it. So we backed out and went two or three miles further north down the creek. We ran into the swamp again and then had to wait for the pontoon train to come up and lay a bridge across the creek before we could get across. While they were doing it we got supper, and had nothing to eat but sweet potatoes, coffee and meat. This brings us back to speak of our hard-tack again. We have told you that on March 28th we drew our last five days' rations of hard-tack, and the time for these to be out was on the 1st of April, the day before we got to Selma; but the country had afforded us an abundance of food up to the last two days, since which time we could get nothing at all but sweet potatoes, and to-day the last hard tack disappeared, and the Lord only knows when we'll see another one. The pontoon was not completed until 1 o'clock in the morning, and it was 2 before we got across the creek. About the time we got across we received the word that Gen. Grant had taken Richmond, and from that on to camp we were a little noisy. It has been nearly a year since he began the siege of that place. We traveled until 3 o'clock in the morning and went into camp 12 miles from where we camped last night, having traveled 16 miles in nearly 24 hours. Dr. Cole says: "The road lies through a swamp and is terrible. Col. Miller suffers severely and I almost regret having started with him."

April 12th. We did not get to sleep more than an hour this morning. Dr. Cole says: "We moved at daylight this morning, crossing the Pintetella and Catoma Creeks, and camped within three miles of Montgomery." We traveled steadily all day over miserable and swampy roads. The country is very level and tolerably rich. We saw over 100 large houses full of cotton and all "a-fire." We are certain we burned 10,000 bales to-day. About noon we got the word that the rebels had evacuated Montgomery and surrendered the city without a fight. This gratifying intelligence seemed a little strange to us, that they should give up the first capital of the Southern confederacy without at least a show of spunk. Here is where the first confederate congress met and swore they would be free and independent of the United States, and all along we expected to have a fight to get into the city. We traveled 25 miles for the day, and hundreds of negroes came to us, all anxious to leave "de old plantation," and become soldiers or do anything for the Yankees. They are fearfully ignorant, but it is surprising how well they understand the cause of the war and the meaning of Lincoln's proclamation. At Selma we saw the only native African negro we ever did see. He was somewhat blacker than the natives, head low and flat, but of more intelligence than his looks indicated. He remembered yet, very distinctly, how he was stolen from Africa and brought to this country. He didn't look to be over 50 years of age, but had no idea how old he was. As soon as we go into camp at night the paroling officers go to work, and every morning a lot of prisoners are paroled and turned loose.

April 13th. Rained hard the most of last night, and this morning we awoke to find ourselves lying around promiscuously in puddles of water two to four inches deep. We went foraging and found thousands of bushels of corn, and food of all kinds in greatest abundance. The sun was two hours high when we started, and two miles from camp we came to the defences of the city of Montgomery. These consisted of a series of forts entirely around the city, some of them large ones, well built, and from the nature of the ground easily defended. They were connected by lines of earthworks; but there were no abattis, stockades or ditches, as at Selma. There was a large fort on the road on which we were moving, and two fine pieces of artillery in it, but their wheels had been cut down. Half way from this line of works to the city we passed another very fine brass 12-pounder, the wheels cut down also. It appears that the governor would not let the rebels fight us here, as he had no hope of their making a successful resistance, and was afraid we would burn the town down if we had to fight. We passed through the city very slowly, giving us time to see nearly every thing of note. There was a broad contrast between the way the people treated us here and at Selma. They all appeared to welcome the Yankee raiders, and many pretty girls and women were upon the streets. The rebels on retreating had taken the road east toward Columbus, Ga., and we moved out on the same road, and four miles out passed the 1st division in camp, and seven and a half miles from Montgomery went into camp on a large plantation, our regiment camping in a young orchard and tying our horses to the trees, which was a joke on the trees. The plantation residence was very fine and stately, and all the outbuildings and negro quarters indicated opulence. The negroes seemed very much afraid of their master, and said he would skin them if he knew they should give us anything to eat, but we found no difficulty in getting what we wanted to eat by going around to the kitchen, some of the negroes staying up all night to cook for us. This was near a station on the Atlanta & Montgomery Railroad, called Meigs. After night some members of Company G went to a plantation for something to eat, and found some molasses in a smoke-house. One of the boys, Sergt. Bolen, had no canteen with him, or anything else to get molasses in, and started out to get something. Just outside he found the crock bench; it was quite dark and he was in a hurry, for fear the rest of the boys should get all and he get none, and he jerked up the first crock he came to, filled it and lit out for camp. He and his mess had a fine supper of "flapjacks and 'lasses." After supper they carefully set the remainder away for breakfast. When daylight came the next morning and they went for their molasses they found the vessel to be one that well regulated families usually keep under the bed.

April 14th. As a new feature of the programme, orders were issued that all sick and wounded who could not stand a march of 30 miles a day were to be left; hence Col. Miller, our brave commander, was left behind. Dr. Cole says: "The sick and wounded were left in Montgomery with Dr. Dome, of the 17th, in charge. Col. Miller's wound having become so painful, and threatening gangrene, we left him at Col. Siebold's. Gen. Long is still being taken along." One large steamboat and three steam ferry boats were burned, also several machine shops, a large amount of commissary and quartermaster's stores, and vast piles of cotton—all that could be burned without setting fire to the town. Private property was not molested. There had been so many negroes pressed to follow us, and so many had voluntarily attached themselves to the different commands, that there were nearly as many negroes in each regiment as there were soldiers, and the negro element was likely to become an elephant on our hands. They were so many non-combatants, likely to encumber our movements in case of battle; so to-day we got strict orders that every negro found in the companies should at once be taken and organized into companies, and, together with those previously organized, should be armed and prepared to take care of themselves. This order caused considerable confusion and dissatisfaction in some of the companies, as nearly every company had about four good, faithful negroes, who had been with us a long time. They had always led our pack mules for us and helped about the cooking, and very materially lightened our labors, and we determined not to give them up. The negroes had become very much attached to us, and had been with us long enough to know that their present position suited them much better than soldiering, and they begged us not to let them be taken away. It was amusing to see the stratagems resorted to by us and them to keep them from being taken away from us. Those that were organized into companies were armed with arms taken from the arsenal in Montgomery, in which there were a vast number of Austrian rifles, that had never been unboxed since shipped from England. They were brought from there by blockade runners. The whole corps, except the brigade of first division which left us at Elyton, camped near here last night, and by noon to-day all had gone, going east toward Columbus, and at one o'clock our regiment went directly north to the Atlanta railroad. As soon as we got to the railroad we began immediately to destroy the telegraph, burn the track, and all culverts and bridges. This business was not new to us, and we knew exactly how to go at it, and when night came we had completely destroyed 12 miles of track, burned at least 40 bridges and culverts, and done more damage than the southern confederacy could repair in a month. This was the one weakness of the rebel government. They seemed to have plenty of all kinds of war material, but their means of repairing damaged railroads were very limited. Their greatest difficulty was in procuring the rails. We went into camp on Line Creek, near the Coosa River, on a very large plantation, where we had abundance for man and beast. In addition to the damage done the railroad, we had also burned several station houses and cars, and a vast amount of corn and cotton, and when night came were fearfully tired, having worked about as hard as we ever did, and we felt pretty well satisfied with our havoc. Sergt. Wilhite, Co. E, says of this day's work: "Lieut. Wise was badly hurt by his horse falling through a bridge, but as we could get no conveyance he was obliged to ride his horse and suffered severely. Charles Haines, Nathaniel Hamilton, and John C. Bible, took a scout on their own hook, captured a lot of rebels, who wanted to know what they were going to do with them. Haines dismounted, took their guns and broke them around a tree, and told them to go home and stay there. As the boys rode off the rebels hallooed after them, 'Good bye, boys; that's much better than we expected.' They next ran on to an old army surgeon riding in a carriage, and took from him a sword branded 1777. They next captured a couple of Texas rangers and a bugle, and got into camp without loss." Dr. Cole says: "I burned my medical wagon to-day on account of its breaking down, and so there is not a wagon in the whole brigade." Think of this, ye who soldiered the first year of the war. Capt. Glaze, Co. C, says: "We burned all the bridges and station houses, and pulled down the telegraph for 20 miles. I applied the torch to the last bridge for the night. It was a substantial, fine trestle, over Line Creek, 400 feet long."

April 15th. Moved this morning at sun-up, but as we could not cross Line Creek anywhere near the railroad we had to go south to get on to the road the division and trains were moving on. In doing this we ran into the worst swamp we ever saw men ride through; many of the horses mired down entirely and had to be stripped and pulled out by hand, one of the muddiest jobs we ever had. When we got to the road we found it full of trains, negroes, &c., and also met a lot of paroled prisoners making their way back to Montgomery and Selma. There were 150 of them, that being about the usual number turned loose every morning. After crossing the creek we went immediately back to the railroad and followed it till sundown. During the day we burned numerous culverts, bridges, depots and cars. The bridge across the Cubehachee was 38 bents long. About the middle of the afternoon we sent out foragers from each company, and it began to rain and rained as hard as we ever saw it. This put an end to burning track, making the boards and rails so wet we could not build fires readily, and as we had no time to lose we confined ourselves to burning culverts, bridges, buildings, cotton and corn. Late in the evening we came to a very extensive lumbering establishment, consisting of saw-mills, planing mills, shingle mills and cooper establishment, all of which were working for the rebel government. We set them on fire, and as there were vast piles of shingles and lumber of all kinds, it made a tremendous fire. We had now totally destroyed 40 miles of the road. Here a detail of 100 men from the regiment (30 from Co. I) was made to go up the railroad eight or ten miles further and burn a long bridge across the Cheehaw. Here the regiment left the road and bore off to the right to go to the brigade. It was now getting dark and raining, and proved to be one of the darkest of nights. The Historian's horse fell down with him and mashed his leg in a horrible manner, and for several days he was on the "lift." We bivouacked not far from a station on the railroad called Cheehaw, six miles from Tuskegee, having made 35 miles for the day. Our foragers and detailed men did not get to camp at all. Capt. Glaze says: "To-day's work was a repetition of yesterday's, except that we had to work in the rain. Company C had all the meat and flour it could take care of, and 10 dozen eggs for Easter." Owing to the excessive rain we had to go to bed without coffee, and as we were scarcely ever more tired, we thought this a hard "slam" on the poor soldier.

Sunday, (Easter) April 16th, 1865. There was a great deal of picket firing during the night, and as we were four miles from the main column, and nearly all of our men were out foraging and on detail, we wanted to be ready for any emergency, and were up and saddled by daylight. We found we had slept near a large pitch pine stump, which burns equal to a tar barrel, and in a few minutes had our coffee. Hard-tack had always been the staff of life to us, but coffee was life itself. We moved early, and four miles from camp came out into the main road the column had moved on. We found the column had moved faster than we had, and we came out right in the camp of the negroes, which all the time moves in the rear of the trains. This negro camp "banged" anything in the way of a camp we ever saw or ever expect to see. They were just getting ready to move. There were negro men, women and children, on horse-back, ass-back, mule-back, cow-back; in carts, wagons, wheel-barrows, and every other way you could think. They seemed to have plenty to eat, and were perfectly happy, thinking, no doubt, that the "year of jubilo" had come. Two miles further on we came to a large town called Tuskeegee, the county seat of Macon County, a most beautiful place, containing a court-house, a college, several churches, and some of the finest evergreens and gardens we ever saw. Two miles further on we came to where our brigade had camped, and our foragers and detailed men caught up with us. We also met another batch of paroled prisoners. About the middle of the afternoon we stopped to feed at a place called Sida-hill, (marked on the map Society Mill.) While we were eating our dinner the whole train moved past us, which shows that everything is being kept carefully closed up. We moved on steadily again till 10 o'clock at night, passing through a town called Crawford, and went into camp 10 miles from Columbus, Ga., making 40 miles for the day, the farthest we had traveled any day yet. Dr. Cole says: "At 5 a. m. we were again in motion. The 2d brigade, of the 1st division, under command of Gen. McCook, moved out along the railroad toward West Point, while the 4th division in the advance, and 2d division next, moved on Columbus. By the kindness of Col. Vail I obtained a company from the 123d Illinois to accompany me on a scout over the country. Went in the direction of Auburn, on the West Point Railroad, and returned to the Columbus road in the evening and joined the command at midnight, just as it went into camp, near Crawford. We captured 40 horses and mules."

April 17. Our trains all closed up on to us last night, and this morning the left wing of the regiment fell in behind them as train guard. The right wing moved early, but instead of taking the direct road to Columbus, took a road leading south and to the right of it, which made the distance 15 miles, instead of 10 by the direct road. We had not gone far till we heard heavy and continued firing east of us. The 1st and 4th divisions had been ahead of us ever since we left Selma, and we, supposing they were having a hard fight at Columbus, hurried forward. In the course of an hour we got the word that our forces had captured the place last night at 11 p. m., and we felt relieved. The heavy artillery firing still continued, and we supposed there must be some mistake, and hurried on again. Pretty soon we could see vast volumes of smoke, black and sulphurous, rising a thousand feet into the air, and we were sure there was a terrible battle raging. By 10 o'clock we were close enough to the city to see that the smoke was not the smoke of battle, but was from burning forts, arsenals, machine shops, steamboats, locomotives, cars, cotton, commissary stores, &c. Columbus is a fine city on the east side of the Chattahoochee river, and on the west side is a station on the railroad called Girard. These two places were connected by three fine covered bridges, two of which the rebels burned yesterday, thinking they could defend one better than they could three. Extensive preparatoins had been made to give the Yanks a warm reception. The remaining bridge had been thoroughly stuffed with cotton, well saturated with turpentine, and a bristling piece of artillery planted in the eastern end ready to blow to atoms any thoughtless Yankee who should set his foot upon it. There were some forts west of the river well filled with artillery and well manned with rebel soldiers, and this bridge was left for them to retreat upon, should they, by any possible chance or misfortune, be driven out of them. Lucky provision! Last night our forces arrived in front of the place about 9 o'clock, formed their lines so quietly that the rebels knew nothing of it until our men began to charge, and as our men paid no attention to the forts, charging right on past them, made a grand rush for the bridge and got there as soon as the rebels did; and charged right on through it with them, capturing the piece of artillery, turning it upon the flying rebels before those in the city were aware of the presence of the hated Yankees. This we regard as one of the best executed movements of the war. The capture of Selma and Montgomery were big things, but in some respects this was bigger, as many things had been moved from those two places to this, only to be overtaken and captured at last. There was so much war material captured that no complete inventory was ever taken of it. Among the trophies were two gun-boats, five steamboats, 15 locomotives, and 250 cars, 52 field-guns mounted and in position, the rebel ram Jackson, mounting six seven-inch guns, four cotton factories, and 115,000 bales of cotton, the navy yard, foundry, armory, sword and pistol factory, accoutrement shops, three paper mills, 100,000 rounds of artillery ammunition, and 1,200 prisoners. The truth is, we already had so many prisoners on our hands that no effort had been made for several days to capture more. Many more might have been captured here but for this very reason.

The rebels had used a great deal of wood in the construction of the forts west of the river, and these had been set on fire. There were arsenals and powder houses connected with the forts, and by the time we got to the bridge this morning the shells were bursting and throwing the fire and dirt a hundred feet high, making the place a thousand times more noisy than pleasant or safe. Columbus, like Selma, seemed to be full of all kinds of ammunition, shells, &c., and as everything had been set on fire that had any rebel property in it, the explosions were constant and almost deafening. We crossed over the bridge and saw the piece of artillery still standing just as our men had fired it at the retreating rebels. We stopped in town long enough to give officers and men time to look over the city. Dr. Cole says: "We reached the city at 10 a. m. and witnessed the burning of the gun-boats, the rolling mills, powder mills, arsenals, manufactories, iron foundries, and government supplies. The *poor* citizens were allowed to carry off all the provisions they desired. The 4th division, to which belongs the honor of capturing Columbus, lost 25 men killed and wounded; 1,500 prisoners were captured, 100 pieces of artillery, and a vast number of small arms, which were distributed among the contraband command, which now numbered over 3,000. We crossed the river and moved through the city to the tune of 'Hail Columbia.' We had given Columbus hail, and the tune was appropriate, but somewhat ironical. We went into camp three miles east of the city. Our sick and wounded were all left in hospital at Columbus. There had been quick work made of this job. In less than 24 hours from the time our men had appeared in front of the place, our whole army, trains, niggers and all, like a besom of destruction, had swept through one of the fairest cities of the South, and left but little of it, and nothing in it, that would be of any benefit to the rebel cause.

Again we said, "*Business.*"

It was about 3 p. m. when we camped, and the Historian was sent back to the city in charge of a detail from the regiment to get rations. After we got there we could find neither bread nor flour; all had been carried off by the citizens except a vast pile of meal in sacks. We loaded up with this and started for camp just at sundown. The southern chivalry are noted for their hospitality and good cheer, and every cellar of any magnitude is generally well stocked with every variety of wines, apple-jack, brandy, and tangle-foot whisky. The boys of our detail managed to find a lot of this stuff, and many laughable and ridiculous incidents occurred on our way back to camp. As so many of the comrades have given incidents of this trip, we shall only give space for two of them. John C. Bible, Co. E, says: "We had just sat down to a good supper of slapjacks and molasses, ham and eggs, when McGraw, who rode a little bit of a sorrel mule, came galloping up the line inquiring for mess No. 5. He had a sack of flour before him and couple of hams strapped to each side of his saddle, and a wooden bucket of pinetop whisky in his hand, and some whisky that wasn't in the bucket. As McGraw sighted the mess seated around the camp fire eating supper, he came for us on the jump. His mule sailed clear over the head of one of the boys and set both hind feet into his tin plate of cakes and molasses. The fellow looked up and said, 'McGraw, I wish you would keep your mule out of my dish,' and went ahead with his supper as though nothing had happened." Sergt. Samuel Johnson, Co. D, says: "One of the boys had secured a dozen "cognac," and as he was making his way to camp we approached him to sell or trade a part of his stock. We made every reasonable overture we could think of, and still he refused. We fell back to the rear and let him get some hundred yards ahead of us; we then gathered all the empty canteens in the crowd that had no covers on, and fixed them so as to rattle and make all the noise we could, fired a few shots, and charged down upon the fellow with the wine. The mule he was riding thought its time was about up and stampeded in a twinkling. The fellow tucked his head down behind the mule's neck, supposing the Johnnys were after him, dropped the box and skinned out for camp. We marched all night, and this medicine, which had been secured at a drug store, was a wonderful help in keeping us awake." Our detail got back to camp just at dark, and expected to stay over night at least, but were not done eating our supper when the bugle blowed "boots and saddles." We thought this was hurrying the thing a little. We moved steadily the whole night in the direction of Macon without ever stopping, and about an hour by sun on the morning of April 18th, stopped to feed at Singleton's plantation, 22 miles from Columbus. After stopping about an hour, we moved on steadily all day, and saw abundant evidence of the rebels' hasty retreat from Columbus. They had left along the road three pieces of artillery, numerous wagons, ambulances, &c. During the day we passed 400 rebels scattered through the woods, off to our left, and could easily have captured them, but we paid no attention to them, as we already had more prisoners than we wanted to be bothered with. Besides, all we cared for now was to scatter them and get them in our rear, where we were sure they would bother us no more. During the day hundreds of horses and mules were captured, and the boys began to exchange their jaded horses for fresh ones. We passed through two little villages, Belleview and Pleasant Hill, crossed Flint river, and went into camp 50 miles from Columbus, making a march of 65 miles without sleep or rest. Dr. Cole says: "By continued and rapid marching we reached Flint river at 12 m., just in time to prevent the enemy's guard from burning the bridge. We captured the bridge guard, consisting of several officers and 45 men; one, whose wound I dressed, says that the report of the surrender of Lee's entire army to Gen. Grant was current in Macon when he left there yesterday. A large body of rebel troops are fleeing before us from Columbus. Our camp to-night is 62 miles from Macon."

April 19th. Captain Glaze says: "My company were on picket last night, and took advantage of being in advance to send out a detachment, under command of Lieut. Geiger, to gather in what horses could be found. He fought all the straggling bands he met, capturing and wounding quite a large number, and brought in 40 horses and mules." The sun was two hours high when we got started; we were so stiff, and sore, and used up generally, that it was hard starting. We moved four miles and came to Big Potato creek. Here we had trouble. There was a dam across the stream, and our bridge was right on top of the dam, and just below the dam was quite an extensive cotton factory which had been prematurelv fired. Its close proximity to the bridge, and very intense heat, came near burning the Historian and several others to death. It was with the utmost difficulty that we saved the bridge by wetting our blankets and dog-tents in the creek and covering it with them. This stopped the column for several hours. Four miles further on we came to a village of considerable importance called Thomaston, the county seat of Upson county. Here two rebels were killed, a locomotive and train of cars captured, with quite a lot of commissary stores. Co. I was detailed as provost guard. Our business was to guard the commissary stores and issue them to the men as they passed through, and not to let any of them take more than their share; as it too frequently occurred that when a soldier found what he wanted, he would take what he could conveniently carry, and set fire to the rest, regardless of the wants of the balance of the command in the rear. This mania for burning had grown very rapidly. Our further business was to keep the column moving, and not let the men scatter over town. It was 10 a. m. when we stopped, and the whole column did not get through till sundown, when we were relieved and went into camp four miles further on.

Just before noon a locomotive came into the place direct from Macon, and all unconscious of the presence of the pestiferous Yankees. We very quietly "took it in out of the wet." It had on board the mail and the morning papers from Macon. This was a treat for us; we had been so long away from God's country, and the civilizing influences of the U. S. Mail, that we devoured the news with the eagerness of hungry wolves; albeit the mail sack was marked C. S., instead of U. S. Among the items of peculiar interest to us was the announcement that Lee, (the commander of the confederate army at Richmond) had actually surrendered to Gen. Grant, and furthermore that Gen. Wilson had captured Columbus and had started eastward toward Macon, and in all probability would reach Thomaston by day after to-morrow, and unless he was checked and harassed by all the means at the command of the Southern confederacy, in all probability would reach Macon in three days more. Oh! but this was good reading for us, as we were now already at Thomaston two days ahead of time, according to the rebel calculation; and according to the same calculation we knew we could get to Macon at least three days ahead of time, which was very encouraging. We got to camp soon after night and had orders to move at half past 3 in the morning. We had made but 12 miles for the day, but the trains, niggers and all, were closed jam up, and all our troops camped "snug" and ready for a fight. Thomaston is due north-east of Columbus and right west of Macon.

April 20th. Moved this morning long before daylight, our regiment in advance of the whole army, which means business. Our brigade has not been in the advance since we left Selma. We moved rapidly till 9 o'clock, when we stopped and had orders to feed and curry our horses as well as we could. These were extra orders, and assured us some extra work was before us. We had made 20 miles. We only rested three-quarters of an hour and then moved on again. Scouting and foraging parties were sent out on all the roads leading in the direction of Macon, Lieut. Clark, in command of the brigade scouts, taking a road several miles to the south of the one the column moved on. As we moved forward this time the 17th Indiana took the advance and our regiment next. Skirmishing soon began in front, but without halting a moment we pushed on rapidly. Just after noon we came to where the road was barricaded. Here some prisoners were captured, from whom we learned that at Montpelier, four miles ahead of us, there was a force of 400 rebels. These we proposed to capture, thinking we would have that many less to fight at Macon. So our regiment was sent on a circuitous route to the south in order to get in the rear of Montpelier. We made a circuit of full 10 miles, most of the time on the keen run, while the column moved steadily forward on the direct road. The country was open and well cultivated, and aside from many deep and miry ditches we had to cross, we got along very fast, not being more than an hour and a half making the 10 miles, but we had been too slow, as we came out into the road right in the center of our brigade, which had moved rapidly forward, and the rebels had evacuated on its approach and had tried to make a stand at a large stream called Echaconee Creek; but a battalion of the 17th made a sabre charge and drove them from the creek, but not till they had set the bridge, a very long one, on fire. The fire was well under way when our boys reached the bridge, and they only saved it by wetting their blankets and slapping them against the bridge. Had we been 10 minutes later the result must have been very disastrous to us, as we could not have crossed the creek without a bridge, and we felt just now that time was everything to us. This was 13 miles from Macon, and it was now 3 p. m. The column never halted at all, and we pushed on after the 17th. A mile from the bridge the advance was met by a real live brigadier, Gen. Anderson, bearing a flag of truce and a dispatch for Gen. Wilson. The General stated that since Lee had surrendered there had been an armistice declared between Gen. Johnston and Gen. Sherman, and that there would be no further fighting, and that we should *halt our forces till the matter was settled.* The latter part of his speech upset the whole arrangement. Lieut.-Col. White, in command of the advance, proposed to halt his forces whenever he got ready. At any rate he did not propose to obey rebel orders, so he took the dispatch, sent it back to Gen Wilson, then several miles in the rear, and gave Mr. Gen. Anderson five minutes to get out of the way. At the end of five minutes the 17th lit out again and our regiment at their heels, running over Gen. Anderson's body guard before they got half way to Macon. Eight miles from the city Gen. Wilson passed us on the full gallop, and we soon got word that the 17th had got into the city and wanted help to take care of the prisoners

We spurred our horses to their utmost speed, and for several miles kept up with the general in chief, but having no load to carry, as we had, he finally outwinded us; but we never stopped till we got into the city. It was getting dark when we got inside the works, having made a march of 55 miles inside of 16 hours, the last 13 of which had been made on a keen run. The 17th had stopped at the main line of works and busied themselves in taking prisoners, and had not gone into the city at all. The rebels had not made any show of resistance, declaring there was an armistice, and would not fight. There were at least a thousand rebels on each side of the road, behind good substantial works, guns in hand, and ready to blow our brains out. Of course the 17th would not dare to go any further and leave this force in their rear. They found it slow work taking the prisoners, as the Johnnies still stood in their places behind the works, and when ordered to throw down their guns, would one at a time, as they were ordered, stand their guns up against the works in proper shape to be speedily taken up again, and then march out, while all those not very near our men would still stand their ground and hold on to their guns. This made slow work for the 17th; but by the time we got inside the works they had collected all the rebs on either side of the road for a distance, we suppose, of a hundred yards, making about 2,000 prisoners, all bunched up, a strong guard around them, and more being brought in every minute. When the general in chief got in he also halted with the 17th and waited till our regiment got in. Then five of our men charged down into the city, Gen. Wilson right after them, and our whole regiment right at his heels. It was quite dark, and we could not tell where we were going to, or what danger we were in; but on we went till near the heart of the city, where we halted, and for three hours waited in a great deal of suspense. We knew nothing of the number and disposition of the rebels in and about the city, but were bound to suppose that there were at least 7,000 to 10,000 troops inside the works, and we knew that our regiment and the 17th were all the Union troops that were inside the works, and that it would be at least two hours before the other two regiments of our brigade could get in, and in all probability Minty's brigade could not get in before morning; and the other two divisions would scarcely get within 25 miles of the city to-night. and so far as any help they could give us in case we should get into a fight was concerned, they might as well be a hundred miles off. Under such circumstances a man can do a great deal of thinking in a short time.

Of course the prisoners told us there was an armistice extending to all the armies; but we had not yet got the idea into our heads just how there could be an armistice with traitors. All we knew about this was just what the rebels had told us, and we further knew that Gen. Wilson had no means of communicating with his superior officers, and how was he to tell but what the whole thing was a grand scheme to trap him and his whole army. It is hard telling just what we did think in those three hours. But one thing we noticed, the men all kept their places remarkably well, when upon ordinary occasions they would have been in every house in town inside of half an hour. It may be proper here to state that during the last two months nearly all the soldiers of the confederate government had been concentrated into two grand armies, one with Lee, at Richmond, and the other with Johnston, at Raleigh, North Carolina. We had heard that Lee had surrendered; this left only Johnston's command that amounted to an army, with 15,000 irregular troops at Montgomery, Columbus and Macon. We had no means of *knowing* the truth of all this, as since we left the Tennessee River all the news we got came through rebel sources, and it might be true, or it might be false; but we were bound to suppose it was false. So we still kept our places and waited. At the end of three hours orders were sent to the 17th to let their prisoners go, and our regiment was ordered to go back and go into camp just inside of the works. We went back and went to bed without knowing whether we really had captured the city, or whether we might not have to fight for it in the morning. It turned out that on the 18th Gen. Johnston, commander of the rebel army near Raleigh, had agreed with Gen. Sherman on an armistice, looking to the termination of the war, and the rebels in Macon had got the word from Johnston himself, who, since Lee's surrender, was now commander in chief, and of course they were bound to obey it; while we could get no such word from Sherman, and were not bound to believe a word of it. A well rested man of ordinary intelligence would scarcely sleep much under such circumstances.

April 21st. It was so dark, and we were so nearly used up, and it was so late, (nearly 12 o'clock), that we just tumbled off our horses and went to sleep without building fires or getting supper. We didn't even know where we were or if anybody was near us. It was sun-up before any of us awoke, and it made us open our eyes wide to see within a few rods of us a heavy line of earthworks and a row of muskets leaned against them, loaded and primed for use, and not 10 rods south of us a very large, well built fort, full of artillery, already loaded with grape and cannister. Some of the pieces in the fort were large siege guns, and as fine ones as we had ever seen, while all along the field works were smaller pieces of artillery, and all loaded, too. It made us feel very glad to think we did not have to face all these in the hands of the Johnnys, especially if they were veteran soldiers and determined to keep us out. We were filled with awe and astonishment at the preparations made to receive us. We did not unsaddle last night, but after we were up a while, and began to look around and had seen something of what the possibilities might have been had we been obliged to fight to get in here, and had fully realized that there might be danger yet, we got orders to unsaddle and feed, which relieved us wonderfully.

We now set to work to get breakfast, and in doing this set out in various directions to get water. We were fully a half mile from the city. Some of our men struck out in a north-east direction, and came to the houses on the west side, not far from where the road from Atlanta enters the main works. The first man to find water we think belonged to Co. G, of our regiment, and when he went to the well, who should he find there but "Johnny," who had come for water also. "Johnny" looked at him a moment in amazement. Our entry into the city on the Columbus road had been so quiet, the night before, that none of the rebel army except what were defending that road knew a thing of it, and "Johnny" was thunderstruck to see a real live Yankee walk up to him, camp kettle in hand, and so unconcerned, too, that he could not believe his senses, and roared out, "Who are you?" Yank paid but little attention to him, but went up to get his water. Neither of them had their guns, but Johnny thought that he had the right of possession, at least, and roared out, "What are you doing here?" "None of your business," says Yank. "You are my prisoner," says Johnny. "Not much," says Yank. "I'll show you," says Johnny, and he started for camp to get his gun. The rebel camp on the Atlanta road was a full half mile from where we slept, and they were entirely ignorant of our presence. As Johnny started out for the gate for his gun, he saw a string of blue coats reaching clear back to our camp. We were all marching up, camp kettles in hand, for water. We met him at the gate, and as he stopped for a moment in utter bewilderment, he exclaimed, "Well, I'll be gosh danged!" He was frightened nearly to death, and broke for his camp as fast as his legs conld carry him, to spread the alarm and to tell his comrades the Yankees had "dun got in, for a fact." This was the first intimation that the rebels on that road had of our presence, and we could not help wondering at the strange spectacle of two hostile armies camped inside the same city—indeed right among each other—and not a fight during the whole day. It was hard to tell which side held the town, for all around the works, except just on the road we came in on, the rebels occupied and picketed all the roads just as they had done before our arrival. We think scarcely a man in our regiment had made up his mind just how things would be when the war should come to an end, but from frequent conversation with the men afterward, we can safely say that scarcely one man in ten had thought of the war coming to an end any other way than for us to just keep on fighting till all the rebels were whipped, or had laid down their arms. In short, we should just keep on fighting till there were no more rebels to fight. But here were at least 5,000 rebels, all with arms in their hands, and many of them still seemed anxious to use them, too, and yet we were right there among them, listening to their curses against the Union and the dear old flag, and their threats, and still were making no effort to crush them. This was a little too much for the good nature of our soldiers, and they began to curse the armistice and damn the rebels. They said there was no needof an armistice. If the rebels were whipped, why did they not lay down their arms. If they were not whipped the best thing we could do would be to go to work and whip them, and the sooner we got at it the better. We were satisfied that nothing but thorough subjugation would answer the purpose. To think of enduring what we had borne for any result short of this, was adding insult to injury, as we verily believed the work, some day, would all have to be done over. About 9 or 10 o'clock companies C, H, E, and K, of our regiment, were detailed for provost guards in the city, and we were made acquainted with the conditions of the armistice. General Howell Cobb was commander of all the forces in this vicinity, and last night he was surprised and wonderfully indignant when General Wilson popped into his headquarters. He did not know there was a Yankee within 20 miles of him, and when he saw Wilson he railed on him terribly, telling him it was not only cowardly but mean to disregard his flag of truce, and pay no attention to the armistice, and took occasion to remark that if it had not been for his perfidy he never could have got into the city. General Wilson simply remarked that if Gen. Cobb was not satisfied with the manner in which he had got into the city, he was prepared to get into it in any manner the General might suggest, and that he already had two regiments inside his works, and two more divisions close at hand, and felt disposed to accommodate him to anything he might wish. When Mr. Cobb found there were already two regiments inside his works, he concluded to make the best terms he could, and these were the terms:

Cobb was to surrender the city and all the troops in it, and also all the munitions of war, with the understanding that everything was to be left just as it was until the truth of the armistice, and also of its results, should be known. Of course Wilson could afford to do this, as he already had two regiments inside the works, and would have a whole division at hand by the time these arrangements were agreed to. There were 17 general officers, including the notorious Robert Toombs, who had declared in the United States Senate that he would some day call the roll of his slaves under Bunker Hill Monument, and 5,000 troops, included in this agreement, and we think this number was in addition to the 2,000 we captured last night, as we already had their arms in our possession. During the night Toombs made his escape. So you see how nicely everything had worked for us, as these 7,000 veteran troops could have slaughtered us terribly had we been compelled to fight them.

As before intimated, it was midnight last night before all our brigade got up, and the 98th and 123d Illinois went into camp just outside the works, while Minty's brigade, of our division, went into camp just at daylight, on the Tobesofkee Creek, three miles back. Lieut. Clark, Company I, in command of the brigade scouts, says:

"On the night before reaching Macon, when five miles south of the main column, at about 10 o'clock at night, we were met by a flag of truce under Col. Leon Von Zinkin. We regarded it as a ruse and played ourselves off as Gen. Upton's command, by which title the boys addressed me. As we had a vast number of lead horses, and the night was quite dark, the ruse was successful. We gave them five minutes to get out of our road, and told them we were going to march right into Macon. When they were well out of our way we started for the command, which we reached some time after daylight."

The capture of Macon, in some respects, equals all the rest of our achievements put together. Some of the most splendid artillery we have yet seen, and such a vast amount of it, too, (60 pieces) all mounted and in the very best fix; and ammunition enough to supply all the armies in the confederate states. This had been hauled out of the arsenals in great loads and piled on the ground beside the guns. We had never seen so much artillery ammunition in all our lives as we saw to-day. Some of the siege guns in the forts were 64-pounders, and it required a gallon of powder for each load. This powder was tied up in flannel sacks, and upon examining them we found the grains of powder to be as large as hulled walnuts, and although we comprehended the reason for this in a minute, we confess we had never thought of it before. A 64-pound gun would throw a conical shell weighing at least 120 pounds, and this vast weight on starting from the gun would start very slowly. Now a gallon of musket powder behind one of these large shells would explode almost instantly, and burst the gun before starting the ball. Coarser grained powder would ignite and explode slowly, and start the ball with less force.

The works around the city are about 12 or 15 miles long, and of very substantial character, though in our judgment some of the field works were badly constructed, the ditches being on the inside instead of the outside, and we believe we could have just charged right over them on horseback. Everything is quiet in the city, and the city government goes on as it used to. There is a paper printed here, and once more we get to read the news, if it is rebel news. This is quite a treat to us; we have been without news so long that we don't know anything that has taken place since we left the Tennessee River. About noon the other two divisions began to come up, and were put into camp on the north east and north-west of the city, just outside of the works.

About the middle of the afternoon all the rebel soldiers around the city marched down into the city, and stacked their arms and surrendered in a body, our brigade and division occupying the same position it did this morning. Our train is coming in, but will not all be up before to-morrow night. Last night Gen. Wilson tried to get a dispatch in cipher through to Gen. Sherman, asking for instructions. It seems the dispatch got through all right, but it had to pass through rebel hands both ways, and he could not get a satisfactory answer, which confused him very much. Late in the afternoon we were ordered to saddle up, but had only begun to move when we were ordered back into camp again. The day wore away and finally died without us knowing anything certain about the armistice, or the result of our occupation of the city. It had been a day of suspense to us, and to relieve the monotony the boys finally got to setting fire to the piles of ammunition for amusement. This made things lively for a few minutes, as the bursting shells sent the old iron flying in every direction, and the burning powder sent up volumes of smoke, and you would have thought a volcano had broken loose. A little nigger belonging to one of the companies lay down and went to sleep; some of the boys took the sacks of powder and poured a ring around him about 10 feet in diameter and set fire to it. The nigger started on the short cut to glory, but after going up about 15 feet came down again, lighting on his feet, and started to run as if Satan were after him. This was more fun than the boys had seen in many a day, but Colonel Thomson thought it cruel, and placed the boys under arrest. Our men went to bed in a very doubtful mood. The discussion ran high at times in regard to the propriety of the whole proceeding, some of the men swearing they would like to see just one more bonfire.

April 22d. One month ago to-day we left Chickasaw landing, on the Tennessee river. Since then the mighty rush of events has left little time to note down, much less to realize and digest, all that has transpired. Since then we had marched 570 miles, fought two hard battles, captured five large and well fortified cities, and done a thousand other things to break up the rebellion. Ten days ago (on the 12th,) we got the news of the surrender of Lee's army, and to-day comes the word that Johnston's army has been surrendered, and yet our men regard all this with the most stoical indifference. One reason for this is that all the news we get comes from the rebels, and the men say "it will not do to tie to." Another is that this army, almost to a man, swears that the rebels have not been half whipped, and in proof of this point to the fact that the citizens are chafing at our occupation of the city, and swearing we have no right to be here, and that we have violated the armistice or we could never have gotten inside the city. This grinds our men almost beyond endurance, and threats of burning "the d—d secesh hole" are very frequent. These remarks apply mostly to the stay-at-home citizens, who bitterly curse the leaders of the rebellion, and the soldiers, for not holding out longer. Nine-tenths of the privates in the rebel army are heartily glad to lay down their arms. About 8 o'clock we saddled up and our whole division began to move. The weather is very warm. Our division went into camp just on the outside of the works, two miles south of the city. It was the middle of the afternoon before we got into camp. The news we get about the armistice is still conflicting, and there are a thousand wild rumors still flying; but there is now very little doubt that the dawn of peace is fast approaching. Some soldiers to-day, prospecting in the grave-yard, dug up four pieces of rifled brass howitzers. Late in the evening the following order was read to us, which proved to be the end of the war, but the very next day came very near upsetting this order and tried our patience wonderfully:

GENERAL WILSON'S ORDER ANNOUNCING ARMISTICE.

HEADQUARTERS CAVALRY CORPS, M. D. M.,
Macon, Ga., April 22d, 1865.

Special Field Order No. 22.

It is hereby announced to the Cavalry Corps of the Military Division of the Mississippi that an armistice has been agreed to between Lieut. Gen. J. E. Johnston and Major Gen. W. T. Sherman, with a view to final peace. The troops of the Cavalry Corps are ordered to refrain from further acts of hostility and depredations. Supplies of all kinds are to be contracted for, and foraging upon the country will be discontinued. The officers of the Cavalry Corps will enforce the strictest discipline in their commands. Guards will be established, private and public property respected, and everything done to secure good order.

The Brevet Maj. Gen. Commanding again takes great pleasure in commending the officers and men of the Corps for their gallantry, steadiness, and endurance in battle, and during the arduous marches to this place. He enjoins them to remember that the people in whose midst they are now stationed are their countrymen, and should be treated with magnanimity and forbearance, in the hope that although the war which has just ended has been long and bloody, it may secure a lasting and happy peace to our beloved country.

By command of BREVET MAJOR-GEN. WILSON.

E. B. BEAUMONT, Major and A. A. G.

Sunday, April 23d, 1865. This Sabbath morning we hasten to thank Almighty God for the preservation of our life and the signs of returning peace. Shortly after breakfast we got the word that President Lincoln had been assassinated. Oh, what a terrible national calamity is this! Can it be that this nation has not yet suffered enough? O, God! can this be the precursor of more war and bloodshed? How this fills us with gloom and strange forebodings. But, oh, Lord, may Thy will be accomplished and peace speedily proclaimed!

This terrible news fell upon us like a thunderbolt, and so stupefied us that we could find no words to express our feelings. Strong men sat dumbfounded, and grief was depicted in every countenance. Could it be possible that this great and good man had been killed? And for what? For two or three days we could scarcely bring ourselves to discuss the subject. We had always called him "Father Abraham," and he had always been a father to us. Who should supply his place? It seemed to us the light of the Nation had gone out. Dr. Cole says: "Several fires have broken out to-day, and last night two squares were burned. Intelligence received to-day *via* Chattanooga and Atlanta of the assassination of President Lincoln. The feelings of this Cavalry Corps are highly wrought upon by this news, and if this should prove true it will be hard to restrain the vengeance of the command." We had inspection to-day and more than usual pains taken to ascertain the exact number of our cartridges and our exact fighting trim. This was our first inspection since leaving Gravelly Springs, and it proved to be the last one we ever had. We went through it with a great deal less complaining than usual, because we realized that, under the circumstances, it was proper and right, feeling that the future was still dark. Dr. Cole says: "Gen. Long, who had been hauled through with us in a carriage, started home to-day, and I took occasion to send some letters home, and also a dispatch to Col. Miller's wife, informing her of his condition. General Croxton's brigade, of the 1st division, which left us at Elyton for Tuscaloosa, Ala., has not been heard from since." Sergeant Remley says: "On provost duty in the city. It requires the utmost vigilance to keep the city from being burned; several fires have already occurred in different parts of the city, and would have destroyed the town had it not been for the soldiers."

CHAPTER XXXIX.

From April 24th to May 22d, 1865.—Repairing Railroads—We Regard the Rumors of Peace with Stoicism—We Still Want to Forage—A Taste of Rebel Corn Bread—We Move From Camp—The Whole Army Searched for Stolen Specie—None Found in the Seventy-Second, or the Lightning Brigade—We March Back to the Same Camp—A Visit to a Plantation, Its Almost Naked Negroes, Some with Small-Pox—Official Information of the Surrender of Gen. Johnston—Rebel Property Turned Over to Union Quartermasters—Rebel Sentiments of Citizens of Macon—Soldiers Still Want to Burn the Town—Almost Out of Coffee—Going to Andersonville to Release Union Prisoners—Sergt. Johnson's Description of the Place—Dead Line, Vermin, Stocks, and Other Instruments of Torture—Talk with Rebel Soldiers who are Glad the War is Over—They Say it has been a Rich Man's War and a Poor Man's Fight—200 Guns Salute in Honor of Victory—Raising a Liberty Pole—Jeff. Davis Heading this way—We Start After Him—Apple Jack Makes Us Too Late—We Almost Get Him, But He Slips Us—Detail of Our Adventures, and Davis' Capture—Lieut. Martin's Story About "Rebel President"—Our Regiment Scattered—We Dig Up Boxes We Suppose to be Full of Gold and Silver, and Lo! they Contain Confederate Bonds and Money, and the Archives of Tennessee—Cory's Story of an Overseer being Whipped Because He Whipped a Mulatto Girl for Trying to Secure Her Freedom—Hard-Tack Once More—Our Mail Comes Up Again—Orders to Get Ready to Go Home—Some Hail the Order with Joy, and Others would Rather Stay—How We Felt and How We Talked About Peace, and Making a Living—Orders Relieving Us From Further Duty—Recapitulation—Comparison of Wilson's March with Sherman's March to the Sea.

April 24th. Our brigade, regimental and company blacksmiths, have taken possession of some shops, and all hands are busy shoeing up ready for a move, or any emergency. A large force of negroes were pressed in to repair the Savannah Railroad, that point being the nearest to any of our own lines or friends. There is a daily paper published in this place, called the Evening *News*, which we read very carefully to see if we can tell anything about what is going on in God's country, the North, but the paper gives forth no "certain sounds," and we are left to conjecture and suspense. We know nothing yet as to the certainty of Johnston's surrender. The rebel citizens here are still in hopes it is not so, and announce in the paper that an officer is on his way from Gen. Joe. Johnston to consult with Gen. Wilson as to the legality of our occupation of the city. Very many of the boys say they hope they will decide it is not legal. They think Macon would make a splendid bonfire, and we think it would burn, too, unless we are permitted to leave the place peaceably just when we get ready.

April 25th. Heavy trains sent out in the country for forage, of which there is an abundance in the country. The intelligence of the assassination of President Lincoln, and the surrender of Lee's army, was officially confirmed, and numbers of soldiers of Lee's army have already made their appearance. The country seems to be full of them; the officers still retain their side arms.

We moved camp to-day nearly four miles south-west of the city, in order to get plenty of water and a more healthy location. Weather getting hot; woods in full leaf, peaches are as large as hulled walnuts, corn knee high and wheat all out in head. We camped on a most beautiful ridge covered with very large pine trees of the long leaved species, and scant undergrowth. It is a most delightfully cool place, water running on both sides of us. We here note the very stoical indifference with which the men treat the many rumors of returning peace. With scarcely a single exception this army thinks the rebels just lacked one fight of getting whipped as badly as they should be before we have a permanent. peace. We are still kept in the very best fighting trim, and picket all the roads, and everything just goes on as though we were on a regular campaign, except we are not allowed to molest anything or to supply our wants from the country. This we think is all wrong. We cannot yet bring ourselves to see the necessity for a truce with rebels.

April 26th. Settled down to camp life again. It is proper here to say that, on the 18th, Gen. Johnston and Gen. Sherman did agree upon an armistice, and terms of surrender for all the armies east of the Mississippi; but Gen. Sherman had to send these conditions from Raleigh, N. C., to Washington, D. C., to have them approved. It took five days for them to go there and come back, and when they finally did come back they were disapproved, and Sherman ordered to resume hostilities, and if possible to get word through to Gen. Wilson to do the same thing. Of course the rebels knew all about this, but did everything they could to keep Gen. Wilson from finding it out. As Savannah, 180 miles from us, was the nearest point from which we could possibly get any reliable information, Gen. Wilson was placed under peculiar circumstances. From the fact that the rebels ceased to fight us he was bound to believe there was some truth in the armistice, but what were its exact terms, when it ceased, or whether Gen. Johnston really had surrendered, he knew nothing certain. Hence he kept his command in good fighting trim. Finally Wilson sent a staff officer, under escort, clear through to Savannah, on purpose to learn the truth. We now began to realize something of what "Johnny's" corn bread was. Since we came to this place we have not been allowed to forage, and all we get is corn meal from the rebel commissary, ground very coarsely, and we have no means of removing the bran, and nothing to mix it with but water and salt, and naturally dyspeptic as we are, we thought this would literally burn us up.

April 28th. Reveille this morning at half past 2 o'clock and ordered to get ready to march immediately. A little strange we had heard nothing of it before. Nobody knew where we were going; but rumor said back to Montgomery. We had breakfast at daylight and at sun-up the bugle blew strike tents. We had just got our bunks well up and our quarters cleaned nicely, and it worried us much to leave them. After the usual amount of fussing and cussing, we moved out about 9 a. m. Went back on the Columbus road three miles west of the city to the Tobesofkee creek, and found all our trains parked in a small field awaiting us. We turned off the road and massed in the little field in column by companies, and the first thing we knew there was a chain guard clear around the field, and we heard the command, "Stand to your horses," and were forbidden to stir. The teamsters were all placed under guard. This made the stragglers and pillagers open their eyes, and the rogues and thieves to swear. It was the sharpest thing we ever saw done. To think that an army of 13,000 men could be taken so completely by surprise, and not a single private soldier know a thing of it. Thus far everything had worked to a "T" and we give our officers credit for doing the sharpest thing ever undertaken. It now turned out that during the recent fires in the city some rogues had taken advantage of them and had broken open the bank of Macon and stolen a vast amount of specie and other valuables, and this method was taken to find the treasure. It further transpired that the whole army had moved on different roads just as we had, and all were thoroughly searched. We understand the idea of the search was originated by Gen. Upton and some of the stolen property recovered from the men of his division. But we are glad to announce that nothing valuable was found on any member of the Seventy-Second. After the search was all over we moved right back to our old camp, where we arrived at 2 p. m., hungry as wolves, and in various moods as to our march to Montgomery and the search.

We insert an incident to show the difference economically and mechanically between living on hard tack and corn bread. After our hard tack had all disappeared and we had to take to corn dodger, we were put to our very wits' ends to find some way to prepare the meal so we could eat it at all. For a long time we could do no better than to make mush and then fry the mush. This did well enough as long as we had the grease, but after the armistice it often occurred that we didn't have grease, and cold mush, or hot either, alone, was poor food. Finally the fates favored us, and in our mess we happened to get hold of a very large skillet, or oven, which served us a *mighty* good purpose as long as we stayed in Macon.

April 29th. One year ago to-day we left Columbia, Tenn., for the front, and the operations of the 2d cavalry division for a single year is a field large enough to furnish food for wonder and thought a lifetime, and the Seventy-Second justly claims a large share of all this. A detail was made this morning from our regiment to go into the country for forage, and the Historian was sent in command. We had 40 wagons. We went down the Ocmulgee River 12 miles and crossed two large streams, the Echaconee and Tobesofkee, and found an abundance of corn, and saw hundreds of negroes. Before the war we had read "Uncle Tom's Cabin," and other stories illustrative of the horrors of slavery, and always had an idea that probably the pictures were overdrawn, but to-day we were almost led to exclaim, in the language of the queen of Sheba, "the half had not been told." On the plantation where we got our corn were 100 negroes, men, women and children; one-third of them were nearly entirely naked. and on the whole hundred there were not clothes enough to entirely cover the nakedness of 10 of them. It was perfectly horrible to see old men try to hoe corn who were bent nearly double with age and hard usage. Their candle of hope had long since been blown out, and the dark pall of despair had settled down over them and forever fastened their eyes upon the ground. They had never heard of "Father Abraham," and of his glorious mandate of "Slave go free," being an exception on this plantation from any we had ever seen or heard of in regard to Lincoln and his Proclamation. A numbur of them had the small-pox and did not know what it meant to be doctored. We pray God we may never see such another spectacle.

April 30th. We are now getting the news we ought to have gotten soon after we came here, and the first official intelligence of Lincoln's death, and Andrew Johnson's assuming the presidency, is received. To-night the men are all busily engaged discussing its bearings upon the country at large, and especially its bearing upon the war. As yet we have no official intelligence that Johnston has surrendered. This suspense from the very first has tended more than everything else to demoralize this army, and threats of pillage and burning are very frequent. The citizens of the place, too, have very indiscreetly added fuel to the flame by their scowls and hisses, and to-night it seems to us that it would require but little effort to convert this whole army into a vast mob, by which Macon would be burned and her rabid secesh citizens murdered.

May 1st. To-day we got the official announcement that Gen

Johnston had surrendered and that the war is ended. Gen. Cobb, commander of the forces here, got an order from Gen. J. E. Johnston to turn all the confederate property over to the Federal quartermaster at this place. It was also announced that Gen. Upton, with the 4th division, would go to Augusta, Ga., and Gen. McCook, with the 1st division, would go to Tallahassee, Florida. (We forgot to state that Gen. Croxton's brigade, of the 1st division, came in all right a few days ago. He had taken a very circuitous route and made the longest march of any expedition during the whole war.) These orders were not received by the soldiers with any demonstrations of joy. The bad blood manifested by the citizens, and the news of Lincoln's death, has so soured many af the soldiers that they would about as leave fight as to quit. We have spoken of our Johnny diet of corn bread; but thus far we have had plenty of coffee, which, however is about exhausted. We started from Chickasaw with 45 days' rations of coffee, which will be out in four more days. The 4th division put their coffee in one of the houses that got burned up, and so we have had to divide with them. The Lord only knows what we will do when we get out of coffee.

May 2d. The pressure by the citizens to recover pressed horses and mules is very annoying to headquarters, and Stephen Aiken, of Company K, says: "1,000 mules and 500 horses belonging to the command were sold. They sold from $5 to $85 in gold and silver, pretty well sold for government stock."

May 3d. Ever since we came here, paroling officers have been busy paroling prisoners, and now the men of both Lee's and Johnston's armies are coming in here every day by the thousand, and as not more than half of them have been paroled, they are kept here until paroled before being allowed to go to their homes. This makes 10,000 or 20,000 rebel soldiers here all the time, and it is a matter of serious import to get rations for them, and it became necessary to send out details on all the railroads to look up commissary stores and have them shipped to Macon.

May 4th. A detail from our regiment along, with some doctors and nurses, started for Andersonville to-day, to rescue any unfortunate Yankee soldier that might still be there. We quote from Sergt. Samuel B. Johnson, Company D: "We boarded a train of old rickety cars at 8 a. m., drawn by a locomotive that looked like it might have been the first one ever invented. We arrived at the pen, 60 miles, at 2 p. m. Not very fast, you would say, but as fast as we cared to go with that train. While the surgeons and nurses looked after the prisoners (they found but few, and they were entirely helpless) we proceeded to inspect the place we had heard so much about, where so many brave men had lost their lives through the cruelty of the worst set of men who ever engaged in war. We first went to the prison, which we found deserted by everything except vermin. Everything was as silent as the grave. The gate was shut and locked. It took us but a short time to demolish the lock (part of which I brought home) and get inside. I suppose that I am the first Yankee to enter the place who was not a prisoner. The ground was bare of everything but five small sheds at the ends of the prison, which were simply posts set up to support the roof, there being no floors or siding, and a very poor shelter for a very small number. We found a great number of wells; some of them dry and some had water in. I think some of them were 50 feet deep, and how the poor fellows dug them with the means at their command is a mystery to me. I had heard men say they didn't believe they had such a thing as a dead line in any of these prisons. But here it was—a row of posts set up about 15 feet from the wall, and a narrow board nailed on top. Between this and the wall were brush, grass, stumps, &c. In fact it was just as when the place was finished, while on the inside there was no more sign of stump than in the best paved street. They had been dug out roots and all for fuel. We next visited the hospital on the outside. It was an old frame building not fit to stable cattle in, if one wished to keep them dry and warm. Next we looked at the forts and earthworks, next through a small enclosure near the railroad in which were a number of appliances for the punishment of prisoners who might offend one of those fiends in human form. There were stocks which would hold several men, with movable slides to close about the neck, wrists and ankles. We fastened each other in and found them effectual for the purpose designed. About this time we found it necessary to build a fire, strip and scorch our garments, in order to get rid of the fleas, which had gotten on to us in countless numbers. One comrade, Wm. W. Hill, wore a white hat which looked like a black one at this time. I then went to Wirz's house, (he gave me a rather cool reception) and upon examination of the prison records I found that three of Company D had met the fate of 15,000 others here, and had gone to their long home. They were as brave as the bravest. Their names were Scott Green, John Fenton and Robt. W. Bennett. Two had been wounded and one left sick on the Mississippi raid, and it was impossible to bring them away. We returned to Macon on the 5th, thankful that we had never fallen into the hands of the brutes who had charge of this death hole." Other details from our regiment were sent down on the same railroad. One detachment, under Lieut. Barnes, Company A, went to Oglethorp, where they found a vast quantity of commissary stores, which were shipped to Macon, or given to the starving poor people in the vicinity. We gawked through Macon to-day and saw but little of interest. During the past year this has become one of the most important cities of the South, and is the head and centre of the military manufactories, and contains a vast amount of military machinery, including railroad shops, arsenals, armories, magazines, &c. We had a long talk with soldiers of both Lee's and Johnston's armies, all veterans, and had seen from two to four years' hard active service They were very sociable and friendly, and say they are sick and tired of the war, and that it never ought to have begun, are glad it is ended, and that from the beginning it has been a rich man's war and a poor man's fight. When Wilson got the official announcement that Johnston had surrendered and the war had ended, he issued an order that our Board of Trade Battery sbould fire a salute of 200 guns in honor of victory to the Federal arms and peace to the country. We were in a good position to witness the firing, which was done at 2 o'clock. The ceremony was grand and imposing, but it called forth nothing but scowls and whispered curses from the citizens.

May 5th. Dr. Cole says: "40 invalids from Andersonville prison were brought up to-day. They are nothing more than living skeletons, and but few of them can recover. They all confirm previous accounts of rebel cruelty and barbarity." There was a liberty pole raised yesterday in front of the Lamar House, Gen. Wilson's headquarters. This again brought forth the hiss of the viper, the citizens represented by the Evening *News*, which said: "*We hope the very bad taste* of the Federals will cause no *serious* disturbance."

About this time we got notice that Jeff. Davis, with his escort, and all that was left of the Southern confederacy, was heading this way, and that we should keep a sharp lookout for him. As the salute was being fired yesterday some mischievous soldier climbed into the belfry of one of the churches, and every time a gun would go off would toll the bell as the death knell of secession and the Southern confederacy. The flag raised was a most beautiful one 24 by 10 feet, and as it went up the bands played the Star Spangled Banner, and other National airs, and also Dixie, while cheer after cheer rent the air and all felt "Gay and Happy," as "Johnny comes marching home."

Saturday May 6th. Last night some of Jeff. Davis' body guard deserted him and came into our division headquarters and reported his whereabouts, and that in all probability he would try to cross the Ocmulgee River to-day somewhere between Macon and Hawkinsville.

Steps were immediately taken to capture him. A detail was immediately started to our regiment for six commissioned officers, six non commissioned officers and 60 men, to report to division headquarters by 3 a. m. It is said that somebody at brigade headquarters had been taking too much apple jack, and hence we did not get the order until nearly sun-up. The detail was taken in equal numbers from A, F, D, I, B and G. The Historian was detailed to go in command of the squad from Company I. The names of the officers on this expedition were Capt. Gross, Co. A, Capt. Cravens, Co. D, Lieut. Maxwell, Co. B, Lieut. Martin, Co. G, all under command of Capt Gates, provost marshal of 2d cavalry division. The sun was an hour high when we got to division headquarters We speak of this because the loss of time resulted in the defeat of the enterprise, and to this day we curse Apple Jack and all of his relations. We were each of us furnished with a description of Jeff. Davis, and instructions to proceed as rapidly as possible down the Ocmulgee River, to find all the crossings and to leave a picket at each one till we got to Hawkinsville, 50 miles distant. We moved down the river at a lively pace, but found no crossing till we had gone 23 miles This brought us to Millbourn's Mill, where there was an old boat landing, and where a ferry had been kept. We found the river lined with impenetrable swamps two to four miles wide. Indeed the whole thing seemed to be a vast swamp two to four miles wide, with a dark, deep stream, meandering back and forth through it, and this was the first place we had found where we could even get into the river. The boats had been destroyed and the ferry discontinued. It turned out afterward that Jeff. Davis' body guard had come to this crossing about the time our advance got there, but seeing our men had turned back and put on down the river as fast as they could. Now, had we been an hour sooner—which we might easily have been had we got the detail as soon as intended—we might very easily have captured Mr. Davis and all his escort. But we were too late. Here the detail from I and G were left, and we will let Lieut. Martin tell what took place at this post. The balance of the command hurried on down the river as rapidly as they could. It was seven miles before they found another crossing. Here again the advance of both parties came to the opposite sides of the river at once, and again Davis and his party put on down the river. Here Capt. Cravens and the detail from Company D were left. Again Capt. Gross and Lieut. Maxwell and their little squads hurried on. The route was circuitous, and they had traveled 20 miles to get to Hawkinsville, the next crossing on the river. It was night. Men and horses had not had a bite to eat since early morn; both were exhausted, and they had done all they had been ordered to do; had done all that brave and determined men could do; and sure enough, there was Davis' body guard once more. All day long they had been traveling on a shorter line than the brave men of the Seventy-Second, and with deepest chagrin and mortification they were compelled to see the prize slip from their grasp. Reader, when you are told that $100,000 was offered by the United States Government for the capture of this party, you may get a faint idea of the terrible disappointment caused to the Seventy-Second by an untimely (it is always untimely) use of apple jack. But the little party will never have any cause for regret. They had done their duty—done it faithfully and done it well—and every member of that detail will, to the last day of his life, be proud to tell to his children, to his grand children, and mayhap to his great grand children, the part he took in the capture of Jeff. Davis, the leader of the most damnable rebellion the world ever saw. Our orders had been to find the crossings and then to secrete ourselves back from the river and let Mr. Davis and his party cross, and then close in on him, and you can readily see how this might have been, had we just been an hour sooner. What a world of thought contained in these four words, "It might have been." With us who had the prize, the reward, and the glory, so nearly in our hands, they are "the saddest words of tongue or pen." Lieut. Martin says: "On arriving at Milburn's Mills I was left with 10 men to patrol the country and guard the river at the landing, while the rest of the command went further down the river. After some reconnoissance I established my headquarters at the house of George M. Feagin, where a road leads off the main Hawkinsville road to the east, down to the old ferry, a mile away. Sunday the 7th passed off quietly, but I found we were in a bitter secesh neighborhood.

"Monday the 8th. The 10 men from Company I reported to me for duty. (This was the Historian's squad.) A dispatch soon came up from the command farther down the river calling for more men, so I sent the detail from Company I, and sent a courier to Macon that all was quiet at my post. We are very vigilant and expect some of the leading spirits of the rebellion to pass this way as they try to escape into the south-west trans-Mississippi department

"May 9th. We are active to-day, have discovered a lot of confederate goods stored in private houses and reported the same to headquarters. At 2 p. m. the 7th Pennsylvania cavalry and 4th Ohio cavalry pass us on their way to Hawkinsville in search of Jeff. Davis.

"May 10th. Early this morning, Corpl. D. P. Howland, who is

in charge of a squad of men guarding the crossing, sent a courier telling me that rebels are near the river on the opposite side and wish to cross. I at once made arrangements to receive them. directed Corpl. Howland to deploy his men in ambush above and below the crossing, leaving a gap in front of the ferry for myself and squad to fill up. Soon we were in our places and the corporal notified that the circle was complete. Corpl. Howland being dressed up for the occasion in rebel uniform, called to the old colored ferryman across the river to send word to the rebels that all was clear now, and to come on with their men and horses. Soon the rebels, three in number, came riding up, dismounted, and gave their horses to two colored men we had secured, for the purpose of swimming them over, which they did in fine style. The old ferryman brought the three men over in his batteau As soon as they nad reached our side and were about ready to mount, our boys closed in on them. They at once realized the situation, and with many curses on the 'd—d nigger,' surrendered. I took their arms, which consisted of two revolvers and a sabre to each man. I started with them to Macon, and in due time delivered them to Col. Minty, at division headquarters. They gave their names as James B. Clay, of Kentucky, a 1st lieutenant; ——Breckenridge, of Kentucky, also a 1st lieutenant, the other man was their hostler and denied being an enlisted soldier. Breckenridge gave me a fine navy revolver in appreciation of his kind treatment; I shook hands with him and bade him good-bye. Taking 10 more men of Company G with me I got back to my post at 2 o'clock at night. Near daylight we had a little excitement, which was interesting to the men who took part in it. The report of a gun and the clatter of horses' feet, as if coming at a terrible rate, were heard when a mile distant. I posted my men to check their advance. In a short time they were upon us; we ordered them to halt, but they could or would not halt, and we opened upon them. Two of them took to the woods, and the third one being in a buggy and having a fleet horse, rushed by us and on toward Macon and escaped unhurt, so far as we could tell. I ordered Simon Harper and another man to mount their horses and if possible capture the man in the buggy. After chasing the man 12 miles and wounding him slightly they captured him. It was a negro trying to get away from his master."

On the morning of the 8th, after leaving Lieut. Martin, our squad went down the river to the next crossing, where Capt. Cravens and the detail from Company D had stopped. We found they had crossed the river at Buzzard Roost Ferry and taken up their quarters at a station on the Brunswick Railroad one-half mile from the river. This was called Buzzard Roost Station. This crossing is of some importance on account of its being the head of navigation on the Ocmulgee. Boats, during high water, do go up as far as Macon, but they can come up to here almost any time, and there is a switch laid from the railroad down to the landing. The details from D and I were on duty here nearly two weeks, and some most interesting incidents took place, of which we will speak further on. After the failure of the Seventy-Second to capture Jeff. Davis, the reader is anxious to know just how and when he was captured. We have the account before us, as authorized by Davis himself, and also accounts from various other sources, but shall give our own version as we understood it and recorded it from day to day at the time, as we find it corresponds exactly with the report of Maj.-Gen. Thomas.

May 7th. Last night, after having done all we could toward capturing the chief of the rebellion, and failed, a courier was started back to Macon to let the authorities know of our failure, and that Davis had attempted to cross the river, and was surely in the neighborhood, and was making a desperate effort to reach the Mississippi. Lieut.-Col. Harnden, of the 1st Wisconsin cavalry, with a detachment of that regiment, struck the trail of Davis and his party at Doublin, on the Oconee, 40 miles east of Hawkinsville, on the evening of the 7th, and pushed on after Davis to Abbeville, on the Ocmulgee, 25 miles below Hawkinsville, where Davis got across the river on the 9th. Early on the morning of the 8th, Lieut.-Col. Pritchard, with the 4th Michigan, was ordered to Hawkinsville to picket the river below that point just as the Seventy-Second had done above, and got to Abbeville about the time that Col. Harnden and his men did. Harnden told Pritchard that Davis had left Abbeville at 1:00 that morning, and had gone in the direction of Irwinville, 25 miles distant. Harnden then pushed on after Davis, and at 9 p. m. went into camp near Irwinville, satisfied that Davis was near by. As soon as Harnden was out of sight Pritchard selected his best mounted men and went to Bowenville, 10 miles south of Abbeville, and then struck straight for Irwinville, 20 miles south-west, and about 2 o'clock on the morning of the 10th came out in the road Davis was on, and to the west or ahead of Davis. They then moved back cautiously until they came upon Davis' camp, and Pritchard deployed his men around the camp without causing alarm. This was done by 3 o'clock, and they awaited daylight. Not long after this the advance of the Wisconsin regiment ran into this line of pickets, and a fight ensued, in which two of the Michigan men were killed and one officer seriously wounded, and five or six of the Wisconsin men wounded, three of them seriously, and it was quite a while before the Michigan men could make the Wisconsin men understand that they were firing on their friends. The Michigan men on the west side of the camp hearing the firing on the east side, supposed that Davis and his party had become alarmed and were trying to make their escape, and they charged right into camp. It was now getting daylight, but a sergeant and 10 men of the 4th Michigan got to Davis' tent before he was up As soon as Davis' wife heard the firing she jumped up and ran to the door, and seeing the blue coats coming into camp, she ran back and helped Davis top ut on *her* water-proof cloak, which was made exactly like a woman's dress with a cape, and told him to take a bucket and start for the spring, while she stood in the door and pretended that Davis was still in the tent, by warning the Yanks not to come in to the tent as they might "irritate the President," and then he might shoot some of them. The president on stepping out of the tent in front of the sergeant, stepped on a brush which raised the bottom of the water-proof sufficiently high to reveal a pair of cavalry boots. The sergeant paid no attention to Mrs. Davis, but walked on down behind the president, and with his sabre lifted up the bottom of the dress and exclaimed, "Mister, you wear pretty large boots for a woman." By this time both regiments were pouring into camp from every side. The Wisconsin regiment was deeply chagrined at having the prize snatched out of their hands, and the Michigan men always said the Wisconsin men fired on them purposely This was on the morning of the 10th of May, and on the evening of the 11th, we saw Davis and his captors pass through Hawkinsville, and one of these same 4th Michigan men told us all we have written as taking place below Hawkinsville. He said he saw the whole of it with his own eyes, and then and there told the same to us; and further this deponent sayeth not.

Again we copy from Lieut. Martin's report:

"Friday, May 12, 1865. This evening the 4th Michigan, Lieut.-Col. Pritchard in command, camped near my headquarters. They had a lot of prisoners, and just before sundown, in company with a lot of citizens, I went to see them; the most prominent among them being Jeff. Davis, accompanied by his wife, three small sons, one daughter, and his sister-in-law, and also Col. Johnson, of Tennessee, Col. Lubbock, of Texas, Maj. Maurie Howell, of the navy, Capt. Madison. Capt. Moody, Judge Reagan, P. M. General, and quite a number of lesser lights. Reagan was very indignant at our Government for offering a reward of $100,000 for the capture of President Davis, and said it would be a lasting shame and disgrace to our Government.

The ladies that went with me from the Feagin house were very demonstrative and overflowing in their sympathy for the captured president, and as we started back to the house they, with tears in their eyes, bade 'Our President' an affectionate farewell, and a short distance from camp asked me if I didn't feel sorry for Mr. Davis. 'Sorry,' said I, 'indeed I do; I am sorry I was not permitted to tie the hangman's knot around his neck and spring the drop from under him and see his old traitor neck broken in the fall.' The ladies dropped the subject." And yet that same Lieut. Martin is one of the gentlest and best men in the world.

While all the foregoing has been transpiring the whole division has been scattered all over the country, scarcely leaving enough of any of our regiment in camp to "take care of the children." Especially was this the case with the Seventy-Second, heavy details from which were scattered along the Macon & Mobile Railroad as far as Cuthbert, 120 miles, and we quote an incident from John B. Davis, Company D: "May 8th. At 11 last night we saddled up and went to the railroad. At 8:00 this morning we put our horses inside box-cars and ourselves on top and pulled out for Cuthbert, Ga. We passed through Oglethorp, Andersonville, Americus and Dawson. By the time we got to Cuthbert the pine smoke from our locomotive had made us quite black. The secesh citizens were 'mad as a rail' because the Union general had sent them a 'nigger' regiment. A little soap and water soon set that all right."

We now go back to the detail from the Seventy-Second which had started down the Ocmulgee River to capture Jeff. Davis. As before stated, we were strung along the river for a distance of 30 miles; Company G at Milburn's Mills, D and I at Buzzard Roost, and A and B at Hawkinsville. As the duty at Buzzard Roost and Hawkinsville was the same, we simply relate some incidents illustrative of what took place at each place. Buzzard Roost, 30 miles below Macon, is the first place in all that distance that there is a regular crossing, and a ferry that amounts to anything. We have spoken about Lee's and Johnston's armies passing through Macon, and of the vast numbers of them who were without paroles. It now appears that each officer and man was to give his individual parole of honor that he would never more take up arms against the United States; but it further appears that all the troops belonging to these two armies, and who were serving on detached duty—that is, away from the main armies—never waited or went to be paroled at all, but just "skinned out" for home as fast as they could travel. Hundreds of them were coming to this crossing every day, and it was our business to stop them, send them up to Macon on the railroad, and make them get their paroles. Most of these soldiers had their arms with them, and they would come in such numbers sometimes as to make it look a little risky to disarm them; but we always did it. There were 14 of us at this crossing now, and not another Yankee within 10 miles of us, and as our men were constantly hunting squirrels in the swamps, or riding over the country for forage, there was very seldom more than three or four of us at the ferry at a time. One day there happened to be but ourself and two others at the ferry, when a colonel and most of his regiment, about a hundred men, came riding up. Most all of them had their guns, and the situation was rather interesting. We told the boys to loosen the boat and push it from shore, and we moved boldly out to meet them; but you don't know how scared we were. We halted them and asked them who they were and where they were going? The colonel told us they were from Florida, and that was all that was left of his once noble regiment, and that they were going home. We explained our business, and asked for their paroles. The colonel showed his, and said his men were all paroled. We then called his attention to the guns. He said it was according to the terms of the surrender that all officers, and men too, should retain their own private property, and that his regiment on going into the service had furnished its own arms. We then knew nothing of the terms of the surrender, but saw that the guns were shot-guns, and concluded to let them pass. Three blue coats against 100 butternuts was too wide a difference for us to be over-nice about the matter.

May 11th. The writer carried a dispatch to Hawkinsville, and enjoyed the privilege of beholding the president of the defunct confederacy. We instinctively grasped our Spencer, and just then wanted to kill one more rebel. The truth is, he is the only one we ever saw that we really did *want* to kill.

May 12th. All hands left the river and went out the Hawkinsville road to see the remnants of the Southern confederacy pass.

May 15th. On the 8th, the same day we came to Buzzard Roost, some negroes came in from the country east of this and told us of some large heavy boxes which they had helped to secrete some time last summer, and they supposed there was gold in them. Capt. Craven, Co. D, sent word up to Macon about them, and got an order to go out and get them. So to-day he went out and pressed in a lot of teams and hauled them into the depot. There were five of them, all about the same size, four feet long and three feet high, and the same in width. They were bound with iron and very strong.

and were so very heavy that treasure was suggested at once. They were all plain on the outside, without marks or brands of any kind, and Cravens determined to see what was in them, and broke them open, and the contents proved to be the archives of the State of Tennessee. When the war broke out Isham G. Harris was governor of Tennessee, and when Grant had captured Forts Henry and Donelson, and was moving on Nashville, Harris gathered up all the money there was in the treasury, school funds, State bonds, &c., and ran away. He went to Memphis; but when our wooden gunboats began to "open up the Mississippi" it got too warm for Harris, and he skipped out for Atlanta, taking his treasure with him. When Sherman captured Kenesaw Mountain, Marietta, and set his army down along the Chattahoochie, Harris again started "on for Dixie." He went to Macon; but when Sherman started for the sea, and the right wing of his army was sweeping down toward Macon, he again loaded up his treasures and moved them down to Buzzard Roost, hauled them out into the country and hid them, but the pesky Yanks "dun got 'm" at last. There was neither gold or silver in the boxes, but they were full of all kinds of bank bills, bonds, and graybacks, or confederate money. Our boys took out all they wanted of these and used them to gamble with, or to buy things of the citizens. They were now worth nothing, and we took a bill and bond of each kind and denomination and brought them home with us, and have them yet. They will be worth as much to our grand children as Continental money now is to us. After we had taken out all we wanted, Capt. Cravens sent the writer in charge of the boxes on the railroad up to Macon, and it is presumed the State of Tennessee got all the boxes contained that was of any real value to the state.

Sergt. A. M. Cory, Co. D, furnishes an incident that took place while we were on duty at the "Roost." Our only object in publishing it is this: our history, and all the histories of the war we have ever consulted, starts out with the assumption that slavery was the cause of the war; and yet you may take any 20 of the best educated children under 16 years of age in the country, and ask them what slavery was, and they can't tell you. As before remarked, we had read Uncle Tom's Cabin and many other stories illustrative of the "sum of all villainies," and we couldn't realize them—couldn't believe them; and our children open their eyes in wonder and astonishment when we tell them of the hellish torment and cruelties of slavery, and they do not, cannot, believe them. But we have seen with our own eyes the negro lash, the whip, the cat-o'-nine-tails, the whipping post, the knout, the stocks, the branding iron, the ball and chain, the negro jail and the negro gallows, and we know that half never has been told, and we insert Cory's incident as a specimen of many others now before us, simply as illustrating *some* of the *milder* forms of human slavery.

"One morning just at daylight a mulatto girl, equally as white as some of our sisters of the North, came to our quarters and asked the protection of the captain till she could be sent to Macon to join the large army of contrabands there. Her master soon came on the hunt of her, and to the utter surprise of every one the captain ordered her to go back with her master. The boys knew the plantation where she belonged, and three or four of them carelessly shouldered their Spencers and started toward the swamp as if going after squirrels. When out of sight they quickened their pace. and soon came in sight of the negro quarters, and when within a quarter of a mile of the place heard the cries of the poor unfortunate girl, as the bloody lash was plied to her naked back. It did not take long for the boys to cross the field and make their appearance at the door of a large log house, or jail, with its different hellish arrangements for the punishment of the poor slave who should offend the majesty of the master's rules. There were the whipping post, the rack on the wall, the cowhide, the cat-o'-nine-tails, and other instruments of torture. In the middle of this room stood the devil's victim securely tied by the wrists, her back laid bare to the waist, and a large, heavy muscled negro man, with whip in hand, and the overseer standing by counting the strokes as they were skillfully applied by the negro. A change in the programme immediately took place. The three boys in blue rushed in, and in language more forcible than elegant ordered hostilities to cease; the bloody victim was released and the overseer ordered to strip to the belt. Prayer meeting immediately commenced, but only the prayers of the righteous are presumed to be heard, and so it was in this case. No mercy was shown, and the heartless brute who a few minutes before gloated over the misery and suffering of his victim, was made to feel the potency of his own treatment, and his victim required to stand and witness the punishment." The girl was also released from these devils and given freedom.

May 17th. Soon after we had taken Macon, and the truth of the armistice was ascertained, a party left Macon and went down to Hawkinsville and captured two steamboats, the Governor Troup and the Comet, and boarded them and went down to the Altamaha Sound, at the mouth of the Ocmulgee, and from there up the coast to Savannah after rations. Gen. Long, our division commander, and several other wounded officers, took this means of getting home.

Well, to-day we at the Roost, about 9 o'clock, heard one of those boats whistle, and the sound came rolling up through the swamp like a harbinger of peace and good will. Although we did not know what was coming we all broke for the landing. In about an hour the Governor Troup come slowly winding up through the trees and landed just below our ferry. She was loaded with commissary stores. You may *never-never*-know how we laughed to see a cracker box once more. It had been nearly two months since we had seen one, and with hearts overflowing with gratitude we felt like showering unnumbered blessings upon the head of the man who invented hard-tack. It took the boat eight days to make the trip from Savannah, and some of our boys who were on the boat as guards had a fine time shooting alligators as they came up. A shot from an ordinary rifle has but little effect on their tough old hides, but our Spencers went to the spot every time. The men had a very large one, eight feet long, on board, which they had just killed.

May 18th. To-day the other boat, "The Comet," came up and landed at the Roost. The boats brought our mail and the first real and reliable information we had received from the outside world. For two months we had been in the heart of what to us was a foreign country—nay, worse than a foreign country—and now these boats more than any other one thing brought us back to our homes and firesides, and just here we feel like launching into an eulogium on the love of home and country, but haven't the space. The 4th of July orators will see that this work is properly done.

On the 19th we left Buzzard Roost, went to Hawkinsville and took up our quarters in a church, a most delightful place. In the afternoon an altercation took place between some conscripting officers and some deserters, in which several were wounded and two fatally stabbed. For once we got to see a fight in which we didn't care a snap which dog got on top. Hawkinsville is the most notorious rebel hole we have ever seen; a perfect den of gamblers, thieves, robbers and rakes, and is a kind of summer resort for the young hot-bloods of the South who come here on purpose to gamble. The citizens say there are at least four men killed here every summer.

May 20th. The two boats that landed at Buzzard Roost had discharged their cargoes and passed down the river. As before stated our regiment was now scattered all over the southern part of Georgia, and on the 21st orders were sent from Macon for all these scattered squads to report at once to Macon and get ready to go home. Of course by a great many this news was hailed with demonstrations of joy, but the thing had come on to us so gradually that we are safe in saying a majority looked upon it as a matter of course. All of us felt we had done our whole duty toward suppressing the rebellion and making peace possible, and for several days had felt that there was but little left for us to do, and that Uncle Sam would no longer need our services; but how different, with many of us, was the reality, to what we had over and over again imagined it would be. "Home!" How many times every man in the regiment had uttered that word in every accent. One would have thought that some little village or farm house in Indiana was Heaven itself, to hear the men speak of "Home." How they talked about the commonest articles of food they were going to eat when they got home. But from the very day we began to write this history we have gradually been approaching a point where we have always felt we could never do the subject justice, and we have come to that point now, and so shall not attempt to aggregate the feelings of the regiment and describe them as a whole, but shall simply give our own individual experience, and beg our comrades to consider in charity, whether it does not correspond with theirs.

Sunday, May 21st, 1865. Last night the writer went to bed very late—much later than usual when lying in camp; but was too restless to sleep. A curious, indescribable feeling came over us, as if something was going to happen. This was very uncommon for us, for when we go to bed it is always to sleep, and we do sleep, too, for all that is out. We got up and moved about. We went out and listened for the accustomed picket-firing; went to the horse-quarters and noted that they were all tied; and then listened again, and wondered if it was not about time to "change the relief;" then went back into the church and found the whole squad in much the same condition as we were; for when we spoke we found them all awake. We lay and talked a while, and at 11 o'clock our Lieut. Foster came down from Macon. We had not seen him for nearly two weeks, and of course had a long talk with him. At 1 o'clock a courier from Macon came down with orders for us to go back to Macon at once. This drove sleep entirely away from us, and we did not sleep a bit the whole night; but, as we lay there till 3 o'clock in the morning, we again went over the whole ground of the war, and discussed the effect of peace upon ourselves and upon the country, and upon our chances of making a living when we got home; and so far as making a living was concerned, we unanimously agreed that it would be better for us to stay in the army. We were all farmers, and this was the case with three-fourths of the regiment; and we had been away from our accustomed labor so long that we would not know where or how to take hold. Harvest had already commenced where we were, and we knew that the time for making a crop or engaging in any other kind of business for the year had just now gone by, and we knew it would be almost a year before we could get into any kind of business that would bring us a living; and in our whole squad we do not think there was a man who seemed anxious, or even glad, we were going home. We could easily appreciate hcw soldiers could grow into a profession. We got all the different squads together, and started for Macon, by sun-up, and had an awful long, lonely tedious, and tiresome ride of fifty miles, without food or rest. The roads the whole way were sandy, and the sun shone extremely hot. From loss of sleep, and from the reflection of the sun off the white sand into our eyes, we were nearly blinded. We think we never marched one-fourth of the distance before and saw as little sociability manifested, or heard as few words spoken. Everybody seemed entirely occupied with his own thoughts, or sound asleep, and the whole distance was made in silence. It was 9 o'clock at night before we got to camp; but it was not long till we once more enjoyed a hospitable supper at home, and that, too, of hard-tack and coffee. It had been 40 days since we tasted hard-tack, and we had been two weeks without coffee. It seemed as though we were taking a new lease of life. We found that not more than one-third of our regiment had got in from the various expeditions upon which it had been sent, and we learned that private Richard Myers, of Co. B, was drowned in a mill-pond on the Tobesofkee Creek on the 15th of May. Private Basil Lamb, of the same company, had been detailed to go to the mill as a safeguard, but was quite unwell, and Myers volunteered to go in his place. While on duty there he had went in the pond to bathe, took the cramp, and drowned. He was a brave soldier, and a most kind and generous comrade, and nothing we can say will add to the esteem in which he was held by his comrades.

We here insert a brief resume, by a member of the Seventy-Second, who knows exactly what he is talking about:

"We left Gravelly Springs, on the Tennessee River, the latter part of March, 1865, the objective point being Andersonville; being in the advance, fought the battle of Ebenezer Church on the 1st of April; stormed the works, which were regarded impregnable, at Selma, Alabama, where Col. Miller was severely wounded, capturing 5,000 prisoners, and destroying the most extensive arsenals and armories in the whole confederacy; moving on through Montgomery, Alabama, and capturing the strongholds of West Point and

Columbus, Georgia. We reached Macon, Georgia, April 20th, late in the evening, where two regiments, the Seventy-Second and 17th Indiana, charged the works and took possession of the city. A strange state of things—a city surrounded by a continuous line of earthworks, manned by 5,000 infantry and 40 field guns, and the enemy, two small regiments, resting on their arms in the streets till the light of morning revealed the true state of the case. But they took possession. Gen. Howell Cobb, who was in command, was immediately interviewed in the evening by Gen. Wilson, and, of course, was indignant at being captured by the Yankees in such a manner, but was assured that if he was not satisfied with the manner of capture, we could take his city in any way he would suggest, as he (Wilson) had a reserve force outside the works of *ten thousand Spencers*. The haughty General concluded that discretion was the better part of valor, and the rebel line was disarmed and paroled.

"In a few days news came (through rebel sources) that an armistice had been agreed upon between Sherman and Johnston, that there would be no more fighting for 60 days. Soon the rebel forces of Gen. Lee were returning and reported the surrender. How the boys shouted when they knew "the cruel war was over!"

"The Union forces were then deployed from Atlanta to the gulf to intercept the President of the confederacy, who was supposed to be trying to escape west of the Mississippi or across the water. A scout of the Seventy-Second regiment who had been sent out in gray uniform had found the distinguished party. He reported, and the regiment was pushing on to the capture; but the 4th Michigan cavalry were fortunate in gaining the prize, and all returned again to Macon, where Jeff. Davis, Capt. Wirz, of Andersonville, and other prominent men of the Southern confederacy, were held a number of days as prisoners. The boys all remember well Mrs. Jeff., the author of the phrase 'Don't irritate the President,' who was a conspicuous member of this distinguished party. A court martial was ordered by the General in command, and Col. C. G. Thomson was detailed as president of the same, with orders to convene the court at once, to dispose of the cases of the prisoners in charge. But the war was over, and the authorities at Washington telegraphed to have the parties forwarded to the Capitol at government expense, and the result is a matter of history. The inferior officer, Capt. Wirz, who was compelled to obey the orders of his superior officer, was hung by the neck till he was dead, and the commander-in-chief is to-day the champion of the lost cause, an aspirant for a seat in the United States Senate, and the idol of many who are prominent in the councils of the nation they sought to destroy. Such partiality for the aristocracy of the rebellion would not have been probable by a court of volunteer soldiery."

May 22d. All the different squads got in to-day except one of Company A, under Lieut. Barnes, which was stationed at Americus, and for some cause had not got orders to report to camp when other detachments got theirs. This evening we were called out in line to listen to orders relieving us from further duty at the front, and that we should start for home in the morning. Before leaving Macon we wish, by way of recapitulation, to further impress upon the mind of the reader the vast importance of what to us has always been called the Wilson raid. Comparisons sometimes are odious, but we know of no better way of bringing the subject clearly before your minds than comparing Wilson's raid with "Sherman's march to the sea," which has so justly been celebrated in song, and which will always live in history. Sherman, in his Memoirs, vol. 2, p. 193, says: "The trains were all in good order and the men seemed to march their 15 miles a day as though it was nothing. No enemy opposed us, and we could only *occasionally* hear the faint reverberation of a gun to our left rear, where we knew that Gen. Kilpatrick was skirmishing with Wheeler's cavalry, which persistently followed him; but the infantry columns had met with no opposition whatever." Page 220: "I only regarded the march from Atlanta to Savannah as a 'shift of base,' as the transfer of a strong army which had no opponent." On page 221 he admits he had an army of 65,000 men. We have recorded from day to day most of the events occurring with us as they happened, and now our only reason for recapitulation is that we think Wilson and his little army never got a tithe of the credit that justly belongs to them. Had the half of this service been performed the second (it would have been impossible the first), year of the war, the participants would have been crowned the greatest military heroes of the age. But the war was just over now; everybody was sick and tired of it and wanted to forget all about it as soon as possible. Another reason why we were never noticed was because no *paid* newspaper correspondent ever, in glowing. colors, gave to the world its grand and triumphant march; while Sherman's march was heralded all over the world by paid correspondence, the press and the people. But here was a much longer march than Sherman's, and made in much shorter time, under vastly greater difficulties, and vastly greater results achieved. Now, in proof of this, let facts speak, and we quote from Sherman's own book to prove every word we say. Sherman was just one month in going from Atlanta to Savannah, and the distance marched was just 285 miles, while we had marched 570 miles in two days less time, and if we take out the eight days we laid at Selma, we marched it in 10 days less time, or just 20 days. Sherman had an army of 65,000 men and nothing in the world to oppose him—did not fight a single engagement, nor did his infantry have even a skirmish, and his cavalry but a few slight ones, while we had (see Sherman's book, page 368) 13,500 men, fought two pitched battles, and were opposed at every point where opposition could be brought to bear. Sherman did not capture or destroy a single point, city or place, of any importance to the rebels, during his whole march from Atlanta to Savannah, while we had captured Selma, Montgomery, West Point, Columbus and Macon, all strongly fortified cities, and the most important cities of the South, too. Sherman, on receiving the surrender of Johnston's army (see his book, page 370) paroled only 36,817 men, while we captured and paroled in Georgia and Florida 52,453 men, beating Sherman by 15,636; this does not include those captured at Selma, Ala., which would swell the grand aggregate of prisoners to 60,000, or more than four to every man in our command. Every soldier who went with Sherman to the sea may well be proud of the honor. How much more, then, has every member of the Seventy-Second reason to be proud that he took part in the great Wilson raid and the capture of Jeff. Davis!

CHAPTER XL.

From May 23d to June 18th, 1865—We Start for Home—Regrets at Leaving the Gallant 17th—This Regiment and the Brigade Band Accompany Us Through the City and Bid Us Farewell—"Home, Sweet Home!"—"Who Will Care for Mother Now?"—"A Time for Memory and for Tears"—Marching Northward—Diary of the March Through Atlanta, Marietta, Kenesaw—The Old Familiar Forts and Fields of Battle—A View of All from the Top of Kenesaw Mountain—Pass through Big Shanty, Ackworth, Allatoona, Hightower, Cartersville, Cassville and Kingston—Allatoona Pass—Still Moving North and Coming to Some Yankee Troops—We Pass through Tunnel Hill and Ringgold, and Visit the Battle-field of Rock Springs—Find the Graves of Capt McMurtry and Other of Our Fallen Comrades, Fill Up the Graves, Set Up a Headboard, and Pray—Looking Over the Chicamauga Battle-field—Bones Scattered All About—To Chattanooga—Expecting to be Mustered Out—Ordered to Come on to Nashville on Horseback, and the Men Swear "Tall"—The Last Look from Old Lookout Mountain at the Historic Ground—Moving North through Decherd, Murfreesboro, and Other Places of Interest—Get to Nashville, and Meet Col. Miller—Glad to See Him and Cheer Him Heartily—Turn Over Horses and Mules—Camp Looks Lonesome and Thin—Making Out Muster Rolls.

Tuesday, May 23d, 1865. This morning at 7 a. m. we started for home. Our command (all that are going along) consists of the 4th Michigan, the Board of Trade Battery, the 98th and 123d Illinois and the Seventy-Second Indiana. We left the 17th Indiana behind. We had served two years and a half with the boys of the 17th, and parted with them with many regrets. It is surprising how common dangers will drive away jealousies, grudges, and little spites. When the 17th was first put into our brigade, with J. T. Wilder as the ranking colonel, it was very natural that every member of the Seventy-Second should feel that he had suffered a personal injury in the wrong done to our own Colonel, A. O. Miller, and for quite a while the men of the two regiments did not harmonize very well. But since Miller had been in command of the brigade all this had long since been forgotten, and we will venture the assertion that no four regiments in the army ever passed over two years of service with such unanimity of feeling or purpose, or with such genuine brotherly love and kindness, as characterized the four regiments of our brigade. No matter how difficult or dangerous the position we got into, if we but knew a regiment of our own brigade was near us, we felt perfectly at ease, and it didn't make a whit of difference which regiment it was. And this morning, when we started, the whole regiment, including our brigade band, escorted us through the city and at the outskirts bade us an affectionate farewell. Our camp was more than three miles from the city, and as we neared the outer line of works, not far from division headquarters, the 2d brigade band took its place at head of column and played us through the streets, the last piece rendered being "Home, Sweet Home." We marched in column of 4's through the principal streets of the city, and passed in grand review in front of the Lamar House, Gen. Wilson's headquarters, the General and his staff, and other distinguished officers, occupying the balcony. Our colors and battle-flags were all flying, and as they came opposite the General they were dipped, and arms presented, and the General with his hat waved us a pleasant adieu. As we got to the outskirts of the city the 17th Indiana formed on the left of the road with its band at its head. As each of our regiments came abreast of the 17th, it presented arms, and its band played "Who Will Care for Mother Now?" Each company of us in turn, as we came opposite, then gave them three rousing cheers and an affectionate good-bye. And so we parted. It was the parting of brothers in arms.

We took the Columbus road, and followed it eight or nine miles, crossing the Tobesofkee, and then turned north toward Forsyth. The day was excessively warm and dusty, nothing of note transpiring. We camped early, having made but 25 miles. The squad from Company A, Lieut Barnes in command, that had been stationed for quite a while at Americus, 65 miles south-west of Macon, had not yet got to camp when we started, and so we had to come off and leave them behind.

May 24th. Reveille this morning at 3 o'clock, and we moved at 4, crossed the Tobesofkee Creek again, and passed through Forsyth, a smart little town of 500 or 600 inhabitants; crossed the Towaliga River, and passed through Liberty Hill. Made 28 miles for the day.

May 25th. Moved to a little station on the Atlanta and Macon Railroad called Millner, we believe, and drew two days' rations and forage, which had been sent from Macon for us. Moved on, and in the afternoon passed through Griffin, a good-sized town on the railroad, and the place where Hood was when Sherman left off following after his retreat from Atlanta. We passed through Fayetteville, and camped early, near a station on the railroad called Pear Creek. It was near this place where McCook made his raid on the railroad last summer. At this time our division was surrounded at Flat Shoals. He burned 500 wagons, killed 800 mules, and in turn got himself badly whipped, losing 600 of his men. Made 25 miles.

May 26th. Moved very early this morning and soon began to pass line after line of earthworks and skirmish pits thrown up by the rebels, and our own men too, last summer; 13 miles from camp we came to

Jonesboro, and at no time during the day did we go far without passing line after line of earthworks, and they will long be remembered by many as the scenes of terrible conflicts. Shortly before noon we came to places very familiar to us, as it was here we struck this railroad on the 1st of September while Sherman was fighting at Jonesboro. About 2 p. m. bivouacked just inside the outer line of works on the south of Atlanta, and three miles from the city. Made 30 miles to-day.

May 27th. Moved early this morning and went into what once was the city of Atlanta; but now nothing but huge and unshapely piles of brick and mortar remain of what was a very beautiful town. The destruction has been so thorough the oldest inhabitant would scarcely recognize the place. We were in the city just after the rebels had been driven out, and then thought it was about as badly knocked to pieces as it well could be, but before Sherman's army started to the sea it hardly left one stone upon another that it did not throw down. Here we drew two days' forage and a little sugar and coffee, but no hard-tack or meat. Our rations have been short ever since starting, and a little strange, too, they have all come from the seacoast. When here last summer we had abundant rations, but they all came from the north. The railroad has just been completed to this place from the south, while there is a gap of five miles toward Chattanooga that is yet entirely destroyed. We moved on to Marietta and went into camp just at the foot of Kenesaw, on the east side of the mountain, and north-west of the town, about 2 p. m., having made 30 miles for the day. Marietta was once one of the most delightful towns in the state, but here, too, were many lasting marks of our earnest efforts to put down the rebellion. The same old story of brick and mortar. We have now been traveling over places that are strikingly familiar to us, and we point out to each other the exact places we were on such a day last summer, and speak of the part each one played in the great game of war then in progress. After eating our dinners nearly the whole command struck out for the top of Kenesaw. We had been all around and on every side of it for several months last summer, but had never been on it. We went up the north end of the ridge two-thirds of the way to the top, where there was a lunette fort dug into the face of the ridge. It had been large enough for an eight-gun battery, and is the one we watched with so much interest on the 17th of last June. Some of the embrasures had been walled up to keep our shells from coming into them. We could plainly see where some of them had come through, struck the back part of the fort and exploded, tearing up wagon loads of earth that must have buried the men working the guns. When we got on top of the ridge we found it extremely narrow, in many places not more than six to ten feet wide, and a full half mile of it nearly even in hight, the west face being very precipitous, while the east face sloped off more gradually, but quite too steep for the rebels to get their guns on top of the ridge, only as they rolled them up by hand from either end of it. Just on the west edge of the ridge there was a line of works of loose rocks, there being very little earth near the top of it. Our shells had literally knocked this line of works to pieces, and some of them, which went just a little too high, landed in Marietta, a mile and a half away. When we first came in sight of this mountain last June there was a large tree on the highest point of it, and on top of the tree a signal station, the light of which at night could be seen 60 miles away. Our shells had cut this tree down, and the stump was as full of bullets, grape, canister, and pieces of shells, as they could stick. The day was perfectly clear and bright, and when we got to the top of the ridge the sun was yet two hours high, and we had the grandest view we ever beheld. We could see as far as our vision would reach in every direction Turning to the east Marietta seemed just under our feet, and so close we might drop a finger stone down into it. Rosswell, 18 miles away, and Stone Mountain, more than 30 miles distant, yet appeared so close that we might ride to either in half an hour. As we looked at the places we spoke of our grand charge through the Chattahoochee, and where we first learned to burn railroad at Gibraltar, and then at Covington, 25 miles beyond. Turning further south we could see Decatur, full 30 miles from where we stood, and we called up our many skirmishes and encounters there. A little further to the right and we could see the battle-field where McPherson was killed; 24 miles south-east of us we could see Atlanta as plainly as if but a half dozen miles distant; could see all its forts and field-works and point out the exact places we had occupied. Four miles this side was the battle-field of Peach-tree Creek. West of Atlanta was the Battle-field of the 28th of July, on the Sand Town road; 30 miles south of us was Sand Town, south-west of us was Powder Springs, with Lost Mountain and Pine Mountains rising up like lone hay-cocks in a meadow between us and the Springs; while 10 miles beyond was Dallas, and New Hope Church, and the place called "Hell Hole" on account of the terrible fighting there. Still further we could trace the course of Pumpkin-vine Creek, with the south end of the Allatoona Mountains. Still beyond, just west of us, were the swamps and head waters of Noses and Noonday Creeks; eight miles away, north-west of us, was Big Shanty, though seeming so close we could count every house in it. Beyond this was Ackworth, and still beyond, and 18 miles away, was Allatoona Pass and Allatoona Station, the scene of the most terrible conflict for the numbers engaged that took place during the war. North of us ran the Noonday Creek, where our brigade had such terrible fights on the 19th and 21st of June. North-east of us was Sweet Mountain and Little River.

But why weary you further? Suffice it to say we had been on nearly every foot of the ground for nearly 40 miles in every direction, and now we could see and point them all out from where we stood. O, what a grand rush of emotions and thoughts hurried through our minds, as we took this all in at once! It was almost worth three years of toil to enjoy what we then did. And then, too, to see the sun sink quietly down behind the Allatoonas, with not a cloud to be seen and not a zephyr to rustle a leaf! Could Paradise furnish anything more sublime? As the shadows came swiftly eastward from the Allatoonas, and gradually climbed to the top of Kenesaw, and the sun suddenly dropped out of sight, a mania almost instantly seized the whole command, and each began to select some memento to take home with him in remembrance of this grand old mountain, and many a cane cut from the brow of the hill, and many a piece of shell or bullet cut from tree or stump, will accompany us to our homes. We had, almost at a single view, seen six of the great battle-fields of the war, and as it was growing dark we went to camp. As we wended our way to the north end of the ridge, we wondered how many of our comrades were sleeping near us. We were going home, but leaving our dead behind, and carrying many sad memories with us. Lieut. Barnes and his squad caught up with us to-day.

May 28th. Moved early, going over the same road we had often moved on before; weather extremely hot, and dust in many places six inches deep and pulverized as fine as flour, and every time our horses would step it would splash like thin mortar; clouds of it constantly rising were absolutely intolerable, settling on our clothes till you could not tell they ever had any color, filling our eyes till we could scarcely see, and our nostrils almost to suffocation. We passed through Big Shanty, Ackworth, Allatoona, Hightower, Cartersville, and Cassville, and camped at Kingston, a march of 35 miles without stopping. As we neared Allatoona Pass the boys waked up from their sound sleep and began to feel an interest in viewing the ground of the most heroic defense of the war. Officers and men were alike interested, and as we neared the place the head of column turned out of the road and wound around over the battle-field and up by the redoubts, so as to give us all a chance to see all that was to be seen. The marks of the terrible conflict were still plentiful and plainly to be seen. After crossing the Etowa we saw a blue coated sentry on a high knob away ahead of us, near Cartersville, and from his motions we judged he was almost frightened to death. We wondered where he came from, and found out afterwards that he really supposed we were rebels, and that he was a real, live Yankee soldier. We wondered what he was doing there. We were nearly 200 miles from our little army at Macon, and had not seen a soldier since leaving there, and we had no means of knowing how far south of the Tennessee River our lines extended, nor when we should reach them. We were yet a long ways from Chattanooga, the farthest point our lines extended south when we left the Tennessee River, but when we got to Cartersville we found a whole regiment of Yankees the 145th Indiana. They were as much surprised to see us as we were to see them. They supposed they had advanced to the very heart and center of the Southern confederacy, and wondered where in the world we could have come from, supposing it absolutely impossible that anybody had gone farther than they had. They were complaining terribly of their hardships, and among many other things said they had not had a bit of light bread for nearly two weeks. We told them there were just dead loads of it down where we come from, and if they wanted easy times and "lots of fun," just go down where we had been. We enjoyed their talk hugely; besides it made us feel like we were getting back towards God's country. When we got to Kingston we found a small brigade of infantry camped there. They were all new troops, had never seen a rebel, and their new clothes and general fresh appearance contrasted sharply with our rags, woe-begone and haggard looks. We went to bed supperless.

May 29th. Moved early this morning, and a mile from Kingston found some cars pushed down to the end of the repaired track with some forage and rations for us. Spent an hour drawing them, and then moved on slowly, passing Adairsville, and camped at Calhoun, making but 20 miles for the day.

May 30th. Moved early this morning, and as the weather was cool made Dalton by noon, having traveled 20 miles. Here we found another brigade of infantry camped in and around the town; all new troops, and we "smole" a very broad smile to see the style they were putting on. They had not yet got the gloss off their clothes, and were still wearing their white gloves and stand-up collars; but you might have supposed from their actions they were born soldiers, and had never done anything but fight all their lives, and we began to ask each other if *we* had ever behaved so foolishly. We unanimously agreed we had not. Perhaps it was because we never had the time. But all we had yet seen or admired was forgotten, when, a few minutes afterwards, we came upon their brigade sutler. Some of the troops were Dutch, and when we got to the sutler's we saw at least 100 kegs of beer, (it would have been a nice thing for our sutler to have kept 100 kegs of beer "ferninst" us on a campaign,) and 15 or 20 Dutch officers, each dressed in the very finest style, with a meerschaum pipe in one hand and a mug of beer in the other. They were jabbering like so many geese, and drinking and smoking as complacently as if they had been in their own beer-gardens at home. This brought to our minds our seven days at Gravelly Springs without a bite to eat, and we wondered who wouldn't be a soldier and always have it just as these fellows were having it.

May 31st. We were camped a mile south of Dalton last night, and as we passed through there this morning the infantry began to blow the sick call. We had heard this but very few times for more than a year, but we knew the sound so well, and it called up so many old recollections, and so many old "play-off's," that we immediately began to cheer most lustily, and to sing our old songs of "Are you all dead? Are you all dead?" "Come and get your quinine! Come and get your quinine!" and a hundred other droll and harsh expressions which were quite offensive to our "broadcloth" troops, and they began to retort with some sharp words. This called forth the cheers and jeers of the whole command, and we never saw a set of fellows get such hectoring It seems natural for old soldiers to treat green ones with a sort of contempt that often amounts to insult.

We passed through Buzzard Roost Gap, Tunnel Hill and Ringgold, all familiar names to us, and bivouacked at noon about two miles west of Ringgold, making 20 miles for the day. We had not been in Ringgold since September 12th, 1863. On the same day four companies of our regiment had a fight at Rock Springs and got badly handled. On the 7th of October, 1863, at Farmington, we captured some of the same fellows that fought us at Rock Springs, and they told us what they had done with our dead, whom we had laid on a porch; where they had buried them, &c. We took all these notes down and still had them with us, and as we came to Tunnel Hill we began to talk of the time we were there before and what happened us; and also the same at Ringgold, we for the first time in a year thought of these notes, and at dinner got them out of our knapsack and read them to our mess, and thought we would like to go out there and see how things looked once more. After dinner we went to Col. Thomson and got permission to take a sqnad and go and see if we could find Capt. McMurtry's grave. There were eight of us, and when within two miles of the place things began to look familiar. John P. Angelly was the man's name who lived in the big white house where we had the fight. He was still living there, and we had no difficulty in finding the place. This man was very clever to us, and told us all about the fight, how many were killed on each side, where they were buried, and a hundred other things of deep interest. He took us out in his orchard and showed us a long trench where he said 17 confederate soldiers were buried. He took us to another, where he said a captain and seven Yankees were buried. Everything corresponded so exactly with our notes that we were sure there could be no mistake about it. We rounded up the grave, set up a well-lettered head-board and built a pen around it. By this time it was getting dark, but we did not feel like leaving the place without rendering thanks to Almighty God, who had preserved us through this great struggle and permitted us to pay this tribute of respect to one we loved so well. So we took off our hats and said, comrades, let us pray! We all knelt down around the grave, and to the very best of our ability, and from the depths of our heart, thanked God for his goodness in protecting our lives, for bringing us once more to honor the dead, for sending peace to the country, and for all his blessings of life; and asked that his protection might still be over us, and that we might do our duty faithfully as citizens as we had done it as soldiers; and that we might all finally meet in Heaven at last. The old gentleman told us many things about the fight, number and disposition of the rebels, we had not known before; told us how the division we had fought followed us in the night, and said he didn't see how we could possibly escape; and further, that the rebels themselves were the worst beat set of fellows he ever saw, as they seemed to be just as certain of capturing us as they were of getting their breakfast the next morning. After our sad but pleasant task had been performed, we went to Chicamauga Creek, opposite Lee & Gordon's Mills, and camped for the night.

Next morning, June 1st, we spent three or four hours riding over the battle-field and verifying everything we have written about that fearful battle. Along on the ridge where Davis' and Sheridan's divisions were slaughtered so fearfully were hundreds of soldiers (that is their bones and clothes) still lying unburied. Right west of this is precisely where our brigade lay, and we found vastly more dead here than on any other part of the field. Every part of the field looked just as familiar as if we had always lived in the neighborhood. Our modest line of logs and rails, though rotted down some, was still there, and behind it thousands of our cartridge shells. We still had a very vivid recollection of a bullet striking a rail right in front of us during the thickest of the fight, and had no trouble going right to the place, picking out the ball, which we brought home as a reminder that just one rail had been between us and certain death. We moved on toward Chattanooga till we got to Rossville, where we laid in the shade an hour; our regiment came along and we fell in with the column, heartily glad of our adventure, and of course had a thousand questions to answer, as the whole command would have been glad to have made the visit. We passed through Chattanooga, crossed the Tennessee River, and camped not far from where we lay in camp the latter part of August, in 1863. All these places, Chattanooga and vicinity, we had seen so often and under so many different circumstances that they failed to excite any interest or passing remark. The regiment had marched 20 miles.

Friday, June 2d. We expected to turn over our horses at this place, and in a few days to be mustered out of the service, and Maj. Kilborn has been sent on to Nashville for the books and papers belonging to our brigade. These we have not seen since we left Gravelly Springs. Time is now hanging heavily upon our hands. Of course we are justly proud of what we have passed through, but somehow or other that does not very much enhance our prospects for the future; at least we cannot expect to make a living off of what has already passed.

Monday, June 5th. We have been here now for several days and still no word from Maj. Kilborn or our books. The men have ceased to take any interest in their horses, and many of them are nearly starving to death. Our trip from Macon to this place has not been a hard one on horses, but just as soon as we got orders to go home the men quit taking care of them, hoping thereby to get to ride on the cars.

June 6th. To-day Maj. Kilborn telegraphed from Nashville that we would not be mustered out here, but that we should come on to Nashville, and we got orders to get ready to march to-morrow morning. This made about half of the men mad as hornets, and they swore they would not ride on horseback any further.

June 7th. Reveille at 3 a. m., and orders to get ready to move immediately. There was some tall swearing done inside the next few minutes. We have full notes on all that transpired, but suffice it to say that about one-half of the whole command moved out and the others didn't. This leaves the thing in bad shape, but in the course of time all who were left behind found their way to Nashville. We were one that moved out, and shall continue the journey. We moved back through Chattanooga and took the road for Shell Moun, struck old Lookout at the north-east corner, wound around over the north end two-thirds of the way to the top, with the railroad hundreds of feet below us, and the river hundreds of feet below that. After we had got up a mile, on looking back to the east, north-east and north, we could see miles and miles of historic ground. We could see the whole of Missionary Ridge, and could point out many prominent points of interest connected with the great battle-field. Looking north we could see up the valley to North Chicamauga, and still away up to where the Wheeler raid began. Turning to our left and looking up we could see the far famed battle-field above the clouds, where Hooker's men swept around the north end of the ridge and drove the rebel hordes down the east side of the mountain. We took a last long look at many of the scenes of our strifes, privations and hardships, passed down into Lookout Valley, over the Lookout Creek, over the Raccoon Mountains, Whiteside, and hundreds of other places of deep interest; but we had seen them all before, settled down to entire indifference, and finally all went to sleep, which we could do on horseback nearly as well as any other way. We bivouacked at Shell Moun, on the very same place we occupied the 6th of May, 1864.

June 8th. Moved early, and when we got to Bridgeport took some pains to ascertain the length of the bridge there. It is the finest wooden bridge we ever saw. The railroad runs on top, and the wagon road immediately under it. There is an island in the river here and the bridge passes over it. The bridge across the east branch of the river is 200 yards long, across the island 50 yards, and across the western branch is 480 yards. Here we found more new troops. Passed through Stevenson and camped three miles north, on Crow Creek.

June 9th. Moved early and camped an hour before noon at a place called Condit.

June 10th. Passed through Tantallon, over the Cumberland Mountains, through Cowan, and camped within two miles of Decherd.

June 11th. Moved early, passed through Decherd; 15 miles north we came to Tullahoma. Here there were a great many troops camped, most of them new ones, and a whole brigade fell out into line of battle, along the side of the street, to do honors to old soldiers by presenting arms and dipping their colors as we passed in front of them, while each company of our brigade, in turn, gave them three cheers and a tiger. This was a very pleasant episode; but we should not be surprised if these new troops were glad the war was over, as our old clothes were so very ragged and dirty that they contrasted sharply with their new and clean ones. We camped near Normandy.

June 12th. Passed through Wartrace, Bellbuckle, Fosterville, and camped near a little station called Christiana, 11 miles from Murfreesboro.

June 13th. Moved at sun-up, passed through Murfreesboro—the name which stands for half of the sufferings of the regiment; moved on over the Stone River battle-field, and were wonderfully interested in the National cemetery started there, and also in the monument erected to the dead heroes of Hazen's brigade. It stands over the grave where they were all buried in one long trench, close by where they fought and fell. The name, company and regiment of each, is inscribed on the monument. This cemetery, when completed, will be of deep interest to all loyal people who have friends buried here who were slain in that fearful conflict. The place is very beautiful. Bivouacked on Stewart's Creek.

June 14th. Moved when the sun was an hour high, and went into camp shortly after noon, four miles from Nashville. We were much impressed with the contrast in the appearance of the country the whole way from Murfreesboro to Nashville, now, with that of January, 1863, just after the battle of Stone River. The whole way is surpassingly rich, and then was in the very highest state of cultivation. The plantations were all fenced with heavy, high fences, of cedar rails, and all cut up into small fields. There were hundreds of fine houses and thousands of negro quarters. Now there were scarcely any houses of any kind left standing, and scarcely a rail between Nashville and Murfreesboro. Then there were thousands of acres of corn still standing. To-day the whole country is one vast sea of old dead weeds, 10 feet high. The only cultivated places that we saw at all were two or three small patches of cotton cultivated by some negroes, and these had no fences at all around them. This country can never be made what it once was, as all the rails are gone and no timber to make others; but worst of all, the people are all gone, and but few of them will ever come back. Such is war.

We had drawn no rations since leaving Decherd, and then but two days'—and were entirely out; hadn't a bite to eat, and the men were cursing mad because we did not go on to Nashville, which we might just as easily have done. After feeding our horse we struck out to see if we could not find something to eat. A mile and a half north of camp we ran on to a brigade of new troops, and inquired of the first soldier we met for something to eat. He said they only drew a day's rations at a time, and they were out. We asked him what kind of rations they got. He said, soft bread. We asked him where they got it. He said they had a brigade bakery. We asked him to show us the place, and we went for it. After finding out where we belonged (they could easily tell by our clothes that we didn't belong to them) they flatly refused to let us have a bite. They had plenty of bread, but could not let it go out of the brigade. We asked how they sold it; they said 10 cents a loaf, but could sell to no one but officers. We hadn't a cent of money, but determined to have something to eat at all hazards. We went back to camp and told the boys what we had found, and after raking around among the whole company, got 60, cents and went back, four of us. The bakers still refused to sell to any but officers. We told them we were officers, and they inquired the names, company, regiment, etc. We told what we pleased, they took it all down in a book; we got the bread and "skinned out," but it will be a long time before they ever find the officers we named, or ever hear tell of the regiments or companies we belonged to.

June 15th. This morning we moved for Nashville, our regiment in the advance, and when we got there we met Col. Miller. Oh! but we were glad to see him, and cheered him heartily. You remember he had been shot in the thigh at Selma, and we had left him at Montgomery. He was still unable to walk, or ride on horseback, but had to be hauled in an ambulance; but we felt proud to have him at the head of column once more. We moved through Nashville, crossed the Cumberland on a steam ferryboat, and went into camp three miles north-east of Edgefield, where the dismounted men we left at Chattanooga had been in camp for two or three days. We were glad to have the family all together once more. In the afternoon, all who rode horses turned them over, and our camp began to look slim. We had four pack mules to each company, and about one-third of the men were riding mules, the Historian included; taking so many horses away made them lonesome, and besides they were very hungry, and made the night perfectly hideous with their braying. They were so very uneasy that for the last time we had to detail a horse guard to mind them.

June 16th. This morning we turned over our mules, and the pack mules, and our camp looks so lonesome and deserted that it doesn't seem like camp at all. For more than two years, now, our horses have been so constantly with us, and seemingly such a very necessary part of our service, that they have grown to be almost a part of ourselves; and no doubt there were many old and tried friends parted when we turned over our horses. We give it as our unqualified opinion that "Old dog Tray," as a friend, has been badly discounted by the affection of the horse for its rider, and the friendship of the trooper for his horse. Our men are busy taking the straps, from their saddles—of course Uncle Sam will have to lose the straps—and buckling them around their knapsacks, blankets, &c., and making them portable, and our camp presents much the same appearance it did on the 1st of November last, when we turned our horses over to Kilpatrick's division. Muster rolls were ordered to be made out immediately. This was worse than going through a hard fight, and we have little doubt but those who had the work to do would much rather a second time take their chances of going through any engagement we had ever passed through than to undertake to make out muster rolls. To get up a muster roll accurately and neatly required three hard days' labor for an expert, or one who was used to making them out; and as two or three correct copies had to be made out each time, you can readily see what a task it was. In our regiment there was nobody used to it; as before intimated nearly the whole regiment was composed of farmers and mechanics, and not accustomed to writing; but suppose the whole of them had been born penmen, and educated in the science up to its highest point, carrying a rifle was not very well calculated to steady their hands to such a degree as to enable them to write gracefully. There was another thing that militated against a proper performance of the task more than all things else, and that was the want of that practice which makes perfect in all things. You will the better understand this when I tell you that during our whole term of service we had been paid but four times, viz: First at Murfreesboro, Tenn., March 10th, 1863; second at Duck River, Tenn., July 16th, 1863; third at Brownsburg, Ala., November 12th, 1863; fourth at Louisville, Ky., November 23d, 1864; and at the last time we had been paid, the government owed us over 13 months' wages, and now owed us over seven months', so that to make out the rolls now, it was like undertaking a task that had never been performed before. This evening we turned over our saddles and spurs, and were simply foot infantry once more. For more than a week the officers and men tugged and toiled away at the company papers and the muster rolls, and it was not until the 26th of June, 1865, that Capt. Hosea declared the regiment ready for mustering out of the service. During this interval there were many things took place that would have been of lasting interest had we been just going into the service instead of going out.

CHAPTER XLI.

ANDERSONVILLE—THE SUM OF ALL MISERIES.

"In the prison cell I sit, thinking, Mother dear, of you,
And the dear, beloved ones, so far away—
Yet my heart will still grow sad spite of all that I can do,
Though I try to cheer my comrades and be gay.
Tramp, tramp, tramp, the boys are marching,
Cheer up, comrades, they will come!
And beneath the starry flag we shall breathe the air again
In the Free land, in our own beloved Home!"

While we are here waiting for our muster rolls to be made out, and before speaking further of the incidents that transpired at this place, we propose to pay our respects to our unfortunate comrades who have fallen into the hands of the enemy. We know of no more fitting tribute we can pay *them*—no more fitting lesson of instruction for our children, to teach them the love of freedom, of loyalty, and the love of country they should ever possess—than to give the actual experience of many of those who were so unfortunate as to get into those Southern prison pens, and yet so fortunate as to escape, as by the skin of their teeth, with their lives to tell the story of their sufferings, their heroic endurance, and their brave attempts to escape.

The God of battles looked kindly upon the Seventy-Second during its entire eventful service. It had, perhaps, fewer men killed, in proportion to the vast number of times it was under the severe and withering fire of the enemy, and the number of men engaged each time, than any other regiment in the service. Being under the command of officers whose ripe judgment, quick perception, and varied experience, enabled them to take advantage of every providential circumstance in our favor, and whose conscientious love of country, and the men they commanded, prevented them from entertaining for a moment any enterprise that seemed rash, or needlessly hazardous; and being composed of men whose judgment and good sense enabled them to take advantage of everything that would shield or protect them from the death dealing missiles of the enemy—we *never* came out of any contest in which we had not inflicted vastly more damage than we received. And we cannot call to mind a single instance where we ever lost a man on account of the carelessness or inefficiency of any officer in our regiment, or of the negligence or want of good sense of the men themselves. But sometimes, while serving with other troops whose officers were less efficient than our own, and whose men did not always evince the same gallantry and "staying" qualities that characterized the men of our brigade, we had some men killed and others captured. The epitaphs of those who were killed are written in the hearts of their surviving comrades, and they sleep well. But no sculptured monument, however costly, or however elaborately carved, can ever tell of the reeking hell through which those who were captured waded in order to find a martyr's grave. You fathers and mothers, who sent forth your noble boys upon whom you doted, and upon whom with just pride you looked as the stay and support of your declining years—you wives, who let your husbands go to fight for their country, whose strong arms you relied upon to build up for you everything you could conceive to be good, great and holy—and you children, who kissed your papas for the last time, and as you all gathered around the old hearthstone, and prayed and waited, and waited and prayed, and hoped with that hope that makes the heart sick, and longed and yearned, for the dear one that came not—picture to yourselves all the horrors of death from pain intensified, from torture long drawn out, from misery multiplied, and from suffering beyond any human tongue or pen to tell, and then multiply them a thousand times, and you may write in these words all this suffering after each loved one's name: DIED IN ANDERSONVILLE PRISON.

Of 21 of our regiment who fell into rebel hands, 15 died thus, and we can think of no way of bringing their heroism, fortitude and suffering, more vividly before your minds, than by giving you a very brief and condensed statement of the experience of those who escaped from those nameless tortures.

We have very frequently spoken of "scouts"—regimental scouts, brigade scouts, and division scouts. These all had their legitimate and proper duties to perform; but there was another class of scouts attached to the army of which we have said nothing, who were called the secret service scouts, or in common parlance, spies. No branch of the service was more risky than this, and it required a talent so very rare that proper persons for this service were extremely hard to get But of the very solid material of which our regiment was composed there was no lack of men to fill any responsible position for which a well regulated army had any need, and of the many of our regiment who at one time or another tried their hands at the secret service, and with varying success, three were unfortunately captured, viz: Sergts. Oscar F. Bryan, Co. C, Theophilus W. Milligan, Co. G, and private Wm. DeStewart McIntyre, Co. H. We condense the following from McIntyre's experience:

STORY OF WILLIAM DE STEWART M'INTYRE.

Scout to the Tennessee River—Taking Massah Picket's Meat—Eating Rebel Ham—Reporting to Gen. Logan—Great Activity—Captured—I'm going to take you out in the morning and Hang you, G—d d—n you—Didn't get Hanged, but Worse Was sent to Andersonville—Closely Guarded—Miseries, Filth and Vermin of Andersonville—Meet Buck Milligan, who says: "Well, old fellow, I'm sorry to see you."—Life in Andersonville—Carrying out the Dead—The Tunnel Diggers—Escape—Blood Hounds on the Trail—Recaptured—Put into the Stocks.

The secret service had two representatives from Company H, viz: Sergt. Henderson Monroe, and McIntyre, better known throughout the regiment and army as "Mack." Mack is of Scotch parentage, his father being an Old School Presbyterian Scotch Clergyman, and it was to this fact Mack always attributed his well known love for confederate horse flesh. Mack was born in Pulaski County, Virginia, but early in life taken by his father to Indiana, and received his education in that State. (He is now living in Mattoon, Illinois.) He entered the service, and at the solicitation of his friend Adjutant Rice, went into Company H, which to him was a company of strangers.

The first year of service was characterized by a love of adventure, and it is safe to say that unless on other regular detail, or sick, no foraging or scouting party went out without him. These traits coming to the knowledge of Gen. George Crook, about the time of the Wheeler raid, Mack was selected for many special services, and was finally regularly detailed, December 26th, 1863, for the secret service. From that time until brought to a sudden and abrupt stop, by capture, he led a most active life. Possessing a vigorous constitution, quick, active mind, and perceptions very acute, he was singularly well adapted to that branch of the service. The 123d Illinois has cause to recollect him with grateful stomachs, if not grateful hearts. He had received orders, while we were in camp at Huntsville, to go down to and along the Tennessee River in search of rebel mail, crossings, &c., and took with him the scout from Company G, known by everybody as "Buck" Milligan. A soldier belonging to the 123d Illinois, learning that their service would take them near Mooresville, where his regiment was then in camp, concluded to go along with them in order to get to his regiment. Toward the close of the day the scouts left their regular work on the river and started to Mooresville to spend the night. When about eight miles from that place they met a man on horseback, who, alarmed by the blue uniform of the 123d man, hastily turned his horse, put spurs to him, and hurried off on a byroad leading to the river. About 200 yards behind him was an ox team drawing an old fashioned Pennsylvania wagon. On coming up to it the boys were very much amused to see the face of the negro driver

—mouth spread from ear to ear—and hear him say, "Ya! Ya!! Massa —Golly, didn't ole Massa run? Ya! ya!! ya!!!" "What have you here, Uncle?" asked the boys. "Some of de finest hams and shol'ers, Cap'n, you eber see in all your bo'n days, and dat was Massa Kurn'l Pickett. De men dun gone haf hour ago, down to de ribber to get de ole boat ready. De Yankees gettin' too close; dey cum down to Mo'sville de odder da', and Massa Pickett cum fo' his meat—oh, ya! ya!! ya!!! Cap'n!" Brightening up with a new and happy thought, he said, "An' dar's an odder wagon loden at de house." "Uncle, how far is it to Mooresville?" "About eight mile, sah." "And how far is it to the river?" "About foah mile, sah." Telling the old man to turn his steers around as quickly as possible and push out for Mooresville, the 123d man moved off with him, while Mack and Buck rode up to the house and around to the rear. There they found four mules hitched to a wagon, already well loaded with well cured meat, just hung up for smoking, a *petite*, black-eyed woman, superintending the loading. When she saw the visitors she ordered one of her servants to go for "Massa Pickett." A Spencer rifle induced the driver to mount the saddle mule and drive out. The boys well knew Col. Pickett would be back as soon as he could go to the river, get his men and return. So Mack directed Milligan to leave with him his Spencer rifle and hurry forward to Mooresville for assistance, while he and the 123d man would keep along with the wagons and fight it out in case Col. Pickett should overhaul them. The Lieutenant in charge of the picket post, when Milligan reported, immediate mounted his reserves and hastened to the assistance of Mack, but his help was not needed. The wagons and all were just inside the picket post when Col. Picket and his men came up. 'Twas too late; niggers, wagons, hams, and all, were forever confiscated. Col. Biggs, of the 123d, Adjt. Hamlin, Capt. Woods, Mack, Milligan, and others, had fried ham for breakfast, and before noon the quartermaster was issuing hams and shoulders to the regiment. While this was going on a barouche was driven into camp and halted in front of Col. Biggs' headquarters. The occupant was the lady of the previous afternoon, and she *wanted a voucher for those things.*

The winter and spring preceding the campaign of 1864 was a busy one for the scouts, and Mack was almost constantly in the saddle, carrying a rebel mail, and other like duties. In the latter part of April, of that year, Mack came into Gen. Thomas' headquarters, and it being inconvenient for him to reach his own headquarters, with the 2d cavalry division, he was ordered to report to Maj.-Gen. John A. Logan, commanding the 15th army corps, until such time as he could regain his own headquarters, then at Columbia, Tenn. May 4th began the advance of the Army of the Tennessee, under McPherson, for the rear of the rebel army, under Jo. Johnston, *via*. Snake Creek Gap. The scouts and signal corps men surprised the guard at the gap, secured it without loss, and chased the few Johnnies guarding it almost into Resaca. The next few days, as indeed throughout the entire campaign, the scouts were in constant demand, and Mack, with the others, found but little rest night or day. Finally, on the morning of the 14th of May, 1864, in attempting to enter the rebel lines before daylight, he was captured and taken to the headquarters of a Gen. Wright, who asked him a few questions and then with a contemptuous expression said: "Do you know what I am going to do with you? I'm going to take you out in the morning and hang you, G—d d—n you; that's what I'll do with you!" And thereupon he ordered the sergeant and soldiers in charge of the prisoner back to their posts. The next morning the rebel picket called across the lines to one of our pickets that they had captured a Yankee spy the night before and would hang him that morning. From this, no doubt, sprang the report which circulated through the army and went home to his friends, that Mack *had been hanged* that morning. (The Historian well remembers of hearing, the next day, that he had actually been hanged,) and for long months he was mourned by comrades and friends as one dead A quiet investigation of the guards and the surroundings at Wright's headquarters satisfied him that any attempt to escape would be futile, and so he settled himself down for some much needed sleep. It was but fairly daylight when he was awakened and told that he was wanted at Gen. Hardee's headquarters. At the investigation which followed there were present quite a number of prominent rebel Generals, and as may well be supposed, Mack was subjected to a most rigid examination, but owing to his "*ignorance of the country, and his misfortune in getting lost (?) in the woods,*" backed by the volunteered statement of an old residenter, "I wouldn't a' tried to a' cut cross through them thar woods arter night myself; I'd a' got loss suah," Gen. Hardee concluded he couldn't be considered a spy, and remarked, "Send him on down for exchange." To say that Mack was happy would be drawing it very mild. Alas! he little knew what sending him on down for exchange meant. It meant exchange of freedom for fetters, of health for disease, of robustness for rottenness, of cleanliness for foulness, filth, loathesomeness, unspeakable starvation of mind and body; gangrened arms and feet, scurvy, swollen arms, SUICIDE, DEATH, ANDERSONVILLE.

Mack, with a few others, were put into an old hotel, and unfortunately employed his time sitting in a window and counting the regiments as they passed, until discovered by that same Gen. Wright, who had given him such cheerful assurance of his intentions a few hours before. Calling the lieutenant in charge of the prisoners to him, and pointing up to Mack, he communicated something to that officer which led him immediately to withdraw Mack from the other prisoners and send him on down to Atlanta by the first train To add to his discomfort, a guard would persist in occupying the same seat with him and would not even allow the window to be opened. A few days of close confinement in Atlanta, a hurried inspection of the brick jail at Macon, and he arrived at that sum of all rebel villainies and cruelties, Andersonville. And who can describe it? Its stockade of pine logs, 18 feet above and six feet below ground; the little sentry boxes perched on the outside and just high enough for a guard to look over inside with ease; its two gates doubly stockaded; its flat, sanded, low hill sides, with a sluggish marsh of concentrated filth, miasma and death, trying to flow between; its merciless heat by day, its unwarmed, chilly night; its hot sand, alive with vermin; its fluid, called by way of apology, water; its mockery of food called rations; and its inhabitants!! Who tells of them? Those moving skeletons, hollow eyes, sunken cheeks, protruding bones, gangrened arms, scurvied mouths, bare, rotting feet, contracted, shrunken limbs, the vacant, idiotic stare; hope! all gone; food! ample food for the dead wagon, with its 10 at a load, and 10 loads per day. It never can be fully described; it never will be fully laid bare in all its enormity. The 13,400 dead in its grave yard cannot tell their sufferings. Of the 20,000 survivors, possibly 7,000 are yet alive, and to them it is but as some horrible nightmare clothed in reality, and they can but guess at the extent of their injuries. While marching around to his detachment between the solid masses on either side, watching eagerly to see if some friend had been equally unfortunate with himself, a well known voice exclaimed, "If there isn't Mack!" It was his old scouting companion, Buck Milligan. There was a depth of meaning in the greeting, "Well, old fellow, I am sorry to see you," which Mack did not then, but afterwards did, appreciate. Then began in reality life in Andersonville. Chaplain Moody has written of the "Lights and Shadows of Libby Prison." There were no lights in Andersonville. 'Twas all shadows, with nothing to relieve the dread, dull monotony, but roll call in the forenoon and drawing rations in the afternoon. The question has often been asked, "How did you put in your time?" In the morning, those who were fortunate enough, or rather provident enough, to save over any part of their rations from the previous day's drawing, would get up from their sand beds and go through the form of eating a breakfast, and this was made as long continued as possible. Then followed roll call—those of a detachment able to do so would form in a regular company line, and answer promptly as their names were called. But squatted on the ground in front and rear were cripples, some with legs drawn up with scurvy, some with feet eaten into by gangrene, some emaciated by diarrhœa, whose feeble "here" would require so much exertion as to almost take the last breath from their bodies. The next thing requiring attention was carrying out the dead. This was a great privilege, and by custom the four sleeping nearest the corpse had a vested right in the matter. It gave an opportunity to procure a few sticks for fuel, or pine brush for bedding or shelter. The remainder of the day, until ration time, was generally spent in aimless wandering about, or talking with old army acquaintances, bewailing their sad lot, and speculating as to how our armies were getting along, what the prospects were for an exchange, &c. The tunnel diggers, however, improved their time by sleeping. The ration drawing was the event of the day. The sergeant in charge of a detachment would detail a certain number of men to go with him to the ration wagon which was driven inside the stockade. In that wagon would be large loaves of bread, innocent of salt or shortening, some meat, and possibly some rice or peas, generally nothing but bread and meat, the latter in very small quantities, and sometimes so small as to be omitted entirely. When the sergeant received the amount due, it was carried to the headquarters of the detachment, where the final distribution took place. As soon as their share was allotted, many, *very* many, of the poor fellows, would sit down and eagerly devour the last crumb. The issue generally began about 4 o'clock p. m., and was completed before dark. From that time on for an hour or more, a low, steady hum, floated through the air, an indefinable dull murmur of voices. No sound of buggy, wagon or dray; no shout of driver, no call of news boy or peddler; no clear ringing note of church bell, or loud screech of locomotive; no flash of gas light or lamp; but by the light of the moon or stars, the last report of a coming exchange would be repeated over and over again, until at last even that dull murmur of voices had died away, and such a heavy, death-like silence, as no pen can describe, would come stealthily over the vast camp, to be relieved only by the cry of the guard: "Post number one, 10 o'clock, and a-l-l-z well!" taken up and repeated by each guard, in turn, until it has made the "grand rounds." Sometimes an aroused sleeper, indignant at the repeated falsehood, would contradict it with, "You lie! you —— rebel!" As the night wore on and the cold chill became more pinching, the thousands of half naked, shivering forms, sleeping side by side on the bare sand, with nothing but the sky or clouds for a covering, would huddle closer and closer together. Now and then might be heard the dreaming delirious mutterings of a husband and father talking to the wife and children at home; or of a boy, in the last delirium of death, upbraiding himself to his mother for leaving her at all. And when the morning light crept softly over the high stockade, here, there, and yonder, all over the camp, would be cold corpses; not bodies, but apologies—semblances—each a residium of what had once been a human body. And oh, my God! All this in the "Land of the free and the home of the brave." What mockery! What blasphemy!!

In October, Martin E. Hogan, one of Gen. Meade's scouts, Payton Shields, James Smith, and Mack, made their escape, and by going through the grave yard and using great care, they succeeded in preventing the stockade blood hounds from finding their trail; but after getting well up in the country they were discovered by a negro-hunting hound and finally recaptured, brought back to Andersonville and put into the "'stocks,—"Hogan and Mack in to the "lay-down stocks," which confined the feet only, and kept them nine inches from the ground. The other two, Shields and Smith, were put into the "upright stocks," which kept the body perfectly erect, and confined both feet and head. This was about 4 o'clock on Monday afternoon, and on Tuesday morning at 6 o'clock they were compelled to exchange places, and were thus changed every 12 hours. This arrangement brought Hogan and Mack into the upright stocks in the daytime, and Shields and Smith into the lay-down stocks in the daytime, and so it was continued until Thursday noon, when the lieutenant in charge of the guards took the responsibility upon himself of releasing them, and turning them back into the stockade.

To stand for 12 minutes in one position is irksome, but to stand for 12 hours with feet fast in the stocks and the head held firmly by a 16-inch board, and exposed to the rays of a Georgia sun, is agony. This is but the merest glimpse of Andersonville. Its full history can never be written. It seemed to be a place over which the cloud of rebel hate hung so dense as to shut out the blessings of Heaven itself.

WM. DESTEWART MCINTYRE.

STORY OF WILLIAM M. SPENCER.

In Prision at Macon—Rats sold for $2 apiece—Renting an Ax and an Oven for Rations—Sent to Savannah—Dead Men in the Cars with Us—11 Frozen to Death at Once—To Black Shear—Paroling—Jump from the Train and Escape—Burying Ourselves to Escape Andersonville—Negro Guides to Prisoners—Shelter them at Night, Secrete and Feed them by Day, Ferry them over Rivers and Save them from Death or Recapture—Coming in Sight of the Old Flag.

Wm. M. Spencer, private Company K, furnishes this:

On the 7th of September, 1864, myself and a man from my company by the name of Albert Weeks, were captured about 16 miles south-east of Atlanta. When taken, Weeks was severely wounded by a gun-shot through the body. This was about 5 o'clock in the afternoon; we were immediately taken 10 miles to brigade headquarters. From there we were sent to division headquarters, arriving there about 11 o'clock at night. The next morning we were sent to Gen. Hood's headquarters, at Lovejoy's Station, on the Atlanta & Macon Railroad, 25 miles from where we were captured, and we had walked all the way. We were then sent to Macon Prison, where we arrived about 3 p. m. on the 9th. When we were put in prison that evening we received one-half pint of corn meal, about four ounces of bacon, and a little rice, for one day's rations; and this was the first we had had to eat since the morning of the 7th. The third day after being in the prison Weeks was taken to the hospital and I got to see him no more until after my escape. Weeks was exchanged in the latter part of November, in the exchange of sick and wounded. When I was captured all my blankets, one suit of clothes, and my boots, were taken from me. On going into the prison I got in with a young man by the name of John W. Richards, of the 98th Illinois, of our brigade. He had one old blanket, which he divided with me. Rations at Macon were short, At this place rats were brought in which sold for $2.00 apiece in confederate money. I frequently saw men buy and eat them, but I never could bring my stomach to the point of eating them. At Macon we stayed about four weeks; then we were sent to Millen. While at Macon we were furnished with bake-ovens to bake our meal in, and when we were moved from there we managed to steal ours through. On arriving at Millen we found the oven a great help to us. When we arrived, there were 9,000 men there. The timber had all been taken off, but we found an old log that was left. There was no shelter of any kind, and we had no ax to work up this old log; so I went around hunting for an ax. I succeeded in finding one in the upper end of the camp. They told me I could have it if I would bring a part of our rations for the use of it. I took it, and we built a shelter; I took the ax home and some corn meal for the use of it, but we loaned our oven the same day—so we made it back. While there our time was spent in studying a plan to make our escape. We were at this place eight weeks, and I met McIntyre, of Company H. He got out in the exchange, in November. I also met "Buck" Milligan, but after we left there I saw him no more. We were next sent to Savannah, in box-cars, 90 to 95 in a car, and when we arrived, we had some dead men in the cars to take out. We were unloaded on the commons, where we had no wood for fire, and by 11 o'clock we had 11 frozen to death. Here we stayed some 10 days with no shelter. Our old blanket had given out long before this, and the sea breezes were very cold. From this place we were sent down the Gulf Railroad to a place called Black Shear, 86 miles from Savannah, and the county seat of Pierce county, Georgia. This was the poorest county in the state, and there were but three or four houses in the town. Here we were camped in the woods with no stockade around us—nothing but a heavy guard. I think we had about 6,000 here. In about a week there were 1,000 taken out and paroled—sent on to Savannah, and from there to Florence, South Carolina. In a few days there were 1,000 more called out—Richards and myself went out in this thousand. We were paroled and expected to be sent through to our lines. They intended to send us to Florence, South Carolina, but by the time we got to Savannah, Gen. Sherman had got in ahead of us and cut the railroad, so they were compelled to send us back to Black Shear, where we stayed some 10 days longer, and were then sent to Thomasville, the end of the Gulf Railroad, 200 miles from Savannah. On the way from Black Shear to Thomasville, Richards and myself jumped the train, about 9 o'clock at night, and started for our blockading fleet at Brunswick. When within about 15 miles of that place, and on the third night after our escape, we were recaptured and taken to Thomasville, where on the 19th day of December, 1864, we made our escape again and made our way to Gen. Sherman's lines, at Savannah, where we arrived on the 21st of January, 1865. Just a few days before making our escape the last time, the officers commanding the prison came in and told us to be ready to move at any time, as they intended to take us back to Andersonville. So Richards, a man by the name of Kennedy, of the 51st Illinois, and myself, dug a hole in the ground, six feet long, three feet deep, and two and one-half feet wide, and let boards down about six inches and covered them with dirt. On the 19th our men were moved. We stayed in our hiding place and they moved off and left us. It was about 9 o'clock that night when we came out of our hiding place, and we were till daylight next morning making six miles. We did not venture in any negro hut for several nights. We traveled only at night and lay by in the day time. After our escape we got plenty to eat. On Christmas Eve, the old boots which the rebels gave me when I was captured in exchange for my new ones, gave out, and I was compelled to march through the swamp barefooted for four or five nights, when a negro gave me a pair of shoes, which I put on, and for which I was very thankful. We had a long trip through the enemy's country of 33 nights out. The last two weeks we were out, and after we found out the negroes would do to trust, we met them every night, and were guarded by them. We went into a little station on the railroad, about 70 miles from our lines, one night, and there were 50 rebel guards there. We took supper in one of the negro houses and then went out and left them. They thought we were some of their own men, as we had on the same colored clothes they had. On New Years eve we went into a negro hut and got our suppers, and after starting on, the rebels got some hounds after us, but the hounds got on our back track and we got into a swamp and thus made a very narrow escape, as the dogs passed within 30 yards of us. About the 12th of January we arrived at the Altamaha River, where we had to lie over three days, as the rebels had the river guarded so the negroes could not get us across. On the fourth night they succeeded in getting a boat, and took us across. Four miles from here was another deep stream that the negroes called Highland. This we had to cross on a log by using poles to push us over. Our poles were 18 feet long, and in some places the water was so deep we could not touch bottom. It took us a day and a half to get across these waters. After getting across this river we came to a plantation where there were a lot of negroes clearing ground, and we dried our clothes by their fires, and that night went to their quarters and got our suppers. We were compelled to stay three days with them on account of rebels guarding a river five miles ahead of us. From where we lay in the swamp we could look into the rebel camp of 50 men, any time in the day. They were not over 300 yards from us. The negroes brought our provisions to us at night. On the third night the negro who brought our supper to us told us we could cross that night, and he went with us as far as the river, saw us safely over, and then started for home. On that night Richards and myself got separated from Kennedy and never saw him again. We still had a great many rebels to pass after we left him, and I think he was taken up again, as we were in Savannah five days and he never reported to headquarters while we were there. When we came in sight of our men and the old flag at King's Bridge, on the

)geechee River, we felt like shouting. When we reported to Gen. herman, with our butternut clothes on, he looked at us, shook his ead, and said he could not send us to our commands without a recom- nendation from some one that knew us. So we had to go to the 92d llinois (this regiment had served in our brigade.) for a recommenda- ion. The Colonel gave us a recommendation, and we were sent rom Savannah to New York, by water. From there we came to ndianapolis, and from there went to Nashville, where we took a boat ind went around up the Tennessee River and got to our regiments at Gravelly Springs, on the 22d of February, 1865.

WM. M. SPENCER.

EXPERIENCE OF HENRY NOBES, PRIVATE COMPANY C.

A Man with Nine Lives and Many Hair-breadth Escapes—A Modern Othello—Leg Broken—Captured by Forest—Cruelty of Forest—A Kind Lady—A Brute of a Doctor—Leg Broken the Third Time—Good Enough for a d—d Yankee—To Andersonville—The Brute and Devil, Wirz—Clothes All Worn Out—The Dead Line—Prisoners Shot Without Warning—30 Days Furlough for Every Yankee Prisoner Killed—A Poor Boy Shot while Asleep—Rations Little and Poor—Beef or Mule meat, Which?—Five days on a Single pint of Meal—Insanity from Hunger —That Lame Leg Again—A Good Surgeon of Union Sentiments—Using Sand for a Splint—Lying on the Back until the Skin is all worn off. and until the Shoulder Blades Cut Through the Skin—Leg Getting Well—The Well Trampling the Sick to Death—Sick Removed—Fearful Rate of Mortality—Rebel Surgeons Aiming to Make Cripples of Union Prisoners for Life—Paroled at Last—Behold the Stars and Stripes—15 Men Die of Joyful Emotion—God's Land and People—Rags Torn Off—Bathed—Smell Coffee and Meat Cooking and Cry for Them like Children—Clean and Dressed in Blue Once More—Start for Annapolis, and 162 out of 480 Die Before We Reach the Place.

We offer no apology for the following preliminaries. Ever since our election to the office of Regimental Historian, we have most assiduously applied ourself to the task of gathering every bit of information that would throw light and lustre upon the achievements of one of the best regiments in the service. or that would bring to light some of the noble and daring deeds of the modest but meritorious members of that command. These are numerous and astounding, and of themselves would fill volumes that would be a credit to any library which recounts the deeds of the heroes of the war. With the above object in view we were anxious to hear from Mr. Nobes' own lips the story of his capture and imprisonment, Mr. Nobes tells his story in such a straightforward, unvarnished way, that it irresistibly carries conviction with it. The fact is, we believe every word of it, nothwithstanding it recounts some of the most horrible sufferings, and it shows the most noble fortitude, and (to use an army phrase) "eternal grit," that challenges the most profound admiration. Mr.

Nobes is small of stature and slight in build, and as he was but [illegible] years old when he enlisted, we have wondered how he could "pass muster." He seemed to bear a charmed life, and yet to the casual observer there are many things that scarcely seem so charming. His father has often said that, like a cat, he had nine lives. And as he has been killed outright but four times, and suffered four long, lingering and horrible deaths, while a captive, he still has one very substantial life remaining. When four years old his clothes caught fire and burned every stitch off of him, and for the next five months he lay flat on his stomach, it being impossible to turn him over. It would have been fatal to do so. Soon after the war he was working on a "header" reaping machine, down on the Wea, was sun-struck, fell between the four horses, the machine passed over him, and for the next 24 hours he was unconscious. Still later he was driving a wild team over the Main Street Levee, at LaFayette, the horses became frightened, ran away, threw him headlong down the steep embankment, his head striking a stone. He was picked up for dead, and from that time has not known what it was to smell anything. Only a few years ago, when the river was so high the water was several feet deep over the levee, Mr. Nobes undertook to ride across to the bridge, the current being so terribly swift that it washed the horse's feet from under him and carried him down stream. The very timely boat picked him up just as he was going under the last time. A vigorous rolling on a barrel relieved him of the surplus water and brought him to his senses. Mr. Nobes is now 36 years old, and unless some very extraordinary accident should happen him he may yet live to a good old age. He was a member of Company C, and on the 20th of February, 1864, while the command was going into camp at 11 p. m., two miles from West Point, Miss., and while closing up at a quick gallop, his horse stumbled and fell, catching the unfortunate man's leg between the animal and a rail, fracturing the thigh bone in a terrible manner. During the night Dr. Cole had him carried to the house of a Mr. Evans and properly adjusted the fracture. Mr. Nobes' sufferings were terrible in the extreme, but by the morning of the 21st he was resting tolerably well, and he supposed everything was going off right; but shortly after daylight Col. Thomson, then Captain of Company D, and Dr. Cole, came to him and gave him $5.00 in greenbacks, got him some meat and coffee, and bade him good-bye. Mr. Nobes says:

"Soon after Col. Thomson left me the fighting began, and for a time the skirmishing was lively, but still coming closer to me. By 8:30 a. m., from where I lay, I could see the rebels advancing. and I realized for the first that my chances for Andersonville were most flatering. In a few minutes the skirmish line passed by the house. The few who came into the house treated me with all the respect one brave man always accords to another. The line passed on and the skirmishing died away, in the distance. About 9 a. m. Gen. Forest and his staff rode up to the house. Mrs. Evans told him I was in the house, and also of my condition. He and his surgeon came in. Forest seemed in a terrible rage and railed out at me, 'You d- d Yankee son of a b—h, where do you belong?' I told him I belonged to the Seventy-Second Indiana. 'Ah, you are one of Wilder's hell hounds!' I told him I was one of Wilder's men, but no hell hound. He then began to curse me most furiously and wanted to know where my gun and accoutrements were. I told him they were where he would never get hold of them. Said he, 'You needn't to be too d—d sure of that; I expect to capture the whole d—d brood before night.' During all this time the surgeon had been examining me. Forest turned to him and ordered me to be put on a horse and started for Cahawba. The surgeon shook his head and said it was a very bad fracture. Forest said, 'I guess the son of a b—h can stand it.' The surgeon said it would be impossible to move me. Robert B. nnett, of Company D, bad sick of typhoid fever, was left at this house with me. They took him out and put him on a horse and started him off, and Forest ordered a guard left over me. About 10 o'clock the lead horses, stragglers and camp followers, came along, and treated me most shamefully, applying to me all the epithets their devilish meanness could invent. They took away my boots, socks, coat and pants, and the money Col. Thomson left me, and then abused me because I had no more. Before night everything was quiet, the rebels had all gone except the two left to guard me, and I began to congratulate myself that crippled as I was, I was keeping two well rebels out of mischief. The woman of the house treated me kindly. Her husband was an officer in Forest's command, and came home once while I was there, and told me I should never be hurt as long as he could help it. At the end of nine days my leg had knit tolerably well, so that I could work my toes a little. Mrs. Evans now gave me a pair of pants and a rebel jacket; I was put into an ambulance and hauled 15 miles over corduroy roads to Starksville. This broke my leg over again, and left me in a much worse fix than at first. There were a good many sick and wounded Yankees here, and the surgeon in charge seemed a brute, paying no attention to my broken leg. At the end of two weeks it had nearly knit again, but this time my toes were turned square in, and at a right-angle from what they ought to be. About this time there came another surgeon to the hospital—evidently of Union sentiments—and seeing the fix my leg was in, seemed much annoyed at the gross carelessness of the surgeon in charge. So the next day he came to see me again, and finding me asleep applied chloroform to my nose, and then gave my leg a vigorous twist and pull, which broke it the third time, and he straightened it out. I soon awoke, and the surgeon in charge coming in, the doctor called his attention to me and explained what he had done. The surgeon said it was good enough for a d—d Yankee. At the end of two weeks my leg had knit for the third time so that I could move about a little, but could not yet bear a bit of weight on it. I was now moved to a little station on the railroad, and was in hospital a week and fared miserably, and was then moved to Cahawba and was there eight days. The officers here were kind to me, but the fare was hard indeed. I was scarcely able to sit up and had nothing but bare boards to lie upon. I was now put on to a boat and started up the river, in the morning, and by 3 p. m. got to Montgomery, Ala About an hour afterwards I was put on the cars and sent right back to Selma, 12 miles from where I started in the morning. I was so weak I could scarcely stand alone, and could not bear any weight on my leg, but helpless as I was the officers and guards tried to force me to walk. I told them they might kill me or do as they pleased, but that I could not and would not walk. I was at Selma four days. Here I was treated most cruelly and got nothing but a little corn bread to eat. I was not able to walk on crutches yet when I was put on the cars and sent direct to Macon, and from there, without stopping, was sent to Andersonville, getting there between the middle of April and the 1st of May. I had no means of keeping dates and only guess at the time. When I got to Andersonville I was searched by Wirz, who pulled and jerked me around violently, and treated me most shamefully, and then put me in the stockade without blanket or shelter. My shirt and drawers—all the Union clothes I had left me when I was captured—had now given entirely out, had been torn away a piece at a time till nothing remained. The pants Mrs. Evans gave me were now old and rotten with filth and dirt. The roundabout she gave me had nice buttons on, but the guards at Selma had cut them off, and it was now ripped and torn in the sleeves, and these were the only clothes I had while in Andersonville. Shoes or socks I had none while there. The bare sand was my bed, and the sky or clouds my only covering. There was an imaginary line running clear around on the inside of the stockade, 20 feet from the wall, over which we were not allowed to pass. As there was nothing in many places to indicate where this line was, in the excessively crowded condition of the stockade many got too near the wall and were cruelly shot without any warning whatever. I heard one of the guards say that for every Yankee soldier they killed they got a 30 days' furlough, and it is no wonder that under these promises many were shot when entirely unconscious of being near the fatal line. I still have a very vivid recollection of one poor boy being shot while he was asleep, and instantly killed; the reason why I so clearly recollect it is that I was lying right beside him, asleep also, and between him and the wall, and had not the report of the gun, the hiss of the bullet, and the thud as it struck the poor boy, aroused me up to see my comrade dying, I should never have thought of being near the line.

"Shortly after I got to Andersonville the stockade began to fill up rapidly with prisoners captured from Sherman on the Atlanta campaign, and from Grant in the battles of the Wilderness and before Richmond. Our rations proportionately diminished. At first our rations consisted of a pint of corn meal, two spoonfulls of rice, and a piece of bacon two inches square. The bacon finally stopped, and they brought in to us what they called beef, but we always believed it to be mule meat, and this, too, finally stopped, as also did the rice. From that time we had nothing but the meal, and immediately after the conspiracy to throw the wall over there were five whole days that I had but a single pint of meal. As the weather grew hotter and the stockade became more crowded, disease and death made sad havoc among us. Many from the effect of raging hunger became insane; scurvy raged to an inconceivable extent; in wounds it became putrid, eating ulcers, while in the case of unwounded it took the form of malignant diarrhœa and carried them off by platoons. In my own case it had entirely eaten away the cartilaginous knitting of my broken thigh, and for a fourth time my leg was limp as a rag, black as a bat, and almost entirely destitute of feeling. I could take my hands and twist it about any way without feeling pain, and the prints of my fingers in the flesh would remain for 12 hours at a time. About this time some of my comrades built me a turf hut, just high enough for me to crawl into, which kept the broiling sun off of me; but in two or three weeks there came a tremendous rain storm which washed my turf house all down, and again left me to the merciless rays of the scorching sun, the heat of which was sufficient to burst open the skin on my feet; while the nights—naked as I was—were so cold that sleeping was out of the question, and all the rest I got was an hour or two in the evening, and a short time after sun-up in the morning.

About three weeks after my turf house was washed down, there came along a surgeon, evidently of Union proclivities, and examined me. He gave me for my scurvy some acid stuff, looking and tasting like scraped potatoes and vinegar, and cautioned me not to let the officers or guards know anything about it. I used this about a week, and the doctor came again. I was so much better, and my leg had come to its feeling and pained me so, that I told the doctor I believed if he would get some splints and tie my leg up it would knit again. He said he would do it in a minute, but that he dare not. He then told me to get some of my comrades to scrape a hole in the sand and bury my whole leg. This we did, and you can never imagine what I suffered for the next two weeks, lying there in the broiling sun, with scarcely a possibility of removing the excretions of my body away from me. The sand wore away all the skin on my hips and back, and my shoulder blades protruded through the skin, and the scars of all remain to this day, some of them as large as a person's hand. [We can verify this, for we have seen them.—ED.] Long before this the surgeons wanted to cut my leg off. I told them no; it would kill me, and if I had to die I would die with my leg on. At the end of two weeks my leg had knit sufficiently to enable me to free myself from the sand and turn over, and not long after I was able to crawl around some. About the middle of September some of my comrades went outside the stockade to cut wood, and brought me a couple of forked sticks for crutches, and these were all the crutches I used till I was exchanged. About this time the stockade had got so full that the well ones were trampling the sick ones to death, and on the 17th of September I and 800 other sick were moved out on to the north side of the stockade, into a grove, where we had tarpaulins to lie under. These tarpaulins were 12x16 feet in size, and 14 to 20 of us were put under each. Our food was a pint of black pea soup and a very small piece of corn bread twice a day. The mortality among us was horrible. From 50 to 100 died every 24 hours, and their places were filled by those taken from the inside. As we lay in a row, three died next to me on one side and two on the other, in one night. Shortly after I was taken outside, three surgeons came around one morning and told me they were going to cut my leg off. Again I told them *no*. They came back in the evening and told me they had orders to amputate all such cases as mine. The only object seemed to be to make cripples, as at this time I had been hobbling around on crutches for two weeks. I told them they might kill me, but should never cut my leg off if I could help it. About the time Sherman left Atlanta and began his march to the sea, they began to move the prisoners from Andersonville to Salisbury, N. C., and by the middle of November but a few thousand were left. During my stay outside Fred. Landis, Co. A, was my nurse, and by his kindness alleviated much of my suffering. On the 16th of November I was put on the train and started for Macon, and although but a few hours on the road, four died on the train. We went from Macon to Millen, and from there to Savannah, and on this whole trip had nothing but sweet potatoes and raw beef to eat. We got to Savannah about noon on the 20th, and as yet did not know where they were taking us, but were immediately called up to sign a paper, and when I saw the heading, "Paroled Prisoners of War," I was only too glad to write my name. You may never know with what feelings of gratitude I contemplated the idea of once more being free. We were immediately put on board a steamer and started for the neutral waters at the mouth of the Savannah River, and in a short time saw the Stars and Stripes waving over boats coming to meet us. The ecstasy of joy was now unbounded, and proved too powerful for many a poor fellow, for before the boats had met 15 had died. As soon as I saw the Stars and Stripes I hobbled to the bow of the boat, determined to be among the first to get aboard. But when the boats "bumped" together, weak and exhausted as I was from suffering and excitement, I tumbled over, and for a time lay almost insensible. The first thing I knew two men, with inscriptions printed in large letters on their caps, "Commissioners for Sick and Wounded Prisoners," picked me up, tore my old rags off and threw them into the water, and carried me to a warm bath. I weighed 83 pounds. While in the bath we smelled coffee and meat cooking, and began to cry piteously for them, and were terribly vexed because they would not give us all we wanted. In a short time we were all cleaned up and dressed in blue once more, and the contrast was so great that none of us recognized our most intimate comrades. There were 480 on the boat, and we started for Annapolis, Md., but before we got there 162 had died.

HENRY NOBES.

EXPERIENCE OF T. W. MILLIGAN, SERGT. COMPANY G.

Captured--Jack Knife only Taken—Money in His Waistband—Started to the Interior—Shoved into Prison with "You d—d Yank, Stay There!"—Clanking of Chains, and Darkness, and Dreadful Noises—Off for Andersonville—Description of the Horrid Place, and How Prisoners were Received—Prison Fare—Lice by the Million—News through Rebel Sources—Fresh, Fresh, Fresh!—McIntyre Come Too—I Shed Many Bitter Tears as I Prepared to Receive Him—Vaccinating with Poison Vaccine—Terrible Sufferings and Mortality Follow—100 to 113 Die Daily—Brutal Surgical Operations, Always Fatal—Eating the Mush Issued for Poultices and Still Dying of Hunger—Catching and Eating the Rats that Ate the Dying—Howell Cobb, the Hyena, Makes a Speech.

Sergt. Milligan says: "In January, 1864, I was taken prisoner, and was taken 20 or 30 miles to the rear to await my first examination. All that my captors relieved me of was my jack knife. I had carefully slipped my money into the waistband of my pants. My uniform was dirty and well worn, and they had no use for it. After five days' confinement in a county jail, I was reinforced by five Yanks and three rebels, and we were started on foot for the interior. We marched very leisurely, and had the best the country afforded—corn bread and bacon—until we reached the Coosa River. Here our first rations were issued to us: two pounds of brown bread for three days' rations It was about 10 o'clock at night when I arrived at Rome, Ga., and I was taken to a large building and led up one flight of stairs. After some fumbling after keys, the door was opened and I was shoved in with "You damned Yank, stay there!" For the first time in my life I felt that the infernal regions were at hand. It was dark as a pocket. I heard a clanking of chains, and a noise like a herd of Texas cattle were crossing a suspension bridge. I crouched down without taking a step from the door, and remained there until daylight, with great drops of sweat standing in beads all over my face. When daylight came, I found at the further end of the building 18 men heavily ironed with ball and chain for deserting from the rebel army; two of them were sentenced to be shot that day. I learned from these men that I was in Rome. About 3 p m. I was put on board the train for Atlanta. Here I found a small number of prisoners comfortably situated, with houses to eat and sleep in and a large yard for amusements. About the 10th of March we had orders to start for Andersonville. We were tired of the monotony, and glad to hear of a change. It was 10 o'clock at night on the 20th of March, 1864, when we arrived at Andersonville, dark and raining. The gate was thrown open, and we were driven in much the same as cattle are driven into a pound. I was struck dumb. By the light of one little fire I saw more real suffering than I had ever seen in all my life. Poor, emaciated, sick, starving, scurvy-eaten, gangrened, and naked! All around was black as Egypt, and for the first time in my life did I truly appreciate the comforts of home. The poor fellows had been at Belle Isle until almost gone, and had been shipped to Andersonville to die. The pine smoke had obscured all the appearance of human beings in their faces, and it wasn't long till we were all alike in appearance. I had taken in the situation by the time the sun was up, and set to work to put me up a bunk At 9 a. m. the gate was thrown open, and a rebel sergeant walked in: "You-all what come in last night, form line" We formed, and Capt. Wirz rode in and said, "Form in 90's and count off, so we can issue rations." The sergeant said, "Can any of you-all read 'ritin?'" After being informed that 89 of our 90 could read "ritin," he stepped back three paces and stared as if he had seen a ghost. "One of you-all take charge of this 90 and call the roll." After roll-call, the rations came. Fare: one-half pint corn meal. I found in my ration one part sand, one part cob and husk, and two parts cracked corn. In a few days our lot was most miserable. The lice were so numerous it was impossible to get rid of them with any means at our command. Often when a man died his few rags were so covered with lice it was with reluctance the naked would appropriate the scanty clothing. The only way we had of replenishing our wardrobe was by appropriating the effects of our dead comrades.

"Shut out as we were from the world, all the news we got was through rebel sources, and purposely manufactured to discourage us as much as possible. The news in their newspapers always ran about this way: '*One of the bloodiest battles of the war* was fought at Resaca yesterday. Gen. Joe Johnston completely whipped and routed Gen. Sherman; but Gen. Johnston fell back for a strategic position.' This was of great importance to us, and every mile our armies advanced was noted with great accuracy, and with joyful voices the entire stockade was informed of our nearest lines. The majority of rebels stationed at Andersonville really believed Sherman was rapidly losing his army.

"When any prisoners were brought in from the front, the cry of 'Fresh! fresh!! fresh!!! fresh!!!!' was sounded over the stockade, and a grand rush was made for the entrance gate. It has often been said that misery loves company, but let me give you my experience: I was one day on the north side of the stockade, when I heard 'Fresh! fresh!!' I arrived just as the 'fresh fish' were being assigned to 90's, and heard Capt. Wirz say, 'McIntyre, you go and draw your rations with 90 No. —.' I was dumbfounded.

D. S. McIntyre, of Company H, Seventy-Second Indiana, st... inside of the most miserable hell on earth that could be imagin... I was truly glad, and yet sorry, to see him, for I knew the ordea... must pass. He was a perfect picture of health, and looked so in... cent of what was expected of an inmate of Wirz's Castle. I show... him where I stayed, and told him to come to me as soon as conv... nient, and without another word turned away and cried; yes, shed many bitter tears, as I made preparations to receive him under my humble shelter of an old blanket stretched over a pole.

"In a few weeks after we arrived at Andersonville, the authorit... thought we were not dying fast enough, and proposed vaccinati... We were called into line by 90's, and none were exempt. Two of the men in the 90 I was in, who had had small-pox till the p... all over their faces might be noticed 100 yards off, had to subm... to the operation. The virus was so poisonous that in many instanc... three hours was sufficient to show a purple spot as large as a dolla... and in a few days the most pitiful groans and sobs were heard all over the stockade. One brave little Michigan boy said death was prefer able to a day's torture of that kind. In many instances the flesh would drop from the bone, until the bone would almost be bare fro... the shoulder to the elbow—a limb girdled to the bone!! Truly, thos... were days of mortality. The dead at the gate numbered from 100 t... 113 per day. No sympathy was shone to the brave fellows wh... offered up their lives as sacrifices for our country. But when one of the poor fellows died, one rebel took him by his head and one too... him by his feet, and they would sing out, *one! two!! throw!!!* a... into the dead cart they were thus piled and hauled away; and simply to keep them from becoming a pest, they are stuck into a hole and cov... ered up. In October, 1864, I was taken to the prison hospital fo... treatment. Tent flies to sleep under and mush for poultices was ... that I could see that was different from the stockade. The ratio... were not sufficient to sustain life. The surgeons would come at 9 a. m. and the stereotyped prescriptions were mush poultices and amput... tion. This operation was brutal in the extreme, and always resulte... in death The patient was held on a table and chloroformed ti... insensible, then the doctors would roll up their sleeves and go to work with all the complacency of city butchers.

We had no blood to spare, and got nothing to eat out of which t... make more, and of course each poor fellow operated upon had to d... From the piles of limbs I saw carted away from day to day, I shoul... judge it was either profitable, or vastly amusing, to cut Yankee prison ers in pieces. At one time there were eight of us under one fly, a...

we were so straightened for food, and all of us so nearly gone, that we would look from one to the other to see who should die first. Diarrhœa and fever set their seal upon a Frenchman, and for two days he was unable to eat, and we took his pittance of corn bread and divided it into seven parts—a small bite for each—yet we scrupulously demanded it. We also ate the mush issued to us for poultices, and were still dying of hunger. One of the boys proposed we set dead-falls and catch the numerous rats that ran over us at night, and often gnawed the poor fellows before they were dead. We set our traps, caught the rats, and ate the rats.

A man by the name of Isham, from Michigan, ate the entire rat to the very tail. This sentence is the gospel truth, and fact unvarnished, and should any of these poor fellows still be living, and ever see this in print, they will remember it well.

In January, 1865, Howell Cobb drew the rebel guards up in line on an eminence overlooking the stockade, so they could look down upon the poor, sick, maimed, naked and miserable Yankees, moving about in every conceivable position, and made a speech to them. In that speech he said: 'Will you surrender to those *things?* They are not men; they are brutes, groveling in their own filth!'

It is true we were groveling in our own filth, and starvation gaunt and lean had almost driven the last spark of humanity out of us, and yet it was hard to say this of men, brave and true, and a full average of the best of the Federal army.

There are a thousand horrors of prison life that I have not spoken of, and never read of, and have not the time to relate, and will conclude by saying that 12 months in Andersonville deprived me of the greatest blessing on earth—health. 40,000 others suffered, and have a history equally cruel, that will never be placed on record."

THEOPHILUS W. MILLIGAN,

Late Sergeant, Co. G, Seventy-Second Indiana Vols.

From other sources we have learned the following facts in regard to comrade Milligan: He was captured near Mooresville, Ala., in January, 1864; arrived at Andersonville March 20th. Took scurvy in June. His foot bursted and his right leg is so contracted that he is a bad cripple for life. Was vaccinated with poisonous virus, causing a sore in which gangrene set in. Was taken to rebel hospital in the fall and remained there till March, 1865, when he started to our lines, on the Mississippi, and was on board the steamboat Sultana when she blew up, and he lost everything. He is still badly crippled. —HISTORIAN.

STORY OF SERGT. HENRY HOOVER, COMPANY B.

Capture near Okolona—A Panic—Detachment of the Seventy-Second Holding Forest's Army in Check—Captured while Kneeling by a Comrade—Gen. Forest Infuriated because His Brother was Killed—Wanted to Get Hold of Wilder's Brigade—Begin to Starve and Freeze at Once—Searched—The Enraged Planters—Wanted All the Prisoners Hung or Shot at Once—Enraged Women—Trading Boots—In Prison at Columbus—To Selma—Fresh Fish! Fresh Fish!—In Prison at Selma—Water from the Street Gutter—Corn Bran—The game of Sock'em—Singing in Prison—Awing Us with Blood Hounds—Catching Prisoners with the Hounds—Allowing the Dogs to Mangle and Tear Our Men—We are Told We are Going to be Exchanged—Started up the Alabama River—Half an Ear of Corn as Rations—Deceived, and into Andersonville—The Brute Wirz Again—Description of Andersonville Prison Stockades—Dead Line—All the Cruelties Repeated—Most Pitiable Suffering—Systematic Starving of Union Soldiers—Wood All Around Us, and We are Permitted to Have None to Cook with, or to Build Fires and Warm By—Rebel Sinks Above Our Camp on the Stream We Get Water from—Horrible Hospitals—How the Miserable Prisoners Died—No Protection from Rain or Sun—Eating Excrement—The Thugs and Robbers Arrested—Tanner Discounted in Fasting—The Swamp of Filth and Maggots Three Feet Deep—The Miserable Sick—No Medicines—They Lie Down in Sun or Rain and Die Without Attention or Sympathy—Waiting for a Man to Die to Get His Clothes—The Wall Street of the Prison—Selling Water and Other Things—A Pint of Beans, and Cholera Morbus—Efforts to Escape—Bloodhounds—Ball and Chain—Guards Deserting—Rebel News—"Eight O'Clock, and Atlanta's Gone to Hell!"—Whisky Defeats Stoneman's Raid to Release the Prisoners—Wirz Threatens to Open on the Camp with Grape and Canister—Sending Prisoners from the Hell Hole—To Florence—A Mere Skeleton—Another Wirz, and Smaller Rations—All Wells Filled Up—Freezing—Three Blankets to Every 100 Men—Exchanging Sick Prisoners—A Brave Boy—Wirz No. 2 will not let Us have Fires, and 20 Freeze to Death—A Miserable Night in Charleston Jail—A Generous Rebel Ex-Prisoner—Once More Under the Old Flag, and We Wave Our Skeleton Arms and Cheer It—Treated as Tenderly as Babes—Throwing Our Old Clothes Overboard—Sea Sickness—Change Clothes Again at Annapolis—Young Ladies, with Paper, Pens, Envelopes, and Stamps—Tobacco as Free as Water—At Home in God's Country Again.

"I was captured on Smith's raid, February 22d, 1864, between Okolona and Pontotoc, Miss. A detachment of the Seventy-Second Indiana, on this occasion, was used as a kind of forlorn hope to hold the whole command of the rebel Gen. N. B. Forest in check, while a conglomerated mass of cavalry, pack mules, ambulances, several hundred confiscated mules, and niggers, which were crowded into a large field, and could neither advance or retreat, could be extricated. About noon Forest had struck our forces near Okolona so unexpectedly as to produce a panic, and for quite a while it was every fellow for himself, and 'devil (rebel) take the hindermost.' Forest had pressed us so hard that we were compelled to cut loose from our artillery, and if something was not speedily done our whole pack and ambulance trains, and all the confiscated property we had collected on a raid through one of the most prolific portions of the Southern confederacy, would also fall into rebel hands.

"Our little detachment, with little more than 10 rounds of ammunition to the man, had all along been kept in reserve for an emergency, and that emergency had at last come to hand. We were ordered to dismount and throw down a cross-fence for breastworks, which we did in much less time than it has taken me to tell it. We did not have long to wait for the enemy, and were soon showing him the superiority of infantry over cavalry, and of rifles over carbines. We held him at bay for quite a while, when he flanked us, and we were compelled to fall back. In falling back John E. Doss, of my company, who was a little in advance of me, fell mortally wounded. I was going on, but the poor fellow plead so hard for me to come back, that I yielded. He was shot through the hips, and must have died soon after I left him. He told me to write to his folks after death, and wanted me to take his watch to them. I had stopped but for a moment, but when I arose from my knees I could see nothing of my company, and rebels were thick in the direction it had gone. I have since learned the rebels had got in our rear before we began to fall back. I started for a strip of woods to my right, and had almost got there, when out stepped a dozen rebels with their guns leveled at me, and calling, 'Halt, you d—d son of a b—h!' This was about sundown. I was placed under guard, and started back toward the rear. On the way back I was taken to Gen. Forest's headquarters. The General was in a bad humor. His brother, commanding a brigade in his army, had been killed back at Okolona, which had infuriated him, and his men said he had fought like a devil, capturing two pieces of artillery with his own hands. He asked me a number of questions about our forces, their number, who was in command, &c. He also asked me if Wilder's Brigade was along. Said I, 'No; if it was you would not see this command making such good time toward Memphis.' He said he had heard so much about Wilder's Brigade that he wanted to get hold of it just once; didn't have a brigade in his command that couldn't whip h—l out of it. (The reader will remember how he did it at Ebenezer Church, and at Selma.—HISTORIAN.) After he had learned how little I knew, I was taken to the train, where I found 75 or 100 poor unfortunates like myself. Most of these were cavalrymen, with a few artillerymen. Sergt. Oscar F. Bryant, of Company C, and myself, were the only representatives of the Seventy-Second. A small piece of corn bread and a very small piece of bacon were considered a square meal for a Yankee prisoner. None of us had blankets or overcoats, and sleep would have been out of the question from no other reason than the cold, but there were many others. Home and loved ones far away, whom we might never see, and *their* mourning us as dead, or starving by inches in some rebel prison.

"In the morning we were marched to the provost marshal's, where we were searched. They were very thorough in their examinations, stripping us to our shirts, and turning our pockets inside out. I did not possess much wealth. A good pocket-knife, an old pocket-book, (empty,) a lead pencil and pocket comb, completed my worldly effects. My old clothes were all I got back, and I felt thankful to get them. We were searched several times afterwards, and it was always amusing to me to see the look of disappointment on the faces of the examining committee after getting through with their task. After being sure we had nothing calculated to give 'aid or comfort,' we were placed under charge of a mounted guard and started back on the same road we had so recently traveled and so thoroughly desolated. We had destroyed everything that would burn, and carried off all the horses, mules, and negroes, that we could find, and lived like princes off the best a most bountiful country could produce. Miles of fencing had been burned, and the whereabouts of the three different columns, on different roads, could be located at any time by the black clouds of smoke. On our way down, one night, a whole picket post of a Tennessee regiment were murdered, and this had so enraged the regiment that it was the supposition that some of that regiment had fired the fences. It was rather trying to be taken back over such a route as prisoners, and have to meet the enraged planters, face to face, who had suffered the wholesale destruction. 'Twas lucky for us we were well guarded, and by old soldiers, too, who did not like the stay-at-home element in the South any more than we did the same element in the North. Some of the planters made every effort to have us hung or shot at once. One old fellow offered a guard a thousand dollars to shoot one of us, remarking that he would just like to see how a d—d Yankee died. The guard told him if he would shoulder his gun and go to the front he could soon get his fill of seeing how they died. The women were worse than the men, and called us all the bad names ever invented. Our guards were poorly shod and clad, and as a consequence, before we had been many days on the march, the Johnnies looked like Yankees, and we like rebels, so far as uniforms were concerned. On the second day after my capture a big fellow took a fancy to my boots, (they were long-legged cavalry boots,) and immediately proposed a trade in about the following style:

"'Say, Yank, them's durned nice boots you war, 'spose you let me try 'm on; if they fit, you may hev mine.' In this way I lost a splendid pair of boots and got the worst pair I ever wore, and the sand that got in at the holes nearly ruined my feet, and I was compelled to throw them away and go barefooted. At Columbus, Miss., we were confined for several days in a female seminary, and from the charcoal inscriptions I saw on the wall I suppose it had been used as a sort of military prison. A part of one of these ran about this way, which I thought quite appropriate: 'Man that is born in the Southern confederacy is of but few days and full of trouble. He cometh forth as a flower and is conscripted.' From Columbus we were taken to Selma, Ala. I was surprised to find a city in the interior of the confederacy so well fortified as this was. We were kept over night here, and the next day taken to Cahawba. We arrived there about 9 o'clock at night, March 7th, 1864. Our march had been long, and we had suffered severely from cold and hunger; and barefooted, as most of us were, our feet were in a wretched plight. Many of the boys had taken sick, and when they could possibly go no further, were left at the houses. One poor fellow, orderly sergeant Co. I, 4th Regular cavalry, marched hard all day and died at night. As we entered the building we were greeted with 'fresh fish! fresh fish!!' from many of the inmates who had not yet gone to bed. Next morning I was surprised to find so many prisoners confined here already. Many of them had spent the entire winter here. They had suffered from cold and had taken up the floor and burned it. The room in which we lived and did our cooking was a very large one, and a large square hole had been cut in the roof to let the smoke out. They always issued green wood to us. We had but two meals a day, and when the fires were started to cook with, the smoke was almost thick enough to cut with a knife Often after a meal have I gone to my bunk and laid with my face in my hat to get rid of some of the smoke, that burned my eyes like fire. Each mess had an old fashioned oven, with a lid, to bake our corn bread, fry our bacon, and boil our beans, when we got such luxuries, which was very seldom. About two pints of corn meal a day was considered a bountiful ration for each man, often it was less. We had plenty of water, which came from an artesian well up town. It followed a street gutter to the building, and was brought inside under ground. It was reported that all manner of filth was thrown into this gutter; but save the fact that it always tasted warm in the middle of the day, I thought it excellent water. The guards were stationed around the walls on the inside of the building, and at night burned pine knots to make a light and to warm by. Many of us were entirely destitute of coats or blankets, and often when it was too cold to sleep on a pine board, I have passed the night around the guards' fire. Notwithstanding our many privations we were a lively lot of Yanks. Of course we had to do something to kill time. Looking over our clothing for 'gray-backs' consumed a large part of it, but not all. Some would play cards, make jewelry out of buttons and bones, and others would spar or wrestle. One of the games they played, called 'sock 'em,' always amused me. One of the boys would place the crown of a hat between his knees and another would place his face in the hat so as to blindfold himself. This brought him just in the right position to be kicked behind. Those who participated in the play were to use only the side of the foot in kicking. If he guessed the party who kicked him the other fellow was to take his place. A great deal of skill was acquired in kicking, and some of the boys could raise a fellow off the ground every pop, and I have seen some of the poor fellows kicked till I really felt sorry for them, before they could guess the right one. This was especially the case where they got hold of a fellow who thought himself extra sharp, when extra pains were taken to keep him from guessing the right one.

"Singing was quite a passtime, and there were many splendid singers among the prisoners, and often at night would we almost raise the roof with 'John Brown's Body,' 'Rally Round the Flag, Boys,' and other soul-stirring and patriotic songs. A pack of bloodhounds were kept near the prison to catch any Yankee who might attempt to escape, and almost every day they were paraded before us to awe us into meek submission, and the dogs would stand around the door and growl, and show their sharp teeth. Only once while I was there were their services called into requisition. One dark night the boys puled off a board from the back of the sink, and quite a number made their escape; but the rebels soon found it out, and there was great excitement in camp. The yelling of the rebels and the baying of the hounds as they struck the fresh trail of our boys, made a most horrid din. As it was very dark and our boys knew nothing of the situation, most all of them were easily captured and brought back. The hounds would soon make them climb out of reach of their jaws, and the rebels would march them back to prison again. However, two of the boys were out several days, and were brought back horribly mangled. Their captors had among their hounds a lot of young dogs they were training for the business of catching men, and formed a circle around the poor fellows and kept the old dogs out, and left them to the mercy of the vicious pups. (This is one of the horrible practices of slavery.—Historian.) If either of those poor fellows are alive to-day they are cripples for life. Withal I must say the keeper of the Cahawba prison was the best man I was under while a prisoner, and a majority of the guards were kind and accommodating, and these were my happiest days of prison life.

"Toward the latter part of April we were ordered to bake a sufficient quantity of corn bread to last several days, the rebels telling us we were going to be exchanged. This was glorious news, and working with a will we soon had the requisite amount, and one fine morning we were put on the Southern Republic, a fine, large steamboat, with a calliope. Some of the boys had brought all their quilts, blankets, skillets, &c., with them. These were all taken charge of by the guards, who told us we would not need them, that we were going to be exchanged in a few days. We were soon on our way up the Alabama River, and on to freedom, as we supposed. We were a jolly crew, and nearly every one had some relic that we knew loved ones would almost venerate on account of association. I never was much of a mechanic, but I had whittled out a spoon that I thought extra in size and style. It never reached 'God's country,' but was worn out with hard service in the Southern confederacy. There were nearly 500 of us on board, and we had plenty to eat while it lasted, but alas! its keeping qualities were short. There was no salt in our bread, and the damp atmosphere caused it to mould, and ere we were many hours on our journey it all had to be thrown overboard, and before we reached Montgomery we were on very short rations. When nearing the city, the man at the calliope began to let himself out on the 'Bonnie Blue Flag,' but he did not get through with the piece. It made the boys furious, and they hooted and hissed until the guard became alarmed and stopped the playing. We landed at noon, and drew about six small hard-tack to the man, the first and last I ever saw in the confederacy. We boarded a train and started east. Columbus, Ga., is a great manufacturing town, and while we were changing cars the factory girls came down to see us. Our clothes were the worse for usage, our hair had not been trimmed, and soap was a stranger to us, and no doubt they thought us a hard set. We again started east, and at a small station called Butler, our engine gave out.

The hard-tack we drew at Montgomery had long since only existed in our memory. We were hungry as wolves, and passed a miserable night of it, and next morning were glad to get as rations half an ear of dry, unparched corn. We ate it with thankfulness, and it tasted good. After waiting, it seemed like an age, we were on our way again. At Fort Valley we turned south, and our faith in the exchange dodge played out entirely. We were soon in sight of the stockade of Andersonville, and our spirits sank within us. We found a regiment of soldiers ready to escort us to the prison, a half mile east of the station. Here I got my first sight of Wirz, who had charge of the prison. I shall never forget his manner, his broken accent, nor the first sentence I ever heard him utter. After getting off the cars, we were formed in line and ordered to count off. We were then ordered to right face, and made a bad job of it. As most of the men were cavalry, and were entirely ignorant of infantry tactics, a soldier can readily imagine the ludicrous mistakes that would occur. Wirz was not well pleased with the way the command was executed, and some of the infantry were twitting the cavalry about their mistakes, as soldiers very naturally would, when Wirz broke forth in these very words: 'You d—d Yankee sons of b—s, when I'm done with you, you won't feel so lively and joky; you'll be of d—d little service to your government.' We were marched between two lines of infantry, and with several pieces of shotted artillery leveled on us, we entered through the north gate into hell. I can think of no other word that comes near expressing that horrid place, and I think that even the infernal regions would be the loser by comparison. At this time the prison contained about 10 acres of ground, situated on two hills, between which ran a small stream of water. On each side of the stream, and especially on the north side, was a swamp which took up fully one-third of the space in the inclosure, and had it not been for the roots and brush that once grew on it, a man could not walk upon it without miring down. Around the prison was a stockade made of large pine logs, 26 feet long, hewn square, and set so closely side by side, in a trench six feet deep, that we could not see through the cracks into the outside world. This made an impregnable wall around us 20 feet high. Sentry boxes were built on top of the wall every 40 or 50 yards. Fifteen feet from the stockade, on the inside, posts were driven into the ground so as to leave them about three feet high. On the tops of these were driven narrow strips of plank. This constituted the dead line. It was an imaginary line in many places, which gave the guards the better opportunity of killing their man; an opportunity they never let pass unimproved. For if the prisoner came too near where the guard thought the dead line should be, the first intimation was the deadly ball from the guard's gun. We never heard of a dead line until we were inside, and the first intimation we had of such a thing was the cry of some of the prisoners, 'Don't go in there! You'll get shot!' when some of our party, seeing unoccupied space, were just on the point of stepping over the line to fix up their bunks. One poor fellow was killed that morning for simply reaching inside the line for a crust of bread. I entered Andersonville May 2, 1864. The prison had been opened the 15th of February the same year. The first inmates had been brought from Belle Isle, where they had spent the fore part of the winter, and many of them frozen frozen to death, and others were cripples from exposure to the cold. Most of them had chronic diarrhœa when they arrived, and as the rebels never issued any cooking utensils here, living on half-cooked mush, or mixing their corn meal with water, and then drinking meal and all, had decimated their ranks until out of over 3,000 who first entered the prison, now only about as many hundred remained. They had huddled around the pine knot fires till they were black as negroes, and had suffered until every vestige of human kindness seemed to have been eradicated from their hearts. Their skeleton forms, not more than half covered with rags; their long hair, uncut and uncombed, a mass of vermin; and the almost fiendish glance from their sunken eyes, made them the most unnatural, as well as most pitiable, objects. I had ever seen. Ask one of them a simple question, and you got nothing but curses in return. They had lost all hope. They had seen their number grow smaller and smaller day by day, and were but waiting their turn, nor cared how soon it might come. There were 18,000 prisoners in the pen when we entered, and these were divided into detachments of three messes of 90 men each, making 270 men to each detachment. Most of us were put in old detachments; 27 were put into the 23d detachment, and among the 27 the nearest thing we had to a cooking utensil was the half of a rebel wooden canteen. We drew from a half to three-fourths of a pint of meal for a day's rations, and for over a month did not draw any wood to cook it with, and of course had an awful time getting something to eat. Many of the prisoners who entered the stockade soon after it was opened had laid in supplies of wood, (the hills each side of the swamp had once been thickly covered with timber,) but they kept an eye on it day and night lest some of us fellows who were destitute should confiscate it. We had to resort to all kinds of strategy to get wood, and when we were so fortunate as to get hold of a small stick we had to break it up right away, so that if the owner should come for it, which he was sure to do, he would recognize none of his private marks. Often we would break it up and put it in our pockets. I ran across an old friend the first day, who owned no share in any wood, but by some streak of good luck had managed to get hold of a large pine chip, which I used to borrow to bake my Johnny cake on. One of us would take our half canteen, go to the brook and get water, mix our Johnny cake, and put it on the chip and bake it. After this operation had been performed 27 times, we could all of us say we had had our breakfast. The last man would scarcely get done before noon. Every stump inside the stockade was dug up, and at any time in the day you could see men wading around in the swamp in search of roots, and every little root, no matter how small, was carefully preserved. I have spent many an hour gathering roots. I could always overlook, to some extent, the rebels giving us short rations and no cooking utensils at all, for I did not know whether they had them to give; but why they could not give us wood, which we so much needed, when we were surrounded on all sides by dense forests, I never could tell, unless that sentence of Wirz's explains the cause. After they began to issue wood we got three sticks of cord-wood to each detachment, or one small stick for 90 men. As every man cooked for himself, these sticks had to be split into 90 splinters, and these were so small that I have often broken mine up and put it in my pocket. They always issued green wood, when the woods were full of old pitch-pine logs that would burn like resin.

"The water we had to use from the branch was filthy in the extreme. There was a brigade of rebels camped just above the prison, and they had their sinks built over the stream, so that we got all their filth. The part of the swamp not too miry, inside the stockade, was used as a sink by the prisoners, and the filth was constantly carried into the stream. I have frequently drank with a pile of excrement not six inches from my nose. I frequently visited the hospital on my side of the brook, which consisted of old tent flies stretched over poles, that would not keep out the sun, let alone the rain. Under these the sick lay on the ground, most of them destitute of covering. When a man died he was stripped of his clothes, if they were worth anything, and he was laid inside the dead line, and I never visited the hospital but I saw from 15 to 20 dead men, their mouths, eyes and nostrils, full of fly-blows. Walking through the hospital streets our eyes and ears were greeted with horrible sights and sounds. Most of the sick were delirious. Some died cursing themselves and the government that would suffer them to endure such damnable cruelty. Others died peacefully and with prayers on their lips; but most of them died entirely unconscious of their surroundings or misery. I remember one poor fellow who labored under the delusion that he had got back home from that hell on earth, and was busy talking to his wife and children, called them by their names and told them of the hardships he had endured, and spoke of the joys of the future now that he had got home once more. I never heard anything half so pathetic before or since. Accustomed as I was to horrid scenes, I could not stand to listen to him long. The next time I went back to the hospital he was gone. Sometimes for days the sick would be without medicines of any kind. There they lay on the ground, you might say eaten up with vermin, and often besmeared from head to foot with their own excrement, with not a particle of covering to protect them from the chilly night air, or pitiless rain. In this manner thousands of as good men, morally, mentally and physically, as the world ever produced, perished. The rebels determined to make Andersonville *the* prison of the confederacy, and all prisoners captured east of the Mississippi were brought here, and by the last of June room inside the stockade began to get scarce. The pen was crowded to its utmost capacity, and after night you could not walk around on the streets without stepping on men, so thick did they lie all over the ground. It was estimated that there were fully 12,000 men inside the stockade, who had no shelter or protection of any kind from sun or rain. I belonged to this class—I never slept under any covering but the sky or clouds while in Andersonville. I occupied a small space of ground in one of the streets about six feet by two that I claimed as my own. Here I lived day and night, rain or shine. In June it rained every day for 23 days, and during all that time my clothes were never dry. Those 23 days soaking rain gave me the rheumatism, and well do I remember how I used to sit on the ground with my pants rolled up to my knees, and scrape my shins with a little stick till the pain caused by friction counterbalanced that caused by the rheumatism. About the last of June they began to issue cooked rations to us. We got a piece of corn bread two by three inches square, and once in a great while a very small piece of bacon. They built the cook house on the brook above the stockade, and all the filth from it was thrown into the brook, which but added to its already filthy composition. Sometimes they would give us rations of what they called 'nigger peas.' They were never half cooked, and were so full of weevil that you never could get the taste of the peas. But the worst trouble about the ration was its small proportions. When our ration was peas, you could see starving men down on the swamp picking the undigested peas out of the excrement and eating them, Sometimes they would issue us mush—and such mush! It would be raw, lumpy and filthy. The barrels they used to issue it out of were never cleaned, but were set inside the dead line, next to the gate, until they were wanted again, and during the interval would be the resort for countless millions of flies that congregated there for a feast. Once in a great while they issued to us what they called cooked beef, which was often so badly spoiled that you could smell it a long distance. It would be full of big live maggots and tasted very similar to the way it smelled. Yet I never knew a man to refuse his rations, however rotten they might be. I remember once of seeing a poor fellow eat some, whose stomach was too weak to retain it. He vomited it up, but before it was cold another fellow downed it with better success. We got so little for a ration that we always ate it as soon as we got it, and then went hungry until the time for drawing rations next day.

"Few people have any just conceptions of genuine hunger. I never was hungry until my experience in rebel prison, although I had often fancied myself almost starved because I happened to miss one or two meals a day. The life we were compelled to live was not conducive to brotherly love. It was every fellow for himself. I have frequently been asked if I did not know so and so, he was in Andersonville so many months, and you must have known him. No! we knew few, and cared not to know more. It was all that any man could do to live. He saw the ration, small as it was, grow smaller and smaller day by day, and his strength grow weaker and weaker, and he knew that a few more days, at the farthest, would put an end to his existence. Thousands of men saw the sun set day by day, not knowing or caring whether they ever saw it rise again. The rebels always excused the short rations by saying that it was all they could do to live, and we fared *almost* as well as they did; and when I got home, a mere shadow, I found numbers of intelligent men who believed such bosh as this.

"There were many desperate characters among the prisoners—thugs and bounty jumpers. These organized themselves into a band for the purpose of robbery, and grew so bold and defiant that no life was safe after night. The case finally became so desperate that even Wirz, destitute of sympathy as he was, interfered, and told us he would issue no more rations to us till the ringleaders were arrested and delivered into his hands outside the stockade. [He kept his word, and for the arrest and conviction of these scoundrels, see McElroy's History of Andersonville.—HISTORIAN.]

"I well remember how hungry we all were at the end of the three days. Just think of men living on next to nothing for months, and then to have that little cut off and not get a mouthful for three long days Dr. Tanner was not the only man who has fasted for weeks.

There are hundreds of men who have doubly discounted his celebrated fast. Of one thing there is no doubt; by issuing that inhuman order Wirz was the direct cause of thousands of deaths. Many a poor fellow began that fast who never lived to see it half completed. I was so very weak that I could walk but a few yards without resting, and staggered as I walked. July and August were the months always to be remembered by surviving Andersonville prisoners. The weather was fearfully hot, the water was simply liquid filth; the swamp was a living, moving mass of excrement, mud and maggots, to the depth of three feet, that poisoned. the air by day and night, and which, if applied to a scratch or sore, would produce gangrene. All these causes, aided by our exposure and miserable rations, produced a frightful mortality. There were not enough able bodied men to help the sick out to sick call. This was at 8 o'clock in the morning, and from that time till noon the street leading to the south gate would be crowded with sick. There was a space just outside the gate alongside the stockade wall allotted to the sick, and there thousands would congregate to be examined and get medicines. Often after waiting hours in the broiling sun, word would come that there was no more medicine, and the poor sufferers would be compelled to hobble back to their miserable quarters as best they could, to be fooled in a like manner the next day. I wish I had the power to describe that army of ragged, hopeless, helpless skeletons. I have never seen a description of it that gave any one not seeing it the faintest idea of the horrible condition of the sick and dying, and I shall not attempt it. Frequently men on their way to or from sick call gave out, lay down by the side of the road and died. Often men living near where some poor sick fellow would give out and lie down, would kick and beat him and tell him to move on, as they did not want him to lie there and die where they would have to carry him out.

"It was no uncommon occurrence to see a crowd of men waiting for a man to die that they might get his clothes. Frequently the clothes were torn off the man before he was dead, and who should own the clothes was settled by a big fight. Naked men were not choice in regard to the kind or quality of the clothes. No matter what kind they were, they were sure to be covered with lice, for the ground was alive with lice and fleas, and at night the air was full of musquitoes. The street running to the north gate of the prison was *the* street of the prison, and was to Andersonville what Wall street is to New York. Along that street the man who had anything to sell or trade, and those who engaged in gambling, held forth. Here you could buy most anything if you had the money; and it took good money, too, as in all prisons I was in. One dollar in greenbacks would buy ten in confederate money. A biscuit with butter was a dollar. One man would have a sack of salt, which he sold for 25 cents a teaspoonful—not large ones at that. Another one had a sack of nigger peas, which he sold at a dollar a pint. Another fellow would have a few plugs of tobacco, and this was the cheapest thing in camp. A small potato was worth 25 cents; an egg the same. After a few wells had been dug in camp another business was added to the list, that of selling water; and you could hear men yelling at the top of their voices, "*Who's got a chew of tobacco for a fresh drink of water?*" As to gambling, I know of no game of chance that was not represented.

"I had no money when captured, and never had an opportunity to make any but once. I helped carry a man out to the dead house, once, and on my way back picked up a small piece of pitch-pine. A fellow who kept a kind of bake-oven offered me a dollar for it. I took it quick; he might have had it for 50 cents. I had brought in a few pine knots besides. So, I invested my dollar in a pint of beans, borrowed a tin can, and had one good square meal. As a result of my indiscretion, I had an awful attack of cholera morbus, and thought for several hours that some other fellow would have a chance of making a raise by getting the job of carrying me out to the dead-house.

"Of course every means was tried to effect an escape from this horrid place, and among the many perhaps tunneling was the most resorted to; but there was no means adopted by any that proved very successful, as they had a pack of bloodhounds here that almost invariably scented the track of every one who attempted to make his escape. It sometimes happened that the guards would take a notion to desert, and a party of prisoners would go with them. When this occurred, the guards would take their guns with them, and then the dogs were never sent after them. Such parties almost always succeeded in reaching our lines. If any man made his escape, and was recaptured, he was compelled to have a ball of iron chained to him weighing 60 pounds. If he made the second attempt and was recaptured, he had two such balls chained to him; and I have seen men in Andersonville compelled to carry 120 pounds of iron just for attempting to be free. The rebel soldiers here were mostly all Georgia home guards, and as soon as one of them would hear that his home had been placed within the Union lines by the advance of Sherman's army, he or they would light out for home. The sentinels had to call the hours of the night. Each sentinel box was numbered, and during the summer they began to call the hour at 8 p. m. The man on the first post would cry out: 'Post No. 1, 8 o'clock, and a-l-l-z well.' Immediately the man on the second post would cry out: "Post No. 2, 8 o'clock, and a-l-l-z well." In this manner every post around the entire stockade would be called in a few minutes. Sometimes the guard would begin to call one hour, and everything would go on smoothly until half the guard had called their numbers, when there would be a skip of five or six numbers. We always knew what was the matter, and wished we could have gone along. We used to get some good news from the guard, and some awful bad news from the rebel newspapers, during the Atlanta campaign. When the rebel papers had anything in them calculated to make us feel worse than we were feeling all the time, they would see that we found it out. Just a few days before the fall of Atlanta, a rebel sheet found its way into camp, which was full of news calculated to dishearten us. Hood had Sherman just where he wanted him; his forces divided; one corps cut off, and probably annihilated; and that in a few days they would be able to publish news that would make the heart of every true Southerner thrill with joy. About a week from that time, at 8 o'clock in the evening, the guard began to call the hour. We could see all through the day that something was up in the rebel camp, but did not know just what. The 'a-l-l-z well' had been repeated by quite a number of the guards, when it came around to a big, burly guard, who, with a voice like thunder, shouted: '*Post No. 4, 8 o'clock, and Atlanta's gone to hell!*' In less than five minutes the whole camp was aroused and cheering. And such a cheering! I did not think that such feeble creatures could make so much noise. After the fall of Atlanta the rebels began to see that Andersonville was not as *secure* a place as they could desire for the 33,000 prisoners confined there at this time, should there be a raid made to release them. Stoneman had started on just such an expedition a short time before the fall of Atlanta, and had reached Macon, and might have succeeded, had not his command captured a train containing a large quantity of whisky, of which the command imbibed so freely as to render them not only unfit to carry out the grand object of the expedition, but to make them an easy prey to a very inferior command of rebels. Stoneman's raid caused a furious commotion at Andersonville. We could see all this in their camp, on the hill above the stockade. Eight hundred negroes were put to work strengthening the forts and digging new rifle pits. We were also excited, and anxious to know what was the matter, and it was very natural we should collect in groups to express and to hear opinions as to the probable cause.

Nearly every man in camp was giving his opinion, or listening to some one else, when our deliberations were cut short by the shriek of a shell just over our heads. We slackened up on the chin music, and Wirz sent in a general order that if the crowds did not immediately disperse he would open on the camp with grape and canister. In the afternoon of the next day a large part of Stoneman's command was brought into Andersonville, and the mystery was solved.

"The latter part of August the rebels began to send their prisoners away from Andersonville, and on the 12th of September I was taken to Florence, a small town 95 miles north-east of Charleston, and I distinctly remember the morning we passed through that city we could hear the old 'Swamp Angel,' (as we called the big Union siege gun,) as she hurled her 300-pound shells into the heart of the city. The stockade at Florence was similar to that at Andersonville. Being among the first prisoners to enter the new pen, we laid in a good supply of wood. Two men (I have forgotten their names) and myself built a mud hut, that seemed like a palace, after living out in all kinds of weather, as we had been doing.

"I cannot remember things that transpired at Florence. When I entered Andersonville I was a man. When I entered Florence I was a mere skeleton, weak in mind and body. I cannot remember the names of the prison officers, nor the names of the men with whom I bunked; but one thing I do remember—the commander was as mean as Wirz, and our rations were even smaller. We never had meat while I was there. Two or three times they issued sorghum molasses, as a substitute, they said, for meat. As we had nothing to eat with it, it didn't amount to much so far as appeasing hunger was concerned. There was a small stream ran through the stockade, but the men preferred digging wells to using the water. A tunnel was started from one of these wells, but the rebels found it out, and we were deprived of rations for three days, every well filled up, and no more allowed to be dug. At the end of the three days I was almost gone. I could walk but a few yards at a time without resting. Dead men lay everywhere. I counted 20 dead bodies on less than an acre of ground, who had died of starvation. In November it was quite cold, and my clothes were played out. I had neither coat, shirt, nor hat. The legs of my pants were worn off above the knees, and all the back part gone. We had roll-call every morning, and I shall never forget how I used to stand from a half to three-quarters of an hour, nearly naked, the ground frozen, and my feet swollen to double their natural size, and as black as a hat from scurvy. As soon as the roll was called we would go to our mud hovel and huddle up like hogs to keep from freezing. On the 24th of November the Christian Commission sent us some blankets, and there were just three distributed to every 100 men. We had to draw lots for them, and I was one of the lucky ones; and wasn't I happy! This was the first stitch or thread I had received from any source since my capture. After I had drawn my blanket the sergeant told me I would have to receipt for it, and asked me if I could write. I told him 'I used to could.' He looked at me as though he doubted my assertion, but after I had signed my name, and he had looked at the signature, he said I had no business to be in there; if I would go outside and write I should have plenty to eat and wear. I told him I would rather rot in prison than to work for such a God-forsaken government as the Southern confederacy.

"Our commissioners and those of the confederate states had made arrangements for the exchange of 10,000 sick, and I was of the number, and on the 8th of December, 14 days after I drew my blanket, I was examined by the surgeons, and a man had to be just a little bit better than dead to pass muster. I shall never forget one incident I witnessed at the surgeons' quarters. A poor boy wasted by disease to a mere skeleton, had been carried down to be examined. He probably would never have lived to reach home even if he had succeeded in getting out. When the surgeon came to him he made some remark about the boy not being able to stand the journey, and then said to him, 'If I let you go home and you get well, you won't fight us any more, will you?' 'Fight you?'—the poor fellow's eyes gleamed as he said it—'I'll fight you till hell freezes over.' The surgeon turned and said to the guard, 'Take this man to his quarters, damned if he shan't die inside the stockade.' The night before we left the stockade a band came out and discoursed some sweet music, and among the pieces played was 'Home, Sweet Home,' and I have never heard it since but it carried me back to prison. One of the men who helped to build our mud hut was fortunate to get out with me. I gave my blanket to our other comrade, it was the only earthly thing I possessed. We bade him good-bye and I do not know what became of him. On the evening of the 8th of December we were taken outside and camped by the stockade. We drew the half of a small loaf of bread to the man. This was more than I had eaten in any day for two months, and I shall never forget how sweet it tasted. We had fires, the weather was warm, and we passed a comfortable night; but the next night was cold and Wirz No. 2 would not let us have fires, and the consequence was, out of the 200 or 300 in our camp, 20 froze to death. That morning we took the train for

Charleston, and that night passed a miserable night in the Charleston jail. On our way to the jail a rebel soldier who had been a prisoner in the North stood on a street corner, and as we passed gave each of us a five or ten dollar bill of confederate money; he had a large roll of it, and said as long as any of it was left we should have it; he said he had been treated like a man while he was a prisoner at the North, and not like a brute. We could see the effects of our 'swamp angel' on every hand. Where a shell would strike the street it left a hole like a cellar, and where one struck a brick wall it made a hole large enough for a cow to jump through. The jail had been struck several times. The second day after we got to Charleston we got aboard the rebel flag of truce boat and steamed out past Fort Sumter, and were not more than a hundred yards from that fort when we were taken aboard the steamer Crescent. I shall never forget my feelings when I once more stood under our old flag, on a United States vessel, a free man. How we waved our skeleton arms and cheered the old flag—that was the happiest hour in my life. How kind all on board were to us. We were treated as tenderly as though we were babes. We were not allowed to eat too much, nor to eat anything that would harm us. We were taken to a large room where there were large stacks of clothing of all kinds, and every man was told to throw his old clothes overboard and help himself to a new suit; and as we steamed along, as far as the eye could see our old rags were floating in our wake. All of us were affected more or less with scurvy, and they allowed us to eat all the onions we wanted. Barrels of them were setting around almost everywhere. There was a great deal of sea-sickness, and I had to laugh at the poor fellows who were troubled with too much bile. There were barrels lashed to the railing at convenient distances for the use of the men, and sometimes there would be as many as three to one barrel, all vomiting at once, and a sudden lurch of the vessel would cause them to vomit all over each other.

"When we got to Annapolis, Md., we were met at the wharf by the Marine Band, which played 'We'll Rally Round the Flag, Boys,' for us. We were taken to the barracks, where we were ordered to throw away the clothes we then had on, have our hair cut, to wash ourselves, and put on new clothes again. After washing and dressing up, we found young ladies on hand with pens, paper, envelopes and stamps. Men were there with tobacco, which they gave to the prisoners as free as water. I could not bear the idea of writing to my parents; they were old, and I did not know but one or both might be dead, as I had not heard a word from them for over 10 months. As fast as we were able to travel we were furnished a 30 days' furlough and transportion home, with orders to report to Camp Chase, Ohio, at the expiration of our furlough. I arrived at home on New Years morning, 1865. It is needless to say I was happy, and that my father, mother, brother and sisters, shared in the happiness. Indeed the word happy hardly expresses it. I never saw my father so affected as upon this occasion. My friends by scores came flocking in to see me, and seemed to vie with each other in their efforts to do me some kind favor, and had I eaten the tenth part of the good things sent to me by kind friends, instead of living to write this narrative my obituary would have been written long years ago.

Respectfully, HENRY HOOVER,
Late Sergeant Co. B, Seventy-Second Indiana Vols.

REMARKS BY THE HISTORIAN AND THE EDITOR.

Conclusion—The Martyrdom of Prisoners—Their Splendid Manhood—Sufferings of Their Parents and Friends—The Case of Mrs. Ogborn—Died of a Broken Heart—Capture Cut Off Promotion—Many Turned Loose to Get Home the Best They Could, at the End of the War, and Perish by the Way—Many Bear the Odium of Desertion, and Cannot Draw Pay, Bounty, or Pension.

The Historian has been compelled, on account of space, to abridge the whole of this most interesting narrative, and to leave out entirely many of the most interesting incidents.

The above, gentle reader, is a true and faithful account of the sufferings of a *few* of the hundreds, who endured and escaped those nameless tortures, nameless because no words will ever describe their agonies and horrible sufferings. It also tells you of the death of thousands of others whose endurance was taxed beyond its limits, and they yielded to a death most painful to contemplate. And all for what? These men all loved their country, saw it in peril and in danger of being destroyed, and because of their love had engaged in its service, and fought for it; and for this, when captured, were made to suffer every privation and torment that savage ingenuity could invent, and face a slow, agonizing death, day and night. These men all tell you they might have gone out of that horrible den of misery, filth and death, at any time. Then why not embrace any proposition that would give them life, and health, and strength, and freedom? Was there any moral obligation that would compel these men to accept a certain death when by simply accepting service in the rebel ranks they might escape? Let each one solemnly answer these questions for himself. Each has answered for himself, and most of them answered the question with their lives—all declaring from the pit of writhing torture and groaning death, that any sort of misery, any sort of lingering, tormenting, horrible death, were preferable to the violation of manhood and a solemn oath; preferable to becoming a traitor and serving the base traitors' cause. Each noble man who died in those rebel hells was a martyr to manhood, liberty and patriotism; each noble man who endured them and escaped, is a martyr saved as by fire. They all reflect glory on their country, and honor on manhood and show how great, how strong, how invincible, was the patriotism which rallied to the rescue of our country in the war of '61—5.

There is another feature of this horrible—and to those who endured it damnable—suffering, that is seldom thought of and never spoken of. For the thousands of unfortunates who died in those dens of damnation, there were other thousands whose hearts bled at home While there were thousands of incidents all over the North, illustrative of this, we shall speak of but one, as coming under our own observation.

William E. Ogborn, of Co. I, was a bright and intelligent boy, a mother's joy and pride. He went into our regiment full of hope and manly aspirations, followed by a mother's love and prayers, and carrying with him needles, buttons, thread, and many little *et ceteras* as reminders of a mother's care. On that terrible New Year's eve, when the regiment started on the four days' scout which lasted three months, he was among the first to get ready. His knapsack, with his name in large letters upon it, was left in our care. When his comrades came back to us at Mooresville, from that fatal scout, Ogborn was not with them, and for the first time we opened his knapsack, and there we found the identical needle-book which his mother gave him; some of the thread and buttons, and many other useful trinkets. Corpl. Records took charge of most of his effects, and at the close of the war carried them to his mother, and in a letter to the author most beautifully and truthfully describes the scene that followed. Comrade Records says: "Ogborn's mother never gave up hoping for 'poor Will,' until the last survivor returned, and I carried to her the few mementoes that Ogborn gave me just a few days before we lost him. Said he: 'Henry, if anything should happen to me, I want you to take charge of my things, and carry them to my mother.' In a few days after I got home I took the things and carried them to his mother, and when I gave them to her she said: 'Oh, I understand, now' (and there was a vacant stare in her eyes as she spoke,) 'that my poor boy is gone! gone!! never, never to return! I have kept myself believing that finally, when the last prisoner was set free, it would be found that my dear boy was alive, and that when all came home, he would come, too; but I see now that there is no hope.' She lived until the next spring, and then died. The neighbors said no one knew what ailed her, but that it was thought to be heart disease. Ah, that was it—a broken-hearted mother! She, too, a victim of Andersonville."

There is one other feature of the case of these poor unfortunates we wish to speak of, and then leave the reader to reflect upon the magnitude, madness, and meanness, of the infernal rebellion. It as often happened as any other way that the "brightest and best" were captured; those who were just as worthy of preference, advancement, and promotion, as any in the army; and many a poor fellow who went into the army in robust health, big with hope, his feet already upon the rounds of the ladder that was to lead him up to the possession of bars, eagles, and stars, and might easily have gained the honors and plaudits attending success, was captured in the very first engagement, and his hopes forever blasted, as no soldier was ever promoted for being captured. Again, after the lines of our armies had been drawn around the confederacy, and like the coils of the anaconda began to tighten and crush the life out of the rebellion, the confederate authorities were put to their wits' end to find a place of safety for their prisoners, and the poor fellows were hurried from one place to another, and finally many of them were turned loose to shift for themselves, or to get home as best they could. These, of course, made their way North as speedily as possible, but owing to the unfortunate circumstances attending their escape, were never regularly discharged from the service, and in addition to their suffering untold horrors from disease, and a broken constitution, they have to bear the odium of desertion from the service, and have never been able to draw the pay and bounty justly due them, or to obtain the pensions which their disability entitles them to. We think it is a shame Government has never been able to devise some means of reaching their cases.

SKETCH OF MAJOR LAWSON S. KILBORN.

[The following sketch should have been inserted in this book with those of Cols. Kirkpatrick, Thomson, and Maj. Pinkerton, but the facts could not be obtained in time. We cannot omit a personal sketch of so brave a man and competent an officer of the Seventy-Second as was Maj. Kilborn, who served with it from first to last. We must say that the Major wanted the sketch omitted, but we would hear to no such thing, and have the satisfaction of presenting it in this out-of the-way place.—THE EDITOR.]

Major Lawson S. Kilborn was born in Kingston, Canada West, now "Ontario," December 28th, 1835. His father was of a roving disposition, and moved from Kingston, shortly after the wife and child were able to bear a journey with safety. The babe was but six weeks old when the family crossed Lake Ontario and settled in

Monroe County, New York. In alluding to his short stay in the Queen's Dominions, the Major has often been heard to declare that it was owing to his dislike to "petticoat government."

The father had once been in quite comfortable circumstances, but frequent movings, and some misfortunes, had reduced him to a renter, and to a dependence upon day labor for the support of a family consisting of five boys and three girls, of whom Lawson was the youngest child. The mother cheerfully bore her part of the privations of poverty, and contributed not a little to the support of the family with her spinning wheel and loom, with both of which she was expert. There were times of severe trial, and the boy often had nothing but a crust of corn bread with which to appease his hunger. At the age of eleven he lost his father, and the older children nobly assisted the mother in keeping the family together; one especially, Hiram, next older than Lawson, taking care that the two youngest of the family, the subject of this sketch and a sister next older, should have all the educational advantages the then recently introduced partially free school system of New York afforded.

When Lawson was 13, Hiram bargained for a little home for the family, then consisting of the mother, two sisters, himself, and Lawson, the eldest daughter being married, and the three older brothers having gone to try their fortunes in the then new and far distant State of Indiana. Lawson was to care for the home and work by the day, all his spare time, and make his labor supply the table of the family, while Hiram, who commanded high wages as a farm hand, worked by the month and applied his earnings, after clothing himself, to paying for the home. The boy's first act of business was to go in debt for a sack of flour, and he has often asserted that he has been in debt for something to eat ever since. Though but a boy he promptly discharged the obligation, and laid the foundation for a good credit, which he has scrupulously maintained ever since. Thus, working summers and going to school winters, the time passed until he reached his 17th year, when it was decided to sell the home, let the two youngest children spend a year in some High School, the mother visit with a married daughter, Hiram go to Indiana, and all the others follow in the following spring. The plan was carried out nearly as proposed: Lawson and his sister Emma attending Riga Academy, in the town of Riga, New York, the winter of 1852-3. In the spring of 1853 he came west, in company with his mother, oldest sister and her family, her husband having gone the previous year with Hiram.

Arrived at LaFayette, Indiana, Lawson at once commenced work for his brothers, who were carrying on the carpenter's trade in that city. In the winter he taught his first term of school, in an old log school-house, about seven miles from LaFayette. It was a subscription school, and netted him about ten dollars a month. While teaching his second term of school, at Linden, Montgomery county, Indiana, he married Miss Samantha Aydelott, the daughter of a farmer living near that village. She came of an excellent family, and has always worthily fulfilled her duties in the battle of life.

In the spring of 1860, Mr. Kilborn was chosen Principal of the Central School, LaFayette, which position he filled with honor and growing popularity until the spring of 1862. The war fever was high at this time, and the young husband longed to be away to the battle-field, but hesitated on account of his young wife, who was soon to become a mother for the third time. At length, when the little new-comer was about a month old, he hesitatingly broached the matter to his wife, who at once, with noble patriotism, replied, "I know how you feel. If I were a man, I should go. I, and the little ones, will be taken care of, never fear." This decided him, and he at once set about recruiting a company, in connection with his brother-in-law, Dr. J. B. Johnson. In about a month's time the company was raised, and mustered into the Seventy-Second Indiana Regiment, with Dr. Johnson as captain, H. B. Wilson first lieutenant, and L. S. Kilborn second lieutenant. Arrived at Indianapolis, the Doctor was promoted to the medical department, Wilson made captain, and Kilborn first lieutenant. From this time until the regiment left Murfreesboro, Tennessee, on the Chattanooga campaign, Lieut. Kilborn's history is that of the regiment. Capt. Wilson's health failing, he resigned at Murfreesboro. Kilborn was promoted to the captaincy of his company, and just before the army moved he was detailed to command the pioneers of the brigade. As this service cut him off from active participation on the battle-field, he chafed under it a good deal; but as Col. Wilder declared he had only one other man in the brigade who could get as much work out of men as he, and that man could not be spared for this position, Capt. Kilborn was compelled to retain that position. After the capture of Gurley, he was relieved of the command of pioneers by Gen. Crook, and detailed to command scouts, to be attached to the General's headquarters. In this position he accompanied Gen. Wm. S. Smith on his raid along the Mobile and Ohio Railroad to West Point and Columbus, Mississippi, being often engaged in severe and perilous secret service. A part of the Seventy-Second Indiana and Kilborn's scouts were all of the Wilder Brigade that went on this expedition.

Returned to the regiment, Capt. Kilborn was granted a furlough through the intervention of Gen. Smith, who esteemed him highly but finding he could not go home and back before the commencement of the Atlanta campaign, upon Gen. Garrard promising to suspend the furlough till the campaign was over, he resolutely silenced the longings in his heart for a sight of the loved ones at home, and turned his face southward with his command. Capt. Kilborn was promoted to the Majority of his regiment November 9th, 1864, and served with credit till the close of the war, going with Gen. Wilson on his famous raid through Alabama and Georgia, resulting in the capture of Selma and Montgomery, Alabama, and Columbus and Macon, Georgia. From the latter place the command was ordered home, and the Seventy-Second was mustered out in June, 1865.

Major Kilborn at once cast about him for something to do, and nothing else offering, he went to work at his old trade of carpentering.

During the war his wife, by frugal management, had bought and nearly paid for a house and lot in the village of Ladoga, Indiana. This he traded for a quarter section of land in Shelby County, Illinois to which he moved in the fall of 1865. He moved to Marion County, Illinois, in the fall of 1866, and, having been unfortunate in his farming operations, he once more entered the school-room as Principal of the Graded School, then but one year established, in Kinmunday. Since that time he has made teaching his profession, devoting himself to it with a zeal and earnestness that has given him a good reputation with educational men in many parts of the State. He has been Principal of the schools of Marshall, Clark County, Illinois, for seven years, and his name was prominently mentioned as a candidate for Superintendent of Public Instruction at the Prohibition Convention at Bloomington, in 1882. Major Kilborn is a man of the best of habits and Christian principles, which were never for a moment prostituted in the service. He has a generous heart, and a clear head for literary work; but, like many others of like endowments, he has not the knack of making money in large quantities; but to compensate for this he has a genial disposition, and has no cravings for large wealth.

There was no better soldier than he—always ready, always cheerful, always brave and cautious, always attentive to the wants of his men. Though not large, he is compactly built, muscular, agile, swift of foot and hand. His quick eye could take in the situation at a glance, on any occasion, and this made him a very valuable officer on the scout or skirmish line, where all that was done had to be done quickly.

Time is making its impression upon the Major, as well as upon all the comrades. His face, almost boyish when he entered the service is now somewhat furrowed. His hair and whiskers, jet black on that memorable August day when he stood up with us all and was sworn into the service, are now sprinkled with gray; but he is yet vigorous and active; the same old fire burning in his eyes, and the same good heart beating in his bosom. In the march of life, in the reunions here below, and in the great camp and reunion above, the comrades all will be glad to meet and greet comrade Maj. Lawson S. Kilborn, one of the bravest and best men of the grand old Seventy-Second.

CHAPTER XLII.

At Nashville—Last Sad Days of Disorganizing—Services by Chaplain De La Matyr to Large Audiences, and the Ministration of the Lord's Supper—Religion in the Army—Faithfulness of Chaplain De La Matyr—Turn Over Our Spencers, and Many of the Men Purchase and Take Them Home—Recruits Turned Over to the 44th Indiana Veteran Regiment for Further Service—Roll Call of the Living and Dead—Answer to Roll Call for the Last Time—Bidding Adieu to the 98th and 123d Illinois—To Louisville, To Indianapolis, and Into Camp Carrington whence We Started to the Service—Welcome Home Dinner by the Ladies—Going Home to Spend the Fourth—The Transition from Soldiers to Citizens—Its Joys and its Sorrows—Paid Off—Good-bye, Old Fellow, I'm Going—Soldiers Begin to Talk Reunion—The Seventy-Second in 52 Battles—Some Under Fire Over 100 Times—Traveled 15,000 Miles—Recapitulation of Number of Enlistments and Losses—Why No More of Us were Killed—Our Manner of Fighting—Final Words by the Editor—The End.

The reader has been through the miserable scenes of Andersonville, and will no doubt be glad to return to the command, at Nashville, and follow the old Seventy-Second in its proper but sad work of disbanding.

Sunday morning, June 18th. About 10 o'clock this morning our bugle blowed for church. This was the first time we had heard this call since leaving Gravelly Springs. Our Chaplain, Isaac De La Matyr, was the only chaplain in the brigade, and to show you how well he was liked by all, we state that to-day nearly the entire brigade, officers and all, came to hear him preach. We should say that there were 2,000 soldiers gathered around him as closely as they could get. They listened to him with rapt attention, and after he was done preaching he announced that he would speak to them again in the evening, and administer the sacrament. When the bugle blowed again in the evening, not only our whole brigade turned out, but also many from the other brigades and regiments, miles away, came to hear him. You may be a little curious to know how this solemn service was performed in the army, and we will try to explain. When our chaplain first came to us, at Brownsburg, Ala,, about the 1st of November, 1863, he went through all the companies and asked every man if he was religious, what church he belonged to, and if he would now like to have his name enrolled with those who were still trying to serve God. The names of all these were taken down in a book, and he called them his class of believers. This class numbered near 300 members John B. Davis, Company D, says: "Perhaps few regiments in the service had so decidedly a religious character as the Seventy-Second Indiana. Organized at a time when the floating population of curiosity seekers had already joined the army under excitement, with the impression that the war would soon be over, the men composing this regiment had time for sober thought, and to realize something of the magnitude of the work before them. The war was not to be a 'little breakfast job,' but it was one that would take time, suffering and blood. Of the 1,000 comprising the regiment at muster in, perhaps 700 of them were professors of religion, or were warm supporters of it, and during our whole term of service a strong religious sentiment predominated." It is one of the most pleasing reflections with the Historian that the God of battles who so kindly presided over the destinies of the Seventy-Second Indiana, is the Christian's God, and it gives us unbounded pleasure to be able to say that a majority of our comrades yet living are firm believers in that God, and are yet enjoying his smiles and favors and the consolations of a Christian faith. Though we were sometimes without the ministration of a commissioned chaplain, we are happy to say there never was a time when the Seventy-Second lacked for men ready and willing at all times, and upon all proper occasions, to stand up and unfurl the glorious banner of the Christian faith. A few of those were P. P. Johnson, Luther Cheader, J. M. Brannan, of Company I; J. B. Davis and Col. Thomson, of D; Maj. Pinkerton and Lieut. Jewell, of G; Maj. Kilborn and Lieut. Priest, of E; and a host of others we might name. Of our commissioned chaplains we have, at the proper place, spoken of Hill and Eddy. Of De La Matyr, Davis says: "He was an earnest, faithful worker, always looking after the spiritual interest of those under his charge, furnishing the best religious reading he could get, and preaching as often as practicable." He was a fine old Presbyterian. Whenever we would stay long enough in a place he would have public preaching, and announce a time and place where he would meet the class of believers, inviting all to come who wished: and upon these occasions we would have bible lessons, or Sunday School, or prayer meeting, and as often as convenient he would administer the sacrament. This was done in this way: The chap lain would prepare a stand or table with a plate of bread and pitcher of water, and after calling attention to the last supper of our Lord Jesus Christ, would invite all present to come forward and take of the bread and of the water, as representing the broken body and the blood of our Lord Jesus, while the chaplain and those present would engage in singing appropriate hymns. Each one who felt so disposed would walk up to the stand, take a bit of bread and a sip of water, and resume his place again. Sometimes when the crowd was dense. and getting to the stand was difficult, the chaplain would ask two of the soldiers present to take the plate and pitcher of water and pass them around through the crowd, when those disposed helped themselves. There was not the least ostentation or display about it, nor yet was there any shrinking or timidity. Among all the walks of life where chance or circumstance has thrown us, the army is the only place where a man really *was* just what he seemed to be. If a man wanted to be religious he could be so in the army just as well as anywhere, as there were none with us so base as to try to make him afraid. If he wanted to curse and swear the whole time, he could do so without let or hindrance. This latter feature, however, was governed by the messes (or families) themselves, and in the Seventy-Second were many messes, the men of which never swore at all, nor was swearing allowed in the mess. We are bold to make the assertion that thousands and thousands of soldiers passed through the war with lives and characters just as pure and blameless as any who stayed at home. Nay, more; we believe that those who made the effort succeeded better than a like number at home, and that the per cent. of those who apostasized or back-slid was far less in the army, and for this reason: There is such a sameness in a soldier's life—one day just like another, so far as the temptations were concerned—one month or one year just like another—that nearly all those who were enabled to hold fast their integrity for a single month were equal to almost any emergency, and came out of the war stronger and better men than when they went into it. The war was simply a rigid school for the development of character, the foundation of which had already been laid. If a man's training at home had been correct, his character well formed, and purposes to do right well fixed, like purest gold he came out in the end all the brighter for the rubbing. On the other hand, if the training had been bad, character unsettled, and purposes weak, the man invariably went to the bad, and it generally took but a short time to tell which way he was going. A month or six months invariably settled it, It is true that there are many things in a soldier's life calculated to blunt the finer feelings. It is also true that many of the best soldiers did things for recreation, amusement or pastime, that would not be proper for them to do at home, and we find, too, that they have no inclination to do them. But we want it distinctly understood that many of the very best men in the world were in the army, and the Northern army, taken as a whole, was equally as good, or perhaps better, than a like number of men any where in the world, and instead of being that cold, unfeeling, selfish and brutalized mob, that we have heard it represented to be, it possessed all the finer feelings and sentiments of our enlightened age, and the verdict of history, as it compares the excesses of our army with those of the Franco-German War, ten years later, or with the excesses of the Russo-Turkish War, more recently, must be largely in favor of our war for the suppression of the rebellion. So much for a general diffusion of knowledge resulting from our free and republican institutions.

Before taking leave of this subject, and especially our chaplain, we want to say that from the time he first came to us, till the close of the war he stuck right to us; and the loudest and best preaching we ever heard at any time was in the thickest and hottest of any engagement we were ever in; and while shot and shell were raining death all around us; we had only to look back a little ways, for we could always see Chaplain De La Matyr, stretcher in hand, ready to assist with the dead and dying. We have often seen him between the skirmish and the main line of battle, and no feeble words of ours can ever express the love, gratitude, esteem, and veneration, which our whole regiment rightly and justly accords to our brave, good and kind chaplain. We must say, all honor to the noble old man, and to all the good and true men of our regiment.

June 23d we turned over our guns and accoutrements, and for the first time in nearly three years went to bed without knowing where our guns were; hitherto we had never lain down of a night without knowing just where to lay our hands on them in a moment. How soon the soldier ceased to be a soldier without a gun! Here was another separation of long united friends, and we had learned, too, to trust our Spencers as we never could trust a friend. Many of our boys had become so attached to them that they desired to retain them, and on the intervention of our officers were permitted to do so on the payment of $10.00 apiece for them. This at the time was considered magnanimous in the Government, as during the war we were required to pay $35.00 apiece for those we lost through negligence or carelessness.

Of the 335 recruits who had joined us, about 245 were still with us. All the rest had died, or been discharged. Those with us had been good soldiers, and we liked them much, and regretted beyond measure to leave them behind. They now comprised over one-third of our regiment, and it began to look like we were parting with so many things that were dear to us, as to spoil half the anticipations of being mustered out at all. There was an order that all recruits for the Seventy-Second Indiana should be transferred to the veteran 44th Indiana regiment. Their descriptive rolls were made out, and when we came away they were left behind. This was a bad "slam" on the recruits, and discouraged them greatly. They went back to Chattanooga, and served with the 44th regiment till the 14th of September, when they were mustered out of service, reaching Indianapolis on the 17th of September.

June 26th. Our muster rolls were done at last, and the most noticeable feature about them was the additional number of names, some of which had been dropped from the rolls for a year, and the owners of which we had not seen for two years. Some had been left behind sick, and had served out their time as cooks and nurses in hospitals, and others in the quartermaster's department; some one way and some another; and still others, who could never tell how or or where they had put in their time. We are glad to say there were but few of this character in the Seventy-Second. But there they were, ready and anxious to be mustered out with the regiment, and when we were finally called up in line, the companies had not been so full for many a day. Ordinarily, "roll-call" was for the living; but when Capt. Hosea came to muster us for discharge, the original roll was produced, and every name that had ever been added from first to last was called, and for the first time we realized how many of our number had already completed their record before the expiration of term of service. A chapter could be written on the emotions of our breasts, as name after name was called of brave men who went forth with us, but whose graves now mark our pathway all over the South.

About noon we answered to our names, for the last time, as soldiers of the Grand Army that had put down the Rebellion, preserved the Union, and rendered this fair land of ours forever free, in deed, as it had been in name. This transition of soldiers to citizens had come on to us so gradually that each one, when his name was called, stepped two paces to the front with the same stolidity, or about as much alacrity, as he ordinarily went to draw rations. Perhaps every man in the regiment realized, to a great extent, the import of the step, yet there was no outward sign of any inward emotion.

Our regiment was the first one of our brigade mustered, and after we were mustered we began to think about what few thought of before, and that was, of leaving behind the 98th and 123d Illinois. As the evening wore away, this subject more and more seemed to engross the minds of the men. We were all camped close together, and Col. Kitchell, of the 98th Illinois, still occupied brigade headquarters as commander of the brigade, Col. Miller staying there without assuming command. So, after supper, nearly every man of the Seventy-Second seemed all at once seized with an irresistible impulse to avail himself of the last opportunity of meeting the other two regiments once more in friendly congratulations. So, with cheers, and calling for the other regiments, the whole of the Seventy-Second started for brigade headquarters. In a few minutes the entire three regiments were densely packed around Col. Kitchell's tent. Of course, Col. Miller was first called on for a speech. From the severity of his wound, it was still difficult for him to get on to his feet; but he arose and thanked the men of the brigade for this, another manifestation of their regard toward him, and took the opportunity of bidding the 98th and 123d an affectionate farewell, telling them that on the morrow we would separate from them, never more to meet as the Lightning Brigade. Col. Kitchell was next called out, and the tremendous burst of eloquence that rolled from his lips told how full he was of the theme that was then uppermost in all our minds. We shall never forget with what prophetic vision and glowing colors he pictured to us that, as the years rolled away, and our numbers year after year became less, what an eager rushing forward there would be to grasp the hands of the few that were left of this brigade! No prophet of old ever saw the approach of the bright and Morning Star more clearly than he seemed to see this and no words of an Isaiah have more certainly been fulfilled. Col Thomson was next called out, and while he seemed to fully comprehend the breaking up of old associations and parting of old friends, he was still young and full of hope, and bright pictures of home, happiness, and prosperity, for everybody, were the theme of his discourse. It was late when the meeting broke up, and we wended our way back to our humble bunks, with a flood of emotions running through our minds.

It was about noon of the 27th when we broke camp for the last time, and bade adieu to the scenes that had, during two years and a half, grown so familiar as to seem almost like home. We moved down through Edgefield, crossed the Cumberland on the railroad bridge, and boarded the cars for Louisville. At 2 p. m. we were pulled back across the river, and from some cause lay in Edgefield until 5 p. m., when we finally got started. Darkness overtook us at Gallatin. We traveled steadily all night, and daylight came upon us at Mumfordsville, and it was nearly noon when we got to Louisville. We took dinner at the Soldiers' Home, and, after resting awhile, marched through the town and crossed the Ohio River, and at 5 p. m. got on the train at Jeffersonville and started for Indianapolis, and had another long ride in the night, arriving at Indianapolis just at daylight on the morning of June 29th. We marched to the Soldiers' Home, where we had a good wash and a good breakfast, and dinner also; after which we marched to Camp Carrington. This is the place where we first camped on going into the service. Then it was bare of everything but dog-fennel and smart-weed; but now was covered with long rows of barracks for soldiers; but most of our boys preferred sleeping in the streets to going into them, as it was more like what we had been used to.

June 30th. We signed the pay-rolls, and were given a reception at the Soldiers' Home by the ladies of Indianapolis, after which, at the signal of a cannon fired in the State House yard, the regiment assembled at the tabernacle and listened to welcoming speeches made by Lieut.-Gov. Baker, Gen. Hovey, and others. After songs and music by a brass band, we were dismissed. As soon as Lieut.-Col. Kirkpatrick heard of our being at Indianapolis, he came over to meet us, and after we were dismissed he invited the boys to partake of his hospitality.

It was found that we could not be discharged for several days, and Col. Miller went to Gov. Morton and got money, and gave each man five dollars who wanted to go home and spend the Fourth of July. All who had home or friends to go to availed themselves of the opportunity, and we suppose the men of the Seventy-Second celebrated the Fourth as they had never celebrated it before. For three years they had been fighting to make the Fourth of July mean something more than a glittering generality, and now they enjoyed this holiday with that ease and complacency that is always a sequence of a work faithfully and well done. But, for all this, there was a peculiarly sad loneliness crept over us that we were utterly unable to shake off.

Much has been written, said and sung, about the "soldiers' return," and with all there has been a strange mingling of all the glory, and pomp, and circumstance, of war, with the quietude and enjoyment of peace; of the glory and honor, and unfading laurels, that should crown the victorious soldier, and of the blessings of prosperity and plenty that should attend him in the pursuits of peace. And 'tis well. The humblest loyal citizen, though "clod-hopper" he may be, who sees his country in peril, and the government that has fostered and protected him in imminent danger of being broken up, and war, like a besom of destruction, sweeping over his fair land, laying all in one vast and wide spread field of ruin, and who takes his life in his hand, springs into the breach, and by his own strong will and strong arms helps to turn back the mighty and overwhelming flood, and causes the return of peace and prosperity again, is deserving of all the honors a country can give, of all the plaudits a grateful people can bestow; and it will be a sad day for any country when her defenders can die unmourned and unhonored. With many of us there was a very noticeable difference between 1862 and 1865—between the going and the coming volunteer. No fluttering handkerchiefs greeted the return of our regiment. No committees of invitation or reception met us at the depot; no loud sounding cannon belched forth thunders of welcome. More than half of the 208,000 Indiana soldiers were already discharged, and the land was full of soldiers then; nearly every other man you met was a soldier. And while we do not think the people felt ungrateful for our services, the country was saved, the cloud of war, which for four long years had overspread our fair land like a pall of darkness and death, had vanished into thin air, and the country's rescuers and defenders had been coming home, and kept coming, till their coming had become monotonous, and ceased to cause remark or ripple in the busy circles of life. By ones, twos and threes we scattered to our homes. While some of us were met with clasping arms and the joyful music of greeting voices, there were many others left in unutterable loneliness. There were many in our regiment who had no homes to go to; five to fifteen of such in each company had stayed at Indianapolis; and still a few others had come along with us in the vain hope of finding something or somebody as remnants of a once loved home; but alas! the mess, the company, the regiment, was all the home they had, and now *it* was broken up and gone.

On the 5th of July all were back again at Indianapolis, but not as the Seventy-Second Indiana. All who had gone home had exchanged the blue and the brass of the soldier for the garb of the citizen. And how changed each one seemed! We scarcely recognized each other; but saddest of all, the unanimity of feeling was all gone. There was a time, when, like a long, thin line of blue, in front of an enemy, as one man we lay down, as one man we got up; as one mighty giant we rushed upon the enemy and overwhelmed him in one terrible death struggle in a minute. We moved, we ate, we slept, at once. Our interests were all the same; we had but one grand object in view—putting down the rebellion; and we doubt if the world ever produced a regiment with that universal unanimity that characterized the Seventy-Second Indiana. No conscript or drafted man marched, fought, or fell, in her ranks; but every man of the regiment, with a loyalty intense, and a purpose well fixed, had volunteered in the country's service. This unanimity was all gone now. Of those who had gone home, some of the farmers had already found the plow they had left sticking in the furrow three long years ago; some of the mechanics had found their tools; some of the merchants had found goods to sell and people to buy; some of the students had found their books, and still others had found places of trust and profit. All such, of course, came back with broad smiles and beaming countenances, and a general air about them that said to their comrades as plainly as words could say, "My comrades, for three long years you have stood by my side and I have stuck to you because I felt I needed you, but now I've got a place, so good-bye, old fellow." How sad to some the change of those five short days! Some who had gone home found father, mother, and wife dead, the household goods scattered, and to them home only existed in memory as a thing forever gone. Some farmers found the ground they once owned and tilled, now owned and tilled by another, and their stock and farming implements scattered as by a breath of destruction. Mechanics and merchants found their tools and shops and places of business in the hands of others, and with many the prospects for home and bread were dark indeed.

Of course, all such came back for their discharges with countenances indicating the sorrow and dark forebodings of their minds. To a person given to the study of character, and reading of human nature, these, and those of our regiment who did not leave Indianapolis at all, presented a picture sad, indeed, to contemplate; and to us it yet seems that of all men, the volunteer soldier is most to be pitied. He first leaves the hearthstone and the family in response to his country's call, with the feeling that he will always continue to be identified with that little domestic circle. The first few months of his service is passed in a struggle between the conflicting forces of public duty and private interest—in other words, love of country and love of home. But, as he works out the problem in his mind, he arrives at a point where the question is squarely put before him: What is home without a country? Then, filled with the vain idea that home will be all the same to him when he returns from the discharge of his duty that it was when he left it, he falls into line. Then come the longings and home-sickness, which in thousands of cases never can be overcome, and the soldier dies, just as surely as if pierced by the deadly Minie, or torn by the exploding shell. But with others the charm is broken, and all unconscious of the change in their nature, they now call the mess, the company, the regiment, their home. To every such soldier, his comrade by his side on the march, in the camp, on picket, in the battle, and in gnawing hunger and raging thirst, has shared the last hard-tack and canteen; and this relationship has existed until the presence and companionship of that comrade is one of the essential elements of his happiness. As before remarked in these pages, what father, mother, wife, child, are to those at home, soldiers must, for the want of these, be to each other. But a change comes. His country's command now is, "Disband and go home." Then, for the first time, he is to realize that he has no home. He is discharged, and in joyful haste returns to his old home. He receives a hearty welcome, to be sure, from those who still live; but how changed! The old are older. The young have grown out of his recognition. All have changed; but none more than himself. Home is a disappointment, and he instinctively turns to his regiment; but that organization, which had become the pride of his heart, and the only one thing on earth to which he feels his identity belongs, has vanished away like a vapor before a morning sun. The iron enters his soul, and he realizes that he has given the best years, and the prime of his life, to preserve and perpetuate a great country, only to find himself as lonely in it as the iceberg in the midst of the Atlantic ocean.

"The cock's shrill clarion," heard across the country in the gray of the morning, sounds melancholy enough to ears accustomed for years to the sound of the reveille. The struggle for work, for bread, comes hard enough; for many of our regiment it has been hard ever since. And when now and then we meet one of the old Seventy-Second comrades, something in the sunken lines of his face, in his hair, in the stoop of his shoulders, tells us that the years of peace have broken him more than all the marches and vigils of the war. With *some*, all these years since the war have been passed without identifying themselves with *any* interest. They seem to be listening for the bugle call, and looking for the well-known ensign and colors. But the bugle has no voice for them, and the banners are folded away. But others, with that same energy which characterized them as soldiers, have adapted themselves to the situation, and have won a new identity. Their families are like little flocks, and to them is *a home* for the third time, where we hope and pray they may peacefully rest until transferred to a better home above.

One more reflection comes to our mind just here. It was our supreme fortune to be one of the very few men of the Seventy-Sec ond who ever got a furlough and came home. This was in the early spring of '64, before Grant moved "on to Richmond;" before the Atlanta campaign; before it was certain in the mind of any one that we should ever be able to "conquer a peace," and while the scales of victory were yet so evenly balanced that the wisest could not tell, and the most loyal could only hope, which side might yet "kick the beam." We shall never forget with what warmth of gratitude old men rushed forward to grasp us by the hand, and to wish us to live to put down the wicked rebellion; and we believe that such men who are yet alive feel that they owe the faithful soldier a debt of gratitude that can scarcely ever be paid. But the ones who fawned on us most, patted us most on the back, and who were the loudest in their protestations that anything the soldier wanted he most surely should have, were the would-be-politicians; those who, instead of going into their country's service and fighting for her rescue, were willing to fatten upon her misfortunes. "O yes," said they, "we who were doing the fighting were really a first-rate set of fellows, and if we really succeeded in putting down the rebellion, and were so fortunate as to get home alive, and there were any places of trust or profit, (not already wanted by themselves,) and we wanted them, all we had to do was to say so, and we should have them. O yes, we were just the very fellows they wanted;" and we still have a very vivid recollection how, after the war was over, and the soldier element carried the balance of power, these same fellows in grand conventions assembled and "resoluted" in favor of the soldier. We have no doubt that some of them really felt that if there was a one-armed or one-legged soldier who wanted to be road supervisor, constable, or country justice of the peace, why, they could really urge no serious objection. How they adored the soldier! How they lifted their hats to him, shook hands with him, and treated him to cigars on election day!

But what a change now! Seventeen short years have rolled away, all too soon, and the soldier element has ceased to be a factor in calculating the chances of an election. No vast assemblage representing the wealth and wisdom of our citizens in mass meetings, or by petitions long-drawn out and numerously signed, ever asks Congress to give even a small pittance toward equalizing the pay and bounties of soldiers, in order that all may share alike.

Were it not for the undying love and friendship, sealed by battle, blood, and death, the old veterans have for each other, and the promptness and certainty with which they meet in their annual reunions, and the persistency with which they gather around their camp fires and fight their battles over, the young of our land, or the stranger coming to our shores, would scarcely ever know that once upon a time, long ago, there was a terrible war for the preservation of this Union.

All these reflections and a thousand others have forced themselves upon our mind while thinking upon the volunteer "soldier's return." Are republics, indeed, ungrateful? Let no one think that the above has been written in a malignant, morose, or selfish spirit. We have never sought office and never expect to be a candidate for any position within the gift of the people. Though quite poor we have a comfortable home and make an honest living by attending to our own business and letting other people alone. Nor would we for one moment have any one think what we have here written is intended to discourage military service; far from it. We would have a spirit of patriotism so fostered, and a loyalty so deeply rooted, that when war does come—and come it may and no doubt will—our country shall never lack for *volunteer* defenders. The martyred Garfield truthfully said, "The *heart* of this country will never let the soldier die." For 17 years we have been thinking upon the "soldier's return," and have never seen, heard, or read, anything that, to our mind, exactly suited the case, and we most painfully realize how utterly we have failed to place the subject just as we have felt it properly before you. We are satisfied, however, that no two persons will look at this matter just in the same light, and have simply given the above as our own individual experience; and to show that we are not partial to our own views we insert the views of another member of the Seventy-Second:

MUSTERED OUT.

The pride, the pomp, the circumstance
Of glorious war at length are done:
The rebs have ceased their devil's dance—
Othello's occupation's gone.
I twirl my thumbs and mope about,
Alas! alas! I'm mustered out.

I joined the service with the thought
I'd quit it with a warrior's name;
For this I suffered, struggled, fought,
All burning with ambition's flame.
My dreams of fame are o'er, no doubt,
For now, alas! I'm mustered out.

Farewell the bars, farewell the stars,
The sparkling leaves and eagles, too,
I love you all, ye gifts of Mars,
And bid you now a sad adieu.
I'm bound for home the quickest route,
I'm mustered out, I'm mustered out!

No more for me the grand array—
  The drill, review, the dress parade,
The fever of the maddening fray,
  The contest fierce of ball and blade,
The carbine's ring, the trooper's shout,
  I'll have no more--I'm mustered out.

The tale, the song, the jocund roar,
  Will pass no more the camp-fire 'round.
"Played out" is "ante," and no more
  Shall commissary's grub abound.
Why couldn't General Lee hold out?
  Confound it all, I'm mustered out!

After he had been home a month he finished thus:

No battle now but that of life—
  (To fight the rebs I'd much prefer)
Sweet IDA said she'd be my wife,
  But forbids me now to think of her.
Whenever I speak she seems to pout.
  My hopes are fled, I'm mustered out!

We spent the forenoon of July 6th sauntering around over the city, and very impatiently waiting for our discharges and the seven months' pay and $75 bounty due us from the Government. Not that we wanted our discharges, or need the money so badly, but like Dick Stinson, who was urgently hurrying the cook to get his dinner ready, and said, "he wasn't so awful hungry, but then he wanted it off his mind." While we believe there was a scrupulous and exact settlement of all accounts, and a perfect willingness to settle the last cent owed by each one, we saw but little disposition to sociability and cheerfulness. Each one seemed totally absorbed in the problem of life before him. The fact that each soldier of the Seventy-Second had come to Indianapolis for the express purpose of getting his pay and bounty, and the piece of parchment with a spread eagle at the top which was to proclaim for all time to come that John Jones or James Smith had served his country faithfully and well, and was now honorably discharged, seemed to be as far from each one's mind as going to Halifax or Congress; and when our names were called, and each one of us walked up to a table and got his discharge, then to another and got his money, to a third and paid Col. Miller the five dollars loaned each of us, we did it with about as much stolidity as we ever performed any military duty in obedience to orders. There was no hurry, no pushing, no jest or loud talking; but all was done in a regular "matter of course" sort of way, as though we had done the same thing a thousand times before and might do it a thousand times again. And we shall never forget how we left that room and went out into the world, and parted from those dear old comrades for the last time, with scarcely a friendly word or parting salute. "Good-bye, old fellow, I'm going," was the nearest approach to friendship we saw or heard. Oh, how could we! how could we be so selfish! and what would we now give if we could but call that time back, that we might take each comrade by the hand—whom we shall never take by the hand again—and bid him an affectionate and a long farewell? Rather, what is there we would not give? Ah! how little we knew with whom we were parting then. All those ties and friendships which we have so often spoken of, and which each one in his mind had declared a thousand times never could be broken—all went for naught then. And so we went out into the world, "one to his farm, and another to his merchandise," and still others out into utter loneliness; and how long it took us to find out our great loss!

Five long years rolled away before soldiers began to talk of reunions. Slowly and gradually soldiers began to wake up to the fact that those dear old comrades were something more to them than kith or kin could ever be, and with this fact came the ever increasing longing once more to take those dear old comrades by the hand. After long years of separation, in which we had ample time to realize the true worth of those companions in arms, how glad we were to meet in our first reunion; and with what increasing warmth of affection, from year to year, we gather around our camp-fires. It requires no prophetic vision to predict that the last two survivors of the noble old Seventy Second shall, in future years, meet for the last time, with a love and affection stronger than that of David and Jonathan.

The seven months' pay due, and the $75 bounty we were to get at the end of our service, made $180 for each private soldier, all of which we took in Uncle Sam's due bills, or promissory notes—in short, greenbacks. Gold was then worth two dollars and forty cents. In other words, it took two dollars and forty cents of the kind of money we got, to buy, or be worth, one dollar in gold. So that, in reality, each private soldier of the Seventy-Second, on being discharged from the service of the Government he had helped to save, got just *seventy-five dollars*. The officers were of course paid in the same money.

Of the History of the Seventy-Second Indiana Regiment there remains but little to be said. Slowly, carefully, and faithfully, step by step, we have taken you through its eventful service, neither boasting nor exaggerating; neither prevaricating nor extenuating, nor setting down aught in malice; and we are glad it is so. In looking back over our work we see almost a thousand instances where we might have pictured the war cloud ten fold more dark, and the many dangers that surrounded us ten times more dangerous, and then not exceed the reality, but we rest our case on the evidence in the hands of the reader. We do not claim that the Seventy-Second Indiana was the *best* regiment in the service, or that it did more to put down the rebellion than any other, but we do claim that it was just as *good* as any, and that it did just as much as any other that was the same length of time in the service. And more: we claim that the Seventy-Second had better *opportunities to do*, than most of the regiments of the service ever possessed. According to Dr. Cole's journal, the regiment was in 52 battles and skirmishes; this is for the regiment, or as much as a battalion of the regiment, and the Historian himself was in 45 of these; that is to say, that number of times under the enemy's fire in which somebody was killed or wounded on one side or the other. The above, of course, does not include the vast number of skirmishes by squads or single companies of the regiment. Neither does it include any part of the siege of Atlanta, in which we were under rebel fire every day, as long as we lay in the trenches; but fortunately no one of our regiment was hurt, so that it has not been counted at all. We are well satisfied we shall not exaggerate one bit when we say there were members of the Seventy-Second Indiana under the enemy's fire over 100 times

Of the vast amount of work actually accomplished by the Seventy-Second there has been no attempt to aggregate. It would simply be to go over the whole history again. It traveled, in straight marches, as measured from point to point on the map, 9 100 miles. Taking into account the extreme crookedness of the roads, especially in Kentucky, and this can safely be increased by 1,000 more, and not exaggerate a foot the distance actually traveled. And as scouting, foraging and picketing, which is not included in the above calculation, comprised three-fourths of all the duty we performed while in the service, it is just as safe to add 5,000 more for this, making a grand total of 15,000 miles.

The Seventy-Second Regiment Indiana Volunteers was raised in what was then the Eighth Congressional District of Indiana, and organized at LaFayette on the 10th day of August, 1862. That is, all the companies were in camp by that time. It was mustered into the service at Indianapolis, on the 16th day of August, and left for the seat of war on the next day. It arrived at Lebanon, Ky., with an aggregate of 978 men. During its service it received 335 recruits, making a grand total belonging to the regiment of 1313 men. On the 26th of June, 1865, it was mustered out of the service at Nash-ville, Tennessee, and on June 29th reached Indianapolis with [illegible] men and 36 officers, or an aggregate of 546 of those who were with the regiment at its first muster; showing a loss of the original muster of 432 men, nearly 44 per cent. Of the 335 recruits, 245 were transferred to the 44th Regiment Indiana Veteran Volunteers, and were mustered out of the service with that regiment on the 14th of September, 1865. This shows a loss of 90 recruits, 37 per cent., a total loss to the regiment of 522 men, 40 per cent. of the whole Strange as it may seem, only 29 of that number were killed dead in battle, and by members of other regiments from this district, less fortunate than our own, we have often been bantered in this way "How is it that your regiment has seen so much service, been in so many battles, and had so few killed, and got home with so many men? The explanation is easy. We have frequently referred to the superior skill and generalship of our officers; to the superior drill and discipline of the men, and to the overwhelming superiority of the arms we carried. But there was one other feature, combining all the above items, which was of great advantage to us, of which we have said but little, and that was our manner of fighting. When we first went into the service, and were armed with the Springfield rifle. (by the way, a most excellent single-shooting gun,) we never thought of facing an enemy unless formed in two ranks, and we felt that the actual touch of the elbow was necessary to impart that confidence which would enable us to charge upon him; and we believe this feeling is universal with all green troops When they lose the "touch," they become confused, and, in their efforts to regain it, "bunch up," and become a target for the deadly Minie, exploding shell, or mowing grape and canister. When we drew the Spencer rifle, the confidence imparted by it enabled us to march in single rank, and never afterward did we face the enemy in two ranks As the war progressed, and we gained confidence in ourselves, in each other, in our commanders, and the balance of the brigade, we always went into battle in single rank, and deployed so wide apart—often as much as five paces—that it took the closest shooting every time on the part of the enemy to hit one of us.

And here we want to pay a parting and a just compliment to the other regiments of our brigade, the 17th Indiana, the 98th and 123d Illinois. There was no difference in any of them; but each one possessed those staying qualities which characterized our own, and which would always stick right to a comrade under any and every circumstance; and we never went into a fight asking which of the three was to be our support. The only question asked, was our support a part of our own brigade? and then we could rush right into the very jaws of death with the assurance that we would have all the help brave men, who never faltered, could give. Often have we gone into battle deployed, as above indicated, and been suddenly and unexpectedly fired upon; our custom was never to "bunch up," but to scatter behind tree, and stump, and log, or to immediately fall flat upon the ground, and sometimes the enemy upon seeing us scatter, have mistaken it for a panic or retreat, and moved upon us only to find an unseen foe ready to mow them down as fast as they should come on. In moving upon the enemy, it was our custom for our long, thin line, to slip forward stealthily and as noiselessly as possible until within charging distance, and then, with a tremendous cheer, to rush upon them like a mighty avalanche and overwhelm them without scarcely giving them time to fire a single shot. So we did at Flat Shoals, at Rome, and Blue Pond; and the rebels were never able to mass a line before us so strong that we could not break it and sweep them before us like chaff before the wind. Such, reader, were the characteristics of the trained soldiery of the Seventy-Second Indiana. Never retreating, never panic stricken, never surprised.

The History of the Seventy-Second Regiment is completed to the best of our ability. As we have before said, we now repeat, that we are painfully sensitive to the fact that it is not all in these pages. Many gallant deeds of many gallant men are omitted because we could not get hold of them at all, or only so vaguely that no true statement of them could be made. Here, perhaps, we should lay down the pen, but for those who read the book—especially for the young, for we flatter ourselves that many young men and women will read it, children, grand children and great grand children of our noble comrades—and for them we feel that a few valuable lessons may be drawn from these pages and summed up in a few words:

The intense loyalty of the loyal, and their intense devotion to their country! They were loyal at home or in the field; whether male or female—from the lisping babe to the form bent and tottering with age. No amount of suffering or sorrow cooled their ardor. Whether a loyal person was a soldier in the front line of battle, or in the horrid hells of Southern prisons, suffering and dying by the inch; or a wife, or a mother, or a father, whose husband or son was so exposed, or so suffering, or had even gone to an unknown grave—still the bright flame of patriotism would but blaze the higher, and shine the brighter from the altars of their suffering hearts. The rebels who sought to quench the patriotism of the loyal by torturing Union prisoners, were as utterly mistaken as was Satan when he sought to traduce the Savior by temptation. Neither the rebels nor Satan—and they are synonymous terms, Satan being the first traitor, and the great element in all subsequent ones—knew the spirit of those they sought to traduce. All those cruelties only made every loyal person more uncompromisingly determined to stamp out any pretense of a government so low, so devilish, so full of savagery.

Every loyal person aided to put down the rebellion. The strong men went to war. The older men were counselors, and also took hold of plows, tools, and business generally, and worked as in the vigor of manhood to fill the places of those gone to the front, and to provide them with supplies. Women and children went to the fields again to toil, as in primitive times, while fathers, brothers and sons were in the army. Old women, whose fingers were stiff and eyes dim, took up the knitting needles, and day after day knit for the boys in the field. In loyal houses we have seen old women who could not rise from their beds, lying with work in hand, day after day, making something for the soldier boys. In cities and villages good women formed organizations for the making of articles of clothing for the sick and the well soldiers; and to pick lint and make bandages and articles for the wounded. Of them the grateful soldiers sang around their camp-fires:

Plying the busy fingers,
Over the vestments old;
Not with the weary needle,
Not for some grains of gold;
Thinking of fainting heroes,
Out in the dreary night,
Smitten in Freedom's battle,
First in the gallant fight.
O, bright are the jewels from love's deep mint,
God bless the fingers while picking the lint!

Quicker the blood is flowing;
Thousands were slain to-day,
And every warm pulsation
Is stealing life away.
"A hundred threads a minute,
A hundred drops of gore,"
The sad and thrilling measure,
We've never learned before.
The shadows are weaving a silver tint.
God bless the fingers while picking the lint!

We've clad the fallen heroes
With garments we have made;
By lint we now are picking,
The fearful tide be stayed.
We lift our eyes to heaven,
Our Father's blessing crave—
Behold our smitten country,
O, bless the fallen brave!
O, bright are the jewels from love's deep mint,
God bless the fingers while picking the lint!

The best men and women of the country organized the Sanitary and Christian Commissions, the objects of which were to collect and forward to the soldiers in the field, especially the sick and the wounded, and those in the rebel prisons, such extra supplies of food, clothing, blankets, and medical supplies, as were necessary for the most careful nursing of the unfortunate men who needed them, and could not get them from the regular supply. In all these efforts the noble President, and the Governors of the loyal States, aided the good people in their work of love. History can never tell how much good these grand commissions did. Thousands are alive to-day who would have died during the service but for the timely aid from the commissions, and who can best testify of the great work they wrought. All this work was voluntary. The supplies were all donated, and so were the services of almost all the agents; the best men and women in the country volunteered their services to go to the front and serve in the hospitals as agents to distribute these extra supplies, and as nurses for sick and wounded. There have we seen aged mothers and young women, Sisters of Charity, and old men, bent with age, working day and night for weeeks after a great battle, doing all that human effort could do to make the wounded as comfortable as possible. These commissions were the very flower and fruit of Christian patriotism—grand and beautiful achievements of united, generous, Christian effort, to reduce to the minimum the sufferings of a great war.

It is painful to write it, but it is true, that these commissions gave their aid most liberally to the rebel wounded and prisoners who fell into Union hands, while the rebels gave no such relief to the Union sick and wounded who fell into their hands, but a cruel treatment, which we have recorded in the chapter on prisons, and do not wish to repeat. Worst and basest of all, the rebel authorities would not permit the Union Government to send the sanitary stores of these commissions to our suffering and perishing prisoners. While our brave men were perishing so miserably in Southern prison-pens, and the Southern confederacy was giving as an excuse for the cruelty, that it had not the means to supply them, both the Union Government and the Christian and Sanitary Commissions stepped forward and said: "Let us send supplies to the Union prisoners; we will at once relieve them, and without a cent of cost to the confederacy." But, like a black demon, the rebel authorities replied: "No; you shall give them nothing!" Not a man in a rebel prison would have starved, or frozen for want of blankets or fuel, or died for want of medicines or medical treatment, had the rebel authorities permitted the supplies, which were piled up and ready, to have been taken to Union prisoners. There is no blacker passage in the wicked rebellion than this.

. We learn from this that patriotism and Christianity combined all the noblest, bravest elements of the Nation, in an effort to save the Union, and to minister to all the wants of the soldiers who fought the battles of those dark and bloody days.

We learn what a poison to heart and soul is slavery. It caused the spirit of treason to spring and grow, and finally to take up the sword and strive to divide the government. It had raised up a section of dealers in the bodies and souls of men, women and children ; some of them so base that they would sell into slavery human creatures in whose veins ran their own blood, in whose faces were indelibly stamped their own likenesses. Many of these slave mongers had become as brutal as Legree is described to have been. When Union prisoners—"Northern mudsills," detested "Yanks," fell into their hands, all their brutal, slave-nourished passions, were stirred, and hence the horrors of the Southern prison pens, a disgrace and shame forever to the slaveocracy. Cursed be slavery as a sin against Almighty God. Cursed be slavery as a sin against mankind. Cursed be slavery as the cause of the rebellion, and cursed be slavery for the brutality of the Southern rebel prison pens. In the name of God and humanity, cursed be slavery, and blessed be they who crushed it out.

We learn that rebellion in this country, to establish wrong, and divide the Union, cannot succeed. The loyal people have decided that the Union is one and indivisible, and free from sea to sea, from north to south.

We learn that the country will ever honor and care for its brave men. No other nation in history has ever so liberally and constantly cared for its soldiers as has the United States. Pensions and artificial limbs have been given to the disabled and maimed. For those not able to make a living, homes have been provided, where they can live in peace and comfort, read books and papers, and "fight their battles o'er," until the tattoo of death is sounded from headquarters above For orphans of soldiers, left in poverty, schools have been provided where they are educated at the expense of the Government their fathers fought and their mothers worked and suffered to maintain. The bones of the dead have been gathered from forest, plain, wayside and battle-field, into great National Cemeteries, buried with care, and at the head of each a neat stone fitted, with name and rank if known —if not known, then marked "unknown"—and those homes of the ashes of our brave are kept with motherly care and neatness. For those whose reasons became dethroned, asylums have been provided, and they are tenderly cared for until the spirit shall go free from its shattered tabernacle, and in its freedom from carnal wreck find joy and reason again.

In a word, most munificently has the government we fought to preserve cared for our unfortunate comrades. However selfish politicians have been, Uncle Sam, dear good heart, has cared for them with fatherly diligence and liberal bounty that has made the old nations of the earth wonder, or say, "no wonder its citizens love and fight for such a government."

It teaches us that no large standing armies are needed in this Nation; that though the people are devoted to peace, make no wars of conquest—never go to war at all unless in defense of the rights of citizens or in self-defense—yet when war must come, and does come, volunteer armies can soon be raised, equipped and drilled that will be a match for any troops on earth. This was done in the war of the rebellion, it had been done before, and it can be done in the future.

It teaches us that ignorance is not the best qualification of a private soldier. Almost every Union soldier was well educated; a large per cent. of rebel soldiers were ignorant of letters. The superiority of the Union soldiers in the service no one can deny; and that superiority sprang mainly from superiority of education. The Union soldiers, as a body, were so intelligent as to fully understand the cause and object of the rebellion, and to comprehend the disastrous consequences of its success. Our volunteer soldiery in the future will be necessarily intelligent, hence efficient men.

The rapidity with which the members of the Seventy-Second were transformed from citizens of various pursuits into a unitized, solid, disciplined body of soldiers, has been told; the rapidity with which they were transformed from veteran soldiers to citizens of various pursuits and objects, has also been told. This proves the wonderful elasticity of the American character; the triumphs of self government in the highest state of civilization. We became soldiers, as it were, at the sound of the bugle, and after years of war became citizens again at the sound of the bugle. A nation of such citizens is invincible.

We learn also that the people of this Nation honor their soldiers. Gens. Grant, Hayes, Garfield and Arthur, have in turn been Presidents of the United States since the war. Congress in both branches has had a large per cent. of soldiers; the National Government has long since passed a law that in the Government Departments Union soldiers, their orphans or widows, shall be preferred, when able to perform the duties required; and a late report shows that the departments have well observed the law. In State, county, and even township, offices, the capable soldier has found wide recognition in offices of trust and profit.

In the various callings of life the soldiers of the Union army have found diversified, useful and profitable employment, and surely the soldiers of the Seventy-Second make a splendid showing in all honorable civil pursuits. We should be happy to state the address and avocation of each, and seriously entertained such a statement as part of the plan of this book, at one time, but find we cannot obtain information complete enough to be satisfactory. Suffice it to say, that from Col. Miller, who is practicing medicine in Lebanon, Ind., through rank and file, there are doctors, lawyers, preachers, bankers, merchants, professors, teachers, farmers, editors, telegraphers, judges, and civil officers of almost every grade. No equal number of men, who have never served a day in the army, can show a better record in civil life than the members of the Seventy-Second Indiana.

We learn that our Nation has large recuperative powers. As soon as the destruction of time and wealth ceased, at the close of the war, industry again began to create wealth, and to restore the wasted resources of the Nation. We need not speak of the great struggle, of the panic, and other difficulties which were overcome; they were overcome, and a public debt, which was $2,756,431,571 about the time the Seventy-Second was mustered out of the service, bearing interest to the amount of $150,977,697 per year, has been cut down to $1,675,023,474, on the 4th of July, 1882, with an annual interest of $57,360,110. The principal of the debt is almost one-half less than at the close of the war, and the annual interest charge is less than one-half what it was at that time. Had not the soldiers of both armies gone promptly to work, and practiced the arts of industry and frugality to the utmost degree, this result could never have been achieved.

We will not weary the reader with statistics of the increase of manufactures, and products of all sorts; with the settlement of the wild lands, and the acres brought under cultivation since the war; of the spread of American manufactures and products of the soil into all parts of the earth; the numbers of miles of new railroads built; the wide-spread use of the wonderful telephone; the improvement in our common school system, &c., &c. None of these results could have followed the war had not the soldiers generally, like those of the Seventy-Second, returned promptly and vigorously to productive labor, and helped to achieve the triumphs of peace.

The Negroes, whom the Emancipation Proclamation, and the triumphs of our arms, freed, have done their part, and behaved very admirably, considering their long bondage, and deep ignorance. During the war they were the steadfast friends of the Union soldiers from the first; they have fed, sheltered, and guided, the fugitives from rebel prison-pens, hundreds of times, for which kindness many a noble black man was brutally murdered. They were finally armed, and showed themselves worthy of freedom, the ballot, and civil rights, since the war. The dire results of freedom to the Negro, predicted by some, have not come. They are pushing their way up from ignorance and base servitude, to the broad, sunny plains, of general intelligence and lofty freedom; and between them and the noblest white men there is no friction. The Negroes are also producing more than when in slavery, and their labor is contributing largely to make one grand aggregate of national wealth and strength. The noble Lincoln, in his Emancipation Proclamation, invoked the considerate judgment of mankind That judgment has been rendered, and is, that he did right in freeing them, and that the Seventy-Second, and all the loyal troops, did right in standing by him, and fighting until the proclamation became an accomplished fact.

The South is rapidly recuperating in both loyalty and wealth. All this every Union soldier is glad to see. We fought to bring them back to the Union, because we believed it would be better for them and for us. For them and their children we fought as much as for ourselves and our own children. We took away slavery, which cursed their States, and gave them free States. Since the war the spirit of the free States has been gradually infusing itself into the Southern States. Quietly have free schools sprung up, large plantations have been broken up into smaller farms; the miserable negro cabins are giving place to neat homes of land owners, white and black; manufactures are springing up all over the sunny land like daisies in the spring All sectional feelings of bitterness are passing away; and, in short, they who erst were "Johnny Rebs," are now almost Yanks, and in a few years will be fully so.

This is all very comforting to the Union soldier, for it is "seeing of the travail of their souls and being satisfied." The noble men of the Seventy-Second rejoice in all this, and heartily wish it may constantly increase until the era of perfect good will is restored, and the South is as rich as the North. Noble Union soldiers are now able to meet those who once were rebel soldiers upon the most cordial terms; not to acknowledge the rebels were right, not to concede a hair's-breadth to treason, or to discount loyalty by the slightest shade;

to acknowledge them as brave men when enemies in the field, and to congratulate them on being once more in the Union and once more on the highway to prosperity. In this is the lesson of magnanimity, a conspicuous trait of the noble soldier. We were right, we were victorious, and we can afford to be magnanimous.

Many other lessons might be drawn, by an acute analyst, from the facts of this book. The final one which occurs to us is, that the world has clearly seen that the United States is not a plaster cast; not a shell; not a thing of temporary being; but that it is solid as granite, firm as the everlasting hills, and is durable as the mountains; that as an intelligent, religious, free people, our motto, "In God we trust," is significant of strength, long national life and grand moral achievement. With great confidence that, brave and noble as our comrades were in the war of the rebellion, their children will be even braver and nobler in any like crisis in the future, we bid our comrades and readers an affectionate ADIEU.

SEVENTY-SECOND REGIMENT---THREE YEARS SERVICE.

FIELD AND STAFF OFFICERS.

NAME AND RANK.	Date of Commission.	Date of Muster.	REMARKS.
Colonel.			
Abram O Miller	Aug. 13, 1862	Aug. 24, '62	Wounded at Selma, Ala., April 2, '65; Brevetted Brig. Gen.: mustered out with Regt.
Lieutenant Colonel.			
John B Milroy	Aug. 14, 1862		Declined.
Sam'l C Kirkpatrick	Oct. 18, 1862	Oct. 23, '62	Resigned September 26, '64.
Chester G Thomson	Sept. 27, 1864	Dec. 6, '64	Mustered out with Regiment.
Major.			
Sam'l C Kirkpatrick	Aug. 13, 1862	Aug. 13, '62	Promoted Lieutenant Colonel.
Henry M Carr	Oct. 18, 1862	Oct. 23, '63	Resigned June 28, '64.
Adam Pinkerton	Sept. 1, 1864	Sept. 16, '64	Resigned November 28, '64.
Lawson S Kilborn	Nov. 29, 1864	Dec. 6, '64	Mustered out with Regiment.
Adjutant.			
Alexander A Rice	July 21, 1862	July 21, '62	Promoted Captain and A. A. G. Mar. 17, '63.
William K Byrns	Mar. 17, 1863	Feb. 24, '63	Resigned December 19, '64.
Jeremiah Anderson	Feb. 23, 1865	Mar. 6, '62	Mustered out with Regiment.
Quartermaster.			
Henry S Dewey	July 21, 1862	July 22, '62	Mustered out with Regiment.
Chaplain.			
Jesse Hill	Sept. 20, 1862	Sept. 30, '62	Resigned April 13, '63.
John R Eddy	May 19, 1863	June 17, '63	Killed at Hoover's Gap, Tenn., June 24, '63.
Isaac DeLaMater	Sept. 19, 1863	Oct. 20, '63	Mustered out with Regiment.
Surgeon.			
James L Morrow	Aug. 14, 1862	Aug. 15, '62	Resigned December 17, '63.
William C Cole	Dec. 18, 1863	Jan. 7, '64	Mustered out with Regiment.
Assistant Surgeon.			
James L Morrow	Aug. 4, 1862	Aug. 4, '62	Promoted Surgeon.
John B Johnson	Aug. 13, 1862	Aug. 14, '62	Resigned May 3, '63.
William C Cole	Aug. 14, 1862	Aug. 15, '62	Promoted Surgeon.
Geo W Kirkpatrick	Jan. 11, 1864	April 1, '64	Mustered out with Regiment.
Elias B Stearns	July 2, 1863	Dec. 25, '63	Mustered out with Regiment.

COMPANY "A."

NAME AND RANK.	Date of Commission.	Date of Muster.	REMARKS.
Captain			
Nathanial Herron	Aug. 1, 1862	Aug. 16, '62	Resigned December 17, '62.
Milton W Newton	Dec. 18, 1862	Dec. 23, '62	Resigned February 1, '63.
Andrew J Klepser	Feb. 2, 1863	Feb. 24, '63	Discharged October 6, '64.
Lewis Gros	Dec. 3, 1864	Dec. 4, '64	Mustered out with Regiment.
First Lieutenant.			
Milton W Newton	Aug. 1, 1862	Aug. 16, '62	Promoted Captain.
Andrew J Klepser	Dec 18, 1862	Dec. 23, '62	Promoted Captain.
Lewis Gros	Feb. 2, 1863	April 3, '63	Promoted Captain.
Mark Aschaffenberg	Dec. 3, 1864		Resig'd as 2d Lieut. to avoid dismis'l, 12-10-64.
James H Barnes	Dec. 29, 1864	Dec. 27, '64	Mustered out with Regiment.
Second Lieutenant.			
Andrew J Klepser	Aug. 1, 1862	Aug. 16, '62	Promoted 1st Lieutenant.
Mark Aschaffenberg	Dec. 18, 1862	Dec. 29, '62	Promoted 1st Lieutenant.
James H Barnes	Dec. 3, 1864	Dec. 11, '64	Promoted 1st Lieutenant.
Richard W Pilling	Dec. 26, 1864	Dec. 27, '64	Mustered out with Regiment.
	RESIDENCE.	1862.	
First Sergeant.			
Aschaffenberg, Mark	LaFayette	July 23	Promoted 2d Lieutenant.
Sergeants.			
Pilling, Richard W	Camden	July 12	Promoted 2d Lieutenant.
Gros, Lewis	Delphi	July 16	Promoted 1st Lieutenant.
Knight, Jonathan L	Delphi	July 20	Promoted 1st Lieutenant.
Stewart, Samuel	Camden	July 15	Mustered out with Regiment.

NAME AND RANK.	RESIDENCE.	Date of Muster. 1862.	REMARKS.
Corporals.			
Barnes, James H.	Delphi	July 15	Promoted 2d Lieutenant.
Stewart, William R.	Camden	July 15	Mustered out July 24, '65, as 1st Sergeant.
Robinson, James T.	Delphi	July 18	Died at Chattanooga, Sept. 16, '63, wounds.
Higginbotham, Jos R.	Delphi	July 16	Died at Corinth, Miss., January 14, '64.
Pilling, Samuel G	State Line.	July 22	Mustered out July 24, '65, as Hospital Steward
Stokes, Marion F.	Danville	July 17	Mustered out July 25, '65, as Sergeant.
Faughty, Samuel	Delphi	July 14	Mustered out July 24, '65, as private.
Huntsinger, Rufus	Rockfield	July 14	Mustered out July 24, '65, as Sergeant.
Musicians.			
Smith, Arthur A	Delphi	July 16	Discharged October 28, '62.
Stoner, George	Delphi	July 16	Discharged May 28, '63.
Wagoner.			
Wallack, Benjamin	Delphi	July 16	Mustered out July 24, '65.
Privates.			
Allen, George W.	Delphi	July 13	Mustered out July 24, '65, as Corporal.
Bailey, George	Idaville	July 18	Died in Andersonville prison, Aug. 8, '64
Barnard, John M	Camden.	July 20	Mustered out July 24, '65, as Sergeant.
Bowers, Daniel	Carroll	July 28	Mustered out July 24, '65.
Boyd, John	Delphi	July 16	Killed at Pilot Shoals, Ga., July 28, '64
Brown, Harvey A.	Mentez	July 21	Transferred to V R C, Sept 16, '63.
Burton, Jeremiah	Lockport	July 21	Mustered out July 24, '65.
Cantner, George W	Poplar Grove.	July 19	Discharged Jan. 31, '63.
Cline, Daniel H.	Camden	July 17	Mustered out July 24, '65.
Cline, Daniel	Camden	July 17	" " "
Cline, Thomas	Camden	July 17	Transferred to V R C, July 1, '63.
Comer, Thomas	Delphi	July 17	Discharged Oct. 11, '62.
Culler, Jacob	Delphi	July 14	Transferred to V R C, July 1, '63.
Culler, George	Delphi	July 14	Transferred to V R C, August 1, '63.
Dimmit, Benoni	Delphi	July 18	Mustered out July 24, '65.
Dimmit, John	Delphi	July 19	" " "
Dimmit, William H	Delphi	July 18	Mustered out July 24, '65, as Corporal.
Etskin, Joseph	Delphi	July 16	Killed at McElmore's Cave, Ga., Sept. 12, '63
Felix, Leonard G.	Feth'rh'f's Mill	July 23	Discharged May 7, '64.
Franklin, Nelson	Delphi	July 22	Discharged June 2, 65, as Sergeant.
Frederick, John	Feth'rh'f's Mill	July 22	Transferred to V R C, January 15, '64.
Gard, Stephen J	LaFayette	July 19	Mustered out July 24, '65, as Corporal.
Ghear, Elijah	Feth'rh'f's Mill	July 12	Discharged May 19, '63.
Gee, Jeremiah	Delphi	July 13	Mustered out July 24, '65.
Gaumer, Harrison	Camden	July 17	" " "
Gaumer, William	Camden	July 19	Died at Nashville, August 13, '63.
Grantham, William H	Camden	July 17	Discharged October 26, '62.
Hare, Joseph L.	Cicero	July 17	Mustered out July 24, '65.
Heiney, Henry	Idaville	July 20	" " " as Corporal.
Huntsinger, Isaac	Rockfield	July 16	" " "
Huntsinger, Samuel K	Rockfield	July 16	" " "
Jones, Daniel H.	Burlington	July 16	" " "
Kahl, Ezra	Shelby	July 17	" " "
King, William J	Delphi	July 20	Must'd out July 24, '65, as Commissary Serg't.
Landis, John R.	Carroll	July 21	Mustered out July 24, '65.
Landis, Frederick	Carroll	July 21	" " " as Corporal.
Lane, Eli	Delphi	July 21	Deserted January 10, '64.
Lathrop, Harrison T.	Christiansbu'g	July 19	Mustered out July 24, '65
Lesler, William	Feth'rh'f's Mill	July 12	Discharged March 28, '63.
Lewis, Wilson	Lockport	July 13	Mustered out July 24, '65.
Martin, Thomas	Delphi	July 12	" " "
Melson, James F	Anderson	July 12	" " "
Mills, Thomas	Camden	July 11	" " "
Mills Daniel	Camden.	July 11	" " " as Sergeant.
Moore, Peter J	Delphi	July 12	Discharged December 15, '63.
Murphy, Francis	Feth'rh'f's Mill	July 13	Mustered out July 24, '65, as Corporal.
McArdle, John	Delphi	July 13	Transferred to V R C, January 15, '64.
McArdle, Philip	Delphi	July 13	Mustered out July 24, '65.
McClurg, Cyrus	Delphi	July 16	Died at Louisville, Ky., Sept. 20, '62.
Neff, James A	Delphi	July 21	Discharged February 17, '63.
Neville, James	Pittsburg	July 21	" " 9, '63.
Nipper, Isaac	Delphi	July 13	Mustered out July 24, '65.
Nokes, William	Camden	July 13	Died at Murfreesboro, Tenn., March 29, '63.
Nye, John P	Delphi	July 21	Discharged March 1, '63.
Oliver, James K	Pittsburg	July 22	Mustered out July 24, '65.
Paxon, John		July 23	Deserted Sept 26, '62.
Pilling, Robert	Camden	July 11	Mustered out July 24, '65.
Pruitt, James H	Delphi	July 15	Transferred to V R C, July 1, '63.
Riley, Dennis	Feth'rh'f's Mill	July 25	Mustered out July 24, '65.
Riley, Daniel	Feth'rh'f's Mill	July 25	" " "
Reigel, Simon	Lockport	July 19	" " "
Scott, William W.	Delphi	July 26	Discharged February 8, '63.
Seagraves, William E	Camden	July 26	Mustered out July 24, '65.
Sance, Isaac	Poplar Grove.	July 19	" " "
Shirar, Peter	Camden	July 17	Transferred to V R C, July 1, '63.

NAME AND RANK.	RESIDENCE.	Date of Muster. 1862.	REMARKS.
Shaw, Henry C.	Delphi	July 15	Mustered out July 24, '65.
Sigars, Albert	Delphi	July 13	Killed at Mooresville, Ala, Nov. 21, 63.
Spittler, Benjamin	Burlington	July 24	Mustered out July 24, '65, as Corporal.
Smith, Samuel H.	Fetn'ehff'sMill	July 24	" " " "
Salsberry, John A	Camden	July 19	Mustered out July 24, '65.
Stoner Philip	Delphi	July 12	Discharged March 26, '63.
Stoley, George	Delphi	July 24	Mustered out July 24, '65.
Tolbey, Berry	Delphi	July 18	Died at Bowling Green, Ky., Nov. 8, '62.
Vick, Lucien A	La Fayette	July 19	Mustered out July 24, '65.
Wasts, Isaac	Delphi	July 20	" " "
Wilkinson, Isaac	Montez	July 17	Died at Murfreesboro, Tenn., April 7, '63.
Yonker, Benjamin F.	Battle Creek	July 25	Discharged March 1, '63.
Recruits.			
Adams, James R		Mar. 22, 64.	Transferred to V R C, Dec. 28, '64.
Brice, Asbury		Mar. 3, '64.	Transferred to 44th Regiment.
Cress, Ira		Feb. 20, '64.	" " "
Chapman, Wyman		Dec 26, '63	" " "
Cranshorn, Elias		Jan. 10, '64.	" " "
Foble, Nicholas		Dec. 24, '63.	" " "
Foust, David		Jan. 4, '34	" " "
Foust, Samuel		Jan. 4, '64	" " "
Foust, George		Dec. 26, '63.	" " "
Grandstaff, James		Dec. 29, '63.	Discharged June 5, '65.
Hawkins, Henry H		Jan. 4, '64	Transferred to 44th Regiment.
Hicks, Thomas B		Jan. 4, '64	" " "
Hall, John		Feb. 6, '64	" " "
Herron, Henry H.		Dec. 29, '63.	" " "
Henderson, Andrew		Mar. 11, '64.	" " "
Irwin, Henry		Dec. 11, '63.	Died at Jeffersonville, Ind., May 22, '65.
Malott, Jacob		Dec. 26, '63.	Transferred to 44th Regiment.
Moses, William F.		Jan. 4, '64	" " "
Montgomery, John		Feb. 11, '64.	" " "
McGlennen, Charles E.		Feb. 29, '64.	" " "
McFarland, David		Dec 26, '63.	Died at Marietta, Ga., Aug. 9, '64.
Noyce, John F		Dec. 24, '63.	Transferred to 44th Regiment.
Newman, Mark A		Dec. 24, '63.	" " "
O'Brien, Christ'ph'r A		Dec. 16, '63.	" " "
Rader, Daniel O		Jan. 15, '64.	" " "
Sinks, David		Feb. 20, '65.	" " "
Thompson, Robert H.			" " "
Thomas, John D.		Feb. 20, '65.	" " "
Timmons, James W		Dec. 29, '63.	" " "
Wilson, Henry		Dec. 26, '63.	" " "
Wickham, George		Jan. '15, '64.	" " "
Woods, James		Jan. 15, '64	" " "
Youngst, John H		Dec. 21, '63.	" " "

COMPANY "B."

NAME AND RANK.	Date of Commission.	Date of Muster.	REMARKS.
Captain.			
Henry M Carr	July 22, 1862	Aug. 16, '62	Promoted Major.
Oliver P Mahan	Oct. 19, 1862	Oct. 24, '62.	Resigned Feb. 16, 1863.
William P Herron	Feb. 17, 1863	Feb. 24, '63	Mustered out with Regiment.
First Lieutenant.			
Oliver P Mahan	July 22, 1862	Aug. 16, '62	Promoted Captain.
Wesley C Gerard	Oct. 19, 1862	Oct. 24, '62.	Resigned Feb. 2, '63.
William P Herron	Feb. 2, 1863		Promoted Captain.
Robert Maxwell	Feb. 17, 1863	Feb. 24, 63.	Mustered out with Regiment.
Second Lieutenant.			
Wesley C Gerard	July 22, 1862	Aug. 16, '62	Promoted 1st Lieutenant.
William P Herron	Oct. 19, 1862	Oct. 24, '62.	Promoted 1st Lieutenant.
Robert Maxwell	Feb. 2, 1863		Promoted 1st Lieutenant.
Charles M Robinson	Feb. 17, 1863	Feb. 24, '63	Resigned April 18, '64.
Nelson Gaskell	May 1, 1864	Jan. 12, '65	Mustered out with Regiment.
	RESIDENCE.	1862.	
First Sergeant.			
Herron, William P.	Crawf'rdsville	July 14	Promoted 1st Lieutenant.
Sergeants.			
Maxwell, Robert.	Crawf'rdsville	July 15	Promoted 1st Lieutenant.
Robinson, Charles M.	Crawf'rdsville	July 27	Promoted 2d Lieutenant.
Grubb, Joseph.	Montg'mery co	July 14	Discharged March 25, '63.
Hauver, Barnett	Crawf'rdsville	July 14	Mustered out July 24, '65, as private.

NAME AND RANK.	RESIDENCE.	Date of Muster. 1862.	REMARKS.
Corporals.			
Green, Thomas C	Waynetown	July 21	Mustered out July 24, '65, as Sergeant.
Herr, Benjamin L	Crawfordsville	July 14	" " " " [Apr. 4, '63
Montgomery, William	Montgomery co.	July 19	Killed by guerrillas near Lebanon, Tenn.
Keese, Thomas	Crawfordsville	July 19	Mustered out July 24, '65.
Bridges, John	Montgomery co.	July 15	Discharged March 9, '63.
Clain, John	Crawfordsville	July 19	Mustered out July 24, '65.
McClean, William C	Montgomery co.	July 17	Died at Gallatin, Tenn., Jan. 17, '63.
Richestine, Jacob G	Wesley	July 19	Mustered out July 24, '65.
Musicians.			
Waldron, James	Crawfordsville	July 19	Mustered out July 24, '65.
Townsley, Charles	Montgomery co.	July 15	Discharged February 20, '63.
Wagoner.			
Christman, Matthias	Darlington	July 19	Mustered out July 24, '65.
Privates.			
Andrews, Joel H	Montgomery co.	Aug. 9	Discharged May 1, '63.
Anderson, Austin B	Crawfordsville	Aug. 9	Mustered out July 24, '65.
Beckner, Marion	Darlington	July 19	" " " [12, '64
Brown, John H		July 18	Died in Rebel prison, Cahawba, Ala., May
Brown, Solon H	Crawfordsville	July 18	Mustered out July 24, '65.
Bannister, William	Whitesville	Aug. 9	" " "
Bannister Enoch	Whitesville	Aug. 9	" " "
Callahan, William H	New Richmond	Aug. 9	" " "
Castor, Franklin	Darlington	July 19	" " "
Cowan, Samuel	Crawfordsville	Aug. 9	" " "
Childers, Robert	Montgomery co.	Aug. 19	Died at Murfreesboro, Tenn., Jan. 26, '63.
Castor, Isaac N	Montgomery co.	July 19	Discharged May 28th, '63.
Carns, Joseph	Montgomery co.	July 22	Discharged May 10, '63.
Dodd, George W	Montgomery co.	July 25	Died at Gallatin, Tenn., Nov. 27, '62.
Doyle, Sanford	Montgomery co.	July 19	Died at Louisville, Ky., Dec. 14, '62.
Doherty, James	Crawfordsville	July 14	Mustered out July 24, '65, as Corporal.
Drennan, John W	Montgomery co.	July 19	Discharged June 10, '63.
Davisson, Nathan	Crawfordsville	Aug. 9	Must'd out July 25, '65. [supposed dead
Doss, John E	Montgomery co.	Aug. 9	Left wounded, Okolona, Miss., Feb. 22, '64;
Eshelman, Peter	Adel	July 22	Mustered out July 24, '65.
Fulwider, William A	Prairie Edge	July 18	" " " as Sergeant.
Goble, Jasper	Montgomery co.	Aug. 9	Discharged June 26, '63.
Goble, Thomas	Montgomery co.	Aug. 9	Transferred to Marine Squadron, July 1, '63.
Gillam, Salathiel J	Burnside	July 19	Mustered out July 24, '65.
Grubbs, Samuel	Montgomery co.	Aug. 9	Died at Camp Dennison, Feb. 11, '63.
Grubbs, John	Montgomery co.	Aug. 9	Discharged January 13, '63.
Goodman, Jacob	Darlington	July 19	Mustered out July 24, '65.
Grist, Alva C	Crawfordsville	July 19	" " "
Hamilton, Sanford	Montgomery co.	July 19	Discharged Feb. 8, '63.
Hancock, Joseph	Coal Creek	July 19	Mustered out July 24, '65, as Corporal.
Hoover, Henry	Darlington	July 19	" " " as Sergeant.
Hatfield, Thomas	Montgomery co.	July 19	Discharged January 15, '63.
Hashberger, Noah	Montgomery co	July 19	Died at Bowling Green, Ky., June 18, '63
Harris, John	Montgomery co.	July 27	Discharged June 10, '63.
Hixson, Theodore	Pleasant Hill	Aug. 9	Mustered out July 24, '65.
Hollingsworth Pinson	Darlington	Aug. 9	" " "
Henshaw, John M	Montgomery co.	Aug. 9	Died at Murfreesboro, Tenn., May 22, '63.
Harris, Jonah	Montgomery co.	Aug. 9	Discharged July 4, '63
Harris, John L	Montgomery co.	Aug. 9	Died at Bowling Green, Ky., Nov. 15, '62.
Henderson, William	Waynetown	Aug. 9	Mustered out July 21, '65, as Corporal.
Ingersoll, Martin	Alamo	July 19	" " "
Johnson, Benjamin	Montgomery co.	July 19	Discharged June 26, '63.
Joyce, Robert T	Mace	July 15	Mustered out July 21, '65
Jackson, Elbridge	Montgomery co.	July 19	Died at Gallatin, Tenn., Jan. 10, '63.
Jackson, Athol	Montgomery co.	Aug. 9	Died at Gallatin, Tenn., Jan. 12, '63.
Lowman, David A	Darlington	Aug. 9	Mustered out July 24, '65.
Landers, John	Laporte	Aug. 9	" " "
Laughlin, Nathan M	Montgomery co.	July 19	Disch'g'd Mar. 15, '64. ['63, supposed dead
Martin, David	Montgomery co.	Aug. 9	Wounded and capt'd, Chicamauga, Sept. 19,
Miller, Enoch	Whitesville	Aug. 9	Mustered out July 24, '65, as 1st Sergeant.
Mills, William H	Montgomery co.	Aug. 9	Died at New Albany, May 15, '63.
Mershon, Shubal	Montgomery co.	Aug. 9	Transferred to Marine Squadron, July 1, '63
Monohan, David	Montgomery co.	July 19	Died at Gallatin, Tenn., Jan. 18, '63.
Martz, Jacob	Montgomery co.	July 19	Discharged March 15, '64.
Miller, Jasper	Montgomery co.	July 17	" May 20, '63.
McCoy, James F	Montgomery co.	Aug. 9	" June 9, '63.
McCoy, Boyd L	Mace	Aug. 9	Mustered out July 24, '65.
Moorman, Miles	Montgomery co.	July 19	Discharged Sept. 8, '62.
O'Harlon, Henry	Montgomery co.	July 19	" March 8, '63.
Patton, Aaron	Montgomery co.	Aug. 9	Killed, accident, Columbia, Tenn., Sept. 5, '64.
Powers, David F	New Richmond	July 19	Mustered out July 24, '65.
Patton, Albert	Crawfordsville	Aug. 9	" " "
Picket, Nathan	Montgomery co.	July 19	Died at Bardstown, Ky., Nov. 16, '62.
Peters, John H	Montgomery co.	July 19	Discharged Feb. 10, '63.
Rhoads, John	Darlington	July 15	Mustered out July 21, '65.

NAME AND RANK.	RESIDENCE.	Date of Muster. 1862.	REMARKS.
Ruckelle, John C F...	Montgomery co.	Aug. 9....	Deserted Oct. 28, '62.
Shurr, John A........	Waynetown. ..	July 22 .	Mustered out July 24, '65.
Sellers, James	Crawfordsville .	Aug. 9....	" " "
Sands, David A......	Darlington.....	Aug. 9.. .	" " "
Strain, Andrew	Darlington.....	July 21 ..	" " "
Smith, Abijah........	Darlington.... ..	Aug. 9 ..	" " "
Smith, Pleasant......	Marion....	July 21.....	" " "
Trickey, David S.....	Montgomery co.	July 19....	Died at Selma, Ala., Oct. 17, '63.
Vance, Isaac R.......	Crawfordsville.	July 15...	Mustered out July 24, '65, as Corporal.
Vance, John W.......	Montgomery co.	Aug. 9 ...	Discharged June 9. '63; wounds.
Wright, Henry F.....	Montgomery co.	July 15 ...	Died at Frankfort, Ky., Nov. 10, 62.
White, Francis A.....	Crawfordsville..	July 16 .	Mustered out July 24, '65.
Wilson, Joseph.	Montgomery co.	Aug. 9....	Discharged June 26, '63.
Wilson, George M....	Clark's Hill.	Aug. 9....	Mustered out July 24, '65.
Wilson, Henry H.....	Clark's Hill.....	Aug. 9 ..	" " "
Wright, Elam P......	Montgomery co.	July 17....	Died at Columbia, Tenn., April 25, '64
Walters, Harvey.....	Darlington	July 19 ...	Mustered out July 24, '65.
Recruits.			
Brady, Oliver B......	....	....	Transferred to 44th Regiment. ....
Bright, Hiram	....	Nov. 12, '64	" " "
Carnutt, John..	....	Oct. 13, '64	" " "
Coble, Nelson J......	....	Nov. 23, '64	" " "
Fisher, William......	....	Mar. 1, '64	" " "
Fulwider, James M..	... .	Oct. 17, '64	" " "
Fincher, Lemuel.....	....	Nov. 29, '64	" " "
Fox, Jonathan B.....	....	Feb. 17, '65	" " "
Gooding, John F	....	Nov. 12, '64	" " "
Gibbons, Michael. .	....	....	" " "
Henry, William......	....	....	" " "
Helton, John..........	....	Feb. 17, '65	" " "
Hoel, John	....	Nov. 12, '64	" " "
Ireland, James.......	....	Nov. 29, '64	" " "
Irwin, John....... ...	....	Dec. 15, '63	" " "
Jamison, Peter M....	....	Feb. 22, '65	" " "
Littleton, William ...	. ...	Feb. 24, '64	" " "
Lazers, William......	....	Oct. 6, '64	" " "
Lamb, Basil.........	....	Nov. 12, '64	" " "
Myers, Hugh H......	....	Nov. 12, '64	" " "
McFarland, Wm. E...	....	....	" " "
Myers, Richard......	Montgomery co.	Nov. 12, '64	Drowned at Macon, Ga., May 8, '65.
Owen, Thomas M....	....	Jan. 20, '63	Transferred to 44th Regiment.
Sink, Lewis C........	....	Mar. 10, '64	" " "
Sellers, John B... .	....	....	" " "
Sellers, Solomon.. ..	....	....	" " "
Small, Nathan........	....	Nov. 11, '64	" " "
Stewart, William F..	....	Dec. 11, '63	" " "
Thrasher, Henry.....	....	Nov. 30, '64	" " "
VanBuskirk, Th'rnt'n	....	Nov. 12, '64	" " "
Weaks, John W.......	....	Nov. 12, '64	" " "
Ward, William.......	....	July 1, '63	" " "
Winter, Henry A... .	....	May 1, '63	" " "
Wakeman, Thomas..	....	Nov. 12, '64	" " "

COMPANY "C."

NAME AND RANK.	Date of Commission.	Date of Muster.	REMARKS.
Captain.			
James E Robinson...	July 26, 1862.....	Aug. 15, '62	Resigned Mar. 28, '64; injuries on "Wheeler Raid."
John Glaze...........	Aug. 8, 1864.... .	Aug. 8 '64	Mustered out with Regiment.
First Lieutenant.			
Frank B Everett.....	July 26, 1862.....	Aug. 11, '62	Resigned Feb. 16, '63.
Edward A Cutshaw..	Feb 17, 1863.....	Mar. 1, '63	Cashiered Aug. 19, '63.
John Glaze...........	Aug. 20, 1863....	Nov. 5, '63	Promoted Captain.
George Geiger...	Mar. 29, 1864....	Aug. 28, '64	Mustered out with Regiment.
Second Lieutenant.			
George Ruger........	July 26, 1862.....	Aug. 11, '62	Resigned Dec. 1, '62; hernia.
Edward A Cutshaw..	Dec. 2, 1862.....	Feb. 24, '63	Promoted 1st Lieutenant.
John Glaze.	Feb. 17, 1863.....	Mar. 2, '63	Promoted Captain.
George Geiger..	Aug. 20, 1863....	Apr. 24, '64	Promoted 1st Lieutenant.
William H Atkinson.	June 1, 1864.....	Sept. 7, '64	Mustered out with Regiment.
	RESIDENCE.	1862.	
First Sergeant.			
Cutshaw, Edward A..	Lafayette	July 18....	Promoted 1st Lieutenant.
Sergeants.			
Harris, John L.......	Lafayette.	Aug. 5....	Discharged Aug. 1, '63.

NAME AND RANK.	RESIDENCE.	Date of Muster. 1862.	REMARKS.
Derby, Aisel J	Lafayette	July 18	Mustered out July 24, '65 as 1st Sergeant
Moore, Daniel W	Lafayette	July 16	Mustered out July 24 '65.
Atkinson, William H.	Lafayette	July 18	Promoted 2d Lieutenant.
Corporals.			
Bryant, Oscar F	Lafayette	July 14	Mustered out May 22, '65.
Glaze, John	Lafayette	July 15	Promoted 2d Lieutenant.
Reese Samuel L	Catlin, Ill	July 17	Mustered out July 24, '65.
Geiger George	Lafayette	Aug. 5	Promoted 2d Lieutenant.
Devault, Strauder	Lafayette	July 26	Mustered out July 24, '65.
Rawles, Marcellus	Lafayette	Aug. 5	" " " as private.
Squires, Sterling	Tippecanoe co	July 26	Discharged Sept. 25, '65.
Fisher, William R	Battle Ground	Aug. 6	Mustered out July 24, '65.
Musician.			
Coddington, Samuel	Lafayette	July 18	Mustered out July 24, '65.
Wagoner.			
Russell, Abram J	Lafayette	Aug. 8	Mustered out July 24, '65.
Privates.			
Andrus, Henry C	Lafayette	Aug. 8	Mustered out July 24, '65.
Armstrong, James M.	Lafayette	July 16	" " "
Bennett John R	Lafayette	July 18	" " "
Brown, George W	Lafayette	Aug. 11	" " "
Basher, Bennett	Transitville	Aug. 11	" " "
Brown, Samuel	Lafayette	Aug. 11	" " "
Brown, William	Lafayette	Aug. 11	" " "
Cory, Thomas	Tippecanoe co	Aug. 11	Discharged Jan. 21, '63.
Cox, William F	Tippecanoe co	July 15	Died at Gallatin, Tenn., Jan. 1, '63.
Cole, James	Transitville	Aug. 12	Mustered out July 24, '65.
Campbell, John	Tippecanoe co	Aug. 11	Killed at Chicamauga, Sept. 19, '63.
Davis, Lewis S	Lafayette	July 18	Mustered out July 24, '65, as Sergeant.
Davis, Martin V	Transitville	Aug. 12	" " "
Davis, Oliver M	Tippecanoe co	Aug. 12	Transferred to V R C Jan. 10, '65.
Davis, William R	Tippecanoe co	July 17	Discharged Jan. 17, '63.
Edmunds, Cyrus	Transitville	Aug. 8	Mustered out July 24, '65.
Fulks, Alexander S	Lafayette	Aug. 5	" " "
Flinn, Michael	Lafayette	Aug 11	" " " as Corporal.
Fiddler, Andrew	Tippecanoe co	Aug. 11	Discharged June 10, '65.
Green, Summer	St. Paul, Minn.	July 18	Mustered out July 24, '65.
Gillum, Anderson	Lafayette	July 29	" " "
Hayne Thomas	Lafayette	Aug. 11	" " "
Hoover, Samuel A	Tippecanoe co	July 12	Discharged Nov. 9, '62.
Henderson, Alex. H.	Tippecanoe co	Aug. 8	Transferred to V R C, Feb. 15, '64.
Hawkins, Milton	Lafayette	Aug. 11	Mustered out July 24, '65.
Hoon, James	Lafayette	Aug. 6	" " "
Henderson, John W	Lafayette	Aug. 11	" " "
Harris, William	Transitville	Aug. 12	" " "
Henderson, James A.	Tippecanoe co	Aug. 11	Discharged April 7, '63.
Jackson, Christ'ph'r C	Lafayette	Aug 6	Mustered out July 24, '65.
Jennings, Harrison	Tippecanoe co	Aug. 6.	Died at Scottsville, Ky., Dec. 2, '62.
Jones, William B	Tippecanoe co	Aug. 5	Discharged March 21, '63.
Jackson, Cavalier	Lafayette	Aug. 11	Mustered out July 24, '65.
Jackson, Samuel A	Lafayette	Aug. 11	" " "
Jones, William L	Lafayette	Aug. 11	" " "
Jones, Charles	Lafayette	July 19	" " "
Jennings, Francis M.	Tippecanoe co	Aug. 6	Discharged March 22, '63.
Kleppinger, Ancil B	Lafayette	July 17	Mustered out July 24, 65.
Kindt, Solomon	Lafayette	Aug. 12	" " " as Corporal.
Lehman, William H	Lafayette	Aug. 7	" " "
Livingston, James	West Point	Aug. 5	" " "
Martin, Munson	Lafayette	July 29	" " "
Moore, Elias C	Stockwell	July 23	" " "
Miller, William	West Point	Aug. 11	" " "
Martin Joseph T.	Transitville	Aug. 6	" " "
Mitchell, Albert	Tippecanoe co	Aug. 9	Died at Scottsville, Ky., Dec. 12, '62.
McKim, John L	Lafayette	Aug. 11	Mustered out July 24, '65.
McCoy, Francis	Stockwell	Aug. 9	" " "
McCann, Michael	Lafayette	July 17	" " "
Martin, Otho J	Brookston	Aug. 11	" " " as wagoner.
Mays, DeWitt	Lafayette	Aug. 6	" " "
Nobes, Henry	Lafayette	Aug. 8	" " "
Neyhard, William H	Dayton	July 17	" " "
North, Richard J	Lafayette	July 29	" " "
Newport, James P	Tippecanoe co	Aug. 17	Died at Cartersville, Ga., June 7, '64.
Patterson, John W	Transitville	Aug. 12	Mustered out July 24, '65.
Quaintance, Thomas.	Tippecanoe co	Aug 11	Died at Gallatin, Tenn., Dec. 28, '62.
Russell, Daniel R	Lafayette	Aug. 11	Mustered out July 24, '65.
Rodefer, Peter B.	Lafayette	Aug. 8	" " "
Relph William	Lafayette	July 26	" " " as Corporal
Robertson, David H	Lafayette	July 18	" " "
Scott, Eleazer H	Lafayette	July 12	" " "

NAME AND RANK.	RESIDENCE.	Date of Muster. 1862.	REMARKS.
Sellers, Thomas	Tippecanoe co	Aug. 8	Transferred to V. R. C.
Shigley, Jacob	Transitville	Aug. 11	Mustered out July 24, '65, as Corporal.
Schnepp, Phillip	Transitville	Aug. 12	Mustered out July 24, '65.
Seibert, Henry	Lafayette	Aug. 12	" " "
Smith Minor	Watseka, Ill.	July 15	" " "
Sprague, Andrew J.	Tippecanoe co	Aug. 5	Discharged March 6, '63.
Smith, Martin V.	Brookston	Aug. 11	Mustered out July 24, '65.
Sellers, John W	Lafayette	Aug. 8	" " "
Smith, Joshua M.	Tippecanoe co	Aug. 11	Died at Murfreesboro May 13, '63.
Swift, William	Tippecanoe co	July 30	Drummed out of service June 9, '63.
Thompson, George P.	Lafayette	Aug. 4	Mustered out July 24, '65, as Serg't.
Thieme, William	Lafayette	Aug. 6	Mustered out July 24, '65
Truett, William S	Tippecanoe co	Aug. 8	Died at Murfreesboro, March 1, '63.
Wimsey, Peter	Lafayette	July 16	Mustered out July 24, '65.
Warner, James	Lafayette	July 29	Mustered out July 24, '65, as Corporal.
Wright, John D	Lafayette	Aug 5	Mustered out July 24, '65.
Williams, James	Transitville	Aug. 6	" " "
Wood, Joshua	Tippecanoe co	Aug. 8	Deserted August 17, '62
Wright, Albert S	Lafayette	Aug. 7	Mustered out July 24, '62
Williams, Robert M	Transitville	Aug. 6	" " "
Recruits.			
Allburns, James		Dec. 23, '63	Transferred to 44th Regiment.
Anderson, Samuel		Dec. 23, '63	" " "
Bronson, William		Dec. 23, '63	" " "
Bates, Joseph		Dec. 11, '63	" " "
Chamberlain, John		Dec. 23, '63	" " "
Carroll, John		Dec. 11, '63	" " "
Dailey, James		Dec. 23, '63	" " "
Dailey, John J		Dec. 2, '63	" " "
Dawson, William A.		Dec. 11, '63	" " "
Fisher, James		Dec. 23, '63	" " "
Folk, Samuel J		Dec. 23, '63	" " "
Glaspy, James		Dec. 11, '63	" " "
Gerard, Mitchell		Dec. 23, '63	" " "
Hoon, Jason		Feb. 21, '63	" " "
Hood, William A		Dec. 2, '63	" " "
Hoon, John		Dec. 11, '63	" " "
Johnson, George L		Nov. 25, '63	" " "
Langdon, William		Dec. 1, '63	" " "
McClatchey, Francis P		Dec. 24, '63	" " "
McCann, James		Dec. 11, '63	" " "
Morris, William		Dec. 11, '63	" " "
McCarty, William		Dec. 23, '63	" " "
Smith, Thomas H		Dec. 2, '63	" " "
Sellers, William		Dec. 23, '63	" " "
Stetler, Silas W		Dec. 23, '63	" " "
Wade Michael.		Dec. 23, '63	" " "

COMPANY "D."

NAME AND RANK.	Date of Commission.	Date of Muster.	REMARKS.
Captain.			
Robert H LaFollett	Aug. 2, '62	Aug. 2, '62	Resigned Dec. 18, '62.
Chester G Thomson	Dec. 19, '62	Feb. 17, '63	Promoted Lieutenant Colonel.
Arius U Craven	Dec. 10, '64	Dec. 11, '64	Mustered out with Regiment.
First Lieutenant			
Chester G Thomson	Aug. 2, '62	Aug. 2, '62	Promoted Captain.
William R Byrns	Jan 1, '63	Feb. 24, '63	Promoted Adjutant.
Robert M Sims	Mar. 17, '63	Apr. 9, '63	Honorably disch'd July 21, '64, acc't wounds.
Arius U Craven	July 22, '64	Sept. 7, '64	Promoted Captain.
Lewis B Garrett	Dec. 10, '64	Dec. 11 '64	Mustered out with Regiment.
Second Lieutenant.			
David H Ashman	Aug 2, '62	Aug. 2, '62	Discharged Sept. 1, '62.
Arius U Craven	Jan. 1, '63	Feb. 24 '63	Promoted 1st Lieutenant.
Lewis B Garrett	July 22, '64	Sept 7, '64	Promoted 1st Lieutenant.
John P Seawright	Dec. 10, '64	Dec. 11, '64	Mustered out with Regiment.
First Sergeant.	RESIDENCE.	1862.	
Craven Arius U	Thorntown	July 17	Promoted 2nd Lieutenant.
Sergeants.			
Ashman George	Thorntown	July 17	Discharged Jan. 17 '63.
Vogan James	Thorntown	Aug. 9	Discharged Jan. 16, '63.
Sims Robert	Thorntown	July 25	Promoted 1st Lieutenant.
Garrett Lewis B	Thorntown	Aug. 9	Promoted 2d Lieutenant.
Corporals			
Johnson Samuel B	Thorntown	July 21	Mustered out July 24 '65, as Sergeant.
Thompson Brainard M	Ladoga	July 21	Mustered out July 24 '65, as Sergeant Major.
Rogers William T	Frankfort	Aug. 8	Mustered out July 24 '65, as Private.

NAME AND RANK.	RESIDENCE.	Date of Muster. 1862.	REMARKS.
Belles David	Thorntown	Aug. 9	Mustered out July 24, '65, as private.
Irwin Robert S	Thorntown	July 17	" "
Brown Joseph	LaFayette	July 23	Transferred to V. R. C. Jan. 18 '64.
Seawright Perry	Thorntown	Aug. 8	Promoted 2d Lieutenant.
Richey James	Thorntown	Aug. 9	Mustered out July 24 '65, as 1st Sergeant.
Musicians.			
Crose Britton R	Thorntown	July 18	Mustered out July 24 '65.
Boyd Wallace J	Thorntown	July 18	Discharged Dec. 1 '62.
Wagoner.			
Hill Hugh W	Thorntown	July 18	Mustered out July 24 '65.
Privates.			
Anderson Jeremiah	Thorntown	Aug. 14	Promoted Adjutant.
Bennett Robert W	Thorntown	July 21	Died in Andersonville prison, Oct. 27 '64
Beach Joseph H	Thorntown	July 21	Mustered out July 24 '65, as Sergeant.
Buntin George A	Thorntown	July 26	Died at Gallatin, Tenn., Jan. 24 '63.
Ball John W	Thorntown	July 29	Mustered out July 24 '65, as Corporal.
Blackburn William A	Thorntown	July 26	Died at Murfreesboro, Tenn., March 11 '63.
Burch William R	Thorntown	July 30	Mustered out July 24 '65.
Billings Nathan	Thorntown	Aug. 4	Discharged March 4 '63.
Ball Perry A	Thorntown	Aug. 1	Discharged Oct. 21 '62.
Burnham Perry C	Thorntown	Aug. 9	Mustered out July 24 '65.
Cory Leander C	Thorntown	July 17	Died at Nashville, Tenn., Dec. 2 '63.
Cory Augustus M	Thorntown	Aug. 6	Mustered out July 24 '65, as Sergeant.
Cosand Samuel W	Thorntown	July 18	Mustered out July 24 '65.
Custer James C	Thorntown	July 29	Died at Scottsville, Ky., Dec. 8 '62.
Cain Joseph	Thorntown	July 30	Killed at Chicamauga, Sept. 19 '63.
Carter John M	Thorntown	Aug. 1	Died at Murfreesboro, Tenn., April 21 '63
Council Milton	Thorntown	Aug. 1	Mustered out July 24 '65, as Corporal.
Cook Edward	Mechanicsburg	July 26	Discharged March 7 '63.
Crose George W	Thorntown	July 29	Discharged June 17 '63.
Coltrain Linden P	Thorntown	Aug. 9	Died at Murfreesboro, Tenn., May 10 '63.
Davis John B	Thorntown	July 19	Mustered out July 24 '65.
Dicks William H	Thorntown	July 17	" " "
Dukes William C	Thorntown	July 29	Died at Gallatin, Tenn., Jan. 4 '63.
Dunwoody Eugenius B	Thorntown	Aug. 14	Mustered out July 24 '65.
Edwards Lemuel B	Thorhtown	July 18	" " "
Eubanks George E	Thorntown	Aug. 19	" " "
Fall John M	Thorntown	Aug. 4	Discharged Feb. 28 '63.
Fall Samuel H	Thorntown	July 25	Died at Nashville, Feb. 9 '64.
Fenton John	Thorntown	Aug. 9	Died at Andersonville prison, Sept. 12 '64.
Flinn George W	Thorntown	Aug. 9	Mustered out July 24 '65, as Corporal.
Frazier Morgan C	Thorntown	Aug. 9	Dischrrged Feb. 9 '63.
Greene Robert S	Thorntown	July 23	Died at Andersonville prison, Sep. 18 '64: w'th
Hill William W	Thorntown	July 17	Mustered out July 24 '65.
Hargraves John W	Thorntown	July 17	" " "
Hall Robert W	Thorntown	July 22	" " "
Hall William H	Thorntown	July 28	Died at Murfreesboro, Tenn., May 10 '63
Hall James M	Thorntown	July 29	Mustered out July 24 '65.
Hall John G	Thorntown	July 26	Mustered out July 24 '65, as Corporal.
Higgason James H	Thorntown	July 30	Mustered out July 24 '65.
Hodgens Isaac N	Thorntown	July 22	Discharged March 1 '63.
Hawkins Simeon B	Linden	Aug. 4	Mustered out July 24 '65.
Hashberger Abraham	Thorntown	July 23	" " "
Hutchens John H	Thorntown	Aug. 9	Died at Gallatin, Tenn., Jan. 14 '63.
Handlen William E	Thorntown	Aug. 9	Discharged March 7 '63.
Handlen Joseph M	Thorntown	Aug. 9	Discharged Dec. 29 '63.
Isrigg Joseph W	Thorntown	Aug. 4	Mustered out July 24 '65.
Kring James M	Thorntown	July 18	Died at Murfreesboro, March 18 '63.
Laverty David W	Thorntown	July 19	Killed near Rome, Ga., Oct. 11 '64.
Long Daniel	Thorntown	July 25	Discharged Feb. 24 '64: wounds.
Mount James A	Thorntown	July 22	Mustered out July 24, '65, as Sergeant.
McKinsey Noah	Thorntown	July 22	Mustered out July 24 '65.
McKinsey Morgan	Thorntown	July 26	Mustered out May 24 '65.
McKinsey Jesse	Thorntown	July 21	Mustered out July 24 '65.
McGraw John	Thorntown	July 22	" " "
Nevels Stephen H	Thorntown	July 21	Discharged Feb. 20, '63.
Parsons John P	Thorntown	Aug. 17	Transferred to V R C, July 1, '63.
Pyke Wesley B	Thorntown	July 17	Killed at Hoover's Gap, Tenn., June 24, '63
Pickerel Benjamin F	Thorntown	July 28	Mustered out July 24, '65.
Park James F	Thorntown	Aug. 4	Discharged May 28, '63.
Phillips Thomas B	Thorntown	July 21	Mustered-out July 24, '65, as Corporal.
Rogers Hugh Y	Thorntown	Aug. 8	Died at Gallatin, Tenn., Feb. 17, '63.
Ryley James L	Thorntown	July 29	Mustered out July 24, '65.
Runyon Albert P	Thorntown	July 21	Discharged Aug. 28, '63.
Sheedy John	Thorntown	Aug. 11	Mustered out July 24, '65.
Sasbe Alexander B	Thorntown	Aug. 11	" " "
Strain Wilson	Thorntown	July 25	Discharged Jan. 12, '63.
Sanders Barnabas	Thorntown	Aug. 9	Mustered out July 24, '65.
Sparks Henry L	Thorntown	July 20	" " "
Shofstall Robert C	Thorntown	Aug. 14	" " "

NAME AND RANK	RESIDENCE.	Date of Muster. 1862.	REMARKS.
Starbuck James M....	Thorntown ...	Aug. 1.....	Mustered out July 24, '65.
Shull David A........	Thorntown ..	Aug. 9	Transferred to V R C, July 1, '63.
Taggart Charles L....	Thorntown ...	July 21...	Mustered out July 24, '65.
Tucker Albert R	Thorntown ...	Aug. 9	" " "
Tull John H	Madison.	Aug. 14...	" " "
Wright Charles.......	Thorntown ...	July 17 .	Mustered out June 7, '65.
Welch Alexander L ..	Dhorntown ..	July 17	Mustered out July 24, '65.
Welch Charles F......	Thorntown . .	July 19....	" " "
Warbritton WilliamM	Thorntown ...	July 21....	Died at Gallatin, Tenn., Jan. 7, '63.
Warbritton John R...	Thorntown ...	July 21 ...	Mustered out July 24, '65.
Woods Alexander .	Time, Ill	July 21. ..	" " "
Watson Lee.	Franklin	Aug. 14 ...	" " "
Watkins Elihu H. ...	Jefferson	Aug. 14 ...	" " " as Corporal.
Recruits.			
Beckheart Benedict..	....	Dec. 23, '63	Transferred to 44th Regiment.
Ball William N.... ...	....	Jan. 12, '64	" " "
Burris Robert T......	....	Dec. 16, '63	" " "
Burris Wesley........	....	Dec. 16, '63	" " "
Burch John B	....	Oct. 26, '64	" " "
Ball James A.	LaFayette.....	Dec. 13, '63	Discharged.
Cook Robert	....	Nov. 16, '63	Transferred to 44th Regiment.
Edwards John G......	....	Dec. 16, '63	" " "
Evans John H	....	Jan. 27, '64	" " "
Grimes Tobias M	....	Jan. 27, '64	" " "
Gibson John C.......	....	Feb. 9, '64	" " "
Hollingsworth Abm R	....	Jan. 12, '64	" " "
Harris William F.....	....	Jan. 12, '64	" " "
Johnson Joel W	....	Jan. 4, '64	" " "
Lewis John	Thorntown ...	Dec. 13, '63	Discharged.
Mathies William	....	Mar. 17, '64	Transferred to 44th Regiment.
McCorkle Thomas H..	....	Feb. 29, '64	" " "
McDaniel William A .	....	Jan. 4, '64	" " "
McDaniel Joseph A..	....	Jan. 4, '64	" " "
Milliken Milton W....	Thorntown ...	Mar. 5, '64	Killed at Leesburg, Ala., Oct. 21, '64.
Moore George W	....	Mar. 28, '64	Died at Gallatin, Tenn., Feb. 21, '65.
Pickard John.........	....	Dec. 23, '63	Transferred to 44th Regiment.
Riley George F	....	Dec. 16, '63	" " "
Simms Alexander W.	....	Sep. 10, '63	" " "
Thompson Martin B .	Thorntown ...	Dec. 5, '63	Musterrd out —— '65, as Q M Sergeant.
Tyson Asher	Thorntown ...	Dec. 22, '63	Transferred to V R C.

COMPANY "E."

NAME AND RANK.	Date of Commission.	Date of Muster.	REMARKS.
Captain			
Harvey B Wilson.....	Aug. 14, 1862..	Aug. 14, '62	Resigned December 14, '62.
Lawson S Kilborn ...	Dec. 15, 1862..	Feb. 17, '63	Promoted Major.
William H Mahan ...	Dec. 3, 1864..	Dec. 10, '64	Mustered out with Regiment.
First Lieutenant.			
Lawson S Kilborn...	Aug. 14, 1862..	Aug. 14, '62	Promoted Captain.
John N Insley	Dec. 15, 1862..	Dec. 17, '62	Resigned February 9, '63.
Lewis C Priest........	Feb. 10, 1863..	April 9, '63	Died June 24, '64.
John P Wise	Dec. 3, 1864..	Dec. 10, '64	Mustered out with Regiment.
Second Lieutenant.			
John N Insley.	Aug. 14, 1862..	Aug. 14, '62	Promoted 1st Lieutenant.
Lewis C Priest	Dec. 15, 1862..	Dec. 17, '62	Promoted 1st Lieutenant.
William H Mahan.....	Feb. 10, 1863..	April 9, '63	Promoted Captain.
John W Plunkett.....	Jan. 1, 1865..	June 21, '65	Mustered out with Regiment.
	RESIDENCE.	1862.	
First Sergeant.			
Priest Lewis C..	....	July 19....	Promoted 2d Lieutenant.
Sergeants.			
Park Elijah..........	Linden	July 19....	Deserted Nov. 21, '62.
Ashby William	Ladoga	July 19....	Died at Gallatin, Tenn., Dec. 26, '62.
Medearis James W ..	Waynetown ..	July 25....	Mustered out July 24, '65, as private.
Plunkett John W.....	Waynetown ..	July 25...	Promoted 2d Lieutenant.
Corporals.			
Cooningham Edw'd H	Ladoga	July 25 ...	Mustered out June —— ,65.
Montgomery Simpson	Linden	July 25...	Transferred to V R C July 1, '64.
Wilhite Lewis E......	Independence.	July 25....	Mustered out July 21, '65, as sergeant.
Maxwell Samuel C...	Ladoga	July 25....	Discharged October 27, '62.
Shelby David	LaFayette.....	July 25....	Mustered out July 24, '65, as sergeant.

NAME AND RANK.	RESIDENCE.	Date of Muster. 1862.	REMARKS.
Mahan William H	Thorntown	July 25	Promoted 2d Lieutenant.
Harris James	Crawfordsvil'e	July 25	Mustered out July 24 '65.
Musicians.			
Greenburg, Johann	Linden	July 25	Mustered out July 24, '65, as Principal Mus'
Webster John	Ladoga	July 25	Died at New Albany.
Wagoner.			
Ellis Alfred P	Whitesville	July 25	Mustered out July 24 '65.
Privates.			
Avery Whiting A	Ladoga	July 25	Mustered out July 24, '65.
Albertson Silas W	Linden	July 25	Transferred to V R C.
Barton Madison	Linden	July 25	Discharged Sept. 30, '63.
Bible John C	Sugar Grove	July 25	Mustered out July 24 '65.
Campbell John F.	Ladoga	July 25	Discharged March 8, '63.
Chambers Andrew J.	Crawford 'vil'e	July 25	Mustered out July 24, '65.
Cobb Uriah	Lafayette	July 25	" " "
Coombes John N.	Linden	July 25	Discharged Nov. 28, '63.
Coombes Denman J.	Pleasant Hill	July 25	Mustered out July 24 '65.
Connell heodore B.	Lafayette	July 25	Mustered out July 24 '65, as Corporal.
Curnutt Henry	Linden	July 25	Discharged —— '63, disability.
Doyle Harrison	Parkersburg.	July 25	Mustered out July 24 '65.
Doyle Allen	Parkersburg	July 25	" " "
Dungan John W	Linden	July 25	Discharged —— '63; disability.
Deans George	Linden	July 25	Mustered out July 24 '65, as Corporal.
Edwards John W	Ladoga	July 25	Discharged February 24, '63.
Edwards Michael H	Whitesville	July 25	Mustered out July 24 '65, as Corporal.
Fletcher Jonathan	Ladoga	July 25	Discharged Nov. 11, '62.
Gannon George W	Linden	July 25	Died at Murfreesboro, April 18, '63.
Gill Jonathan	Ladoga	July 25	Transferred to V. R. C. July 1 '63
Harney Richard H	Lebanon	July 25	Mustered out July 24, '65.
Haines Charles G	Blue Grass Ills	July 25	" " "
Haywood Thomas	Sugar Grove.	July 25	" " "
Hobbs Horatio	Linden	July 25	Died at New Albany, Dec. 7, '63.
Hamilton Nathaniel	Pleasant Hill	July 25	Mustered out July 24, '65.
Insley William A.	Sugar Grove	July 25	" "
Insley David W	Linden	July 25	Died at Murfreesboro, Tenn, April 27, '63
Jones John E B	Ladoga	July 25	Mustered out July 24, '65.
Johnson Presley J	Ladoga	July 25	Discharged.
Keeny John	Linden	July 25	Mustered out July 24 '65.
Keeny James	Linden	July 25	" " "
Keys William G	Linden	July 25	Died in Andersonville prison, July 26, '64
Kirkpatrick Milton	Sugar Grove	July 25	Mustered out July 24, '65.
Kendall James K.	Sugar Grove	July 25	" " "
Kesterson George S.	Linden	July 25	Discharged Sept. 8, '63.
Leffland Alfred.	Romney	July 25	Mustered out July 24 '65.
Miller Henry	New Richmo'd	July 25	" " "
Montgomery Geo W.	Linden	July 25	" " "
McClemrock Lemu'l B	Crawfordsvil'e	July 25	Mustered out July 24, '65, as Sergeant
Mason Omer W.	Crawfordsvil'e	July 25	Mustered out July 24, '65.
Menagh Robert J.	Sugar Grove	July 25	" " "
Meadows William J	Sugar Grove	July 25	" " "
Mason Francis M.	Linden	July 25	" " "
Nutt James H	Ladoga	July 25	Transferred to Marine Brigade, ——, '63
Nicholson William W	Ladoga	July 25	Discharged Feb. 2, '63.
Newkirk Abner M.	Linden	July 25	Mustered out July 24 '65.
Neely John A	Ladoga	July 25	Died at Murfreesboro, Tenn, May 28, '63
O'Neil John	Ladoga	July 25	Discharged February 24, '63.
Plunkitt Abram	Vevay	July 25	Mustered out July 24 '65.
Peters Henry S	Ladoga	July 25	Died at New Albany, Oct. 27, '62.
Piggott Joseph	Linden	July 25	Mustered out July 24, '65.
Plunkitt George W.	Waynetown	July 25	" " "
Plunkitt Levi H	Linden	July 25	Transferred to V R C, July 1, '63.
Pointer William	Ladoga	July 25	Discharged January 17, '63.
Quick Stebbins	Linden	July 25	Discharged Feb. 2, '63.
Quick Harrison	Linden	July 25	Discharged Nov. 11, '62.
Randel Abram B.	Ladoga	July 25	Mustered out July 24 '65.
Romley Ambrose	Crawfordsvil'e	July 25	Mustered out July 24 '65, as Sergeant.
Reed Henry	Linden	July 25	Discharged November 3, '62.
Ross James	New Richmo'd	July 25	Mustered out July 24, '65.
Roush William	Homer Ill.	July 25	" " "
Rice Henry E.	Sugar Grove	July 25	" " "
Savage Patrick	Urbana Ill	July 25	Mustered out July 24, '65, as Corporal.
Swindler Calvin E.	Crawfordsvil'e	July 22	Mustered out July 24 '65.
Shepherd Israel H	Ladoga	July 25	" " "
Shepherd John T	Sugar Grove	July 25	Mustered out July 24 '65, as Corporal.
Strater Daniel	Attica	July 25	Mustered out July 24 '65.
Stockton Theodore	Linden	July 25	" " "
Slavins John W	Linden	July 25	Died at New Albany, Nov. 20, '62.
Stewart John J.	Linden	Aug. 16	Died at Louisville, July 21, '63.
Totten Jasper	Linden	July 25	Mustered out July 24 '65.
Thorpe George B.	Linden	July 25	Died at Gallatin, Tenn., Jan. 11, '63.

NAME AND RANK.	RESIDENCE.	Date of Muster. 1862.	REMARKS.
Tennery Tristom B	Linden	July 25	Discharged July 10, '64; wounds.
Winter Daniel W	Ladoga	July 25	Mustered out July 24, '65.
Wright James W	Ladoga	July 25	Died at Murfreesboro, Tenn., June 5, '63.
Warbritten Andy	Ladoga	July 25	Discharged March 23, '63.
Wood John O	Linden	July 25	Killed at Chickamauga, Sept. 19, '63
Wise John P	Lewisville	July 25	Promoted 1st Lieutenant.
Walton James W	Linden	July 25	Discharged February 17, '63.
Williams James H	Sugar Grove	July 25	Mustered out July 24, '65.
Zoller George F	Sugar Grove	July 25	" " "
Recruits.			
Allen James		Oct. 16, 64	Transferred to 44th Regiment.
Adwell James H		Mar 14, 65	" " "
Andrews Horace		Mar. 14, 65	" " "
Burnett Flavius J		Oct. 6, 64	" " "
Bacheldor Ira D		Mar. 4, 65	" " "
Berry James M		Mar. 8, '65	" " "
Bell Ransom H		Oct. 5, '62	" " "
Clark Jackson		Mar. 8, '65	" " "
Carter William H		Mar. 27, '65	" " "
Cavanaugh John		Mar. 24, '65	" " "
Fry Samuel		Mar. 8, '65	" " "
Hamilton Andrew		Oct. 5, '64	" " "
Haywood Curtis B		Oct. 6, '64	" " "
Haynes George U		Apr. 20, '64	" " "
Hickon Israel		Feb. 1, '65	" " "
Haywood Curtis D		Oct. 6, '64	" " "
Kesterson William H			" " "
Kesterson George S		Oct. 6, '64	" " "
Kinsell William B		Oct. 6, '64	" " "
Kiger Mordecai M		Mar. 22, '65	" " "
Liberger Isaac			" " "
Lyon William		Mar. 23, '65	" " "
Miller James L		Mar. 4, '65	" " "
Parker Henry A		Mar. 14, '65	" " "
Rifer Thomas		Oct. 19, '64	" " "
Shaw William L		March 8, '65	" " "
Self Hiram		March 8, '65	" " "
Tiffeny William W		Oct. 6, '64	" " "
Thayer Caleb		Oct 6, '64	" " "
Westfall John W		Oct. 16, '64	" " "

COMPANY "F."

NAME AND RANK.	Date of Commission.	Date of Muster.	REMARKS.
Captain.			
Moses Birch	Aug. 9, '62	Aug. 9, '62	Resigned Mar. 23, '63.
James L Dalton	Mar. 24, '63	Apr. 9, '63	Mustered out with Regiment.
First Lieutenant			
James L Dalton	Aug. 9, '62	Aug. 9, '62	Promoted Captain.
Johnson Parker	Mar. 24, '63	Apr. 9, '63	Mustered out and honorably disch'd June 8, '65; cause service no longer req'd & disablity.
Second Lieutenant.			
Orrin E Harper	Aug. 9, '62	Aug. 9, '62	Dishonorably dismissed March 1, '63.
Johnson Parker	Mar. 2, '63	Mar. 24, '63	Promoted 1st Lieutenant.
Moses Nowls	Mar. 24, '63	Apr. 9, '63	Mustered out with Regiment.
	RESIDENCE.	1862.	
First Sergeant.			
Parker Johnson	Williamsport	Aug. 26	Promoted 2d Lieutenant.
Sergeants.			
Nowls Moses	Williamsport	Aug. 28	Promoted 2d Lieutenant.
Andrew Charles	Warren co	Aug. 28	Discharged Jan. 25, '63
Parker Thomas C	Williamsport	Aug. 26	Mustered out July 24, '65.
Cadwallader Elisha	Warren co	Aug. 25	Died at Bowling Green, Ky., Nov. 16, '62.
Corporals.			
Schoonover Martin	Warren co	Aug. 28	Discharged Jan. 12, '63.
Jordan Levi	Marshfield	Aug. 4	Mustered out July 24, '65, as private.
Andrew William	Warren co	July 28	Discharged February 13, '63
Burch Charles J	Warren co	July 25	Died at Gallatin, Tenn., Jan. 20, '63.
Van Reed Milton H	Williamsport	July 28	Mustered out July 24 '65, as sergeant.
Schoonover William H	Williamsport	July 29	Mustered out July 24 '65, as 1st Sergeant.
Briggs Seth S	Williamsport	Aug. 8	Mustered out July 24 '65, as Private.
Spies John	Williamsport	July 28	" " " "

NAME AND RANK.	RESIDENCE.	Date of Muster. 1862.	REMARKS.
Musicians.			
Jones James E	Williamsport	July 28	Mustered out July 24, '65.
Etnire Samuel M	Williamsport	Aug. 8	Mustered out July 24, '65, as corporal.
Wagoner.			
Mabee Pinkney	Warren co	July 28	Discharged May —— '63.
Privates.			
Abott John	West Lebanon	Aug. 3	Mustered out July 24, '65.
Adams Jesse M	Warren co	July 28	Discharged Jan 17, '63.
Adams William H	Bl'Gr'sGrve Ill	Aug. 8	Mustered out July 24, '65.
Alburn Henry	Marshfield	July 28	" " "
Aldridge David	Warren co	Aug. 8	Died at Scottsville, Ky., Dec. 10, '62.
Brenner Ephraim L	West Lebanon	Aug. 8	Mustered out July 24, '65.
Briar Luther	Warren co	July 28	Died at Murfreesboro, April 20, '63.
Briggs Elisha	Williamsport	July 30	Mustered out July 24, '65.
Buckley William P	Ash Grove, Ill	July 26	" " "
Caldwell James	Warren co	July 28	Discharged May 26, '63.
Cole George	Rainsville	July 28	Mustered out July 24, '65.
Correll Valentine	Attica	July 28	Mustered out July 24, '65, as Corporal
Cozod Thomas	Warren co	July 28	Killed at Rock Spring, Ga., Sept. 12, '63.
Crawford James H	Williamsport	Aug. 8	Mustered out July 24, '65.
Crowell Daniel	Warren co	July 28	Died at Louisville, Ky., April 18, '65.
Campton King B	Marshfield	Aug. 3	Mustered out July 24, '65.
Davis George W	Williamsport	Aug. 8	" " "
Dimitt Sylvester	Jordan, Ill	July 28	" " "
Fleming David W	West Lebanon	Aug. 3	" " "
Frame Samuel H	West Lebanon	Aug. 4	Mustered out July 24, '65, as Corporal.
Gillett Alfred	Williamsport	Aug. 3	Mustered out July 24, '65
Goodwine Wesley	Warren co	Aug. 3	Discharged August 31, '63.
Gray John W	West Lebanon	Aug. 8	Mustered out July 24, '65.
Hardy Joseph	Williamsport	July 28	" " "
Horrier William D	Warren co	July 28	Discharger Jan. 23, '63.
Horrier Samuel	Williamsport	July 28	Mustered out July 24, '65.
Hewitt John M	Warren co	Aug. 4	Died at Castillian Springs, Tenn. Dec 9, '62
Hobaugh Nelson	West Lebanon	Aug. 8	Mustered out July 24, '65.
Holycross Elisha J	Warren co	July 28	Killed at Rock Spring, Ga. Sept 12, '63.
Hornaday John H	Williamsport	Aug. 11	Mustered out July 24, '65, as corporal.
Horner Thomas F	Lafayette	July 29	Mustered out July 24, '65
Hunter James H	Williamsport	July 28	" " "
Jordan Miles	Marshfield	Aug. 4	" " "
Keister David L	Williamsport	July 28	" " "
Kennedy Thomas	Williamsport	Aug. 9	" " "
Labau Benjamin F	Warren co	July 28	Died at Bowling Green, Ky, Dec 30, '62
Leak William	Warren co	Aug. 8	Discharged February 26, '64.
Liggett Samuel M	Warren co	Aug. 8	Died at Gallatin, Tenn. Dec 8, '62.
Long Henry C	Warren co	Aug. 3	Transferred to Marine Brigade March 21, '63.
Lutz Henry C	Williamsport	Aug. 11	Mustered out July 24, '65, as Corporal.
Mathis George W	Warren co	July 28	Killed at Rock Spring, Ga, Sept 12, '63.
Mayhall George W	Williamsport	July 28	Mustered out July 24, '65.
McKnight James A	Williamsport	Aug. 3	" " "
Millhollin Henry E	Warren co	July 26	Died at Murfreesboro, March 5, '63.
Millhollin Jasper N	Warren co	July 26	" " " 4, '63.
Moody George W	Warren co	July 26	Deserted December 29, '62.
Moore James C	Warren co	July 28	Died at Scottsville, Ky, Dec 1, '62.
Moore Morris	Williamsport	Aug. 9	Mustered out July 24, '65.
Morgan George T	Warren co	Aug. 8	Discharged Feb 22, '63.
Munson John	Attica	July 28	Mustered out July 24, '65.
Nixon John A	Warren co	July 28	Killed at Rock Spring, Ga, Sept 12, '63.
Parent Hiram	Attica	July 28	Mustered out July 24, '65.
Patterson James B	Williamsport	July 29	" " "
Pine George M	Warren co	July 26	Transferred to V. R. C, August 25, '63.
Pruden Ebenezer	Carbondale, Ill	Aug. 11	Mustered out July 24, '65.
Pugh Benjamin F	Warren co	July 28	Died at Gallatin, Tenn Feb 11, '63.
Pugh William S	Williamsport	Aug. 8	Mustered out July 24, '65.
Pugh William	Warren co	Aug. 8	Died at Louisville, Nov 19, '62.
Pugh Josephus M	Warren co	Aug. 8	Died at Bardstown, Ky, Nov 13, '62.
Pugh George W	Warren co	Aug. 8	Died at Louisville, Nov 23, '62.
Reid Richard	Williamsport	July 28	Mustered out July 24, '65, as Corporal.
Reed Nathan J	Williamsport	Aug. 3	Mustered out July 24, '65.
Reed Daniel W	Williamsport	Aug. 8	" " "
Rice John T	Warren co	July 28	Discharged Nov 20, '62.
Riggs James	Independence	July 28	Mustered out July 24, '65.
Romine Daniel C	Jordan, Ill	July 28	" " "
Schoonover Harvey	Warren co	July 28	Died at Chattanooga, Sept. 26, '63, wounds
Schoonover James S	Williamsport	Aug. 8	Mustered out July 24, '65, as Sergeant.
Shuter Peter S	Warren co	Aug. 8	Discharged April 4, '63.
Smith George W	Rainsville	Aug. 2	Mustered out July 24, '65.
Stearns Zura T	Williamsport	Aug. 9	Mustered out July 24, '65, as Sergeant.
Stratton Daniel M	Warren co	July 28	Discharged Feb 24, '63.
Stump George B	Warren co	July 28	Transferred to V R C, March 21, '64.
Swarner John	West Lebanon	July 26	Mustered out July 24, '65.
Swisher Joseph	Williamsport	July 26	" " " as Corporal.

NAME AND RANK.	RESIDENCE.	Date of Muster. 1862.	REMARKS.
Totheroh Martin	Williamsport	Aug. 3	Mustered out July 24, '65.
Tyler Hiram B	Williamsport	Aug. 1	" " "
Volkel Henry	West Lebanon	July 28	" " "
Wakley Daniel	Warren co.	July 28	Discharged August 8, '63
Warbritton John	Williamsport	July 29	Mustered out July 24, '65.
Warbritton William	Warren co.	Aug. 13	Died at Scottsville, Ky, Dec. 9, '62.
Wood Ephraim H	West Lebanon	Aug. 11	Mustered out July 24, '65, as Corporal.
Recruits.			
Adams John Q		Jan 6 64	Transferred to 44th Regiment
Bengarner Stephen		Jan 6, 64	Mustered out May 35, '65.
Byers Samuel B		Feb 29, 64	Transferred to 44th Regiment.
Bottorff David		Mar 26, 64.	Discharged Feb 24, '65.
Briggs William P		Nov 30, 64.	Transferred to 44th Regiment.
Bowlus Samuel H		Jan 6, 64	Died at Columbia, Tenn, July 8, '64.
Cannutt Levi		Feb 11, 64	Transferred to 44th Regiment.
Darling Ezekiel P		Oct 30, 64	" " "
Etnire Daniel		Jan 6, 64	" " "
Etnire Jacob L		Jan 6, 64	" " "
Flemmings Thomas C		Jan 6, 64	" " "
Gillette Hardin		Jan 6, 64	" " "
Javell Levi		Feb 27, 64	" " "
Kendall Matthew M		Oct 29, 64	" " "
Lattimore Absolom		Jan 6, 64	" " "
Mershon William J		Oct 20, 64	" " "
Mallott John		Jan 6, 64	" " "
Mabee Pinckney		Oct 25, 64	" " "
Mullin LaFayette		Oct 20, 64	" " "
Morton Richard		Mar 5, 64	" " "
McCowan John		Oct 21, 64	" " "
Nourse Henry S		Mar 1, 64	Discharged May 9, '65.
Porter Alonzo N		Dec 5, 64	Transferred to 44th Regiment.
Pomeroy Ashley C		Jan 6, 64	" " "
Quick Charles		Jan 6, 64	" " "
Ransom William L		Nov 30, 64.	" " "
Schlosser Frederick A		Jan 6, 64	Discharged May 12, '65.
Sewell David		Feb 27, 64	Transferred to 44th Regiment.
Sewell Hiram		Feb 27, 64	" " "
Search Thomas		Feb 23, 64.	" " "
Swisher Jesse		Jan 6, 64	" " "
Safford Andrew		July 1, 63	" " "
Tyler Lopher		Apr 21, 64	" " "
Tegarden John		Dec 15, 64	" " "
Wineland John F		Jan 26 64	" " "
Welsh Whitfield		Mar 20, 64	" " "
Windsor Alvin R		Jan 6, 64	Discharged Jan. 4, '65.

COMPANY "G."

NAME AND RANK.	Date of Commission.	Date of Muster.	REMARKS.
Captain.			
Adam Pinkerton	Aug. 6, 1862	Aug. 8, '62	Promoted Major.
John B Crick	Sept. 1, 1864		Resigned as 1st Lieutenant, Dec. 5, '64.
Jacob W Gladden	Dec. 13, 1864	Dec. 15, '64	Mustered out with Regiment.
First Lieutenant.			
John B Crick	Aug. 6, 1862	Aug. 8, '62	Promoted Captain: resigned Dec. 5, '64.
Jacob W Gladden	Sept. 1, 1864		Promoted Captain.
Ephraim B Martin	Dec. 13, 1864	Dec. 15, '64	Mustered out with Regiment.
Second Lieutenant.			
William R Jewell	Aug. 6, 1862	Aug. 8, '62	Resigned May 19, '63.
Jacob W Gladden	Mar. 20, 1863	April 9, '63	Promoted 1st Lieutenant.
Ephraim B Martin	Sept. 1, 1864		Promoted 1st Lieutenant.
Augustus W Lane	Jan. 1, 1865	May 16, '65	Mustered out with Regiment.
	RESIDENCE.	1862.	
First Sergeant.			
Stehrns Elias P	Tippecanoe co	July 19	Promoted Assistant Surgeon.
Sergeants.			
Byrns William K	Tippecanoe co	July 24	Promoted Adjutant.
Gladden Jacob W	Tippecanoe co	July 15	Promoted 2d Lieutenant.
Martin Ephraim B	Tippecanoe co	July 26	Promoted 1st Lieutenant.
Barksdoll George W	Tippecanoe co		Deserted Oct. —— '63.
Corporals.			
Gault Frank M	Tippecanoe co	July 21	Died at Gallatin, Tenn., Dec. 23, '62.
Blickenstaff Jacob	Tippecanoe co	Aug. 8	Died at Nashville, Tenn., May 26, '63.
Reed James O	Tippecanoe co	July 26	Died at Murfreesboro, Tenn., July 3, 63; w'ds.

NAME AND RANK.	RESIDENCE.	Date of Muster. 1862.	REMARKS.
Thompson William J	Tippecanoe co	July 21	Discharged February 15, '64.
Lane Augustus W	Reynold's St'n.	July 21	Mustered out July 24, '65, as 1st Sergeant.
Milligan Theophilus W	Clark's Hill	July 26	" " " as Sergeant.
Loveless Sylvester C.	Tippecanoe co	July 23	Discharged Dec. 26, '62.
Wilson Sylvanus C	Tippecanoe co	Aug. 8	Missing in action, Chicamauga, Sept. 20, '63.
Musicians.			
Lenker William P.	Culver's St'n.	Aug. 8	Mustered out July 24, '65.
Robison Jonathan W.	Tippecanoe co	Aug. 9	Transferred to V R C, Feb. 5, '64.
Wagoner			
Burns George B	Tippecanoe co	July 23	Mustered out July 24, '65.
Privates.			
Anderson Rufus H	Tippecanoe co	Aug. 8	Discharged Feb 8, '63.
Armstrong Samuel	Tippecanoe co	Aug. 1	Transferred to V R C, July 1, '63.
Ashe James	Culver's St'n	Aug 6	Mustered out July 24, '65, as Sergeant.
Ashley George	Culver's St'n	Aug. 7.	Mustered out July 24, '65.
Brewer Thomas	Stockwell	Aug. 2	" " "
Bolen William S.	Stockwell	July 23	Mustered out July 25, '65, as Sergeant.
Bailey William T.	Culver's St'n	Aug. 8	Mustered out July 24, '65.
Bryan Andrew	Clark's Hill	Aug. 6	" " "
Bush John S.	Tippecanoe co	Aug. 7	Discharged December 18, '62.
Barcus Enoch G	Tippecanoe co	July 23	Transferred to V R C, Apr. 30, '64.
Boyles George W	Stockwell	July 26	Mustered out July 24, '65.
Baer David	Dayton	July 21	" " "
Bull Robert T.	Dayton	July 21	" " "
Bails William	Clark's Hill	Aug 5	" " "
Conson John	Dayton	July 26	" " "
Connell Wesley	Tippecanoe co	Aug. 8	Discharged Nov. 21, '62.
Corkins Egbert C	Tippecanoe co	Aug. 11	Died at Murfreesboro, Tenn., Jan. 19, '63.
Clark Francis M	Clark's Hill	Aug. 8	Mustered out July 24, 65.
Cann Robert	Culver' St'n	Aug. 11	" " " as Corporal.
Chenoweth Isaac N	Tippecanoe co	July 26	Died at Bowling Green, Ky., Nov. 18, '62.
Craig William W	Melville, Iowa	Aug. 7.	Mustered out July 24, '65, as Corporal.
Derrick Albert	Tippecanoe co	July 19	Discharged Jan. 27, '63.
Davis Daniel C	Lafayette	Aug. 7	Mustered out July 24, '65.
Driskell James	Clark's Hill	Aug. 2	" " "
Duddleson William	Colfax	July 26	" " "
Fowler William H	Clark's Hill	July 23	" " "
Gouth George W	Tippecanoe co	July 15	Deserted Feb. 25, '63, from hospital
Goldsberry George W	Tippecanoe co	July 19	Transferred to V R C July 24, '63.
Howland Dennis P	Dayton	Aug. 9	Mustered out July 24, '65, as Corporal.
Helmboldt Edward	Lafayette	Aug. 6.	Mustered out July 24, '65.
Handley David	Hebron	Aug. 8	" " "
Harper Simeon	Stockwell	Aug. 6	" " "
Hunter John	Stockwell	Aug. 8	" " "
Hunter Daniel	Stockwell	Aug. 8	" " "
Hoffman Martin P	Clark's Hill	Aug. 8	" " "
Hann Granville	Clark's Hill	Aug. 6	" " "
Hann John	Clark's Hill	Aug. 6	" " "
Hudson Ira	Tippecanoe co	Aug. 5	Deserted Sept. —— '62.
John Jeremiah	Colfax	July 27	Mustered out July 24, '65.
Knight Henry R.	Tippecanoe co	Aug. 11	Died at Gallatin Tenn., Dec. 21, '62.
Reese Willis T.	Pennville	July 26	Mustered out July 24, '65.
Keese William G.	Clark's Hill	Aug. 5	" " "
Kirkpatrick John A.	Tippecanoe co	July 22	Discharged Jan 14, '63; wounds.
Lindsey Francis	Clark's Hill	July 22	Mustered out July 24, '65, as corporal.
Loveless Lysander	Tippecanoe co	Aug. 11	Discharged March 17, '63.
Lackey Thomas	Clark's Hill	Aug. 6	Mustered out July 24, '65, as corporal.
Lock George	Wyandotte	Aug. 5	Mustered out July 24, '65.
Love Alfred	Stockwell	Aug. 5	" " "
Martin Thomas A	Dayton	Aug. 8	" " " as Corporal.
Moore Greenberry	Pettys, Ill	Aug. 2	" " "
McRiddle John	Stam'g Gr'd Ky	July 22	" " " as Corporal
Oglebay John C.	Stockwell	Aug. 7	" " "
Passale George	Lafayette	July 24	" " "
Parker William P	Tippecanoe co	Aug. 1	Transferred to V R C April 10, '64.
Peterson Gastus	Tippecanoe co	Aug. 6	Died at Louisville, Ky., Oct. 17, '62.
Peterson Martin B	Tippecanoe co	Aug. 9	Transferred to V R C, July 1, 63.
Rinehart Samuel H	Tippecanoe co	Aug. 2	Discharged August 13 '63; wounds.
Rose William	Clark's Hill	July 26	Mustered out July 24, '65.
Rubofett Henry	Tippecanoe co	July 21	Discharged October 10, '63.
Stingley Francis M.	Tippecanoe co	July 25	Discharged July 18, '63.
Smith William	Tippecanoe co	July 26	Deserted October —— '62.
Stephenson William H	Tippecanoe co	July 19	Discharged January 31, '63.
Stiers Andrew G	Tippecanoe co	July 19	Died at Gallatin, Tenn., March 6, '63.
Strawn Simeon	Oxford	Aug. 8	Mustered out July 24, '65.
Smith James R	Tippecanoe co	Aug. 11	Transferred to V R C September 1, '64.
Sassonon Cyrus	Lafayette	Aug. 6.	Mustered out July 24, '65, as Sergeant.
Scheerer Lewis	Tippecanoe co	July 21.	Deserted December 10, '62
Talby James F	Lafayette	Aug. 6	Mustered out July 24, '65, as corporal.
Travis William	Tippecanoe co	July 23	Discharged May 1, '63.

NAME AND RANK.	RESIDENCE.	Date of Muster. 1862.	REMARKS.
Vanhorn Alexander B	Tippecanoe co	Aug. 2	Mustered out July 24, '65.
Vance Joseph R	Culver's St'n	Aug. 6	" " "
Wagoner John W	Wyandotte	Aug. 6	" " "
Wiltshire Samuel	Dayton	July 21	" " "
Watts Austin	Dayton	Aug. 8	" " "
Young William H	Tippecanoe co	July 22	Discharged February 8, '63.
Young James B	Tippecanoe co	Aug. 11	Discharged Dec. 29, '62, as 1st sergeant.
Yeager John W.	Stockwell	Aug. 11	Mustered out July 24, '65.
Recruits.			
Armstrong George D		Mar. 8, '65	Transferred to 44th Regiment.
Asley George		Dec. 11, '63	" " "
Best Josiah		Oct. 17, '64.	" " "
Cann Peter H.		Mar. 9, '64	" " "
Ford William H H		Mar. 8, '65	" " "
Hall James W		Dec. 29, '63	" " "
Jackson George T		Oct. 19, '64.	" " "
Long William		Mar. 6, '64	" " "
Lucus Barton		Dec. 23, '63	" " "
Moorehouse Silas O		Feb. 21, '65	" " "
Miller Thodore A		Mar. 29, 65.	" " "
Mitchell George		Mar. 14, '65	" " "
Oshel Jesse		Dec. 26, '63.	" " "
Payton Philip		Apr. 17, '63	" " "
Reeser Henry C		Dec. 17, '63	" " "
Reed Isaac		Mar. 2, '65	" " "
Ramey Joshua J		Mar. 6, '65	" " "
Riggs Avery	Tippecanoe co	Oct. 17, '64	Died at Gravelly Springs, Ala., Feb. 2, '65.
Sharp George P		Mar. 3, '65	Transferred to 44th Regiment.
Smith David J		Mar. 31, '64	" " "
Sovereign William P.			" " "
Todd John		Dec. 17, '63	" " "
Wagner Andrew J		Oct. 8, '64	" " "
Weldon John		Mar. 7, '65	" " "
White Randolph	Tippecanoe co	Mar. 5, '64	Discharged Feb. 27, '65.

COMPANY "H."

NAME AND RANK.	Date of Commission.	Date of Muster.	REMARKS.
Captain.			
Robert B Hanna	Aug. 9, 1862	Aug 9, '62	Resigned December 16, '63.
John C Scott	Dec. 17, '63	Mar. 13, '64	Mustered out with Regiment.
First Lieutenant.			
James M Stafford	Aug. 9, 1862	Aug. 9, '62	Resigned June 11, '63.
John C Scott	June 12, 1863	Aug. 31, '63	Promoted Captain
Hugh H Stafford	Dec. 17, '63	Mar. 13, '64.	Mustered out with Regiment.
Second Lieutenant			
George F Ward	Aug. 9, 1862	Aug. 9, '62	Resigned November 26, '62.
John C Scott	Nov. 27, 1862	Dec. 9, '62	Promoted 1st Lieutenant.
Hugh H Stafford	June 12, 1863		Promoted 1st Lieutenant.
Charles D McClure	Jan. 1, '65		Mustered out with Regiment, as 1st sergt.
	RESIDENCE	1862.	
First Sergeant.			
Griffith William	Fountain co	July 28	Discharged October 13, '62.
Sergeants			
Scott John C	Fountain co.	July 21	Promoted 2d Lieutenant.
Healy Joseph	Fountain co.	July 25	Discharged September 10, '64.
Zerse Augustus	Fountain co.	July 16	Discharged February 4, '63.
Stafford Hugh H		July 25	Promoted 1st Lieutenant.
Corporals.			
Bromley Joseph	Fountain co.	July 25	Discharged Jan. 30, '65; wounds.
Toms Perry	Attica	July 23	Mustered out July 21, '65, as sergeant.
McClure Charles D	Newtown	July 28	Mustered out July 24, '65 as 1st sergeant.
Beeks, James M	Attica	July 16	Mustered out July 21, '65, as sergeant.
Beckley James H.	Newtown	July 28	" " " "
Stowe Theodore E	Attica	July 21	" " " as corporal.
Musician.			
Lane James W	Fountain co.	July 26	Discharged January 27, '63.
Wagoner.			
Smith Isaac	Newton	July 26	Mustered out July 24, '65.
Privates.			
Allen Edward	Fountain co	Aug. 6	Died at Nashville, Tenn., Nov. 16, '63.

NAME AND RANK.	RESIDENCE.	Date of Muster. 1862.	REMARKS.
Anderson John L.....	Attica.........	Aug. 6....	Mustered out July 24, '65.
Anderson John......	Attica.........	July 22 ..	" " "
Anderson Andrew....	Attica.	Aug. 9....	" " "
Adams William	Fountain co...	July 23....	Discharged May 19, '63.
Bottenburg Joseph...	Newtown	July 29....	Mustered out July 24, '65.
Bourison Andrew....	Attica.........	July 22 ...	" " "
Batteral Michael . ..	Fountain co...	Aug. 1....	Discharged Sept. 25, '65.
Cubberly Thomas	Fountain co...	July 29 ..	Died at Murfreesboro, Tenn., April 6, '63
Curtis WilliamN	Hillsboro......	Aug. 1 ..	Mustered out July 24, '65.
Cook Samuel	Newtown	July 28....	" " "
Castle James M.......	Fountain co...	Aug. 9....	Transferred to V R C February 15, '64.
Clark William R.	Rob Roy	Aug. 5	Mustered out July 24, '65.
Clark Nathan W. ...	Fountain co..	July 29....	Transferred to V R C February 15, '64.
Clifton Houson	Fountain co...	Aug. 2....	Transferred to V R C. Sept. 30, '63.
Cox Joseph H	Fountain co...	Aug. 15....	Discharged June 4, '63.
Dixon Simon Y E.....	Newtown	Aug. 4....	Mustered out July 24, '65.
Dawson John E	Westville	July 29....	" " " as corporal
Edwards Hamilton S .	Hillsboro......	Aug. 9....	" " "
Ellis James W........	Hillsboro	Aug. 2....	" " " as corporal.
Frankenfield Jared...	Newtown	July 25....	" " " "
Griffith Horace	Fountain co,..	Aug. 5....	Died at Murfreesboro, Tenn., Jan. 15, '63.
Hatton Richard A....	Newtown	July 28....	Missing at Chicamauga, Sept. 20, '63.
Hays John L..	Attica	Aug. 9....	Mustered out July 24, '65, as corporal.
Hobson John C	Fountain co...	Aug. 2....	Deserted October 6, '62.
Hiestand Samuel.....	Fountain co...	Aug. 1....	" " "
Horr William....	Fountain co...	July 23....	Discharged September 1, '62.
Homes Anthony V....	Attica	Aug. 5....	Mustered out July 24, '65.
Haas William.........	Newtown	Aug. 4. ..	" " "
Helms John M........	Rob Roy	Aug. 8....	" " "
Johnson John	Fountain co...	July 21....	Died at Memphis, Tenn., Mar. 11, '64, w'ds.
Johnson Frederick...	Paxton, Ill....	Aug. 9....	Mustered out July 24, '65.
Johnson Andrew.....	Paxton, Ill ...	July 22.. :	" " "
Keister Daniel	Williamsport .	July 24....	" " "
Keister George H ...	Fountain co...	July 24....	Discharged May 16, '63.
Kerr James A	Newtown	Aug. 9....	Mustered out July 24, '65.
Laman William H....	Indianapolis ..	July 26....	" " "
Leatherman John W.	Newtown	July 28....	" " "
Lellis Patrick..... ..	Fountain co...	July 28.....	Discharged Nov. 30, '64.
Leas William.	St Joseph, Ill .	Aug. 7....	Mustered out July 24, '65.
McIntyre DeStewart..	Fountain co..	Aug. 13....	Mustered out May 22, '65.
McCollum Thomas B.	Fountain co..	Aug. 4....	Discharged February 15, '63.
Miller Benjamin.. ...	Attica	July 29....	Mustered out July 24, '65.
Meaker John M . ..	Fountain co...	Aug. 7....	Discharged January 30, '63.
Monroe Henderson W	Attica.........	Aug. 9....	Mustered out July 24, '65, as sergeant.
Miller Phillip A	Hillsboro	Aug. 9....	Mustered out July 24, '65.
Nevil Moses	Bl Gr's Gr'e, Ill	Aug. 13....	" " "
Ogle John	Bruce's Lake .	Aug. 4....	" " "
Oliver John W........	Fountain co...	July 26....	Deserted December 1, '62
Pine William	Fountain co...	Aug. 5 ..	Deserted third time July 30, '64.
Petro Henry C...	Westville	Aug. 2....	Mustered out July 24, '65.
Parrot Samuel B	Rob Roy	July 20....	" " "
Price Joseph H.......	Newtown . ..	July 26....	" " "
Peterson John A.......	Fountain co...	July 21....	Transferred to V R C July 1, '63.
Peterson John P ....,	Fountain co...	Aug. 11 ...	Died at Bowling Green, Ky., Dec. 6, '62.
Peterson John........	Attica	Aug. 11 ...	Mustered out July 25, '65.
Powel Thomas M	Fountain co...	July 17...	Discharged January 23, '63.
Rothermel William ..	Treverton, Pa.	July 25 ...	Mustered out July 24, '65.
Scamrel Benjamin P.	Hillsboro	Aug. 9....	" " "
Stephens John N	Fountain co...	Aug. 7....	Died at Scottsville, Ky., Dec. 24, '62.
Stafford William H...	Fountain co...	July 25....	Discharged February 8, '63.
Shields James H ...	Newtown	July 26.. .	Mustered out July 24, '65.
Shafer Peter A.......	Rob Roy......	July 20....	" " "
Scott Nathan	Fountain co...	Aug. 9 ...	Discharged Feb. 15, '63.
Stephens Peter S	Fountain co...	Aug. 6....	Discharged May 28, '63.
Smith Joel C P	Fountain co...	Aug. 6 ...	Died at Frankfort, Ky., Nov. 6, '62.
Tanner George	Paxton, Ill....	Aug. 4....	Mustered out July 24, '65.
Town Edward R	Attica	Aug. 9....	" " " as corporal.
Town Lewis..........	Attica	Aug. 9....	" " "
Town Charles........	Fountain co...	July 23....	Died at Louisville, Nov. 22, '64; accid'l w'ds
Whitesel Tobias	Union City ...	July 25...	Mustered out July 24, '65.
Ward Julius C	Fountain co...	Aug. 6....	" " "
Whiccar John M.. ..	Attica	Aug. 9...	" " "
Wilson Jasper N.....	Attica	Aug. 1....	Sentenced to make up 1 year lost by deser'n.
Yeasel William.	Fountain co...	Aug. 1....	Died at Rome, Ga., July 13, '64.
Zimmerman James W	Attica	Aug. 9....	Mustered out July 24, '65.
Zimmerman Michael	Attica	Aug. 6....	" " "
Recruits.			
Brier Asbury.........	....	....	Transferred to 44th Regiment.
Coon Eli	....	Jan. 10, '64	" " "
Crumley Hezekiah ...	....	Mar 11, '64	" " "
Chenne Hamilton A..	....	Nov. 28, '64	" " "
Coulter William	....	Dec. 5, '64	" " "

NAME AND RANK.	RESIDENCE.	Date of Muster. 1862	REMARKS.
Davidson William....	Fountain O ...	Oct, 13, '64	Died at Jeffersonville, March 29, '65.
Douglas Joseph H....	Fountain O ...	Jan. 12, '64	Discharged January 19, '65; wounds.
Earp Wesley...	Trenton Ga ..	Sep. 8, '63	Promoted Lieutenant 1st Alabama Cavalry.
Hines James J........	....	Jan. 12, '64	Transferred to 44th Regiment.
Holstead James A....	....	Oct. 13, '64	" " "
Lyon Napoleon B.....	....	Jan. 12, '64	" " "
Lonbergen Henry H..	....	Jan. 12, '64	" " "
Stup Joseph L	....	Mar. 3, '64	" " "
Smith James A.	....	Dec. 5, '64	" " "
Swanson John.......	....	Dec. 5, '64	" " "

COMPANY "I."

NAME AND RANK.	Date of Commission.	Date of Muster.	REMARKS.
Captain.			
Jesse Hill............	Aug. 11, 1862..	Aug. 11, '62	Resigned Sept. 30, '62.
John Watts...	Nov. 8, 1862	Nov. 8, '62	Dishonorably dismissed Jan. 19, '63.
William H McMurtry.	Jan. 20, 1863..	Mar. 1, '63	Killed at Rock Spring, Sept 12, '63.
Robert A Vance ..	Mar. 1, 1864..	Mar 17, '64	Mustered out with Regiment.
First Lieutenant.			
Ira Brown	Aug. 11, 1862..	Aug. 11, '62	Resigned Nov. 21, '62.
William H McMurtry.	Nov. 21, 1862..	Feb. 20, '63	Promoted Captain.
Robert A Vance......	Jan. 20, 1863..	Mar. 1, '63	Promoted Captain.
Richard C Clark......	Mar. 1, 1864..	April 25,'64	Mustered out with Regiment.
Second Lieutenant.			
John Watts	Aug. 11, 1862..	Aug. 11, '62	Promoted Captain.
William H McMurtry.	Nov. 8, 1862..	Nov. 22, '62	Promoted 1st Lieutenant.
Robert A Vance	Nov. 21, 1862..	Feb. 20, '63	Promoted 1st Lieutenant.
Henry C Cassel.	Jan. 20, 1863..	Mar. 1. '63	Honorably discharged May 27, '64.
George J Foster	Sept. 1, 1864..	Sept. 27, '64	Mustered out with Regiment.
	RESIDENCE.	1862.	
First Sergeant.			
Cassell Henry C	... ...	Aug. 4....	Promoted 2d Lieutenant
Sergeants.			
McMurtry William H.	Poolesville....	Aug. 4....	Promoted 2d Lieutenant.
Foster George J	Poolesville	Aug. 4 .	Promoted 2d Lieutenant.
Anderson Eli W... ..	Homer, Ill....	Aug. 4....	Discharged Feb. 29, '64; wounds.
Taylor Samuel	Pine Village ..	July 24....	Mustered out July 24, '65.
Corporals.			
McGee Benjamin F ..	Montmorenci .	Aug. 4....	Mustered out July 24 '65 as Sergeant.
Kelley Robert.........	Rainsville.....	Aug. 4....	Discharged January 1, '63.
Dawson Charles	Poolesville....	July 24....	Discharged Jan. —'63.
Ogborn James W. ..	Pine Village..	Aug. 4 ...	Discharged Dec. 31, '62.
Drummond James ...	Pine Village..	July 24....	Mustered out July 24 '65.
Odle Richard G	Pine Village..	July 24....	Discharged January 31, '63.
Johnston Peter P.. ..	Oxford	July 24 ...	Mustered out July 24, '65 as private.
Wakeman William S.	Pine Village..	July 24....	Mustered out July 24, '65, as Sergeant.
Musicians.			
Young John H........	Chambersburg	July 24....	Discharged April 21, '64.
Hooker Henry H . ..	Rainsville ...	July 24....	Discharged June 30, '63.
Wagoner			
Munson Restana......	Poolesville ..	July 24...	Mustered out July 24 '65.
Privates.			
Adams John	Independence.	July 24....	Transferred to V R C, Nov. 10, '63.
Allen Jacob..........	Poolesville...	July 24 .	Discharged April 9, '64.
Allen Archibald	Poolesville...	July 24....	Discharged Dec. 31, '62.
Allen David W	Poolesville....	July 24....	Mustered out July 24 '65.
Ashcraft Joseph......	....	July 24....	Died at Louisville, Ky., —, '63.
Barber Alfred	Pine Village..	July 24....	Mustered out July 24, '65.
Barker Thomas J....	Pine Village..	July 24....	" " " as corporal.
Brannan Joseph M ..	Pine Village..	July 24 ...	" " "
Beaver Anson	Rainsville.....	July 24....	" " "
Brooks George.	Rainsville	Aug. 4.....	Killed at Rock Springs, Ga., Sept. 12, '63.
Brown Levi D	Pond Grove ..	Aug. 4. ..	Discharged February 18, '65; wounds.
Brooks John	Rainsville	Aug. 4....	Mustered out July 24 '65.
Cheadley Martin L...	Remington ...	Aug. 4....	" " "
Chenowith Wm E T..	Montmorenci .	Aug. 4....	Transferred to V R C, Sept. 30, '63.
Citizen James S.......	Pine Village..	Aug. 4 ...	Mustered out July 24 '65.
Clark Richard C.....	....	Aug. 4....	Promoted 1st Lieutenant.
Cowgill Jesse.........	Remington ..	Aug. 4....	Mustered out July 24, '65.

Name and Rank.	Residence.	Date of Muster. 1862	Remarks.
Courtney Oren	Pine Village	Aug. 4	Dropped as deserter June 30, '64.
Collins John D	Lafayette	Aug. 15	Mustered out July 24, '65.
Dawson Francis M.	Remington	Aug. 4	Discharged June 30, '63.
Day Abraham	Independence	Aug. 4	Mustered out June 3, '65.
Dunwiddie Abraham	Newton	Aug. 4	Mustered out July 21, '65.
Fail Samuel T	Remington	Aug. 4	Died at Louisville, Ky. Dec. 3, '62.
Fisher William R	Pine Village	Aug. 4	Discharged Nov. —, '62
Foster Joshua D	Remington	Aug. 4	Mustered out July 24, '65.
Freeman Jasper	Rainsville	Aug. 4	" " "
Franklin John	Poolesville	Aug. 4	" " "
Harmond Christian R	Remington	Aug. 4	" " " as corporal.
Harvey William	Poolesville	Aug. 4	" " "
Hamilton John	Montmorenci	Aug. 4	" " "
Hawkins James H	Catalpa Grove	Aug. 4	" " "
Hawkins John T	Catalpa Grove	Aug. 4	Discharged Jan. 15, '63.
Haynes John T	Remington	Aug. 4	Mustered out July 24, '65, as sergeant.
Haynes David	Remington	Aug. 4	Mustered out July 24, '65.
Hollenback Thomas	Montmorenci	Aug. 4	Transferred to V R C October 7, '64.
Hoover Andrew J	Brookston	Aug. 4	Mustered out July 24, '65.
Jervis Amos	Oxford	Aug. 4	Discharged April 18, '63
Kelley Albert D	Rainsville	Aug. 4	Mustered out July 24, '65, as corporal.
Killin Jeddiah F	Montmorenci	Aug. 4	Sent'd to make up 21 months lost by desertion
Keys William T	Independence	Aug. 4	Discharged Sept. 19, '62.
Kenada Barney	Montmorenci	Aug. 4	Mustered out July 24, '65.
Kidney John A	Pine Village	Aug. 4	" " " as Corporal.
Lewis Joseph J	Poolesville	Aug. 4	Discharged Jan. 13 '63.
McKinney Albert M	Pond Grove	Aug. 4	Mustered out July 24, '65.
Melton Paten	Pine Village	Aug. 4	" " "
Miller George W	Rainsville	Aug. 4	" " "
Morris John H	Attica	Aug. 4	Died at Chattanooga, Tenn., Nov. 17, '64.
Melton Allen K	Pine Village	Aug. 4	Mustered out July 24, '65.
McKinzie John	Rainsville	Aug. 4	" " "
McCoy Richard M	Delphi	Aug. 16	Discharged Jan. 6, '63.
Nowlen Payton S		Aug. 16	Died at Castillian Springs, Tenn., Dec. 6, '62.
Odle James W	Pine Village	Aug. 4	Mustered out July 24, '65.
Odle James H	Pine Village	Aug. 4	" " "
Ogborn Henry	Pine Village	Aug. 4	Died at Murfreesboro, April 27, '63.
Owens Jeremiah	Remington	Aug. 4	Died at New Albany, Jan. 11, '63.
Ogborn William E	Montmorenci	Aug. 4	Died in Andersonville prison, Sept. 18, '64.
Pike Benjamin	Independence	July 7	Mustered out July 24, '65.
Rater Andrew	Independence	Aug. 4	Died at Gallatin, Tenn., Feb. 12, '63
Records William H	Montmorenci	Aug. 4	Mustered out July 24 '65, as Corporal.
Records Elisha	Montmorenci	Aug. 4	Mustered out June 6, '65.
Rider Thomas N	Fairfield, Iowa	Aug. 4	Mustered out July 24, '65, as corporal.
Roach John A	Warren co	Aug. 4	Died at Gallatin, Tenn., Mar. 6, '63.
Roberts Jordan B.	Oxford	Aug. 4	Mustered out July 24, '65.
Sargent John M	Oxford	Aug. 4	" " "
Shaw William	Montmorenci	Aug. 4	Discharged May 12, '63.
Southard George W	Remington	Aug. 4	Discharged Jan. 13 '63.
Southard James	Remington	Aug. 4	" "
Smith James B	Rainsville	Aug. 4	Mustered out July 24, '65.
Smith George M	Pine Village	Aug. 4	Transferred to V R C.
Sale William W	Pine Village	Aug. 4	Mustered out July 24, '65.
Stanfield Abraham M	Pine Village	Aug. 4	Mustered out July 24 '65, as Corporal.
Stuckey Simon	Warren co	Aug. 4	Mustered out July 24, '65.
Stuckley William	Warren co	Aug. 4	" " "
Stevenson Hiram S	Lafayette	Aug. 4	" " "
Taylor George	Montmorenci	Aug. 4	Died at Gallatin, Tenn., Dec. —, '62.
Talbert James K	Poolesville	Aug. 4	Dropped as deserter June 30, '64.
Vance Robert A	Warren co	July 24	Promoted 2d Lieutenant.
Vance Alfred	Lafayette	Aug. 5	Mustered out July 24, '65.
Vick Noah	Lafayette	Aug. 5	Discharged September 19, '62.
Wakeman George W	Pine Village	July 7	Mustered out July 24, '65.
Wyatt Harmon H	Poolesville	July 7	" " "
Yarbrough Andrew J	Oxford	July 7	" " "
Recruits.			
Anderson Samuel E		Dec. 23, '63	Transferred to 44th Regiment.
Brookall Charles		Dec. 29, '63	" " "
Benson James C		Dec. 23, '63	" " "
Brown George D	Pine Village	Nov. 17, '64	Discharged May 31, '65.
Burt Alfred	Pine Village	Feb. 20, '64	Died at Chattanooga, Jan. 25, '64; wounds.
Coffin Seth		Mar. 29, '61	Transferred to 44th Regiment.
Cook Daniel C		Dec. 23, '63	" " "
Connell Joseph		Feb. 20, '64	" " "
Clark William H		Dec. 23, '63	Died at Wilmington, N. C., March 12, '65.
Dunwiddie Isaac		Feb. 27, '63	Transferred to 44th Regiment
Dickens William	Pine Village	Feb 20, '64	Discharged Feb. 16, '65.
Foster Richard		Dec. 23, '63	Transferred to 44th Regiment.
Frazier Davie		Jan. 16, '64	" " "
Gerard Simon		Dec. 26, '63	Deserted Feb. 23, '64.
Hooker Abram W		Jan. 16, '63	Transferred to 44th Regiment.
Hatcher Jesse	Rainsville	Nov. 2, '64	Died Jan 1, '65.

NAME AND RANK.	RESIDENCE.	Date of Muster. 1862.	REMARKS.
Killin Jeddiah		Aug. 10, '62	Transferred to 44th Regiment.
Kidney James	Pine Village	Feb. 20, '64	Died at Marietta, Ga., Aug. 28, '64.
Miklejohn Andrew J.		Dec. 23, '63	Transferred to 44th Regiment.
Montgomery James		Dec. 23, '63	" " "
Moffit Joab		Feb. 20, '64	" " "
Ryan John N		Dec. 23, '63	" " "
Ryan Jesse		Dec. 23, '63	" " "
Rozelle Zachariah		Feb. 20, '64	" " "
Seargeant Joseph W		Dec. 23, '63	" " "
Thomas Samuel		Feb. 20, '64	" " "
Turman William H H	Pine Village	Dec. 23, '63	Discharged March 6, '63.
Webb Rufus		Mar. 21, '64	Transferred to 44th Regiment.
Winchel Isaac		Dec. 9, '63	" " "

COMPANY "K."

NAME AND RANK.	Date of Commission.	Date of Muster.	REMARKS.
Captain.			
Hiram B Collins	Aug. 22, 1862	Aug. 26, '62	Resig'd Apr. 21, '63; re-ent. service as Capt. in 15th Regt.
Richard H McIntire	April 22, 1863	May 2, '63	Honorably disch'ged, May 26, '64.
George W Brown	July 1, 1864	Nov. 26, '64	Mustered out with Regiment.
First Lieutenant.			
George W Ross	Aug. 22, 1862	Aug. 26, '62	Resigned Nov. 13, '62.
Richard H McIntire	Nov. 14, 1862	Nov. 18, '62	Promoted Captain
James W Davis	April 22, 1863	May 2, '63	Resigned January 14, '64.
George W Brown	Jan. 25, 1864	April 20, '64	Promoted Captain
James T Quick	July 1, 1864	Nov 26, '64	Mustered out with Regiment.
Second Lieutenant			
James H Whitcomb	Aug. 22, 1862	Aug. 26, '62	Resigned Dec 19, '62: re-entered service as 1st Lieutenant in 11th Cavalry.
John W Gaskill	Dec. 20, 1862		Died at Murfreesboro, Tenn., Feb. 20, '63.
James W Davis	Feb. 20, 1863	Feb. 24, '63	Promoted 1st Lieutenant.
Carey M Lane	April 22, 1863	May 2, '62	Resigned Jan 23, '64; re-entered service as Captain in 150th Regiment
James T Quick	Jan. 25, 1864	Mar. 26, '64	Promoted 1st Lieutenant.
Wm F Hendrickson	Jan. 1, 1864	Nov. 26, 64	Must'd out and honorably disch'd May 15, '65: cause, service no longer req'd and disability
	RESIDENCE.	1862.	
First Sergeant.			
McIntire Richard H	Frankfort	July 17	Promoted 2d Lieutenant.
Sergeants.			
Davis James W.	Frankfort	July 17	Promoted 1st Lieutenant.
Lane Carey M	Lafayette	Aug. 3	Promoted 2d Lieutenant.
Quick James T	Frankfort	July 19	" "
Sea Henry A.	Clinton co.	July 19	Deserted Dec. 20, '62.
Corporals			
Gaskill John W	Frankfort	Aug. 13	Promoted 2d Lieutenant.
Brown Amos G	Clinton co.	Aug. 13	Died at Gallatin, Tenn, Dec 29, '62.
Reed William P.	Clinton co.	July 23	Discharged Feb 2, '63.
Rourk Daniel	Frankfort	Aug. 10	Mustered out July 24 '65.
Hendrickson Wm F	Frankfort	Aug. 1	Promoted 2d Lieutenant.
Phillips James	Clinton co	Aug. 13	Deserted Sept 20, '62.
Fogle John	Colfax	July 19	Mustered out July 24 '65.
Wimborough Wm H.	Frankfort	July 22	" " "
Musicians.			
Brady Edward F	Clinton co.	Aug. 14	Deserted August 28 '62.
Fuell James B	Clinton co.	Aug. 19	Discharged Sept 12, '62.
Wagoner.			
South George W	Michigantown	July 17	Mustered out July 24, '65.
Privates.			
Anderson William J.	Michigantown	Aug. 9	Mustered out July 24 '65.
Allen Ashbrook J	Clinton co.	Aug. 9	Died at Murfreesboro, Tenn., April 9, '63.
Byers George	Frankfort	July 20	Mustered out July 24, '65.
Benjamin Francis E.	Frankfort	July 21	" " "
Brown George W.	Frankfort	July 23	Promoted 1st Lieutenant.
Ball Jackson S	Lafayette	Aug. 12	Mustered out July 24 '65, as Sergeant.
Beard Jesse	Frankfort	Aug. 13	Mustered out July 24, '65.
Bales Joseph	Clinton co.	Aug. 6	Discharged June 9, '63.
Boohar Jacob	Lafayette	Aug. 6	Mustered out July 24, '65.
Cue William J	Clinton co.	July 27	Discharged August 8, '64.
Cloninger John W	Clinton co.	July 25	Died at Chattanooga, Nov. 9, '64.

NAME AND RANK.	RESIDENCE.	Date of Muster. 1862.	REMARKS.
Cooley Willis	Battle Ground	Aug. 6	Mustered out July 24, '65.
Choate Erasmus M	Clinton co	Aug. 13	Killed at Okolona, Miss., Feb. 22, '64.
Critchfield James	Colfax	July 19	Mustered out July 24, '65.
Clark William A	Rossville	Aug. 8	" " "
Cloe John L	Clinton co	Aug. 11	Died at Gallatin, Tenn. Feb. 6, '63.
Dethl William H	Frankfort	July 15	Mustered out July 24, '65.
Davis Joseph	Kirk'sCr'sR'ds	July 25	" " "
Fraser William W	Frankfort	Aug. 13	" " "
Gresmar William	Rossville	July 31	" " "
Gaskill Benjamin F	Rossville	July 25	" " "
Gaskill Ansell B	Clinton co	Aug 13	Discharged March 27, '63.
Herchert Henry O	Clinton co	July 21	Discharged Sept. 23, '64.
Herr John	Rossville	Aug. 15	Mustered out July 24, '65.
Harbaugh John H	Frankfort	July 18	" " "
HarnsbergerGeorgeM	Clinton co	July 21	Died at Murfreesboro, Tenn , April 5, '63.
Huff Eli	Clinton co	Aug. 7	Died at Louisville, Dec. 4, '62.
Hollingsworth Jos B	Clinton co	July 17	Died at Gallatin, Tenn., Dec. 1, '62.
Herr George	Rossville	Aug. 11	Mustered out July 24 '65.
Heffner Samuel H	Rossville	Aug. 9	Mustered out July 24, '65 as Sergeant.
Hollingsworth Amos	Clinton co	July 24	Mustered out June 3, .65.
Johnson William L	Thorntown	Aug. 14	Mustered out July 24 '65.
Keys James S	Frankfort	Aug. 13	Mustered out July 24, '65, as 1st sergeant.
Kelley John	Clinton co	Aug. 9	Died at Louisville, Ky., Oct. 26, '62.
Kreisher Henry S	Middle Fork	Aug. 13	Mustered out July 24, '65.
Lipp Samuel	Clinton co	July 26	Discharged June 11. '64.
La Croix Jules	Clinton co	Aug. 15	Deserted August 28, '64.
Lucas Richard J	Clinton co	Aug. 9	Discharged February 8, '63.
Magan Alfred	E.Not'gh'm,Pa	Aug. 20	Mustered out July 24, '65.
Mead William	Clinton co.	Aug. 20	Transferred to V. R. C. August 31, '63.
Martin Thomas M	Michigan town	July 8	Mustered out July 24 '65.
Mendenhall Wm A	Union St'n, Mo	Aug. 15	" " "
Ostler William	Clinton co	Aug. 15	Died at New Albany, Ind., May — '65.
Pierce William	Frankfort	July 20	Mustered out July 24, '65.
Parish James H	Lafayette	Aug. 7	" " "
Purner John H	Rossville	Aug. 9	" " "
Peake Samuel	Fraukfort	Aug. 12	" " "
Petre Daniel	Clinton co	Aug. 9	Discharged Dec. 11. '62.
Russell William	Clinton co	July 23	Died at Louisville, Ky.. Nov. 25, '62.
Rogers John C	Clinton co	Aug. 8	Discharged December 8, '62.
Stoddard James O	Clinton co	Aug. 6	Discharged Jan 21, '63.
Shepperd Joseph	Rossville	July 23	Mustered out July 24, '65.
Shaw Albert	Clinton co	July 22	Died at Murfreesboro, March 18, 63.
Sheets James K	Frankfort	Aug. 13	Mustered out July 24, '65.
Sheets John	Frankfort	Aug. 13	" " "
Sale ilbert G	Frankfort	Aug. 9	Mustered out May 15, '65.
Scott Francis M	Clinton co	July 17	Mustered out July 24, '65.
Sheets James	Frankfort		" " " as corporal.
Spencer William M	Frankfort	July 15	" " "
Thompson Ephraim W	Elbridge, Ill	Aug. 15	" " "
Tourney Peter	Clinton co	Aug 15	Deserted August 28, '62.
Trowbridge Aaron M	Frankfort	Aug. 15	Mustered out July 24. '65, as sergeant.
Waldron Joseph D	Delphi	Aug. 15	Mustered out July 24, '65.
Wakeland James M	Rossville	July 25	Mustered out July 24 '65, as Sergeant.
Williams George	Clinton co	July 20	Deserted Dec. 22, '64.
Youkey William P	Frankfort	July 14	Mustered out July 24, '65.
Recruits.			
Aiken Stephen		Mar 5, 64	Transferred to 44th Regiment,
Beaum John C		Mar 9, 64	" " "
Bailey Henry J		Dec. 26, 63	" " "
Bowen Alfred		Mar 5, 64	" " "
Brandon Jesse		Feb 27, 64	" " "
Brown Sandford	Clinton co	Mar 10, 64	Discharged Jan. 29, '65.
Culver Edward	Clinton co.	Jan 6 64	Discharged June 30, '64.
Clark Joseph M		Dec 26, 63	Transferred to 44th Regiment.
Cunningham Thomas		Mar. 11, '64	" " "
Cox Carlton C		Feb 27, 65	" " "
Clark William S		Mar. 5, '64	" " "
Camfield Amos		Jan 6, 64	" " "
Davis Albert		Mar. 5, '64	" " "
Davidson Henry L		Dec 26, 63	" " "
Eaton George W		Jan 6, 64	" " "
Ford James E	Clinton co	Mar. 5, '64	Died at Mound City, Ill., May 9, '65.
Gilbert William	Sugar Crove	Mar. 9, '64	Died at home, Dec. 27, '64.
Gillespie Cornelius		Dec 26 63	Transferred to 44th Regiment.
Goff George W		Mar. 23, '64	" " "
Goff William R		Feb 13, 64	" " "
Hughes Thomas E		Jan 6, 64	" " "
Hileman Jacob		Dec. 26, 63	" " "
Hardy Scott		Feb 27, 65	" " "
Hutchinson James R.		Dec 26, 63	" " "
Johnson Erastus D		Dec. 26, '63	" " "
Jackson William T		March 5, '64	" " "

NAME AND RANK.	RESIDENCE.	Date of Muster. 1862.	REMARKS.
Kriesher Daniel		Jan 6, 64	Transferred to 44th Regiment.
Lough Joseph R.		Dec. 26, '63	" " "
Livingston William T		March 5,'64	" " "
Marsh James W		Dec. 26, '63	" " "
Miller John		Jan 6, 64	" " "
Musgrave Jacob		Jan 6, 64	" " "
McClintock William W		Mar. 9, '64	" " "
Parvis Joseph S		Dec. 26, '63	" " "
Richardson Francis M		Jan 6, 64	" " "
Richardson Silas		Jan 6, 64	" " "
Reed William P		Feb 22, 65	" " "
Rutter David		Mar. 5, '64	" " "
Rice Samuel	Clinton co.	Aug. 30, '62	Died at Murfreesboro, April 22, '63.
Spalding James S.		Dec. 26, 63	Transferred to 44th Regiment.
Spalding William C		Dec. 26, '63	" " "
Sigars Louis	Clinton co.	Mar. 5, '64	" " "
Vice Henry	Clinton co.	Jan 6, 64	Died at Nashville, Tenn., Jan. 14, '65.
Williams John J	Clinton co.	Mar. 5, '64	Died at Nashville, Tenn., July 26, '64; w'ds.
Westfall William		Mar. 5, '64	Transferred to 44th Regiment.
Weeks Allen	Decherd, Tenn	Aug. 5, '63	Captured Sept. 7, '64.

UNASSIGNED RECRUITS.

NAME AND RANK.	RESIDENCE.	Date of Muster. 1862.	REMARKS.
Anderson John		Feb 25, 64	
Conner James		Mar 26, '64	
Coulter David J		Dec 15, '64	
Catterline James M		Dec 1, '63	
Cloyd William W		Mar 24, '63	
Colliers Charles		Sept 12, '64	
Cannatt Henry F		Feb. 22, '64	
Downs Henry D		Dec 19, '63	
Diel John A		Dec 12, '63	
Freeman Ezekiel		Dec 5, '64	
Gardner Charles		Dec 31, '63	
Killfeather Michael		Aug. 10, '64	
Maher Thomas		Jan 26, 64	
McDowell Andrew J.		Jan 4, 64	
Poynsett William B.		Oct. 4, '64	
Patchett Isaac M.		Jan 1, 64	
Potts Stephen		Oct 24, 64	
Redman George T.		Mar 10, '64	
Sipes James		Jan 5, 64	
Sipes George W		Dec 29, '63	
Shadell Levi R		Dec 19, '63	
Saunders James F		Aug 12, 64	
Thrasher Nat A		Mar 29, '64	
Webster Johnson G		Dec 24, '63	
Williams Charles E		Feb 26, 64	
Weborn David J.		Feb 29, '64	
Welch John.		Mar 22, '64	

ERRATA.

Preface, page VIII, end of 14th line from bottom, should read "of whom she was mother of ten."

Page 17, 13th line from bottom, should read "and one month's pay."

Page 38, 10th line from bottom, should read neatly instead of newly.

Page 57, 11th line from top, should read bought instead of brought.

Page 71, 12th line from top, should read Rousseau instead of Rosecrans.

Page 71, 6th line from bottom, should read 12 instead of 25.

Page 76, 21st line from top, should read our instead of over.

Page 83, 9th line from bottom, should read without, instead of with.

Page 98, 13th line from bottom, should read Triune, instead of Trinne.

Page 104, 1st line from bottom, should read Readyville, instead of Reddyville.

Page 127, 15th line from top, should read Manchester, instead of Winchester.

Page 129, 15th line from top, should read Beech Grove, instead of Beech.

Page 132, 22d line from top, should read Long, Co. D, instead of Co. E.

Page 138, 2d line from bottom, two lines are left out: "Each non-commissioned officer was allowed to take all his men but two, who were left in the main road with the pack train," &c.

Page 140, 3d line from the bottom, should read Roweshill, instead of Roseville.

Page 296, 9th line from top, should read Vilanau, instead of Vilanan.

Page 301, 13th line from top, should read Euharlee, instead of Enhartee.

Page 301, 15th line from top, should read Euharlee, instead of Enhartee.

Page 316, last line, should read 20th, instead of 10th.

Page 324, 21st line from bottom, should read right, instead of left.

Page 385, last line, should read houses, instead of horses.

Page 424, 4th line from bottom, should read Vi anau, instead of Vilanan.

Page 416, 3d line from top, should read Chattooga, instead of Chattanooga.

Page 422, 1st line from top, should read Chattooga, instead of Chattanooga.

Page 425, 6th line from top, should read Vilanau, instead of Vilanan.

Page 440, 21st line from bottom, should read 98th, instead of 29th.

Page 454, 12th line from top, should read last of November, instead of September

Page 458, 14th line from top, should read were not, instead of were.

Page 467, 21st line from bottom, should read Co. I, instead of Co. D.

Page 526, 19th line from top, should read south-east, instead of north-east.

Page 564, 11th line from top, should read Trunions, instead of Trimmings.

CPSIA information can be obtained
at www.ICGtesting.com
Printed in the USA
BVHW091754170119
538094BV00003B/62

9 781147 209105